AN

INDEX

TO

PRINTED PEDIGREES,

CONTAINED

IN

County and Local Histories,

the Heralds' Visitations,

AND IN THE

MORE IMPORTANT GENEALOGICAL COLLECTIONS.

BY

CHARLES BRIDGER,

HON. MEM. SOC. ANTIQUARIES OF NEWCASTLE-UPON-TYNE.

CLEARFIELD

Originally Published
London, 1867

Reprinted
Genealogical Publishing Company
Baltimore, 1969

Reprinted for
Clearfield Company, Inc. by
Genealogical Publishing Co., Inc.
Baltimore, Maryland
1997

International Standard Book Number: 0-8063-0049-3

Library of Congress Catalog Card Number 69-20050

Made in the United States of America

TO

SIR THOMAS PHILLIPPS, BART., M.A., F.R.S., F.S.A.,

OF THIRLESTANE HOUSE, CHELTENHAM,

ONE OF THE TRUSTEES OF THE BRITISH MUSEUM,

&c. &c. &c.

This Volume

IS, IN ACKNOWLEDGMENT OF FRIENDLY FAVOURS,

RESPECTFULLY DEDICATED BY

THE COMPILER.

PREFACE.

In the autumn of 1863 I announced my intention to pub-
lish a volume on the Bibliography of Heraldry and Genealogy,
and in the following spring, in *Notes and Queries* and in the
Herald and Genealogist, I promised to add to it an " Index
to the Pedigrees contained in the County Histories, and other
topographical works."

Partly in consequence of the extent of the materials I have
collected for that work, and partly on account of the produc-
tion of a hastily prepared compilation of a similar nature to the
present Index, I have been compelled to postpone for a time
the publication of the bibliographical manual, and to issue my
Index as a separate work.

In submitting it to the genealogical student, I can only
express a hope that the trifling errors which may have escaped
notice, in over sixteen thousand references, in duplicate, will
not militate against the general adoption of it as a guide to
printed genealogies.

I am aware that much more might have been done had time
and circumstances admitted ; and I shall be willing to con-
sider any suggestions which may be made to me, with the view
of publishing an appendix, embodying additions, and the
amendment of errors of omission and commission. It might
then be desirable to add a list of Pedigrees contained in Scotch
and Irish topographical works, and in our biographical lite-
rature.

To Sir Thomas Phillipps, Bart., I am indebted for permission to index his privately printed Heralds' Visitations; and to him, as well as to many friends and correspondents who have taken a kindly interest in the progress of the work, I beg to offer my sincere thanks.

CHARLES BRIDGER.

Witley, Surrey,
Jan. 30, 1867.

AN

INDEX TO THE BOOKS,

CONTAINING PEDIGREES.

BEDFORDSHIRE.

1.—Collections towards the History and Antiquities of Bedfordshire. (No. 8, Bibliotheca Topographica Britannica.) *London*, 1783, 4to.

Napier, 55, 56.

2.—An Historical Account of the Parish of Odell, in the County of Bedford. (No. 44, Bibliotheca Topographica Britannica.) *London*, 1783, 4to.

Wahul and Chetwode, folding at 31.

BERKSHIRE.

3.—The Antiquities of Berkshire. By ELIAS ASHMOLE. *London*, 1719, 3 vols. 8vo.; 2nd ed. *London*, 1723, 3 vols. 8vo.; 3rd ed. *Reading*, 1736, folio.

Annesley (*Maidenhead*), iii. 33 ; 2 ed. *ib.*

Berington *of Reading*, iii. 297 ; 2 ed. *ib.*; 3 ed. 335.

Blagrove *of Bullsnashe Court*, iii. 329 ; 2 ed. *ib.*; 3 ed. 338.

Booth *of Fawler Court*, iii. 308 ; 2 ed. *ib.*

Bulstrode *of Upton*, iii. 310 ; 2 ed. *ib.*

Cater *of Letcomb Regis*, iii. 286 ; 2 ed. *ib.*

Carmond, iii. 42 ; 2 ed. *ib.*

Cheek *of Avington*, iii. 318 ; 2 ed. *ib.*

Couper, iii. 19 ; 2 ed. *ib.*

Delahyde *of Brimpton*, iii. 296; 2 ed. *ib.*; 3 ed. 340.

Everard *of Reading*, iii. 291 ; 2 ed. *ib.*

Eyston *of East Hendred*, iii. 361 ; 2 ed. *ib.*

Fettyplace, *of North Denchworth*, iii. 307 ; 2 ed. *ib.*

Fettyplace, iii. 306 ; 2 ed. *ib.*

Forster *of Aldermarston*, iii. 311 ; 2 ed. *ib.*; 3 ed. 337.

Gayer *of Foxley*, iii. 316 ; 2 ed. *ib.*; 3 ed. 334.

Gerard *of Shinfield and Lambourn*, iii. 320 ; 2 ed. *ib.*

Gunter *of Kingsbury*, iii. 315 ; 2 ed. *ib.*

Hildesley *of Benham*, iii. 317 ; 2 ed. *ib.*

Hinton *of Stanswyke*, iii. 327 ; 2 ed. *ib.*

Holloway *of Maidenhead*, iii. 298 ; 2 ed. *ib.*; 3 ed. 331.

Hulse *of Sutton Courtney*, iii. 303 ; 2 ed *ib.*; 3 ed. 332.

Hyde *of South Denchworth*, iii. 322 ; 2 ed. *ib.*

Iermonger *of Couldingfeild*, iii. 290 ; 2 ed. *ib.*

Latton *of Chilton*, iii. 361; 2 ed. *ib.*

Lenthall, i. 157 ; 2 ed. *ib.*

Loveden *of Lambourn*, iii. 289 ; 2 ed. *ib.*; 3 ed. 338.

Maunsell *of Newbury*, iii. 304; 2 ed. *ib.*

Moore *of Cookham*, iii. 314; 2 ed. *ib.*

Nooke (*Bray*), iii. 20 ; 2 ed. *ib.*

Pleydell *of Coleshill*, iii. 319 ; 2 ed. *ib.*

B

Plott *of Sparsholt,* iii. 285; 2 ed. *ib. ;* 3 ed. 331.

Pusey *of Sparsholte,* iii. 294; 2 ed. *ib. ;* 3 ed. 336.

Redyshe *of Binfield,* iii. 293 ; 2 ed. *ib.*

Shottesbrooke *of Shottesbrooke,* iii. 301; 2 ed. *ib. ;* 3 ed. 333.

Snell *of Hampsted Marshall,* iii. 287 ; 2 ed. *ib.*

Standysh *of Wantage,* iii. 288; 2 ed. *ib.*

Stanshall *of Reading,* iii. 328 ; 2 ed. *ib.*

Staverton *of Staverton and Shiplake,* iii. 326; 2 ed. *ib.*

Tyghall, *originally of Tyghall, co. Somerset,* iii. 335 ; 2 ed. *ib.*

Unton *of Faringdon,* iii. 313; 2 ed. *ib.*

Vachell *of Colley and Warfield,* iii. 312 ; 2 ed. *ib.;* 3 ed. 339.

Ward *of Hurst,* iii. 309 ; 2 ed. *ib.*

Welisburne *of West Hanny,* iii. 299 ; 2 ed. *ib.*

White *of Reading,* iii. 323, 324; 2 ed. *ib.;* 3 ed. 335, 341.

White *of Fyfield,* iii. 325 ; 2 ed. *ib.* ; 3 ed. 336.

Winchcombe *of Newbury,* iii. 300; 2 ed. *ib.;* 3 ed. 333.

Wyrdham *of Farneborough,* iii. 291 ; 2 ed. *ib.*

Yate *of Stanford,* iii. 295: 2 ed. *ib.*

Yate *of Charnay,* iii. 320; 2 ed. *ib.*

4.—Some Account of the Parish of Great Coxwell, in the County of Berks. (No. 13, Bibliotheca Topographica Britannica). *London,* 1783, 4to.

Collier, 6.

Mores *of Great Coxwell,* folding at 2.

Pleydell and Pratt, folding at 2.

5.—Collection towards a History of Berkshire. (No. 16, Bibliotheca Topographica Britannica). *London,* 1783, 4to.

Fettyplace, facing 67.

6.—Parochial Topography of the Hundred of Wanting, and other Miscellaneous Records relating to the County of Berks. By WILLIAM NELSON CLARKE. *Oxford,* 1824, 4to.

Fetyplace, *of Childrey, East Shefford and Besils' Legh,* folding at 68.

Fetyplace *of North Denchworth,* folding at 107.

Hyde *of Denchworth,* folding at 86.

Keate (*East Lockinge*), folding at 151.

Musard (*Spersholt*), 171.

Sherwood (*East Hendred*), facing 128.

Wiseman (*West Hendred*), folding at 144.

7.— County Genealogies. Pedigrees of Berkshire Families, Collected by WILLIAM BERRY. *London,* 1837, folio. *(Published with Bucks and Surrey.)*

Allin, 103.
Allingham, 45.
Aphugh, 131.
Arches, 23.
Audeley, 34.
Barker, 40.
Barlow, 77.

Bassett or Bassnet, 65, 94.
Benyon, 139.
Berington, 23.
Berry, 59.
Blackstone, 97.
Blagrave, 147.
Blandy, 50, 144, 153.

Bockett, 78.
Bouchier, 53, 85.
Brabazon, 10.
Bradney, 67.
Bresworth, 129.
Buckeridge, 49, 153.
Bunny, 46.
Burnaby, 100.
Butcher, 41.
Carne, 122.
Cheke, 43.
Cherry, 73.
Clare, 34.
Clarke, 130.
Clayton, 9.
Congreve, 27.
Cox, 37.
Danvers, 40.
Dawson, 125.
Deans, 32.
Delahyde, 106.
Dewe, 92.
Dickinson, 10, 43.
Dokenvelt, 74.
Dudley, 67.
Dukinfield, 75.
Dundas, 31.
East, 9.
Eyston, 22.
Fines, 40.
Fowke, 27.
Gardiner, 41.
Green, 41.
Hamilton, 61.
Hartley, 149.
Hawkins, 59.
Hawthorne, 41.
Hayward, 37.
Hope, 90.
Hungerford, 35.
Hunter, 126.
Innes, 109.
Jeames, 2.
Jenner, 90.
Keverell, 2.
Kibblewhite, 49, 145, 153.
Knevet, 52.
Langford, 97.
Lee, 98.
Lenthall, 60.
Loder, 33.
Lodge, 8, 146.
Long, 8.
Maclane, 68.

Merriman, 58, 71.
Millett, 58.
Mitford, 12.
Molyneux, 10.
Monke, 13.
Moore, 79.
Mott, 91.
Moyne, 13.
Nind, 11.
Norris, 10.
Palmer, 63.
Perfect, 39.
Perott, 40.
Perry, 84.
Phillimore, 135.
Plantagenet, 53.
Pocock, 119.
Powlett, 138.
Price, 100.
Pride, 16.
Pye, 131.
Rennell, 98.
Richards, 136.
Roos, Lord de, 34.
Sainsbury, 71.
Sandys, 43.
Saunders, 50, 153.
Sawyer, 88, 104.
Scoles, 101.
Seton, 115.
Sharpe, 10.
Slocock, 71.
Smith, 87.
Southby, 36, 140.
Stafford, 34.
Stapylton, 78.
Steavens, 41.
Stephens, 21, 92.
Stowe, 23.
Strange, 35.
Taylor, 45.
Thompson, 84.
Thorpe, 65, 94.
Tipping, 43.
Tonge, 10.
Torriano, 86.
Tuberville, 23.
Venour, 126.
Walcot, 150.
Walcott, 100.
Watlington, 80.
Whitley, 33.
Whyte, 49, 145, 153.
Wilder, 153, 154.

Willes, 2.
Williams, 41, 86, 152.
Winchcombe, 149.
Winchester, Marq. of, 38

Wiseman, 128, 129.
Wright, 68, 138.
Zouche, Lord, 35.

8.—History and Antiquities of the Hundred of Bray in the County of Berks. By CHARLES KERRY. *London*, 1861, 4to.

Atmore, or Atte-More *of Bray*, 124.

Cherry *of Maidenhead and Bray*, 64.

De Sancto Philiberto, or Philibert *of Bray, Eaton Hastings, Sulham, De la Hyde, East Hanney, Eton and Sotwell*, 86.

Foxle, or Foxley *of Bray, Apuldrefield, Kent, Bramshill, &c.* 104.

Hayes *of Cookham, Maidenhead, Holyport, and Clewer*, 48.

Norreys *of Bray*

Page *of Bray*.

Philibert ; see De Sancto Philiberto.

Powney *of Old Windsor and Bray*, 148.

Stafferton, or Staverton *of Bray, Winkfield, &c.* 96.

Winch *of Bray*, 126.

BUCKINGHAMSHIRE.

9.—The History and Antiquities of the Hundred of Desborough, and Deanery of Wycombe, in Buckinghamshire, &c. By THOMAS LANGLEY, M.A. *London*, 1797, 4to.

Borlase (*Little Marlow*), folding at 317.

Duffield, 481.

Goodwin (*Wooburn*), folding at 442.

10.—The History and Antiquities of the County of Buckingham. By GEORGE LIPSCOMB, ESQ., M.D. *London*, 1847, 4 vols. 4to.

Abell and Verney (*East Clayton*), i. 164.

Albini (*Towersey*), i. 455.

Alta Ripa (*Ellesborough*), ii. 192.

Anderson (*Fleet Marston*), i. 325.

Annesley (*Newport Pagnell*), iv. 280.

Antonie (*Hartwell*), ii. 309.

Ap Rees *of Brecknock*, allied with Bray and Latimer (*Crawley*), iv. 126.

Apsloy (*Iver*), iv. 520.

Argentein (*Ashendon*), i. 13.

Ardes (*Sherrington*) ; see Sherrington.

Aubrey *of Boarstall, Brill, Dorton, Chilton, Oakley, &c.*, i. 74.

Avenel, Earls of Devon ; see Redvers.

Awbrey, Jane, wife of Thomas A. *of Cantreff*, i. 67.

Awbrey Amabel, great-grand-mother of Dame Mary A. i. 70.

Awbrey, Dame Mary, wife of Sir Thomas, A. Knt. i. 69.

Backwell (*Tyringham*), iv. 376.

Badcock (*Bledlow*) ; see Lovell.

Baker (*Iver*) ; see Tower.

Banastre (*Boarstall*) ; see Fitz Nigel.

Barre or Barry *of Staunton-Barry*, iv. 345.

Barrington (*Ashton-Clinton*) ; see Montacute.

Barry *of Stanton Barry* ; see Barre.

Basset and Stafford (*Newton Blossomville*), iv. 258.

Beauchamp (*Grendon Underwood*) ; see St. Amand.

Beauchamp (*Iver*) ; see Tower.

Beauchamp *of Hacche, co. Somerset, and of Dorton*, i. 240.

Beaulieu ; see Bellâ-Aquâ.

Bedford, Earls and Dukes of; see Russell.
Beke, Lee and Antonie (*Hartwell*), ii. 309.
Bellâ Aquâ or Beaulieu, Neyrnut and Harvey (*Fleet Marston*), i. 326.
Belson (*Brill*), i. 103.
Benet *of Beachampton and Calverton*, ii. 529.
Bennet (*Chilton and Easington*); see Colebrooke.
Bernard and Bernard-Morland, Barts. i. 521.
Bernard *of Nether Winchendon*; see Goodwyn.
Bertie *of Notley Abbey*, i. 234.
Bertie *of Notley Abbey*; see Norris.
Bett *of Tetchwick*, i. 315.
Blanks, Crosse, Hayton, and Whitbread *of Bledlow*, ii. 116.
Bohun, Earls of Hereford, Essex, and Northampton, i. 206.
Bolebec *of Whitchurch*, iii. 510.
Bolebec *of Weston Turville*, ii. 493.
Bolebec *of Beachampton*, ii. 526.
Borard Reignes (*Clifton Reynes*), iv. 105.
Borlace; see Burlacy.
Borlace-Warren; see Burlacy.
Boscawen, Viscount Falmouth, i. 447.
Boteler or Butler, Earls of Ormonde, and Boleyn or Bullen, Earl of Wiltshire, ii. 7.
Bottetourt, Barons of Newport Pagnell, iv. 276.
Bowyer *of Denham*, iv. 446.
Braose (*Crendon*); see Newmarch.
Bray (*Crawley*); see Ap Rees.
Breose (*Quainton*); see Golafre.
Brereton, Trelawny-; see Trelawny.
Brerewood (*Horton*), iv. 511.
Brightwell (*Chearsley*), i. 122.
Brock (*Quainton*), i. 399.
Browne-Willis, iv. 11.
Brudenell *of Stoke Mandeville*, ii. 447.
Bruyn (*Boarstall*); see Fitz Nigel.
Buckingham, Earl of; see Giffard.
Buckingham, Duke of; see Grenville.
Buckinghamshire, Earls of; see Hobart.
Bulstrode (*Hedgerley*), iv. 503.

Bulstrode *of Upton*, iv. 572.
Burghersh (*Kinsey*); see Marney.
Burlacy or Borlace, and Borlace-Warren *of Ludgershall and Little Marlow*, i. 309.
Busby *of Addington*, ii. 507.
Butler (*Sherrington*); see Sherrington.
Butler, see Boteler.
Cadogan, Earl Cadogan, i. 353.
Calvert and Verney (*Middle Clayton*), i. 184.
Cantilupe *of Middle Clayton*; see Greseley.
Carter *of Chilton*, i. 133.
Cary (*Easington*), i. 152.
Chaker, Chequers, or Alta Ripa (*Ellesborough*), ii. 192.
Chaloner *of Claydon*, iii. 80.
Chaucer (*Kingsey*); see Marney.
Chequers (*Ellesborough*); see Chaker.
Chernocke (*Chilton and Easington*); see Hervey.
Chesterfield, Earl of; see Stanhope.
Chetwode *of Chetwode*, iii. 2.
Churchill, Duke of Marlborough, i. 563.
Clare *of East Clayton*; see De Burgh.
Claver or Cleaver *of Oving*, i. 376.
Cleaver *of Oving*; see Claver.
Clerke *of Shabbington*, i. 446.
Colebrooke and Bennet (*Chilton and Easington*), i. 134.
Corbet *of Fulbrook*; see Lacy.
Cornwall (*Brill*), i. 112.
Cottrell-Dormer *of Chearsley*; see Dormer.
Courtenay, Earls of Devonshire, i. 471.
Courtenay; see Redvers.
Cowdray *of Moulsoe*, iv. 251.
Cressi (*Chearsley*), i. 120.
Croke *of Chilton and Easington*, i. 131.
Croke *of Chequers*, ii. 189.
Croke *of Studley*, i. 368.
Croke (*Ellesborough*), ii. 194.
Crosse *of Bledlow, &c.*; see Blanks.
Cutts (*Ellesborough*); see Thurbane.
Danvers, Harrison, Snell and Hood, (*Ickford*), i. 280.

Dayrell *of Lillingston Dayrell*, iii. 32.
Dashwood *of Halton, &c.*, ii. 222.
De Beauchamp and Foster *of Hanslape*, iv. 174.
De Burgh, Clare, Plantagenet, and Mortimer (*East Clayton*), i. 159.
De Burgh (*East Clayton*); see Mandeville.
De Grenville, Richard, (*Wotton Underwood*), i. 589.
De Grey *of Rotherfield*, i. 160.
De la Pole (*Boarstall*); see Fitz Nigel.
Dell *of Aylesbury and Walton*, ii. 71.
Denton *of Hillesden*, iii. 17.
Devereux, Lord Ferrers of Chartley, Viscount Hereford and Earl of Essex, iv. 258.
Devereux, Ancestors of Sir Walter, iv. 258.
Devon, Earls of; see Redvers.
Deyncourt and Lovell *of Woburn*, iii. 634.
Digby (*Gayhurst*), iv. 145.
Dormer *of Chearsley, Dorton and Kimbrell*; and Cottrell-Dormer *of Chearsley*, i. 118.
Dormer *of Lee Grange and Quainton*, i. 415.
Doily or D'Oyley (*Iver*), iv. 516.
Drake *of Amersham*, iii. 154.
Drayton (*Policott*); see Talbot.
Dublin, Kings of, (*Boarstall*), i. 67.
Duncumbe or Duncombe; see Lee.
Dynham (*Boarstall*); see Fitz Nigel.
Elmes (*Quainton*); see Golafre.
Essex, Earls of; see Bohun.
Essex, see Devereux.
Eyre *of Burnham*, iii. 211.
Fawconer (*Ashendon*), i. 16.
Fermanagh, Viscounts; see Verney.
Ferrers (*Grendon Underwood*), i. 252.
Fleetwood *of Missenden*, ii. 377.
Fleetwood *of the Vache in Chalfont*, iii. 227.
Flemyng, Earls of Wigtoun *of Wyrardisbury*; see Smijth.
Fiennes, Fiendles or Fines (*Wendover*), ii. 470.
Fiott (*Hartwell*), ii. 309.
Fitz Nigel, Handlo, De la Pole, Bruyn, Rede, Dynham, Banastre, and Lewis (*Boarstall*), i. 66.

Fitz-Piers (*East Clayton*); see Mandeville.
Foster *of Handslape*; see De Beauchamp.
Frankland, Bart. (*Ellesborough*), ii. 197.
Frome (*Quainton*); see Golafre.
Gerard (*Aston-Clinton*); see Montacute.
Giffard, Earl of Buckingham, and Clare, Earl of Clare and Hertford, i. 200.
Giffard *of Twyferd*; see Wenman.
Giffard *of Fulbrook*; see Lucy.
Godolphin, Earl of, iv. 559.
Golafre or Gulafre, Missenden, Frome, Breose, Spigurnell, Iwardby, and Elmes (*Quainton*), i. 394.
Goldington (*Stoke Goldington*), iv. 352.
Goodwyn or Goodwin, Tyringham, Winlowe, and Bernard *of Nether Winchendon*, i. 519.
Green (*Policott*); see Vere.
Grenville, Elizabeth, second wife of Eustace, G. Esq. *of Wotton*, i. 596.
Grenville, Duke of Buckingham, i. 599.
Greseley, Cantilupe and Zouche *of Middle Clayton*, i. 176.
Greville, Earl of Warwick, i. 267.
Grey de Ruthyn (*Great Brickhills*), iv. 60.
Grubb *of Princes Risborough*, ii. 444.
Grubb *of Horsenden*, ii. 332.
Gulafre *of Quainton*; see Golafre.
Gyll *of Wyrardisbury*, iv. 598.
Gyll *of Buckland and Wyddiall Hall, co. Herts., of Yeoveny Hall, co. Midd., and of Wyrardisbury Hall, co. Bucks*, iv. 606.
Hale (*Iver*); see Tower.
Hampden *of Great and Little Hampden, &c.* ii. 302.
Hampden, Trevor-, Viscount Hampden, ii. 296.
Hampden (*Great Missenden*), ii. 374.
Hampden (*Kingsey*); see Marney.
Handlo (*Boarstall*); see Fitz Nigel.
Hanmer *of Simpson*, ii. 341.
Harcourt *of Ankerwycke*, iv. 589.
Harrison (*Ickford*); see Danvers.
Hassel *of Wyrardisbury*, iv. 604.

Hastings (*Aston Clinton*); see Montacute.

Haversham (*Haversham*), iv. 187, 188.

Hawtrey (*Ellesborough*); see Thurbane.

Hawtrey *of Hedsor, &c.* iii. 212.

Hayton *of Bledlow;* see Blanks.

Herbert *of Kinsey,* and Wenman and Wykeham *of Tythorp,* i. 297.

Hertford, Earls of, (*Clare*); see Giffard.

Hertford, Viscounts; see Devereux.

Hertford, Earls of; see Bohun.

Hervey; see Bellâ Aquâ.

Hervey and Chernocke (*Chilton and Easington*), i. 132.

Hickman *of Aylesbury,* ii. 52.

Hoare *of Walton and Wavendon,* iv. 390.

Hobart and Hobart-Hampden, Earls of Buckinghamshire, ii. 276.

Hoby (*Wyrardisbury*); see Stonor.

Hood (*Ickford*), i. 280.

Hood (*Ickford*); see Danvers.

Hopkins *of Oving,* and Northey-Hopkins, i. 377.

Hughes *of Quainton,* i. 402.

Ingoldsby *of Waldridge, &c.* ii. 169.

Iwardby (*Quainton*); see Golafre.

Jeffreys (*Hedgerley*), iv. 505.

Jekyll (*Stoke Goldington*), iv. 356.

Jenkinson (*Ludgershall*), i. 315.

Jervoise (*Shalston*), iii. 71.

King *of Wyrardisbury;* see Sharowe.

King *of Wormenhall,* i. 585.

Knapp *of Linford,* iv. 231.

Knollys *of Nether Winchendon, and of Thame, co. Oxon.* i. 527.

Lake (*Aston Clinton*); see Montacute.

Lane and Pigot *of Hogshaw,* i. 266.

Latimer (*Crawley*); see Ap Rees.

Lee and Duncumbe or Duncombe *of East Clayton,* i. 163.

Lee *of Hartwell,* ii. 307, 309.

Lee *of Quarendon,* Earls of Litchfield, ii. 404.

Lewis (*Boarstall*); see Fitz Nigel.

Lipping *of Shabbington,* i. 450.

Litchfield, Earls of; see Lee *of Quarendon.*

Longueville *of Wolverton,* iv. 415.

Louet, Lovet, or Lovett *of Liscombe,* iii. 457.

Lovell, and Badcock and Lovell (*Bledlow*), ii. 115.

Lovell *of Woburn,* iii. 634.

Lowndes andSelby(*Winslow*),iii.544.

Lucy, Vaux, Corbet, Percy, Throgmorton and Giffard *of Fulbrook,* i. 271.

Lucy (*Haversham*), iv. 188.

Lynford (*Sherrington*); see Sherrington.

Mackworth and Praed (*Tyringham*), iv. 378.

Mandeville, Say, Fitz Piers, and De Burgh (*East Clayton*), i. 158.

Marlborough, Dukes of; see Churchill.

Marney *of Kingsey,* allied with Burghersh, Chaucer, Hampden, &c. i. 295.

Martyn *of Ludgershall,* i. 310.

Martyn *of Nether Winchendon, and of Pertenhall, co. Bedford,* i. 529.

Mead *of Prince's Risborough,* ii. 444.

Minshull *of Bourton, &c.* ii. 590.

Missenden or Nowers (*Great Missenden*), ii. 365.

Missenden (*Quainton*); see Golafre.

Molins *of Stoke Poges,* iv. 547.

Monchensie (*Marsworth*), iii. 410.

Monchensy (*Dinton*), ii. 141.

Montacute, Nevill, Plantagenet, Pole, Hastings, Barrington, Gerard, and Lake Viscounts Lake (*Aston-Clinton*), ii. 75.

Morland, Bernard-; see Bernard-Morland.

Mortimer (*Crendon*), i. 203.

Mortimer. (*East Clayton*); see De Burgh.

Moyle *of Caversfield,* ii. 595.

Mulso (*Gayhurst*); see Nowers.

Murroy *of Stanhope;* see Smijth.

Musard (*Quainton*), i. 398.

Nevill, see Montacute.

Nevill (*Gayhurst*); see Nowers.

Newmarch, Braose, &c. (*Crendon*), i. 202.

Neyrnut; see Bellâ-Aquâ.

Norris, Williams, and Bertie (*Notley Abbey*), i. 233.

Northampton, Earls of; see Bohun.

Northey, Hopkins- ; see Hopkins.
Nowers (*Great Missenden*) ; see Missenden.
Nowers, Nevile, and Mulsho (*Gayhurst*), iv. 143.
Olney (*Weston Underwood*), iv. 398.
Ormonde, Earls of; see Butler.
Ouseley (*Beconsfield*), iii. 188.
Paganel (*Newport Pagnell*), iv. 275.
Pakington *of Aylesbury*, ii. 14.
Penn (*Stoke Poges*), iv. 555.
Percy *of Fulbrook ;* see Lucy.
Peyvre (*Lavendon*), iv. 210.
Plantagenet (*Aston Clinton*) ; see Montacute.
Plantagenet (*East Clayton*) ; see De Burgh.
Pigot *of Ickford and of Aston Rowant, co. Oxon.* i. 278.
Pigot or Pigott *of Chetwynd, co. Salop, and of Doddershall, co. Bucks,* i. 409.
Pigot *of Colwich in Waddesdon,* i. 486.
Pigot *of Doddershall,* i. 406.
Pigot *of Beachampton,* ii. 527.
Pigot *of Beachampton and Loughton,* iv. 237.
Pigot *of Hogshaw ;* see Lane.
Pigott *of Shenley,* iv. 326.
Pigott *of Chetwynd,* &c.; see Pigot.
Pote ; see Montacute.
Proctor (*Iver*) ; see Tower.
Purefoy and Jervoise (*Shalston*), iii. 71.
Rede (*Boarstall*) ; see Fitz Nigel.
Redman *of Oving,* i. 375.
Redvers, Avenel, and Courtenay, Earls of Devonshire, i. 466.
Revett (*Ellesborough*) ; see Thurbane.
Reynolds *of Prince's Risborough ;* see Stone.
Risley *of Chetwode and Barton,* iii. 3.
Russell (*Ellesborough*), ii. 194.
Russell *of Chenies,* Earls and Dukes of Bedford, iii. 248.
Russell *of Chequer's Court,* ii. 195.
Ruthall of Moulsoe, &c., iv. 416.
Sackville *of Fawley,* iii. 560.
Saunders *of Pitchcott,* i. 385.
Sauuders *of North Marston,* i. 336.
Say (*East Clayton*) ; see Mandeville.
Selby (*Whaddon*), iii. 497.

Selby (*Winslow*) ; see Lowndes.
Seymour *of Langley,* iv. 533.
Sharowe, allied with King (*Wyrardisbury*), iv. 620.
Sherrington, Lynford, Butler, and Ardes (*Sherrington*), iv. 334.
Smijth *of Hill Hall, co. Essex,* Wyndham *of Norfolk,* Fleming, Earls of Wigtoun, and Murray *of Stanhope,* allied with Gyll *of Wyrardisbury, and of Shenley, Herts.* iv. 598.
Smijth *of Great Linford,* iv. 223.
Snell (*Ickford*) ; see Danvers.
Snell (*Brill*), i. 102.
Spencer, Earls, iii. 342.
Spencer, Earls of Sunderland, i. 565.
Spigurnell (*Quainton*) ; see Golafre.
Stafford ; see Talbot.
Stafford ; see Vere.
Stafford ; see Basset.
St. Amand, Beauchamp, and West (*Grendon Underwood*), i. 255.
Stanhope, Earls of Chesterfield, i. 479.
Stanhope, Earls Stanhope, iii. 379.
Stone *of Princes Risborough,* allied with Mead, Grubb, and Reynolds, ii. 444.
Stonor, Hoby, and Walshe (*Wyrardisbury*), iv. 609.
St. Walery (*Studley*), i. 367.
Sunderland, Earls of ; see Spencer.
Sullivan (*Iver*), iv. 519.
Tash (*Iver*), iv. 530.
Talbot, Valence, and Stafford (*Policott*), i. 27.
Temple *of Stowe,* iii. 85.
Thompson Baron Haversham, iv. 188.
Throgmorton *of Fullbrook ;* see Lucy.
Throgmorton (*Weston Underwood*), iv. 399.
Thurbane, allied with Hawtrey, Croke, Cutts, Revett, and Russell (*Ellesborough*), ii. 194.
Tipping *of Shabington and Wormenhall,* i. 450.
Tower, allied with Hale, Proctor, Tash, Baker, and Beauchamp *of Iver,* iv. 530.
Tracy (*Worminghall*), i. 575.
Trelawney and Trelawney-Brereton (*Quainton*), i. 400.

Trevor and Trevor-Hampden, Viscount Hampden, &c. ii. 296.
Turville *of Weston Turvile*, ii. 493.
Tyringham *of Nether Winchenden;* see Goodywn.
Tyringham (*Tyringham*), iv. 373.
Tyrrel or Tyrrell *of Thornton*, iii. 119.
Tyrrell *of Oakley*, i. 352.
Vachell (*North Marston*), i. 336.
Valence ; see Talbot.
Vaux *of Fulbrook;* see Lucy.
Vere, Drayton, Green, and Stafford (*Ashendon*), i. 29.
Verney *of Fleet Marston*, Viscounts Fermanagh, Earls of Verney, &c. i. 178.
Verney *of Middle Clayton*, i. 184.
Verney ; see Abell.
Vernon (*Pitchcott*), i. 383.
Wake (*Crawley*), iv. 126.
Waller *of Beaconsfield*, iii. 182.
Walshe (*Wyrardisbury*), iv. 609.
Warren, Borlase- ; see Burlacy.
Warwick, Earls of ; see Greville.
Waterhouse (*Whitchurch*), iii. 512.

Webb *of Stoke Mandeville*, ii. 450.
Wenman, allied with Giffard *of Twyford*, iii. 131.
Wenman *of Tythorp ;* see Herbert.
West (*Grendon Underwood*) ; see St. Amand.
Wharton *of Winchendon and Wooburn*, i. 543.
Whitbread *of Bledlow;* see Blanks.
Whittewrong *of Stanton Barry*, iv. 347.
Wilkes (*Aylesbury*), ii. 44.
Williams (*Notley Abbey*) ; see Norris.
Willis, Browne-, iv. 11.
Wiltshire, Earls of ; see Boteler.
Winlowe *of Nether Winchendon ;* see Goodwin.
Wotton (*Eton*), iv. 480.
Wrighte (*Gayhurst*), iv. 151.
Wykeham *of Tythorp ;* see Herbert.
Wyndham *of Norfolk (Wyrardisbury)*, iv. 598.
Zouche *of Middle Clayton ;* see Greseley.

11.—County Genealogies. Pedigrees of Buckinghamshire Families. By WILLIAM BERRY. London, 1837, folio. (*Published with Berks and Surrey.*)

Albini, 65.
Alesburge, 20.
Alford, 82.
Allen, 5.
Alta Ripa, 38.
Andrews, 47.
Awbrey, 87.
Bagot, 15.
Barker, 95.
Blackwell, 24.
Boteler, 11.
Boseville or Boswell, 32.
Bromley, 86.
Brudenell, 16.
Bulleyne, 21.
Burlacy, 81.
Bexley, Lord, 52.
Carington, 83.
Cave, 10.
Chanworth, 20.
Cheney, 20.
Chester, 10.

Clayton, 77.
Clifford, 17.
Colet, 46.
Croke, 39.
Cromwell, 9, 40.
Dashwood, 98.
Dawney, 60.
Dayvell, 18.
Duffield, 45.
Duncombe, 92, 100, 102.
Eagles, 95.
Fines, 95.
Fitzmaurice, 59.
Fox, 78.
Gardiner, 95.
Goodwin, 71.
Gorges, 63.
Gray, 18.
Greenhill, 41.
Grenville, 86.
Guldeford, 2.
Hamilton, 59.

c

Hampden, 9.
Hastings, 18.
Hawtrey, 38.
Hippesley, 80.
Howard, 63.
King, 99.
Lechmere, 99.
Mackworth, 28.
Mowbray, 63, 65.
May, 48.
Neale, 53.
Norfolk, Duke of, 21.
Orkney, Earl of, 59.
Ouseley, 63.
Pabenham, 19.
Pauncefort, 101.
Penn, 73.
Perrott, 95.
Peyton, 11.
Phipps, 6.
Pinfold, 31.
Praed, 28.

Rokes, 82.
Russell, 37.
Sackville, 82.
Segrave, 62.
Smith, 83.
Smyth, 42.
Stokes, 1.
Stonhouse, 53.
Swabey, 56.
Thurban, 39.
Tipping, 81.
Tyrringham, 18.
Van Sittart, 51.
Uthwatt, 49.
Waller, 16.
Wallur, 1.
Warren, 80.
West, 96.
Wharton, Lord, 71.
Wilcocks, 48.
Windsor, 47.
Wollaston, 11.

12.—Ædes Hartwellianæ, or Notices of the Manor and Mansion of Hartwell. By Captain W. H. SMYTH, R.N., K.S.F., D.C.L., F.R.S., &c. *London*, 1851, 4to. (*Privately printed*).

Lee of *Hartwell*, 96.

13.—The History of Wraysbury, &c. co. Bucks. By GORDON WILLOUGHBY JAMES GYLL, ESQ. *London*, 1862, 4to.

Apsley and Bathurst, 281.
Ashbrook, 91.
Atkinson; see Scawen.
Aubrey and Carter, 229.
Bathurst; see Apsley.
Blagrove, 24.
Blount, 234.
Blunt; see Scawen.
Bowser, 234.
Brecknock; see Stonor.
Brierwood, 227.
Brome; see Sandford.
Brudenell of *Stoke Mandeville*, 206.
Buckingham, 273.
Bulstrode and Croke, 217.
Burnel, 13.
Carleton, 95.
Carter; see Aubrey.
Conyers; see Lee.

Croke; see Bulstrode.
De Walden, 9.
Digby, 209.
Fleming, Earl of Wigtoun, 101.
Fray, 16.
Gaynsford and Whethill, 205.
Goade, 284.
Gosset, 230.
Gould, 75.
Gyll, 99, 125.
Hale; see Tower.
Harcourt and Powell, 128.
Harcourt of *Ankerwycke*, 45.
Hassell, 77.
Hearne, 233.
Howard; see Vere.
Howard, Wyndham, and Smyth of *Hill Hall*, 102.
Irby, Lord Boston, 78.

Jodrell ; see Lee.
Kederminster, 89.
King ; see Sharowe.
Knyvett, 212.
Lee, Conyers, Jodrell, Nourse, and Weyland, 23.
Meale, 282.
Milton, 242.
Montagu and Scott, 69.
Mountfitchet, 6.
Neville, 82.
Nicholls ; see Salter.
Nicholls ; see Urwin.
Norris of Wraysbury, 17.
Nourse ; see Lee.
Norwode ; see Vere.
Oxenbridge, 64.
Paulet, 15.
Peters ; see Salter.
Pitt, 274.
Powell and Ringer, 86.
Powell ; see Harcourt.
Pynchon. 21.
Ringer ; see Powell.

Salter, 43.
Salter, Peters, Nicholls and Slocomb, 233.
Sandford and Brome, 22.
Scawen, Blunt, and Atkinson, 223.
Scott; see Montagu.
Sharowe with King, 19.
Shorter, 275.
Slocomb ; see Salter.
Smijth ; see Howard.
Smijth of Ankerwycke, and Hill Hall, Essex, 41.
Spencer, 29.
Stonor and Brecknock, 59.
Tower and Hale, 62.
Trumball, 71.
Tyrrell, 236.
Unwin and Nicholls, 83.
Vere, Norwode, Howard, &c. 7.
Weyland ; see Lee.
Williams, 228.
Windsor, 208.
Whethill ; see Gaynsford.
Wyndham ; see Howard.

CAMBRIDGESHIRE.

14.—The History and Antiquities of the Conventual and Cathedral Church of Ely, &c. By JAMES BENTHAM, M.A., &c. *London*, 2nd ed. *Norwich*, 1812, 4to.

Bentham, 2 ed. folding at 20.

15.—The History and Antiquities of Barnewell Abbey, and of Sturbridge Fair. (No. 38, Bibliotheca Topographica Britannica.) *London*, 1786, 4to.

Butler, 9, Appendix.

16.—The Cambridgeshire Visitation. By HENRY ST. GEORGE, 1619, from MSS. Phillipps, No. 63. Edited by Sir T. P. Bart (Sir THOMAS PHILLIPPS, Bart). *Typis, Medio Montanus*, 1840, fcap. folio.

Adam, of Tidd St. Giles.
Allen and Bettes of Chateriz.
Alington of Batersham.
Amy of Abbington.
Arkinstall of Ely.
Aunger.
Ayre of the Isle of Ely.
Backus of Trumpington.
Ball.

Barnes of Some.
Barret of Chippenham and Deforden.
Barrow.
Bettes ; see Allen.
Buck of Wisbeach.
Borough of Borough Greene.
Brakyn of Chesterton.
Buckworth of Wisbeach.
Butler of Fendrayton.

Burgoyne *of Long Stanton.*
Bury *of Mildreth.*
Carleton *of Linton.*
Cage *of Long Stanton.*
Castell *of Cambridge.*
Castell *of East Hatley.*
Cuttes *of Benigbery.*
Chalderton *of Queen's College, Cambridge.*
Chamberlayn *of Gedding.*
Chapman *of Ely.*
Chapman *of Wickham.*
Creke *of Cartlinge.*
Chicheley *of Wynpull*
Colvile *of Tadlowe.*
Colvile *of Newton.*
Daye *of Wisbeach.*
Cotton *of Cotton Landwade, Swafham, &c.*
Craye *of Wichford.*
Hastings *of Landwade.*
Drurey *of Swafham.*
Cracroft *of Cotenham.*
Dalton *of West Wratting.*
Edwards *of Wisbiche.*
Dockwra *of Foulbourne.*
Flower *of Ely.*
Foxton *of Cambridge.*
Gardner *of Histon*
Fincham *of Outwell.*
Fitz *of Elsworth.*
Gervais *of Ely.*
Glapthorne *of Whittlesey.*
Goodrick *of Ely.*
Goodwyn *of Stonham.*
Gouldwell *of Wisbiche.*
Gouldwell *of Magna Shelford*
Gottes.
Grange *of Swafham.*
Hagger *of Bourne.*
Hall *of Stretham.*
Hamond *of Winchingham.*
Harvey *of Cambridge.*
Hatley *of Cotton.*
Hawford *of Cambridge.*
Higham *of Ely.*
Holland *of Ely.*
Holford *of Stepford.*
Holmes *of Borough.*
Holte *of Samston (Sawston).*
Hound *of Cambridge.*
Humphrey *of Burrough.*
Hudleston *of Cambridge.*

Ithell *of Cambridge.*
Jarvis *of Pracling.*
Jawdrell *of Sutton.*
Kempton *of Mordon.*
Larkyn *of Cambridge.*
Latham *of Papworth.*
Lawrence *of Cambridge.*
Leedes *of Croxton.*
Leetes *of Kingston.*
Legge *of Cambridge.*
Lound *of Tokesford.*
Love *of Wisbich.*
Lund *of Shelford.*
Lynne *of Bassingbourne.*
Mallory *of Papworth.*
Maningham *of Fendrayton.*
March *of Ely.*
Martyn *of Steple Mordon.*
Massey *of Ely.*
Meade *of Cambridge.*
Nightingall *of Knesworth.*
Norton *of Hinxton.*
Orrell *of Ely.*
Pepis *of Cotenham.*
Parris *of Little Linton.*
Parsonne *of Wisbish.*
Payton *of Isham.*
Pelsett *of Milton.*
Perne *of Cambridge.*
Piers *of Cambridge.*
Pigot *of Allington.*
Pledgerd *of Bostham (Bottesham ?).*
Pooley *of Cambridge.*
Potkyn *of Skleton (sic).*
Proctor *of Wisbich.*
Rivett *of Chippenham.*
Rudston *of Ely.*
Sandford *of Wisbich.*
Sandes *of Wilverton.*
Sgargill *of Knockwell (Knapwell ?).*
Scriven *of Stapleford.*
Sedgwick *of Wisbish.*
Shutes *of Hollington (?).*
Sewster *of Steple Morden.*
Sherman *of Littleington.*
Slegge *of Cambridge.*
Sterne *of Stokequi.*
Stokes *of Cambridge.*
Stotevill *of Brinkley.*
Steward *of Stantney.*
Sutton *of Durford.*
Symonds *of Wittlesford.*
St. George *of Hatley St. George.*

Taver, or Taber *of Cambridge.*
Taylor *of Wisbich.*
Taylor *of Stret Church.*
Thornton *of Some.*
Thorold *of Chesterton.*
Tilney *of Wisbich.*
Towers *of Ely.*
Trowle *of Linton.*
Turpin *of Bassingborne.*
Ventris *of Hokington.*

Vescy *of Islam.*
Walter *of Crawdon.*
Ward *of Little Abbington.*
Watson *of Conington.*
Webbe *of Botesham.*
Wendy *of Haslingfield.*
Wilbore *of Foxton.*
Wilkes *of Wisbich.*
Wise *of Hinton.*
Wood *of Foulbourne.*

CHESHIRE.

17.—The History of the County Palatine and City of Chester, &c. &c. By GEORGE ORMEROD, LL.D., F.R.S., and F.S.A. *London,* 1819, 3 vols. folio.

Aldelym; see De Aldelym.
Aldersey *of Aldersey,* ii. 404.
Allen *of Brindley,* iii. 196.
Alport *of Overton,* ii. 368.
Antrobus *of Antrobus,* i. 487.
Ardern *of Dorfold,* iii. 183.
Arderne, ii. 134, 135.
Arderne *of Timperley,* i. 413.
Arderne *of Aldford, Alvanley and Harden,* ii. 41.
Arderne and Stanley *of Aldford and Elford,* iii. 301.
Ashley *of Ashley,* i. 419.
Ashton *of Hefferston Grange;* see Warburton.
Astbury *of Astbury;* see Somerford.
Aston *of Aston,* i. 535.
Baggiley *of Baggiley,* i. 415.
Barnston *of Churton,* ii. 408.
Baskervyle *of Old Withrington,* iii. 355.
Bebington *of Bebington,* ii. 251.
Beeston *of Beeston,* ii. 145.
Bellst *of Great Moreton;* see Moreton.
Berington *of Bradwell;* see Venables.
Birchles *(Birtles),* iii. 353.
Bird *of Broxton,* ii. 371.
Birkenhead *of Glegg and Backford,* ii. 199.
Bold *of Upton,* ii. 266.
Booth *of Twemlowe,* iii. 78.
Booth *of Mollington,* ii. 207.
Booth *of Dunham Massey,* i. 406.

Booth *(Honford and Bosden),* iii. 325.
Bostock *of Bostock,* iii. 135.
Boydell *of Dodleston and Gropenhall,* ii. 458.
Boydell *of Pulcroft,* iii. 190.
Bradshaw and Isherwood *of Marple and Wyberslegh,* iii. 408.
Bradwell *of Bradwell,* iii. 65.
Brereton *of Shocklach and Malpas,* ii. 377.
Brereton *of Ashley,* i. 418.
Brereton *of Tatton,* i. 346.
Brereton *of Wettenhall and Eccleston,* ii. 106.
Brereton *of Honford;* see Honford.
Brereton and Holt *of Brereton,* iii. 51.
Brock *of Upton,* ii. 404.
Bromley *of Hampton,* ii. 358.
Bromley *of Badington,* iii. 195.
Brooke *of Mere,* i. 360.
Brooke *of Norton,* i. 504.
Brooke *of Leighton,* iii. 241.
Broughton *of Doddington;* see Delves.
Bruen *of Bruen Stapleford,* ii. 175.
Bruen *of Tarvin,* ii. 166.
Bruen and Oliver (Appendix), iii. 446.
Bulkeley *of Eaton and Alstanton,* iii. 138.
Bulkeley *of Bulkeley,* ii. 363.
Bunbury *of Bunbury and Stanney,* ii. 216.
Burganey *of Pulford,* ii. 462.
Caldecote *of Caldecote,* ii. 380.

Calveley *of Lea*, ii. 419.
Calveley and Davenport *of Calveley*, ii. 153.
Carington *of Carington*, i. 412.
Catheral *of Horton*, ii. 188.
Chanu (*Willaston*), iii. 256.
Chester, Saxon and Norman Earls of, i. 47.
Chetwode *of Agden and Nether Whitley*, i. 489.
Cholmondeley *of Holford*, i. 496.
Cholmondeley *of Cholmondeley*, ii. 356.
Cholmondeley *of Vale Royal*, ii. 78.
Clieveland and Price *of Birkenhead*, ii. 257.
Clive *of Huxley*; see Huxley.
Coghull *of Coghull*, ii. 442.
Coudray (*Worleston*), iii. 189.
Corona; see De Corona.
Cottingham *of Little Neston*, ii. 298.
Cotton *of Cotton Edmunds*, ii. 428.
Cotton *of Combermere*, iii. 212.
Cotton (Appendix), iii. 449.
Cotton *of Cotton*, iii. 72.
Cowper *of Chester and Overleigh*, i. 293.
Cranach, Ermitage, Haslington, and Winnington *of Hermitage*, iii. 74.
Crewe *of Crewe*, iii. 169.
Crewe *of Aston in Mondrem*, iii. 193.
Crue (*Worleston*), iii. 189.
Croxton *of Ravenscroft*, iii. 111.
Croxton and Mainwaring *of Croxton*, iii. 114.
Croxton and Egerton-Warburton *of Norley*, ii. 68.
Currie *of Boughton*; see Davenport.
Daniel *of Tabley*, i. 365.
Daniell *of Daresbury*, i. 540.
Davenport *of Calveley*; see Calveley.
Davenport, Hand, Foulkes and Currie *of Boughton*, ii. 421.
Davenport *of Davenport*, iii. 39.
Davenport *of Chorley*, iii. 312.
Davenport *of Henbury*, iii. 352.
Davenport *of Woodford*, iii. 346.
Davenport *of Wheltrough*, iii. 357.
Davenport *of Bramhall*, iii. 401.
Davis or Davies (*Marton*), iii. 359.
De Aldelym (*Audlem*), iii. 246.
De Corona (*Adlington*), iii. 332.

Delves and Broughton *of Doddington*, iii. 268.
De Masey-Massie (*Backford*), ii. 198.
Dod *of Broxton*, ii. 370.
Dod *of Edge*, ii. 374.
Dod *of Shocklach*, ii. 378.
Domville *of Brunstath and Oxton*, ii. 240.
Domville *of Lymme*, i. 436.
Done *of Crowton*, ii. 64.
Done *of Utkinton, Flaxyards and Duddon*, ii. 133.
Downes *of Downes and Taxal*; and Downes *of Shrigley and Worth*, iii. 379.
Drake *of Malpas and Shardeloes*, ii. 334.
Duckenfield *of Duckenfield*, iii. 397.
Dutton *of Dutton*, i. 476.
Dutton *of Hatton*, and Hatton *of Hatton*, ii. 433.
Dyve; see Wydville.
Eaton *of Eaton*, and Grosvenor *of Eaton*, ii. 454.
Egerton *of Tatton*, i. 348.
Egerton *of Egerton*, ii. 350.
Egerton Grey, *of Egerton and Oulton*, ii. 118.
Egerton *of Ridley*, ii. 162.
Egerton *of Warburton*; see Croxton.
Elcocke and Massey *of Whitepoole*, iii. 188.
Elton and Frodsham *of Elton*, ii. 22.
Ermitage *of Hermitage*; see Crewe.
Feilden *of Mollington*, ii. 206.
Fitton *of Bollin and Dunham*, i. 400.
Fitton *of Pownall*, and Newton *of Newton and Pownall*, iii. 310.
Fitton *of Bollin*, and Fitton *of Gawsworth*, iii. 292.
Ford *of Ford Green, co. Stafford*, and Ford *of Abbey Field, co. Chester*, iii. 59.
Foulkes *of Broughton*; see Davenport.
Frodsham *of Elton*; see Elton.
Fulleshurst *of Crewe and Baithomley*; see Praers.
Gamul *of Buerton*, iii. 250.
Gamul *of Crabwall*, ii. 318.
Gerard *of Riddings*, i. 414.

Gerard, Lords Gerard *of Gerards Bromley*, i. 483.
Gerard *of Kingsley*, ii. 61.
Gerard *of Crewood*, ii. 61.
Glasier *of Lea*, ii. 209.
Glegg *of Grange*, ii. 270.
Glegg *of Gayton*, ii. 285.
Golborne *of Overton*, ii. 369.
Grafton, Milneton, and Massey *of Grafton*, ii. 387.
Green *of Poulton Lancelyn*; see Lancelyn.
Gregg *of Hapsford and Bradley*, ii. 24.
Grey, *Earl of Stamford*, i. 406.
Grey-Egerton; see Egerton.
Griffin *of Barterton*, iii. 258.
Grosvenor *of Eaton*; see Eaton.
Grosvenor *of Little Budworth*, ii. 116.
Grosvenor *of Hulme*, and Shakerley *of Hulme and Somerford*, iii. 87.
Hall *of Hermitage*, iii. 74.
Hand *of Broughton*; see Davenport.
Harcourt *of Wincham*, i. 465.
Hardware *of Peele and Bromborough*, ii. 181.
Haslington *of Hermitage*; see Crewe.
Hassal *of Hassal*, iii. 159.
Hatton *of Hatton*; see Dutton.
Haughton *of Haughton*, ii. 157.
Hellesby *of Hellesby*, ii. 35.
Henry *of Hefferston Grange*, ii. 94.
Henshaw *of Henshaw*; see Thornycroft.
Hibbert *(Marple)*, iii. 407.
Hinton *of Rushton*, ii. 131.
Hockenhull *of Duddon*, ii. 171.
Hockenhull *of Prenton*, ii. 293.
Hockenhull *of Hockenhull and Shotwick*, ii. 171.
Holcroft *of Vale Royal*, ii. 75.
Holford *of Holford*, i. 494.
Holford *of Davenham*, iii. 127.
Hollinshed *of Hollinshed*, iii. 375.
Holme *of Tranmore*, ii. 253.
Holt *of Brereton*; see Brereton.
Holt *of Wimbaldsley and Newton*, iii. 116.
Honford and Brereton *of Honford*, iii. 327.
Hooton *of Hooton*, ii. 228.

Hough *of Leighton and Thornton Hough*, ii. 304.
Hough (Appendix), iii. 447.
Hulgreve *of Minshull-Vernon*, iii. 118.
Hulse *of Norbury*, iii. 245.
Hurleston *of Hurleston, Picton, and Newton*, ii. 441.
Huxley, Clive, and Tilston *of Huxley*, ii. 435.
Hyde *of Norbury and Hyde*, iii. 394.
Isherwood; see Bradshaw.
Jodrell *of Yeardsley*, iii. 282.
Kelsall *of Bradshaw*, iii. 323.
Kingsley *of Kingsley*, ii. 44.
Lancelyn *of Poulton*, and Green of *Poulton and Lancelyn*, ii. 248.
Latham *of Bradwell*, iii. 66.
Lathom or Latham *of Astbury and Congleton*, iii. 14.
Lawton *of Lawton*, iii. 11.
Leche *of Mollington*, ii. 207.
Leche *of Carden*, ii. 385.
Lee *of Lea*, afterwards *of Dernhall and Wincham*, and Townshend *of Wincham*, i. 466.
Legh *of Baggiley*, i. 415.
Legh *of East Hall*, i. 358.
Legh *of Knutsford Booths*, i. 383.
Legh *of Adlington*, iii. 333.
Legh *of Lyme*, iii. 338.
Legh *of Ridge*, iii. 374.
Leicester *of Tabley*; see Wylme.
Leigh *of Oughtrington*, i. 439.
Leigh *of West Hall*, i. 356.
Leftwich *of Leftwich*, i. 465.
Leftwich *of Leftwich*, iii. 140.
Leversage *of Whelock*, iii. 140.
Leycester *of Toft*, i. 388.
Leycester *of Nether Tabley*, i. 456.
Littler *of Wallerscote*, ii. 66.
Lostock *of Lostock Gralam*, i. 494.
Lowe *of Moreton and Wood*, iii. 99.
Lymme *of Lymme*, i. 352.
Mainwaring *of Over Pevver*, i. 373.
Mainwaring *of Bromborough*, ii. 239.
Mainwaring *of Croxton*, iii. 114.
Mainwaring and Trussel *of Warmincham*, iii. 122.
Maisterson *of Nantwich*, iv. 231.
Mallory *of Mobberley*, i. 329.
Malpus *of Hampton and Bickley*, ii. 358.

Manley *of Manley*, ii. 49.
Manwaring *of Merton;* see Merton.
Manwaring *of Kermincham*, iii. 46.
Marbury *of Marbury*, i. 470.
Massey *of Rosthorne*, i. 342.
Massey *of Dunham Massey*, i. 398.
Massey *of Tatton*, i. 344.
Massey *of Sale*, i. 424.
Massey *of Podington*, ii. 308.
Massey *of Broxton*, ii. 372.
Massey *of Grafton;* see Grafton.
Massey *of Whitepoole;* see Elcocke.
Massey *of Audlem and Denfield*, iii. 247.
Massie *of Coddington*, ii. 399.
Massie; see De Masey.
Massy *(Hough)*, iii. 259.
Meoles *of Meoles*, ii. 272.
Merbury *of Walton*, i. 542.
Mere *of Mere*, i. 362.
Meredith *of Henbury and Ashley*, iii. 352.
Merton *of Merton*, and Manwaring *of Merton*, ii. 96.
Millington *of Millington*, i. 349.
Milneton *of Grafton;* of Grafton.
Minshull *of Erdswick Hall*, iii. 118.
Minshull *of Minshull*, iii. 181.
Mobberley *of Mobberley*, i. 326.
Montalt, Barons of, i. 55, 148.
Moreton and Bellot *of Great Moreton*, iii. 25.
Moreton *of Moreton*, iii. 29.
Moreton, iii. 99.
Newnham *of Thornton*, ii. 14.
Newton *of Newton and Pownall;* see Fitton.
Nuthal *of Cattenal*, ii. 47.
Oldfield *of Bradwell;* see Venables.
Oldfield *of Somerford;* see Somerford.
Oliver (Appendix), iii. 446.
Olton *of Wrenbury;* see Wrenbury.
Ormerod *of Chorlton*, ii. 204.
Orreby *of Gaworth*, iii. 290.
Oulton *of Oulton*, and Starkey *of Oulton*, ii. 104.
Page *of Erdsham and Drakelow*, iii. 95.
Poole *of Poole*, ii. 235.
Powel *of Birkenhead and Horsley*, ii. 256.

Praers *of Barthomley*, and Fullershurst *of Crewe and Barthomley*, iii. 162.
Prestland *of Prestland and Wardle*, ii. 155.
Price *of Birkenhead;* see Clieveland.
Pulford *of Pulford*, ii. 461.
Raby *of Raby*, ii. 302.
Rode *of Rode*, iii. 30.
Rope *of Rope and Stapeley;* see Stapeley.
Rutter *of Kingsley*, ii. 45.
Sandbach *of Sandbach*, iii. 56.
Savage, Earl Rivers, i. 530.
Savage *of Rock Savage*, i. 526.
Shakerley *of Shakerley, Hulme, and Somerford*, iii. 87.
Sherd *(Disley Stanley)*, iii. 403.
Smethwick *of Smethwick*, iii. 53.
Smith *of Oldhaugh*, iii. 123.
Smith *of Hough*, iii. 260.
Somerford *of Somerford*, iii. 297.
Somerford and Oldfield *of Somerford*, and Astbury *of Astbury*, iii. 33.
Spurstow *of Spurstow*, ii. 158.
Stanley *of Hooton and Storeton*, ii. 230.
Stanley *of Aldford and Elford;* see Arderne.
Stanley *of Alderley*, iii. 306.
Stapeley *of Rope*, and Rope *of Rope and Stapeley*, iii. 237.
Starkey *of Stretton*, i. 491.
Starkey *of Oulton;* see Oulton.
Starkey *of Wrenbury;* see Wrenbury.
Starkie *of Bamton, co. Chester*, and *of Huntroyde, co. Lanc.* i. 474.
Steele, iii. 450.
Stockton *of Stockton*, ii. 454.
Stokeport, Barons of, iii. 388.
Storeton *of Storeton*, ii. 250.
Sutton *of Sutton*, iii. 373.
Swetenham *of Somerford Booths*, iii. 298.
Swettenham *of Swettenham*, iii. 43.
Sylvester, iii. 447.
Swynnerton; see Whelton.
Tarleton *of Bolesworth*, ii. 372.
Tatten *of Withamshaw*, iii. 315.
Thornton *of Thornton*, ii. 15.
Thornycroft *of Thornycroft*, and Henshaw *of Henshaw*, iii. 362.
Thurstanton *of Thurstanton*, ii. 278.

Tilston *of Huxley*, ii. 435.
Titherington and Worth *of Tither-ington*, iii. 350.
Touchet *of Nether Whitley and Bug-lawton*, i. 489.
Townshend *of Wincham ;* see Lee.
Trafford *of Bridge Trafford*, ii. 30.
Trafford *of Knutsford*, i. 378.
Traylebew *(Audlem)*, iii. 246.
Troutbeck *of Dunham*, ii. 28.
Trussel *of Warmincham*, iii. 122.
Tuchett, iii. 144.
Tremlowe *of Arclyd*, iii. 69.
Vawdrey *of Riddings and Bank*, i. 414.
Venables *of Agden and Horton*, i. 409.
Venables *of Antrobus*, i. 487.
Venables and Venables-Vernon *of Kinderton*, iii. 106.
Venables Berington, and Oldfield *of Bradwell*, iii. 67.
Venables *of Bollin and Dunham*, i. 398.
Vernon, Venables- *of Kinderton ;* see Venables.
Vernon *of Shipbrook*, iii. 133.
Vernon *of Haslington*, iii. 171.
Walthall *of Wistaston*, iii. 178.
Warburton *of Warburton and Arley*, i. 430.
Warburton Egerton *of Norley ;* see Croxton.
Warburton, Henry, and Ashton *of Hefferston Grange*, ii. 94.
Ward *of Copesthorne*, iii. 358.
Wareing *of Ince*, ii. 13.
Warren *of Poynton*, iii. 353.

Waschet *(Church Coppenhall)*, iii. 174.
Wa-teneys *of Wincham and Tyrall*, i. 464.
Weever *of Weever*, ii. 114.
Weld *of Eaton*, ii. 131.
Werden *(Burton)*, ii. 179.
Wettenhall *of Hankelow*, iii. 251.
Wettenhall *of Wettenhall*, ii. 106.
Whelock and Leversage *of Whelock*, iii. 70.
Whitmore *of Thurstanton*, ii. 278.
Wicksted *of Nantwich*, iii. 233.
Wigland *of Wigland*, ii. 366.
Wilbraham *of Townsend and Dela-mere Lodge*, ii. 65.
Wilbraham *of Rode*, iii. 31.
Wilbraham *of Dorfold*, iii. 184.
Wilbraham *of Woodhey*, iii. 199.
Winnington *of Winnington*, ii. 112.
Winnington *of Hermitage ;* see Crewe.
Winnington *of Birches*, iii. 93.
Wood, iii. 99.
Woodnoth *of Shavinton*, iii. 262.
Worleston ; see Coudray.
Worth *of Titherington ;* see Tither-ington.
Wrenbury, Olton, and Starkey *of Wrenbury*, iii. 205.
Wright *of Offerton, Mottram, and Nantwich*, iii. 348.
Wright *of Bickley and Stretton*, ii. 389.
Wydville, Wylde, and Dyve, i. 160.
Wylme and Leigh *of Oughtrington*, i. 439.
Wynington *of Offerton*, iii. 402.

18.—The History of the Hundred of Wirral, with a Sketch of the City and County of Chester. BY WILLIAM WIL-LIAMS MORTIMER. *London*, 1847. 4to.

Cleveland and Parry-Price *of Birkenhead*, 321.

19.—Miscellanea Palatina. By GEORGE ORMEROD, Esq. D.C.L., F.R.S., &c. *Not published*. 1851, 8vo. *See also Lancashire.*

Arden *of Alvanley and Harden*, with Arden *of Walford, co. Northamp-ton ;* Arderne *of Aldford Castle, Cheshire, and Elford, Stafford-shire*, folding at 90.

De Montalt, 106.
Lathom *of Astbury, co. Cheshire*, folding at 68.

D

CORNWALL.

20.—The History of Cornwall. By the Rev. R. POLWHELE.
London, 1816. 7 vols. 4to.

Carmino, ii. facing 43.
Carnsew *of Bokelly in St. Kew,* iv.
facing 112.
Code *of Morvall,* iv. 112.
Courtenay, iv. 9.
Davies ; see Noye.
Flamock *of Bokarne,* ii. 44.
Haweis, Kempe, Tanner, Taunton,
Tregarthyn, Tregian, and Wol-
verton, iv. facing 112.
Kempe ; see Haweis.
Kestell *of Kestell,* ii. facing 43.
Lanion *of Lanion in Maderne,* ii.
facing 42.
Lower *of St. Winnow,* iv. facing 112.
Noye, Sandys and Davies, iv. fold-
ing at 94.

Polwhele *of Polwhele,* ii. facing 42.
Roscarrock *of Roscarrock,* ii. facing
42.
Sandys ; see Noye.
Tanner ; see Haweis.
Taunton ; see Haweis.
Tregian ; see Haweis.
Tregarthyn ; see Haweis.
Trefusis *of Trefusis,* ii. facing 42.
Trevanion *of Trevanion,* ii. facing
42.
Tucker, iv. facing 112.
Vyvyan *of Trevidren and Trelowa-
nen,* iii. facing 42.
Wolverton ; see Haweis.

21.—Visitation of Cornwall, made in the year 1620, by W.
CAMDEN and ST. GEORGE. (Edited by Sir NICHOLAS
HARRIS NICOLAS). Foolscap folio. Printed in 1838 ?

Aleigh, or Leigh, 1.
Arundell *of Trerice,* 1.
Arundell *of Lanherne,* 2.
Arundell *of Camborne,* 2.
Ayre, or Eyre, 3.
Barrett *of St. Tudy,* 3.
Barret, 4.
Bassett, 5.
Bastard, 5.
Battersby, 6.
Byll, 6.
Beauchamp *of Binnerton,* 7.
Beauchamp *of Chiton,* 8.
Bere *of Barlawren,* 9.
Bere *of Trevedo,* 9.
Bennet, 10.
Blackhall, 10.
Billinge, 11.
Blake, 12.
Bosavern, 12.

Bligh *of Botadon,* 13.
Bligh *of Bodmin,* 14.
Bond *of Holewode,* 15.
Bond *of Earth,* 16.
Bonithon, 17.
Boscawen, 18—20.
Bonatre, 21.
Bossawsach, 22.
Bosustowe, 23.
Bray, 24.
Bugan or Bogans, 24.
Buller, 25.
Burell, 26.
Burgess, 27.
Burvargus, 27.
Byrd, 28.
Carew *of Anthony,* 28.
Eyre ; see Ayre.
Leigh ; see Aleigh.

CUMBERLAND.

22.—The History and Antiquities of Cumberland, &c. By
WILLIAM HUTCHINSON, F.A.S. *Carlisle,* 1794. 2 vols.
4to.

Aglionby *of Nunnery,* i. 195. | Blencowe *of Blencowe,* i. 413.

Boyvill *de Levington*, ii. 568.
Brisco *(Thursby)*, ii. 459.
Brougham *(Brougham)*, i. 301.
Carleton *of Carleton Hall*, i. 340.
Christian *(Workington)*, ii. 146.
Curwen *of Workington*, ii. 143.
Dacre *of Lanercost*, i. 60.
Dacre *of Dacre*, i. 468.
Dacre *of Kirklevington*, ii. 568.
Dalston *of Dalston*, ii. 447.
Derwentwater *of Castle Rigg upon Derwent*, ii. 227.
Featherstonhaugh *(Kirkoswald)*, i. 207.
Fletcher *of Hutton in the Forest*, i. 508.
Graham *of Netherby*, ii. 531.
Greme *(Nunnery)*, i. 190.
Harrington *of Harrington*, ii. 101.
Hasell *of Dalemain*, i. 467.
Huddleston *of Millum*, i. 527.
Hudleston *of Hutton*, i. 416.
Howard *of Corby*, i. 165.

Howard, Duke of Norfolk, i. 353.
Hutton *of Hutton Hall*, i. 339.
Irton *(Irton)*, i. 573.
Kirkbride *(Hesket)*, i. 504.
Lamplugh *(Lamplugh)*, ii. 95.
Latus *of the Beck*, i. 530.
Lawson *of Osworth and Isel*, ii. 241.
Musgrave *of Edenhall*, i. 272.
Musgrave *of Hayton*, ii. 289.
Orfeur *(Plumbland)*, ii. 350.
Pattenson *(Melmerby)*, i. 218.
Pennington *(Muncaster)*, i. 566.
Porter *of Ulwardby*, and Porter *of Weary*, ii. 303.
Richmond *of Highhead Castle*, ii. 429.
Salkeld *of Whitehall*, ii. 360.
Skelton *of Armathwaite*, i. 494.
Stuteville *of Lyddal Barony*, ii. 528.
Threlkeld *(Melmerby)*, i. 218.
Tilliol *(Allhallows)*, ii. 359.
Wake, Lord of Wake, ii. 529.
Warwick *(Warwick)*, i. 154.

23.—The History and Antiquities of Cumberland. By SAMUEL JEFFERSON. *Carlisle*, 1840. 2 vols. 8vo. [Vol. I. Leath Ward, Vol. II. Allerdale Ward, above Derwent.]

Aglionby *of Nunnery*, i. 243.
Blencowe *of Blencow*, i. 383.
Boyvill or De Millom, ii. 152.
Carleton *of Carleton Hall*, i. 95.
Curwen *of Workington Hall*, ii. 251.
Dacre, i. 167, 175, 345.
Dacre *of the North*, 172.
Dacre *of the South*, 170.
De Millom ; see Boyvill.
Fetherstonhaugh *of Kirkoswald*, i. 290.
Fitz Duncan, ii. 36.
Fletcher *of Cockermouth and Hutton*, i. 427.
Fletcher-Vane *of Hutton and Armathwaite*, i. 430.
Graham *of Nunnery*, i. 239.
Harrington *of Harrington*, ii. 7.
Hasell *of Dalemain*, i. 193.
Howard, i. 346.
Hudleston *of Hutton John*, i. 372.
Hudleston, Lords of Millom, ii. 155.
Hutton *of Hutton Hall*, i. 89.
Irton *of Irton*, ii. 195.

Kirkbride *of Ellerton*, i. 217.
Lamplugh *of Lamplugh*, ii. 84, 437.
Latus *of the Beck*, ii. 172.
Lewthwaite *of Broadgate in Millom*, ii. 440.
Lowther, Earl of Lonsdale, ii. 369.
Lucy, ii. 37, 40.
Multon, ii. 38.
Musgrave *of Musgrave, Hentley and Edenhall*, i. 411.
Nevill, Earl of Westmorland, i. 68.
Pattenson *of Melmerby*, i. 302.
Pennington, Lord Muncaster, ii. 228.
Percy, ii. 49.
Ponsonby *of Ponsonby Hall*, ii. 435.
Seymour, ii. 45.
Skelton *of Armathwaite and Branthwaite*, i. 221.
Stanley *of Dalegarth and Ponsonby*, ii. 281.
Threlkeld *of Melmerby*, i. 300.
Vaux *of Catterlen*, i. 145.
Veteriponte, Lords of Alston, i. 112.
Wyndham, ii. 46.

24.—Heraldic Visitation of the Northern Counties in 1530, by THOMAS TONGE, Norroy, &c. *Surtees Society*, Vol. 41. 1863. 8vo. See *also Durham, Nottinghamshire, Northumberland, Yorkshire and Westmoreland.*

Curwen *of Camerton*, 97.
Curwyn. 100.
Lovell, 98.
Pekeryng *of Therkell*, 97.

Skelton *of Bramford*, 98.
Thoattes *of Thoattes*, 96.
Warcop *of Smordall*, 100.

DERBYSHIRE.

25.—An History of the Manor and Manor House of South Winfield, in Derbyshire. By THOMAS BLORE. (No. 3, Miscellaneous Antiquities, [Nichols]). *London*, 1791. 4to.

Ferrers, Earl of Derby, 13.
Halton, 78.

Leacroft, 73.
Peverel and Pavely, 81.

26.—The Peak Guide, &c. By STEPHEN GLOVER; edited by THOMAS NOBLE, Esq. *Derby*, 1830. 8vo.

Arkwright *of Willersley*, 122.
Cavendish, Duke of Devonshire, folding at 53.

Manners, Duke of Rutland, folding at 100.

27.—The History and Gazetteer of the County of Derby, &c. Collected by STEPHEN GLOVER; edited by THOMAS NOBLE, Esq. *Derby*, 1831-33. 2 vols. 4to.

Allsop *of Allsop in the Dale*, ii. folding at 21.
Allsop *of Burton*, ii. folding at 21.
Bainbrigge *of Lockington, co. Leicester, of Derby, and of Rochester and Woodseat, co. Stafford*, ii. 575.
Bagshaw *of Ford and Banner Cross*, ii. 245.
Bassano *of London, Hale End, co. Essex, Stone and Litchfield, co. Stafford, and Derby*, ii. 592.
Beaumont *of Gracedieu and Barrow*, ii. 97.
Bentinck ; see Cavendish.
Berkeley ; see Segrave.
Beresford *of Bentley Grange, Newton Grange, Ashbourn, &c.* ii. 46.
Boothby, Barts., ii. 43.
Borough *of Derby, and of Chetwynd Park, co. Salop*, ii. 581.
Bourne *of Ashover*, ii. facing 64.

Bowden *of Southgate House in Clown, and Beighton Fields in Barlborough*, ii. 338.
Bower and Potter *of Darley Hall*, ii. 391.
Bradshaw *of Barton Blount*, ii. 101.
Bradshaw *of Bradshaw, in Chapel in Frith*, ii. 248.
Bradshaw, ii. 249.
Browne *of Hungry Bentley and Chesterfield*, ii. 320.
Buckston *of Bradbourn*, ii. 155.
Burton *of Chesterfield, Dronfield, &c.* ii. 324.
Cavendish, Dukes of Devonshire, ii. 276.
Cavendish, Holles, Harley, and Bentinck, ii. 140.
Chadwick *of Callow, Ridware, &c.* ii. 220.
Chesterfield, Earls of; see Stanhope.

Cokaine *of Ashbourn*, ii. 41.
Cotton ; see Peche.
Cox *of Brailsford, Culland, Derby, and Spondon*, ii. 163.
Crewe *of Calke Abbey ;* see Harpur.
Crompton *of Derby*, ii. 593.
Curzon *of Croxall*, ii. 365.
Curzon *of Derby and Breedon,* `co. Leicester`, ii. 587.
Curzon ; see Dunne.
Dakeyne *of Darley in the Dale,* ii. 393.
Dale *of Ashbourn*, ii. 53.
Dale *of Nottingham and Wirkworth*, ii. 54.
Darwin *of Cleatham, co. Lincoln, Elston, co. Notts, and Breadsall Priory, co. Derby*, ii. 178.
Derby, Earls of, of the Royal House of Plantagenet, ii. 545.
Derby, Earls of ; see Stanley.
Dethick ; see Dunne.
Devonshire, Dukes of ; see Cavendish.
Dunne, Curzon, Dethick, and Harpur *of Breadsall*, ii. 179.
Edwards *of Derby*, ii. 589.
Evans *of Allestree, Darley, Mathfield, &c.* ii. 19.
Fawne ; see Fowne.
Foljambe, Plumpton, Sotehill, and Rocliffe *of Darley in the Dale*, ii. 392.
Forester *of Derby ;* see Pulter.
Fowne or Fawne, ii. 5.
Fox *of Derby*, ii. 596.
French *of Derby ;* see Pulter.
Gisborne *of Derby, Yoxall, Chapel-en-le-Frith, and Darley-in-the Dale*, ii. 246.
Gisborne *of Darley-in-the-Dale*, ii. 392.
Grey and Zouche *of Codnor*, ii. 342.
Harley ; see Cavendish.
Harpur ; see Dunne.
Harpur, now Crewe *of Calke Abbey*, ii. 216.
Heathcote *of Stancliffe Hall in Darley Dale*, ii. 393.
Holden *of Darley Abbey, co. Derby, and of Nuttall Temple, co. Notts*, ii. 384.
Holden *of Aston*, ii. 68.
Holles ; see Cavendish.

Hope *of Derby*, ii. 585.
Hurt *of Ashbourn, Alderwasley, Wirksworth, &c.* ii. 5.
Leaper *of Derby*, ii. 601.
Le Hunt, &c. ii. 587.
Lockett *of Derby*, ii. 598.
Lowe *of Denby*, ii. 398.
Lucas *of Chesterfield*, ii. 325.
Master *of Codnor*, ii. 346.
Maynard *of Chesterfield*, ii. 326.
Mellor *of Ideridgehay and Derby*, ii. 584.
Meynell *of Meynell Langley, Wellington and Badley*, ii. 158.
Milnes *of Ashover*, ii. 64.
Milnes *of Mansfield*, ii. 65.
Milnes *of Chesterfield, Tapton, and Brimington*, ii. 322.
Moore, Lords of Appleby Parva, ii. facing 28 and 29.
Morewood *of the Oaks in Bradfield, and Alfreton*, ii. 14.
Moubray ; see Segrave.
Okeover *of Atlow, Okeover, and Oldbury*, ii. 70.
Peche, Ridware, and Cotton, Lords of Boylstone, ii. 152.
Pegge *of Beauchief*, ii. 109.
Plumpton *of Darley in the Dale ;* see Foljambe.
Pole ; see Wakebrigge.
Potter *of Darley Hall ;* see Bower.
Pulter, French, and Forester *of Derby*, ii. 599.
Ridware ; see Peche.
Rocliffe *of Darley in the Dale ;* see Foljambe.
Rodes *of Barlborough*, ii. 91.
Segrave, Moubray, and Berkeley *of Bretby,* ii. 195.
Soresby *of Chesterfield*, ii. 327.
Sotehill *of Darley in the Dale ;* see Foljambe.
Stanhope, Earls of Chesterfield, ii. 190.
Stanley, Earls of Derby, ii. 565.
Streatfield *of Beauchief*, and Pegge *of the same*, ii. 109.
Strelley *of Beauchief*, ii. 109.
Strutt *of Derby, Belper, &c.* ii. 591.
Turner *of Swanswick and Alfreton*, ii. 13.
Twigge *of Broadlow Ash*, ii. 196.

Wakebrigge and Pole *of Wake-bridge*, ii. 356.
Waller *of Chesterfield*, ii. 326.
Walthall *of Darley in the Dale*, ii. 395.
Watkinson *of Brampton*, ii. 168.
Whitby *of Derby*, ii. 598.

Wilkinson *of Hilcote Hall in Black-wall*, ii. 124.
Wilmot *of Chaddesden*, ii. 239.
Wright *of Nottingham and Lenton*, ii. 201.
Zouch *of Codnor ;* see Grey.

28.—The History of Melbourne, in the County of Derby, &c. By JOHN JOSEPH BRIGGS. *Derby.* 2nd edition. 8vo.

Cantrell *of King's Newton*, 175.
Coke and Melbourne, 161.

Hardinge, 167.

DEVONSHIRE.

29.—A View of Devonshire in 1630, with a Pedigree of most of its Gentry, by THOMAS WESTCOTE, Gent. Edited by the Rev. GEORGE OLIVER, D.D., and PITMAN JONES, Esq. *Exeter*, 1845, foolscap 4to.

Ameredith *of Crediton and Slapton*, 596.
Arscot *of Arscot*, 489.
Arscot *of Annery*, 490.
Arscot *of Tidwell*, 490.
Arscot *of Holsworthy*, 490.
Arscot *of Tetcot*, 491.
Arundell *of Talvern*, 476.
Arundell *of Lanhern*, 477.
Ashford *of Ashford*, 481.
Atwill *of Kenton and Mamhead*, 612.
Babington *of Knoll*, 473.
Bampfield *of Poltimore*, 491.
Barry *of Winscot*, 656.
Basset *of Umberlegh*, 485.
Battishill *of Westwyke*, 540.
Bear *of Hunsham*, 461.
Beaumont *of Gittesham*, 498.
Becket, 458.
Becket *of Menwyngæ*, 459.
Bennet *of Chudleigh*, 619.
Berry *of Barley*, 497.
Berry *of Croscombe*, 496.
Berry *of Berry Nerber*, 497.
Bishop *of Choldash*, 557.
Bluet *of Holcombe-Rogus*, 512.
Bodleigh, (*alias* Bodley) *of Duns-combe*, 499.
Bonvile *of Comb-Ralegh*, 465.
Bourchier, Earl of Bath, 460.
Bowerman *of Hemyock*, 518.

Broughton *of Warbrightleigh*, 632.
Brown *of Brownlarsh*, 589.
Budokeside *of Budokeside*, 465.
Bullon, Earl of Ormond and Wilt-shire, 482.
Burgoin *of South Tawton*, 476.
Burgoin *of Bideford*, 551.
Burneby *of Burneby*, 494.
Bury (*alias* Berry) *of Berry-Nerber*, 495.
Bury (*alias* Berry) *of Coleton*, 496.
Butler, Earl of Ormonde and Wilt-shire, 483.
Callard *of Callard*, 582.
Calwodeley *of Calwodeley*, 514.
Cary *of Castle-Cary*, 507.
Cary *of Hunsdon*, 509.
Cary *of Cockington*, 510.
Carey *of Clovelly*, 510.
Carew *of East Anthony*, 528.
Carwithan *of Carwithen*, 552.
Challons, 614.
Charles *of Moreton and Tavistock*, 541.
Cheyney *of Pinhoe*, 518.
Chichester, Viscount Carrickfergus, 608.
Chichester *of Ralegh*, 604.
Chichester *of Arlington*, 607.
Chichester *of Hall*, 608.
Chichester *of Widworthy*, 609.

Chudleigh *of Ashton*, 462.
Cloberry *of Bradston*, 555.
Clotworthy *of Clotworthy*, 480,563.
Cole *of Slade*, 519.
Colins *of Baron's Down*, 562.
Colleton *of Exeter*, 619.
Cooke *of Thorne*, 555.
Copleston *of Copleston and Warlegh*, 503.
Copleston *of Bow*, 505.
Copleston *of Copleston and Eggesford*, 505.
Copleston *of Otterham and Woodland*, 506.
Copleston *of Bowdon*, 506.
Copleston *of Wyke*, 506.
Cottle *of Sampford Peverell*, 475.
Courtenay, Earl of Devon, 570.
Courtenay *of Powderham*, 573.
Courtenay *of Molland*, 574.
Courtenay *of Wotton and Ladock*, 575.
Courtenay *of Upcott*, 576.
Courtenay *of Ugbrook*, 576.
Crocker *of Lynham*, 550.
Cruwys *of Cruwys-Morchard*, 516.
Culme *of Chamston*, 515.
Davils *of Balston*, 611.
Davy *of Sandford*, 598.
De Aubernon *of Daubernon*, 517.
Dennis *of Holcombe-Burnell and Bicton*, 615.
Dennis *of Orlegh*, 616.
Dennis *of Colliscomb*, 617.
Dennis *of Malcot*, 617.
Desmond, Earl of, 477.
Dillon *of Chimwell*, 549.
Dinham, 494.
Donne *of Donne Ralph*, 515.
Dowrish *of Dowrish in Sanford*, 618.
Dowrish *of Heath-Barton, Whitestone*, 618.
Drake *of Ash*, 467.
Drew *of Sharpham*, 582.
Drew *of Drew's Cliff*, 583.
Duke *of Poer-Hayes*, 559.
Edgcombe *of Stonehouse*, 494.
Edmonds *of Salisbury and Plymouth*, 524.
Ellacot *of Exeter*, 479.
Esse (or Ash) *of Thuborough*, 633.
Esse (or Ash) *of Clist Fomison*, 633.
Eston *of Eston*, 565.

Evelegh *of West Evelegh*, 563.
Farringdon *of Farringdon*, 464, 609.
Fitz *of Fitz Ford*, 466.
Floyer *of Floyers Hayes*, 556.
Forde *of Chagford*, 527.
Ford *of Fordmoor*, 528.
Fortescue *of Filleigh*, 498.
Fortescue *of Wimpston*, 625.
Fortescue *of Buckland Filleigh*, 625.
Fortescue *of Fallopit*, 626.
Fountain *of Bawcombe*, 521.
Fowel *of Fowelscombe*, 521.
Franccis *of Combe Flory*, 462.
Frankcheyney *of Clist Gerard*, 517.
Fry *of Exeter and Pawlet*, 562.
Fulford *of Fulford*, 612.
Fursland *of Bickington*, 598.
Gale *of Dartmouth and Crediton*, 567.
Gay *of Goldsworthy*, 564.
Geare *of Heavitree*, 565.
Giffard *of Brightlegh*, 627.
Giffard *of Weare*, 628.
Giffard *of Tiverton*, 628.
Gilbert *of Compton*, 566.
Giles *of Bowden and Dean Prior*, 530.
Godwine *of Clistwill and Godwine*, 540.
Gove (*alias* Gough) *of Woodbury*, 547.
Grenville *of Penheale*, 631.
Grenville *of Stow, Cornwall*, 630.
Hakewell *of Exeter*, 545.
Handcock *of Comb Martin*, 560.
Harris *of Hayne*, 531.
Harris *of Lanrest*, 532.
Harris *of Radford*, 532.
Hatch *of Aller*, 603.
Haydon *of Lympstone, &c.* 579.
Hele *of South Hele*, 533.
Hele *of Wisdom*, 533.
Hele *of Wembury*, 533.
Hele *of Holbeton*, 534.
Hele *of Exeter and Fleet*, 535.
Hele *of Newton Ferrers*, 535.
Hele *of Brixton*, 535.
Henscot *of Henscot*, 589.
Herle *of West Herle*, 514.
Hext *of Kingston*, 503.
Hill *of Shilston*, 503.
Hillersdon *of Hillersdon, &c.* 529.
Holbeam *of Holbeam*, 502.
Holcomb *of Holcomb*, 531.

Hone *of Ottery St. Mary*, 538.
Honychurch *of Tavistock, &c.* 591.
Hoper *of Blackmore*, 525.
Huckmore *of Bokeyt*, 501.
Huddisfield *of Shillingford*, 500.
Huish *of Denniford*, 488.
Huish *of Sand*, 488.
Hull *of Larkbear*, 517.
Hurst *of Exeter and Oxton*, 487.
Jewell *of Bowden*, 536.
Kelly *of Kelly*, 540.
Kenisham *of Brixton*, 566.
Kendal *of Treworgy, &c.* 598.
Kildare, Earl of, 477.
Kirkham *of Blackdon, &c.* 523.
Kirkham, 458.
Knolles *of Little Hempston*, 474.
Langford *of Langford*, 462.
Larder *of Pynes*, 624.
Le Hart *of Yarnacombe*, 603.
Levermore *of Exeter*, 597.
Lippincot *of Lippincot, &c.* 554.
Loveis *of Ogberd in Tamerton*, 629.
Lowman *of Uplowman, &c.* 580.
Lumen or De Lumine *of Uplowman*, 579.
Lutton *of Cofford*, 478.
Lynne *of Exeter*, 457.
Mallock *of Axmouth*, 548.
Marshall *of Teigngrace*, 502.
Marshall *of Exeter*, 502.
Martin *of Comb Martin*, 594.
Marwood *of Westcot*, 604.
Mathew *of Dodbrook, &c.* 599.
Melhuish *of Witheridge*, 623.
Mohun *of Hall in Cornwall*, 610.
Molford *of Chulmlegh, &c.* 603.
Montague, Lord Chief Justice, 633.
More *of Moorhays*, 624.
Munck *of Potheridge*, 468.
Newcombe *of Great Worthy*, 531.
Newcourt *of Pickwel*, 478.
Noble *of Exeter and Belston*, 561.
Norris *of Chulmlegh*, 541.
Norris *of Winkleigh*, 626.
Northcote *of Uton, &c.* 599.
Parker (*alias* Jorden) *of Northmolton*, 538.
Parker *of Exeter*, 564.
Passemere *of Passemere Hayes*, 525.
Paulet *of Sampford-Peverel*, 488.
Pawlet *of Rode Hinton, &c.* 474.
Perriam *of Exeter, &c.* 584.

Pery *of Water in Membury*, 545.
Petre *of Tor-Brian*, 546.
Pointingdon *of Meryfield*, 547.
Pointingdon *of Pennycott*, 547.
Pollard *of King's-Nymet*, 493.
Pollard *of Way and Horwood*, 552.
Pollard *of Knowston-Beauple*, 553.
Preston *of Up Ottery, &c.* 588.
Prestwood *of Exeter, Nooth-Huish, &c.* 545.
Prideaux, Sir Edmund, *of Farway*, 472.
Prideaux *of Orchardton and Thuborough*, 470.
Prideaux *of Orchardton*, 471.
Prideaux *of Soldon*, 472.
Prideaux *of Nutwell*, 486.
Prouse *of Exeter*, 597.
Prowz *of Gidley and Chagford*, 568.
Prye *of Horwell in Colebrook*, 611.
Putt *of Gittisham*, 629.
Pyne *of East Down, &c.* 544.
Ralegh *of Fardel*, 535.
Reynell *of Trumpington, &c.* 576.
Reynell *of Malston*, 578.
Reynell, Sir Richard, 578.
Reynell *of Creedy-Widger*, 578.
Risdon *of Bableigh*, 507.
Roberts *of Comb-Martin*, 609.
Rolle *of Stevenstone*, 593.
Roskimer *of Haylford, Cornwall*, 632.
Rouse (*alias* Le Rouse) *of Modbury*, 580.
Sainthill *of Sainthill*, 537.
Samuel *of Restormel*, 533.
Samuel *of Cornwall*, 623.
Sapcotts, 551.
Saverey, *of Totness*, 562.
Seward *of Stokeinteignhead*, 559.
Seymour *of Berry-Pomeroy*, 479.
Shapcott *of Exeter*, 602.
Shillingford *of Shillingford*, 468.
Skinner *of Cowley*, 599.
Slader *of North Tawton, &c.* 524.
Slanning *of Ley*, 563.
Somaster, 551.
Somaster *of Painsford*, 551.
Somaster *of Widecombe*, 500.
Southcote *of Mohun's Ottery*, 537.
Staplehill *of Bremble in-Ashton*, 624.
Staveley *of East Buckland, &c.* 562.
St. Leger *of Annery*, 483.
Stowford *of Stowford*, 592.

Strode *of Ermington and Newnham,* 542.
Strechlegh *of Strechlegh,* 514.
Stukeley *of Kenn and Faringdon,* 579.
Stukeley *of Affeton,* 585.
Sture *of Marridge,* 512.
Thorn *of Thorn in Holsworthy,* 525.
Todenham *of Church Taunton,* 478.
Tothill *of Exeter and Peamore,* 520.
Trelawney *of Pool in Menhenniot,* 561.
Tremayne *of Collacomb,* 587.
Trevillian *of Nettlecombe,* 558.
Tucker *(alias* Tooker) *of Exeter,* 526.
Upton *of Puslinch and Trelaske,* 519.
Vowel *(alias* Hooker) *of Exeter,* 526.
Wadham *of Edge,* 634.
Waller *of Sidbury and Hampshire,* 623.
Walrond, 484.
Waltham *of Brenton, &c.* 583.
Warr *of Hestercombe,* 491.
Westcote *(alias* Lyttleton or Luttleton) *of Frankley,* 621.
Westcote *of Westcote and Raddon,* 622.

Whitlock *of Frithelstock,* 583.
Whyddon *of Chagford, &c.* 581.
Wichalse *of Chudleigh,* 627.
Williams *of Stowford,* 521.
Willoughby *of Knoll Adrian, Wiltshire,* 619.
Willoughby, Lord Brook, 620.
Willougby *of Payhembury,* 620.
Wise *of South Sydenham,* 553.
Wivell *of Credition,* 611.
Wollacomb *of Comb,* 539.
Wood *(alias* de Bosco) *of North Tawton,* 589.
Wood *of Lewtreanchard,* 590.
Wood *(alias* Atwood) *of Hareston,* 591,
Worth *of Exeter,* 561.
Worthal *of Cotley,* 629.
Wrey *of Wrey, &c.* 567.
Wykes *of North Wyke,* 557.
Wykes *of Bindon,* 558.
Yard, *of Bradley, &c.* 601.
Yeo *of Heanton Sachville,* 592.
Yeo *of Huish,* 593.
Yeo *of Hatherleigh,* 593.
Yerworth *of Ipplepen,* 524.
Young *of Axminster,* 600.
Zouch, Lord John, 475.

30.—The History of Newenham Abbey in the County of Devon. By JAMES DAVIDSON. *London,* 1843. 12mo.

Andrews, 168.
De Shapwick, 161.
De Tynten, 163.
Mohun, 203.
Prince, 215.
Rhodes, 169.

31.—Devonshire Pedigrees. Recorded in the Heralds' Visitation of 1620; with Additions from the Harleian Manuscripts, and the printed Collections of Westcote and Pole. By JOHN TUCKETT. (No. 1—12 *in progress.*) *London.* 4to.

Acland, 153.
Amory, 23.
Atwill, 88, 95.
Ayshe, 80.
Bamfield, 161.
Barby, 130.
Bastard, 182.
Bellew, 157.
Bellott, 186.
Belmain, 192.
Bennett, 88.
Berry, 41.
Beryman, 127.
Blackall, 89.
Bogan, 96.
Burnby, 134.
Bury, 9.
Buryngton, 55.
Cabell, 110.
Carew, 121.

E

Cary, 141.
Champernowne, 129.
Colleton, 168.
Collings, 119.
Collyns, 118.
Coplestone, 165.
Cruis, 177.
Davy, 97.
Davye, 93.
Delves, 169.
Dowriche, 113.
Drew, 62, 63, 64.
Duck, 146.
Dyer, 100.
Dynham, 135.
Edwards, 29.
Eliot, 192.
Ellacott, 36.
Ford, 156.
Fountayne, 109.
Fursland, 72.
Garland, 140.
Geere, 173.
Gilbert, 87, 95.
Giles, 126.
Glanville, 133.
Goodridge, 94.
Gould, 27.
Hakewell, 127.
Harrys, 120, 126.
Hele, 187.
Hillersdon, 136.
Holway, 86.
Huckmore, 181.
Hunt, 146.
Incledon, 11.
Isaak, 5.
Isaake, 11.
Kelley, 1.
Kendall, 16.
Kirkham, 19.
Knapman, 7.
Lande, 16.
Langesford, 6.
Lante, 13.
Larkworthy, 16.
Leach, 5.
Leigh, 17, 33.
Levermore, 24.
Longe, 104.
Lowis, 5.
Lowman, 15.
Luscombe, 24.

Lutton, 40.
Luttrell, 49, 54.
Lynn, 15.
Mace, 23.
Mallet, 35.
Manning, 80.
Menifie, 48.
Minshull, 124.
Mohun, 77.
Mylford, 112.
Newcomb, 39.
Newton, 168.
Northcot, 29.
Osmond, 175.
Pasmere, 39.
Peter, 125.
Plumleigh, 108.
Pomeroy, 160.
Poyntington, 31.
Prestwood, 112.
Prouse, 85.
Prowse, 85.
Prouz, 81.
Prye, 55.
Pyncombe, 22.
Reynell, 147.
Risdon, 107.
Roope, 180, 182.
Rowe, 175, 176.
Sanford, 145.
Savery, 101.
Segar, 173.
Seymour, 91.
Shapcote, 152.
Skynner, 32.
Smyth, 99.
Snellinge, 21.
Somaster, 111.
Southcot, 57, 61.
Southmedde, 76.
Spurway, 184.
Staplehill, 119.
Strobridge, 128.
Strode, 185.
Sture, 169.
Symonds, 40.
Tawley, 125.
Tothill, 163.
Tremayne, 117.
Upton, 73.
Wakeman, 56.
Walrond, 137.
Waltham, 69.

Webbe, 128.
Weekes, 37.
Wilkes, 25.
Willesford, 178.
Willoughby, 71.
Wolfe, 170.

Wolston, 183.
Wotton, 133.
Whyghte, 32.
Yard, 65.
Yeo, 103.
Yonge, 31, 53.

32.—The History and Antiquities of Clyst St. George, Devon. By the Rev. H. T. ELLACOMBE, M.A. 1865. 4to.

Champernon *of Clisse Champernon*, 65.
Gibbs (2), folding at 70.
Lee *of Winslade*, 66.
Osborne *of Kenniford*, 67.

Pomerai, Lord of Beri, 68.
Prideaux *of Nutwell*, 70.
Seaward, 67.
Trosse, 69.
Wynard, 67.

DORSETSHIRE.

33.—The History and Antiquities of the County of Dorset, &c. By JOHN HUTCHINS, M.A. *London,* 1774. 2 vols. folio ; 2nd ed. 1796-1815, 4 vols. folio ; 3rd ed. Vol. I. (*in progress.*)

Abington *of Over Compton*, ii. 350; 2 ed. iv. 43.
Anketil *of Anketil's Place*, ii. 34; 2 ed. ii. 447.
Anketil *of East Almer and Stour Provest*, ii. 490 ; 2 ed. iv. 318.
Arnold *of Ilsington*, i. 489 ; 2 ed. ii. 203.
Arnold *of Armswell*, 2 ed. 262.
Ashley-Cooper, Earls of Shaftesbury, ii. folding at 216 ; 2 ed. iii. 175.
Arundel, Earls of ; see Fitzalan.
Attwater *(Hanford)*, ii. 304 ; 2 ed. iii. 342.
Ayle *of Gussage St. Andrew*, ii. 201 ; 2 ed. iii. 152.
Bancks *of Milton Abbas*, ii. 433 ; 2 ed. iv. 211.
Bankes *of Kingston Hall*, i. 87 ; 2 ed. ii. 567.
Barnes *of Duntishe*, ii. 256 ; 2 ed. iii. 259.
Bartlett *of Holwell and Cranbourne*, 2 ed. iii. 73.
Baskett *of Divelish*, i. 485 ; 2 ed. ii. 196.
Baskett *of Salisbury*, 2 ed. ii. 527.
Battiscomb ; see Bettiscomb.

Bayley and Paget *(Stalbridge)*, 2 ed. iii. 239.
Berkeley-Portman *of Bryanston*, and Burland *of Stock Gayland*, 2 ed. i. folding at 154; 3 ed. i. 253.
Bertie ; see Gigger.
Bettiscomb or Battiscomb *of Vere Wotton*, i. 320; 2 ed. i. 536.
Bingham *of Melcomb Bingham*, ii. folding at 426 ; 2 ed. iv. folding at 202, and 203.
Bishop *of Chilcomb*, i. 542 ; 2 ed. ji. 293.
Blount, Lords Mountjoy, ii. 106; 2 ed. iii. 7.
Bond *of Grange*, i. 205 ; 2 ed. i. 326; 3 ed. i. 603.
Bower *of Ewern Minster*, ii. 198 ; 2 ed. iii. 149.
Brett *of South Maperton*, 2 ed. i. 281.
Bristed *of Sherbourne*, 2 ed. iv. 21.
Brodrepp *of South Maperton*, i. 282 ; 2 ed. i. 476.
Browne *of Frampton*, i. 350 ; 2 ed. i. 583.
Browne *of Godmandston and Blandford St. Mary*, i. 53 ; 2 ed. i. 100 ; 3 ed. i. 165.

Browne *of Bradle*, 3 ed. i. 583.

Brune *of Plumber*, ii. 358 ; 2 ed. iv. 61.

Bryan *of Woodsford*, i. 169 ; 2 ed. i. 271 ; 3 ed. i. 448.

Buckler *of Causeway*, i. 417.

Burland ; see Berkeley Portman.

Burland (*Stok Gaylard*), 2 ed. iii. 250.

Butler *of Handley*, ii. 100 ; 2 ed. iii. 150.

Byrte *of Candel Marsh*, ii. 342 ; 2 ed. iv. 22.

Calcraft *of Rempston*, 3 ed. i. 534.

Cammel *of Shipwick ;* see Plecy.

Cartwright ; see Disney.

Chafin *of Chettle*, ii. 211 ; 2 ed. iii. 166.

Chaldecott *of Quarrelston and East Whiteway*, i. 119 ; 2 ed. i. 199 ; 3 ed. i. 591.

Champayne *of Shapwick Champagne, and* Tournay *of same*, i. 67 ; 2 ed. ii. 516.

Chaunterell (*Swanwich*), 3 ed. i. 667.

Checkford *of Leeson*, 3rd ed. i. 633.

Cheverel *of East Stoke and Chant-marle*, i. 153 ; 2 ed. i. 251; 3 ed. i. 414.

Chidiock *of Chidiock*, i. 326 ; 2 ed. i. 547.

Churchill *of Colliton and Muston*, i. 397 ; 2 ed. ii. 59.

Churchill *of Compton Abbas*, 2 ed. iii. 325.

Chudleigh (*Catstock*), 2 ed. iii. 298.

Clavell *of Smedmore*, i. 196 ; 2 ed. i. 314, 316 ; 3 ed. i. 570.

Clavell *of Quarr*, 3 ed. i. 695.

Clavell ; see Gigger.

Clavil *of Steple*, i. 203 ; 2 ed. i. 324.

Clare *of Tarent Rushton*, ii. 167 ; 2 ed. iii. 105.

Clinton ; see Disney.

Cockram *of the Isle of Purbeck*, 3 ed. i. 672.

Cockram *of Newton, Whitecliff, and Bucknoll*, 3 ed. i. 673.

Coker *of Ashbosam*, i. 105 ; 2 ed. i. 182 ; 3 ed. i. 310.

Coker, *late of Maponder*, ii. folding at 263 ; 2 ed. iii. folding at 273.

Collier *of Piddle Trenthide*, ii. 481 ; 2 ed. iv. 290.

Constantine *of Doddington*, ii. 109 ; 2 ed. iii. 11.

Coplestone *of Shipton Gorges and Nash*, i. 340 ; 2 ed. ii. 569.

Culliford *of Encomb*, i. 187 ; 2 ed. i. 292 ; 3 ed. i. 516.

Daccomb *of Winterbourne-Kingston*, 3 ed. i. 146.

Daccomb *of Stepleton*, i. 103 ; 2 ed. i. 179 ; 3 ed. i. 299.

Dackombe ; see Gigger.

Dacombe *of Corfe Castle and Buck-noll*, i. 183 ; 2 ed. i. 287 ; 3 ed. i. 510.

Damer, Earls of Dorchester, ii. 434 ; 2 ed. iv. 43.

De Isney, Deisney or Disney *of Norton Disney and Swinderby, co. Lincoln, and Corscombe, co. Dorset*, 2 ed. iv. 389-396.

Derby, Earls of ; see Ferrers.

De Vivonia (*Stourminster Marshal*), ii. 121 ; 2 ed. iii. 28.

De Warmwell, 3 ed. i. 428.

Digby, Earls of Digby, ii. folding at 427 ; 2 ed. iv. folding at 133.

Disney, Amandeville, *alias* Humferies, Hussey, Clinton, Woolhouse, Hacker, and Cartwright, 2 ed. 389 and 393.

Disney ; see De Isney.

Dolling *of Downshay*, i. 227 ; 2 ed. i. 364 ; 3 ed. 693.

Dolling and Pyke *of Downshay*, 3 ed. i. 693.

Dorchester, Earls of ; see Damer.

Eggerdon *of South Eygerdon*, i. 288 ; 2 ed. i. 488.

Ekins ; see Gigger.

Erle *of Charborough*, ii. 184 ; 2 ed. iii. 126.

Ettericke (*Wimbourne Minster*), ii. 89 ; 2 ed. ii. 571.

Eureaux and Longspee, Earls of Salisbury, ii. 101 ; 2 ed. iii. 2.

Fane ; see Gigger.

Farquharson *of Langton*, 3 ed. i. 285.

Fauntleroy *of Fauntleroy's Marsh*, ii. 353 ; 2 ed. iv. 54.

Ferrers, Earls of Derby, ii. 120; 2 ed. iii. 27.

Filiol *of Woodlands*, ii. 61 ; 2 ed. ii. 508.

Filiol *of Knightstreet*, ii. 398 ; 2 ed. iv. 161.

Fitz-Alan, Earls of Arundel, ii. 114 ; 2 ed. iii. 20.

Fitz-Herbert *of Mayne and Hinton Martel*, i. 449 ; 2 ed. ii. 145.

Fitz-James *of Lewston*, ii. 337.

Floyer *of Athelhampston*, i. 473 ; 2 ed. ii. 180.

Foliot *of Melbury Osmund*, ii. 464 ; 2 ed. iv. 258.

Fox *of Failey*, 2 ed. ii. 611.

Frampton *of Moreton*, i. 145 ; 2 ed. i. 238 ; 3 ed. i. 398.

Freke *of Shroton*, ii. 318.

Fry *of Ewern Minster and Gunvill*, ii. 197 ; 2 ed. iii. 148.

Fulford *of Toller Fratrum and Great Fulford, co. Devon*, 2 ed. ii. 261.

Fyler *of Heffleton*, 3 ed. i. 418.

Gerard *of Hide*, 3 ed. i. 609.

Gigger *of Bucks and Dorset ;* with Dackcombe, Lovell, Clavell, Twyn-yhoe, Lisle, Tytherley, Chaldecott, Ekins, Malie, Greene, Piers, Bertie and Fane, 2 ed. i. folding at 61 ; 3 ed. at 122.

Glyn *of Gaunts House* ; and Lewen *of Hinton Parva*, 2 ed. iv. 418.

Gollop *of Berwick*, i. 669 ; 2 ed. ii. 332.

Gollop *of Bowood and Strode*, i. 265 ; 2 ed. i. 434.

Goodden (*Over Compton*), 2 ed. iv. 44.

Gorges *of Bradpole*, i. 279 ; 2 ed. i. 471.

Gorges *of Wraxall, co. Somerset, and Stourminster Marshal*, 2 ed. iii. 33, 35.

Gould *of Upway*, i. 596 ; 2 ed. ii. 378.

Greene ; see Gigger.

Grey *of Kingston-Maureward, and Askerswell*, i. 461; 2 ed. ii. 162.

Guldene of Langton, i. 97 ; 2 ed. i. 171 ; 3 ed. i. 282.

Hacker ; see Disney.

Hanham *of Purse Candel*, ii. 344 ; 2 ed. iv. 24.

Hanham *of Deans Court*, ii. 76; 2 ed. ii. 562.

Hardy *of Wolcomb-Maltravers and Toller Welme*, ii. 462; 2 ed. iv. 255.

Hardy *of Up Sydling*, 2 ed. iv. 306.

Havelland *of Wilkswood*, 3 ed. i. 640.

Hawles *of Upwinbourne*, ii. 144 ; 2 ed. iii. 59.

Hayter *of East Creech*, 3 ed. i. 587.

Helton *of Helton*, ii. 418 ; 2 ed. iv. 191.

Henley (*Wotton Glanvile*), ii. 275 ; 2 ed. iii. 287.

Henning *of Pokeswell*, i. 151 ; 2 ed. i. 151 ; 3 ed. i. 408.

Henville *of Looke*, 2 ed. ii. 283*.

Hody *of Pillesdon*, i. 317 ; 2 ed. i. folding at 531.

Horsey *of Clifton-Maubank, and Melcomb-Horsey*, ii. 459 ; 2 ed. iv. 249.

Hoskins *of Beminster*, i. 268 ; 2 ed. i. 441.

Hose ; see Husee.

Humfines ; see Disney.

Hungerford (*Folke*), 2 ed. iv. 49.

Husee, Huse, Hose, Hussey or Husee, iii. folding at 68.

Husey *of Sydling St. Nicholas*, 2 ed. iv. 301.

Husey *of Stour Payne*, 3 ed. i. 302.

Hussey *of Shapwick and Thompson*, ii. 68.

Hussey *of Marnhull*, ii. 397 ; 2 ed. iv. 160.

Hussey *of Edmundsham and Bland-ford St. Mary*, ii. 151 ; 2 ed. iii. 80.

Hyde (*Gussage St. Michael*), 2 ed. ii. 495.

l'Anson *of Corfe Castle*, 2 ed. i. 267 ; 3 ed. i. 546.

Ironside (*Burton Bradstock*), i. 339; 2 ed. i. 568.

Ironside *of Durham and Dorset*, 2 ed. i. folding at 586.

Janssen *of Owre Moyne*, i. 232 ; 2 ed. i. 371 ; 3 ed. i. 458.

Jessop *of West Chickerel*, i. 423 ; 2 ed. ii. 113.

Kaynes *of Tarent Kayneston*, i. 110 ; 2 ed. i. 188 ; 3 ed. i. 320.

Keylway *of Lillington*, ii. 360 ; 2 ed. iv. 65.

Kymer *of West Chelbury*, i. 500 ; 2 ed. ii. 219.

Larder *of W. Chelbury and Loders*, i. 501.

Latimer *of Duntishe*, ii. 255 ; 2 ed. iii. 258.

Laurence *of Grange*, i. 204 ; 2 ed. i. 325 ; 3 ed. i. 599.

Laurence *of Winterbourne Stapleton*, i. 565 ; 2 ed. ii. 325.

Lewen *of Hinton Parva ;* see Glyn.

Lewston *of Lewston*, ii. 336 ; 2 ed. iv. 10.

Lewys *of Stoke Gaylard*, ii. 249 ; 2 ed. iii. 243.

Lisle (*Winterbourne Abbas*), 2 ed. ii. 506.

Lisle ; see Gigger.

Long *of Draycot*, 2 ed. ii. 179.

Lovell ; see Gigger.

Lovell *of Tarent Rawson*, i. 112 ; 2 ed. i. 191 ; 3 ed. 325.

Lymbergh (*Hanford*), ii. 304 ; 2 ed. iii. 342.

Malie ; see Gigger.

Maltravers *of Litchet Maltravers*, ii. 113 ; 2 ed. iii. 19.

Maltravers *of Hooke*, i. 291 ; 2 ed. i. 492.

Mandeville *of Marshwood*, i. 329 ; 2 ed. i. 551.

Mansel *of Smedmore*, 3 ed. i. 574.

Martin *of Athelhampston*, i. 471 ; 2 ed. ii. 177.

Martin *of Park Pale*, i. 498 ; 2 ed. ii. 215.

Meere *of Chaldon Boys*, i. 123 ; 2 ed. i. 207 ; 3 ed. i. 343.

Meggs *of Bradford Peverel*, i. 444 ; 2 ed. ii. 139.

Meller *of Little Bridy*, i. 296 ; 2 ed. i. 497.

Michel *of Kingston Russel*, i. 300 ; 2 ed. i. 501.

Mintern of Newland, ii. 456 ; 2 ed. iv. 245.

Mohun *of Fleet*, i. 545 ; 2 ed. ii. 297.

Mohun *of Ham Mohun*, i. 92 ; 2 ed. i. 163.

Molam and Myldmore, i. 357.

Mompesson *of Durnford*, 3 ed. i. 632.

Montacute, Earls of Salisbury, ii. 104 ; 2 ed. iii. 4.

Moore and Wyndham *of Wild Court*, 2 ed. iii. 332.

Morgan *of South Maperton*, i. 282 ; 2 ed. i. 472.

Morton *of Milbourne S. Andrew*, i. 478 ; 2 ed. ii. 187.

Morton *of Henbury*, ii. 119 ; 2 ed. iii. 37.

Myldemore ; see Molam.

Napier *of Puncknole*, i. 560 ; 2 ed. ii. 319.

Napier *of More Crichel*, ii. 48 ; 2 ed. ii. 485.

Napier (*Great Mintern*), ii. folding at 447 ; 2 ed. iv. folding at 286.

Napper *of Baglake*, i. 295 ; 2 ed. i. 497.

Napper *of Swyre and Oxford*, i. 567 ; 2 ed. ii. 328.

Newburgh *of Warmwell, and Berkeley, co. Somerset*, i. 158 ; 2 ed. i. 259 ; 3 ed. i. 429.

Newburgh *of East Lulworth*, i. 135 ; 2 ed. i. 222 ; 3 ed. i. 366.

Newman *of Fifehide Magdalen*, ii. 302 ; 2 ed. iii. 338.

Oglander *of Parnham*, i. folding at 271 ; 2 ed. i. 450.

Paget, Earls of Uxbridge ; see Bayley.

Pelham *of Compton Valence*, i. 347 ; 2 ed. i. 580.

Penne (*Corscomb*), 2 ed. i. 421.

Peverel *of Bradford Peverel*, i. 443 ; 2 ed. ii. 138.

Piercy *of Shaftesbury and Manston*, ii. 309 ; 2 ed. iii. 349.

Piers ; see Gigger.

Pitt *of Dorsetshere*, ii. folding at 318 ; 2 ed. iii. folding at 360.

Pitt *of the Down*, i. 54 ; 2 ed. i. 99 ; 3 ed. i. 164.

Plecy and Cammel *of Shapwick*, ii. 70 ; 2 ed. ii. 520.

Pleydell *of Milbourne St. Andrew*, i. 480 ; 2 ed. ii. 189 ; 3 ed. i. 198.

Portman ; see Berkeley-Portman.

Poyntz *of Sutton Poyntz*, i. 592 ; 2 ed. ii. 373.

Pybus ; see Symonds.

Pyke ; see Dolling.

Radcliffe *of Foxenton Hall, Lancashire, and Hyde, co. Dorset,* 3 ed. i. 141.

Radford *of Divelish,* i. 485; 2 ed. ii. 196.

Rawles *of Fifehide Neville,* 3 ed. i. 269.

Rempston *of Goldingston ;* see Talbot.

Rogers *of Brianston,* i. 86; 2 ed. i. 153; 3 ed. i. 250.

Roy *of Piddleton,* i. 487; 2 ed. ii. 201.

Russel *of Tyneham,* 3 ed. i. 615.

Russell *of Kingston-Lacy,* 2 ed. ii. 568.

Russell *of Kingston-Russell,* i. 298; 2 ed. i. 499.

Russell *of Berwick,* i. 668; 2 ed. ii. 329.

Russell ; see Montacute.

Russell, Earls of ; see Eureaux.

Ryves *of Damory Court,* ii. folding at 320 ; 2 ed. iii. 366.

Salkeld *of Fifehide Neville,* 3 ed. i. 270.

Salter *of Coombe Raynes,* 3 ed. i. 347.

Sampford *of Melbury Samford,* i. 509.

Samways *of Toller Fratrum and Winterbourne St. Martin,* i. 524 ; 2 ed. ii. 260.

Savage *of Bloxworth,* i. 59 ; 2 ed. i. 105 ; 3 ed. i. 180.

Scott, Earls of Eldon, 3 ed. i. 522.

Seymer (*Handford*), ii. 305.

Shaftesbury, Earls of; see Astley-Cooper.

Skinner *of Dewlish,* 2 ed. ii. 199.

Slymer (*Hanford*), ii. 305 ; 2 ed. iii. 343.

Small ; see Symonds.

Smith *of Sydling,* 2 ed. iv. 303 ; 3 ed. i. 166.

Squibb *of Whitchurch,* 3 ed. i. 198.

Stafford *of Hooke,* i. 292 ; 2 ed. i. 493.

Stagg *of Little Hinton,* ii. 55 ; 2 ed. ii. 497.

Still *of Anketil's Place, East Knoyle, and Mere,* ii. 35 ; 2 ed. ii. 448.

Stillingfleet *of Cranbourne,* 2 ed. iii. 78.

St. Loe *of Little Fontmel,* ii. 314; 2 ed. iii. 353.

Stoke (*East Stoke*), i 153 ; 2 ed. i. 251 ; 3 ed. i. 412.

Strode (*Beminster*), i. 270 ; 2 ed. i. 446.

Strangewayes (*Melbury Sampford*), i. 511 ; 2 ed. ii. 237.

Strangewayes *of Muston,* i. 46 ; 2 ed. i. 87 ; 3 ed. i. 149.

Swain *of Kingston, Dorchester and Upway,* i. 186 ; 2 ed. i. 29 ; 3 ed. i. 515.

Swayne *of Gunville,* ii. 164 ; 2 ed. iii. 99.

Sydenham *of Winford Eagle,* i. 526 ; 2 ed. ii. 263.

Sydenham ; co. *Somerset,* 2 ed. ii. 264.

Symonds, Small, and Pybus, *of Pillesdon,* folding at 531.

Symonds *of Cliff,* i. 495.

Talbot *of Broad Maine,* i. 449 ; 2 ed. ii. 146.

Talbot and Rempston *of Goldingston,* 3 ed. i. 667.

Thornhull *of Thornhull and Wolland,* ii. 451 ; 2 ed. iv. 240.

Thornhurst *of Winfrith,* i. 161 ; 2 ed. 263 ; 3 ed. i. 438.

Tournay *of Shapwick ;* see Champagne.

Tregonwell *of Milton and Anderson,* i. 52, ii. 432 ; 2 ed. i. 96, iv. 210 ; 3 ed. i. 161.

Trenchard *of Litchet Maltravers,* ii. 115, and folding at 116 ; 2 ed. iii. 22.

Trenchard *of Warmwell,* i. 159 ; 2 ed. i. 260 ; 3 ed. i. 430.

Turbervill *of Bere Regis,* i. 42 ; 2 ed. i. 83 ; 3 ed. 138.

Turberville *of Winterborn Whitchurch,* i. 67 ; 2 ed. i. 113.

Twynhoe ; see Gigger.

Tytherley ; see Gigger.

Uvedale *of Horton,* ii. 58 ; 2 ed. ii. 503, 503*.

Uvedale *of Little Crichel,* ii. 49 ; 2 ed. ii. 487.

Uxbridge, Earls of ; see Bayley and Paget.

Wadham *of Catherston,* i. 313 ; 2 ed. i. 523.

Wallis *of Langton Wallis and Chickerel*, 3 ed. i. 637.
Warham *of Osmington*, i. 429 ; 2 ed. ii. 121.
Watkins *of Holwell*, ii. 495 ; 2 ed. iv. 324*.
Webb *of Great Canford*, ii. 106 ; 2 ed. iii. 8.
Weld *of Lulworth Castle*, i. 139 ; 2 ed. i. 226 ; 3 ed. i. 373.
Wells *of Bambridge, co. Hants, and of Goldingston, Isle of Perbrek*, 3 ed. i. 668.
West *of Hinton Martel*, 2 ed. ii. 500.
West *of Shillingston*, 2 ed. iii. 97.
Whitaker *of Motcomb*, ii. 231.
White *of Fittleford*, ii. 413 ; 2 ed. iv. 183.
Whitfield (*Frome Whitfield*), i. 395 ; 2 ed. ii. 57.

Willett *of Merly*, 2 ed. iii. 14.
Williams *of Shitterton*, i. 44 ; 2 ed. i. 85.
Williams *of Tyneham*, i. 210 ; 2 ed. i. 333 ; 3 ed. i. 617.
Williams *of Herringstone*, i. 438 ; 2 ed. ii. 132.*
Williams, *late of Spittesbury*, 2 ed. iii. 136.
Willoughby *of Silton*, ii. 323 ; 2 ed. iii. 368.
Woolhouse ; see Disney.
Wyndham *of Norfolk, Wilts and Somerset*, 2 ed. iii. folding at 330.
Wyndham *of Wild Court;* see Moore.
Wyot *of East Kemeridge*, 3 ed. i. 616.
Yeatman *of Stock House*, 2 ed iii. 251.

DURHAM.

34.—The History and Antiquities of the County Palatine of Durham. By WILLIAM HUTCHINSON, F.A.S. 1785-1794, 3 vols. 4to.

Baliol (*Bernard Castle*), iii. 232.
Beauchamp, iii. folding at 240.
Bellasis *of Morton or Murton, and of Oughton or Owton*, ii. facing 575.
Bellasis, ii. facing 574.
Biddic, iii. xxv.
Billingham *of Crook Hall*, ii 318.
Birtley *of Birtley*, ii. 411.
Blakeston *of Blakeston*, iii. 119.
Booth *of Old Durham*, ii. 306.
Bowes *of Streatham*, iii. folding at 253.
Brackenbury, iii. folding at 223.
Bulmer, iii. xxvi.
Carrowe, (Chester-le-Street) ; see Coniers.
Chancellor *of Brafferton*, iii. xxiv.
Chaytor *of Butterby*, ii. 327.
Clavering *of Calleley, Tilmouth, Axwell and Berrington*, ii. folding at 442.
Claxton *of Claxton, Horden and Fishburne*, ii. 579 ; iii. xxxi.
Coniers, Lisle, and Carrowe (*Chester-le-Strand*) ii. folding 447.

Coniers ; see Langton.
Croyser *of Newbiggen*, iii. 165.
Cuthbert (*Witton*), iii. 305.
Darlington, Earls of ; see Vane.
Davison *of Blakiston*, iii. 120.
Dethick *of Gretham*, iii. 101.
Eden, Bart. *of Windlestone and West Auckland*, iii. folding at 339.
Elstob *of Foxden*, iii. 71.
Eure *of Witton*, iii. folding at 304.
Featherstonhaugh (*Stanhope*), iii. 291.
Forcer, ii. 335.
Frevill *of Hardwick*, iii. 68.
Fulthorp *of Tunstall*, iii. 45.
Gilpin (*Houghton - le - Spring*), ii. 549.
Haggerston, iii. 378.
Hagthorp *of Nettleworth*, ii. 415.
Hansard, iii. xxiv.
Harpyn and Trollop *of Thornlaw*, iii. (folding at 339).
Heath *of Kepier*, ii. 302.
Hebborne *of Hardwick*, iii. 67.
Hedworth, iii. xxi.

Heron *of Thickley*, iii. 206.

Hilton, iii. xvii.

Hutton, Bishop of Durham, i. 470.

Hutton *of Houghton-le-Spring*, iii. folding at 522.

James, Bishop of Durham, i. 479.

Kendal *of Thorpthewles*, iii. 89.

Killinghall *of Middleton St. George*, iii. 142.

Lambton *of Lambton*, ii. 413, iii. 32.

Langton and Coniers *of Winyard*, iii. 88.

Liddel *of Ravensworth*, ii. folding at 417.

Lilburn (*Shildon*), iii. 342.

Lisle (*Chester le Street*); see Coniers.

Lumley, Earls of Scarborough, ii. folding at 398.

Maddison (*Forsterley*), iii. 296.

Maire *of Hardwick, co. Durham*, and Appleby *of Lartington, co. York, N.R.* iii. folding at 3.

March *of Redworth*, 205.

Matthew, Bishop of Durham, i. 472.

Middleton *of Silksworth*, iii. folding at 339.

Millot *of Whitehill*, ii. 416.

Ord *of Longridge in Norham*, iii. folding at 304.

Pemberton *of Aislaby*, iii. 138.

Perkinson *of Whessey in Haughton*, iii. folding at 339.

Pilkington, Bishop of Durham, i. 447.

Playse or Place *of Egton and Dinsdale*, iii. 147.

Pollard *of Pollard Hall*, folding at iii. 351.

Ratcliff *of Tunstall*, iii. 45.

Riddell *of Ardnamuicham and Sunart*, Bart. iii. i.

Saltmarsh *of Saltmarsh, and of Newby Wick, co. Ebor*, iii. 461.

Salvin *of Croxdale*, ii. 329, 330.

Scarborough, Earls ; see Lumley.

Scrope (*Lanchester*), ii. 383.

Shaftoe *of Tanfield Leigh*, ii. 424.

Surtees *of Middleton*, iii. 145.

Surtees *of Dinsdale*, iii. 145.

Tempest *of Stella*, ii. 440 ; iii. xxx.

Tonge *of Thickley*, iii. 206.

Tonge (*Gainford*), iii. 218.

Trollope ; see Harpyn.

Tunstall *of the Bishopric of Durham*. iii. folding at 228.

Vane, Earls of Darlington, iii. folding at 264.

Whittingham *of Holmside*, ii. 378.

Williamson *of Monkwearmouth*, iii. folding at 339.

35.—The Parochial History and Antiquities of Stockton-upon-Tees, &c. By JOHN BREWSTER, M.A. *Stockton*, 1796, 4to.

Bordon, 46.

36.—The Visitation of the County Palatine of Durham, taken by RICHARD ST. GEORGE, Esquire, Norroy Kinge of Armes, &c. In the Year of Our Lord, 1614. *Sunderland*, 1816. Folio.

Bainbridge *of Wheatley*, 24.

Barnes *of Bedborne*, 20.

Beckwith *of Nutwithcoat*, 86.

Bellasis *of Morton*, 69.

Blakeston *of Gibside*, 75.

Blakeston *of Great Chilton*, 65.

Blakeston *of Seaton*, 74.

Blackett *of Woodcroft*, 9.

Brandling *of Felling*, 3.

Booth *of Silksworth*, 103.

Bower *of Oxenfield*, 52.

Bowes *of Biddick*, 84.

Bowes *of Streatlam*, 70.

Bulmer *of Tursdale*, 21.

Bunny *of Ryton*, 90.

Butler *of Fishburn*, 100.

Calverley *of Littleburn*, 39.

Chamber *of Cleadon*, 28.

Cheytor *of Butterby*, 34.

Claxton *of Claxton*, 18.

F

Clopton *of Sledwiche*, 102.
Colmore *of Durham*, 47.
Comyn *of Durham*, 16.
Conyers *of Sockburne*, 12.
Conyers *of Wooley*, 104.
Cooper *of Durham*, 55.
Crosier *of Newbiggin*, 25.
Dawson *of Unthanke*, 73.
Dearham *of Brimelawe*, 54.
Dethick *of Amerstone*, 26.
Dixon *of Ramshaw*, 105.
Dodsworth *of Stranton*, 56.
Downes *of Evenwood*, 53.
Dudley *of Chopwell*, 60.
Elstob *of Foxton*, 101.
Ewbanke *of Durham*, 13.
Featherstonhaugh *of Stanhope*, 78.
Fulthorpe *of Tunstall*, 82, 83.
Garnett *of Egglescliffe*, 10.
Gifford *of Darlington*, 87.
Hall *of Birtley*, 59.
Hall *of Hollenbushe*, 51.
Halliman *of Lumley*, 30.
Heath *of Kepier*, 7.
Heighington *of Greystones*, 95.
Hilliard *of Durham*, 92.
Hilton *of Dyons*, 80.
Hodgson *of Hebburn*, 91.
Hutton *of Durham*, 62, 72.
Hutton *of Hunwick*, 57.
James, Bishop of Durham, 99.
Johnson *of Twissell*, 85.
Lambert *of Stockton*, 105.
Lambton *of Lambton*, 27.
Lee *of Fishburn*, 23.
Liddell *of Ravensworth*, 11.
Lilburne *of Thickley*, 31.
Machell *of Pitfield*, 68.
Maddison *of Unthanke*, 35.
Madokes *of Skirmingham*, 36.
Martyne *of Durham*, 44.

Middleton *of Seaton*, 61.
Middleton *of Silksworth*, 96.
Millot *of Whitehill*, 77.
Morgan *of Millhouses*, 89.
Orde *of Fishburn*, 6.
Pemberton *of Aisleby*, 88.
Place *of Dinsdale*, 22.
Porter *of Shield Row*, 45.
Punshon *of West Herrington*, 41.
Richardson *of Durham*, 40.
Riddell *of Gateshead*, 43.
Robson *of West Morton*, 66.
Salvin *of Croxdale*, 2.
Sanderson *of Brancepath*, 17.
Scruteville *of Kibblesworth*, 46.
Selby *of Whitehouse*, 14.
Shaftoe, 8.
Shaftoe *of Tanfield Leigh*, 42.
Skepper *of Durham*, 49.
Smith *of Durham*, 98.
Surtees *of Ravensworth*, 5.
Tempest *of Stella*, 15.
Thomlinson *of Gateshead*, 58.
Tonge *of Thickley*, 38.
Trollop *of Thornley*, 37.
Trotter *of the Ashes*, 64.
Trotter *of Helmden*, 67.
Tunstall *of Ootham Mundeville*, 32.
Vasey *of Newlands*, 4.
Ward *of Bishop Middleham*, 93.
Ward *of Trimdon*, 1.
Watson *of Whitworth*, 76.
Wharton *of Wingate Grange*, 94.
White *of Redheugh*, 33.
Wilkinson *of Harpley*, 81.
Williamson *of St. Helen Auckland*, 29.
Wortley *of Langley*, 48.
Wrenn *of Binchester*, 97.
Wright *of Durham*, 63.
Wycliffe *of Offerton*, 50.

37.—The History of Hartlepool.   By Sir Cuthbert Sharp,
Knight, F.S.A., Mayor of Hartlepool.   *Durham*, 1816.
8vo.; 2 ed. *Hartlepool*, 1851.   8vo.

Allison *of Hartlepool*, 83 ; 2 ed. 95.
Baker *of Crook*, 83 ; 2 ed. 95.
Brus, folding at 14 ; 2 ed. at 16.
Clavering, 83 ; 2 ed. 95.
Clifford, folding at 28 ; 2 ed. at 34.
Darlington, Earls of ; see Vane.

Davison *of Blakiston*, 76 ; 2 ed. 88.
Eden, 76 ; 2 ed. 88.
Greveson *of Hartlepool*, 78 ; 2 ed. 90.
Lambton, 79 ; 2 ed. 91.
Liddel, 81 ; 2 ed. 93.

Lumley, Earls of Scarborough, 46 ;
2 ed. 55.
Pocock, 53 ; 2 ed. 63.
Romaine, 77 ; 2 ed. 89.
Rafton *of Hartlepool*, 78 ; 2 ed. 90.
Scarborough, Earls of; see Lumley.

Smith *of Hartlepool*, 75 ; 2 ed. 87.
Tempest *of Old Durham*, 72; 2 ed. 86.
Vane, Earls of Darlington, 82 ; 2 ed. 94.
Wilson *of Hartlepool*, 80 ; 2 ed. 92.
Wright, 68 : 2 ed. 80.

38.—The History and Antiquities of the County Palatine of Durham, &c. &c. By ROBERT SURTEES, of Mainsforth, Esq., F.S.A. *London*, 1816-1840. 4 vols. folio.

Addison *of Offerton ;* see Scurfield.
Allan *of Darlington and Blakewell Grange.* iii. 373.
Alwent ; see Graystanes.
Amcoats (*Houghton-le-Spring*) ; see Thirkeld.
Anderson and Simpson *of Bradley*, ii. 269.
Anderson *of Haswell Grange*, i. 122.
Anderson (*Kelloe*), i. 98.
Andrews, iv. 145.
Appleby *of Lathington, - N.R. co. York ;* see Maire of Hardwick.
Applynden ; see Epplyngden.
Ashmall *of Amerston,* iii. 87.
Ayscough *of Middleton-one-Row*, iii. 227.
Ayscough ; see Hansard.
Ayton *of West Herrington*, i. 186.
Baker *of Elemore ;* see Hall.
Baker *of Crook Hall and Elemore*, ii. 358.
Baliol *of Cavers*, iv. 59.
Baliol, iv. 60.
Barnes, i. lxxxii.
Barnes *of Darlington*, iii. 355.
Baxter *of Whitworth ;* see Watson.
Baynbrigg *of Snotterton*, iv. 141.
Baynbrigg *of Wheatley Hill*, i. 101.
Beauchamp *of Barnard Castle*, iv. 65.
Beaumont, i. xlv.
Bedford, iv. 99.
Belasyse *of Morton House, co. Pal.* i. 203.
Bewick *of Urpeth*, ii. 193.
Billingham *of Billingham*, iv. 139.
Bindloss *of Borwick Hall, co. Lancaster*, i. 106.
Birkbeck *of Morton Tynemouth*, iv. 25.

Birkbeck *of Moreton Tynemouth ;* see Graystaynes.
Birtley and Blenkinsop *of Birtley*, ii. 189.
Blakiston *of Farnton Hall*, i. 246.
Blakiston *of Gibside*, ii. 255.
Blakiston *of Shieldrow ;* see Porter.
Blakiston *of Blakiston*, iii. 162.
Blakiston *of Newton Hall, co. Pal. and Old Malton, co. York*, iii. 163.
Blakiston *of Seaton*, i. 276.
Blenkinsop *of Birtley ;* see Birtley.
Booth *of Old Durham*, iv. 92.
Booth *of Herefordshire*, iv. 92.
Booth *of Silksworth*, i. 246.
Bower *of Oxenfield*, iii. 367.
Bowes *of Barnes*, i. 236 ; iv. 116.
Bowes *of Thornton*, iii. 383.
Bowes *of Streatlam*, iv. 107.
Bowes *of Bradley and Biddic Waterville*, iv. 110.
Boynton *of Ravensworth ;* see Lumley.
Brakenbury *of Burnhall*, iv. 19.
Brakenbury *of Geddington, co. Northants.* iv. 20.
Brakenbury *of Killerby*, iv. 20.
Brandling *of Hoppen and Newcastle, and Little Eden, co. Pal.* ii. 92.
Brandling *of Newcastle-on-Tyne, and Ipswich, co. Suffolk*, ii. 92.
Brandling *of Felling, co. Pal. and Alnwick Abbey and Gosforth, co. Northumberland*, ii. 90.
Brandling *of Leathley, co. York*, ii. 91.
Brasse *of Broome, Whitwell House, &c.* i. 82.
Bright and Stonehewer, iv. 145.
Bristow *of Great Lumley*, ii. 167.
Bromley (*Hesleden*), i. 48.

Brunskill *of Barnard Castle*, iv. 93.
Brus *of Skelton and Annandale*, iii. 94.
Buck *of Sadberge*, iii. 269.
Bulmer *of Tursdale*, i. 79.
Bunny *of Newsham*, iv. 41.
Burdon, iii. 416.
Burleston *of Trimdon*, i. 110.
Burnopp *of Hamsteels*, ii. 334.
Burnynghill *of Newbiggen;* see Bynchestre.
Burnynghill (*Houghton le Spring*), i. 199.
Burwell, iv. 168.
Busby *of Cassop and Millfield*, i. 75.
Butler *of Old Acres*, iii. 49.
Byerley *of Midridge Grange*, iii. 313.
Byers *of Newbottle*, i. 180.
Bynchestre, Burnynghill and Crosier *of Newbiggin*, iii. 310.
Carrow (*Stanton*), iii. 131.
Carlele (*Houghton-le-Spring*), i. 196.
Carnaby (*Ryton*) *;* see Horsley.
Carr *of Cocken*, i. 208, 209.
Chamber *of Cleadon, co. Pal. and Dagenham, co. Essex*, ii. 55.
Chandler, i. cxxi.
Charron, Monboucher, Harbotel, and Percy, Lords of Beamish and Tanfield, ii. 225.
Chaunceler, *of Brafferton*, iii. 329.
Chaytor *of Butterby and Croft*, iv. 111.
Clavering *of Chopwell;* see Dudley.
Clavering *of Axwell*, ii. 248.
Clavering *of Gateshead and Cawsey*, ii. 228.
Claxton *of Old Park*, iii. 299.
Claxton *of Burnhall*, iv. 97.
Claxton, Lords of Horden; see Menvill.
Claxton (*Hulam*), i. 57.
Claxton; see Langton.
Clopton *of Sledwish*, iv. 48.
Colley (*Houghton-le-Spring*), i. 198.
Collingwood *of Dalden, Eppleton, and Hetton-on-the-Hill*, i. 7.
Conyers *of Cotham Conyers*, iii. 219.
Conyers *of Elemore;* see Hall.
Conyers, Lords of Horden; see Menvill.
Conyers *of Layton*, iii. 37.
Conyers *of Sockburne*, iii. 247.

Conyers; see Langton.
Cooper *of Durham*, iv. 150.
Cosyn, i. cxiv.
Coundon *of Nesham, co. Pal. and Willerby, co. York*, iii. 262.
Cradock *of Gainford*, iv. 13.
Crosier *of Newbiggin;* see Bynchestre.
Dalden (*Dalton-le-Dale*), i. 6.
Dale *of Tunstall*, i. 251.
Dale *of Staindrop, co. Pal. and Gillfield, Yorksh.* iv. 145.
Darcy, Co-Heirs of, i. 182.
Davenport (*Houghton-le-Spring*), i. 170.
Davison *of Blakiston*, iii. 166.
Davison *of Thornley Gore, and Elvet*, iii. 167.
Davison *of Beamish*, ii. 227.
Dearham *of Brimelawe*, iv. 152.
De Denum *of Offerton*, i. 192.
Dent *of Piersbridge*, iv. 33.
Dethick *of Amerston*, iii. 87.
Dodsworth *of Stranton*, iii. 123.
Dolphanby (*Gateshead*) ii. 117.
Doubleday *of Butterby*, iv. 112.
Dowthwaite *of Westholme*, iv. 42.
Dovre, *of Chilham*, iv. 61.
Draper *of Headlam*, iv. 31.
Duck, Heslop, and Nicholson, iv. 156.
Dudley and Clavering *of Chopwell*, ii. 280.
Egleston *of Hunstanworth*, ii. 367.
Ellison *of Hebburn*, ii. 78, 79.
Elmeden *of Elmeden*, iii. 55.
Elstob *of Foxton*, iii. 47.
Emildon (*Silksworth*), i. 243.
Epplyngden, or Applynden *of Eppleton*, i. 217.
Errington (*Elton*), iii. 209.
Ettricke *of High Barnes*, i. 238.
Ettricke *of Silksworth;* see Middleton.
Ewbanke, iv. 141.
Farrer *of Mainsforth and Bradbury*, iii. 43.
Fawcett (*Boldon*), ii. 60.
Fayrehare *of Ford*, ii. 317.
Felton (*Medomsley*), iii. 285.
Fenwick (*Houghton-le-Spring*), i. 193.
Fenwick (*Newton Garths*), ii. 64.

Forcer *of Kelloe and Harberhouse*, i. 65.
Forster *of Darlington*, iii. 357.
Forster *of Durham*, iv. 152.
Frevile and Lambton *of Hardwick*, iii. 36.
Fulthorpe *of Fulthorpe and Tunstall, co. Pal. and Hipswell, co. York*, iii. 126.
Garnett *of Egglescliffe*, iii. 198.
Garth *of Bolam*, iv. 29.
Garth *of Headlam*, iv. 28.
Gascoigne *of Ravensworth ;* see Lumley.
Gategang (*Gateshead*), ii. 116.
Gifford *of Darlington*, iii. 356.
Gildeford (*Lanchester*), ii. 359.
Goodchild *of Pallion*, i. 240.
Gower (*Elton*), iii. 209.
Graystaynes, Alwent, and Birkbeck, *of Morton Tynemouth*, iv. 24.
Greenwell *of Ford and Kibblesworth*, ii. 318.
Grey *of Southwick, co. Pal.* ii. 19.
Griffith (*Houghton-le-Spring*), i. 151.
Gyll *of Houghton-le-Skene*, iii. 338.
Hadham *of Seaham*, i. 273.
Hagthorpe *of Nettlesworth*, ii. 204.
Hall *of Wingate*, i. 99.
Hall *of Elemore*, i. 121.
Hall, Conyers, and Baker *of Elemore*, i. 121.
Hall *of Hollenbush*, ii. 215.
Hall (*Medomsley*), ii. 291.
Hall *of Consett*, ii. 297.
Hall *of Greencroft*, ii. 323.
Hall *of Durham and Flass*, iv. 154.
Hall *of Newsham and Great Chilton*, iii. 207.
Halliman *of Lumley*, ii. 397.
Hancock *of Frereside ;* see Rawe.
Hansard and Ayscough *of Walworth, co. Pal. and of South Kelsey, co. Lincoln*, iii. 318.
Harbart (*Chester-le-Street*), ii. 205.
Harbotel (*Tanfield*) ; see Charron.
Harding *of Hollingside*, ii. 252.
Harpyn (*Kelloe*), i. 85.
Harrison *of Stubhouse ;* see Holmes.
Harrison *of Biermoor and Briansleap*, ii. 257.
Hawyk (*Little Eden*), i. 36.
Hagthorpe *of Nettleworth*, ii. 204.

Heath *of Kepyer*, iv. 70.
Heath *of Little Eden*, i. 38.
Hebborne *of Hardwick*, iii. 35.
Hedlam *of Stainton*, iv. 99.
Hedworth *of Chester Deanery*, ii. 151.
Hedworth *of Harraton*, ii. 184.
Hedworth *of Pokerley*, ii. 197.
Hedworth *of Ryton Woodside*, ii. 261.
Heighington *of Greystones*, iii. 275.
Heighington *of Windgate and Milnburngate*, i. 99.
Heron *of Eppleton*, i. 218.
Heslop ; see Duck.
Hickes (*Whitburn*), ii. 54.
Hildyard, *of Durham*, iv. 151.
Hilton *of Hilton*, ii. 26 ; iv. 167-170.
Hilton *of Swyne*, ii. 28.
Hilton *of South Shields, and of Sussex, London, and Leicester*, ii. 29.
Hilton *of Monkwearmouth*, ii. 35.
Hodgson *of Hebborne*, ii. 77.
Hodgson *of Manor House* (*Lanchester*), ii. 319.
Holmes and Harrison *of Stubhouse*, iv. 93.
Horsley and Carnaby (*Ryton*), ii. 266.
Howard *of Tursdale and Sunderland Bridge, co. Pal.* i. 80.
Hull *of Ousterley Field*, ii. 331.
Hunter *of Medomsley*, ii. 289.
Hutchinson *of Bitchburn and Dryburn*, iv. 155.
Hutchinson *of Framwellgate*, iv. 155.
Hutton, i. lxxxv.
Hutton *of Houghton-le-Spring*, i. 149.
Hutton *of Mainsforth*, iii. 19.
Hutton *of Woodham*, iii. 333.
Ile *of Darlington*, iii. 355.
Ironside *of Houghton-le-Spring*, i. 150.
Jackson (*Haugton-le-Skerne*), iii. 271.
Jackson *of Harraton*, ii. 183.
Jakson *of Farrington Hall*, i. 246.
James *of Washington and Hetton-le-Hole*, i. 216.
Jefferson *of Durham*, iv. 156.
Jenison *of Low Walworth*, iii. 320.

Jenison *of Hurworth and Nesham Abbey*, iii. 263.
Jenison *of Elswick, co. Northumberland*, iii. 322.
Johnson *of Twysel*, ii. 200.
Johnson *of Kibblesworth*, ii. 218.
Johnson *of Whorlton*, iv. 45.
Kendal *of Thorpthewles*, iii. 81.
Kennet *of Sellendge, in Kent, and of Coxhoe, co. Pal.* i. 72.
Killinghall *of Middleton St. George*, iii. 222.
Lambe *of West Herrington*, i. 186.
Lambton *of Lambton*, ii. 174.
Lambton *of Tribley*, ii. 201.
Lambton *of Newham*, ii. 397.
Lambton *of Hardwick;* see Frevile.
Lambton *of Great Stainton, Belsis, and Haughton Field*, iii. 62.
Lambert *of Owton*, iii. 133.
Langton, Conyers, and Claxton, Lords of Winyard, iii. 79.
Latimer and Nevill, iv. 162.
Laton, Tylliol, and Musgrave, Owners of Hetton, i. 215.
Lawson *of Usworth*, ii. 47.
Lawson *of Nesham Abbey*, iii. 264.
Lawson *of Thorp-Bulmore*, i. 61.
Lee *of Fishburn*, iii. 52.
Lee *(Monk Wearmouth)*, ii. 7.
Liddell *of Farnacres*, ii. 245.
Liddell *of Ravensworth*, ii. 212.
Lister *(Trimdon)*, i. 110.
Loyzelure *of Coatsay Moor*, iii. 315.
Lumley, Earl of Scarborough, ii. 162.
Lumley *of Great Lumley*, ii. 168.
Lumley, Boynton, and Gascoigne *of Ravensworth*, ii. 241.
Machell *of Pittfield*, iii. 38.
Machon *of Sherburn House*, i. 143.
Maddison *of Saltwellside and Newcastle-upon-Tyne*, ii. 135.
Maire *of Hartbushes, co. Pal.* i. 52.
Maire *of Hardwick, co. Durham,* and Appleby *of Lartington, N.R. co. York*, i. 53.
March *of Redworth*, iii. 308.
Marley *of Gibside and Marley Hill*, ii. 256.
Marshall *of Selaby*, iv. 21.

Martin *of Durham*, iv. 149.
Mascall *of Eppleton, co. Pal.* i. 220.
Meaburne *of Pontop*, ii. 351.
Meisnell *of Stainton*, iv. 47.
Menvill, Claxton, and Conyers, Lords of Horden, i. 28.
Metcalfe *of Alwent*, iv. 22.
Mickleton *of Crookhall*, iv. 140.
Middleton *of Offerton*, i. 195.
Middleton, Ettricke, and Robinson *of Silksworth*, i. 245.
Middleton *of Barnard Castle*, iv. 70.
Middleton, iv. 168.
Midford *of Pespoole*, i. 21.
Milbanke *of Halnaby, co. Ebor.; and of Seaham and Dalden, co. Pal.* i. 274.
Millot *(Chester-le-Street)*, ii. 153.
Monboucher ; see Charron.
Moorcroft, iii. 415.
Morland *(Haughton-le-Skerne)*, iii. 276.
Morpeth *of Stillington*, iii. 74.
Mountaigne, i. xci.
Mowbray *of Ford*, i. 242.
Musgrave ; see Laton.
Neile, i. lxxxix.
Nesham *of Houghton-le-Spring*, i. 151.
Nevill ; see Latimer.
Neville *of Raby*, iv. 158.
Neville *of Thornton Bridge*, iv. 163.
Neville *of Weardale*, iv. 163.
Nicholson ; see Duck.
Norton, i. clx. clxi.
Norton *of Stranton*, iii. 125.
Ord and Wright *of Bradbury*, iii. 41.
Orde *of Fishburn*, iii. 53.
Parke *(Lanchester)*, ii. 320.
Parkinson *of Haghouse*, iv. 144.
Pattison *of Hedworth*, ii. 81.
Paule *of West Hartburne*, iii. 220.
Peacock *of Burnhall*, iv. 99.
Peareth *of Usworth*, ii. 45.
Pemberton *of Bainbridge-Holme and Barnes*, i. 237.
Pemberton *of Aislaby and Middleton St. George*, iii. 205.
Percy *(Tanfield)* ; see Charron.
Perkynson *of Beaumond Hill and Whessoe*, iii. 347.
Phillip *of Morton Tynemouth*, iv. 24.

Pilkington, i. lxxix.
Place *of Dinsdale, co. Pal. and Halnaby, co. York*, iii. 236.
Porter and Blakiston *of Shieldron,* ii. 231.
Prescott *of Darlington,* iii. 370.
Punshon *of West Herrington,* i. 182.
Radclyffe *of Dilston and Derwentwater,* Lords of Hawthorne, i. 32.
Radcliffe *of Tunstall and Newton Hansard,* iii. 129.
Rand, iii. 417.
Ravensworth (*Gateshead*), ii. 115.
Rawe and Hancock *of Frereside,* ii. 234.
Rayne *of Gainford,* iv. 15.
Redheugh and White *of Redheugh,* ii. 132.
Reed *of Cassop,* i. 75.
Richardson *of Cater House,* iv. 145.
Richardson *of Durham,* iv. 151.
Ridell *of Gateshead, Fenham, Swinburne Castle and Felton,* ii. 128.
Robinson *of Herrington,* i. 190.
Robinson *of Silksworth;* see Middleton.
Robson *of West Morton,* iii. 57.
Roper *of Trimdon,* i. 107.
Rowe *of Plawsworth,* ii. 203.
Rudd *of Shincliffe,* iv. 107.
Salvin *of Croxdale,* iv. 117.
Salvin *of Sunderland Bridge,* iv. 120.
Sampson (*Pelawe*), ii. 187.
Sanderson *of Hedleyhope,* iii. 343.
Sayer *of Worsall;* see Seton.
Scarborough, Earls of; see Lumley.
Scurfield and Addison *of Offerton,* i. 194.
Scurfield *of Kibblesworth,* ii. 218.
Scurfield *of Elstob,* iii. 65.
Sedgwick *of Thorpthewles,* iii. 82.
Selby *of Winlaton,* ii. 274.
Seton (*Castle Eden*); see Thorp.
Seton and Sayer *of Worsall and Preston-on-Tees,* iii. 190.
Shadforth *of Eppleton,* i. 221.
Shadforth (*Wardon*), i. 227.
Shafto *of Benwell, co. Northumberland,* iii. 296.
Shafto *of Wickham and Swalwell,* ii. 246.

Shafto *of Tanfield,* ii. 220.
Shafto *of Whitworth,* iii. 294.
Shipperdson *of Merton and Bainbridge-holme,* i. 114.
Shipperdson *of Piddinghall Garth ;* see Sympson.
Silvertop *of Minsteracres, co. Northumberland,* i. 52.
Simpson *of Bradley ;* see Anderson.
Skepper *of Durham,* iv. 150.
Smart *of Snotterton,* iv. 142.
Smith *of Burnhall,* iv. 98.
Smith *of West Herrington,* i. 187.
Smythe *of Eshe and Nunstainton,* ii. 338.
Somerset *of Cleatham,* iv. 33.
Spearman *cos. Durham, and Northumberland,* i. 94.
Spearman *of Hetton-le-Hole, Thornley and Bishop Middleham,* i. 95.
Spearman *of Oldacres,* i. 96.
Stevenson *of Byerside and Manor House,* ii. 292.
Stonehewer; see Bright.
Story *of Bishopwearmouth,* i. 233.
Straithmore, Earls of; see Bowes.
Surtees *of Dinsdale,* iii. 234.
Surtees *of Durham and Ravensworth,* iv. 168.
Swinburn *of Chopwell,* ii. 278.
Swinburne (*Kelloe*), i. 71.
Sympson and Shipperdson *of Piddinghall Garth,* i. 115.
Tailbois (*Hurworth*), iii. 254.
Tailbois *of Thornton,* iii. 382.
Talbot, i. cxx.
Teasdale *of Whitwell Grange and Newbrough,* i. 82.
Tempest *of Stella and Stanley,* ii. 271.
Tempest *of Thornley,* ii. 275.
Tempest *of Holmeside,* ii. 327.
Tempest *of Old Durham,* iv. 93.
Thirkeld and Amcoats (*Houghton le Spring*), i. 197.
Thomlinson *of Gateshead,* ii. 117.
Thorp and Seton (*Castle Eden*), i. 43.
Thursby *of Woolhouse,* iv. 95.
Tonge *of West Thickley,* iv. 4.
Toode *of Eppleton,* i. 219.
Trayne *of Streatlam,* iv. 100.
Trollop *of Thornley,* i. 92.
Trollop *of Crossgate,* i. 93.

Tunstall *of Cotham Mandeville,* iii. 272.

Tunstall *of Thurland,* i. lxvi.

Tweddell *of Thorpthewles,* iii. 82.

Tylliol ; see Laton.

Umfraville *(Lanchester),* ii. 325.

Umfraville, ii. 394.

Vane *of Long Newton,* iii. 214.

Vasey *(Coniscliffe),* iii. 381.

Walker *(Hesleden),* i. 47.

Walton *of Durham,* iv. 154.

Ward *of Bishop Middleham,* iii. 13.

Warde *of Trimdon,* i. 110.

Wardell *(Edmondsley),* ii. 198.

Watson and Baxter *of Whitworth,* iii. 292.

Welbury *of Castle Eden,* i. 43.

Wharton *(Houghton-le-Spring),* i. 194.

Wharton *of Old Park,* iii. 300.

Wheler *(Houghton-le-Spring),* i. 176.

White *of Redheugh ;* see Redheugh.

Whittingham *of Holmside,* ii. 330.

Whytehed *of Monkwearmouth,* ii. 8.

Widdrington *of Monkwearmouth,* ii. 8.

Wilkinson *(Kelloe),* i. 81.

Wilkinson *of Harpley and Kyo,* ii. 349.

Wilkinson *of Kirkerigg, co. York,* iv. 3.

Wilkinson *of West Layton,* iv. 3.

Williamson, *of East Markham, co. Notts. and Monkwearmouth, co. Pal.* ii. 9.

Willey *(Jarrow),* ii. 74.

Willy *of Haughton-le-side,* iv. 5.

Wilson *of Seaton and Cassop,* i. 276.

Wilson *of Field House, afterwards of Lumley Castle,* ii. 133.

Wray *of Beamish,* ii. 226.

Wright *of Bradbury ;* see Ord.

Wright *of Durham,* iv. 153.

Wycliffe *of Offerton,* i. 194.

Wycliffe *of Whorlton,* iv. 46.

Wyvill, *of Nesham,* iii. 263.

Yeland, *of Seaham,* i. 273.

Young *of Edderacres,* i. 22.

39.—An Historical and Descriptive View of the Parishes of Monkwearmouth and Bishopswearmouth, and the Port and Borough of Sunderland. By GEORGE GARBUTT. *Sunderland,* 1819. 8vo.

Hilton *of Hilton Castle,* folding at 99.

40.—The Heraldic Visitatione of yᵉ Countye Palatyne of Durham, in the Yeare of our Lord God, 1575. *Newcastle,* 1820. Folio.

Baynbrige *of Wheteley-hill,* 47.

Baynbrigge *of Snotterton,* 5.

Billingham *of Crook Hall,* 40.

Blackett *of Woodcrofte,* 17.

Blaykeston *of Blaykeston,* 19.

Blaykeston *of Sadbery,* 50.

Blaykeston *of Thornton Hall,* 51.

Blenkinsoppe *of Byrtley,* 48.

Boothe *of Old Durham,* 52.

Bowes *of Streatlam,* 2.

Brackenbury *of Sellaby,* 7.

Butler *of Bishope Aukland,* 49.

Cheytor *of Butterby,* 30.

Claxton *of Wynyard,* 55.

Conyers *of Horden,* 53.

Croyser *of Newbigginge,* 20.

Eden *of West Aukland,* 12.

Elstobbe *of Foxton,* 27.

Fetherstonhaughe *of Stanhope Hall,* 9.

Forser *of Kellow,* 31.

Hagthorpe *of Nettlesworthe,* 41.

Hall *of Greencroft and Byrtley,* 44.

Hardinge *of Holmsyde,* 32.

Hebborne *of Shotton,* 24.

Hedworth *of Harverton,* 42.

Heron *of Est Thickley,* 15.

Hull *of Ousterleyfield,* 43.

Hutton *of Hunwyke,* 14.

Kendall *of Thorpthules,* 25.

Lambert *of Owlton,* 57.

Lambton *of Belsis,* 28.

Lambton *of Lambton*, 38.
Lawson *of Usworthe*, 35.
Madysonne *of Unthanke*, 10.
Marche *of Redworthe*, 16.
Midleton *of Bernard Castell*, 8.
Millot *of Whittell*, 33.
Mydleton *of Silkesworthe*, 56.
Perkinson *of Beaumondhill*, 11.
Pilkington, Bishop of Durham, 1.
Playse *of Dynsdell*, 23.
Porter *of Shildroe*, 39.

Preston *of East Morton*, 21.
Punshon *of West Herrington*, 46.
Ratcliffe *of Newton*, 29.
Shaftoe *of Anvill*, 45.
Surtees *of Midleton one Row*, 22.
Thomlinson *of Gateside*, 37.
Tonge *of West Thickeley*, 4.
Trollope *of Morden*, 26.
Tunstall *of Stockton*, 34.
White *of Redheughe*, 36.
Wrenne *of Billyhall*, 13.

41.—The Antiquities of Gainford, in the County of Durham, &c. By JOHN RICHARD WALBRAN. *Ripon*, 1846, 8vo. Part 1. *All published.*

Alwent, 50.
Baliol, Barons of Gainford, folding at 147.
Blaxton, 49.
Birkbeck *of Headlam and Morton Tynmouth ;* with Draper, Mossock and Brockett *of Headlam*, folding at 106.
Brockett *of Headlam;* see Birkbeck.
Dent, 58.
Draper *of Headlam ;* see Birkbeck.

Eden, 51.
Fotherby, 87.
Garth *of Headlam and Bolam, co. Durham*, folding at 110.
Headlam, 56.
Malet, 88.
Mossock *of Headlam ;* see Birkbeck.
Swainston, 57.
Vane *of Raby Castle*, unpaged, in some copies only.

42.—The History and Antiquities of North Durham, &c. (Now a part of Northumberland.) By the Rev. JAMES RAINE, M.A. *London*, 1852. Folio.

Alder *of Horncliffe*, 301.
Askew *of Goswick ;* see Watson.
Blake *of Twisell*, 316.
Cary, Lord Hunsdon, 30.
Cheswick, Strangeways, and Donaldson *of Cheswick*, 228.
Clavering *of Berrington*, 213.
Donaldson *of Cheswick ;* see Cheswick.
Forster *of Thornton, Bamborough Castle, &c.* 306.
Forster *of Cornhill*, 322.
Goswick and Middleham *of Goswick*, 182.
Gregson *of Lowlinn*, 206.
Grey *of Heaton, Chillingham, Howick, Bitchfield, &c.* folding at 326.
Grey *of Kyloe*, 327.
Haggerston *of Haggerston*, faces 224.
Heron *of Ford Castle, Thornton, &c.* 304.

Lawson *of Scremerston;* see Swinhoe.
Manners *of Etal*, 209.
Manors *of Etal Castle and Bering.ton*, 211.
Manners *of Cheswick*, 230.
Middleton *of Goswick ;* see Goswick.
Muschamp (*Norham*), 266.
Muschamp *of Barmoor*, 267.
Nicholson *of Loan End*, 302.
Oglo *of Choppington*, 371.
Orde *of Holy Island*, 159.
Orde *of Orde*, 248.
Orde *of East Orde and Berwick*, 250.
Orde *of West Orde*, 253.
Orde *of Longridge*, 303.
Orde *of Newbiggin*, 311.
Orde *of Grindon*, 320.
Reade or Reede *of Fenham*, 179.
Reveley *of Ancroft, Berwick, Tweedmouth, &c.* 221.

G

Riddell *of Tillmouth*, 325.
Selby *of Beal*, 338.
Selby *of Lowlinn*, 206.
Selby *of Twisell*, 315.
Selby *of Holy Island and Swans-field*, 338.
Strangeways *of Cheswick*; see Cheswick.
Swinhoe *of Goswick*, 184.

Swinhoe and Lawson *of Scremerston*, 237.
Watson and Askew *of Goswick*, 186.
Watson *of Grindon Ridge*, 319.
Wilkie *of Ladythorne and Broomham in Islandshire, and Eland Hall in Hetton, Northumberland*, 233.

43—The History and Antiquities of the Parish of Darlington, in the Bishoprick. By W. HYLTON DYER LONG-STAFFE, Esq., F.S.A. *Darlington*, 1854. Royal 8vo. and 4to.

Allan *of Buckenhall and Brockhouse in Staffordshire, Darlington and Blackwell in Durham, and Boston in Yorkshire*, (not paged.)
Backhouse, xciii.
Barnes *of Darlington*, lxxxi.
Bower *of Oxenfield*, lxxxv.
Bowes, xcii.
Clervaux *of York city*; and Croft and Cowton *in Richmondshire, and Darlington, co. Pal.*; and Chaytor *of Croft and Butterby*, (not paged.)

Daykins, xcii.
Emerson, xcii.
Helton, Hylton, or Hilton, *of Helton Bacon, Burton, and Ormside, in the co. Westmoreland, Hilton in Staindropshire, Stranton and Darlington in the co. Palatine*, (not paged.)
Ile, lxxxvii.
Ornsby, xciv.
Pease, xciv.
Prescott *of Darlington and Blackwell*, (not paged.)

44.—Heraldic Visitation of the Northern Counties in 1530. By THOMAS TONGE, Norroy, &c. *Surtees Society*, Vol. 41. 1863, 8vo. *See also Cumberland, Nottinghamshire, Northumberland, Yorkshire, and Westmoreland.*

Brakynbury *of Denton*, 41.
Hedworth, 37.
Hilton, 36.
Lumley, Lords, 26.

Nevill, Earl of Westmoreland, 27.
Rokeby, 40.
Tonge *of Ekilsall*, 39.
Wyclyff *of Wyclyf*, 40.

ESSEX.

45.—The History of Essex. By N. TINDAL, *London, n. d.* 4to. Parts 1 and 2, *all published.*

Rich, 24.

46.—The History of Audley End, to which are appended, Notices of the Town and Parish of Saffron Walden, in the County of Essex. By RICHARD, LORD BRAYBROOKE. *London*, 1836, 4to.

Audley, 24.
Buckingham, Dukes of; see Stafford·
Byrde *of Saffron Walden*, 292.

Smijth *of Saffron Walden and Hill Hall, Essex*, 285.
Stafford, Earls of Stafford and Dukes of Buckingham, 7.

47.—The Proceedings of the Essex Archæological Society. *Colchester*, 8vo. Vols. 1—3. Commenced in 1855.

Durward or Doreward, and Yngoe, iii. 100.
Marney, iii. 9.
Shakspere *of Stratford on Avon*, and Shakspere *of Essex*, folding at 74.

Strangman or Strangeman *of Hadleigh Castle, Essex*, 99.
Yngoe ; see Durward.

48.—County Genealogies. Pedigrees of Essex Families collected by WM. BERRY, &c. *London*, no date, folio.

Abdy, 7.
Adams, 16.
Albini ; see De Albini.
Alleyn, 88.
Amundeville ; see De Amundeville.
Anderson, 19.
Andrewes, 114.
Archer, 161.
Arundel, Earl of, 67.
Astle or Astley, 79, 135.
Audley, 134.
Balston, 117.
Barrington, 124.
Bayles, 37.
Bindon, Viscount, 73.
Bodle, 87.
Bonham, 78, 167.
Boyne, Viscount, 65.
Boys ; see De Boys.
Bramston, 49.
Brise, 84.
Brown, 110.
Bullock, 105.
Callis, 92.
Carington, 129.
Carwardine, 114.
Caswall, 33.
Chenow, 70.
Chichley, 71.
Clarendon, 11.
Conyers, 140.
Copdow, 64.
Corsellis, 44.
Cressener, 121.
Dacre, Lord, 166.
Dare, 76.
De Albini, 67.
De Amundeville, 1.
De Boys, 161.
De Isney, 1.
Derham, 86.

Derwentwater, Earl of, 138.
Disney, 5.
Drury, 72.
Du Cane, 14.
Du Quesne, 45.
Eaton, 76.
Eccles, 18.
Elgar, 87.
Estleigh, 135.
Eyre, 162.
Fitch ; see Fytch.
Fitz Alan, 67.
Fizt Flal, 67.
Fitz Gerald, 43.
Fitz Walter, 43.
Flemyng, 64.
Flytche, 4.
Freeland, 29.
Fytch or Fitch, 146.
Gent, 88.
Gerard, 43.
Goodday, 117.
Gough, 47.
Grafton, 77.
Grand ; see Le Grand.
Green, 110.
Grymston, 148.
Hall, 77.
Hamilton, 65.
Hankey, 110.
Harlakenden, 113.
Harvey, 24.
Havens, 37.
Hervey, 68, 126.
Higham, 104.
Hills, 81.
Holgate, 115.
Honywood, 72.
Houblon, 164.
Howard, Lord, 73.
Hutchinson, 37.

Isney ; see De Isney.
Jesse, 5.
Jocelyn, 119.
Le Grand, 70.
Le Neve, 155.
Lennard, 166.
Lescher, 20.
Lockwood, 169.
Lockwood-Percival, 169.
Lovekin, 37.
Lovibond, 65.
Luard, 101.
Marlow, 62.
Marney, 73.
Maydwell, 169.
Maynard, 103.
Mildmay, 69, 149.
Miller, 47.
Mitchel, 117.
Neave or Le Neve, 155.
Nerwyt, 68.
Neville, 71.
Nichol e or Nicholl, 46, 47.
Northumberland, Earl of, 71.
Nowell, 18.
Onley, 127.
Onley, Savill- ; see Savill-Onley.
Osborne, 39.
Paisley, Lord, 65.
Papillon, 22.
Percy, 71.
Perry, 110.
Petre, Lord, 138.
Plantagenet, 66.
Quarles, 114.
Quesne ; see Du Quesne.
Radcliffe, 18.

Rahn, 47.
Rayleigh, Baron, 117.
Rawstone, 23.
Raymond, 26.
Rebow, 16.
Rebow ; see Slater.
Round, 31.
Ruggles, 84.
Rush, 82.
Rutherforth, 9.
Savill-Onley, 127.
Scott, 85.
Shirley, 91.
Slater, now Rebow, 16.
Smith, 14, 129, 158, 160.
Smijth, 11, 34, 130.
Sparrow, 53.
Strutt, 117.
Sulyard, 64.
Tendering. 142.
Thompson, 88.
Thynne, 117.
Tufnaile or Tuffnell, 121.
Tyrell, 57.
Tyssen, 63.
Walmesley, 39.
Warren, 66, 96.
Watson, 108.
Western, Lord, 91.
Westmoreland, Earls of, 71.
Weymouth, Viscount, 117.
White, 35, 144.
Wiltshire, 70.
Windsor, 43.
Wood, 11.
Wright, 100.
Wrottesley, 162.

GLOUCESTERSHIRE.

49.—Graphic Illustrations, with Historical and Descriptive Accounts of Toddington, Gloucestershire, the Seat of Lord Sudeley. By JOHN BRITTON, F.S.A. *London,* 1840. 4to.

Sudeley *of Sudeley,* extinct in the male line, 1441, v.
Tracy *of Toddington,* i.
Tracy, first branch of the Stanway line, iv.

Tracy, second branch, seated at Stanway, iv.
Tracy, Coscombe branch, v.
Vere, issue of Lord, and Mary, sister of Viscount Tracy, iv.

HAMPSHIRE.

50.—County Genealogies. Pedigrees of Families in the County of Hants. By WM. BERRY. *London*, 1833, folio.

Abarow or Abarrow, 284.
Alchorne, 197.
Allexander, 316.
Alphe, 247.
Andrews, 330.
Arnwood, 247.
Asheldam, 210.
Ashman, 177.
Attehooke, 97.
Austen, 48.
Ayliffe, 284.
Aylward, 177.
Bacon, 305.
Banbury, 90.
Banester, 81.
Baring, 345.
Barkley, 209.
Barloe, 235.
Barnham, 167.
Barthelmew, 49.
Baskervile, 7.
Basket, 160.
Baskett, 197.
Bassett, 194.
Bayley, 239.
Bayly, 8.
Beach, 257.
Beausarvire, 234.
Beckford, 105, 266, 274.
Bee, 9.
Beeston, 290.
Bellamy, 157.
Belsonn, 316.
Benett, 157.
Berkeley, 125.
Beronsaw, 124.
Bethell, 300.
Bettesworth, 208.
Betts, 244.
Bill, 216.
Blachford, 79.
Blake, 145, 306.
Boileau, 66.
Bonham, 111, 160.
Bostock, 13.
Bourne, Sturges-; see Sturges-Bourne.
Bowreman, 78.
Bowyer, 9, 250.

Boys, 129.
Bramston, 258.
Braybuff, 287.
Brereton, 209.
Bretton, 41.
Bridgman, 137.
Brigstocke, 159.
Broad, 197.
Brocas, 90, 197, 271.
Brockholes, 210.
Brodnax, 46.
Brokas, 197.
Brooke, 339.
Brudnell, 109.
Bulkler, 21.
Burley, 289.
Burrard, 154.
Button, 33.
Campbell, 139.
Campton, 177.
Capel, 342.
Cary, 196.
Chamberlyn, 337.
Champanti, 233.
Champion, 311.
Chandler, 52.
Cheeke, 98.
Chute, 117.
Clare, Earl of, 125.
Clarke-Jervoise, 341.
Clerke, 315.
Cobb, 292.
Colnett, 16.
Colt, 293.
Compton, 328.
Conway, 287.
Cope, 301.
Copley, 271.
Corham, 172.
Cotton, 52.
Cowdrey, 324.
Creswell, 24, 248.
Cuffold, 281.
Dalridgecourt, 70.
Davies, 207.
Dawley, 321.
Dawtry, 106, 112.
De Alta Ripa, 112.
Deane, 20, 270, 183.

De Clare, Earl of, 125.
De Insula, or Lisle, 173, 193, 271.
Delamore, 70.
De la Warr, Lord, 198, 219.
Dene, 20, 283.
Denefield, 20.
Denmead, 41.
Denys, 197, 271.
Dering, 219.
De Roches, 90.
De Worting, 234.
Dickonson, 351.
Dillington, 116, 308.
Dingley, 17, 213.
Dottin, 10.
Doughty, late Tichborne, 31.
Dowse, 12.
Drew, 53.
Durant, 281.
Earlsman, 309.
Edmonds, 120.
Effingham, Earl of, 277.
Eliot, 126.
Estwicke, 12.
Etterick, 282.
Fane, 113.
Fashin, 129.
Fawknor, 239, 297.
Fell, 127.
Fellowes, late Wallop, 42.
Fisher, 234.
Fitz-Gilbert, 125.
Fitz-Hugh, 144.
Fleming, 126, 259.
Flower, 37.
Foyle, 334.
Freeland, 108.
Frere, 12.
Fulwer, or Fuller, 286.
Gardiner, 170.
Gaynsford, 242.
Giffard, 125.
Gifford, 285.
Glynn, 132.
Goddard, 186.
Goldsmith, 88.
Goodlad, 197.
Goodwyn, 111.
Gorges, 125.
Gray, 253.
Guilford, 200.
Gunter, 177.
Guy, 210.

Haggerston, 169.
Hamilton and Brandon, Dukes of, 276.
Hamlyn, 287.
Hanbury, 133.
Harris, Earl of Malmesbury, 332.
Harris or Heirres, 25, 28.
Harrison, 48.
Hawley, 340.
Hawte, 219.
Haydock, 216.
Heathcote, 82.
Hellier, 77.
Henley, 251.
Herbert, 157, 209.
Hertford and Pembroke, Earls of, 125.
Herward, 280.
Hewett, 325.
Hicks, 79, 119, 254.
Hill, 185, 319.
Hobbs, 158.
Hobson or Hobsonn, 269.
Holcroft, 304.
Holmes, Lord, 350.
Holowell, 283.
Holt, 209, 210.
Hooke, 212.
Horkett, 116.
Houghton, 236.
Howard, Earls of Effingham, 277.
Howard, 125.
Hulse, 342.
Hulton, 150.
Hungerford, 215.
Hurlbatt, 322.
Hussey, 160.
Hyde, 264.
Ingpen, 220.
Iremonger, 14.
Irton, 116.
James, 188.
Jephson, 264.
Jervoise, Clarke- ; see Clarke-Jervoise.
Jones, 11.
Kedwelley, 51.
Kelloway, 338.
Kempe, 89.
Kingsmill, 44, 224.
Kingston, 53, 174.
Kingswell, 322.
Kirkby, 267, 268.

Knight, 17, 46, 261, 306, 320.
Knowles, 40.
Lambert, 77, 180, 330.
Langrish, 236.
Lawrens, 248.
Leeds, 272.
Leg, 357.
Leigh, 79, 123, 294.
Lewkenor, 46.
Lillingston, 10.
Limbrey, 68.
Lind, 159.
Lisle ; see De Insula.
Lisley, 193, 271.
Lister, 240.
Lloyd, 246.
Lobb, 119.
Long, 22, 149.
Love, 266.
Ludlow, 161.
Luther, 113.
Lyndhurst, 106.
Lyne, 344.
Lys, 69.
Lyssley, 177.
Manners, Lord Roos, 54.
March, 175, 176, 196, 354.
Marshal, 72.
Martin, 46.
Mathew, 68.
May, 46.
Meeres, 114.
Meller, 8.
Meux, 54, 135.
Mildme or Mildmay, 225.
Miller, 139, 147.
Mompesson, 111.
Moningham, 215.
Monk, 47.
Moody, 95.
Moore, 73, 192, 296.
Mordaunt, Baron, 206.
Morley, 157, 246.
Morris, 288.
Mowbray, 125.
Neale, 149, 155.
Nicholas, 93.
Norris, 178.
North, 245.
Norton, 106, 194.
Oglander, 130.
Okeden, 329.
Owen, 219.

Oxenbridge, 214.
Palmes, 298.
Parmiger, 349.
Pawlett, 148, 268.
Pelham, 137.
Penris, 71.
Peper, 222.
Pepsall, 333.
Pescod, 328.
Pesmeade, 272.
Pexsall, 90.
Phillipps, 176.
Pigeon, 115.
Pistar, 262.
Pitt, Lords Rivers, 101.
Player, 159.
Plessitis, 261.
Pollen, 66.
Poole, 168.
Popham, 181, 197.
Pounde, 194.
Puttenham, 288.
Rennell, 1.
Rice, 121.
Rich, 13.
Richards, 18.
Ricketts, 163.
Rider, 167.
Riggs, 306.
Ringwood, 237.
Rivers, Lord, 101, 276.
Roberts, 352.
Robye, 235.
Rogers, 193, 271.
Rolfe, 210, 279.
Romsey, 49.
Roos, Lord; see Manners.
Rotherfeld, 106.
Rous, 11.
Rudiard, 50.
Sadleir, 95.
St. Barbe, 4.
St. John, 67, 148, 232.
Salmon, 12.
Samborne, 271.
Samon, 278.
Savage, 291.
Scardeville, 112.
Sclater, 68.
Scroope, 64.
Shipley, 207.
Silver, 92.
Simeon, 100.

Simpson, 137.
Skilling, or Skylling, 299.
Smythe, 169.
Sompter, 210.
South, 145.
Sowle, 353.
Sprinte, 217.
Stapleton, 207.
Staunton, 61.
Staverton, 178.
Stewkley, 310.
Stockwith, 114.
Strangeways, 54, 135.
Stringfellow, 233.
Strode, 196.
Stuart, 189.
Sturges-Bourne, 336.
Stylleman, 60.
Surrenden, 219.
Talbot, 235.
Talk, 224.
Talke, 324.
Tame, 287.
Tanke, 234.
Thornburgh, 86.
Tichborne, 28.
Tichborne ; see Doughty.
Tisted, 29.
Titherleigh *of Tytherleigh*, 273.
Troughear, 352.
Trussell, 143.
Tutt, 38.
Twyne, 223.
Tyllington, 116.
Tytherleigh ; see Titherleigh.
Unwin, 59.
Urry, 79, 357.
Uvedall, 74.
Vaughan, 300.
Venables, 221.

Verney, 168.
Wadham, 196.
Wall, 65, 317.
Waller, 109, 358.
Wallop, 41.
Wallop ; see Fellowes.
Walter, 10.
Warham, 252.
Warnford, 314.
Watson, 331.
Wayte, 80, 110.
Wells, 110.
West, 191.
West, Lords De la Warr, 204, 219.
Westrow, 342.
Whalley, 171.
Whitchurch, 25.
White, 185, 194, 241, 260, 295.
Whitehead, 194.
Whithed, 287.
Wiggett, 119.
Williams, 73, 191.
Willis, 128.
Willoughby, 238.
Wilmott, 121.
Wiltshire, 177.
Windsor, 36.
Wither, 256, 326.
Wolff, 319.
Wolveridg, 313.
Wood, 71, 112.
Worsley, 84, 134, 353.
Worting ; see De Worting.
Wright, 323, 335.
Wylde, 127.
Wyndham, 196.
Wynyard, 205.
Yarborough, Lord, 137.
Yong, 318.
Yonge, 207.

51.—Brief Historical Notices of the Parishes of Hurstbourn
   Priors and St. Mary Bourn, &c. Hampshire. *London,*
   1861.   8vo.

Oxenbridge, 44, 46.

HEREFORDSHIRE.

52—A View of the Ancient and Present State of the
   Churches of Door, Home-Lacy, and Hempsted, &c.
   By MATTHEW GIBSON, M.A. *London,* 1727.   4to.

Scudamore, 54, 116.

HERTFORDSHIRE.

53.—The Historical Antiquities of Hertfordshire. By Sir HENRY CHAUNCY, Knt. *London*, 1700, folio; 2nd edition. *Bishop's Stortford*, 1826. 2 vols. 8vo.

Alington, 363 ; 2 ed. ii. 114.
Austen, 414 ; 2 ed. ii. 212.
Barrington, 366 ; 2 ed. ii. 120.
Berners, 160 ; 2 ed. i. 316.
Billers, 172 ; 2 ed. i. 338.
Blunt, 495 ; 2 ed. ii. 388.
Boteler, 333 ; 2 ed. ii. 57.
Bourstal and Bristow, 324; 2 ed. ii. 40.
Brograve, 227 ; 2 ed. ii. 445.
Capel, 158 ; 2 ed. ii. 313.
Cecil, 308 ; 2 ed. ii. 10.
Chauncy, 60 ; 2 ed. i. 120.
Cock, 296 ; 2 ed. ii. 580.
Coningsby, 462, 531 ; 2 ed. ii. 312, 441.
Dacre, 301 ; 2 ed. i. 586.
Denny, 300 ; 2 ed. i. 584.
Docwra, 406 ; 2 ed. ii. 196.
Elwis, 118 ; 2 ed. ii. 235.
Fairclough, 375 ; 2 ed. ii. 136.
Flyer, 142 ; 2 ed. i. 282.
Fountain, 531; 2 ed. ii. 441.
Frowick, 462 ; 2 ed. ii. 312.

Gardiner, 264 ; 2 ed. i. 519.
Jocelin, 183 ; 2 ed. i. 359.
Lee, 459 ; 2 ed. ii. 304.
Leventhorpe, 182 ; 2 ed. i. 358.
Lytton, 353 ; 2 ed. ii. 136.
Maynard, 40, 602 ; 2 ed. i. 82.
Mildmay, 179 ; 2 ed. ii. 351.
More, 534 ; 2 ed. ii. 448.
Moryson, 484 ; 2 ed. ii. 354.
Nevil, 281 ; 2 ed. i. 551.
Nicholl, 496 ; 2 ed. ii. 376.
Pilkington, 413 ; 2 ed. ii. 210.
Poultney, 535 ; 2 ed. ii. 450.
Pulter, 73 ; 2 ed. i. 146.
Robinson, 302 ; 2 ed. i. 588.
Sadleir, 398 ; 2 ed. ii. 180.
Sherburne, 62 ; 2 ed. i. 125.
Shotbolt, 61 ; 2 ed. i. 123.
Spencer, 405 ; 2 ed. ii. 195.
Taverner, 518 ; 2 ed. ii. 418.
Throckmorton, 368 ; 2 ed. ii. 123.
Tredenham, 208 ; 2 ed. ii. 409.
Waterhouse, 548 ; 2 ed. ii. 474.

54.—History and Antiquities of the County of Hertford. By ROBERT CLUTTERBUCK, Esq. *London*, 1815-27. 3 vols. folio.

Aguillon, Bardolf, Phelip, Beaumont, Lovell, Norreys and Stapilton (*Walton at Stone*), ii. 484.
Alington ; see Tecon.
Altham (*Watford*), i. 248.
Anderson and Harcourt (*Aldbury*), i. 285.
Ansell (*Ickleford*), iii. 57.
Argentine ; see Tecon.
Arnold *of Childwick*, i. 99.
Ashton and Buck (*Watford*), i. 251.
Aston ; see Sadleir.
Atkins (*Essenden*), ii. 131.
Austen (*St. Paul's Walden*), iii. 139.
Averenges (*Aldbury*), i. 280.
Babthorpe and Plumpton (*Sacomb*) ii. 424.
Bachesworth ; see Sumery.

Bacon (*Gorhambury*), i. 93.
Badlesmere and Tibetot, or Tiptoft (*Offley*), iii. 102.
Baesh (*Stansted Abbot's*), iii. 243.
Baliol (*Hitchin*), iii. 17.
Bardolf ; see Aguillon.
Bardolf ; see Cressy.
Barley ; see De la Lee.
Barlye ; see Bibbesworth.
Barrington (*Chisfield*), ii. 299.
Bassingburne and Gawdy (*Bishop's Hatfield*), ii. 345.
Beauchamp (*Flamsted*), i. 358.
Beauchamp (*Elstree*), i. 159.
Beaufort (*Hitchin*), iii. 31.
Beaumont ; see Aguillon.
Belasyse (*Sacomb*), ii. 425.
Belfield (*Studham*), i. 497.

H

Bellomonte; see Grentemaisnil.
Bennet (*Harpenden*), i. 411.
Benstede (*Benington*), ii. 280.
Berkley; see Mowbray.
Bibbesworth and Barlye (*Kimpton*), ii. 67.
Billers (*Thorley*), iii. 270.
Bisse; see Poyner.
Blackwell (*Bushey*), i. 335.
Blount, and Yorke, Earl of Hardwicke (*Ridge*), i. 211.
Blount; see Stalworth.
Blount; see Heron.
Bolebec; see Montfitchet.
Bovil (*Aldbury*), i. 280.
Boleyne; see Hoo.
Borough; see Cobham.
Boteler (*Wotton at Stone*), ii. 475.
Boteler and Hutchinson (*Bishop's Hatfield*), ii. 347.
Boteler and Villiers (*Bramfield*), ii. 46.
Botreaux; see Moels.
Bowles (*Wallington*), iii. 596.
Brand, Lord Dacre, iii. 73.
Braybrooke; see Reinbudicurt.
Brittany, Earls and Dukes of, and Earls of Richmond (*Cheshunt*), ii. 84.
Briscoe (*Elstree*), i. 158.
Bristow (*Great Ayot*), ii. 254.
Brocket and Reade (*Bishop's Hatfield*), ii. 360.
Brograve (*Braughing*), iii. 154.
Bromley (*Ware*), 304.
Broughton; see Peyver.
Browne (*North Mimms*), i. 448.
Browne (*Essenden*), ii. 130.
Brydges, Duke of Chandos, ii. 450.
Buck; see Ashton.
Bucknell and Grimston (*Watford*), i. 247.
Butler (*Tewin*), ii. 222.
Byde (*Ware*), iii. 297.
Byng (*Elstree*), i. 160.
Cæsar (*Benington*), ii. 286.
Calvert (*Albury*), iii. 335.
Calvert (*Hunsdon*), iii. 182.
Capel, Earl of Essex (*Watford*), i. 243.
Carnarvon, Earl of; see Dormer.
Cary (*Aldenham*), i. 129.

Cary, Lord Hunsdon, iii. 181.
Cecil, Marq. of Salisbury, ii. 339.
Chamberlayn (*Great Gaddesden*), i. 376.
Chandos, Duke of; see Brydges.
Chauncy (*Little Munden*), ii. 400.
Chelrey and Darell (*Lilley*), iii. 86.
Chester (*Barkway*), iii. 363.
Chesterfield, Earl of Stanhope, i. 494.
Cheyney, Willoughby, Greville, and Verney (*Cottered*), iii. 512.
Cheyney (*Aldenham*), i. 133.
Clare, De Burgh and Mortimer (*Standon*), iii. 225.
Clerke and Throckmorton (*Chisfield*), ii. 301.
Cliderowe (*Pirton*), iii. 121.
Clinton; see Limesi.
Clitheroe (*Little Wymondley*), ii. 551.
Clutterbuck (*Ware*), iii. 300.
Child (*Abbot's Langley*), i. 171.
Churchill (*Sandridge*), i. 217.
Clerke and Throckmorton (*Chisfield*), ii. 301.
Clinton; see Limesi.
Cobham and Borough (*King's Walden*), iii. 131.
Cocks; see Somers.
Coke; see Leventhorpe.
Combe (*Hemel Hempsted*), i. 418.
Comyn; see Fitz Walter.
Coningsby (*North Mimms*), i. 444.
Cowper (*Hertford*), ii. 194.
Cock and Monson (*Broxbourn*), ii. 55.
Coxe of Beaumonts, i. 114.
Coppin (*Caddington*), i. 347.
Creke and Vauncy (*Welwyn*), ii. 495.
Cressy and Bardolf (*Harpenden*), i. 407.
Crevequer (*Aldbury*), i. 280.
Criol (*Aldbury*), i. 280.
Cromwell (*Cheshunt*), ii. 95.
Crouch (*Layston*), iii. 429.
Dacre, Lord; see Brand.
Dacres (*Cheshunt*), ii. 101.
D'Arci (*Bovingdon*), i. 324.
Darell; see Chelrey.
Dauntsey and Langford (*Hitchin*), iii. 33

De Burgh ; see Clare.
De Burgh ; see Lanvallei.
De la Lee, Barley, Leventhorpe, and Frank (*Albany*), iii. 333.
De la Mare (*Offley*), iii. 100.
Denny (*Cheshunt*), ii. 107.
Derby, Earl of ; see Stanley.
Devereux (*Watford*), i. 245.
Devereux, Longespe, La Zouch and Holand (*Great Gaddesden*), i. 371.
D'Eschalers (*Widial*), iii. 471.
Dimsdale (*Little Birkhamsted*), ii 35.
Docwra and Warburton (*Lilley*), iii 82.
Dormer, Earl of Carnarvon ; and Stanhope, Earl of Chesterfield, i. 494.
Downshire, Marq. of ; see Hill.
Drake (*Wheathampsted*), i. 514.
Duncombe (*Sarret*), i. 222.
Dunster ; see Gardiner.
Egerton (*Little Gaddesden*), i. 391.
Elwes (*Throcking*), iii. 465.
Engaine (*Hunsdon*), iii. 178.
Ewer (*Watford*), i. 255.
Fanshawe (*Ware*), iii. 294.
Featherstone (*Ware*), iii. 299.
Feilde (*Stansted Abbot's*), iii. 243.
Ferrers (*Flamsted*), i. 360.
Fiennes, Lord Say and Sele, ii. 9.
Filmer (*Abbot's Langley*), i. 172.
Fitz Gerold (*Sawbridgeworth*), iii. 198.
Fitz Walter and Comyn (*Sacomb*), ii. 432.
Fitz Walter ; see Lanvallei.
Fitz Walter ; see Valoines.
Flyer (*Brent Pelham*), iii. 446.
Foliot ; see Reinbudccurt, iii. 58.
Forester ; see Pulter.
Fortescue (*Bishop's Hatfield*), ii. 348.
Fortibus ; see Montfichct.
Fotherley (*Rickmansworth*), i. 188.
Frank ; see De la Lee.
Franklyn (*Rickmansworth*), i. 194.
Fray, Say, and Waldegrave (*Great Munden*), ii. 391.
Freman (*Aspeden*), iii. 348.
Freville ; see Scalers.
Frowick (*Shenley*) i. 476.
Furnival ; see Lovetot.
Grape (*St. Peter's*), i. 112.

Gardiner and Dunster (*Hertford*), ii. 183.
Gardiner (*Thundridge*), iii. 279.
Garrard and Drake (*Wheathampsted*), i. 514.
Gatesdene (*Great Gaddesden*), i. 376.
Gawdy ; see Bassingburne.
Gobion (*Stapleford*), ii. 217.
Gore (*Gilston*), iii. 170.
Gore (*Tring*), i. 502.
Gould ; see Morgan.
Goulston (*Widial*), iii. 472.
Greene and Vaux (*Lilley*), iii. 80.
Grentemaisnil, Bellomonte, Quincy, La Zouch, Wake, Holand, Montacute, Neville, Earl of Salisbury, and Pole (*Ware*), iii. 287.
Greslei ; see Lavellei.
Greville ; see Cheyncy.
Grimston and Luckyn (*Gorhambury*), i. 95.
Grimston ; see Bucknall.
Hale (*King's Walden*), iii. 132.
Halsey (*Great Gaddesden*), i. 378.
Harcourt ; see Anderson.
Hardwicke, Earls of ; see Yorke.
Hare (*Bishop's Hatfield*), ii. 353.
Hare (*Totteridge*), ii. 454.
Harby (*Aldenham*), i. 130.
Harold, King of England, iii. 14.
Harrison and Townshend (*Hertford*), ii. 186.
Helder ; see Spicer.
Heron, Blount, &c. (*Sawbridgeworth*), iii. 195.
Hewett (*Sawbridgeworth*), iii. 202.
Heydon (*Watford*), i. 250.
Heysham ; see Woodhall.
Hide ; see Osborne.
Hill, Marq. of Downshire (*Hertford*), ii. 196.
Holand ; see Devereux.
Holand ; see Grentemaisnil.
Holes and Troutbeck (*Watford*), i. 246.
Holles and Pelham (*Aldenham*), i. 131.
Hoo and Boleyne (*Offley*), iii. 94.
Hoo and Keate (*Kimpton*), iii. 72.
Horsey ; see Perient.
Howe (*Shenley*), i. 479.
Hunsdon, Lord ; see Cary.
Hutchinson ; see Boteler.

Jekyll (*North Mimms*), i. 458.
Jenkyn ; see Kentish.
Jennings (*Sandridge*), i. 217.
Jocelyn (*Sawbridgeworth*), iii. 203.
Keate ; see Hoo.
Kendale (*Hitchin*), iii. 18.
Kentish (*Codicote*), ii. 308.
Kentish and Jenkyn (*St. Stephen's*), i. 229.
Kingesley (*Sarret*), i. 223.
Knighton (*Beyford*), ii. 42.
Lake (*Tring*), i. 505.
Langford ; see Dauntsey.
Lanvallei, De Burgh, Greslei, Fitz Walter, Mareschal, Morlé, Lovell, and Parker (*Walkern*), ii. 463.
Lawes (*Harpenden*), i. 411.
Lawndey, Sparhauke, and Parkins (*Chisfield*), ii. 302.
La Zouch ; see Devereux.
La Zouch ; see Grentemaisnil.
Ledet ; see Reinbudcurt.
Lee (*St. Peter's*), i. 105.
Lee (*Totteridge*), ii. 453.
Lee ; see De la Lee.
Leman (*Northaw*), ii. 414.
Le Mareschal (*Studham*), i. 492.
Leventhorpe and Coke (*Sawbridgeworth*), iii. 208.
Leventhorpe ; see De la Lee.
Limesi, Pinkeney, Odingsells, and Clinton (*Pirton*), iii. 119.
Longespe ; see Devereux.
Lovell ; see Lanvallei.
Lovell ; see Aguillon.
Lovetot and Furnival (*Great Mundon*), ii. 390.
Luckyn ; see Grimston.
Lucy (*Little Gaddesden*), i. 395.
Lyde (*Great Ayot*), ii. 255.
Lytton, Strode, and Robinson (*Knebworth*), ii. 377.
Magnaville and Say (*Sawbridgeworth*), iii. 194.
Mareschal ; see Le Mareschal.
Mareschal ; see Lanvallei.
Marlborough, Dukes of; see Spencer.
Matham (*Clothall*), iii. 503.
Maynard (*Caldecote*), iii 497.
Mayne (*Bovingdon*), i. 324.
Meautys (*Gorhambury*), i. 93.
Meetkerke (*Rushden*), iii. 572.
Miller and Mundy (*Sandon*), iii. 580.

Moels and Botreaux (*Little Berkhamsted*), ii. 32.
Monson ; see Cock.
Montacute, Earl of Salisbury, i. 481.
Montacute ; see Grentemaisnil.
Montfichet, Bolebec, Fortibus, and Playz (*Little Ayot*), ii. 261.
More (*North Mimms*), i. 452.
Morgan and Gould (*Hertford*), ii. 189.
Morlé ; see Lanvallei.
Morrison (*Watford*), i. 238.
Mortimer ; see Clare.
Mountchensy ; see Sumery.
Mounteney ; see Sumery.
Mowbray and Berkley (*Weston*), ii. 516.
Mundy ; see Miller.
Nedham (*Little Wymondley*), ii. 550.
Neville, Earls of Salisbury ; see Grentemaisnil.
Newcome (*Shenley*), i. 485.
Newport (*Brent-Pelham*), iii. 445.
Nodes (*Sheephall*), ii. 433.
Norfolk, Earls of; see Strongbow.
Norreys ; see Aguillon.
Odingsells ; see Limesi.
Onslowe (*Bishop's Hatfield*), ii. 353.
Osborne and Hide (*North Mimms*), i. 447.
Oxford, Earls of; see Vere.
Parker ; see Lanvallei.
Parkins ; see Laundey.
Pateshull, ii. 296.
Peachey, Baron Selsey, iii. 365.
Pelham ; see Holles.
Pembroke, Earls of; see Strongbow.
Penne (*Codicote*), ii. 306.
Penrice ; see Spencer.
Perient and Horsey (*Digswell*), ii. 321.
Peyver and Broughton (*Willian*), ii. 529.
Phelip ; see Aguillon.
Pilkington (*St. Paul's Walden*), iii. 138.
Pinkeney ; see Limesi.
Playz ; see Montfitchet.
Plomer (*Radwell*), iii. 550.
Plumer (*Gilston*), iii. 171.
Plumpton ; see Babthorpe.
Pole ; see Grentemaisnil.

Poultney (*Shenley*) i. 474.
Poyner and Bisse (*Codicote*), ii. 307.
Poyntz ; see Taverner.
Prestley (*Essenden*), ii. 129.
Preston (*Childwick*), i. 99.
Puckeringe (*Weston*), ii. 521.
Pulter and Forester (*Cottered*), iii. 517.
Pym (*Norton*), iii. 545.
Pycot ; see Sumery.
Quincy ; see Grentemaisnil.
Radcliffe (*Hitchin*), iii. 23.
Rawling (*Lilley*), iii. 84.
Raymond (*Abbot's Langley*), i. 171.
Reade ; see Brockett.
Reinbudecurt or Reincourt, Foliot, Braybrooke or Braibroc, and Ledet (*Ickleford*), iii. 58.
Revett (*Baldock*), ii. 269.
Richmond, Earls of ; see Brittany.
Robinson ; see Lytton.
Robotham (*St. Peter's*), i. 106.
Rokesley (*Albury*), i. 280.
Rolt (*Sacomb*), ii. 426.
Roos (*Buckland*), iii. 393.
Rowlatt and Jennings (*Sandridge*), i. 217.
Russell, Earls of Bedford, i. 193.
Ryder (*Bovingdon*), i. 325.
Sadleir (*Hitchin*), iii. 28.
Sadleir and Aston (*Stanton*), iii. 229.
Salisbury, Marq. of ; see Cecil.
Salisbury, Earls of ; see Grentemaisnil.
Salisbury, Earls of ; see Montacute.
Saltonstall (*Barkway*), iii. 362.
Salusbury ; see Spencer.
Salusbury (*Offley*), iii. 98.
Sambrooke ; see Vanacker.
Saunders ; see Sebright.
Say ; see Magnaville.
Say ; see Fray.
Say and Sele ; see Fiennes.
Scalers and Freville(*Little Mundon*), ii. 398.
Sebright and Saunders (*Flamsted*), i. 362.
Sedley (*Dingwell*), ii. 322.
Selsey, Barons ; see Peachey.
Shaw (*Cheshunt*), ii. 103.
Smith (*Essenden*), ii. 131.
Smyth (*Harpenden*), i. 412.
Snagg (*Letchworth*), ii. 386.

Snell (*Shenley*), i. 483.
Soame (*Throcking*), iii. 464.
Somers and Cocks (*North Mimms*), i. 457.
Sparhauke ; see Lawndey.
Spencer (*St. Peter's*), i. 107.
Spencer, Dukes of Marlborough, ii. 356.
Spencer, Penrice, and Salusbury (*Offley*), iii. 96.
Spicer, *alias* Helder (*Offley*), iii. 107.
Stalworth, Blount, and Woodhall (*Bishop's Hatfield*), ii. 350.
Stanhope, Earls of Chesterfield, i. 494.
Stanley, Earls of Derby, i. 374.
Stapilton ; see Aguillon.
Steward (*Braughing*), iii. 151.
Strode ; see Lytton.
Strong and Strange (*Abbot's Langley*), i. 170.
Strongbow and Mareschal, Earls of Pembroke ; and Bigot, Earls of Norfolk, ii. 510.
Sumery, Bachesworth, Mounteney, Mountchensy, and Pycot (*North Mimms*), i. 442.
Taverner and Poyntz (*Hexton*), iii. 8.
Tecon, Argentine, and Alington (*Great Wymondley*), ii. 541.
Throckmorton ; see Clerke.
Tiptoft ; see Badlesmere.
Tony (*Flamsted*), i. 354.
Tooke (*Bishop's Hatfield*), ii. 351.
Townshend (*Datchworth*), ii. 315.
Townshend ; see Harrison.
Troutbeck ; see Holes.
Valoines or Valoignes, and Fitz Walter (*Benington*), ii. 277.
Vanacker and Sambrooke (*North Mimms*), i. 453.
Vauncy ; see Creke.
Vaux ; see Greene.
Vere, Earls of Oxford, iii. 104.
Verney ; see Whityngham.
Verney ; see Cheyney.
Vernon (*Hertingfordbury*), ii. 200.
Villiers ; see Boteler.
Villiers (*Watford*), i. 252.
Wake ; see Grentemaisnil.
Waldegrave ; see Fray.
Walker (*Bushey*), i. 336.

Waller (*Coleshill*), i. 351.
Warburton; see Docwra.
Waterhouse (*Hemel Hempsted*), i. 418.
Watts (*Ware*), iii. 305.
Weld (*Bishop's Hatfield*), ii. 358.
West (*Bushey*), i. 338.
Wittewronge, Bennet, and Lawes (*Harpenden*), i. 411.
Whichcote (*Totteridge*), ii. 449.
Whitfeld (*Rickmansworth*), i. 189.
Whityngham, and Verney (*Aldbury*), i. 284.

Williams (*Sarret*), i. 224.
Willis (*Hertford*), ii. 184.
Willoughby; see Cheyney.
Willymot (*Kellshull*), iii. 533.
Wilshere (*Great Wymondley*), ii. 544.
Wilson (*Willian*), ii. 530.
Wingate (*Welwyn*), ii. 496.
Woodhall; see Stalworth.
Woodhall and Heysham (*Little Munden*), ii. 399.
Wolley (*St. Peter's*), i. 111.
Yorke, Earl of Hardwicke, i. 211.

55.—The History and Description, with Graphic Illustrations, of Cassiobury Park, Hertfordshire, the seat of the Earl of Essex. By JOHN BRITTON, F.S.A. *London*, 1837. Folio.

Capel, Lords of the Manor of Casso, 29.

Morrison, Lords of the Manor of Casso, 18.

56.—County Genealogies. Pedigrees of Hertfordshire Families. Collected by WM. BERRY. *London*, 1846. Folio.

Alston, 10.
Altham, 172.
Amherst, 94.
Amyand, 83.
Ashe, 54.
Aspland, 58.
Aston, 10.
Atkinson, 65.
Attegare, 155.
Bagott; see De Bagott.
Baker, 84.
Barley, 75.
Barnard, 124.
Bateson, 27.
Bennet, 205.
Benyon, 93.
Bolles, 39.
Bosanquet, 255.
Bownest, 226.
Bowyer, 54.
Bradshaw, 99.
Bridges, Lord Chandos, 239.
Brocket, 132.
Brograve, 31.
Bromley, 131.
Broome, 64.

Bruce, 53.
Buggin, 219.
Bulwer-Lytton, 7.
Bulwer, 7.
Burghley, Lord, 208.
Butt, 41.
Byde, 11.
Calverd, or Calvert, 17.
Canon, 56.
Capel, Earl of Essex, 1.
Carington, 124.
Carter, 100.
Cecil, Marquis of Salisbury, 208.
Chandos, Lord; see Bridges.
Chase, 26.
Chester, 82.
Clarke, 112.
Clifford, Lord, 239.
Clotterbooke, or Clutterbuck, 178.
Cock, 120.
Coldham, 48.
Coningsby, 2, 161.
Cooke, 95, 188, 189.
Cormick, 99.
Cowper, 167.
Cowper, Earl, 168.

Crakenthorpe, 241.
Cromwell, 77, 106.
Dacre, 66.
Daniel, 95.
De Bagott, 162.
De la Lee, 74.
Delawood, 225.
Delmé-Radcliffe, 113.
Derby, Earl of, 239.
Dering, 38.
Dewhurst, 66.
Dickinson, 93.
Dimsdale, 211.
Dormer, 68.
Drake, 158.
Ellis, 225.
Essex, Earl of; see Capel.
Fevre; see Le Fevre.
Field, 107.
Filmer, 135.
Finch, 43.
Fleming, or Flemyng, 53.
Flyer, 146.
Fortescue, 42.
Frank, 75.
Gape, 114.
Garrard, 156, 160.
Gascoigne, 26.
Gill, or Gyll, 56.
Gille, 56.
Glothian, Lord of Powis, 106.
Goodwyn, 111.
Goodyer, 185.
Gosselin, 52, 192.
Gott, 98.
Gough, 220.
Goulston, 202.
Granado, 82.
Greene, 228.
Grenville, 152.
Grimsditch, 176.
Grimston, 140.
Grimston, Earls of Verulam, 144.
Gyll, 53, 56, 57, 68.
Hadsley, 52.
Hale, 35.
Halsey, 88.
Hampden, 77.
Harrison, 250.
Harrison, Rogers-; see Rogers.
Harrowby, Earls of, 231.
Heygate, 166.
Heysham, 91, 92.

Hewitt, 215.
Hibbins, 26.
Hoo, 148, 213.
Horner, 30.
Horsey, 201.
Howard, 54.
Howe, 116.
Hunter, 256.
Hyde, 58.
Jackson, 49.
Keate, 149, 214.
Lawes, 205.
Landon, 46.
Lee; see De la Lee.
Le Fevre, 78.
Little, 4.
Lloyd, 27.
Lomax, 103.
Luckyn, 143.
Lumley, 216.
Lytton, 4.
McIntosh, 251.
Madan, 170.
Manners, 55.
Mayo, 48.
Meetkirke, 190.
Meux, 55.
Miller, 220.
Mills, 217.
Monox, 174.
Monro, 79.
Monson, 120.
Mowbray, 54.
Murray, 53, 69.
Neville, 42.
Newce, 175, 176.
Newcome, 117.
Nicholl, 222.
Norland, 226.
Norton, 226.
Oteby, 151.
Oxenbridge, 120.
Page, 250.
Palmer, 42.
Parr, 25.
Patrick, 25.
Paxton, 62.
Pellew, 29.
Peryent, 200.
Perry, 238.
Pert, 189.
Pigott, 57.
Plantagenet, 54.

Plomer, 198.
Plumer, 198.
Polley, 42.
Powis, Lords of, 106.
Prescott, 105.
Price, 26.
Pride, 239.
Radcliffe, 109, 113.
Radcliffe, Delmé-, 133.
Rainsford, 188.
Rayment, 52.
Reade, 134.
Rider, 83.
Robinson, 7, 229.
Rogers, 252.
Rogers-Harrison, 245, 252.
Russell, 108.
Russell, 6.
Ryder, Earl of Harrowby, 231.
Sadleir, 7.
St. Leger, 55.
Sanders, 62.
Savile, 142.
Shaw, 48.
Sherwerd, 241.
Sitsilt, 207.
Smith, 78, 124.
Smyth, 54, 151.
Stacey, 101.
Stanley; see Earls of Derby.
Stanley, 26.
Sterne, 227.

Steward, 53.
Stonor, 42.
Strangways, 55.
Strode, 7.
Thomson, 50.
Thompson, 235.
Thornton, 92.
Toke or Tooke, 70.
Tyssen, 96.
Verney, 21.
Vernon, 200.
Verulam, Earls of; see Grimston.
Von Rahn, 220.
Walker, 137.
Waller, 76.
Warburton, 7.
Warde, 27.
Watlington, 233.
Wedd, 242.
Wentworth, 42.
Western, 98.
Willaby, or Willarby, 151.
Williams, 2, 106.
Wilsher, or Willsher, 246.
Winnington, 134.
Winthrop, 29.
Wiseman, 216.
Wittewrong, 206.
Woodhall, 92.
Wright, 25, 93.
Wyndham, 54.
Wyndout, 225.

HUNTINGDONSHIRE.

57.—The Visitation of the County of Huntingdon, under the Authority of William Camden, &c. Edited by Sir HENRY ELLIS, K.H. Printed by the Camden Society, 1849. Small 4to.

Ap Rhese, 31.
Astrie, 98, 99.
Audley, 54.
Baldwyn, 58.
Beaumys, 16.
Bedell, 38.
Bellay, 122.
Best, 65.
Bevill, 8, 9, 116.
Beumes, 77, 78.
Bolton, 55.

Broughton, 81.
Browne, 95.
Calton, 40.
Castle, 111.
Clifton, 4.
Cotton, 26, 27, 28.
Crespin, 54.
Cromwell, 79, 80.
Cropley, 59.
Deyer, 69, 70, 71.
Edwards, 113.

Fawkener, 36.
Folvile, 76.
Forster, 56.
Fowberge, 104.
Germin, 106.
Grace, 21.
Herbert, 17.
Herne, 97.
Hetley, 108.
Holcot, 21.
Hullock, 108.
Jackman, 105.
Jawdrell, 66.
Kaye, 33.
Knowles, 101.
Kryell, 113, 114.
Leete, 67.
Louthe, 11.
Luke, 60, 61.
Marshall, 34.
Moyne, 78.
Nailour, 96, 109, 110.
Paris, 62.
Payne, 64.
Pikering, 19.
Pratt, 37.

Pulter, 101.
Rooe, 92.
Rous, 103.
St. John, 2.
Sapcotts, 12.
Skeggs, 63.
Slade, 20.
Stones, 101.
Taylarde, &c. 87—91.
Throckmorton, 123.
Torkyngton, 102.
Tryce, 107.
Turbervill, 57.
Tyringham, 115, 116.
Walden, 18.
Whalley, 35.
Whitbrooke, 72.
Williams, 20.
Wingfield, 112.
Wingfield *of Wingfield Castle*, 125.
Wingfield *of Upton in Lincolnshire*, 128.
Wingfield *of Dunham in Norfolk*, 129.
Wingfield *of Brantham*, 130.
Wingfield *of Kimbolton*, 131.

KENT.

58.—History and Antiquities of Tunstall in Kent. By the late EDWARD ROWE MORES, F.A.S. (No. 1, Bibliotheca Topographica Britannica). *London,* 1780. 4to.

Arsic, 11.
Cheyney, 38.
Clifford, 40.
Crowmer, 22.
De Burgo, 14.
De Meduana or Mayney, 19.
Gore, 40.

Grey, 114.
Grove, 115.
Hales, 36.
Harlakenden, 39.
Mores, folding at xvii.
Port, 7.
Tong, 116.

59.—Collections for an History of Sandwich in Kent. By WILLIAM BOYS, Esq., F.A.S. *Canterbury,* 1792, 4to.

Conant, folding at 274.
Hougham or Huffam, 367.
Manwood, folding at 246.

Rutten or Rutton, folding at 273.
Thurbarne, 350.

60.—County Genealogies. Pedigrees of the Families of Kent. By WILLIAM BERRY. *London,* 1830. Folio.

Alchorne, 176.
Alde, 179.

Aldersey, 290.
Allen, 76, 192.

Amherst, Earl, 494.
Amherst, 191.
Ashfeild, 424.
Astley, 372.
Aucher, 222.
Austen, 127, 350.
Aylesford, Earl of ; see Finch.
Ayleworth, 312.
Bachellor, 47.
Badbye, 436.
Baker, 216, 353.
Ball, 46.
Bannister, 278.
Bargrave, 2, 12, 106.
Barkeley, 197.
Barnes, 356.
Barham, 404.
Barnham, 394.
Bathurst, 198, 200.
Beale, 18, 22, 204.
Beard, 423.
Beaumont, 140.
Beauvoir, 182.
Beckingham, 223.
Beer, 327.
Belcher, 16, 39, 281.
Benger, 228.
Benson, 223.
Bere, 33.
Beresford, 437.
Berry, 264.
Best, 14, 382.
Bestwick, 381.
Bettenham, 265, 456.
Billington, 202.
Bird, 10.
Bix, 284.
Blackmore, 316.
Blomer, 223.
Blondell, 85.
Blunt, 417.
Bode, 136.
Booth, 484.
Bosvile, 424.
Bosville, 480.
Bourne, 128.
Bowle, 357.
Boys, 16, 182, 441, 453.
Bradley, formerly Dyne, 452.
Breton, 205.
Brett, 325.
Bridges, 491.
Brockhull, 106.

Brockman, 118.
Brodnax, 50, 126.
Brograve, 272.
Brome, 289.
Bromley, 57.
Brooke, 45.
Brooker, 224.
Brown, 494.
Browne, 352, 377.
Bryan, 5.
Brydges, 378, 410, 492.
Buck, 98, 100.
Bufkin, 470.
Bunce, 378.
Bungay, 319.
Burr, 193.
Burt, or Byrt, 40.
Butler, 83, 229.
Butts, 257.
Byrchet, 346.
Byrte ; see Burt.
Cadman, 116.
Cadwell, Caldwell, or Kadwell, 314.
Cæsar, 489.
Cage, 273.
Caldwell ; see Cadwell.
Carkeredge, 137.
Cartell, 123.
Carter, 414.
Chambers, 360.
Chambre, 367.
Champneys, 39.
Chapman, 98.
Charleton, 352.
Cheney, Lord, 125.
Cheney, 125, 429.
Cheyney, 429.
Chilborne, 461.
Chisholm, 204.
Chowne, 85.
Chute, 173, 491.
Clark, 7.
Clarke, 131.
Clerke, 84.
Cleybrooke, 148.
Clive, 111.
Cobb, 149.
Colepeper, 78.
Colfe, 368.
Collett, 328.
Collier, 427.
Collins, 433, 458.
Colwell, 320.

Constable, 350.
Cooke, 472.
Coppin, 409.
Corbett, 223.
Cottam, 83.
Cotton, 476.
Couchman, 260.
Courthop, 476.
Coutry, 45.
Covert, 428.
Cowper, 122.
Cozens, 404.
Craford, 109.
Crayford, 133.
Cripps, or Crispe, 154, 491.
Crompe, 165, 294.
Crux, 363.
Culpeper, 56.
Curling, 5.
Curteis, 66.
Dade, 460.
D'Aeth, or Death, 429.
Dalison, 182.
Dane, 196.
Daniel, 122.
Darell, 102.
Davie, 373.
Deane, 154.
Death ; see D'Aeth.
De Exherst, 179.
De Gatton, 269.
De Goodhurst, 177.
Denew, 359.
Denne, 154, 194, 269.
Denton, 451.
Dering, 12, 397.
De Rosier, 35.
Dig, or Diggs, 142.
Dine, 452.
Dingley, 120.
Dixon, 392.
Dixwell, 469.
Dobree, 59.
Dom, or Doon, 39.
Doon ; see Dom.
Douce, 176.
Dowel, 216.
Drake, 119.
Draper, 450.
Dray, 427.
Dudlow, 176.
Dyne, 452.
Dyne, now Bradley ; see Bradley.

Edgbury, 339.
Edingham or Engham, 141.
Edmed, 271.
Edolphe, 124.
Ellis, 64, 179.
Elsley, 403.
Elwin, 378.
Elwyn, 300.
Engham ; see Edingham.
Espinesse, 333.
Estday, 145.
Evering, 262.
Faussett, 138.
Ferby, 365.
Feversham, Earl of, 244.
Fifield, alias Lowe, 450.
Filmer, 13, 186.
Finch, 165.
Finch, Earl of Aylesford, 207.
Finch, alias Herbert, 207.
Finch, Baron, 206.
Finet, 449.
Fineux, 110.
Fisher, 324.
Fleete, 169.
Fletcher, 200, 488.
Flint, 202.
Flud, 304.
Fludd, 448.
Foche, 132.
Fogge, 471.
Folkes, 286.
Foote, 26.
Forster, 44.
Fotherby, 268.
Fowle, 112.
Fowler, 121.
Gaynsford, 451.
Gibbon, 181, 378, 408, 410.
Gibbs, 418.
Gilbert, 341.
Gilborne, 345.
Gildart, 366.
Gillow, 487.
Gipps, 462.
Glydd, 119.
Godfrey, 146, 205, 396.
Gokin, 113.
Goodhurst ; see De Goodhurst.
Goulding, 160.
Gouldsmith, 432.
Greaves, 332.
Grebbel, 487.

Greenland, 217.
Griling, 120.
Gull, 294.
Hadd, 217.
Hales, 12, 210.
Hall, 25, 285.
Halle, 39.
Hallett, 246.
Hames, 267.
Hammond, 94, 182.
Hamon, 245.
Handvile, 117.
Hanington, 131.
Hardwick, Earl of, 411
Hardy, 248.
Harlakenden, 465.
Harleston, 408.
Harlstone, 4.
Hart, 424.
Harty, 52.
Harvey, Harvy, and Hervy, 252.
Hasling, 99.
Haule, 311.
Hawking, 267.
Hayward, 133.
Henden, 436.
Hendley, 174, 175.
Hervy ; see Harvey.
Hill, 320, 427.
Hilton, 255.
Hodgson, 38.
Holbrooke, 73.
Holden, 363.
Hollingbery, 196.
Honywood, 226.
Hooper, 477.
Hopper, 7.
Horne, 175.
Horsmonden, 287, 363.
Horspoole, 318.
Hougham, 164.
Howard, 87.
Howell, 384.
Hubble, 176.
Hugeson, 329.
Hughes, 38, 93, 247.
Hulke, 300.
Hulse, 326.
Hunt, 260.
Hunt, 101.
Hussey, 220, 315, 401.
Jacob, 132.
James, 209.

Jemmett, 315.
Jenkin, 482, 484.
Jennings, 181.
Johnson, 153, 366, 384, 487.
Jordan, 431, 463.
Judd, 39.
Jull, 396.
Juxon, 464.
Kadwell ; see Cadwell.
Kempe, 1, 87, 97, 486.
Kenwrick, 457.
Kingsley, 306.
Knatchbull, 297.
Knevet, 359.
Knight, 127.
Lad, Ladd, Lade, or Ladde, 342.
Lake, 218.
Lamb, 288.
Lambard, 349.
Langworth, 469.
Lee, 172.
Lefroy, 17.
Leicester, Earls of; see Sidney.
Lemins, 371.
Lemon, 87.
Lethieullier, 358.
Leversedge, 455.
Levesey, 197.
Lewin, or Lowin, 212.
Lloyd, 189.
Loftie, 404.
Lone, 305.
Lord, 427.
Love, 176.
Lovelace, 474.
Lowe, *alias* Fifield, 450.
Lowndes, 468.
Lowin ; see Lewin.
Lushington, 330.
Lynch, 282.
Maccaree, 17.
Mace, 72.
Man, 1, 92.
Manley, 463.
Maningham, 32.
Manning, 406.
Mantell, 185, 332.
Manwood, 356.
Maplesden, 322.
Marche, 132.
Marler, 405.
Marsh, 75, 460.
Marsham, 94.

Mason, 328.
Master, 24, 25, 122.
Maude, 315.
May, 50, 130.
Mennis, 338.
Merriweather, 348.
Merryweather, 468.
Middleton, 17.
Mildenhall, 142.
Milles, 7, 309.
Milner, or Mylner, 82.
Mirfine, 39.
Monckton, 490.
Monins, 179, 311, 415.
Monk, 127.
Monypenny, 313.
Moore, 160.
Morland, 367.
Moyle, 205.
Mulcaster, 63.
Multon, 76.
Musgrave, 186.
Mylner ; see Milner.
Narborough, 248.
Naylor, 97.
Nethersole, 104, 403.
Nevill, 185.
Nevinson, 390.
Newington, 93, 374.
Newman, 314, 468.
Nicholson, 329.
Nisell, 327.
Norreys, 129.
Northey, 277.
Northwood, 50.
Norton, 158, 181.
Norwood, 59.
Notbene, 179.
Nottingham, Earl of; see Finch
Nowell, 430.
Oliver, alias Quinton, 393.
Ombersley, Baron, 42.
Osborne, 28.
Ower, 447.
Oxenden, 224.
Oxford, Earls of; see Vere.
Packenham, 46.
Palmer, 188, 258, 429.
Papillon, 114.
Paramour, 49.
Paramor, 156.
Parr, 404.
Parbo, 96.

Payler, late Turner, 274.
Pattenson, 204, 315.
Payne, 425.
Paynter, 337.
Pearson, 493.
Peek, 189.
Peirce, 74.
Peirs, 464.
Peke, 116, 357.
Pershall, 347·
Petitt, 157.
Petley, 232, 388.
Pett, 86, 328.
Pettit, 6, 227.
Peyton, 213, 424.
Pigeon, 455.
Pilcher, 7.
Pix, 364.
Plumptre, 89.
Polhill, or Polley, 334.
Polley ; see Polhill
Poole, 415.
Pope, 434.
Porcas, 35.
Porker, 271, 373.
Porter, 321.
Post, 20.
Prendreth, 159.
Preston, 449.
Proude, 51.
Pym, 35.
Quinton ; see Oliver.
Radcliffe, 130.
Ralfe, 55.
Randolph, 278.
Reade, 413.
Richardson, 53.
Rider, 395.
Roberts, 181, 379, 177.
Roberts, alias Rockhurst, 177.
Robinson, 37, 47.
Rokeby, Lord, 47.
Rolfe, 427, 449, 455.
Rolte, 385.
Rooke, 301.
Roper, 214.
Roper, Lords Teynham, 215.
Rosier ; see De Rosier.
Round, 191.
Ruck, 16.
Rutten, or Rutton, 161, 184.
Sabin, or Savin, 461.
Sackett, 203.

St. Leger, 287.
Saker, 144.
Sanders, 159.
Sands, 244.
Sandys, 41, 43.
Sandys, Lord, 42.
Sare, 420.
Savage, 176.
Savin, see Sabin.
Sayer, 496.
Scott, 161, 170.
Scudamore, 34.
Selby, 465, 494.
Selling, 107.
Shakerley, 261.
Sharp, 470.
Shawe, 248.
Shovell, 248.
Short, 61.
Sidley, 230.
Sidney, Earl of Leicester, 478, 480.
Simons, 459.
Simpson, or Sympson, 173.
Simpson, 6.
Skeffington, 371.
Skinner, 271, 286.
Smith, 64, 113, 248, 250, 325, 428, 454.
Smythe, 10, 250.
Solly, 196.
Somer, 121.
Sondes, Viscount, 244.
Southland, 317.
Spencer, 38, 318, 473.
Spracklyn, 369.
Springett, 242, 243, 256.
Stacey, 190.
Stafford, 336.
Stanley, 140.
Starkey, 37.
Steede, 105.
Stephens, 487.
Steward, 257.
Stockett, 303.
Stokes, 110.
Stone, 473.
Stonehouse, 206.
Stoughton, 108.
Strangman, 136.
Streatfeild, 236, 238.
Streynsham, 122.
Stringer, 46, 127, 308.
Studley, 425.

Style, 412.
Suliard, 87.
Sumer, 81.
Swan, 293.
Sympson; see Simpson.
Tappenden, 487.
Taylor, 106, 133, 162, 193, 277, 391.
Tenche, 145.
Terry, 487.
Teynham, Lord; see Roper.
Thatcher, 328.
Thomas, 416.
Thompson, 328.
Thomson, 16, 293, 459.
Thornhill, 466.
Thursby, 429.
Thurston, 98, 202, 203.
Tichborne, 361.
Tilghman, 70, 71, 165.
Tillesley, 100.
Tilly, 181.
Timms, 248.
Toke, 167.
Tolson, 181.
Tonge, 73.
Tornay, or Tournay, 107.
Trench, 178.
Trippe, 88.
Tritton, 202.
Tucker, 36.
Tufton, 352.
Turner, 11, 169, 274
Twisden, or Twysden, 310.
Twysden; see Twisden.
Tylden, 30, 204, 427.
Upton, 152.
Vaile, 292.
Venour, 370.
Vere, Earls of Oxford, 424.
Violett, 257.
Wage, 98.
Waller, 296.
Walsingham, 176, 192, 356.
Walter, 380.
Walthew, 340.
Ward, 101.
Warren, 60.
Watmere, or Watmoughe, 144.
Watmoughe; see Watmere.
Watton, 8, 13, 477.
Webb, 302.
Wecherlin, 457.
Weller, 46.

Wenlock, 449.
Wevell, 293.
Wheeler, 345.
Whelden, 427.
White, 467.
Whitfeld, 54.
Whittaker, 53.
Whitton, 386.
Wichalse, 362.
Wilcock, 130.
Wilde, 108.
Wildes, 189.
Wilkinson, now Edgbury, 339.
Williamson, 143.
Wilmott, 280.

Wilsford, 134, 496.
Wilson, 421.
Winchester, 80.
Windsor, 350.
Wing, 424.
Winne, 471.
Withen, 389.
Wombwell, 57.
Woodward, 52, 180.
Worley, 129.
Wraight, 16.
Wright, 264.
Wyat, 295.
York, 411.
Young, 461.

61.—Bibliotheca Colfanæ Catalogus. Catalogue of the Library of the Free Grammar School at Lewisham, &c. By W. H. BLACK, 1831, 8vo. *Privately printed.*

Colfe.

62.—Some Account of Maidstone, in Kent, &c. By J. H. BAVERSTOCK, F.S.A. *London*, 1832, 8vo.

Bosville *of Eynsford* (12 tables), 14—22.

63.—The Visitor's Guide to Knole, in the County of Kent, &c. By JOHN H. BRADY, F.R.A.S. *Sevenoaks*, 1839, 8vo.

Sackville, folding at 19.

64.—Excerpta Cantiana. By the Rev. T. STREATFEILD, F.S.A. (1836.) Folio.

De Burghersh, Paveley, D'Aldone, and Nevill, 6.
Elryngton, folding at 44.
Tryvet, 6.

65.—The Archaeological Mine ; a Collection of Antiquarian Nuggets, relating to the County of Kent, &c. By ALFRED JOHN DUNKIN. *London*, 1845, 8vo. Vols. 1 and 2.

Apylton, Appulton, or Appleton *of Dartford, Kent, and Jervis Hall, Essex*, i. folding at 142.
Chester, i. 92.

66.—Archæologia Cantiana ; being Transactions of the Kent Archæological Society. Commenced in 1858. Vols. 1—5.

De. Crevecœur and D'Avrenches, ii. folding at 142; iii. 273.
De Segrave, ii. 39, 139 ; and folding at 142.

Fogge, v. folding at 125.
Gatton, v. folding at 222.
Grandison, coheirs of, ii. folding at 36.
Hardres, iv. folding at 56.

Northwode, Sir John; coheirs in Gavel Kind of, ii. folding at 36.
Northwode, ii. folding at 42.
Twisden *of Newenden*, iv. 112.

67.—The Visitation of the County of Kent, taken in the year 1619. By JOHN PHILIPOTT, Rouge Dragon, &c. Published with the Archæologia Cantiana. Some copies separate.

Bargrave *of Bargrave*, iv. 252.
Bere *of Gravesend*, iv. 250.
Best *of Allington Castle*, iv. 268.
Bryan *of Wrotham*, iv. 244.
Clerke *of Wrotham*, iv. 246.
Contry *of Reculver*, v. 235.
Culpeper *of Aylesford*, iv. 264.
Forster *of Borden*, iv. 269.
Hall *of Ashford*, iv. 267.
Harlestone *of Fordwich*, iv. 257.
Hasling *of Mepham*, iv. 254.
Holbrooke *of Newington*, v. 225.
James *of Ightham*, iv. 242.
Lambarde *of Sevenoaks*, v. 247, and folding at 248.

Manningham *of East Malling*, iv.255.
Master *of Willesborough*, iv. 259.
Master *of Woodchurch*, iv. 266.
Master *of East Langdon*, v. 238.
Moulton *of St. Clere's*, v. 243.
Osborne *of Hartlip*, v. folding at 227.
Robinson *of Gravesend*, iv. 251.
Thomson, or Thompson *of Lenham*, iv. 261.
Tripp *of Wingham*, v. 236.
Tucker *of Gravesend*, iv. 248.
Watton *of Addington*, iv. 258.
Willoughby *of Ditton*, iv. 256.
Wombwell *of Northfleet*, iv. 253.

LANCASHIRE.

68.—An History of the Original Parish of Whalley, and Honor of Clitheroe, in the Counties of Lancaster and York. By THOMAS DUNHAM WHITAKER, LL.D., F.S.A. *Blackburn*, 1801, 4to.; 2nd edition, *London*, 1806, 4to.; 3rd edition, *London*, 1818, 4to.

Altham and Banastre *of Altham*, 385, 2 ed. ib.; 3 ed. 402.
Assheton *of Great Lever, Whalley and Middleton*, folding at 218, 2 ed. ib.; 3 ed. at 244.
Assheton *of Downham and Ouerdale*, 218; 2 ed. ib.; 3 ed. 299.
Banastre; see Altham.
Barcroft *of Barcroft*, 351; 2 ed. ib.; 3 ed. 363.
Birtwistle *of Huncote*, 392; 2 ed. ib.
Blackburn, 241; 2 ed. ib.; 3 ed. 260.
Braddyll, folding at 218; 2 ed. ib.; 3rd. 244.
Catteral *of Catteral in Amunderness, and of Little Mitton*, 3 ed. 254.

Emmot *of Emmot*, 379; 2 ed. ib.; 3 ed. 397.
Greenacres *of Worston*, 284; 2 ed. ib.; 3 ed. 295.
Grimshaw *of Clayton Hall*, 389; 2 ed. ib.; 3 ed. 406.
Habergham *of Habergham*, 316; 2 ed. ib.; 3 ed. 337.
Halsted *of Rowley*, 3 ed. 383.
Halsted, 363; 2 ed. ib.; 3 ed. 329.
Harrington *of Hornby Castle*, 456; 2 ed. ib.; 3 ed. 476.
Haydock *of Hesandforth*, 311; 2 ed. ib.; 3 ed. 333.
Hoghton *of Pendleton*, 240; 2 ed. ib.; 3 ed. 259.

Holden *of Palace House,* folding at 408 ; 2 ed. ib. ; 3 ed. 418.

Holt *of Little Mitton,* 236 ; 2 ed. ib. ; 3 ed. 254.

Johnson *of Rushton Grange,* 3 ed. 152.

Legh *of High Legh,* 262 ; 2 ed. ib. ; 3 ed. 275.

Merclesden, 380 ; 2 ed. ib. ; 3 ed. 397.

Nowell *of Read,* folding at 247 ; 2 ed. ib.; 3 ed. at 264.

Nowell *of Morley,* 278, 282; 2 ed. ib. ; 3 ed. 291, 293, 533.

Ormerod *of Ormerod,* 353 ; 2 ed. ib. ; 3 ed. folding at 364.

Parker *of Extwisle,* 357 ; 2 ed. ib. ; 3 ed. 377.

Parker *of Browsholme,* folding at 209 ; 2 ed. ib.; 3 ed. at 241.

Paslew *of Wiswall Hall,* 242 ; 2 ed. ib.; 3 ed. 261.

Radcliffe *of Clitheroe,* 270 ; 2 ed. ib ; 3 ed. 283.

Radcliffe *of Todmorden and Merley,* folding at 278; 2 ed. ib.; 3 ed. (2) 292.

Radcliffe *of Radcliffe Tower,* folding at 401 ; 2 ed. ib. ; 3 ed. at 412.

Radcclive, De, 3 ed. folding at 414.

Sherburn *of Little Mitton,* 236 ; 2 ed. ib. ; 3 ed. 254, 256.

Shuttleworth *of Gawthorp,* 320 ; 2 ed. ib. ; 3 ed. 256, 339.

Stansfield, 360; 2 ed. ib. ; 3 ed. 381.

Starkie *of Huntroyd,* 251 ; 2 ed. ib.; 3 ed. 266, 529.

Starkie *of Twiston,* 294 ; 2 ed. ib. ; 3 ed. 320.

Townley *of Royle,* 313 ; 2 ed. ib. ; 3 ed. 335.

Townley *of Townley,* folding at 324 ; 2 ed. ib. ; 3 ed. at 344.

Townley *of Hurstwood,* 364 ; 2 ed. ib. ; 3 ed. 384.

Townley *of Barnside,* folding at 376 ; 2 ed. ib. ; 3 ed. 396.

Walmesley *of Dunkenhalgh,* 390 ; 2 ed. ib. ; 3 ed. 407.

Whalley, Gardiner, and Smythe, folding at 235 ; 2 ed. ib.; 3 ed. at 252.

Whitaker *of Holme,* 2 ed. folding at 336 ; 3 ed. 352.

Whitaker *of Henthorn,* 231 ; 2 ed. ib. ; 3 ed. 257.

Worsley *of Twiston,* 294 ; 2 ed. ; 3 ed. 320.

69.—A Portfolio of Fragments relative to the History and Antiquities of the County of Lancaster. By MATTHEW GREGSON. *Liverpool,* 1817. Foolscap folio.

Anderton ; see Lydiate.

Bankes *of Bank Newton and Winstanley,* 234.

Blackburne *of Orford, Hale, Liverpool, Hawford, Lynn Regis, &c.* 200.

Blackburne *of Orford and Hale,* 216-219.

Blackburne ; see Lydiate.

Blundell *of Little Crosby,* 225.

Blundell ; see Lydiate.

Bold *of Prescot,* 188.

Buccleuch, Dukes of; see Montague.

Case ; see Clayton.

Charlemagne, the Great Emperor of the West, and King of France, faces 51.

Clayton *of Fullwood,* connected with the families of Tarleton, Hough ton, Case, Hardman, Earle, &c. *of Liverpool,* and with Leigh *of Oughterington, co. Chester,* 175.

Deiri or Lancashire, Kings of, faces 50.

Earle ; see Clayton.

Farington *of Shaw Hall,* 256.

Hardman; see Clayton.

Harrison *of Lancaster.* 268.

Houghton ; see Clayton.

Ireland ; see Lydiate.

Lancaster, Kings of; see Deiri.

Lancaster, Earls and Dukes of, of the House of Anjou and Plantagenet, folding at 6*.

K

Lancaster ; see York.

Latham and Tarboks or Tarbocks, 244.

Leigh *of Oughtrington, co. Chester ;* see Clayton.

Lydiate *of Lydiate,* with Blackburne, Ireland, Anderton, and Blundell.

Montague, Dukes of Montagu, and Dukes of Buccleuch, 273.

Norreys *of Speke,* 204 to 207.

Ogle *of Whiston,* 182.

Patten *of Bold,* 190-194.

Pictavensis, Roger, Lord of the House of Lancaster, 44.

Smith *of Peel House, Prescot,* 185.

Tarboks or Tarbocks ; see Latham.

Tarleton ; see Clayton.

Walmesley *of Westwood House in Ince,* 241.

Wilbraham, *cos. Lancashire and Cheshire,* 246.

York and Lancaster, union of the Houses of, folding at 6* and 40.

70.—A History of Lancashire. By J. CORRY. *London,* 1825. 2 vols. 4to.

Braddyll *of Braddyll, Brockhole, Portfield, and Conishead Priory, with* Dodding, Gale, and Richmund, i. 449-456.

Chadwick *of Chadwick,* ii. 542-552.

Chadwick *of Healey, Ridware, Callow, and Leventhorp,* ii. 553-651.

Crossley *of Crossley,* ii. 653-655.

Dodding *of Conishead Priory ;* see Braddyll.

Farington *of Shaw Hall,* ii. 721-724.

Gale *of Whitehaven and Cleator ;* see Braddyll.

Lloyd *of Manchester, Hulme, and Liverpool,* ii. 480.

Moseley *of Rolleston,* ii. 478.

Richmund *of Highhead Castle, co. Cumb. ;* see Braddyll.

Shuttleworth *of Clithero,* ii. 655.

Trafford, ii. 660-667.

Walmesley, ii. 715, 716.

Winstanley, ii. 717.

Winstanley *of Braunston,* ii. 718.

71.—The History of the County Palatine and Duchy of Lancaster. By EDWARD BAINES, Esq., M.P. *London,* 1836. 4 vols. 4to.

Anderton *of Euxton and Lostock,* iii. 452, folding.

Ashton *of Ashton-under-Lyne,* ii. 532.

Ashton *of Middleton,* ii. 596.

Ashton *of Chadderton,* ii. 591.

Ashton *of Lever and Whalley,* iii. 190.

Atherton *(Aughton),* iv. 228.

Banister *of Bank,* iii. 406.

Barlow *of Barlow,* ii. 396.

Bigland *of Bigland,* iv. 734.

Birch *of Birch,* ii. 531.

Blundell *of Crosby,* iv. 218.

Bold *of Bold,* iii. 717.

Bootle *of Skelmersdale,* iv. 247.

Bothe or Booth *of Barton,* iii. 113, folding.

Bradshaigh *of Haigh,* faces iii. 553.

Butler *(St. Michael's le Wyre),* iv. 450.

Butler *of Kirkland,* iv. 471.

Butler *of Bewsey,* iii. 660.

Chadwick *of Chadwick,* ii. 655.

Chester, Earls of, iv. 155.

Chetham *of Chetham,* ii. 395.

Clayton *of Clayton,* iii. 467.

Clifton *of Clifton,* iv. 404, folding.

Crossley *of Crossley,* ii. 649.

Dalton *of Thurnham,* iv. 543.

De Lacy, Lord of Clitheroe, iii. 207.

De Poictou, Roger, ii. 119.

Egerton *of Heaton House,* ii. 563.

Eland *of Savile,* ii. 620.

Entwisle *of Entwisle,* iii. 95.

Essex, Earls of, i. 156.

Farynton *of Farington,* iii. 446, folding.

Fleetwood *of Poulton,* iv. 440.

Fleming *of Aldingham,* iv. 648.

Gerard *of Bryn,* iii. 641.

Harrington *of Aldingham and Hornby*, iv. 648.
Hereford, Earls of, i. 156.
Hesketh *of Rufford*, iii. folding at 426.
Heywood *of Little Lever*, iii. 85.
Hoghton *of Hoghton Tower*, iii. 348.
Hoghton *of Pendleton*, iii. 230.
Holcroft (*Eccles*), iii. 130.
Hopwood *of Hopwood*, ii. 611.
Hulme *of Hulme*, ii. 394.
Hulton *af Hulton*, iii. folding at 40.
Hyde *of Denton*, iii. 157.
Ireland *of Hutte*, iii. 753.
Johnson and Ormerod *of Tildesly*, iii. 609.
Kenyon *of Kenyon*, iii. 634.
Lacy; see De Lacy.
Lancaster, Royal House of, iv. 155.
Lancaster, Dukes of, iv. 751,
Langley (*Prestwich*), ii. 561.
Langton, Barons of Newton, iii. 642.
Langton *of Broughton Tower, Cockenham*, iv. folding at 409.
Latham *of Parbold*, iii. 479.
Legh *of Lyme and Haydock*, iii. 644.
Lever *of Alkrington*, ii. 566.
Lincoln, Earls of, i. 155.
Manchester, Barons of, ii. 172.
Molyneux, Earl of Sefton, iv. folding at 216.
Mosley *of Ancoats*, ii. folding at 352.
Norreys *of Davy Holme*, iii. 128.

Norreys *of Speke*, iii. 754.
Northampton, Earls of, i. 156.
Nowell *of Read*, iii. 303.
Ormerod *of Tildesley*, iii. 609.
Orrell *of Orrell*, iii. 91.
Osbaldeston *of Osbaldeston*, iii. 343.
Pilkington *of Pilkington*, iii. 104.
Pilkington *of Rivington*, iii. 105.
Plumbe-Tempest *of Aughton*, iv.230.
Preston *of Cockerham*, iv. 658.
Prestwich *of Hulme*, ii. 393.
Radcliffe *of Ordsall*, ii. folding at 353.
Radcliffe *of Radcliffe Tower*, iii. 6.
Rigby *of Harteoake*, iii. 481.
Russell, Earls of, i. 155.
Savile, ii. 620.
Scarisbrick (*Aughton*), iv. 228.
Scarisbrick (*Ormskirk*), iv.258.
Sefton, Earls of; see Molyneux.
Sherburne *of Stonyhurst*, iii. folding at 372.
Southworth *of Samlesbury*, iii. 354.
Standish *of Duxbury*, iii. 519.
Stanley (*Aughton*), iv. 228.
Starkie *of Hunbroyd*, iii. 309.
Tempest, Plumbe- *of Aughton*, iv. 230.
Tildesley *of Tildesley*, iii, 608.
Tarbock (*Huyton*), iv. 9.
Tounley (*Whalley*), iii. 254.
Trafford *of Trafford*, iii. folding at 110.
Tunstal *of Thurland Castle*, iv. 616.
Wall *of Preston*, iv. 375.
Westby, *of Mowbreck*, iv.452.

72.—Historic Society of Lancashire and Cheshire. Proceedings and Papers. Commenced in 1849.

Honford *of Honford*, ii. 54.
Minshull, ii. 92.
Le Noreis or Norreys *of Sutton and Daresbury*, ii. 143.
Norres *of Speke*, ii. folding at 148 at 160 and at 170.
Wade, ii. 100.

73.—Miscellanea Palatina. By GEORGE ORMEROD, D.C.L. F.R.S., &c. *Not published.* 1851. 8vo. See also Cheshire.

Lathom *in Lancashire*, folding at 68.
Le Noreis or Norreys *of Sutton and Daresbury*, facing 8.
Norres *of Speke*, folding at 14, at 26, at 36 and at 47.

74.—The History and Antiquities of the Town of Lancaster. By the Rev. ROBERT SIMPSON, M.A. *Lancaster*, 1852, 8vo.

De Poicton, Earl of Lancaster, folding at 212.

Plantagenet, Earls of Lancaster, folding at 212.

75.—History of the Ancient Chapel of Blackley, in Manchester Parish. By Rev. JOHN BOOKER. *Manchester*, 1854. Foolscap 4to.

Booth *of Salford*, 26.
Booth *of Blackley*, 27.
Chadderton *of Nuthurst*, 147.
Chetham *of Nuthurst*, 155.
Chetham *of Crumpsall*, 204.
Diggles *of Booth Hall*, 38.

Lightbowne *of Salford*, 174.
Lightbowne *of Moston and Manchester*, 172.
Sandford *of Nuthurst*, 160.
Shacklock *of Moston*, 183.

LEICESTERSHIRE.

76.—The Description of Leicestershire. By WILLIAM BURTON, Esq. *London*, 1622, folio ; 2nd ed. *Lynn*, 1777, folio.

Appleby ; see De Appleby.
Ashby, 224 ; 2 ed. 213.
Astley, 58 ; 2 ed. 55.
Basset, 241 ; 2 ed. 228.
Beaumont, 120 ; 2 ed. 111.
Beaumont, 209 ; 2 ed. 199.
Beaumont ; see De Quincy.
Belgrave, 40 ; 2 ed. 38.
Berkeley, 312 ; 2 ed. 291.
Bingham ; see Charnels.
Blunt ; see De Wichard.
Boivile, Southill, &c. 272. ; 2 ed. 256.
Bruyn, 205 ; 2 ed. 186.
Bugg ; see Champaine.
Burdet, 201 ; 2 ed. 182.
Burdet and Stafford ,141 ; 2 ed. 129.
Burton, 177 ; 2 ed. 161.
Cave ; see Malory.
Champaine and Bugg, 289 ; 2 ed. 272.
Charnels and Bingham, 194 ; 2 ed. 177.
Charnels and Trussel, 99 ; 2 ed. 93.
Clarenaulx and Faunt, 107 ; 2 ed. 99.
Cotton ; see Faulconer.
Cuiley ; see De Cuiley.
Danvers, De Amary, Wolfe, De Walshall, and Staresmore, 111 ; 2 ed. 102.

De Amary ; see Danvers.
De Appleby, 13 ; 2 ed. 12.
De Bois, 74 ; 2 ed. 69.
De Camvile ; see Marmion.
De Cuiley, 230 ; 2 ed. 219.
De Esseby, 24 ; 2 ed. 23.
De Hastings, 20 ; 2 ed. 19.
De Houby, 137 ; 2 ed. 125.
De la Zouch ; see Zouch.
De la Zouch, 186 ; 2 ed. 168.
De Maureward, 117 ; 2 ed. 109.
De Odingsells, &c. 255 ; 2 ed. 240.
De Quincy and Beaumont, 37 ; 2 ed. 35.
De Shepey, 253 ; 2 ed. 238.
De Staunton, 268 ; 2 ed. 251.
De Temple, 283 ; 2 ed. 264.
De Walshall ; see Danvers.
De Wellesburgh, 303 ; 2 ed. 283.
De Wichard, Sutton, Blunt, and Pope, 221 ; 2 ed. 201.
Erdington ; see Somery.
Esseby ; see De Esseby.
Farnham, 227 ; 2 ed. 215.
Faulconer, De Ridware, and De Cotton, 287 ; 2 ed. 270.
Faunt ; see Clarenaulx.
Fitzherbert, 294 ; 2 ed. 276.
Fitzherbert ; see Meignell.

Grey, 123; 2 ed. 113.
Hardwick, 176; 2 ed. 160.
Harington; see Moton.
Hastings; see De Hastings.
Herle, 151; 2 ed. 138.
Heselrig, 213; 2 ed. 194.
Houby; see De Houby.
Keble, 140; 2 ed. 128.
Knight, Welsh, Littleton, &c. 299; 2 ed. 280.
Leicester, Earls of, 167; 2 ed. 153.
Littleton; see Knight.
Malory, 153; 2 ed. 140.
Malory, Vincent, Cave, and Mulsho, 279; 2 ed. 262.
Marmion, and De Camvile, 204; 2 ed. 185.
Maureward; see De Maureward.
Meignell, and Fitzherbert, 65; 2 ed. 61.
Moton, Vincent, and Harington, 219; 2 ed. 209.
Mounteagle, Lord; see Stanley
Mulsho; see Malory.
Neal, 223; 2 ed. 212.
Odingsells; see De Odingsells.
Pope; see De Wichard.

Poultney, 193; 2 ed. 174.
Purefey, 93; 2 ed. 86.
Ridisare; see Faulconer.
Shepey; see De Shepey.
Somery, and Erdington, 31; 2 ed. 30.
Southill; see Boivile.
Stafford; see Burdet.
Staresmore; see Danvers.
Staunton; see De Staunton.
Sutton; see De Wichard.
Temple; see De Temple.
Trussel; see Charnels.
Turvile, 208; 2 ed. 188.
Verdon, Lords, 196; 2 ed. 179.
Villiers, 55; 2 ed. 53.
Vincent; see Moton.
Vincent; see Malory.
Wake, Lords, 27; 2 ed. 26.
Walshall; see De Walshall.
Wellesburgh; see De Wellesburgh.
Welsh; see Knight.
Wichard; see De Wichard.
Wolfe; see Danvers.
Woodford, 23; 2 ed. 22.
Youch, or De la Youch, 19; 2 ed. 18.

77.—The History and Antiquities of Hinckley, Stoke, Dadlington, Wykin, and The Hyde. (No. 7, Bibliotheca Topographica Britannica.) *London*, 1790. 4to.

Cleiveland *of Hinckley*, folding at 134.

Onebye, 142, 143, 144.
Wright, 151.

APPENDIX TO THE ABOVE.

Breton, 348*.
Bliss; see Bromhead.
Bromhead, Pulton, Bliss, Moore, Walker and Gifford, 350*.
Chapman and Robarts, folding at 360*.
Cradock; see Morris.
Ferrers, folding at 300.
Giffard; see Bromhead.

Grentmesnill, 299.
Moore; see Bromhead.
Morris and Cradock, 349*.
Oneby, 347*, and folding at 347.
Pulton; see Bromhead.
Roberts; see Chapman.
Walker; see Bromhead.
Wright, folding at 348*.

78. —The History and Antiquities of Aston Flamville, and Burbach, &c. (No. 43 Bibliotheca Topographica Britannica.) *London*, 1790, 4to.

Turvile *of Normanton*, and Flamvile *of Aston Flamvile*, folding at 252.

79.—Collections towards the History and Antiquities of the Town and County of Leicester. (No. 50. Bibliotheca Topographica Britannica.) *London*, 1790. 4to.

Grey *of Barwell*, 428.

80.—The History and Antiquities of the County of Leicester. By JOHN NICHOLS, F.S.A. *London*, 1795-1807. 4 vols. in 8, folio.

Abney *of Willesley and Newton Burguland*, iii. faces 1032.
Albini (*Belvoir*) ; see Todeni.
Alfounder *of Thurcaston*, iii. 1049,
Allen *of Whetstone*, iv. 163.
Allen *of Markfield*, iv. 804.
Allington *of Burbach*, iv. 468.
Alsop *of Church Langton*, ii. 694*.
Alsopp *of Markfield*, iv. 802.
Andrews *of Great Bowden*, ii. 473.
Andrewes, iii. 455.
Appleby *of Appleby*, iv. 442.
Armeston *of Burbach*, iv. 467.
Ashby *of Loseby*, iii. 298.
Ashby *of Quenby* (in 3 parts), iii. 299.
Asheton, *co. Leicester*, iv. 370.
Astley, *of Broughton Astley*, iv. 59.
Astley *of Nailson*, iv. 811.
Andley (*Great Ashby*). iv. 17.
Aylmer *of Knight Thorpe, co. Leicester and Claydon, co. Suffolk*, iii. 908.
Babington, 4 pages inserted at iii. 954.
Babington *of Derby*, iii. 967.
Babington *of Dethick*, iii. 964.
Babington *of co. Oxford*, iii. 967.
Babington *of Temple Rothley*, iii. 965.
Bacon *of Hinckley*, iv. 711.
Baghott *of Leicester*, i. 548.
Bainbridge *of Ashby de la Zouch*, iii. 632.
Bainbrigge *of Hugglescote Grange and London*, iii. 883.
Bainbrigge *of Lockington, co. Leicester and Rocester, co. Stafford*, iii. 882.
Bainbridge *of Woodseat in Rocester*, iii. 883*.

Bale *of Sadington and Carleton Curliew*, ii. 539.
Ballard *of Wimeswould*, iii. 507.
Banaster *of Bosworth and Upton*, iv. 505.
Banastre *of Kirby Muxloe*, iv. 621.
Bankes *of Peckleton*, iv. 876.
Barford *of Shawell*, iv. 343.
Barrett *of Wimeswould*, iv. 407.
Barwell *of Kegworth and Garendon*, iii. 853.
Bate *of Ashby de la Zouch*, iii. 636.
Bath, Earl of ; see Pulteney.
Basset *of Sapcote*, iv. 904.
Basset *of Drayton*, iv. 905.
Basset *of Blore, Grendon, and Hints*, iv. 906.
Basset *of Sapcote and Stoney Stanton ;* see Zouch.
Beaumont *of Barrow, co. Derby*, iii. 663*.
Beaumont (*Barrow-upon Soar*); see Quincy.
Beaumont *of Gracedieu*, iii. 661*.
Beaumont *of Cole Orton*, iii. 743.
Beaumont *of Glenfield*, iv. 621.
Beaumont *of Stoughton Grange*, ii. 861.
Beaumont *of Whitley, near Wakefield, co. Ebor.* iii. 662*.
Boler *of Eye Kettleby and Kirkby*, ii. 278.
Belgrave *of Preston, co. Rutland*, iv. 207.
Belgrave (*Belgrave*), iii. 177.
Belgrave *of North Kilworth*, iv. 201.
Bennett *of Welby*, ii. 285.
Bent *of Enderby*, iv. 162.
Bent *of Leicester*, iv. 150.
Bent *of Cosby*, iv. 144.

Beresford *of Barkby and Shakerston,* iii. 51.
Berkeley *of Wymondham and Coston,* ii. 413.
Bickerton *of Beby,* iii. 170.
Billers *of Burstall,* iii. 188.
Blaby *of Blaby ;* see Lodbroke.
Blount (*Osbaston*), iv. 524.
Blount *of Osbaston ;* see Wichard.
Bliss *of Market Harborough and Church Langton,* ii. 693*.
Bodle *of Markfield,* iv. 802.
Boothby *of Broadlow,* iv. 418.
Boothby *of Broadlow Ash, co. Derby,* Bart. iv. 179.
Boothby *of Tolley Park and Foston,* iv. 178.
Boothby *of Friday Hill, co. Essex,* Bart. iv. 179.
Boothby, Clopton, and Walker (*Foston*), iv. 171.
Boothby *of London, Potter's Marston, and Huncote,* iv. 177.
Borard, Reigne, and Tailard *of Stathern,* ii. 360.
Bouge *of Normanton Turvile ;* see Champagne.
Boughton *of Lawford, co. Warwick, and of Moorbarns, co. Leicester,* iv. 302.
Boun and Smyth *of Warwick and Norwich,* iv. 644.
Bourne *of Ayleston and Waltham, co. Leicester, and Ashover, &c. co. Derby,* iv. 34.
Bowden *of Melton Mowbray,* ii. 262*.
Boyville and Southill (*Stockerston*), ii. 816.
Bozon (*Claxton*) ; see De Rohaud.
Brabazon *of Eastwell, Moseley, Garthorpe, and Sproxton,* ii. 171.
Bracebridge *of Kingsbury, Atherston, and Lindley,* iii. 1145, 1146.
Bradgate *of Little Peatling, Bruntingthorpe, Ullesthorpe, and Wibtoft,* iv. 122.
Bradgate *of Little Peatling,* iv. 330.
Bradgate *of Great Peatling,* iv. 330.
Bradshaw *of Morebarne,* iv. 853*.
Breton *of Barwell,* iv. 484.
Brett *of Rotherby,* iii. 400.

Briggs *of Burrow,* ii. 529.
Brocas *of Beaurepaire, co. Southampton, and of Horton Vale, co. Bucks.* ii. 832.
Brooke *of Luffenham,* ii. 698.
Brokesby *of Stoke Golding, with Parr and Foster,* iv. 725.
Brokesby *of Shouldby,* iii. 406.
Browne *of Wistow and Kilby,* ii. 874.
Browne ; see Tate.
Browne *of Stretton-en-le-Field,* iii. faces p. 1029.
Brudenell *of Staunton Wyvile, and Dene ;* see Wyvile.
Brudenell *of Staunton* (a younger branch), ii. 913.
Bruyn (*Newton*), iii. 349.
Burdet *of Huncote,* iv. 820.
Burdet *of Burton Overy,* iv. 630*.
Burdet *of Loseby, Newton, Burdet, Bramcote, Seckington, and Formarke,* iii. 351.
Burdett and Harvey *of Elmesthorpe,* iv. 608.
Burdett *of Mowsley,* iv. 866.
Burrow *of Burrow ;* see Stockton.
Buswell *of Cadeby ;* see Pelsant.
Burton *of Coventry,* iv. 644.
Burton *of Stockerston, co. Leicester, and of Tolthorpe, Braunston, &c. co. Rutland,* ii. 820.
Burton *of Higham and Lindley,* iv. 635.
Byerley *of Belgrave,* iii. 178.
Byrd *of Cleybrook,* i. 614.
Calcott, or Caldecote *of Catthorpe,* iv. 79.
Caldwell, iv. 370.
Camvile (*Newton*), iii. 350.
Cantilupe, Lords, *of Bowden and Harborough,* ii. 493.
Carington, Smith, or Smyth *of Ashby Folvile,* iii. 29.
Cave *of Barrow,* iii. 68.
Cave *of Pickwell,* iii. 293.
Cave *of Horsepool Grange,* iii. 293.
Cave *of Bagrave and Ingarsby,* iii. 290.
Cave, co. Leicester, iv. 371.
Cave *of Worcestershire,* iv. 420.
Cave *of Worcestershire,* iv. 359.
Cave ; see Tate.

Chamber (*Gaddesby*); see Dannett.
Chamberlaine *of Newton Harcourt*, ii. 881.
Chamberlaine *of Tilton*, iii. 475.
Chambre (*Hothorpe*), ii. 831.
Champagne, Foucher, and Bouge *of Normanton Turvile*, iv. 1006.
Champernon (*Claxton*) ; see De Rohaud.
Charnell *of Muston*, ii. 295.
Charnells *of Snareston*, iii. 1047*.
Charnells *of Elmesthorpe, Swebston, &c.* iii. 1049*.
Charnells (*Snareston*), iv. 984*.
Chatham, Earl of ; see Pitt.
Cheselden *of Allexton*, iii. 19.
Cheselden *of Leicester*, iv. 408.
Cheslyn *of Langley*, iii. 864.
Chester *of Blaby*, iv. 52.
Chevercourt *of Wyfordby*, ii. 396.
Cheverel (*Wimeswould*), iii. 510.
Chippingdale *of Humberston*, iii. 278.
Christian *of Harborough*, ii. 494.
Clarke-Jervoise, (*Drayton*), iv. faces 602.
Clarke *of Tilton*, iii. 468.
Clerke *of Hoby*, iii. 266.
Clerke *of Hoby*, iv. 407.
Cleiveland *of Hinckley*, iv. 707, 708.
Cleiveland, or Cleveland, iv. 727.
Clopton (*Foston*) ; see Boothby.
Cockshutt (*Osbaston*); see Twistleton.
Coke *of Melbourne*, iii. 784*.
Colbrand, iv. 394.
Cole *of Lutterworth*, iv. 272.
Comin (*Barrow upon Soar*) ; see Quincy.
Conyers *of Wakerley and Blaston*, ii. 456.
Conyers *of Walthamstow and Blaston* ii. 457.
Cooke *of Sketchley*, iv. 468.
Corbett *of Barton*, iv. 520.
Corbett *of Wanlip*, iii. 1100.
Cotes *of Ayleston and Burbach*, iv. 35.
Cotes (*Cotes Devile*), iv. 212.
Coton, or Cotton *of Ridware, co. Stafford*, iv. 636.
Cotton *of Conington, co. Hunts.* ii. 834.
Cotton *of Broughton Astley*, iv. 64.

Cotton *of Laughton*, ii. 694.
Cotton *of Dadlington*, iv. 724.
Cowper, or Cooper *of Sapcote and Stoney Stanton*, iv. 974.
Cox *of Lea Grange*, iv. 864.
Cradock *of Markfield*, iv. 802.
Cradock, alias Newton (*Markfield*), iv. 807*.
Cradock *of Durham*, iv. 807*.
Cradock *of Richmond, co. York*, iii. 1150.
Cradock *of East Farndon, co. Northampton and Leicester*, iii. 1150.
Cradock *of Leicester*, iii. 1149.
Cradock *of Swanzy*, iii. 1150.
Cradocke *of Husbands Bosworth*, ii. 466.
Creon and Vaux (*Belvoir*), ii. 28.
Crewe *of Crewe Hale, Cheshire and Misterton, co. Leicester*, iv. 303.
Crewe *of Stene, and Newton Verdon*, iv. 839.
Criol (*Croxton*), ii. 147.
Croft *of Barwell and Peckleton*, iv. 483.
Croft, Wightmam and Jee *of Peckleton*, iv, 876.
Culey *of Ratcliffe Cuily*, iv. 911.
Curl and Wilcox *of Melton Mowbray*, ii. 262*.
Cutler *of Blackfordby*, iii. 634.
Danet *of Bromkinsthorpe*, iv. 571.
Dannet *of South Croxton*, iii. 235.
Dannett and Chamber (*Gaddesby*), iii. 969.
D'Anvers *of Shakerston and Swithland*, iv. 189.
D'Anvers, De Aumari, Wolfe, and Walshall (*Frolesworth*), iv. 188.
Dawes *of Stapleton*, iv. 484.
Dawson *of Newbold and Whatton*, iii. 1106.
DeAumari ; see D'Anvers.
Deene (*Claxton*) ; see De Rohaud.
De Bois, and La Zouche *of Thorpe Ernald*, ii. 372.
De Ferrars, i. 545.
Denbigh, Earl of ; see Feilding.
Derby and Eyton *of Gaddesby*, iii. 968.
De Rohaud, Goldington, Champernoon, Bozon, and Deene (*Claxton*), ii. 132.

Devereux (*Cottesbach*), iv. 147.
Digby *of Tilton, Eye Kittleby, Sisonby, North Luffenham, and Welby*, ii. 261.
Digby *of Tilton*, iii, 473,474.
Digby *of London and Garendon*, iii. 475.
Digby *of Oulney*, iii. 475.
Digby *of Cotes and Luffenham*, iii. 475.
Digby (*Raunston*), iii. 933.
Dillingham *of co. Beds.*, and Ord, i. 615.
Dixie *of Market Bosworth*, iv. 506.
Dixon *of Rolleston* (*add.*), ii. 891.
Draper *of Melton Mowbray*, ii. 263.
Dudley, and of Sidney, Earls of Leicester, i. 544.
Duncumb (*Orton on the Hill*), iv. 853.
Duncombe (*Dalby on the Woulds*), iii. 255.
Duport *of Shepeshed*, iii. 1023.
Duranthorp, (*Donisthorpe,*) iii. 997.
Edwards *of Kilworth and Welham*, ii. 868.
Elkington *of Shawell*, iv. 342.
Erdington *of Barrow*, iii. 67.
Espec (*Belvoir*) ; see Todeni.
Estwick *of Old Hays*, iv. 888.
Everard *of Shenton and Hether*, iv. 522*.
Eyre *of Hassop and Eastwell*, iv. 398.
Eyre *of Belton*, iii. 649.
Eyrick *of Great Stretton*, ii. 615.
Eyrick or Heyrick *of Houghton, London, and Leicester*, ii. 615.
Eyton *of Gaddesby* ; see Derby.
Falconer *of Thurcaston*, iii. 1056.
Farmer *of Ratcliffe Cuily*, iv. 950, 951.
Farmour *of Hugglescote* ; see Warde.
Farnham *of the Nether Hall, in Quorndon*, iii. 104.
Farnham *of Quorndon*, iii. 103.
Farrent or Farren, *of Lutterworth*, iv. 272.
Faunt, *alias* Fawnt *of Wistow, co. Hunts, and Foston, co. Leicester*, iv. 173.
Feilding, *co. Dorset, and co. Middlesex;* see Fielding.

Feilding *of Lutterworth and Missterton*, afterwards Earls of Denbigh, iv. faces 293.
Ferrars ; see De Ferrars.
Fielding or Feilding, *co. Dorset and co. Middlesex*, iv. 394.
Fiennes (*Markfield*) ; see Snell.
Firebrace *of Stoke Golding*, iv. 726.
Fitton *of Shawell*, iv. 343.
Fitzherbert *of Twycross*, iv. 853.
Fitzherbert *of Upton;* see Jakes.
Flanders *of Flanders, co. Warwick;* see Limsey.
Flamvile *of Aston Flamvile*, iv. 447.
Folvile *of Ashby Folvile*, iii. 23.
Fortescue, with Furvile (*Aston Flamvile*), iv. 451.
Foster *of Hinckley*, iv. 726.
Foster *of Stoke Golding;* see Brokesby.
Foucher *of Normanton Turvile;* see Champagne.
Fox *of Bosworth, and Ratcliffe Cuiley*, iv. 504.
Frewen, now Turner *of Cold Overton, and of Northiam, co. Sussex*, ii. 142.
Fullwood *of Hemington*, iii. 860*.
Gage *of Bentley, co. Sussex*, iii. 149.
Gaunt (*Saltby*); see Paynell.
Gee (*Rothley*); iii. 954.
Gerveis, Jerveis, or Jarvis, *of Thorpe Langton and Great Peatling*, ii. 671.
Gery, *co. Bedford*, iii. 1041.
Gery *of Swebston*, iii. 1041.
Gifford *of Burstall*, iii. 188.
Glover (*Sewstern*), ii. 129.
Gobion and Turpin *of Knaptoft*, iv. 225.
Goddard *of Beby*, iii. 170.
Goldington ; see De Rohaud.
Goodall *of Earl Shilton*, iv. 780.
Goodman *of Blaston and Easton*, ii. 455.
Gore *of Ullesthorpe and Lutterworth*, iv. 128.
Gray *of Langley*, iii. 863.
Green and Iliffe *of Hinkley*, iv. 709.
Greene *of Rolleston*, ii. 446*.
Greene *of Kegworth*, iii. 851.
Gregory *of Asfordby*, iii. 19.

L

Gregory *of Askover, co. Derby and of St. Martin's, Leicester,* i. 587.

Grentemaisnell, i. 21.

Gresley *of Drakelow and Nether Seale,* iii. 1009*.

Grey *of Barwell and Basset,* iv. 481.

Grey *of Wilton, Lords, (Leire),* iv. 245.

Grey, Earl of Stamford and Warrington, iii. 682.

Grey *of Enville, co. Staffordshire,* iii. 683.

Griffin *of Gumley, Braybroke and Dingley,* ii. 592.

Griffith *of Barrow,* iii 67.

Groby, Lords of the Manor of, iv. 633*.

Hacket *of Penterry, Abkettleby, and South Croxton,* iii. 238.

Halford *of Lutterworth,* iv. 272.

Halford *of Edithweston, co. Rutland,* ii. 876.

Halford *of Welham,* ii. 864.

Halford *of Wistow,* ii. 874.

Hall *of Asfordby,* iv. 402.

Harborough, Earls of, (*Sherard*), ii. 346.

Harcourt *of Market Bosworth, Stanton Harcourt, and Ellenhall,* iv. 519*—521*.

Harcourt *of Dadlington and Rowden,* iv. 723.

Harley *of Osgathorpe, Oddeston, and Loughborough,* iii. 923.

Harpur *of Calke, Bilston, &c.* iii. 885*.

Harpur *of Littleover,* iii. 885*.

Harpur *of Rushall, Swarkston, and Hemington,* iii. 884.

Harrington *of Glooston,* ii. 584.

Harringworth, iii. 1146.

Harte *of Freby, Stapleford, Hartshall, and Leicester,* ii. 281.

Hartopp *of Freathby and Buckminster,* ii. 128.

Hartopp *of Little Dalby,* ii. 159.

Hartopp *of Burton Lazars,* ii. 267.

Harvey *of Elmesthorpe ;* see Burdett.

Haselwood ; see Marmion.

Hastings *of Kirby, Ashby de la Zouch, and Donington Park,* iii. 607.

Hastings *of Kirby Muxloe ;* see Herle.

Hastings, Earls of Pembroke, iv. 447.

Hastings *of Humberston and Belgrave,* iii. 278.

Hayes *of Burton Lazars,* ii. 271.

Heathcote *of Chesterfield and Sileby,* iii. 428.

Henslie or Inslie *of Lutterworth,* iv. 272.

Herdwicke *of Lindley ;* see Rodvile.

Hereford, Earl of ; (De Bohun), i. App. 33.

Herle and Hastings *of Kirby Muxloe, Braunston, &c.,* iv. 627.

Herrick *of Beaumanor,* iii. 148.

Herrick *of Knighton,* iii. 148.

Hesilrige *of Noseley ;* see Martival.

Hewett *of Dunton and Stretton,* ii. 581.

Hewett *of Dunton Basset,* iv. 156.

Heygate *of Husbands Bosworth,* iv. 628.

Heyrick ; see Eyrick.

Hill *of Norton by Twycross, Measham and Leicester,* iii. 1144.

Hill *of Nether Seale,* iii. 1012*.

Hilton *of Newbold Verdon,* iv. 865.

Hodges *of Syston,* iii. 516.

Holden *of Shepey and Erdington,* iv. 935.

Holled *of Bareby,* and Smith *of Leire and Normanton Turvile,* iv. 342.

Hood *of Bardon Park,* iv. 806.

Houby *of Houby ;* see Kirkby.

Houby (*Hoby*), iii. 264.

Hubert (*Stapleford*), ii. 353.

Hudson *of London and Wanlip,* iii. 1102.

Hudson *of Melton Mowbray,* ii. 264.

Hunter *of Lichfield,* iv. 333.

Hutton, i. lxxxv.

Humphrey *of Barton Segrave and Swebston,* iii. 1050*.

Hyde *of Sundrish and Quorndon,* iii. 109.

Iliffe *of Hinckley ;* see Green.

Ingwardeby (*Willesley*), iii. 1034.

Inslie *of Butterworth ;* see Henslie.

Jakes *of Wellesburgh ;* and Fitzherbert *of Upton,* iv. 964*.

Jarvis; see Gerveis.

Jee *of Peckleton*; see Croft.

Jeffreys (*Broughton*), ii. 114.

Jennens *of Gopsal*, iv. 859.

Jerveis; see Gerveis.

Jervis *of Great Peatling*, iv. 334.

Jervoise, now Purefoy *of Herriard, co. Southampton*, iv. 602.

Jervoise, now Clarke; see Clarke-Jervoise.

Keble (*Humberston*), iii. 273.

Kendall *of Twycross and Thornton*, iv. 985.

King *of Kirby Muxloe*, iv. 626.

Kingston *of Rothley*, iv. 408.

Kirkby *of Kirkby and Melton*; and Houby *of Houby*, ii. 224.

Lacy (*Castle Donington*), iii. 771.

Lacy *of Melton Mowbray*, ii. 264.

Lacy *of Melton Mowbray*; see Ruskin.

Langham *of Gopsal*, iv. 855.

Lany *of Leicester and Reresby*, iii. 400.

Lathbury *of Cadeby and Eggington, co. Derby*; see Soulby.

Latimer *of Foxton, Gumley, and Braybroke*, ii. 566.

Lassells *of Woodhouse*, iii. 169*.

Laurence, iv. 370.

Law *of Keythorpe*, iii. 1137.

Lawrence *of Long Whatton.* iv. 408.

La Zouche *of Thorpe Ernald*; see De Bois.

Legard, *co. Leicester*, iv. 369.

Leicester, Saxon Earls of; i. 18.

Leicester, Earls of (*Montfort*), i. 212, and App. 119.

Leicester, Earls of; see Dudley.

Leicester, Earls of; (*Bellomont*) i. 98.

Leigh *of Ashfordby*, iii. 406.

Leigh *of Cadeby*; see Soulby.

Levinge *of Shepey*, iv. 952.

Le Warre *of Harby*, ii. 211.

Leyntclere (*Luffenham*), ii. 697.

Limsey, Odingsells, and Flanders *of Flanders, co. Warwick*, iv. 636.

Lincoln, Earls of; (De Lacy), i. App. 33.

Lister *of Thorpe Ernald*, ii. 376.

Lodbroke, Blaby, and Savile *of Blaby*, iv. 51.

Ludford, Newdigate-; see Newdigate-Ludford.

Madan *of Ilstock*, iv. 760.

Maior *of Leicester, Barwell, Glen Parva, and Blaby*, iv. 482.

Malory *of Walton-on-the-Woulds*, iii. 501.

Malory, Revell, and Vincent *of Swinford*, iv. 364.

Malory *of Kirkby Malory*, iv. 761.

Malvesyn (*Sadington*), ii. 776.

Manners, Earls and Dukes of Rutland, ii. 48, 67.

Marmion (*Newton*), iii. 350.

Marmion and Haselwood (*Galby*), ii. 569.

Marmion *of Galby*, ii. 569.

Marshall *of Worthington, Whitwick, and Diseworth*, iii. 1122.

Marston *of Slawston*, ii. 798.

Martival and Hesilrige *of Noseley*, ii. 756.

Mason *of Leicester*, iii. 1148.

Maureward *of Godeby*, ii. 194.

May *of Sutton Cheynell, Mayfield, &c.*, iv. 548.

Meade *of Narborough*, iv. 818.

Meignell *of Burton Overy*, ii. 532.

Meysnil (*Staunton Harold*), iii. 707.

Miles *of Leicester*, i. 587.

Moore *of Appleby Parva*, iv. 443.

Moore *of Kentwell House, co. Suffolk, &c.* iv. 444.

Moton, and Vincent *of Peckleton*, iv. 870.

Mordaunt *of Medbourne*, ii. 694*.

Morris *of Lodington*, iv. 401.

Morton (*Wyfordby*), ii. 397.

Morton *of Bosworth*, iv. 505.

Mounteney *of Newbold Verdon*, iv. 848*.

Mowbray (*Melton Mowbray*), ii. 263.

Mundy *of Osbaston, Allestry, Marketon, and Shipley*, iv. 526*.

Mundy *of Marketon, co. Derby, and of Osbaston Hall, co. Leicester*, iv. 525.*

Napton (*Misterton*), iv. 306.

Naunton (*Twyford*), iii. 493.

Neale (*Abkettleby*), ii. 11.

Nedham *of Allexton*, iii. 14.

Nedham *of Gaddesby*, iii. 976, 408.

Nedham *of Cole Orton*, iii. 742.
Nele *of Great Glen*, ii. 575.
Nele *of Prestwould*, iii. 362.
Nevill, *of Holt;* and Smyth who took the name of Nevill, ii. 730.
Nevill of *Wimeswould*, iii. 501.
Nevill *of Enderby and Whetstone*, iv. 167.
Newdigate-Ludford *of Ansley Hall*, co. *Warwick*, iv. 1025.
Newton (*Markfield*), iv. 807*.
Nicolls *of Tilton, co. Leicester, and of Hardwick, co. Northampton*, iii. 480.
Noble *of Frolesworth*, i. 617.
Noble *of Reresby and Leicester*, i. 616.
Noble *of Thussington and Reresby*, iii. 461,
Noel *of Old Dalby*, iii. 254.
Noel, Viscount Wentworth, iv. 770.
Noone (*Walton-on-the-Woulds*), iii. 498.
Norwich *of Bringhurst, and of Bampton*, ii. 519.
Nowers, otherwise Wilcocks *of Knossington*, ii. 655.
Oldershaw *of Kegworth, and of Longborough Old Park*, iii. 859*.
Oneby *of Barwell*, i. App. 145.
Oneby, or Ondeby *of Stoke Dry, Sadington, Oadby, Newton Burguland, Hinckley, and Barwell*, iii. 1147.
Odingsells *of Flanders, co. Warwick;* see Limsey.
Okeover *of Oldbury*, iv. 1039.
Ord; see Dillingham.
Orton, or Overton *of Lea Grange*, iv. 864.
Orton *of Reresby*, iii. 395.
Overton *of Lea Grange;* see Orton.
Pace *of Leicester*, i. 548.
Packe *of Cotes and Prestwould*, iii. 362.
Packe *of Kettering and London*, iii. 557.
Paget *of Barwell*, iv. 481.
Palmer *of Carleton Curlieu*, ii. 543.
Palmer *of Stoke Doyle, and Withcote*, ii. 550.
Palmer *of Osgathorpe, and of the Newark, Leicester*, iii. 923.

Palmer *of Wanlip*, iii. 1101.
Palmer *of Stoney Stanton*, iv. 973.
Palmerston, Visct.; see Temple.
Palmes, *of Melton Mowbray*, ii. 295.
Paramore *of Bagworth*, iii. 988.
Parr *of Kendall, co. Westmoreland, Green Norton's, co. Northampton*, iv. 725*.
Parr *of Stoke Golding;* see Brokesby.
Pate *of Eye Kettleby*, iii. 524.
Pate *of Eye Kettleby and Sisonby*, ii. 283.
Paynell, Gaunt, and Stuteville (*Saltby*), ii. 303.
Peche, iv. 370.
Peck *of Fleckney, Enderby, and Earl's Shilton*, iv. 167.
Peck *of Wakefield and Knossington*, ii. 879.
Peck *of Fleckney*, ii. 879.
Pelsant and Buswell *of Cadeby*, iv. 578.
Pembroke, Earls of; see Hastings.
Pembruge *of Ayleston and Glen Parva*, iv. 36, 422.
Pepper *of Thurmaston*, iii. 187.
Percy, Earls of Northumberland, iv. 174.
Perin *of Ashby de la Zouch*, iii. 633.
Perkins *of Orton-on-the-Hill*, iv. 854*.
Pestell *of Packington and Revenston*, iii. 940.
Pexall *of Beaurepaire, co. Southampton*, ii. 833.
Phelps (*Coston*); see Tufton.
Phillipps *of Garendon*, iii. 804.
Pickering; see Stanton.
Pilkington (*Leicester*), i. 606.
Pilkington *of Worthington*, iii. 650.
Pipe; see Rydeware.
Pitt, Earls of Chatham, iv. 962.
Plumbe *of Potters Marston*, iv. 484.
Pochin *of Barkby*, iii. 51, 52, 62*.
Popham *of Rolleston*, ii. 445*.
Poultney *of Poultney*, iv. 319.
Powell *of Belvoir*, ii. 85.
Power *of Barleston and Barwell*, iv. 517.
Pratt *of Cottesbach*, iv. 152.
Prestwiche *of Luffenham*, ii. 698.

Pulteney, *of Longhborough;* see Tomlinson.

Pulteney, Earls of Bath, iv. 320.

Purefoy; see Jervoise.

Purefoy *of Misterton, Burbach, Drayton, Coldecote, Shalston, &c.,* iv. 599-601.

Quincy, Comin, and Beaumont (*Barrow-upon-Soar*), iii. 66.

Rayson, *of Barrow-upon-Soar,* iii. 135.

Reigne *of Stathern;* see Borard.

Revell *of Swinford;* see Malory.

Roberts *of Thorpe Langton,* ii. 671.

Roberts *of Willesdon, co. Midd.,* iv. 450.

Roberts *of Sutton Cheynell,* iv. 547.

Robinson *of Stretton, co. Leicester, and Cranford St. Andrew, co. Northampton,* ii. 583.

Robinson *of Long Whatton,* iii. 1106.

Rodvile and Herdwike *of Lindley,* iv. 643.

Rooe *of Normanton Turvile,* iv. 1005.

Ross (*Belvoir*); see Todeni.

Ruding *of Westcotes,* iv. 568.

Ruskin and Lacy *of Melton Mowbray,* ii. 264.

Rutland, Earls and Dukes of; see Manners.

Rydeware, Pipe, Stafford, Vernon, Swynfen, &c., iii. faces 982*.

Sacheverell *of Sadington and Kibworth,* iii. 220.

Sacheverell *of Radcliffe upon Sore,* iii. 220.

Sacheverell *of Hopwell, Wimeswould, and Old Hays,* iii. 394.

Sacheverell *of Reresby,* iii. 395.

Sacheverell *of Wimeswould,* iii. 509.

Sacheverell *of Smiterton, and of Irwell, co. Notts,* iii. 513.

Sacheverell *of Newhall,* iii. 1140.

St. John *of Knossington, Cold Overton and Sapcote,* ii. 656.

St. Nicholas *of the Isle of Thanet, Ashe, Knoll, Lutterworth, Skelton, Burbach, &c.,* iv. 269.

Salisbury *of Revenston, Newton, Burguland, and Snibston,* iii. 940.

Saunders *of Shankton,* ii. 792.

Saunders *of Foxton and Sibbertoft,* ii. 564.

Savage *of Walton-on-the-Woulds,* iii. 501.

Savile *of Blaby,* iv. 421.

Savile *of Blaby;* see Lodbroke.

Scarsdale, Ancestors of the Earls of, ii. 217.

Scotland, the Twelve Competitors for the Crown of, iv. 448.

Scrope, *of Masham and Upsal,* iii. 477.

Scrope, Lords, *of Bolton,* ii. 447.

Sedley *of Wymondham, Southfleet, Aylesford, &c.,* ii. 415.

Segrave *of Scalford,* ii. 314.

Segrave (*Segrave*); iii 413.

Segrave *of Cadeby,* iv. 577.

Serjeant *of Melton Mowbray,* ii. 262*.

Sharpe *of Rolleston,* ii. 443.

Shenton *of Barwell,* iv. 483.

Shepey, with Wheathill or Whithull *of Shepey,* iv. 932.

Sherard *of Stapleford,* ii. 343.

Sherard *of Lopthorpe,* ii. 353.

Sherard *of Glatton,* ii. 353.

Sherman *of the Newark, Leicester,* i. 504.

Shipward *of Melton Mowbray,* iii. 523.

Shirley *of Staunton Harold,* iii. 715*,.719*.

Shirley *of Wistenston or Wistoneston, co. Sussex,* iii. 721*.

Shirley *of Preston, co. Sussex,* iii. 727; iv. 1050.

Skeffington (*Skeffington*), iii. 437-448, 459, 450.

Skipwith *of Cotes,* iii. 368.

Skrymsher, *of Aqualate,* iv. 421.

Slorey *of Braunston,* iv. 621.

Smalle or Small *of co. Gloucester, and Lewisham, co. Kent,* iii. 94.

Smalley *of Thorpe Ernold, Barrow, Mountsorell, Newbold, &c.* iii. 93.

Smart *of Ashby de la Zouch,* iii. 636.

Smith *of Ashby Folvile;* see Carington.

Smith *of Normanton Turvile;* see Holled.

Smith, alias Heriz *of Withcock*, ii. 184.

Smith *of Somerby, Husbands Bosworth, Frolesworth, and Edmondthorpe*, ii. 185.

Smith *of Gaddesby*, iii. 971.

Smyth; see Boun.

Smyth; see Nevill.

Smyth; see Carington.

Snell with Wickham, and Fiennes, (*Markfield*), iv. 805.

Soulby, Lathbury (*of Cadeby and Egginton, co. Derby*), and Leigh, iv. 577.

Southill; see Boyville.

Stafford, Lord, *of Dunton Basset*, iv. 154.

Stafford, Lord, *of Ibstock and Huncote, and of Blatherwick, co. Northampton*, iv. 760.

Stafford; see Rydeware.

Stamford and Warrington, Earls of; see Grey.

Stanford *of Barkby Thorpe*, iii. 51.

Stanley *of Cottesbach*, iv. 152.

Stanton, and Pickering *of Langton*, i. 614.

Stanton; see Staveley.

Staresmore *of Frolesworth*, iv. 190.

Starkey *of Tonge*, iii. 728.

Staunton (*Staunton Harold*), iii. 704.

Staveley and Stanton *of West Langton*, ii. 664.

Steele (*Morebarne*), iv. 853.

Stephens *of Leicester*, i. 586.

Stephens *of St. Martin's Leicester*, i. 588, 607.

Stockton or Stockden, afterwards Burrow *of Burrow*, ii. 520.

Stoke *of Boresworth*, ii. 461.

Stourton *of Narborough*, iv. 818.

Strelley *of West Langton*, ii. 663.

Strete *of Hallaton*, ii. 602.

Stretton (*Stretton en le Field*), iii. 1025, 1028.

Stuteville; see Paynell.

Sutton *of Osbaston;* see Wichard.

Swillington *of Kirkby, Somerby and Newhall*, ii. 227.

Swynfen *of Sutton Cheynell and Cadeby*, iv. 546.

Swynfen; see Rydeware.

Tailard *of Stathern;* see Borard.

Talbot *of Swinnington*, iii. 1123.

Tamworth (*Halsted*), iii. 477.

Tate, Cave, and Browne (Add.), ii. 888.

Tatteshall (*Abkettleby*), ii. 17*.

Temple *of Temple Hall*, iv. 958.

Temple *of Temple Hall, Witney and Stowe*, iv. 959-961.

Temple, Visct. Palmerston, iv. 962.

Thame, iv. 370.

Thanet, Earls of; see Tufton.

Thickbrome *of Ashby de la Zouch*, iii. 636.

Todeni, Albini, Espec, and Ross (*Belvoir*), ii. 27.

Tomlinson *of Durham*, Pulteney *of Shepey and Loughborough*, and Pulteney *of Poulteney*, iv. 304.

Toone *of Belton and Osgathorpe*, iii. 650.

Trymnell *of Stoke Golding*, iv. 726.

Tufton, Earls of Thanet, and Phelps (*Coston*), ii. 144.

Turner, Frewen-; see Frewen.

Turner *of Leicester*, i. 548.

Turpin; see Gobion.

Turvile *of Aston Flamvile*, iv. 451.

Turvile *of Thurleston, Newhall, and Normanton Turvile*, iv. 1004.

Turville *of Normanton Turvile, Aston Flamvile, and Husbands Bosworth*, iii. 465.

Twistleton and Cockshutt(*Osbaston*), iv. 524.

Tyringham *of Barkby*, iv. 407.

Vaux *of Shankton*, iii. 1129.

Vaux; see Creon.

Verdon (*Belton*), iii. 640.

Vernon; see Rydeware.

Villiers (*Brooksby*), iii. 197.

Vincent *of Shepey*, iv. 933, 934, 952.

Vincent; see Moton.

Vincent; see Malory.

Vowe *of Hallaton*, ii. 602.

Wadland *of Medboume*, ii. 719.

Wake *of Atterton*, iv. 1026.

Walcote (*Walcote*), iv. 318.

Waldron *of co. Leicester*, iv. 325.

Waldron *of Oadby*, iv. 325.

Walker *of Harborough*, ii. 494.

Walker (*Foston*) ; see Boothby.

Walsh, or Waleys *of Wanlip*, iii. 1100.

Wallers *of Swithland*, iii. 1047.

Walshall (*Frolesworth*); see D'Anvers.

Ward *of Hinckley*, iv. 710.

Warde alias Farmour *of Hugglescote*, iv. 760.

Warde *of Carleton Curlieu*, ii. 539.

Wase *of Rotherby*, iii. 400.

Wells *of Thurmaston and Thrussington*, ii. 60.

Wells *of Great Bowden*, ii. 472.

Wentworth, Viscount; see Noel.

Whalley *of Norton-juxta-Galby*, ii. 736.

Whatton *of Loughborough Oldparks*, iii. 912.

Wheathill *of Shepey ;* see Shepey.

Whellesburgh *of Wellesburgh*, iv. 963*.

Whitaphe *of Reresby*, iv. 407.

Whithull *of Shepey ;* see Shepey.

Whiting *of Desford*, iv. 571.

Wichard, Sutton, and Blount *of Osbaston*, iv. 523*.

Wickham (*Markfield*) ; see Snell.

Wightman *of Peckleton* ; see Croft.

Wigley *of Wirksworth and Scraptoft*, ii. 787-789.

Wigston *of Leicester*, i. 504.

Wilcocks ; see Nowers.

Wilcox *of Melton Mowbray ;* see Curl.

Wileman, or Wildman *of Burton-on-the-Woulds*, iii. 379.

Wilmot *of Chaddesden, Shawell, and Osmaston*, iv. 344.

Wilmot *of Little Shepey, and of Duffield, co. Derby*, iv. 937.

Wilson *of Knight Thorpe*, iii. 907.

Wilson *of Keythorpe and Didlington*, iii. 514.

Wincoll *of Leicester*, i. 548.

Winstanley *of Lancashire*, iv. 629*.

Winstanley *of Braunston*, iv. 629*.

Winter *of Worthington*, iii. 650.

Wolfe (*Frolesworth*) ; see D'Anvers.

Wollaston *of Shenton*, iv. 531, 541.

Woodcock *of Keame*, iii. 983.

Woodford *of Brentingby*, ii. 376.

Woodford *of Ashby Folvile*, iii. 24.

Wright *of Sutton*, iv. 64.

Wrighte *of Brooksby*. iii. 219.

Wyvile and Brudenell *of Staunton Wyvile and Dene*, ii. 807.

Yarde *of Cosby*, iv. 145.

Zouch, Lords, *of Ashby de la Zouch,* iii. 635.

Zouch *of Harringworth*, iii. 1146.

Zouch *of Lubbesthorpe*, iv. 38.

Zouch *of Harynworth*, iv. 780.

Zouch with Basset, *of Sapcote and Stoney Stanton*, iv. 968.

Zouche ; see La Zouche.

81.—Select Views in Leicestershire, &c. By J. THROSBY. *London*, 1789. 2 vols. 4to.

Skeffington, ii. folding at 210.

LINCOLNSHIRE.

82.—Collections for the History of the Town and Soke of Grantham, &c. By EDMUND TURNOR, F.R.S., F.S.A. *London*, 1806. 4to.

Archer *of Coopersale and Great Paunton*, 132.

Brownlow, Viscount Tyrconnel, 100.

Cholmeley *of Easton*, 152.

Cust, Lord Brownlow, 101.

De Ligne *of Harlaxton*, 113.

Gregory *of Harlaxton*, 114.

Harrison *of Bolls, co. Herts*, 146.

Manners, 61.

Newton, 69, 168.

Newton *of Haydor*, 85.

Pakenham *of North Witham*, 100.

Porter *of Belton*, 99.

Turnor *of Stoke Rochford, and Panton House*, 147.

Welby *of Denton*, 124.

Williams, 125.

83.—The History and Antiquities of Gainsburgh, &c.   By
ADAM STARK. *London*, 1817. 8vo. 2nd Ed. 1843.
8vo.

Burgh, 2 ed. 369. | Valence, 2 ed. 440.
Hickman, 1 ed. folding at 123. |

84.—Sketches illustrative of the Topography and History
of New and Old Sleaford. *Sleaford*, 1825. 8vo.

Ashby, Lords of, 140. | Hussey, folding at 108.
Carr, 112. | Kyme, Barony of, 274.

85.—A Topographical and Historical Account of Wainfleet,
&c., in the County of Lincoln. By EDMUND OLDFIELD.
London, 1829. 8vo. and 4to.

Dymoke (*Friskney*), 190. | Langton (*Gunby*), 207.

86.—The History and Topography of the Isle of Axholme,
being that part of Lincolnshire which is west of
Trent. By the Rev. W. B. STONEHOUSE, M. A. *London*,
1839. 4to.

Belwood (*Temple Belwood*); see | Ryther, Popplewell, Johnson, and
  Vavasour. | Steer (*Temple Belwood*), 344.
De Turre ; see Torre. | Sheffield, Lord of Butterwick, fold-
Ferne (*Beltoft*), 350. | ing at 276.
Johnson ; see Ryther. | Stanhope (*High Melwood*), 260.
Maw (*Tetley*), 436. | Steer ; see Ryther.
Mowbray, facing 141. | Stovin *of Tetley*, *Whitgift*, *&c.*
Neville (*Althorpe*) ; see Newmarsh. | folding at 427.
Newmarsh, and Neville (*Althorpe*), | Torre, or De Turre (*Haxey*), 308.
  374. | Vavasour and Belwood (*Temple
Pindar (*Owston*), 244. | Belwood*), 343.
Popplewell ; see Ryther. | Waterton (*Garthorpe*), faces 454.

87.—On account of the Parish of Lea with Lea Wood, in
the Hundred of Corringham, Lincolnshire. *London*,
1841, 8vo.

Anderson, folding at 17. | Trehampton, 12.
Estsax, 21. | Wood *of Longley, co. York*, 21.

88.—The History and Antiquities of Boston, &c. By PISHEY
THOMPSON. *London*, 1820, royal 8vo. 2nd edition.
Boston, 1856, royal 8vo. and folio.

Hussey, 248 ; 2 ed. 398. | Tilney, folding at 248 ; 2 ed. at 373.
Irby, 236 ; 2 ed. 391. |

LONDON AND MIDDLESEX.

89.—Sketches of the History and Antiquities of the Parish of Stoke Newington. (No. 9, Bibliotheca Topographica, Britannica.) *London,* 1790. 4to.

Fleetwood, folding at 28.

90.—The History and Antiquities of Canonbury House at Islington, &c. By JOHN NICHOLS, F.S.A. Edin. and Perth. (No. 49, Bibliotheca Topographica Britannica.) *London,* 1790. 4to.

Dennys, 28.

91.—The History and Antiquities of the Parish of Saint Leonard, Shoreditch, &c. By HENRY ELLIS. *London,* 1798. 4to.

Bowyer and Draper, 329.
Draper; see Bowyer.
Gernon and Montfichet, 98.
Lovell, 196.
Montfichet; see Gernon.

Shorditch, 93, 94.
Vaughan, 326.
Weld, 128.
Wheler, 346.
Whitmore, 129.

92.—An Historical and Topographical Account of the Parish of Fulham, including the Hamlet of Hammersmith. By T. FAULKNER. *London,* 1813. 8vo.

Mordaunt, folding at 88.

93.—The History of Merchant Taylors' School, from its Foundation to the present time. By the Rev. H. B. WILSON, B.D. *London,* 1814. 4to.

Dee, Bedo, 1169.
Dee, Arthur, 1170.
Dee, David, *of Salop,* 1171.
Urrey *of Gatcombe, Isle of Wight,* 1172.

Heneage *of Cadeby, Linc.,* 1173.
Brockholes *of Claughton,* 1173.
Fitzherbert *of Norbury, co. Derby,* 1173.

94.—The Topography and Natural History of Hampstead, in the County of Middlesex. By JOHN JAMES PARK. *London,* 1818. 8vo.

Atye; see Hungerford.
Games; see Langhorne.
Hicks and Noel, folding at 117.
Hungerford, St. John, Atye and Roberts, 198.
Langhorne, Warren, Games, Maryon, and Wilson, folding at 124.
Maryon; see Langhorne.

Noel; see Hicks.
Roberts; see Hungerford.
St. John; see Hungerford.
Ward *of Belsize,* 137.
Warren; see Langhorne.
Wilson; see Langhorne.
Wroth, 115.

M

95.—History and Antiquities of Kensington, &c. By
THOMAS FAULKNER. *London*, 1820. 8vo.

Cope and Rich, faces 62.
De Vere, Earls of Oxford, folding
at 39.

Rich ; see Cope.

96.—The Visitation of Middlesex, began in the year 1663.
By WILLIAM RYLEY, ESQ., Lancaster, and HENRY
DETHICK, Rouge Croix, &c. *Salisbury*, 1820. Folio.

Audley ; see Bonfoy.
Avery *of Enfield*, 25.
Awsiter *of Southall*, 21.
Banister *of St. John's*, 45.
Barrell *of Isleworth*, 15.
Beaumont *of Hackney*, 20.
Benning *of Willesdon*, 5.
Bird *of London*, 7.
Blinckarne *of London*, 51.
Blosse *of Stratford Bow*, 33.
Bonfoy *of Hese*, descended from
Audley, 19.
Bonnell *of Isleworth*, 2.
Bothby *of Tottenham*, 14.
Brigginshaw *of Hese*, 20.
Bronker *of Littleton*, 23.
Browne *of Stepney*, 36.
Brunskill *of Hadley*, 17.
Burnell *of Stanmore Magna*, 25.
Caswell *of Hampton*, 22.
Chambers *of Hackney*, 32.
Chilcot ; see Comyn.
Clerk *of Edmonton*, 18.
Collet *of London*, 47.
Collet *of Chelsea*, 4.
Comyn, alias Chilcot, *of Isleworth*,
12.
Cropley *of Clerkenwell*, 8.
Dixon *of Enfield*, 6.
Drax *of Hackney*, 33.
Dycer *of Hackney*, 29.
Evington *of Enfield*, 17.
Eyre *of Sarum*, 1.
Farmer *of London*, 50.
Finch *of Kensington*, 10.
Fuller *of Thistleworth*, 11.
Garfield *of Tuddington*, 22.
Gomeldon *of Chiswick*, 9.
Gorge *of Hillingdon*, 5.
Hamond *of Tuddington*, 23.
Hampton *of Norwood*, 11.

Harvey *of London*, 42.
Hawkesworth *of Chiswick*, 13.
Hinson *of Fordham*, 30, 31.
Hodges *of Hanwell*, 15.
Holliday *of Bromley*, 38.
Jackson *of Bromfield, in Edmonton*,
26.
Jacob *of Gamlingay*, 13.
Johnson *of Hackney*, 40.
Johnson *of Blackwall*, 37.
Jones *of Chiswick*, 19.
Jones *of Stratford Bow*, 38.
Kearsley *of London*, 51.
Kempe *of the Inner Temple*, 46.
Marsh *of Edmonton*, 4.
Mayo *of Tottenham*, 16.
Meggs *of Whitechapel*, 39.
Merrick *of Norcot*, 20.
Mildmay *of Barnes*, 3.
Milner *of Lylleston Green*, 44.
Nelson *of Gray's Inn*, 48.
Newman *of St. Giles's*, 45.
Otger *of London*, 9.
Page *of London*, 39.
Pagitt *of Hadley*, 24.
Parker *of Tottenham*, 27.
Pawlett *of Wilsdon*, 3.
Pearce *of Fulham*, 50.
Pitfield *of Hoxton*, 40.
Powell *of Fulham*, 42.
Pye *of the Charter House*, 43.
Raynton *of Enfield*, 12.
Richards *of Isleworth*, 14.
Rogers *of Edmonton*, 2.
Row *of Conington*, 16.
Sheffield *of Kensington*, 1.
Shelbury *of St. Clement Danes*, 49.
Smith *of Hammersmith*, 28.
Smith *of St. Giles's*, 41.
Stanley *of Cursitor's Alley*, 47.
Swanley *of Poplar*, 37.

Swynerton *of London*, 28.
Symcotts *of Isleworth*, 18.
Thomas *of Islington*, 44.
Thorowgood *of Kensington*, 34, 35.
Tracy *of Mile End*, 36.
Treswallen *of Hillingdon*, 21.
Turner *of Cursitor's Court*, 49.
Walker *of Hillingdon*, 6.
Walters *of Edmonton*, 26.

Ward *of Lincoln's Inn*, 48.
Webb *of St. James's*, 41.
Weld *of Edmonton*, 27.
Wicks *of Staines*, 24.
Wilding *of Hackney*, 32.
Wiltshire *of St. John's*, 7.
Woodward *of Hampstead*, 8.
Wright *of Marybone*, 46.

97.—Some Account of the Worshipful Company of Grocers, of the City of London. By JOHN BENJAMIN HEATH, Esq. *London*, 1829. Not published. 8vo.

Cannynge, 201.
Crosbie, 204, 291.

Cutler, 253.
Weld, 224.

98.—The History and Antiquities of the Parish of Hammersmith, &c. By THOMAS FAULKNER. *London*, 1839. 8vo.

Bennet ; see Leman.
Capel ; see Leman.

Latymer *of Ipswich and Freston, co. Suff.*, 184.
Leman, Bennet and Capel, 183.

99.—The History and Antiquities of the Parish of Tottenham, in the County of Middlesex. By WILLIAM ROBINSON, LL.D., F.S.A. *London*, 1840. 2 vols. 8vo.

Bothby or Botheby *of Tottenham*, ii. 162.

Mayo *of Tottenham*, ii. 163.
Parker *of Tottenham*, ii. 163.

100.—The History and Antiquities of the Parish of Hackney, in the County of Middlesex. By WILLIAM ROBINSON, LL.D., F.S.A. *London*, 1842. 2 vols. 8vo.

Beaumont *of Hackney*, i. 299.
Brooksbank, i. 447.
Chambers *of Hackney*, i. 299.
Cæsar *of Hackney*, i. 302.
Drax *of Hackney*, i. 300.
Dycer *of Hackney*, i. 300.

Hern *of Hackney*, i. 302.
Johnson *of Hackney*, i. 301.
Rowe *of Hackney*, ii. folding at 11.
Tyssen *of Hackney*, i. folding at 323.
Weld, i. 159.
Wilding *of Hackney*, i. 301.

101.—Some Account of the Worshipful Company of Ironmongers. Compiled by JOHN NICHOLL, F.S.A. *London*, 1851. Royal 8vo. Privately printed by the Company.

Avenon, 545.
Beckford, 581.
Cambell, 554.
Canning, 570.

Clitherow, 552.
Rowe, 550.
Thorold, 572.
Walton, Isaac, 568.

102.—Part of the Visitation of. *London*, 1634. Foolscap
folio. No date. Privately printed by Sir THOMAS
PHILLIPPS, Bart.

Abells *of London*, 1.	Banks *of London*, 4.
Abdy *of London*, 1.	Bard *of London*, 4.
Adams *of London*, 1.	Barksted *of London*, 4.
Alcock *of London*, 1.	Bassano, an Italian, 5.
Amory *of London*, 2.	Basse *of London*, 5.
Angell *of London*, 2.	Bateman *of London*, 5.
Anjou *of London*, 2.	Bayley *of London*, 5.
Anthony *of London*, 2.	Bayning *of London*, 5.
Ashwell *of Ashwell*, 2.	Bennet *of London*, 6.
Atkinson *of London*, 3.	Bewley *of London*, 6.
Atkinson *of London*, 3.	Bicklife *of London*, 6.
Austen *of London*, 3.	Bidulphe *of London*, 6.
Backhouse *of London*, 3.	Blacknall *of London*, 6.
Ball *of London*, 4.	

103.—Transactions of the London and Middlesex Archæological Society. *London*. Vols. 1 and 2. Commenced
in 1856.

Le Strange, i. 125.	Monoux, ii. 145.

104.—The Visitation of London, taken by Robert Cooke,
Clarenceux, A.D. 1568, &c. Edited by JOSEPH JACKSON
HOWARD, Esq., F.S.A., and JOHN GOUGH NICHOLS,
Esq., F.S.A. Published with the Transactions of the
London and Middlesex Archæological Society.

Chester, 2.	Champion, 8.
Martyn, 6.	White, 10.

MONMOUTHSHIRE.

105.—The History of Monmouthshire. By DAVID WILLIAMS.
London, 1796. 4to.

Beaufort, App. 129.	Jones *of Lanarth and Clytha*, 156.
Hanbury, App. 192.	Walters *of Piercefield*, App. 197.
Herbert, App. folding at 129.	Williams *of Lanffwyst*, App. 194.

106.—An Historical Tour in Monmouthshire, &c. By
WILLIAM COXE, A.M., F.R.S., F.S.A. *London*, 1801.
4to.

Hanbury, 244.	Nevill, Barons Abergavenny, facing 181.
Herbert, 131.	Van, 41.
Morgan, facing 66.	Williams, 119.

NORFOLK.

107.—An Essay towards a Topographical History of the County of Norfolk, &c. By FRANCIS BLOMEFIELD, Rector of Fersfield. *Fersfield and Lynn*, 1739-1775; 5 vols. folio. 2nd edition, *London*, 1805; 11 vols. royal 8vo. and 4to.

Adams (*Sprouston*), v. 1374; 2 ed. x. 461.

Athow (*Bichamwell*), iv. 61; vii. 293.

Bacon (*Ryburgh Magna*), iii. 841; 2 ed. vii. 165.

Batchcroft (*Bexwell*), iv. 71; 2 ed. vii. 308.

Beaupre, Bell, &c. (*Upwell*), iv. 183; 2 ed. vii. 460.

Bedingfeld (*Wigton*), v. 785; 2 ed. ix. 206.

Bell (*Upwell*); see Beaupre.

Berney (*Reedham*), v. 1484; 2 ed. xi. 125.

Bexwell (*Bexwell*), iv. 71; 2 ed. vii. 307.

Blomefield *of Fersfield*, 2 ed. i. faces 101.

Brampton (*Norton*), i. 162; 2 ed. i. 245.

Briggs (*Norwich*), ii. faces 640; 2 ed. iv. faces 220.

Bulmer (*South Wooton*), iv. 779; 2 ed. ix. 199.

Calthorpe *of East Barsham*, iii. 762; 2 ed. vii. 58.

Calthorp (*Hickling*), v. 859; 2 ed. ix. 305.

Calthorp (*Ingham*), v. 871.

Castello (*Raveningham*), iv. 263; 2 ed. viii. 47.

Catleyn (*Kirkeby Kam*), iv. 251; 2 ed. viii. 31.

Clere (*Ormesby*), v. 1572; 2 ed. xi. 234.

Clippesby (*Clippesby*), v. 1514; 2 ed. xi. 160.

Cocket (*Brunsthorp*), iii. 726; 2 ed. vii. 6.

Coke (*Holkham*), v. 807; 2 ed. ix. 237.

Coningsby (*Wallington*), iv. 147; 2 ed. vii. 413.

Corbet (*Sprouston*), v. 1373; 2 ed. x. 459.

De Lerling (*Rushworth*), i. 191; 2 ed. i. 285.

De Limesi, and Odingsells (*Oxburgh*), iii. 475; 2 ed. vi. 170.

De Lisle (*Mundford*), i. 535; 2 ed. ii. 243.

De Ridlesworth (*Ridlesworth*), i. 187; 2 ed. i. 279.

Dethick (*Wireham*), iv. 217; 2 ed. vii. 505.

Drury (*Ridlesworth*), i. 186; 2 ed. i. 278.

Du Bois (*of Fersfield*), i. 3; 2 ed. i. 78.

Felbrigg *of Felbrigg*, iv. 306; 2 ed. viii. 108.

Felbrigg, the younger branch, iv. 307; 2 ed. viii. 110.

Fincham *of Outwell*, iv. 185; 2 ed. vii. 462.

Fowler (*Weting*), i. 482; 2 ed. ii. 167.

Gawsell (*Watlington*), iv. 206; 2 ed. vii. 491.

Godsalve (*Bokenham Ferry*), iv. 5; vii. 213.

Goldwill (*Norwich*), ii. 385; 2. ii. 542.

Gonville (*Rusworth*), i. 192; 2. i. 286.

Guybon (*North Lynn*), iv. 623; 2. viii. 539.

Harbord (*Gunton*), iv. 315; 2. viii. 121.

Hare *of Stow Bardolph*, i. 280; 2. i. faces 414.

Havers (*Thelton*), i. 100.

Herling (*East Herling*), i. 215; 2. i. 319.

Hewar (*Emneth*), iv. 524; 2. viii. 410.

Hobart (*Hales*), iv. 241; 2 ed. viii. 19.

Holland *(Redenhall)*, iii. faces 251; 2. i. faces 344.

Hollis *(Flitcham)*, iv. 529; 2. viii. 417.

Hoo *(Scarning)*, v. 1055; 2. x. 40.

Hovell *(Hillington)*, iv. 566; 2. viii. faces 466.

Howard *of Fersfield*, i. 6; 2. i. 81.

Howard, Duke of Norfolk, i. 12; 2. i. 91.

Jerningham, or Jernegan *of Cossey*, i. 661; 2. ii. faces 416.

Kervile (*Wallington*), iv. 205; 2. vii. 490.

Latimer, Lord, i. 9; 2. i. 86.

Le Gross *(Crostwick)*, v. 1396; 2. xi. 10.

L' Estrange *(Hunstanton)*, v. folding at 1265; 2. x. at 314.

Lovell *(East Herling)*, i. 218; 2. i. 323.

Maundeville *(Shouldham)*, 153; 2. vii. faces 420.

Mordaunt *of Massingham Parva*, iv. 643.

Mundeford *of Hockwold*, i. 493; 2. ii. 182.

Mundeford *of Feltwell*, i. 501; 2. ii. 193.

Odingsells; see De Limesi.

Oxford, Earls of; see Vere.

Pakenham *(Dersingham)*, iv. 518; 2. viii. 403.

Paris, coheirs *of Norton*, iii. 805; 2. vii. 116.

Pepys *(South Creak)*, iii. 779; 2. vii. 81.

Pettus *(Rackheath Magna)*, v. 1363; 2. x. 448.

Read *(Massingham Magna)*, iv. 632; 2. ix. 4.

Repps *(North Repps)*, iv. 336; 2. viii. faces 150.

Repps, the younger branch, iv. 337; 2 ed. viii. 150.

Repps *(West Walton)*, iv. 734; 2 ed. ix. 137.

Richardson, Lord *(Huningham)*, i. folding at 684; 2. ii. faces 449.

Rugge *(Felmingham)*, v. 1416; 2. xi. 36.

Sharington *(Cranworth)*, v. 1178.

Shouldham *(Kettleston)*, iii. 802; 2 ed. vii. 113.

Sotherton *(Haylesdon)*, v. 1353; 2 ed. x. 429.

Southwell *(Wood Rysing)*, v. 1236; 2 ed. x. 275.

Sparham *(Sparham)*, iv. 413; 2 ed. viii. 259.

Stannard *(Oby)*, v. 1527; 2. xi. 178.

Stapleton *(Ingham)*, v. 869; 2. ix. 320.

Strabolgi *(Poswick)*, iv. 31; 2. vii. 250.

Steward *(Marsham)*, iv. 125.

Steward *(Geystwick)*, iv. 387.

Thoresby *(Gaywode)*, iv. 533; 2. viii. 422.

Tindale *(Hockwold)*, i. 493; 2. ii. 181.

Trusbutt *(Holme)*, iv. 141; 2. vii. 405.

Tudenham *(Oxburgh)*, iii. 477-478; 2. vi. 174.

Vere, Earl of Oxford, i. 7; 2 ed. i. 84.

Waldgrave *(Staninghall)*, v. 1377; 2. x. 465.

Walpole *of Houghton*, iii. 799; 2. vii. faces 109.

Warde *(Broke)*, v. 1107; 2. x. 106.

Weyland *(Oxbrugh)*, iii. 477; 2. vi. 173.

Wingfield *of Fersfield*, i. 8; 2 ed. i. 85.

Wodehouse *(Kimberley)*, i. 765-770; 2 ed. faces 558.

Woodhouse *(Waxham)*, v. 894; 2. ix. 353.

Wright *(Kilverstone)*, i. folding at 368; 2. i. faces 545.

Wyndham *of Felbrigg*, iv. 309; 2 ed. viii. 311.

108.—Sepulchral Reminiscences. Church of St. Nicholas, Great Yarmouth. By DAWSON TURNER, Esq., M.A., F.R.S., &c. *Yarmouth*, 1848. 8vo.

Cory, 108.

England, folding at 111.

Ferrier, folding at 116.

Grice; see Le Grys.

Ives *of Norfolk*, 129.
Johnson, 47.
Lacon, folding at 131.
Leake, facing 133.
Le Grys, 133.
Loveday, 135.
Manby, 136.
Palgrave, folding at 142.
Ramey, facing 144.

109.—An Analysis of the Domesday Book of the County of Norfolk. By the Rev. GEORGE MUNFORD. *London*, 1858. 8vo.

Alan, Counts, 11, 12.
Bainard, 45.
Bigot, 22.
Bohun, 50.
Dapifer (*Godric*), 25.
Dapifer (*Eudo*), 38.
De Burgh, 8.
De Valoines, Peter, 48.
Eustace, Count, 14.
Ferrariis, Hermer de, 26.
Fitz-Richer, Gilbert, 51.
Giffard, Walter, 39.
Grenon, 47.
Limesi, 42.
Lupus, Hugh, 16.
Montfort, 36.
Montaigne, 8.
Peverell, 46.
Reams of Overstrand, 52.
Spiruwin, 42.
Tailgebosc, 40.
Todeni, 34.
Warren, Earl, 19.

110.—Historical Notices and Records of the Village and Parish of Fincham, in the County of Norfolk. By the Rev. WILLIAM BLYTH, M.A. *King's Lynn*, 1863. 8vo.

Fincham *of Fincham*, folding at 110, at 113, and facing 124.
Fincham *of Outwell*, folding at 124, and at 126.
Fincham *of Suffolk*, folding at 130.
Fincham *of Diss*, facing 132.
Fincham *of Kenninghall*, facing 134.
Fyncham, facing 108.

NORTHAMPTONSHIRE.

111.—The History and Antiquities of Northamptonshire. By the Rev. PETER WHALLEY. *Oxford*, 1791. 2 vols. folio.

Andrew and Andrews (*Charwelton*), i. 38.
Arden (*Watford*), i. 587.
Aylesbury; see Keynes.
Baskerville (*Hellidon*), i. 72.
Beaufort (*Ufford*), ii. 602.
Belchier (*Nortoft*), i. 570.
Berford (*Clendon*), ii. 15.
Bernard (*Abington*), i. 401.
Blencowe (*Merston St. Laurence*), i. 182.
Bray (*Hinton*), i. 176.
Braybroke (*Braybroke*), ii. 10.
Bridgewater, Dukes of; see Egerton.
Brooke (*Oakley Parva*), ii. 326.
Browne (*Walcot*), ii. 497.
Brudenell (*Dene*), ii. 302.
Burnaby (*Watford*), i. 587.
Butler (*Preston Capes*), i. 82.
Cantilupe (*Barby*), i. 24.
Cartwright (*Aynho*), i. 137.
Catesby (*Ashby Legers*), i. 16.
Cave (*Stanford*), i. 580.
Cecil (*Burghley*), ii. 592.
Chauncey (*Edgcote*), i. 119.
Chetwode (*Warkworth*), i. 217.

Cheyne (*Cogenho*), i. 348.
Chichele (*Higham Ferrers*), ii. 179.
Clendon (*Clendon*), ii. 15.
Compton (*Castle Ashby*), i. 344.
Coumbemartyn (*Stoke Bruere*), i. 324.
Cost (*Clendon*), ii. 15.
Cranesley (*Cranesley*), ii. 89.
Crew (*Stene*), i. 198.
Danvers (*Culworth*), i. 163.
De Burgh (*Wakerley*), ii. 342.
De Clare (*Rothwell*), ii. 61.
De la Mare (*Norborough*), ii. 528.
De la Warre (*Wakerley*), ii. 342.
Dene (*Dene*), ii. 300.
Dene (*Staniern*), ii. 337.
De Ros (*Braunston*), i. 29.
De Welton (*Welton*), i. 96.
Drayton (*Strixton*), ii. 197.
Drayton (*Drayton*), ii. 251.
Dryden (*Ashby Canons*), i. 226.
Dudley (*Clopton*), ii. 370.
Egerton, Dukes of Bridgewater, i. 149.
Ekins (*Weston Favel*), i. 469.
Elmes (*Lilford*), ii. 242.
Engaine (*Blatherwick*), ii. 275.
Fartho (*Fartho*), i. 297.
Favel (*Western Favel*), i. 467.
Fermor (*Eston Neston*), i. 290.
Ferrers (*Higham Ferrers*), ii. 171.
Fitz William (*Marham*), ii. 517.
Foliot (*Cheping Warden*), i. 114.
Fowlehurst (*Hellidon*), i. 72.
Garnon (*Plumpton*), i. 254.
Gauntkort (*Clopton*), ii. 369.
Greene (*Ashby Mares*), ii. 137.
Greene (*Drayton*), ii. 251.
Grevill (*Ravensthorp*), i. 535.
Griffin (*Cheping Wardon*), i. 114.
Harvey (*Hardingstone*), i. 362.
Harwedon (*Plumpton*), i. 254.
Harwedon (*Stoke Bruere*), i. 324.
Hastings (*Yardley Hastings*), i. 397.
Hatton (*Holdenby*), i. 528.
Hertwell (*Preston*), i. 381.
Holand (*Ufford*), ii. 602.
Holdenby (*Holdenby*), i. 528.
Hothum (*Collyweston*), ii. 434.
Hotot (*Clopton*), ii. 369.
Humfrey (*Barton Segrave*), ii. 218.
Isham (*Lamport*), ii. 112.

Keynes, Aylesbury, Stafford, Wyrley, &c., i. 52.
Knightley (*Fawesley*), i. 66.
Knightley (*Plumpton*), i. 254.
Kynnesman (*Lodington*), ii. 43.
Latimer (*Cheping Wardon*), i. 114.
Latimer, Lords (*Bosiate*), ii. 160.
Ledet (*Cheping Wardon*), i. 114.
Leeson (*Sulgrave*), i. 128.
Le Poer (*Lichborow*), i. 75.
Leye (*Ashby Canons*), i. 224.
Lewknore (*Harrowden Magna*), ii. 102.
Limesi (*Collyweston*), ii. 434.
Lovel (*Tichmersh*), ii. 382.
Lovett (*Astwell*), i. 215.
Lumley (*Harleston*), i. 512.
Lynne (*Southwick*), ii. 470.
Lyons (*Warkworth*), i. 217.
Mallory (*Winwick*), i. 604.
Markham (*Cheping Warden*), i. 115.
Marmion (*Lutton*), ii. 462.
Mathewe (*Braden*), i. 237.
Montagu (*Boughton*), ii. 352.
Montagu (*Horton*), i. 368.
Mordaunt (*Drayton*), ii. 252.
Mountgomery (*Ecton*), ii. 142.
Mulso (*Thingden*), ii. 259.
Nevill *of Bosiate*, ii. 160.
Newmarch (*Braybroke*), ii. 10.
Newbottle (*Clenden*), ii. 15.
Norwich (*Brampton*), ii. 282.
Osborne (*Kelmarsh*), ii. 40.
Oxenford (*Stoke Bruere*), i. 324.
Palmer (*Carlton*), ii. 292.
Pragiter (*Gretworth*), i. 124.
Pavely (*Sulby*), i. 597.
Pedwardyn (*Clipston*), ii. 18.
Pemberton (*Rushden*), ii. 191.
Peveril, or Pavely (*Sulby*), i. 597.
Pickering (*Tichmersh*), ii. 384.
Pinkeney (*Wedon Pinkeney*), i. 255.
Plantagenet, Holand, and Beaufort (*Ufford*), ii. 602.
Plumpton (*Plumpton*), i. 254.
Prayers (*Strixton*), ii. 197.
Pulton (*Desborough*), ii. 26.
Ridel (*Wittering*), ii. 607.
Ros; see De Ros.
Russell (*Worthorp*), ii. 596.
St. Medard or Semare (*Worthorp*), ii. 596.

St. John (*Woodford*), ii. 2GG.
St. John (*Plumpton*), i. 254.
Samwell (*Upton*), i. 539.
Seinliz (Braybroke), ii. 10.
Semare; see St. Medard.
Seyton (*Maidwell*), ii. 47.
Shirley (*Astwell*), i. 215.
Spencer (*Althorp*), i. 481.
Stafford (*Rothwell*), ii. 61.
Stafford (*Blatherwick*), ii. 277
Stafford ; see Keynes.
Stokes (*Bosiate*), ii. 158.
Stotesbury (*Sulgrave*), i. 128.
Tanfield (*Gayton*), i. 263.
Tate (*Delapre*), i. 365.
Thornton (*Newenham*), i. 22.
Throckmorton (*Paveli's Pery*), i. 312.
Tresham (*Newton*), ii. 323.

Trist (*Maidford*), i. 248.
Trussell (*Merston Trussell*), ii. 51.
Vavasour (*Weekley*), ii. 345.
Vaux (*Harrowdon Magna*), ii. 103.
Vere (*Drayton*), ii. 251.
Verney (*Ravensthorp*), i. 535.
Wake (*Cranesley*), ii. 89.
Wake (*Blisworth*), i. 335.
Ward (*Braffield*), i. 339.
Welton (*Welton*), i. 96.
Willoughby (*Raventhorp*), i. 535.
Wingfield (*Upton*), ii. 508.
Wolverton (*Wykehamon*), i. 332.
Woodhull (*Warkworth*), i. 217.
Woodhull (*Thenford*), i. 205.
Worsley (*Maxey*), ii. 525.
Wydville (*Grafton*), i. 300.
Wyrley ; see Kynes.
Zouche (*Harringworth*), ii. 318.

112.—The History and Antiquities of the County of Northampton. By George Baker. London, 1822-1841. 2 vols. folio.

Adams *of Charwelton*, i. 298.
Adams *of Welton*, i. 459.
Adams *of East Haddon and Morton Pinkeney, and of Anstey, co. Warwick*, ii. 52.
Agar-Ellis, Viscount Clifden, i. 199.
Albemarle, Earl of, ii. 59.
Albemarle, Earls of, i. 672.
Aldham, or Audcham *of Preston*, i. 432.
Alneto *of Maidford ;* see Burdet.
Andrew *of Charwelton*, i. 295.
Andrew *of Harleston*, i. 1G7.
Annesley *of Bletchington, co. Oxon. and of Eydon*, i. 502.
Arden, Chambre, Maxe, and Inguersby, i. 66.
Armenters, Lisle Baron Lisle ; Nevill Baron Latimer ; Danvers, Earl of Danby ; Wharton, Marquis of Wharton, &c. i. 143.
Arnold *of Ashby Lodge*, i. 247.
Arundel *of Stoke Park*, ii. 243.
Arundel, Earl of, i. 54.
Ashley *of Ashby Ledgers*, i. 246.
Audeham ; see Aldham.
Aylesbury (*Dodford*), i. 355.
Ayote (*Dodford*), i. 355.

Bagot (*Woodford*), i. 355.
Bagot ; see Stafford.
Banastre *of Passenham and Maynard*, Viscount Maynard, ii. 190.
Barker *of Astrop*, i. 704.
Barker *of Lyndon ;* see Kynne.
Barnardiston ; see Jennens.
Baron and Dickinson *of Pateshull*, ii. 295.
Barre or Barry *of Great Billing*, i. 19.
Basset ; see Engaine.
Baskerville and Foulshurst *of Hellidon*, i. 397.
Bassingburn ; see Engaine.
Bathurst, Earl Bathurst, ii. 203.
Beauchamp, Earl and Duke of Warwick ; Nevill, Earl of Warwick and Salisbury ; and Plantagenet, Earl of Warwick, and Duke of Clarence, ii. 218.
Beaufort, Duke of Somerset, i. 55.
Beaufoy ; see Whelton.
Bellomont Earl of Leicester, Quincy Earl of Winchester ; Baron Zouch *of Ashby de la Zouch, co. Leicester,* and Baron Holand, i. 563.

N

Bennet *of Beachampton, co. Bucks, and of Hanley Park*, Bart. ii. 342.

Benson *of Charwelton and Dodford*, i. 297.

Benson ; see Keynes.

Bereford *of Steane and Farthingho*, i. 682.

Bernard *of Abingdon ;* see Lillyng.

Betun, Earl of Albemarle ; Mareshall or Marshall, Earl of Pembroke ; and Mareschall, or Marshall *of Hengham co. Norfolk and Norton*, ii. 59.

Betun ; see Cioches.

Betune ; see Romelli.

Bevill *of Wood Preston, and Little Preston*, i. 433.

Biggin *of Cosgrave*, ii. 131.

Billing *of Astwell*, i. 736.

Blake *of Gayton*, ii. 277.

Blencowe *of Marston St. Lawrence*, i. 640.

Boketon or Green *of Boughton and Green's Norton*, i. 32.

Botiller or Boteler, *of Grimsbury*, i. 747.

Botry *of Marston St. Lawrence, and Grimsbury*, i. 641.

Bowles *of Brackley and Evenley*, i. 612.

Bradden *of Bradden and Easton Neston*, ii. 36.

Braose ; see Bruere.

Bray *of East Haddon*, i. 162.

Bray *of Whitfield ;* and Imworth *of Whitfield and Great Oakley*, i. 751.

Bray and Dyve *of Harleston*, i. 169.

Bray *of Steane*, i. 685.

Braybrook ; see Reinbudcurt.

Breton *of Norton*, i. 416.

Breton *of Teton*, i. 220.

Bridgewater, Earl and Duke of, i. 564.

Bruere or Briwere, Braose or Brewse, Wake, Ferte or Feritate, and Cadurcis or Chaworth, Mohun, and Percy, ii. 239.

Buckingham, Duke of, i. 734.

Buckland *of Sewell ;* see De la Hay.

Buckland, Whittingham and Clarell *of Edgcote and Sewell*, i. 493.

Burdet and Alneto *of Maidford*, ii. 44.

Butler *of Appletree*, i. 475.

Butler (*Aston*), i. 470.

Butler *of Preston Capes*, i. 427.

Cadurcis ; see Bruere.

Camvill and Longspé (*Sutton*) i. 694.

Candler *of Callan, co. Kilkenny and Morton Pinkeney*, ii. 51.

Candler ; see Cope.

Capes *of Fawsley and Preston Capes*, i. 378.

Carter *of Edgcote*, i. 494.

Cartwright *of Aynho*, i. 548.

Catesby *of Hinton and Althorp*, i. 538.

Catesby ; see Cranford.

Cave *of Drayton*, i. 348.

Chacomb, Baron Segrave, Mowbray, Duke of Norfolk, &c. i. 588.

Chambre ; see Arden.

Chastillon ; see Combemartin.

Chaunceux ; see Fitz Sewen.

Chauncy and Carter *of Edgcote*, i. 494.

Chaworth ; see Bruere.

Chenduit *of Middleton Chenduit*, i. 649.

Cheney ; see Cheyne.

Cheshunt ; see Combemartin.

Chester, Earl of ; see Morton.

Chetwode *of Warkworth*, i. 739.

Cheyne *of Thenford*, i. 712.

Chokes ; see Cioches.

Churchill, and Spencer-Churchill, Duke of Marlborough, i. 198.

Cioches, or Chokes, and Betun, ii. 273.

Clarell *of Edgcote and Sewell*, i. 493.

Clarke and Plomer-Clarke *of Welton*, i. 460.

Clavering, Baron Clavering, i. 546.

Clifden, Viscount ; see Agar-Ellis.

Cobham, Viscount, i. 734.

Coke *of Melbourne, co. Derby*, and Lamb, Viscount Melbourne, i. 141.

Coker *of Bicester, co. Oxford, and of Althorp*, ii. 266.

Colepeper *of Ashton*, ii. 124.

Coles, Bevill, &c., *of Wood Preston, and Little Preston*, i. 433.

Colville ; see Engaine.

Combemartin, Oxenford, Cheshunt, St. John, Chastillon, and Wolverton, ii. 241.

Cope *of Brewerne*, co. *Oxon and Morton Pinkeney*, and Candler *of Callan*, co. *Kilkenny and Morton Pinkeney*, ii. 51.

Cope *of Denshanger and Grimsbury*, i. 748.

Cope *of Canons Ashby and Eydon*, ii. 13.

Corbet ; see Gozelin.

Cornwall *of Burford*, i. 415.

Courci or Curcy ; Fitz Gerold, Ripariis, or Rivers, Earl of Devon ; and Baron Lisle de Rubeo Monte, i. 619.

Crane *of Stoke Park*, Bart., and Arundel *of Stoke Park*, ii. 243.

Cranford and Catesby *of Ashby Ledgers*, i. 244.

Crawley *of Heyford ;* see Lloyd.

Cressy *(Dodford)*, i. 355.

Creswell *of Purston*, i. 668.

Crewe, Baron Crewe, i. 685.

Culpeper *of Ashton*, ii. 124.

Culworth or Coleworth *of Culworth and Sulgrave*, i. 607.

Danby, Earl of *(Danvers)*, i. 443.

Danvers *of Culworth*, i. 605.

Danvers, Earl of Danby, i. 443.

Darker, Nash and Blake *of Gayton*, ii. 277.

De Daventre ; see Fitz Walter.

Daventre *of Daventry, and Grimscote*, i. 309.

De la Hay ; see Treaunt.

De la Hay, Buckland and Whittingham *of Sewell*, ii. 35.

De la Pole and Langley *of Grimscote and Higham*, ii. 286.

De Lichborowe *(Litchborough)*, i. 406.

Denys *of Stratford Place*, co. *Midd.* ii. 142.

Derby, Earl of, i. 564.

Despenser *of Dallington ;* see Gozelin.

Devereux, Baron Ferrars, and Earl of Essex ; see Ferrars.

Devon, Earl of, i. 619.

Dickinson *of Pateshull*, ii. 295.

Dillon *of Farthingho*, i. 621.

D'Oilly or D'Oyley *of Hooknorton*, co. *Oxon, and Thenford*, i. 709.

Dormer *of Lee Grange*, co. *Bucks*, and *of Purston*, i. 667.

Dormer *of Farthingho*, i. 620.

Downe, Earl of, i. 707.

D'Oyley ; see D'Oilly.

Drury *of Overston*, Bart. i. 57.

Dryden *of Canons Ashby*, ii. 6.

Duck and Harbord *of Grafton Park*, ii. 172.

Dudley, Baron de *(Sutton)*, i. 470.

Dudley, Baron Someri de, i. 479.

Dudley, Duke of Northumberland, &c. ii. 32.

Duras, Baron of Holdenby and Earl of Faversham in Kent, i. 197.

Duston *of Duston*, and Baron Grey *of Rotherfield*, co. *Oxon*, i. 140.

Dyve, St. Andrew, Mucegros, and Ratinden, i. 160.

Dyve *of Harleston ;* see Bray.

Dyve and Picot *of Brampton*, i. 82.

Dyve *of Wicken*, ii. 254.

Dyve ; see Ragon.

Echingham *of Preston*, i. 432.

Edmondes ; see Smyth.

Egerton, Earl and Duke of Bridgewater, i. 564.

Egerton *of Egerton*, co. *Cest. and Farthingho*, Bart. and Earl of Wilton, i. 621.

Ekins *of Weston Favell*, i. 73.

Emson, or Empson *of Easton Neston, Towcester, &c.*, ii. 141.

Emyley *of Helmdon*, i. 629.

Engaine, Lizures, Bassingburn, Colville, Basset, Gernon, &c. i. 9.

England and Adams *of Welton*, i. 459.

Enyon *of Flore*, i. 153.

Esseby *of Catesby*, i. 277.

Essex, Earl of ; see Ferrars.

Eyre *of Hassop and Warkworth ;* see Holman.

Eyton *of Brockhole*, i. 114.

Falwesle or Fawsley *of Fawsley*, i. 379.

Fauconberg *(Boddington)*, i. 478.

Fauconberg, Baron, ii. 296.

Favell and Griffin *of Weston Favell*, i. 73.

Faversham, Duras, Earl of, i. 197.

Fawsley *of Fawsley*, i. 379.

Felton Baron Felton, Fauconberg and Hastings (*Boddington*), i. 478.

Fermor *of Tusmore, co. Oxon,* i. 599.

Fermor, Earl of Pomfret; and Denys *of Stratford Place, co. Midd.,* ii. 142.

Ferrars, Baron Ferrars of Chartley; and Devereux, Baron Ferrars of Chartley, and Earl of Essex, i. 123.

Ferrars Baron Ferrars of Groby, and Grey Marquis of Dorset, i. 103.

Ferrars, Earl, i. 732.

Ferte; see Bruere.

Fienles, Fiennes, Fenys, and Fenes (*Gayton*), ii. 273.

Finch, Earl of Winchelsea and Nottingham, i. 307.

Fitz Alan or Arundel, Earl of Arundel, i. 547.

Fitz Duncan; see Romelli.

Fitz Gerold; see Courci.

Fitz-John; see Fitz-Piers.

Fitz-Piers or Mandeville, Earl of Essex, and Baron Fitz John, i. 47.

Fitz Roy, Lord Southampton, ii. 71.

Fitz Roy, Duke of Grafton, ii. 169.

Fitz Sewin and Chaunceux *of Upton,* i. 224.

Fitz Walter or De Daventre *of Daventry,* i. 306.

Fitz Walter, Baron and Earl; see Smyth.

Foliot; see Reinbudcurt.

Foulshurst *of Hillidon,* i. 397.

Fox and Wykeham - Martin *of Chacomb,* i. 590.

Foxley *of Foxley and Blakesley,* ii. 31.

Freeman *of Great Billing,* i. 20.

Freeman *of Whilton,* i. 233.

Furnival; see Reinbudcurt.

Furtho *of Furtho,* ii. 157.

Gastrell *of Slapton,* ii. 101.

Gaunt, Baron Gaunt and Earl of Lincoln, i. 440.

Gayton *of Gayton,* ii. 275.

Gent *of Norton,* i. 416.

Gernon; see Engaine.

Ghianes; see Gynes.

Gifford *of St. James's Abbey,* i. 151.

Gifford *of Hellidon.* i. 396.

Gilbert *of Tiffield,* ii. 308.

Gisnes; see Gynes.

Golafre *of Norton,* i. 417.

Golafre *of Blakesley and Adston,* ii. 22.

Gore *of Brampton,* i. 84.

Gostelow *of Thorp Mandeville,* i. 719.

Gower, Leveson-, Marquis of Stafford, i. 564.

Gozelin *of Slapton,* Despencer, Lucy, Corbet, and Wallop *of Dallington,* i. 130.

Grafton, Duke of, ii. 160.

Grant *of Litchborough,* ii. 339.

Green *of Boughton;* see Boketon.

Grentemaisnil, i. 241.

Grey, Baron Grey *of Codnor,* i. 658.

Grey, Duke of Kent, i. 685.

Grey, Baron, *of Rotherfield;* see Duston.

Griffin; see Favell.

Guildford, Earls of, i. 526.

Gynes, Ghisnes, Gisnes, or Guisnes, ii. 273.

Handslope, and Mauduit *of Handslope,* Earl of Warwick, ii. 129.

Harbord *of Grafton Park,* ii. 172.

Harby *of Adston,* ii. 19.

Harcourt; see Peverel.

Hardreshull, Baron Hardreshull and Colepeper of Culpeper *of Ashton,* ii. 124.

Harvey-Thursby *of Abingdon,* i. 11.

Harvey; see Hervey.

Hastings (*Boddington*), i. 478.

Hastings *of Hinton,* i. 538.

Hausted *of Harpole and Denshanger,* i. 177.

Hauton, Risley, and Shuckburgh *of Pitsford,* i. 62.

Hawley *of Leybourne Grange, co. Kent,* ii. 276.

Heber; see Jennens.

Herbert, Marquis of Powis; see Morgan.

Hervey or Harvey of *Weston Favell*, i. 74.

Heyford, Morewick, and Lumley of *Harleston*, i. 167.

Hodges of *Sulgrave*, i. 515.

Holand, Baron, i. 563.

Holbech of *Farnborough, co. Warwick, and Radstock*, i. 674.

Holden-Rose of *Daventry and Whilton*, i. 317.

Holdenby and Hatton of *Holdenby*, i. 196.

Holdenby, Baron of; see Duras.

Holman of *Warkworth and Weston Favell*, and Eyre of *Hassop, co. Derby and Warkworth*, i. 740.

Hosier, Sharp, Prowse, and Mordaunt of *Wicker Park*, ii. 255.

Hulcote of *Hulcote*, ii. 153.

Imworth of *Whitfield and Great Oakley*, i. 751.

Inguersby; see Arden.

Isham of *Barby*, i. 264.

Isham of *Braunston*, i. 270.

Ives of *Braddon*, ii. 38.

Janson of *Ashby Ledgers*, i. 245.

Jekyll and Wrighte of *Dallington*, i. 132.

Jennens of *Thorpe Mandeville and Weston by Wedon*; Peareth, Barnardiston and Heber, i. 720.

Keble or Kebyll of *Newbottle*, i. 659.

Kenn of *Grimsbury*, i. 747.

Kent, Earl of; see Moreton.

Kent, Earl of, ii. 296.

Kent, Duke of, i. 685.

Kenwrick of *Sutton*, i. 694.

Keynes, Ayote, Purefoy, Cressy, Aylesbury, Stafford, Wyrley, Benson, &c. (*Dodford*), i. 355.

Kirton of *Thorpe Mandeville*, i. 719.

Knightley of *Byfield and Charwelton*, i. 299.

Knightley of *Fawsley*, i. 381.

Knightley of *Plumpton*, ii. 96.

Kynne, Puleston, Tryst or Trist of *Maidford*; and Barker of *Lyndon, co. Rutland*, ii. 45.

La Leye or Lega of *Canons Ashby*, ii. 5.

Lamb, Viscount Melbourne, i. 141.

Lamport; see Langport.

Lane of *Dodford*, i. 297.

Langley of *Grimscote and Higham*, ii. 286.

Langport or Lamport, Newnham, &c. (*Thenford*) i. 711.

Langton of *Teton*, i. 221.

Latimer; see Reinbudcurt.

Latimer, Baron (*Nevill*), i. 443.

Ledet; see Reinbudcurt.

Leeson of *Sulgrave*, i. 517.

Leicester, Honour of i 350.

Leicester, Earls of, i. 563.

Le Lou, Lupus or Wolfe, of *Ashton and Easton Manduit*, ii. 124.

Leukenor of *Gretworth, and Stoke Doyle*, i. 508.

Leveson-Gower, Marquis of Stafford, i. 564.

Lexington, Sutton Baron de Dudley, Butler and Plowden (*Aston*), i. 470.

Leycester and Poher, i. 426.

Lillyng and Bernard or Barnard of *Abingdon*, i. 10.

Lloyd and Crawley of *Heyford*, i. 185.

Lincoln, Earls of, i. 440.

Lisle of *Barby*, i. 263.

Lisle and Bowles of *Brackley and Evenley*, i. 612.

Lisle, Baron Lisle of *Wodyton and Walton*, i. 706.

Lisle, Baron de; see Courci.

Lisle, Baron, i. 443.

Lizures; see Engaine.

Longspé (*Sutton*), i. 69.

Longueville of *Little Billing*, i. 27.

Longueville of *Cosgrave*, ii. 131.

Lovell of *Harleston*, i. 168.

Lovell of *Preston*, i. 432.

Lovell of *Helmdon*, i. 628.

Lovell, Baron Morley, i. 683.

Lovett of *Rushton*; and Shirley, Earl Ferrars, i. 732.

Lovett; see Turville.

Lucian of *Brockhole*; see Wake.

Lucy of *Dallington*; see Gozelin.

Lumley; see Heyford.

Lunell, Sydenhale, and Shuckburgh (*Farthingston*), i. 371.

Lupus or Wolfe *of Ashton and Easton Mauduit*, ii. 124.
Lyons and Chetwode *of Warkworth*, i. 739.
Makepeace *of Sulgrave*, i. 514.
Mandeville, and Fitz Piers, Earls of Essex, and Bohun, Earls of Hereford, Essex and Northampton, i. 545.
Manners; see Peverel.
Manny, Barons, i. 54.
Mansel, Longueville, and Biggin *of Cosgrave*, ii. 131.
Markes *of Pateshull*, ii. 294.
Marlborough, Dukes of; see Churchill.
Marmion *of Aynho*, i. 548.
Marshall *of Hougham, co. Norfolk, and of Norton*, ii. 59.
Martin, Wykeham- *of Chacomb*, i. 590.
Matthew *of Bradden*, ii. 37.
Mauduit *of Handslope*, ii. 129.
Mauntell *of Heyford*, i. 183.
Maxe; see Arden.
Maynard, Viscount, ii. 190.
Melbourne, Viscount; see Coke.
Melbourne; see Coke.
Mellent, Earls of; and Newburgh, Plessetis, and Mauduit, Earls of Warwick, i. 414.
Meschines; see Romelli.
Mildmay; see Smyth.
Missenden or Mussenden *of Culworth and Croughton*, i. 604.
Mohun; see Bruere.
Montacute, Echingham, Aldham or Audeham, St. Clere or Seynclere, Lovell, etc. *of Preston*, i. 432.
Montalt and Trafford *of Sulgrave*, i. 516.
Monte or Montibus *of Whitfield*, i. 751.
Mordaunt *of Wicken Park*, ii. 255.
Moreton, Earl of; Chester, Earl of; and Kent, Earl of; i. 121.
Morewick; see Heyford.
Morgan, Preston, and Herbert Marquis of Powis, i. 184.
Morgan *of Kingsthorpe*, i. 40.
Morley, Baron, i. 683.
Mount Faltrel, Salceto, Thorp, &c. *of Harpole*, i. 176.

Mowbray, Duke of Norfolk; see Chacomb.
Mucegros; see Dyve.
Munchensi, Baron, and Valance, Earl of Pembroke, ii. 315.
Murdak *of Edgcote*, i. 492.
Mussenden; see Missenden.
Nash *of Gayton*, ii. 277.
Nedham *of Litchborough*, i. 406.
Nevill; see Treaunt.
Nevill; see Whelton.
Newnham *of Newnham*; and Thornton *of Brockhole*, i. 115.
Newnham *of Newbold*, i. 293.
Newnham *(Thenford)*, i. 711.
Newport *of Welton*, i. 459.
Norfolk, Dukes of, i. 588.
North, Earls of Guildford, i. 526.
Northampton, Marquis of, ii. 61.
O'Brien, Earls of Thomond, i. 21.
Onley *of Catesby*, i. 287.
Orme *of Brampton*, i. 84.
Owen *of Welton*, i. 458.
Oxenford; see Combemartin.
Pabenham, and Cheyne or Cheney *of Thenford*, i. 712.
Paganell or Paynell, and Someri or Sumeri Baron Someri de Dudley, co. Stafford, i. 479.
Pargiter *of Gretworth*, i. 409.
Pargiter *of Wappenham*, i. 726.
Park, Botiller or Boteler, and Kenn *of Grimsbury*, i. 747.
Parkhurst *of Catesby*, i. 288.
Parr, Marquis of Northampton, ii. 61.
Pateshull, Baron; Fauconberg, Baron; and Nevill, Earl of Kent, ii. 296.
Pavely *of Paulerspury and Great Houghton*, ii. 200.
Paynell; see Paganell.
Peareth; see Jennens.
Pembroke, Earls of, ii. 59.
Pembroke, Earls, ii. 315.
Percy; see Bruere.
Pettyfer or Pettifer; see Watts.
Peverel *of Brunne, co. Camb.*; Harcourt, Trusbut, Ros or Roos *of Hamlake, co. York*; and Manners, Earls and Dukes of Rutland, i. 269.
Peverel *of Nottingham*, i. 139.
Picot; see Dyve.

Pigge *of Flore;* see Tame.

Pinkeney, Baron Pinkeney *of Wedon;* Pinkeney *of Morton Pinkeney,* etc. ii. 107.

Pittesford *of Pitsford,* i. 61.

Plowden (*Aston*), i. 470.

Plumpton, St. John, Harwedon, Skenard or Skennerton, and Knightley *of Plumpton,* ii. 96.

Poher, or De Lichbarowe, (*Litchborough*), i. 406.

Poher; see Leycester.

Pope, Earls of Downe, i. 707.

Powis, Marquis of; see Morgan.

Preston; see Morgan.

Prowse *of Wicken Park,* ii. 255.

Puleston *of Maidford;* see Kynne.

Purefoy (*Dodford*), i. 355.

Quincy, Earl of Winchester, i. 563.

Ragon, Wylde, and Dyve *of East Haddon,* i. 163.

Ratinden; see Dyve.

Raynsford *of Dallington,* i. 131.

Reinbudcurt, Foliet, Ledet, Braybrook, Furnival, Latimer, Lords of the Barony of Wardon, i. 525.

Ripariis or Rivers; see Courci.

Risley; see Hauton.

Romelli or Rumelli; Meschines; Fitz Duncan; Le Gros; Betune; and Fortibus, Earls of Albemarle; and Baron Lacy, etc. i. 672.

Ros or Roos; see Peverel.

Rose; see Holden-Rose.

Rumelli; see Romelli.

Rush *of Farthingho,* i. 622.

Russell and Capes *of Fawsley and Preston Capes,* i. 378.

Rutland, Earls and Dukes of; see Peverel.

St. Andrew; see Dyve.

St. Clere or Seyncler *of Preston,* i. 432.

St. John; see Combemartin.

St. John *of Plumpton,* ii. 96.

Salceto *of Harpole;* see Mount Faltrel.

Saltonstall, and North Earl of Guildford, i. 526.

Samwell *of Upton,* i. 224.

Sandys, Baron Sandys; Bray *of Steane;* Crewe, Baron Crewe; Grey, Duke of Kent, etc. i. 685.

Saunders *of Flore,* i. 153.

Saunders *of Newbold,* i. 293.

Sawbridge *of East Haddon,* i. 161.

Segrave, Baron, i. 588.

Severne *of Wallop Hall, co. Salop, and Thenford,* i. 712.

Shakerley and Marmion *of Aynho,* i. 548.

Sharp *of Wicken Park,* ii. 255.

Shirley, Earls Ferrars, i. 732.

Shuckburgh; see Hauton.

Shuckburgh; see Lunell.

Skennerton *of Plumpton,* ii. 96.

Smyth, Wood, Edmondes, and Mildmay Baron and Earl Fitzwalter, i. 56.

Someri or Sumeri; see Paganell.

Southampton, Lords, ii. 71.

Spencer, Earls, i. 108.

Spencer *of Yarnton, co. Oxon. and of Whitfield,* i. 752.

Spencer *of Badby and Everdon,* i. 364.

Spencer-Churchill; Dukes of Marlborough; see Churchill.

Stafford (*Dodford*), i. 355.

Stafford and Bagot (*Woodford*), i. 532.

Stafford, Marquis of, i. 564.

Stanley, Earl of Derby; Egerton, Earls and Dukes of Bridgewater; and Leveson-Gower, Marquis of Stafford, i. 564.

Steward *of Pateshull and Cotterstock,* ii. 298.

Stotesbury and Leeson *of Sulgrave,* i. 517.

Strafford; see Wentworth.

Stratford *of Overston,* i. 57.

Stutovill, i. 230.

Sutton, Baron de Dudley, i. 470.

Swynnerton; see Whelton.

Sydenhale; see Lunell.

Tame, Pigge, &c. *of Flore,* i. 152.

Tanfield *of Gayton, Harpole,* etc. ii. 275.

Temple, Viscount Cobham, and Grenville-Nugent-Temple-Bridges-Chandos, Dukes of Buckingham, i. 734.

Thanet, Earls of; see Tufton.

Theed *of Staverton,* i. 435.

Thornton *of Brockhole;* see Newnham.

Thorp *of Harpole;* see Mount Faltrel

Throckmorton *of Paulerspury,* ii. 202.

Tirwhit *of Brockhole,* i. 114.

Trafford *of Sulgrave,* i. 516.

Treaunt, De la Hay, and Nevill *of Brampton,* i. 83.

Trist *of Maidford ;* see Kynne.

Trist or Tryst *of Culworth and Whitfield,* i. 752.

Trusbut ; see Peverel.

Trussel *of Flore,* i. 154.

Tryst ; see Kynne.

Tryst ; see Trist.

Tudenham *of Hayford,* i. 186.

Tufton, Earls of Thanet, i. 606.

Turville and Lovett *of Helmdon,* i. 628.

Tyringham *of Weston Favell,* i. 74.

Vernon-Wentworth *of Stoke Park,* ii. 244.

Vieleston *of Althorp,* i. 105.

Vyse *of Boughton ;* see Wentworth.

Wake and Lucien *of Brockhole,* i. 113.

Wake ; see Bruere.

Wakelyn *of Eydon, Trafford and Boddington,* i. 504.

Wale *of Eydon,* i. 502.

Wale *of Wedon Pinkeney,* ii. 108.

Wallop *of Dallington ;* see Gozelin.

Warwick, Earls of, i. 414.

Warwick, Earls of, ii. 129.

Warwick, Dukes of; see Beauchamp.

Washington *of Sulgrave,* i. 513.

Watts, Pettyfer or Pettifer, and Wight *of Blakesley,* ii. 23.

Wauncy *of Astwell,* i. 731.

Wentworth, Vernon-, *of Stoke Park,* ii. 244.

Wentworth, Earls of Strafford, and Vyse *of Boughton,* i. 33.

Wharton, Marquis of, i. 443.

Whelton, Nevill, Swynnerton and Beaufou or Beaufoy, i. 232.

Whittingham *of Edgcote and Sewell,* i. 493.

Whittingham *of Sewell ;* see De la Hay.

Wideville or Wydeville, Earl Rivers, ii. 166.

Wight *of Blakesley ;* see Watts.

Wilbraham, and Tufton Earls of Thanet, i. 606.

Willes *of Astrop,* i. 695.

Wilton, Earls of, i. 621.

Winchelsea, Earls of, i. 307.

Winchester, Earls of, i. 563.

Wodhull, Barons, i. 711.

Wolfe ; see Le Lou.

Wolverton *of Wolverton, co. Bucks, and Wicken,* ii. 252.

Wolverton ; see Combemartin.

Wood ; see Smyth.

Wrighte *of Dallington,* i. 132.

Wykeham-Martin *of Chacomb,* i. 590.

Wylde ; see Ragon.

Wyrley *(Dodford),* i. 355.

Zouch, Lords, *of Ashby de la Zouch,* i. 563.

Zouche, Baron Mortimer *of Ricard's Castle,* and Cornwall *of Burford,* i. 415.

113.—The History and Antiquities of the Town, College, and Castle of Fotheringay, in the County of Northampton. (No. 40. Bibliotheca Topographica Britannica.) 1786. 4to.

Crews *of Fodringhey,* 112.

114.—A Comment upon the Fifth Journey of Antoninus through Britain . . . . . By the Rev. KENNET GIBSON . . . . . With the Parochial History of Castor, &c. (Miscellaneous Antiquities in continuation of Bibliotheca Topographica Britannica.) 1800. 4to. Second Edition, 1819.

Fitzwilliam, 206, 207 ; 2 ed. 127. | Wingfield *of Orford,* 2 ed. 143.

115.—A Guide to Burghley House, in Northamptonshire. (By T. BLORE.) *Stamford*, 1815. 8vo. and 4to.

Cecil, Marquis of Exeter, 7.

116.—Burghley. By the Rev. W. H. CHARLTON. *Stamford*, 1847. 8vo.

Cecil, Marquis of Exeter, folding at 1.

117.—The Ruins of Liveden. By T. BELL. *London*, 1847. 4to.

Tresham *of Rushton, Liveden, Geddington, Newton, Wold, &c.* folding at 66.

NORTHUMBERLAND.

118.—Archæologia Æliana; or, Miscellaneous Facts relating to Antiquity, published by the Society of Antiquaries of Newcastle-upon-Tyne. *Newcastle*, Ist series. 1822—1844, 3 vols. 4to; IInd series, 8vo. commenced in 1857.

Calverley; see Thompson.
Dawes; see Jackson.
Hilton, II. s. iii. 144.
Jackson and Dawes, I. s. ii. 139.
Killinghall *of Holy Island*, II. s. ii. 106.
Maisnell, Menel, or Menil, II. s. iii. 81.

Meschens; see Tailbois.
Tailbois and Meschens, I. s. ii. 384.
Thirkeld, II. s. ii. 97, 99.
Tison, II. s. iii. 133.
Thompson and Calverley, I. s. ii. 176.
Walworth, II. s. ii. 74.

119.—A History of Northumberland. By JOHN HODGSON, Clerk. *Newcastle*, 1827—1840. 4to. 3 vols. in 6.

Askew *of Ellington and Linton*, II. ii. 198.
Atkinson *of Linemouth*, II. ii. 193.
Aynsley and Tweddell *of Threapwood*, III. ii. 370.
Aynsley, Murray-; see Murray-Aynsley.
Aynsley *of West Shaftoe, and Little Harle Tower*, I. ii. 210.
Bacon *of East Bellasis;* see Ellison.
Bacon (*Walltown*); see Ridley.
Bacon *of Staward, and of Newton Cap. co. Durham*, III. ii. 374.
Balliol; see Valence.

Barker and Purvis *of Earston*, II. ii. 353.
Bell *of Bellasis*, and Spearman *of Eachwick*, II. ii. 290.
Bennet; see Grey.
Bertram *of Milford*, II. ii. 89.
Bertram, Lords of Bothal, II. ii. 125.
Bigge *of Linden*, II. ii. 97.
Blackett *of Wallington*, I. ii. 258.
Blenkinsop and Coulson (*Haltwhistle*), III. ii. 131.
Blenkinsop *of Bellister*, III. ii. 345.
Bolam, Lords of, I. ii. 333.
Bolbeck, Harle *of Kirkharle*, Greystock, Hastings, etc. I. ii. 239.

o

Borough; see Valence.
Cambo, Lords of, I. ii. 285.
Charron, Monboucher, Harbottle, and Fitton, Lords of Horton, II. ii. 260.
Clayton *of Chesters*, III. ii. 419.
Clifford; see De Clifford.
Corbet *of Stanton*, II. ii. 112.
Coulson (*Haltwhistle*); see Blenkinsop.
Cresswell *of Cresswell*, II. ii. 200.
Cumin; see Valence.
Dacre; see Merlay.
Davidson *of Ridley Hall*; see Lowes.
De Clifford, III. ii. 28.
Denom *of Meldon*, II. ii. 15.
De Veteriponte, Vipont, or Vipond, Lords *of Alston*, III. ii. 26.
Ekins (*Morpeth*), II. ii. 527.
Ellison, Wren, and Bacon *of East Bellasis*, II. ii. 291.
Ellison, Lords *of Bellister and Hartley Burne, co. Northumberland; and of Helburn Hall, co. Durham*, III. ii. 346.
Errington *of Walwick Grange, Chesters and High Wardon*, III. ii. 413.
Fenwick *of Meldon*, II. ii. 17.
Fenwick *of Shortflat*, I. ii. 368.
Fenwick *of Langshaws and Nunriding*, II. ii. 75.
Fenwick *of Wallington*; see Strother.
Fenwick *of Stanton*, II. 113.
Fenwick *of Brinkburne, East Hedwin, Hallaton, &c.* II. ii. 115.
Fenwick *of West Harle*, I. ii. 200.
Fenwick, I. ii. 205.
Fenwick *of Little Harle*, I. ii. 209.
Fetherstonhaugh *of Fetherstonhaugh Castle*, III. ii. 353.
Fielding *of Bebside*; see Johnson.
Fitton; see Charron.
Gibson *of Corbridge, Stonecroft, and Stagshaw-Close House*, III. ii. 393.
Gobyon *of Northampton, Bedford, and Leicestershire*, II. ii. 452.
Greene *of Stannington Bridge*, II. ii. 333.
Grey and Bennet *of Chillingham*, II. ii. 331.

Grey, Ward, and Orde *of Nunnykirk*, I. ii. 330.
Greystock; see Bolbeck.
Greystock; see Merlay.
Hall *of Catcleugh and Otterburne*, I. ii. 154.
Harbottle; see Charron.
Harle *of Kirkharle*; see Bolbeck.
Hastings; see Bolbeck.
Hedley *of West Hartford*; see Reed.
Hepple *of West Bellasis*, II. 292.
Heron *of Meldon*, II. ii. 16.
Hick *of West Hartford*; see Reed.
Horsley *of Thernham*, II. ii. 103.
Horsley *of Scranwood and Long Horsley*, II. ii. 104.
Horsley *of Milburn Grange and Bolam*, I. ii. 335.
Howard; see Merlay.
Howard *of Corby Castle*, II. ii. 477.
Johnson, Fielding, and Ward *of Bebside*, II. ii. 277.
Lawson *of Longhurst and Old Moor*, II. ii. 161.
Leadbitter (*Wardon*), III. ii. 409.
Lisle *of Woodburne*, I. ii. 174.
Loraine *of Kirkharle*, I. ii. 246.
Lowes and Davidson *of Ridley Hall*, III. ii. 337.
Merlay, Greystock, Dacre, and Howard, Lords *of Morpeth*, II. ii. 375.
Middleton and Monck *of Belsay Castle*, I. ii. 353.
Mitford *of Mitford*, II. ii. 44.
Mitford, Lord Redesdale, I. ii. 152.
Monboucher; see Charron.
Monck *of Belsay Castle*; see Middleton.
Murrey-Aynsley *of Little Harle Tower*, I. ii. 209*.
Northumberland, Earls of, III. ii. 12.
Ogle *of Cawsey Park*, II. ii. 135.
Ogle *of Bebside*, II. ii. 276.
Ogle *of Choppington*, II. ii. 365.
Ogle *of Ogle Castle*, I. ii. 380-387.
Ord *of Fenham, Newminster Abbey, and Whitfield*, III. ii. 107.
Ord *of Nunnykirk*; see Grey.
Percy; see Valence.
Plessis *of Plessis*, II. ii. 295.

Piriton, Vescy, and Welles (*Ellington*), II. ii. 196.
Purvis *of Earsdon ;* see Barker.
Raymes *of Shortflat,* I. ii. 367.
Redesdale, Descent of the Lordship of, I. ii. 6.
Reed, Hick, and Hedley, *of West Hartford,* II. ii. 276.
Revel, Warren, and Vernon, Lords *of Widdrington,* II. ii. 239.
Reveley *of Ancroft and Newton Underwood,* II. ii. 70.
Ridley *of Willimoteswick, Hadriding, Heaton, and Blagdon,* II. ii. 322.
Ridley, Marshall, Bacon, and Wastal (*Walltown*), III. ii. 323.
Ridley *of Ridley,* III. ii. 339.
Ridley *of Woodhall,* III. ii. 329.
Spearman *of Eachwick ;* see Bell.
Strabolgie ; see Valence.
Strother and Fenwick *of Wallington,* I. ii. 254.
Stutteville ; see Valence.
Swinburne *of Capheaton,* I. ii. 231.
Swinburne *of Longwitton,* I. ii. 310.
Swinburne *of Swinburne ;* see Widdrington.
Thirlwall (*Haltwhistle*), III. ii. 145.
Thorngrafton, III. ii. 329.
Thornton and Trevelyan *of Netherwitton,* I. ii. 316.
Thorpe *of Thorpe,* III. ii. 336.
Tindale, Lords, III. ii. 9.
Tindale, III. ii. 364.

Trevelyan *of Netherwitton ;* see Thornton.
Trevelyan *of Wallington, co. Northumberland ; and of Nettlecombe, co. Somerset,* I. ii. 262.
Tweddell *of Threapwood;* see Aynsley.
Umfreville, I. ii. 35.
Valence, Balliol, Stutteville, Cumin, Strabolgie, Percy, and Borough, Lords *of Mitford,* II. ii. 41.
Vernon ; see Revel.
Vescy ; see Piriton.
Vipond or Vipont ; see De Veteriponte.
Wallace *of Asholme, Knaresdale, and Featherstone Castle,* III. ii. 91.
Ward *of Nunnykirk;* see Grey.
Ward *of Bebside;* see Johnson.
Warren ; see Revel.
Wastal (*Walltown*); see Ridley.
Watson *of North Seaton,* II. ii. 191.
Welles ; see Piriton.
Whitfield *of Whitfield,* III. ii. 100.
Whitfield *of Randal Holme,* III. ii. 104.
Widdrington *of West Harle,* I. ii. 200.
Widdrington *of Widdrington,* and Swinburne *of Swinburne,* II. ii. 230.
Wilson *of Walwick,* III. ii. 418.
Woodman (*Morpeth*), II. ii. 468.
Wren *of East Bellasis;* see Ellison.

120.—Pedigrees from the Heraldic Visitation of Northumberland, taken by RICHARD ST. GEORGE, Esq., Norroy King of Arms, and HENRY ST. GEORGE, Esq., Bluemantle Pursuivant of Arms. Anno Domini 1615. *Typis Medio Montanis,* 1858. Foolscap Folio. Privately printed by Sir Thomas Phillipps, Bart.

Anderson *of Newcastle,* 1.
Bedenell *of Lemington,* 4.
Carnaby *of Halton,* 2.
Carr *of Heaton and Woodhull,* 3.
Clennell *of Clennell,* 4.
Collingwood *of Eslington,* 4.
Collingwood *of Little Harle,* 4.
De la Val *of Seaton Delaval,* on a separate leaf.
Fenwicke, 1.
Grey *of Chillingham,* 4.

Hebborne *of Hebborne,* 3.
Hebborne *of Newton,* 3.
Lisle *of Felton,* 1.
Ogle *of Cawsey Park,* 2.
Proctor *of Shandon,* 3.
Radcliffe *of Derwentwater,* 3.
Read, 1.
Rodham *of Rodham,* 4.
Warmouth *of Newcastle,* 2.
Whittingham, 2.
Whitwange *of Dunstan,* 1.

121. – Heraldic Visitation of the Northern Counties in 1530, by Thomas Tonge, Norroy, &c. Surtees Society, Vol. 41, 1863, 8vo. *See also Cumberland, Durham, Nottinghamshire, Yorkshire and Westmoreland.*

Middleton *of Newcastell of Tyne*, 34.

NOTTINGHAMSHIRE.

122.—The Antiquities of Nottinghamshire. By Robert Thoroton. *London*, 1677. Folio. Second Edition. *London*, 1790. 3 vols. 4to.

Armstrong (*Thorpe*), 39 ; 2 ed. i. 76.
Arnall (*Carcolston*), 124 ; 2 ed. i. 238.
Aslacton and Cranmer (*Aslacton*), 138 ; 2 ed. i. 262.
Ayscough ; see Cokefield.
Babington (*Kinston*), 15 ; 2 ed. i. 20.
Babington ; see Stanhope.
Baker (*Aldesworth*), 244 ; 2 ed. ii. 251.
Bardolf, Stapleton and Norreys (*Stoke Bardolf*), 280 ; 2 ed. iii. 11.
Barret (*Thoroton*), 118 ; 2 ed. i. 227.
Barry and Pendock (*Tollerton*), 85 ; 2 ed. i. 171.
Barry and Molyneux (*Teversalt*), 269 ; 2 ed. ii. 304.
Basset (*Colston Basset*), 80 ; 2 ed. i. 162.
Basset (*Fledborough*), 365 ; 2 ed. iii. 188.
Bekering (*Tuxford*), 381 ; 2 ed. iii. 220.
Bevercotes (*Bevercotes*), 441 ; 2 ed. iii. 356.
Bingham (*Carcolston*), 125 ; 2 ed. i. 242.
Bingham (*Bingham*), 144 ; 2 ed. i. 272.
Bosom (*Screveton*), 128 ; 2 ed. i. 247.
Boteler (*Hockerton*), 332 ; 2 ed. iii. 123.
Botiller (*Crophill Butler*), 96 ; 2 ed. i. 191.
Boun (*Hockerton*), 335 ; 2 ed. iii. 126.

Brinsley and Lewes (*Brinsley*), 248 ; 2 ed. ii. 260.
Bugg and Turvile (*Leke*), 24 ; 2 ed. i. 47.
Burdon (*Maplewick*), 337 ; 2 ed. iii. 130.
Burgh ; see Strabolgy.
Butler ; see Hussey.
Byron (*Papplewick and Newstede*), 261 ; 2 ed. ii. 285.
Calz, Everingham, Roos, &c. (*Laxton*), 374 ; 2 ed. ii. 207.
Cantelup (*Greyseley*), 239 ; 2 ed. ii. 240, 246.
Carleton (*Carleton*), 467 ; 2 ed. iii. 414.
Cartwright (*Osington*), 355 ; 2 ed. iii. 173.
Chaworth (*Titheby and Wiverton*), 101 ; 2 ed. i. 198.
Clifford, 3 ; 2 ed. i. 4.
Clifton (*Clifton*), 53 ; 2 ed. i. 104.
Clifton ; see Vilers.
Cokefeld, Taylboys and Ayscough (*Nuthall*), 245 ; 2 ed. ii. 253.
Compton (*Hawton*), 180 ; 2 ed. i. 354.
Conyers ; see Darcy.
Cooper (*Thurgarton*), 305 ; 2 ed. iii. 59.
Copley ; see Fitz William.
Cortingstock (*Costock*), 28 ; 2 ed. i. 55.
Cranmer ; see Aslacton.
Cressy, 468, 470 ; 2 ed. iii. 416, 419.
Crumwell and Knyvet (*Crumwell*), 354 ; 2 ed. iii. 170.
Cryche (*Hockerton*), 334 ; 2 ed. iii. 125.

Cukeney (*Cukeney*), 448 ; 2 ed. iii. 878.

Darcy and Conyers (*Kirkby*), 264 ; 2 ed. ii. 293.

Dayncourt (*Granby and Sudton*), iii.; 2 ed. i. 212.

De Bella (*Kertlington*), 321 ; 2 ed. iii. 97.

De Roos (*Orston*), 115 ; 2 ed. i. 221.

Draper ; see Hussey.

Everingham ; see Calz.

Eyr ; see Stanhope.

Eyre (*Ryton*), 461 ; 2 ed. iii. 404.

Eyre and Wastney, 2 ed. iii. 248.

Fenton (*Fenton*), 415 ; 2 ed. iii. 295.

Fitz Hugh (*Carleton*), 465 ; 2 ed. iii. 412.

Fitz Randolph (*Kirkby*), 266 ; 2 ed. ii. 296.

Fitz William and Copley (*Plumptre*), 68; 2 ed. i. 133.

Fitz William, Flower, &c. (*Hayton*), 412 ; 2 ed. iii. 286.

Flower ; see Fitz William.

Foliot and Hastings (*Welley*), 371 ; 2 ed. iii. 202.

Foljambe ; see Vilers.

Frecheville (*Boney*), 43 ; 2 ed. i. 86.

Gascoigne (*Whatton*), 141 ; 2 ed. i. 266.

Gascoigne and Musters (*Truswell*), 403 ; 2 ed. iii. 266.

Gregory (*Nottingham*), 498; 2 ed. ii. 41.

Grey and Leek (*Hickling*), 74 ; 2 ed. i. 144.

Grey (*Toueton*) 208 ; 2 ed. ii. 183.

Goushill (*Hoveringham*), 306 ; 2 ed. iii. 62.

Handley (*Bramcote*), 210 ; 2 ed. ii. 187.

Harbotell ; see Sutton.

Hastings ; see Foliot.

Hercy, Nevill, &c. (*Grove*), 401 ; 2 ed. iii. 262.

Heriz and Swillington (*Gunnolston*), 300 ; 2 ed. iii. 50.

Heriz (*Stapleford*), 211 ; 2 ed. ii. 191.

Hodesak (*Hodsok*), 469; 2 ed. iii. 418.

Hussey, Draper and Butler (*Flintham*), 133 ; 2 ed. i. 253.

Hutchinson (*Owthorpe*) 79 ; 2 ed. i. 159.

Hollis (*Houghton*), 443 ; 2 ed. iii. 358.

Hotot (*Flintham*), 134; 2 ed. i. 254.

Illingworth (*Boney*), 45 ; 2 ed. i. 89.

Kelsolt (*Kelham*), 330 ; 2 ed. iii. 116.

Kirketon, Leek and Whalley (*Screveton*), 129 ; 2 ed. i. 248.

Langford (*Knapthorp*), 343 ; 2 ed. iii. 145.

Lascells (*Elston*), 114 ; 2 ed. i. 338.

Leek (*Normanton*), 320 ; 2 ed. iii. 94.

Leek (*Leke*), 25 ; 2 ed. i. 49.

Leek (*Hickling*) ; see Grey.

Leek ; see Kirketon.

Linley (*Skegby*), 268 ; 2 ed. ii. 302.

Loudham, Cheyneys, &c. (*Loudham*), 289 ; 2 ed. iii. 28.

Lovetot (*Wishou*), 28 : 2 ed. i. 63.

Lutterell, Hilton and Thymilby (*Bridgeford*), 62 ; 2 ed. i. 118.

Markham (*Cotham*), 114 ; 2 ed. i. 344.

Markham (*Allerton*), 438 ; 2 ed. iii. 348.

Marsey ; see Monboucher.

Meeres (*Balderton*), 184 ; 2 ed. i. 360.

Mering (*Mering*), 189 ; 2 ed. i. 371.

Monboucher, Marsey, &c. (*Gamston*), 397 ; 2 ed. iii. 254.

Muskham (*South Muscham*), 348 ; 2 ed. iii. 155.

Musters ; see Gascoigne.

Nevill ; see Hercy.

Nevill (*Thorney*), 194 ; 2 ed. i. 383.

Nevill (*Stoke-by-Newark*), 178 ; 2 ed. i. 348.

Norfolk, Duke of (*Worksop*), 455 ; 2 ed. iii. 388.

North (*Walkeringham*), 428 ; 2 ed. iii. 326.

Odingsells (*Eperston*), 294 ; 2 ed. iii. 37.

Outhorpe (*Owthorpe*), 78 ; 2 ed. i. 158.

Palmes ; see Stapleford.

Pavely (*Rodinstone*), 65; 2 ed. i. 124.

Pendock ; see Barry.

Pierpont (*Basingfeild*), 87 ; 2 ed. i. 174.

Pigot (*Ratcliffe-on-Sore*), 11 ; 2 ed. i. 24.

Plumptre (*Nottingham*), 496 ; 2 ed. ii. 80.

Plumptre ; see Vilers.

Poutrell (*Thrumpton*), 19 ; 2 ed. i. 31.

Poutrell (*Wishou*), 29 ; 2 ed. i. 66.

Rempeston (*Rempeston*), 30 ; 2 ed. i. 59.

Rideware (*Bulcote*), 287; 2 ed. iii. 24.

Roos ; see Calz.

Rosel (*Ratcliffe*), 93 ; 2 ed. i. 184.

Rutington (*Rodintone*), 66 ; 2 ed. i. 125.

Sacheverell (*Barton*), 50 ; 2 ed. i. 97.

Sacheverell (*Ratcliffe-on-Sore*), 12 ; 2 ed. i. 27.

Scrimshire and Whalley (*Cotgrave*), 83 ; 2 ed. i. 168.

Scrope (*Langar and Barneston*), 104; 2 ed. i. 204.

Scrope (*East Bridgeford-on-the-Hill*), 149 ; 2 ed. i. 293.

Scrope (*South Muskam*), 346 ; 2 ed. iii. 150.

Serleby (*Serleby*), 474 ; 2 ed. iii. 431.

Shipman (*Scarington*), 120 ; 2 ed. i. 228.

Sibthorpe (*Sibthorpe*), 168, 169 ; 2 ed. i. 327, 329.

Salmon (*Nottingham*), 494 ; 2 ed. ii. 39.

Saunderson (*Blith*), 474 ; 2 ed. iii. 427.

St. Andrew (*Goteham*), 19 ; 2 ed. i. 39.

Stanhope (*Shelford*), 146 ; 2 ed. i. 288.

Stanhope, Babington, Eyr, &c. (*Rampton*), 392 ; 2 ed. iii. 243.

Stapleford, Teverey, and Palmes (*Stapleford*), 213 ; 2 ed. ii. 194.

Staunton (*Staunton*), 157 ; 2 ed. i. 306.

Stirap (*Styrap*), 472 ; 2 ed. iii. 423.

Stotevill (*Kirkby*), 263 ; 2 ed. ii. 291.

Strabolgy, Burgh, &c. (*Dunham*), 389 ; 2 ed. iii. 237.

Strelley (*Woodborough*), 292 ; 2 ed. iii. 33.

Strelley (*Strelley*), 230 ; 2 ed. ii. 220.

Stringer (*Eaton*), 400 ; 2 ed. iii. 260.

Sutton (*Aram*), 327 ; 2 ed. iii. 110.

Sutton, Monboucher and Harbotell (*Sutton-upon-Trent*), 359 ; 2 ed. iii. 177.

Swillington ; see Heriz.

Taylboys ; see Cokefeld.

Teverey ; see Stapleford.

Thornhaugh (*Fenton*), 416 ; 2 ed. iii. 296.

Thoroton (*Carcolston*), 122 ; 2 ed. i. 235.

Tuke (*Kelham*), 329 ; 2 ed. iii. 114.

Turvile (*Leke*) ; see Bugg.

Vilers, Foljambe, Plumpton, Clifton, &c. (*Kinalton*), 76 ; 2 ed. i. 152.

Walker (*Burton Torz*), 284 ; 2 ed. iii. 19.

Walur (*Hockerton*), 332 ; 2 ed. iii. 121.

Wastney ; see Eyre.

Wastney (*Headon*), 395 ; 2 ed. iii. 251.

Watnow (*Watnow*), 242 ; 2 ed. ii. 246.

Whalley ; see Scrimshire.

Whalley ; see Kirketon

Whatton (*Whatton*), 142 ; 2 ed. i. 268.

White (*Cotgrave*), 84 ; 2 ed. i. 169.

Widmerpole (*Widmerpole*), 40 ; 2 ed. i. 78.

Williamson (*Esat Markham*), 386 ; 2 ed. iii. 230.

Willoughby (*Wollaton*), 221 ; 2 ed. ii. 209.

Willoughby (*Normanton-upon-Sore*), 5 ; 2 ed. i. 12.

Wimondefold (*Southwell*, 318; 2 ed. iii. 86.

Wiverton (*Titheby and Wiverton*), 99 ; 2 ed. i. 196.

Wood (*Woodborough*), 292; 2 ed. iii. 34.

123.—A History of the Antiquities of the Town and Church of Southwell in the County of Nottingham. By W. DICKINSON RASTALL, A.M. *London*, 1787. 4to. Second Edition, by WILLIAM DICKINSON, ESQ. *Newark*, 1801. 4to.

Babington ; see Rampton.
Barton, 2 ed. facing 170.
Beecher, 476 ; 2 ed. facing 344.
Birkin ; see Calz.
Burnell, 2 ed. facing 308.
Calz, Birkin, Everingham, Etton, and Roos, 351 ; 2 ed. folding at 274.
Cantalupe, 2 ed. facing 314.
Clay, 473 ; 2 ed. facing 344.
Cooper, 2 ed. folding at 302.
Dickinson, 2 ed. folding at 165.
Etton ; see Calz.
Everingham ; see Calz.
Eyre ; see Rampton.
Lowe *of Southwell*, 474 ; 2 ed. folding at 344.

Maluval ; see Rampton.
Middleton, Lord ; see Willoughby.
Pocklington, 124 ; 2 ed. facing 164.
Rampton, Maluval, Stanhope, Babington and Eyre, 129 ; 2 ed. foldat 177.
Saville *of Rufford*, 2 ed. folding at 304.
Sherbrook *of Orton*, 110 ; 2 ed. facing 156.
Stanhope ; see Rampton.
Stenton, 478 ; 2 ed. facing 344.
Sutton, 135 ; 2 ed. folding at 183.
Welby, 2 ed. folding at 166.
Willoughby, Lord Middleton, 121 ; 2 ed. facing 162.

124.—The History and Antiquities of the Town of Newark, in the County of Nottingham. By WILLIAM DICKINSON, Esq. *Newark*, 1816. 4to.

Bettison, folding at 106.
Leek *of Newark*, 213.
Jenison, 219.
Sikes, folding at 221.
Brough, folding at 276.
Handley *of Newark*, folding at 291.

Milnes *of Newark*, folding at 295.
Heron *late of Newark*, folding at 303.
Twentyman, folding at 315.
Rastall *of Newark*, folding at 322.
Markham, folding at 328.

125.—The History and Antiquities of Blyth, cos. Nottingham and York. By the Rev. JOHN RAINE, M.A. *Westminster*, 1860. 4to.

Clifton *of Clifton and Wilford*, 138.
Clifton *of Clifton and Hodsock*, 139.
Cressy *of Hodsock and Risegate*, 135.
De Builli, 174.
De Lizors, 160.
De Stirap, 161.
Mellish *of Blyth and Hodsock*, 83.

Moncton-Arundell, Viscounts Galway, 112.
Mowbray, 102.
Saunderson *of Blyth and Searlby*, 75.
Stansfield, 73.
Shuttleworth, 153.
Vane *of Bilby*, 96.
Plantagenet (*de Brotherton*), 102.

126.—Heraldic Visitation of the Northern Counties in 1530, by THOMAS TONGE, Norroy, &c. Surtees Society, vol. 41, 1863. 8vo. *See also Cumberland, Durham, Northumberland, Yorkshire, and Westmoreland.*

Byron, 5.
Donham *of Kerlyngton*, 6.
Hercy *of Grove*, 7.
Stapleton, 1.

Thirland *of Gamston*, 8.
Wassenes *of Heydon*, 8.
Willoughby, 4.

OXFORDSHIRE.

127.—The History and Antiquities of the Colleges and Halls in the University of Oxford. By ANTHONY à WOOD, M.A. Edited by JOHN GUTCH, M.A. *Oxford*, 1786. 2 vols. 4to.

Chichele (*All Souls Coll.*), i. 259.
Cookes (*Worcester Coll.*), i. 632.
Pope (*Trinity Coll.*), i. 532.
Smith (*Brasenose*), i. 353.

Sutton *of Brasenose Coll.*, i. 356.
Wadham (*Wadham Coll.*), i. 592.
Wykeham, William (*New Coll.*), i. 172.

128.—Oxfordshire Visitation, by Lee, in 1574. In No. 1 of the Topographer. 1821. 8vo.

Arderne, 37.
Ashfield, 39.
Bampfield, 58.
Beckingham, 33.
Beauforest, 19.
Bowrne, 25.
Butler, 26.
Callcott, 28.
Carleton, 17.
Cave, 29.
Chamberlain, 44.
Cogan, 24.
Cursone, 22.
Danvers, 28.
Doyley *of Merton*, 51.
Doyley *of London*, 52.
Doyley *of Lincoln's Inn*, 52.
Doyley *of Chiselhampton*, 51.
Doyley *of Hundeston*, 52.
Egerley, 31.
Frere, 23.
Gainsford, 31.
Gibons, 36.
Harman, 36.
Hastings, 33.
Hawtton, 27.
Hildesley, 18.

Hitch, 46.
Holte, 21.
Horseman, 15.
Lee, 26.
Lench, 49.
Levins, 21.
Light, 27.
Littcote, 16.
Lybbe, 19.
Moore, 45.
Ogellthorpe, 17.
Owen, 24.
Pennystone, 32.
Perrot, 20.
Petty, 50.
Pope, 29.
Power, 42.
Poyntz, 45.
Rainsford, 41.
Savage, 37.
Seymor, 35.
Smith, 24.
Snappe, 25.
Stompe, 15.
Stoner, 16.
Stretley, 33.
Throgmorton, 39.

Typping, 29.
Warcuppe, 39.
Wayneman, 40.

Whitton, 31.
Wintershull, 17.
Yate, 34, 38.

129.—The History and Antiquities of the Hundreds of Bullington and Ploughley. By JOHN DUNKIN. *London*, 1823. 2 vols. 4to.

Bourne (*Chesterton*), i. 273.
Cottesford (*Launton*), i. 316.
Denton (*Blackthorn*), i. 85.
Doyley (*Merton*), ii. 27.
Dynham (*Piddington*), ii. 137.

Moyle (*Bucknell*), i. 199.
Tipping (*Merton*), ii. 47.
Turner, Page- (*Ambrosden*), i. folding at 58.

130.—Visitation of Oxfordshire, 1574. *Typis Medio Montanis*, 184. Foolscap folio. Privately printed by SIR THOMAS PHILLIPPS, Bart. The same volume contains the Visitations of Oxfordshire, 1634, and of Sussex, 1570.

Arderne *of Enstone*, 1.
Ashfield *of Heithorp*, 1.
Beauforest *of Dorchester*, 1.
Beckingham *of Stonesfield*, 1.
Bourne *of Chesterton*, 1.
Bustard *of Adderbury*, 2.
Butler *of Northington*, 2.
Calcott *of Wilcott*, 2.
Carleton *of Baldwin Brightwell*, 2.
Cave *of Walerstoke*, 3.
Cogan *of Oxford*, 3.
Curson *of Water Pery*, 3.
Danvers *of Oothorpe*, 3.
Doyley *of Adderbury*, 3.
Egerley of Mylton, 3.
Frere or Fryer *of Oxford*, 4.
Gainsford *of Idbury*, 4.
Gibbons *of Ditchley*, 4.
Harman *of Teynton*, 4.
Hastings *of Elford*, 4.
Hawtton *of The Ley*, 5.
Hildesley *of Cromers Gifford*, 5.
Hitch *of Wendlebury*, 5.
Holt of Stoke Lynde, 5.
Horseman *of Haseley*, 5.
Lee *of North Aston*, 5.
Levinz *of Oxford*, 6.

Lybbe *of Chekenden*, 6.
Lyght *of Henley or Horley*, 6.
Lytcott *of Chekindon*, 6.
More *of Clanfield*, 6.
Oglethorp *of Newington*, 7.
Owen *of Oxford*, 7.
Peniston *of Bampton*, 7.
Perrott *of Drayton*, 7.
Petty *of Tettesworth*, 7.
Pope *of Wroxton*, 8.
Power *of Blechington*, 8.
Raynsford *of Tew*, 8.
Savage *of Clanfield*, 8.
Seymour *of Burton*, 9.
Smyth *of Oxford*, 9.
Suape *of Oxford* (? 1574), 9.
Snappe *of Stanlake*, 9.
Stampe *of Fyfield*, 9.
Stonor *of North Stoke*, 10.
Stretley *of Weld*, 10.
Typping *of Whitfield*, 10.
Throckmorton *of Chastleton*, 10.
Wainman *of Fringford*, 10.
Warcup *of English*, 10.
Whitton *of Nethercott*, 11.
Wintershall *of Little Stoke*, 11.
Yate *of Witney*, 11.

P

131.—Visitation of Oxfordshire, 1634. (This Copy has
Additions by Peter Le Neve, the Herald.) Privately
printed by Sir Thomas Phillipps, Bart. The same
volume contains the Visitations of Oxfordshire, 1574,
and of Sussex, 1570.

Annesley *of Cornwell*, 12.
Archer *of Netherthorpe*, 12.
Ashfield *of Shipton*, 12.
Ashcombe *of Alvescott*, 12.
Ashworth *of Heyford Warren*, 12.
Aylway *of Oxford*, 13.
Barber *of Adderbury*, 13.
Barry *of Thame*, 13.
Baugh *of Milcombe*, 13.
Berowe *of Elford*, 13.
Blunt *of Wigginton*, 14.
Bourne *of Wendlebury*, 14.
Brasey *of Thame*, 14.
Bray *of Barrington*, 14.
Brigham *of Cannon Jude*, 14.
Brome *of Clifton*, 15.
Browne *of Kidlington*, 15.
Bull *of Hedington*, 15.
Butler *of Alstone*, 15.
Carleton *of Baldwin Brightwell*, 15.
Carleton *of Oxford*, 16.
Chamberlaine *of Sherborne*, 16.
Chamberlaine *of Stratton Audley*, 16.
Cobb *of Adderbury*, 16.
Coghill *of Blechingdon*, 17.
Corney *of Steple Barton*, 17.
Cottesford *of Lanton*, 17.
Crooke *of Marston*, 17.
Curson *of Water Pery*, 17.
Danvers *of Adderbury*, 17.
Denton *of Blackthorne*, 18.
Doyley *of Chiselhampton*, 18.
Doyley *of Hamilton*, 18.
Doyley *of Adderbury* (entered by mistake in the Visitation of 1574), 18.
Durant *of Yarnton*, 19.
Ewre *of Heyford Warren*, 19.
Fiennes *of Oxford*, 19.
Fitzherbert *of Bagbrooke*, 19.
Greenwood *of Norton*, 19.
Griffeth *of Bloxham*, 20.
Hall *of Banbury*, 20.
Hampshire *of Crawley*, 20.
Hamson *of Bradwell*, 20.

Harbourne *of Tackley*, 20.
Hawtrey *of Bodicott*, 21.
Hercy *of Oxford*, 21.
Hester *of Thame*, 21.
Holloway *of Oxford*, 21.
Hord *of Coate*, 21.
Hughes *of Middle Stoney*, 22.
Hungerford *of Farley Castle*, 22.
Huntingdon *of Stanton Harcourt*, 22.
Ivye *of Oxford*, 23.
Jenkenson *of Walcott*, 23.
Jones *of Castleton*, 23.
Jones *of East Hall*, 23.
Kenyon *of East Hall*, 23.
Lacy *of Shipton*, 24.
Lenthall *of Burford*, 24.
Libbe *of Hardwicke*, 24.
Lukin *of Oxon*, 24.
Lyde *of Coddesdon*, 24.
Martin *of Witney*, 24.
Medhope *of Aston*, 25.
Mese *of Over Worton*, 25.
Molines *of Monkeswell*, 25.
Morecroft *of Churchill*, 25.
Napper *of Hallywell*, 25.
Norris *of Islip*, 26.
Norris *of Weston on the Green*, 26.
Nourse *of Wooddeaton*, 26.
Odell *of Mollington*, 26.
Osbaldeston *of Chadlington*, 26.
Perrot *of North Leigh*, 26.
Petty *of Stoke Talmage and Tetsworth*, 27.
Phetiplace *of Swinbroke*, 27.
Pinke *of Oxford*, 27.
Pollard *of Newenham*, 27.
Plowden *of Shiplake*, 28.
Pope *of Oxford*, 28.
Powell *of Sandford*, 28.
Pudsey *of Ellesfield*, 28.
Rolles *of Lewknor*, 29.
Sacheverell *of Oxford*, 29.
Say *of Blechendon*, 29.
Scroope *of Wormesley*, 29.
Shepard *of Roulwright*, 29.
Shillingford *of Beckley*, 30.

Sonibanck *of Haseley*, 30.
Stampe *of Fyfield*, 30.
Standard *of Whitehill*, 30.
Taylor *of Williamscot*, 30,
Thimblethorp *of Henley on Thames*, 31.
Typping *of Whitfield*, 31.
Vazie *of Oxford*, 31.
Vyne *of Piddington*, 31.
Warcupp *of English*, 31.
Wharton *of Chipping Norton*, 32.

Wenman *of Soulderne*, 32.
Wheate *of Glympton*, 32.
Whorwood *of Oxford*, 32.
Wickham *of Swallcliffe*, 32.
Williams *of Oxford*, 33.
Willmot *of Stodham*, 33.
Wallascott *of South Stoke*, 33.
Wray *of Oxford*, 33.
Yate *of Stanlake*, 33.
Annesley *of Broke*, 33 (omitted in page 1.)

132.—Oxfordshire Pedigrees. No. 1557, Harl. MSS. Folio. No date. Not paged, but consists of 4 pages. Privately printed by Sir Thomas Phillipps, Bart., to accompany Parochial Collections for the County of Oxford (1825).

Ashcomb *of Alvescot*.
Barber *of Adderbury*.
Bethome *of Adwell*.
Cobb *of Adderbury*.
Danvers *of Adderbury*.

Denton *of Ambroseden*.
Doyley *of Adderbury*.
Jones *of Asthall*.
Kenion *of Asthall*.

133.—Historical Notices of the Parishes of Swyncombe and Ewelme in the County of Oxford. By the Hon. and Rev. HENRY ALFRED NAPIER, M.A. *Oxford*, 1858. 4to. *Privately printed.*

Ashfield *of Heythorp, Oxon. and Chesham, Bucks*, folding at 346.
Avelyne, 255.
Bacon, Sir Edmund, and his descendants, folding at 42.
Burgate, 66.
Cokesey, 46.
Danvers, 43.
De la Pole, folding at 322.
Fetyplace *of Swyncombe*, folding at 408.
Fortescue *of Salden*, folding at 390.
Grey *of Rotherfield*, 389.

Holland, Duke of Exeter, folding at 323.
Norris, 255, 346.
Norwich, 286.
Paston, 124.
Sackville, 296.
Suffolk, Descent of William Duke of, and Anne Countess of Warwick, 67.
Suffolk, Descent of Alice, Duchess of, and of Lady Margaret Beaufort, 68.
Ufford, Earl of Suffolk, 288.

134.—A History of Henley-on-Thames, in the County of Oxford. By JOHN SOUTHERDEN BURN. *London*, 1861. 8vo.

Freeman, folding at 254.
Hales, 270.

Marmyon, 270.
Whitelock (2), folding at 248.

RUTLANDSHIRE.

135.—The History and Antiquities of the County of Rutland. By JAMES WRIGHT. *London,* 1684. Folio.

Andrews *(Bysbrook)*, 34.
Barker *(Lynden)*, 84.
Beauchamp, Earl of Warwick, 39.
Bodenham *(Ryall)*, 112.
Brandon *(Tixover)*, 126.
Brown *(Stretton)*, 117.
Brown *(Tolethorp)*, 128.
Brudnell *(Thistleton)*, 119.
Burton *(Braunston)*, 25.
Cecil *(Ezendon)*, 63.
Chesilden *(Braunston)*, 24.
Colly *(Glaiston)*, 65.
Digby *(Stokedry)*, 114.
Digby *(Luffenham)*, 77.
Durant *(Cotsmore)*, 40.
Fawkener *(Uppingham)*, 131.
Feilding *(Martinsthorp)*, 89.
Flower *(Whitwell)*, 135.

Halford *(Edyweston)*, 42.
Harington *(Exton)*, 51.
Houghton *(Kelthorp)*, 71.
Hunt *(Lynden)*, 83.
Johnson *(Clipsham)*, 37.
Mackworth *(Normanton)*, 93.
Manners, Earls and Dukes of Rutland, 7.
Noel *(Ridlington)*, 109.
Palmes *(Ashwell)*, 17.
Plessington *(Burley)*, 28.
Sherard *(Tighe)*, 121.
Sherard *(Whitsundine)*, 135.
Stafford *(Tixover)*, 127.
Verney *(Belton)*, 22.
Villiers *(Burley)*, 30.
Wingfield *(Tickencote)*, 124.

136.—The History and Antiquities of the County of Rutland. By THOMAS BLORE, of the Society of the Middle Temple, and F.S.A. *Stamford,* 1811. Folio.

Albini and Moubray, 114.
Armyne *(Ketton)*, 176.
Basynges ; see Normanville.
Bellairs *of Stanford, co. Lincolnshire*, 53.
Benyon and Pitt *(Ketton)*, 170.
Bladen and Tinker *(Ketton)*, 180.
Bodenham *of Ryhall*, 49.
Bottetourt, Barons of Newport Paganell, 90.
Bottetourt (4 Tables), 209—211.
Browne *of Tolethorpe*, 93.
Buisly ; see Espec.
Bullingham *of Ketton*, 180.
Burghershe, *add.* 204.
Burrell and Foster *of Dowsby, co. Lincolnshire, and of Ryhall*, 50.
Burton ; see Tolethorpe.
Burton *of Tolethorpe*, 91.
Bussew ; see Espec.
Cecil (2 Tables), 24, 25.
Cecil (2 Tables), 80, 82.
Dale ; see Daneys.

Daneys, Dale, Fettiplace, Wollescott, Lynne, and Gresham *(Tickencote)*, 61.
De Clifford ; see Espec.
D'Eincourt ; see De la Hay.
De la Hay, and D'Eincourt *(Kelthorpe)*, 150.
Despenser, *add.* 200.
Digby *of Tickencote*, 62.
Douglas-Hamilton *(Ketton)*, 181.
Edmund Plantagenet, Earl of Kent's Descendants *(Ryhall)*, 37.
Edwards *(Ketton)*, 182.
Espec, Bussew, Buisly, and Vipont, and of the Barons de Clifford, 15.
Fane *(Casterton Magna)*, 222.
Fane *(Great Casterton)*, 103.
Fettiplace ; see Daneys.
Foster ; see Burrell.
Grelley, La Warre, and West *(Great Casterton)*, (4 Tables), 100, 101, 102.
Gresham ; see Daneys.

Grey *of Codnoure, co. Derby, &c.* (*Ketton*), 10 Tables, 162-167.
Gyney and Inglose (*Pickworth*), 188.
Haddon *of Essendine,* 28.
Hall (*Empingham*), 131, 225.
Hamilton, Douglas- *(Ketton) ;* see Douglas.
Hatcher *of Careby, co. Lincoln, and of Empingham, co. Rutland,* 134.
Hercy, Leeke, Towers, and Talbot (*Empingham*), 130.
Hopton, Ralph, Lord (*Empingham*), 133.
Houghton (*Kelthorpe*), 156.
Humet ; see Humez.
Humez, or Humet (*Ketton*), 158.
Hurst (*Ryhall*), 52.
Hussey (*Gt. Casterton*), (4 Tables), 107—109.
Hyde *of Langtoft, co. Lincoln,* 50.
Inglose ; see Gyney.
Kent, Earl of (*Plantagenet*), descendants of, 37.
Lancaster, Earls and Dukes of, 98.
Lane (*Ketton*), (3 Tables), 169.
Le Despenser, 16.
La Warre ; see Grelley.
Leeke ; see Hercy.
Lovell (*Ryhall*), 47.
Lynne ; see Daneys.
Mackworth *of Rutland,* 128.
Mackworth *of Salop,* 129, 226.
Mackworth, 225.
Middleton (*Ketton*), 180.
Mortimer (*Ryhall*), 42, 230.
Moubray ; see Albini.
Nele (*Empingham*), 132.

Normanvill and Basynges (*Empingham*), 127.
Normanvill, *add.* 223.
Paganell or Paynell, and Someri or Sumeri, Barons of Dudley, 90.
Pitt ; see Benyon.
Radclyffe *of Tickencote,* 63.
Rushout (*Ketton*), 171.
Scrope *of Bolton Castle,* (6 Tables), 5.
Scrope, *add.* 198.
Someri or Sumeri ; see Paganell.
Stace (*Pickworth*), 189.
Strange (2 Tables), 228.
Sutton, &c. (3 Tables), Barons of Dudley, 206, 207.
Talbot ; see Hercy.
Tamworth *of Ryhall,* 55.
Thompson (*Ketton*), 117.
Tinker ; see Bladen.
Tiptoft ; see Tybetot.
Tolethorpe and Burton *of Tolethorpe,* 217.
Toller *of Billingborough, co. Lincoln, and of Ryhall,* 51.
Towers; see Hercy.
Tredway (*Ketton*), 175.
Trollope *of co. Lincoln and Rutland,* (4 Tables), 94, 95.
Tybetot, or Tiptoft (*Ryhall*), 44.
Vipont ; see Espec.
Wallescott ; see Daneys.
Ward *of Hallaton, co. Leicester,* 54.
Welby (*Woodhead*), 192.
West; see Grelley.
Wingfield (10 Tables), 65-70.
Wotton *of Ketton,* 177.

SHROPSHIRE.

137.—Antiquities of Shropshire. By the Rev. R. W. EYTON, *London.* 1854 to 1860. 12 vols. Royal 8vo.

Astley *of Astley and King's Nordley,* iii. 154.
Baskerville *of Bradwardine,* (Herefordshire), and *of Pickthom, Newton, Northwood and Lawton,* (*Salop*), v. 102.
Basset ; see De L'Isle.
Beggesovere ; see De Beggesovere.
Belmeis and La Zouche, ii. 208.

Botreaux, Barons of, as coheirs of Robert Fitz Corbet, &c. vii. 159.
Broc ; see De Broc.
Brompton *of Kinlet, and Brompton Brian,* iv. 244.
Burford, and Richard's Castle, Descent of Barony of, iv. 303.

Burnel *of Castle Holgate, and Acton Burnell*, vi. 134.
Castello; see De Castello.
Castle Holgate, Descent of, iv. 56.
Clifford *of Clifford Castle, and Corfham*, v. 147.
Corbet, *of Wattlesborough and Moreton Corbet*, x. 182.
Corbet *of Caus*, vii. 40.
Corbet *of Tasley, Hadley, High Hatton, and King's Bromley*, i. 100.
Cothercote; see De Cothercote.
De Beggesovere *(Badger)*, ii. 65.
De Bohun, Coheirship of, iv. 184.
De Broc, descendants of, i. 190.
De Castello, or De Castro, i. 375.
De Cothercote, vi. 264.
De Lacy *of Ewias, Weobley, and Ludlow*, v. 240.
De Upton *of Upton Cresselt*, i. 144.
De Wililey, ii. 51.
Fitz Aer, ix. 318.
Fitz Alan and Stuart, vii. 228.
Fitz Herbert, Family and Barony of, vii. 148.
Fitz Odo, *of Rushbury, Stanway, Gretton, &c.* vi. 83.
Fitz Robert, *of Brug*, i. 381.
Fitz Warin *of Burwardsley*, descendants of, ii. 12.
Fitz Warin *of Whittington and Alberbury*, xi. 39.
Fleming; see Le Fleming.
Gorram, Turnham, and Leybourn, x. 220.
Hastings, Descent of Barony of, v. 135.
Helgot, *of Bobbington*, iii. 183.
Hodnet and Ludlow, ix. 334
Lacy; see De Lacy.

La Zouche; see Belmeis.
Le Fleming, Walter, Coheirs of, x. 302.
Le Palmer *of Brug*, i. 365.
Le Strange, Guy, Coheirs of, iii. 142.
Le Strange *of Ness and Cheswardine*, x. 262.
Leybourn; see Gorram.
Ludlow; see Hodnet.
Malvoisin *of Berwick Malvoisin;* and Malvoisin *of Ashfield*, viii. 397.
Mortimer *of Chelmarsh*, iii. 44.
Mortimer *of Wigmore*, iv. 196.
Musson, Roger, *of Uppington*, Coheirs of, viii. 160, 165, 176, 184.
Palmer *of Brug;* see Le Palmer.
Pembruge and Vernon *(Tong)*, ii. 226.
Peverel *of Dover, of Bourne, and of High Ercall*, Coheirs and Kindred of, ix. 69.
Pichford *of Albrighton, Pichford, &c.* 270.
Pierpoint *of Glazeley*, i. 218.
Powis, Princes of; see Sutton.
Rodington, Conjectural descent of the two Families of, vii. 380.
Sandford *of Sandford*, ix. 236.
Stanton *of Stanton Hineheath, &c.;* and Lee *of Lea-near-Pimhill,·&c.* ix. 294.
Strange; see Le Strange.
Stuart; see Fitz Alan.
Sutton, Lords of, as deriving from the Princes of Powis, ii. 111.
Turnham; see Gorram.
Upton; see De Upton.
Vernon; see Pembruge.
Wililey; see De Wililey.
Zouche; see Belmeis.

SOMERSETSHIRE.

138.—The History of Taunton, in the County of Somerset. By JOSHUA TOULMAN, D.D. New edition, by JAMES SAVAGE. *Taunton*, 1822. 8vo.

Bonvile and Grey, 69.
Bourchier; see Fitzwarine.

Fitzwarine and Bourchier, 70.
Grey; see Bonvile.

139.—The History and Antiquities of Somersetshire. By the Rev. W. PHELPS, A.B., F.S.A. *London*, 1836-1839. Vols. 1 and 2. 4to.

Colston (*West Lydford*), i. 470.
Davis and Sherston (*Wells*), ii. 24.
Dickinson (*King Weston*), i. 481.
Dyer *of Sharpham*, i. 563.
Fownes and Somerville (*Dinder*), ii. 194.
Fox, Earls of Ilchester (*Redlynch*), i. 253.
Gould of Sharpham, i. 564.
Hartgill *of Kilmington*, i. 177.

Hobhouse (*Pitcombe*), i. 259.
Hunt (*Compton Pauncefort*), i. 409.
Ilchester, Earls of; see Fox.
Medlycott *of Vere House*, i. 298.
Mildmay *(Queen Camel)*, i. 437.
Sherston (*Wells*); see Davis.
Somerville (*Dinder*); see Fownes.
Wickham, *co. Somerset*, folding at 320.

140.—The Visitation of Somersetshire. 1623. With additions from earlier Visitations and Continuations by R. MUNDY. *Typis Medio Montanis*. 1838. Privately printed by Sir Thomas Phillipps, Bart.

Abarough, 1.
Allen, 2.
Allett, 3.
Ashcombe, 4.
Ashe or Esse, 5.
Avery, 6.
Baber, 7, 8, 9.
Balche, 10.
Bamfield *of Hardington*, 11.
Barnard, 12.
Beresford, 13.
Berkley, 14.
Bifleete, 15.
Billingsley, 16.
Bisse, 17, 18.
Blanchard, 19.
Blewett, 20.
Bonner, 21.
Boteler, 22.
Bourne, 23.
Boureman, 24.
Bower, 25, 26.
Bowcher, 27.
Boys, 28.
Brereton, 29.
Brice, 30.
Bridges, 31.
Brooke, 32.
Broughton, 33.
Buller, 34.
Calthorp, 35.
Capell, 36.

Cary, 37.
Caulx, 38.
Chalke, 39.
Champness, 40.
Chappell *of Portishead*, 41.
Cheek *of Bruton*, 42.
Chelworth and Cockes *of Rode*, 43.
Cockes; see Chelworth.
Chilcot *of Stowcumber*, 44.
Clark *of Thornbury*, 45.
Claxton *of Bedminster*, 46.
Cogan *of Churd*, 47.
Cole *of Nailsea*, 48.
Colborne *of Braton*, 49.
Colles *of Barton*, 51.
Colmore *of Colmore*, 52.
Comb *of Tisbury*, 53.
Compton *of Pederton*, 54.
Cottington *of Frome*, 55.
Coward *of Wells*, 56.
Cox *of Churchill*, 57.
Cuffe *of Crich*, 58.
Culliford *of Queen Camel*, 59.
Cupper *of Lodington*, 60.
Clavelshey *of Corey Rivel*, 61.
Dane *of Bristol*, 62.
Davies *of Ticknam*, 63.
Doddington *of Doddington and Loxton*, 64.
Dyer of Sharpham, 65.
Esse; see Ashe.
Every *of Cothay*, 66.

Ewens *of Luddon*, 67.
Faber *of Nunnie*, 68.
Farewell *of Holbrook*, 69.
Floyer *of Marlinch*, 70.
Fort *of Corey Rivell*, 71.
Foster *of Weeke*, 72.
Foster *of Luxborough*, 73.
Francis *of Comb Flory*, 74.
Freake *of Brenham*, 75.
Fry *of Canington*, 76.
Galley *of Bath*, 77.
Gawen *of Horsington*, 78.
Glisson *of Brislington*, 79.
Glynn, 80.
Godwyn *of Wokey and Wells*, 81.
Gorge *of Wraxall*, 82.
Gough *of Meriet*, 83.
Greene *of Milton Clifton*, 84.
Harkshaw *of Hinton St. George*, 85.
Hales *of Highchurch*, 86.
Halswell *of Wells*, 87.
Hancock *of Gregory Stoke*, 88.
Hartgill *of Kilmington*, 89.
Harvy *of Brockley*, 90.
Hayward *of Charleton*, 91.
Herle *of Prideaux, co. Cornwall; and of* ——, *co Som.* 92.
Henley *of Leigh*, 93.
Hewish *of Donyford*, 94.
Hext *of Netherham*, 95.
Hill *of Spaxton*, 96.
Hill *of Poundford*, 97.
Hippesley *of Camleigh and East Pennard*, 98.
Hobbs *of Stokegursey*, 99.
Hodges *of Wedmore*, 100.
Hodges *of Lofton*, 101.
Holbeach *of Filton*, 102.
Holway *of Taunton*, 103.
Hooper *of Stowell*, 104.
Howper *of Meryet*, 104.
Hopton *of Witham*, 105.
Hourd *of Kingsdown*, 106.
Horner *of Wells*, 107.
Huddy *of Stowell*, 108.
Hughes *of Wells*, 109.
Hyett *of Wooton*, 109.
Irish *of Yatton*, 109.
Isham *of Ilbruars*, 110.
Ivery, 110.
Jackson *of Combhayes*, 110.
James *of Minchin Barrowe*, 110.
Jennings *of Burton*, 111.

Jerrard *of Samford*, 111.
Jones *of Wraxhall*, 110.
Kenn *of Kenn*, 111.
Kingston *of Weeke*, 112.
Knoell *of Samford Orcas*, 112.
Lacy *of Hackhowe*, 112.
Linde *of Wells*, 112.
Lancaster *of Milverton*, 113.
Leigh *of Wells*, 113.
Leversedge *of (Frome) Vallis*, 113.
Lewes *of Wincanton*, 114.
Lickland, 114.
Lisle *of Compton Darvill*, 114.
Lottisham *of Chipley*, 114.
Long *of Stratton*, 115.
Lucar *of Maidenbroke*, 115.
Lyte *of Lytes Cary*, 115.
Marshal *of Ivythorne*, 115.
Malet *of Enmore*, 116.
Malet *of St. Audries*, 117.
Martyn *of Seaborough*, 117.
Mauncell *of Mauncell's Place in North Pederton*, 117.
Maudeley *of Wells*, 118.
Mawdley *of Nunny*, 118.
Maye *of Charterhouse Hydon*, 118.
Merifield *of Crewkhorne*, 118.
Milburn *of Dunkerton*, 119.
Milward *of Batcombe*, 119.
Mitchael *of Gornshet*, 119.
Moleyns *of Bridgewater*, 119.
Morgan, 120.
Morgan *of Wells*, 120.
Morgan *of Easton*, 120.
Muttlebury *of Jurdens*, 120.
Moore *of Taunton*, 121.
Napper *of Tittenhull*, 121.
Nevile *of Bathwick*, 121.
Newborow *of Berkley*, 121.
Newman *of Wincanton*, 122.
Newton, 122.
Newton *of Compton Darvill*, 122.
Northover *of Aller*, 122.
Norris *of Splate*, 123.
Oldmixon *of Oldmixon*, 123.
Orange *of Foscott*, 123.
Ormerod *of Huntspill*, 123.
Overton *of Badcary*, 124.
Owen *of Wells*, 124.
Palton *of Palton*, 124.
Pauncefoote *of Compton Pauncefoot*, 124.
Palmer *of Fairfield*, 125.

Pawlett *of Gotehust*, 125.
Payne, 125.
Pennington *of Thornecombe*, 126.
Percivall, 126.
Percival *of Weston Gordan*, 126.
Perry *of Jarberston*, 126.
Philips *of Yeovill*, 126.
Philips *of Thorne*, 127.
Pine *of Stawell*, 127.
Pierce *of Bruton*, 127.
Pitt *of Crykin Malherbe*, 127.
Popham *of Huntworth*, 128.
Popham *of Porlock*, 128.
Pollard *of Kelve*, 129.
Portman *of Orchard*, 129.
Prowse *of Clyffe*, 129.
Preston *of Crickett*, 129.
Pyke *of Mourlynch*, 129.
Pymme *of Brymore and Cannington*, 130.
Pyne *of Curry Malet*, 130.
Radbard *of Lambrooke*, 131.
Raleigh *of Nettlecomb*, 131.
Raymond *of Ilchester and Chard*, 131.
Ritherton *of Langford Budville*, 131.
Rivett *of Wells*, 132.
Rodney *of Stoke Rodney*, 132.
Romsey *of Madford Toine*, 133.
Rosse *of Shepton and Somerton*, 133.
Rouswill *of Dunkerton*, 133.
Roynon *of Axbridge*, 133.
Salisbury, 134.
Samborne *of Tinsbury*, 134.
Samford *of Brecknoler*, 134.
Sandys *of South Petherton*, 134.
Sedborough *of Porlock*, 134.
Shaft *of Charterhouse Hinton*, 135.
Skinner *of Dewlish*, 135.
Smithes *of Wrenton*, 135.
Smith *of Long Ashton*, 136.
Somersett *of South Brent*, 136.
Southworth *of Wickehampflory*, 136.
Speake *of Whitlackington*, 137.
St. Aubyn *of Alfoxton*, 137.
Steyning *of Honycote*, 137.
Still *of Durley*, 138.
Stocker *of Chilcompton*, 138.
Stone *of Wedmore*, 138.
Strode *of Shepton Malet*, 138.
Stowell *of Cotheleston*, 139.

Sidenham *of Brimpton*, 139.
Sydenham *of Langford*, 140.
Sydenham *of Whetstow*, 140.
Sydnam *of North Quarum*, 140.
Sidenham *of Chelworthy*, 140.
Toose *of Wells*, 141.
Trevilian *of Nettlecombe*, 141.
Tynte *of Chelvey*, 141.
Upton *of Frome Selwood*, 141.
Vaughan *of Charlinch*, 143.
Verney *of Ferefield*, 142.
Vernai *of Fairfield*, from the Palmer MS. Hist. of Somersetshire, 142.
Waldron *of Langridge*, 143.
Walker *of Stowey*, 143.
Walton *of Compton Dando*, 143.
Walrond *of Bradfield, co. Dor., and of Sey, co. Som.*, 144.
Walsh *of Cathanger*, 144.
Le Warre *of Chipley*, 144.
Watts *of Wells*, 145.
Watkins *of Holwall*, 145.
Whitington *of Ivithorne*, 145.
Wikes *of Wells*, 146.
Worth *of Worth*, 146.
Worth *of Luckecombe*, 146.
Wyke *of Nynehed Florye*, 146.
Wornele *of Yeatton*, 147.
Wrothe *of Petherton Park*, from the Palmer MS. Hist. of Somersetshire, 147.

OMITTED AND CONTINUED.

Gorge *of Wraxhall* (*cont.*), 148.
Prowse *of Tiverton, co. Devon; and of Taunton, co. Somerset* (*omit.*), 148.
Richards *of Bagborough* (*omit.*), 148.
Rouswell *of Dunkerton* (*cont.*), 148.
Speake *of Whitlackington* (*cont.*), 149.
Gournay *of Harptre* (*cont.*), 150.
Philips *of Montacute* (*cont.*), 150.
St. Aubyn *of Alfoxton* (*cont.*), 151.
Le Warre *of Brislington* (*omit.*), 151.
Montacute, 151.
Moeles, 152.

141.—Guide to Farleigh Hungerford. By the Rev. J. E. JACKSON, M.A. *London*, 1853. 8vo.

Hungerford, 19. Q

STAFFORDSHIRE.

142.—A Survey of Staffordshire. By SAMPSON ERDESWICKE, Esq. *London*, 1717 and 1723. 8vo. Second Edition. *Westminster*, 1820. 8vo. Third Edition. *London*, 1844. 8vo. The first edition does not contain any tabulated pedigrees.

Ashmole, 3 ed. xlix.
Beaumont, 2 ed. 291; 3 ed. 396.
Colclough, 2 ed. 378; 3 ed. 506.
Crewe, 2 ed. 75; 3 ed. 85.
De Blurton, 2 ed. 378; 3 ed. 506.
Degge, 2 ed. xliii.; 3 ed. lx.
De Quincey, 2 ed. 291; 3 ed. 396.
Draycott, 2 ed. 190; 3 ed. 253.
Dyott, 2 ed. 232; 3 ed. 310.
Endesore *of Comberford*, 2 ed. 327; 3 ed. 444.
Ferne, 2 ed. 381; 3 ed. 510.
Ferrers, 2 ed. 394; 3 ed. 525.
Foley, 2 ed. 274; 3 ed. 374.
Grey, 3 ed. 380.
Grey, 2 ed. 391; 3 ed. 522.
Heronville, 2 ed. 291; 3 ed. 396.
Lawton, 2 ed. 89; 3 ed. 106.
Ley, 3 ed. 488.
Lydiat, 2 ed. 273; 3 ed. 370.
Norman, 2 ed. 199; 3 ed. 261.

Orme, 2 ed. 183; 3 ed. 243.
Plot, 2 ed. xlii.; 3 ed. liii.
Pipe, 2 ed. 288; 3 ed. 393.
Ruggeley, 2 ed. 318; 3 ed. 431.
Shelton, 2 ed. 290; 3 ed. 394.
Shirley, 2 ed. 397; 3 ed. 529.
Sprott, 2 ed. 180; 3 ed. 241.
Stanley, 2 ed. 290; 3 ed. 395.
Tixall, 2 ed. 198; 3 ed. 260.
Turton, 2 ed. 290; 3 ed. 395.
Weston *of Weston under Lizard*, 2 ed. folding at 136; 3 ed. 164.
Weston *of Rugeley*, 2 ed. folding at 136; 3 ed. 164.
Weston *of Roxwell and Welford*, 2 ed. folding at 136; 3 ed. 164.
Weston *of Lichfield*, 2 ed. folding at 136; 3 ed. 165.
Whittington, Lord Mayor of London, 3 ed. 381.

143.—The History and Antiquities of Staffordshire. By the Rev. STEBBING SHAW, B.D., F.A.S. *London*, 1798. 2 vols. folio.

Arblaster (*Longdon*), i. 225.
Arden (*Yoxall*), i. 102.
Astley (*Patteshull*), ii. 284.
Aston and Welles (*Yoxall*), i. 105.
Barnesley (*Trysull*), ii. 209.
Basset (*Drayton Bassett*), ii. 12.
Biddulph *of Elmhurst*, i. 352.
Bishbury and Grosvenor, ii. 178.
Bradney; see Pershouse.
Bray; see Grendon.
Brook and Girdler (*Haselor*), i. 389.
Chichester *of Raleigh*, i. 374.
Comberford (*Tamworth*), i. 434.
Corbyn (*Swinford Regis*), ii. 230.
Cotton (*Hamstall Ridware*), i. 157*.
Croxall; see Lacy.
Deane (*Codsall*), ii. 289.
De Tocka (*Rolleston*), i. 35.

Dickins (*Bobington*), ii. 278.
Dyott (*Lichfield*), i. 362.
Ferrers (*Tutbury*), i. 39.
Floyer (*Hints*), ii. 21.
Foley *of Prestwood, &c.* ii. 235.
Fowler *of Pendeford*, ii. 203.
Girdler (*Haselor*); see Brook.
Gough *of Oldfallings and Perry Hall*, ii. folding at 188.
Grendon and Bray (*Shenston*), ii. 34.
Griffith (*Whichnor*); see Somervile.
Grosvenor; see Bishbury.
Harpur; see Rushall.
Hill *of Little Pipe*, i. 355.
Huntbach (*Byshbury*), ii. 187.
Hussey (*Norton*); see Powke.
Inge (*Thorpe Constantine*), i. 409.

Jevon *of Sedgley*, ii. app. 19.
Jordan ; see Lacy.
Lacy, Wylde, Tennant, Sanders, Jordan, Croxall, Scott, &c. *(Aldridge)*, ii. 107.*
Lane *(Bentley)*, ii. 97.
Leigh ; see Bushall.
Leveson *(Wolverhampton)*, ii. 169.
Mollesley, or Moseley, *(Byshbury)*, ii. 184, 276.
Mynors *(Tattenhall)*, i. 117.
Paget *(Longdon)*, i. 220.
Pershouse, and Bradney *(Over Penne)*, ii. 222.*
Pershouse *(Sedgeley)*, ii. 222.
Pipe *of Bilston*, ii. folding at 172.
Powke and Hussey *(Norton)*, ii. 60.
Pyott *(Lichfield)*, i. 364.
Randyll ; see Morgan.
Robinson *(Drayton Bassett)*, ii. 5.
Rushall, Harpur and Leigh *(Rushall)*, ii. 69.
Sanders ; see Lacy.
Scott *of Great Barr*, ii. 107.*

Scott ; see Lacy.
Shareshull *(Patteshull)*, ii. 281.
Skeffington *(Lichfield)*, i. 372.
Somervile and Griffith *(Whichnor)*, i. 126.
Stamford *of Stanford*, ii. 109.
Stanley *(West Bromwich)*, ii. 128.
Strethay *(Lichfield)*, i. 363.
Swynfen *of Swynfen*, ii. 28.*
Tennant; see Lacy.
Turton *(Alrewas)*, i. 132.
Vernon, i. 404.
Welles *(Yoxall)* ; see Aston.
Whorwood *(West Bromwich)*,ii.129.
Whorwood *(Enville)*, ii. 276.
Whorwood *(Bobington)*, ii. 278.
Wightwick *(Tettenhall)*, ii. 201.
Wilkes *(Willenhall)*, ii. 149.
Wolferstan, i. folding at 416.
Woodhouse *(Womburne)*, ii. 216.
Wrottesley *(Tettenhall)*, ii. 205.
Wylde ; see Lacy.
Wyrley *(Handsworth)*, ii. 115.

144.—A Topographical and Historical Description of the Parish of Tixall, in the County of Stafford. By Sir Thomas Clifford, Bart., and Arthur Clifford, Esq. *Paris*, 1817. 4to.

De Frevile, Joyce, wife of Sir Robert Aston, Knt. folding at 144.
Howard, Lady Mary, wife of Walter, fourth Lord Aston, folding at 144.
Talbot, Lady Barbara, wife of James, fifth Lord Aston, folding at 144.

145.—The Borough of Stoke-upon-Trent, &c., &c. By John Ward. *London*, 1843. 8vo.

Audley, 148.
Bagenhall *alias* Bagnall, 346.
Bateman, 181.
Biddulph *of Biddulph*, 278.
Bowyer *of Knypersley* ; see Gresley.
Brindley and Williamson, 177.
Broade *of Fenton Vivian*, 550.
Burslem *of Burslem*, 194.
Child *of Newfield*, 87.
Clayton ; see Lovatt.
Colclough *of Staffordshire*, 340.
Fenton, 422.
Gresley *of Gresley and Drakelow*, Bowyer *of Knypersley*, and Heathcote *of Longton*, folding at 563.

Heathcote *of Longton* ; see Gresley.
Lovatt, Clayton, and Wyse, 523.
Mainwaring *of Whitmore*, 519.
Parker *of Parkhall*, 561.
Smith *of Great Fenton and Elmhurst*, 543.
Sneyd *of Keel*, 82.
Twemlow, 423.
Wedgwood *of Harracles*, 197.
Wedgwood *of Burslem* (5 tables), 199-202.
Wood and Wedgwood, 153.
Wyse ; see Lovatt.

146.—Visitation of Staffordshire, 1663-4. Ex. MSS. Phillipps. *Typis Medio Montanis*, 1854. Foolscap folio. Privately printed by SIR THOMAS PHILLIPPS, Bart.

Abney *of Audley*, 1.
Adderley *of Blackhough*, 1.
Adderley *of Cotton*, 1.
Allen *of Fulford*, 1.
Alport *of Gray's Inn*, 1.
Arbalester, 1.
Arden *of Leacroft*, 1.
Ashmole *of Lichfield*, 1.
Astley *of Wood Eaton*, 1.
Astley, 2.
Aston, 2.
Babington, 2.
Bamfield *of Wolverhampton*, 2.
Barboure *of Flashbrook*, 2.
Barboure, 2.
Barnsley *of Tresley*, 2.
Best *of Apleton*, 2.
Biddulph *of Biddulph*, 2.
Birde *of Field*, 2.
Boothby *of Trowley Park*, 2.
Bowes, 2.
Brandreth *of Shenston*, 2.
Bowyer *of Sidway*, 3.
Brereton *of Halton*, 3.
Brett, 3.
Broughton *of Whittington*, 3.
Broughton *of Longdon*, 3.
Bulkeley *of Stoke*, 3.
Caldwell *of Rolleston*, 3.
Chadwick, 3.
Chetwood *of Okeley*, 3.
Coleclough *of Delfthouse*, 3.
Collier *of Darliston*, 4.
Congreave *of Stretton*, 4.
Cope *of Hanwell*, 4.
Cotton *of Crakendish*, 4.
Coyney, 4.
Digby *of Tilton*, 4.
Diot, 4.
Ducy, 4.
Edge *of Horton*, 4.
Eld *of Siford*, 4.
Ferne *of Chester*, 5.
Fletewood, 5.
Flyer *of Inner Temple*, 5.
Foden *of Fulford*, 5.
Fowke, 5.
Fowler *of Penford*, 5.

Fowler *of Berthomley*, 5.
Gamull *of Alton*, 5.
Gaywood *of Ofley*, 5.
Gifford, 5.
Gilman *of Sutton*, 5.
Gough *of Hampton*, 5.
Grene *of Stone*, 5.
Grey *of Groby*, 6.
Grosvenor *of Bishbury*, 6.
Harecourt *of Milwadse*, 6.
Haw *of Caldmore*, 6.
Hill *of Gorscot*, 6.
Hoo *of Bradley*, 6.
Hopkins *of Wedgebury*, 6.
Huit *of London*, 6.
Huntbach *of Seawell*, 6.
Hurte *of Casterne*, 6.
Inge *of Thorpe*, 6.
Jarvis *of Catrull*, 6.
Jeninges *of Tenby, co. Pembroke*, 6.
Lathorpe *of Bramshall*, 6.
Leacroft *of Walton*, 7.
Lutwich *of Blacklaw*, 7.
Lydeat *of Enville*, 7.
Leveson *of Hampton*, 7.
Macclesfield, 7.
Manley *of Northon*, 7.
Manlor, 7.
Minors *of Uttoxeter*, 7.
Moreton *of Ingleton*, 7.
Moseley *of Bilston*, 7.
Mountford *of Bescote*, 7.
Noble *of Lichfield*, 7.
Orme *of Haunchall*, 7.
Pargiter *of Ridware*, 8.
Parker *of Wedgebury*, 8.
Parker *of Audley*, 8.
Pershouse *of Sedgeley*, 8.
Pipe, 8.
Piot *of Strethay*, 8.
Porte *of Ileham*, 8.
Pudsey *of Seisdon*, 8.
Purcell *of Onslere*, 8.
Rode *of Rushton Quatermaine*, 8.
Rudiard *of Barnswood*, 8.
Rugeley *of Bedford*, 9.
Sanders *of Branston and Barton*, 9.

Scot *of Barr and Allrich,* 9.
Shelton *of Bringham,* 9.
Short *of Ashley,* 9.
Skrimshire *of Aquilate,* 9.
Skrimshire *of Norbury,* 9.
Smith *of Newcastle,* 9.
Sneide, 9.
Somerford, 9.
Stafford *of Pipe,* 9.
Stanford *of Packington,* 9.
Stanley *of West Bromwich,* 10.
Tirrick *of Clayton Griffith,* 10.
Trafford, 10.
Turton *of Alderways,* 10.
Unwyne *of Cloughouse,* 10.
Villiers *of Burton Grange,* 10.
Vise *of Standon,* 10.

Walker *of Raynalds Hall,* 10.
Ward, 10.
Wedgewood *of Hawles,* 10.
Wellis *of Hore Cross,* 10.
Weston, 10.
Whitehall *of Parkhall,* 10.
Whitgrave *of Mesley,* 10.
Whitwick, 11.
Wilbraham, 11.
Wilkes *of Willenhall,* 11.
Wirley *of Houndsworth,* 11.
Wollaston *of Walsall,* 11.
Wolverston *of Shotfield,* 11.
Wolrich *of Copehall,* 11.
Wood *of Uttoxeter,* 11.
Woodhouse *of Woodhouse,* 11.
Wright *of Frodswall,* 11.

147.—A History of Wednesbury, in the County of Stafford. *Wolverhampton,* 1854. 8vo.

Comberford, 161.
Hoo, 163.
Holden, 173.
Hopkins, 169.

Parkes *of Wednesbury,* 165.
Perkes or Parkes, 165.
Rose, 171.

148.—A History of the Ancient Parish of Leek. By JOHN SLEIGH. *Leek,* 1862. 8vo.

Bateman, Parker, Levinge, folding at 108.

SUFFOLK.

149.—The History and Antiquities of Hawsted, in the County of Suffolk. By the Rev. Sir JOHN CULLUM, Bart., F.R. and A.L.S. (No. 23, Bibliotheca Topographica Britannica,) 1784. 4to. 2nd edition. *London,* 1813. 4to.

Clopton, folding at 101; 2 ed. at 112.
Cullum *of Hawsted,* folding at 152; 2 ed. at 179.

Drury (4 Tables), 115; 2 ed. 128-134.

150.—An Historical Account of Lowestoft. By EDMUND GILLINGWATER. *London,* (1790.) 4to.

Mighells, 401.

Wilde, 245.

151.—The History and Antiquities of Hengrave in Suffolk. By JOHN GAGE, Esq., F.S.A., of Lincoln's Inn. *London*, 1822. 4to.

De Hemegrave, folding at 80.
De Hethe, facing 95.

Gage, folding at 240.
Kytson, folding at 212.

152.—The History and Antiquities of Suffolk. Thingoe Hundred. By JOHN GAGE, F.R.S., Dir. S.A. *London*, 1838. 4to.

Ashley (*Fornham All Saints*), 254.
Aspale; see De Aspale.
Badlesmere (*Barrow*), 4.
Blagge *of Horningsherth*, 521.
Blakeham; see De Blakeham.
Bokenham (*Hawsted*); see Talmach.
Boldero (*Fornham All Saints*), 253.
Charman (*Risby*) 75.
Cranmer; see Wood.
Croftes *of Little Saxham*, 134.
Cullum *of Hawsted and Hardwick*, 478.
De Aspale and Geddyng (*Lackford*), 47.
De Blakeham (*Lackford*), 32.
De Hemegrave, 167.
De Ickworth, 276.
De Ligne (*Nowton*), 493.
De Rede, 371.
De Risby, 76.
De Saxham, 372.
De Sopesfeld (*Little Saxham*), 123.
De Walsham (*Brockley*) 351.
Drury *of Hawsted*, 429.
Eldred (*Great Saxham*), 106.
Gage *of Hengrave*, 205.
Geddyng; see De Aspale.
Gipps (*Horningsherth*), 522.
Goodday (*Fornham All Saints*), 244.
Hammond (*Whipsted*), 395.

Heigham *of Barrow*, 9.
Hemegrave; see De Hemsgrave.
Hethe *of Little Saxham*, 126.
Hervey *of Ickworth*, 287.
Houghton (*Westley*), 93.
Ickworth; see De Ickworth.
Kent (*Lachford*), 51.
Kytson *of Hengrave*, 184.
Ligne; see De Ligne.
Lucas (*Little Saxham*), 130.
Lucas (*Horningsherth*), 515.
Metcalfe (*Hawsted*), 446.
Mills (*Great Saxham*), 110.
Noel, &c. Lords of Hawsted, 410.
Oakes (*Nowton*), 494.
Payne (*Nowton*), 489.
Rede; see De Rede.
Risby; see De Risby.
St. Philibert (*Lackford*), 43.
Saxham; see De Saxham.
Shardelow (*Flempton*), 60.
Southwell (*Hardwick*), 475.
Sturgeon (*Manston*) 385.
Talmach and Bokenham (*Hawsted*), 427.
Thomas (*Brockley*), 359.
Topesfeld; see De Topesfeld.
Walsham; see De Walsham.
Wood, Cranmer, &c. (*Whipsted*), 391.

153.—The History and Antiquities of the County of Suffolk. By the Rev. ALFRED SUCKLING, LL.B. *London*, 1846-1848. 2 vols. 4to.

Adair *of Flixton*, i. 201.
Barett (*Blythborough*), ii. 160.
Barne *of Sotterley*, i. 95.
Blennerhasset *of Barsham*, i. 37.
Clarke *of Henstead*, ii. 377.
Cuddon *of Dunwich*, ii. 294.

De Norwich and Ufford, Earls of Suffolk, i. 171.
Duke *of Brampton*, ii. 186.
Farr *of North Cove*, i. 50.
Fastolft *of Oulton*, ii. 41.
Garneys *of Little Redisham*, i. 64.

Gonville *of Blundeston*, i. 314.
Gooch *of Benacre*, ii. 125.
Heveningham *of Heveningham*, ii. 386.
Hopton *of Blythborough*, ii. 137.
Hunt *of Oulton*, ii. 41.
Jerningham and Stafford, folding at ii. 46.
Leathes *of Herringfleet*, ii. 14.
Leman *of Brompton*, ii. 184.
Luson *of Gunton*, ii. 7, 454.
Noion *of Worlingham*, i. 105.

North *of Benacre*, ii 123.
Norwich ; see De Norwich.
Playters *of Sotterley*, i. 86.
Rede *of Beccles*, i. 30.
Rous *of Henham*, ii. 366.
Stafford ; see Jerningham.
Suckling *of Barsham*, i. 40.
Suffolk, Earls of ; see De Norwich,
Sydnor *of Blundeston*, i. 311.
Tasborough *of Flixton*, i. 198.
Ufford, Earls of Suffolk ; see De Norwich.

154.—Proceedings of the Suffolk Institute of Archæology. Commenced in 1849. *Bury St. Edmunds.* 8vo.

De Donzi, Barons, and Lords of St. Aignan in Berri, ii. 407.

Hervey, ii. 412.

155.—The Visitation of Suffolke, made by WILLIAM HERVEY, Clarenceux King of Arms. 1561. Edited by JOSEPH JACKSON HOWARD, LL.D., F.S.A. Published with the East Anglian, and also as a separate work. *Lowestoft.* 4to.

Clopton, 134.
Crane, 163.
Daniel, 241—243.

Eden, 18.
Martin, 227—230.
Spring, 167, 201—206.

SURREY.

156.—The History and Antiquities of the County of Surrey. By the Rev. OWEN MANNING, S.T.B., and WILLIAM BRAY, Esq., F.S.A. *London*, 1804-1814. 3 vols. folio.

Abdy *of Chobham*, iii. 203.
Agmondesham and Muschamp (*East Horsley*), iii. 29.
Albany (*Farnham*), iii. 141.
Albemarle and Devon, Earls of, iii. 496.
Alkstede, Rob. Descendants of, (*Merstham*), ii. 258.
Aperdale ; see Mickleham.
Arpe or Orby, (*Chertsey*), iii. 231.
Arundel, Earls of, i. 27.
Arundel, Earls of, (*Dorking*), i. 553.
Arundel, William Earl of, Descendants of (*Cheam*), ii. 471.
Ashurst (*Mickleham*), ii. 656.
Aston ; see Montfort.

At Hull (*Hambledon*), ii. 56.
Atkins *of Clapham*, iii. 362.
Atwood (*Sandersted*), ii. 570.
Austen *of Shalford*, ii. 100.
Aylesford, Earl of ; see Finch.
Barclay, iii. cxxxi.
Beaumont (*Leigh*), ii. 182.
Beecher *of Bletchingly*, ii. 309.
Berners (*West Horsley*), iii. 37.
Bish (*Burstow*), ii. 288.
Bludder (*Reygate*), i. 306.
Bohun (*Walton*), ii. 762.
Boteler (*Shire*), i. 533.
Boulton, Fuller, and Bruere, (*Letherhead*), ii. 670.
Bouverie ; see Harvey.

Bowyer (*Camberwell*), iii. 409.
Braose (*Bramley*), ii. 77.
Bray (*Shire*), i. folding at 523.
Brocas (*Peperharrow*), ii. 29.
Brocas (*Compton*), ii. 4.
Brodrick, Viscount Midleton, ii. facing 33.
Brown *of Betchworth*, i. 560.
Browne (*Pirbright*) ; see Nevill.
Browne (*Leigh*), ii. 182.
Bruere ; see Boulton.
Bryant (*Caterham*), ii. 437.
Buckle (*Bansted*), ii. 587.
Budgen (*Newdigate*), ii. 173.
Bures ; see De Bures.
Burnel (*Rotherhithe*), i. 222.
Burrell (*Reygate*), i. 308.
Burton (*Carshalton*), ii. 509.
Byne (*Carshalton*), ii. 513.
Byshe *of Burstow*, ii. 318.
Calvert (*Epsom*), ii. 613.
Carew *of Beddington*, ii. folding at 533.
Carleton (*Thames Ditton*), i. 458*.
Carter (*Guildford*), i. 15.
Caryl *of Tangley*, ii. 109.
Cecil (*Wimbledon*), iii. 274.
Clare, Earls of, ii. 299.
Clare ; see Fitz Hamon.
Clarke (*West Moulsey*), ii. 783.
Clarke (*East Moulsey*), i. 474*.
Clarke, iii. cxli.
Clayton *of Marden*, ii. 304.
Cocks ; see Sommers.
Coldham (*Farnham*), iii. 153.
Copley *of Gatton*, ii. 231.
Covert *of Slaugham, co. Sussex* (*Chaldon*), ii. folding at 441.
Covert (*Hascomb*), ii. 65.
Cowper *of Temple Elphant, Capel*, i. 597.
Cranmer *of Mitcham*, ii. 497 ; iii. clii.
D'Abernon (*Stoke D'Abernon*), ii. 721.
Dammartin (*Godstone*), ii. 324.
D'Amorie (*Kennington*), iii. 485.
De Acstede or Ocstede, Roland, descendants of (*Oxted*), ii. 383.
De Bradeston, descendants of (*Shalford*), ii. 97.
De Branche (*Peperharrow*), ii. 25.
De Breose (*Thames Ditton*), i. 455.

De Broc, descendants of, i. 85.
De Bures (*Bansted*), ii. 584.
De Burstow, ii. 286.
De Creoun (*Kingston*), i. 359.
De Fay, descendants of (*Bramley*), ii. 84.
De Gatton, Herefred, descendants of, ii. 228.
De la Poyle (*Seale*), iii. 174.
De Tonbridge, descendants of, (*Shalford*), ii. 90.
Devon, Earls of ; see Albemarle.
De Windsore *of Hurtmere*, i. 627.
Dolshills (*Camberwell*), iii. 413.
Dorril (*Merton*), i. 244.
Downe (*Cobham*), ii. 735.
Drake (*Reygate*), i. 310.
Duckworth (*Letherhead*), ii. 682.
Duncomb (*Godalming*), i. 629.
Duncomb *of Weston House and Shalford*, ii. folding at 127.
Dunstanville (*Shalford*), ii. 97.
Edwin ; see Stydolf.
Effingham, Earls of ; see Howard.
Eliot (*Godalming*), i. 619.
Elwill (*Egham*), iii. 252.
Emily (*Sutton*), i. 143.
Evelyn *of Long Ditton*, iii. 14.
Evelyn *of Godstone*, add. iii. cxliv.
Evelyn of *Wotton*, ii. 150.
Evelyn (*Godstone*), ii. 329.
Fanshawe, iii. cxxvi.
Fanshawe (*Chipsted*), ii. 246.
Farindon (*Lingfield*), ii. 349.
Ferrers, William, Earl of Derby, descendants of, (*Woodmansterne*), ii. 461, add. clxiv.
Fienes (*Carshalton*), ii. 507.
Finch, Earl of Aylesford (*Albury*), ii. 125.
Fitz Alan (*Woking*), i. 116.
Fitz Alan, Earl of Arundel, (*Reygate*), i. 282, 311.
Fitz Hamon, Clare, &c. (*Rotherhithe*), i. 220.
Fitz Pain and Poynings *of Wisley*, iii. 117.
Fitz Piers, descendants of, (*Shalford*), ii. 92.
Fox-Lane (*East Horsley*), iii. 32.
Frederick (*Walton*), ii. folding at 767.
Freeman ; see Harvey.

Freville ; see Montfort.
Fromond (*Cheam*), ii. 473.
Fromonds (*Burstow*), ii. 284.
Frowick (*Betchworth*), ii. 211.
Fulham (*Compton*), ii. 5.
Fuller ; see Boulton.
Gainsford *of Lingfield, Crowhurst, &c.*, iii. folding at 174.
Gardiner *of Camberwell*, iii. 415.
Garret (*Little Bookham*), ii. 706.
Garth (*Morden*), iii. 488.
Gatwick (*Charlwood*), ii. 188.
Gavell (*Cobham*), ii. 734.
Gaynsford (*Carshalton*), ii. 512.
Glover and Bryant (*Caterham*), ii. 437.
Glydd (*Bletchingly*), ii. 307
Glynn of *Henley Park*, iii. 72.
Gore *of Leatherhead*, ii. 664.
Gresham (*Titsey*), ii. 403.
Guildford, Earls of ; see North.
Gwynn, Richard, descendants of, (*Wonersh*), ii. 112.
Harding (*Cranley*), i. 537.
Hardinge (*Kingston*), i. 383.
Harrington, Earls of ; see Stanhope.
Harvey *of Comb*, i. 402.
Harvey, Freeman, Bonverie, &c. (*Betchworth*), ii. 208.
Hawkins : see Shudd.
Hele (*Reygate*), i. 306.
Heath of *Hatchland*, iii. 47.
Heath *of Gomsele*, i. 498.
Heath (*Limpsfield*), ii. 395.
Hervey (*Richmond*), i. 407.
Holles (*Peperharrow*), ii. 32.
Holman (*Bletchingly*), ii. 307.
Hopkins (*Wimbledon*), iii. 278.
Hoskins (*Oxted*), ii. 386.
Howard *of Ashted*, ii. 630.
Howard, Earls of Effingham, ii. 355, 690.
Howard, Lord Effingham, i. 302.
Howard, Earls of Suffolk, ii. 631.
Howland *of Streatham*, iii. 381.
Hull ; see At Hull.
Hull *of Godalming*, i. 607.
Hungerford *of Camberwell*, iii. 422.
Hussey (*Gumsele*), i. 497.
James *of Reygate*, i. 326.
Kenrick (*Bletchingly*), ii. 306.
King *of Ockham*, iii. 124.
Ladbroke (*Reygate*), i. 311.

Lambert, Wood, &c. (*Coulsdon*), ii. 453.
Lambert (*Bansted*), ii. 589.
Lampard (*Farnham*), iii. 141.
Latton ; see Wadham.
Lechford (*Leigh*), ii. 181.
Leigh, Wight, &c. (*Bletchworth*), ii. 211.
Leigh (*Addington*), ii. 560.
Leigh (*Walton*), ii. 764.
Leigh (*Thorpe*), iii. 248.
Leigh (*Stockwell*), iii. 497.
Lewen (*Ewell*), i. 470.
Lumley (*Ewel*), i. 456.
Manship (*Mitcham*), ii. 498.
Mareschal, Earl of Pembroke, descendants of, i. 577.
Merland (*Bansted*), ii. 586.
Merston and Mynn (*Epsom*), ii. 612.
Mickleham and Aperdale, ii. 653.
Montacute (*Pirbright*) ; see Nevil and Browne.
Montfort, Freville, and Aston (*Ashted*), iii. 627.
Moore (*Fetcham*), i. 483.
Moore (*Chertsey*), iii. 229.
More *of Loseley*, i. 99.
More *of Larden, Salop, &c.*, i. 628.
Morgan and Randyll *of Chilworth*, ii. 118.
Mortimer (*Pirbright*), i. 148.
Moys (*Bansted*), ii. 590.
Munchensi (*Nutfield*), ii. 269.
Muschamp *of Camberwell*, iii. 414.
Muschamp ; see Agmondesham.
Mynn (*Epsom*), ii. 612.
Nevil and Browne, Lords Montacute (*Pirbright*), i. 149.
Newdigate (*Newdigate*), ii. 173.
Newland (*Gatton*) ; see Turgis.
Nicholas (*West Horsley*), iii. 41.
North, Earls of Guildford, i. 47.
Northey *of Woodcote*, ii. 615.
Ocstede ; see De Acstede.
Oglethorpe *of Westbrook*, i. 614
Orby (*Chertsey*) ; see Arpe.
Onslow, Earl of, iii. folding at 54.
Paganel (*Dorking*), i. 570.
Parkhurst (*Pirford*), i. 157.
Parvish (*Stoke*), i. 172.
Parvish (*Shalford*), ii. 99.
Pembroke, Earls of ; see Mareschal.
Petre, Lords (*Chertsey*), iii. 228.

Phiffard *(Merton)*, i. 255.

Platt *of Westbrook*, i. 609.

Plescy *(Hedley)*, ii. 638.

Poynings *of Wisley;* see Fitzpain.

Rochdale, Richard, descendants of, *(Warlingham)*, ii. 429.

St. John *(Godstone)*, ii. 324.

Sands, iii. cxxxii.

Sander *of Charlwood*, ii. 190.

Sanders *(Ewell)*, i. 459.

Sandes *(Letherhead)*, ii. 671.

Scawen *(Carshalton)*, ii. 510.

Scot *(Cambermell)*, iii. 406.

Shudd, Stilwell, Hawkins, &c. *(Witley)*, ii. 46.

Skinner *of Reygate*, i. 325.

Smith and Webb *(Witley)*, ii. 44.

Somerie *(Dorking)*, i. 570.

Sommers and Cocks *(Reygate)*, i. 286.

Sonde *of Dorking*, i. 567.

Southcote *(Merstham)*, ii. 260.

Southwell *(Merstham)*, ii. 256.

Stanhope, Earl of Harrington, i. 440.

Stilwell ; see Shudd.

Stoughton *of Stoughton*, i. folding at 171.

Stydolf and Edwin *(Hedley)*, ii. 640.

Stydolf ; see Wymeldon.

Sydney *(Loseley)*, i, 94.

Talmache *of Ham*, i. folding at 368.

Temple *(Farnham)*, iii. 139.

Tichesey and Uvedale *(Titsey)*, ii. 400.

Thurlow *(Streatham)*, iii. 385.

Tryon ; see Wymeldon.

Turgis and Newland *(Gatton)*, ii. 232.

Turnour, Earls of Winterton, *(Compton)*, ii. 7.

Uvedale *(Titsey)*, ii. 400.

Vincent *(Stoke D'Abernon)*, ii. 725.

Wadham and Latton *(Esher)*, ii. 753.

Walmesley *(Burstow)*, ii. 284.

Walsingham *(Croydon)*, ii. 540.

Warren, Sir George *(Fetcham)*, i. folding at 482.

Warren, *(Dorking)*, i. folding at 553.

Webb *(Witley)* ; see Smith.

Westbrook *(Witley)*, ii. 45.

Weston *of Sutton*, i. 135, 136.

Weston *of West Horsley*, iii. folding at 41.

White *of Worplesdon*, iii. 94.

White *of Farnham*, iii. 177.

Wight *of Brabœuf*, i. 88.

Wight *(Betchworth)* ; see Leigh.

Windsor and Berners *(West Horsley)*, iii. 37.

Wilson *(Merton)*, i. 263.

Winterton, Earls of; see Turnour.

Wood *(Coulsdon)*, ii. 453.

Woodroffe *(Seale)*, iii. 176.

Wyke of *Worplesdon*, iii. 93.

Wymeldon, Stydolf, and Tryon, *(Mickleham)*, ii. 651.

Zouch, Lords, i. 125.

157.—The History and Antiquities of the Parish of Lambeth. By Thomas Allen. *London*, 1827. 8vo.

Albemarle and Devon, Earls of, facing 274.

Leigh *of Stockwell*, facing 277.

158.— County Genealogies. Pedigrees of Surrey Families. Collected by William Berry. *London*, 1837. Folio. *Published with Berkshire and Buckinghamshire.*

Atwood, 44.

Austen, 94.

Avelyn, 75.

Batley, 10.

Beaumont, 81.

Bedford, Duke of, 61.

Benyon, 11.

Boothby, 58.

Boscawen, 77.

Brahm ; see De Brahm.

Brander, 92.

Bray, 37, 59.

Brooke, 58.
Browne, 81.
Buckle, 18.
Budgen, 64.
Burgatt, 23.
Burnett, 91.
Byne, 83.
Camell, 56.
Carew, 1.
Cave, 60.
Chandos, Lord, 61.
Chicheley, 103.
Codington, 28.
Copley, 85.
Crowe, 18.
Dawson, 27.
De Brahm, 69.
Dorril, 30.
Duncannon, Visct. 14.
Duncombe, 47.
Dyke, 61.
Eliott, 23.
Emily, 89.
Evelyn, 75.
Fassett, 92.
Garth, 73.
Gee, 8.
Glover, 106.
Gould, 8.
Hackett, 11.
Hallowell, 9.
Harcourt, Visct. 78.
Hart, 60.
Holman, 71.
Hoskins, 32.
Hussey, 57.
Ingram, 49.
Jordan, 28.

Kenrick, 96.
Lambert, 52, 97, 98.
Lee, 34.
Leigh, 102.
Lifield, 62.
Lovett, 60.
Margetson, 15.
Molyneux, 87.
Moore, 87.
Mulcaster, 67.
Nash, 93.
Northey, 53.
Otho, or Other, 1.
Plecy or Plessey, 56.
Pinchon, 54.
Ponsonby, 14.
Reeves, 18.
Reynes, 47.
Richardson, 17.
Rowed, 107.
Saunder, 40.
Scawen, 43.
Skinner, 25.
Smyth, 65.
Steere, 34.
Sturt, 48.
Throckmorton, 6.
Verney, 59.
Vincent, 62.
Warren, 39.
Webb, 54, 66.
Weston, 55.
Wigsell, 44.
Wilks, 27.
Windsor, 1.
Witts, 34.
Wolffe, 54.
Wycker, 15.

159.—A Topographical History of Surrey. By EDWARD
WEDLAKE BRAYLEY, F.S.A. *Dorking,* 1841-1848.
5 vols. royal 8vo., and 4to.

Austen *of Shalford,* v. 139.
Evelyn *of Wotton,* v. 25.
Gaynsford, Zouch, Tate and Long,
   v. 301.
Long; see Gaynsford.

Tate; see Gaynsford.
Warren and Surrey, Earls of, i. 113.
Weston *of West Horsley,* ii. 81.
Zouch; see Gaynsford.

160.—The History and Antiquities of Lambeth. By JOHN
TANSWELL. *London,* 1858. 8vo.

Leigh *of Stockwell,* 40.

124

161.—Surrey Archæological Collections. Published by the
Surrey Archæological Society. *London*, 1858-1865.
3 vols. 8vo.

Barker, ii. 105.
Cobham *of Sterborough Castle*, ii.
folding at 169.
Lumley, John Lord, paternal descendants of, iii. 332.

Parker, ii. 209.
Uvedale *of Titsey, and of Wickham,
Hants*, iii. 185.
Whitgift, ii. 202.

162.—Genealogical and Heraldic Memoranda relating to the
County of Surrey. Published with the Surrey Archæological Collections, by the Surrey Archæological Society.
8vo. At the end of each volume, but not paged.

Abbot *of Guildford*, ii.
Alleyn *of Dulwich*, ii.
Angell *of Crowhurst*, iii.
Banester *of Croydon*, ii.
Benet *of Morden*, ii.
Bludder *of Reigate*, iii.
Boteler *of Croydon*, iii.
Bowyer *of Camberwell*, iii.
Bradbridge *of Lambeth*, ii.
Brereton *of Mitcham*, ii.
Burton *of Carshalton*, ii.
Bynd *of Carshalton*, ii.
Bysh *of Burstow*, iii.
Carew *of Beddington*, i.
Clifton *of Worplesdon*, ii.
Cole *of Petersham*, ii.
Copley *of Gatton*, iii.
Digges *of Reigate*, i.
Drake *of Reigate*, ii.
Duke *of Camberwell*, iii.
Farrant *of Mitcham*, ii.
Finch *of Croydon*, ii.
Garthe *of Morden*, ii.

Harris *of Kingston*, ii.
Harris *of Croydon*, ii.
Hobbes *of Tootingbecke*, ii.
Hoskins of *Oxsted*, iii.
James *of Reigate*, iii.
Kemp *of Croydon*, ii.
Knightley *of Kingston*, ii.
Lloyd *of Cheam*, ii.
Litton *of Wallington*, ii.
Morton *of Croydon*, ii.
Onslow *of Knoll*, iii.
Parkhurst *of Guildford*, ii.
Polsted *of Albury*, ii.
Ryther of *Reigate*, iii.
Smithe *of Mitcham*, ii.
Thompson *of Streatham*, iii.
Thurland *of Reigate*, ii.
Tichborne *of Reigate*, ii.
Tirrell *of Reigate*, ii.
Tonstall *of Addiscombe*, ii.
Waterer *of Woking*, iii.
Wyvell *of Croydon*, ii.

SUSSEX.

163.—A History of the Western Division of the County
of Sussex. Vol. 1, Rape of Chichester. By JAMES
DALLAWAY, M.B., F.A.S. Vol. 2, Part 1, Rape of
Arundel. By JAMES DALLAWAY, M.B., F.A.S. 2nd
edition. Edited by EDM. CARTWRIGHT, M.A., F.A.S.
Vol. 2, Part 2, Rape of Bramber. By EDM. CART-
WRIGHT, M.A., F.A.S. *London*, 1815-1830. Royal 4to.

Alcocke *of Trotton*, i. 219.
Alford (*Broadwater*), II. ii. 30.
Att Milne, or Mille *of Gretham*, II.
i. 239; 2 ed. 271.

Apsley *of Thakeham*, II. ii. 243.
Apsley *of Pulborough*, II. i. 320;
2 ed. 356.

Arundel, Earls of, II. i. 109; 2 ed. 117.
Att Fenne, or Fenner *of West Wittering*, i. 16.
Aylwin *of Treyford*, i. 200.
Bartelott *of Stopham*, II. i. 312; 2 ed. 348.
Bartelott *of Ernley*, i. 28.
Belingham; see Power.
Bellingham; see Clothall.
Bellingham (*Old Shoreham*), II. ii. 116.
Benion *of Aldingbourn*, i. 77.
Bettesworth *of Chithurst*, i. 226.
Bettesworth *of Fyning Rogate*, i. 212.
Bettesworth *of Fitz Hall*, i. 228.
Bettesworth *of Milland*, i. 220.
Bickley *of Chidham*, i. 83.
Biddulph *of Burton*, II. i. 251; 2 ed. 282.
Bisshop *of Parham*, Barons Zouche, II. i. 204; 2 ed. 235.
Blake *of Horsham*; see Goble.
Blount (*Slynfold*), II. i. 254; 2 ed. 390.
Blunt *of Crabbet*; see Sheppard.
Bohun, Lords of Midhurst, i. 282.
Bohun and Cooke, II. i. 23; 2 ed. 22.
Bowyer *of North Mundham*, i. 61.
Bradbridge and Hussey (*Slynfold*), II. i. 355; 2 ed. 391.
Braose (*Bramber*), II. ii. 174.
Bridger (*Ashurst*), II. ii. 265.
Brodnax; see Lewknor.
Browne, Viscounts Montagu, i. 241.
Browne *of Cowdray*, i. 251.
Burrell *of Knepp Castle*, II. ii. 295.
Butler and Clough *of Warminghurst*, II. ii. 255.
Byne (*Washington*), II. ii. 131.
Camoys *of Trotton*, i. 217.
Carrell or Caryll *of Harting*, i. 190.
Cawley *of Chichester*, i. app. to Chichester.
Challen; see Comber.
Chapman; see Rose.
Chatfield *of Oving*, i. 69.
Churcher (*Slynfold*), II. i. 359; 2 ed. 394.
Clothall, Bellingham, Boys and Ferris (*Thakeham*), II. ii. 245.

Colbrond *of Chichester*, i. app. to Chichester.
Coldham *of Stedham*, i. 230.
Colebrooke *of Arundel*, II. i. 52; 2 ed. 54.
Combre and Challen *of Shermanbury*, II. ii. 323.
Cooke (*Goring*), II. i. 36; 2 ed. 39.
Cooke; see Bohun.
Cooke *of West Burton*, II. i. 236; 2 ed. 268.
Copley; see Hoo.
Cowper (*Slynfold*), II. i. 356; 2 ed. 392.
Cowper *of Ditcham*, i. 194.
De Alta Ripa, or Dawtrey, II. i. 261; 2 ed. 292.
De Alta Ripa, De Haut Rey, or Dawtrey, II. i. 296; 2 ed. 232.
Dawtrey; see De Alta Ripa.
De Michelgrove; see Fauconer.
Dennett *of Woodmancote*, II. ii. 284.
Devenish; see Tawke.
Devenish *of Chichester*, i. app. to Chichester.
Doning *of Chichester and Rye*, i. app. to Chichester.
Drury *of Stoughton*, i. 161.
Edmundes and Elliot (*Yapton*), II. i. 43; 2 ed. 46.
Elliot; see Edmundes.
Elson *of Oving*, i. 68.
Ernley *of Ernley*, i. 25.
Fagg and Goring *of Wiston*, II. ii. 151.
Farrington *of Chichester*, i. app. to Chichester.
Fauconer, alias De Michelgrove, II. ii. 75.
Ferris; see Clothall.
Fitz Aucher (*Bosham*), i. 87.
Fitz Roger (*Mundham*), i. 65.
Ford *of East Harting*, i. 192.
Forster (*Trotton*), i. 219.
Frankland *of Muntham*, II. ii. 90.
Garton, Orme and Sargent, II. i. 244; 2 ed. 275.
Garway (*Ford*), II. i. 48; 2 ed. 50.
Goble and Blake (*Horsham*), II. ii. 342.
Goring *of Goring, Lancing and Bodecton*, II. i. 249; 2 ed. 281.
Goring ((*Washington*), II. ii. 133.

Goring; see Fagg.
Gounter *of Racton*, i. 154.
Gratwick (*Tortington*), II. i. 79; 2 ed. 85.
Gratwicke *of Angmering*, II. i. 66; 2 ed. 69.
Grey (*Woolbeding*), i. 235.
Gunter *of Chichester*, i. app. to Chichester.
Hamper (*West Tarring*), II. ii. 4.
Henshaw (*Billinghurst*) II. i. 345; 2 ed. 381.
Higgins; see Hygons.
Hilton (Billinghurst), II. i. 348; 2 ed. 384.
Hinton and Baverstock (*Lyminster*), 2 ed. II. i. facing 53.
Hoese; see Hosatus.
Holmes (*Burpham*), 2 ed. II. i. facing 213.
Hosatus, Hoese or Hussey, Lords of Harting, i. 188.
Howard, House of, II. i. 142; 2 ed. 161.
Howard, II. ii. 185.
Hoo and Copley (*Horsham*), II. ii. 339.
Hussey; see Hosatus.
Hussey; see Bradbridge.
Hygous or Higgins (*Bury*), II. i. 236; 2 ed. 267.
Jenman (*North Marden*), i. 186.
Jerman (*Racton*), i. 155.
Juxon (*Albourne*), II. ii. 289.
Juxon *of Chichester*, i. app. to Chichester.
Kempe, Archbishop of Canterbury, i. 59.
Kempe *of Slyndon*, i. 150.
Knight and Martin (*Lyminster*), II. i. facing 51; 2 ed. 53.
Knight; see Lewknor.
Lee and Steere (*Kirdford*), II. i. 334; 2 ed. 371.
Lee *of Fittleworth*. II. i. 308; 2 ed. 343.
Lewes *of Tortington*, II. i. 79; 2 ed. 85.
Levitt *of Fittleworth*, II. i. 309; 2 ed. 345.
Lewknor *of West Dean*, i. folding at 167.

Lewknor, May, Brodnax and Knight (*Lyminster*), II. i. facing 50; 2 ed. 53.
Lewknor *of Trotton*, i. 218.
Lloyd *of Lancing*, II. ii. 46.
Maltravers, Barony of, II. i. 132; 2 ed. 143.
Martin; see Knight.
May *of Rawmere in Mid Lavent*, i. 114.
May; see Lewknor.
Merlott *of Mundham*, i. 65.
Mervyn *of Durford*, i. 213.
Michell, Shelley and Pilfold (*Warnham*), II. ii. 367.
Middleton (*Horsham*), II. ii. 337.
Mille *of Camoys Court and Wolbeding*, i. 233.
Mille; see Att Milne-
Miller *of Chichester*, i. app. to Chichester.
Montacute, with Neville and Pole i. 250.
Montague, Viscounts; see Browne.
Morley (*Boxgrove*), i. 132.
Mowbray (*Bramber*), II. ii. 181.
Naldrett (*Rudgwick*), II. i. 350; 2 ed. 386.
Nash (*Walberton*), II. i. 73; 2 ed. 77.
Neville; see Montacute.
Oneley (*Pulborough*), II. i. 319; 2 ed. 354.
Onslow *of Dungewick*, II. i. 340; 2 ed. 376.
Orme; see Garton.
Owen (*Easebourn*), i. 242.
Page *of Donnington*, i. 54.
Palmer *of Angmering*, i. 53, II. i. 62; 2 ed. 66.
Palmer *of Parham*, II. i. 204; 2 ed. 232.
Peachey (*South Bersted*), i. 44.
Peachey, Barons Selsey, i. folding at 166.
Peckham *of Chichester*, i. app. to Chichester.
Peckham *of Nyton*, i. 78.
Peckham *of Boxgrove*, i. 143.
Peckham *of Little Green in Compton*, i. 180.
Peckham *of Up Marden*, i. 183.
Pellatt (*Bognor*), II. i. 217; 2 ed. 248.

Pellatt (*Steyning*), II. ii. 160.
Peverel (*Sompting*), II. ii. 97.
Percy (*Petworth*), II. i. 269 ; 2 ed. 302.
Pilfold (*Warnham*) ; see Michell.
Pole ; see Montacute.
Power and Belingham (*Lyminster*), II. i. 51; 2 ed. 54.
Poyntz *of Cowdray*, i. 284.
Richardson *of Ferring, Goring, and Findon*, II. i. 30 ; 2 ed. *ib.*
Riggs *of Hollest*, i. 240.
Rishton *of Ernley, (from Lanc.)* i. 28.
Rose and Chapman *of Eastergate*, i. 120.
Ryman ; see Tawke.
St. John, Lords of Halnaker, i. 124.
Sandham, i. 70.
Sargent ; see Garton.
Selsey, Barons ; see Peachey.
Shelley *of Castle Goring*, II. i. 38 ; 2 ed. 40.
Shelley (*Clapham*), II. ii. 76.
Shelley (*Warnham*) ; see Michell.
Shelley (*Thakeham*), II. ii. 244.
Sheppard and Blunt (*Horsham*), II. ii. 342.
Shirley *of West Grinstead*, II. ii. 307.
Shirley *of Wiston*, II. ii. 139.
Sidney *of Kingsham House*, i. 195.
Smyth *of Binterton*, i. 167.
Stanley *of Fittleworth*, II. i. 309 ; 2 ed. 344.
Steere ; see Lee.

Stoughton *of Chichester*, i. app. to Chichester.
Tawke and Ryman with Devenish; i. 96.
Thomas *of Yapton*, II. i. 44; 2 ed. 46, Thomas *of Dale Park*, II. i. 187. 2 ed. 216.
Threel *of Loxwood*, II. i. 341; 2 ed. 377.
Tudcroft *of Horsham*, II. ii. 341.
Tregos alias Tregoze (*Goring*), II. i. 35 ; 2 ed. 37.
Turner (*Bignor*), II. i. 217 ; 2 ed. 249.
Turnour, Earls of Winterton, (*Compton*), II. i. 332; 2 ed. 369.
Tutt or Tutte, i. app. to Chichester.
Ward *of West Grinstead*, II. ii. 311.
Warren and Surrey, Earls of, II. ii. 121; 2 ed. 128.
Wase *of Sullington*, II. ii. 123.
West (*Broadwater*), II. ii. 27.
West (*Woodmancote*), II. ii. 284.
Westbrooke (*Ferring*), II. i. 29; 2 ed. *ib.*
Williams *of Chichester*, i. app. to Chichester.
Winterton, Earls of ; see Turnour.
Wolf (*Ashington*), II. ii. 260.
Wyndsor (*South Harting*), i. 191.
Wyseman (*Mid Lavent*), i. 113.
Yaldwyn *of Blackdown*, II. i. 326 ; 2 ed. 363.
Young (*South Ambresham*), i. 280.
Zouche, Barony of, II. i. 203 ; 2 ed. 234.

164.—The History and Antiquities of Lewes. By the Rev. T. W. HORSFIELD, F.S.A. *Lewes*, 1824-1827. 2 vols. 4to.

Bridger *of Ashurst and Coombe*, ii. 130.
Burrell, i. folding at 329.
Campion *of Combwell, Kent, and Danny, Sussex*, ii. facing 171.
Challenor *of Chiltington and Stantons*, ii. 246.
Chichester, Earls of ; see Pelham.
Chowne of Alfreston, ii. 7.
De la Chambre *of Rodmill*, ii. 203.
Gage, i. folding at 340.

Hampton, Trevor-, Viscount Hampton, ii. facing 116.
Hay *of Glynde Bourne*, ii. 122.
Hay *of Tickeridge*, ii. 134.
Jefferay *of Chiddingly*, ii. 66.
Jenkinson *of Buxted, and of Pitchford, co. Salop*, ii. facing 44.
Law *of Horsted Parva*, ii. 135.
Medley *of Buxted, Friston, Coneybarrows*, ii. facing 54.

Michelborne *of Broadhurst and Stanmer*, ii. folding at 217.

Middleton *of Alceston*, ii. 15.

Morley and Morley- Trevor *of Glynde*, ii. facing 117.

Newton *of Southover*, i. facing 247.

Pelham, Earls of Chichester, i. folding at 340.

Ridge (*Iford*), ii. facing 138.

Shelley *of Michelgrove and Maresfield*, ii. facing 176*.

Shelley *of Patcham and Lewes*, ii. folding at 180*.

Shurley *of Isfield*, ii. 145.

Spence *of South Malling*, ii. folding at 172.

Springett *of Ringmer and Plumpton*, ii. 194.

Stapley *of Framfield and Patcham*, ii. 110.

Thatcher *of Ringmer*, ii. 189.

Warnett *of Framfield*, ii. 106.

165.—County Genealogies. Pedigrees of the Families in the County of Sussex. By WILLIAM BERRY. *London*, 1830. Folio.

Acland, 76, 206.
Alchorne, 96, 274.
Alcock, 108.
Alford, 302.
Alfrey, 244, 245.
Allfray, 29.
Allen, 361.
Alman, 81.
Alwin, or Aylwin, 167.
Amherst, or Amhurst, 212.
Anstey, 361.
Ap Howell, 324.
Ap Rhese, 203.
Apsley, 150.
Archer, 235.
Arderne, 267.
Ashburnham, 28, 185.
Aylwin ; see Alwin.
Aynscombe, alias Ayniscamp, 98.
Baker, 194, 225.
Ballard, 116.
Barlow, 164.
Bartlett, Bartlott, Bartelott, 178, 201.
Baskett, 218.
Bathurst, 151.
Bayley, 235.
Bayton, 54.
Beale, 26.
Beard, 111. 211.
Beauclerk, 1.
Bellingham, 190, 318.
Benion, 119.
Bennett, 52.
Bettesworth, 34, 104, 134.
Bettsworth, 76, 92.

Bickley, 77.
Biddulph, 219.
Bind, or Byne, 186.
Birch, 25.
Birsty, or Birchanstey.
Blachford, 161.
Blaker, 86.
Blount, or Blunt, 285.
Bonville, 61.
Boord, 270.
Booth, 252.
Bowyer, 134, 363.
Boys, 190, 318.
Bradbruge, 287.
Brand, 174.
Bridger, 109.
Brodnax, 21.
Brooke, 144, 274.
Browne, 237, 254, 350.
Bryan, 110.
Buckle, 22.
Bufkin ; see Buskin.
Bulman, 361.
Bungey, 319.
Burrell, 41.
Burton, 333.
Busbridge, 3.
Busking, or Bufkin, 103.
Butler, 176.
Butterwicke, 271.
Butts, 31.
Byndlos, 48.
Byne ; see Bind.
Bysshe, 199.
Bysshopp, 213.
Bythesea, 236.

Camber, 256.
Campion, 9, 82.
Caarleton, 232.
Carr, 40.
Carrell, 237.
Carrill, 359.
Carryll, 72.
Cawley, 284.
Challenor, 73, 345.
Chapman, 88.
Charleton, 237.
Chatfield, 5.
Chichester, Marquis of Donegal, 6.
Chisim, 30.
Chowne, 133.
Churchar, 48.
Clark, 86.
Clerke, 337.
Clothall, 318.
Colbrand, 183.
Coldham, 2.
Cole, 307.
Colebrook, 94.
Colepeper, 136.
Collins, 89.
Colwell, 320.
Comber, 142.
Commerell, 93.
Compton, 50, 364.
Constable, 369.
Cooke, 105, 373, 374.
Cooper, 99, 377.
Cooper or Cowper, 145.
Copley, 296.
Courthope, 216.
Coventry, 260.
Covert, 18, 321.
Cowper, 194, 276.
Cox, 8.
Cradock, 218.
Crips or Crispe, 360.
Cromer, 318.
Crump, 337.
Curteis, 214.
Culpepper, Culpeper or Colpeper, 341.
Dalbiac, 65.
Dalrymple, 151.
Darrell, 165.
Davies, 153.
Dawtry, 46.
De Alta Ripa, 46.
De Capell, 274.

Dee, 161.
De Haia, 61.
De Hoese, 344.
De Kendale, 173.
De la Chambre, 17, 274.
Derby, Earl of, 76.
Dering, 138, 241.
Dicker, 277.
Dickins, 367.
Dobell, 166.
Donegal ; Marquis of ; see Chichester.
Donynge, 260.
Douce, 96.
Drury, 202.
Dunmoll, 100.
Dyke, 138, 148, 196.
Dyne, 162.
Edmonds, 44.
Edwards, 116, 325.
Elfred, 19.
Ellis, 342.
Elson, 40.
Ernley, 46.
Evelyn, 74.
Eversfield, 154.
Fagg, 255, 262.
Fane, 47.
Farendon, 372.
Farington, 41.
Fenner, 139.
Fermor, 180.
Ferris, 319.
Fetherston, or Fetherstonhaugh, 233.
Finch, 336.
Fitz Pons, or Poyntz, 352.
Ford, 182.
Forster, 7, 192, 320, 329, 375.
Foster, 154.
Fowle, 194, 230.
Fowler, 104.
Franck, 326.
Frebody, 327.
Freeland, 52.
Freeman, 291.
Fuller, 279.
Fynes, 331.
Gage, 295.
Gardner, 334.
Garth, 368.
Garton, 152.
Gason, 283.

8

Gee, 368.
Gelderidge, 155.
Giddy, 153.
Gilbert, 154, 320.
Goch, 324.
Godman, 347.
Goodwin, 332.
Goring, 138, 154.
Gott, 242.
Gratwick, 146, 168, 169, 170, 256.
Gray, or Grey, 208.
Gresham, 238.
Grey, Lord, 182.
Grey, 374.
Grey ; see Gray.
Griffin, 233.
Gunter, or Gounter, 13.
Guy, 54.
Hall, 32, 106.
Hawley, 272.
Hawtayne, 234.
Hay, 118, 311.
Heath, 256.
Henshaw, 53.
Hepden, 303.
Herbert, *alias* Finch, 336.
Hever, 330.
Higgens, 71.
Higham, 338.
Hill, 320.
Hilton, 103.
Hodgson, 339.
Holland, 185, 190, 379.
Honywood, 38, 137.
Hooke, 193.
Horspoole, 318.
Hosatus, De Hoese, or Hussey, 344.
Houghton, 163.
Hubble, 96.
Humpbry, 52.
Hurly, 71.
Hussey, 126, 287, 344.
Inskipp, 246.
Isted, 129.
Jefferay, 156.
Jenkin, 250, 252.
Jenkinson, 248.
Jenner, 275.
Jermin, or Jermyn, 184.
Kemp, 236.
Kempe, 75.
Kendale, 173.

Kingstone, 61.
Kinleside, 169.
Knight, 21, 130, 131.
Lade, 247.
Lamb, 319.
Langham, 273.
Law, 121.
Ledgard, 267.
Lee, or Leigh, 340.
Leech, 7.
Leicester, Earls of ; see Sidney.
Leigh ; see Lee.
Leland, 306.
Lenox, Dukes of Richmond, 1.
Le Power, 318.
Levett, 229.
Levitt, 373.
Lewes, 104, 169.
Lewknor, 130, 343.
Lipping, 53.
Littleboys, 166.
Long, 206.
Love, 96.
Luck, 187.
Lunsford, 312.
Luther, 47.
Lyndsay, 317.
Lyston, 340.
Manning, 260.
Mantell, 20.
Margesson, 258.
Markwick, 155.
Marlborough, Duke of ; see Spencer.
Marlott, 122.
Marshall, 357.
Martyn, 131.
Mascall, 328.
Matthew, 9.
Maunser, 309.
May, 21, 29, 36, 56.
Medley, 74.
Meeres, 255.
Melward, 156.
Meres,, 81.
Mervyn, 92.
Michelborne, 50.
Michell, 123, 124, 137, 346.
Middleton, 4, 107, 231.
Mill, 90, 146.
Miller, 142, 292.
Minshull, 376.
Molyneux, Visct., 359.
Monk, 105.

Monke, 102.
More, 119.
Morley, 76, 134, 173.
Morton, 322.
Naldrett, 92.
Nash, 103.
Newbury, Earl of; see Radcliffe.
Newcastle, Duke of, 314, 315.
Newington, 158.
Newman, 207.
Newton, 24, 128.
Noell, 134.
Norden, 286.
North, 221.
Nowell, 334.
Noye, 153.
Olliver, 170.
Oneley, 197.
Osbaldeston, 76.
Oxenham, 206.
Page, 141.
Palmer, 206, 276.
Panton, 371.
Parker, 12, 249.
Parnell, 81.
Paul, 1.
Pay, 113.
Payne, 164.
Peachey, 54, 106.
Peck; see Pecke.
Pecke, or Peck, 97.
Peckham, 58, 305.
Peirs, 261.
Pelham, 313.
Pellatt, 177.
Phipps, 305.
Pickering, 362.
Pigott, 192.
Pilfold, 123.
Polhill, 264.
Polsted, 243.
Pope, 365.
Porter, 200.
Powell, 243, 324.
Power; see Le Power.
Powis, 27.
Powlett, 61.
Poynings, 61.
Poyntz, 352.
Radcliffe, Earls of Newbury, 75.
Radcliffe, 108, 204.
Raines, 235.

Ralfe, 223.
Raper, 95.
Ravenscroft, 32.
Rayman; see Ryman, 57.
Relfe, 282.
Reve, 110.
Reynell, 233.
Rhese, Ap, 203.
Richardson, 49, 259.
Richmond, Duke of; see Lenox.
Ridge, 11.
Rigges, or Riggs, 190.
Rishton, 306.
Roberts, 29.
Rootes, 242.
Rose, 25.
Rowe, 117.
Russell, 235.
Sackvill, 300.
St. John, 61, 138.
Sandham, 51, 71, 307.
Saris, 149.
Savage, 96.
Scardeville, 46.
Scott, 310, 370.
Scras, or Scrase, 366.
Selwin, 114.
Sergeant, 358.
Shadwell, 369.
Sharp, 220.
Sheldon, 25.
Shelley, 62.
Sheppard, 308.
Shiffner, 109.
Shirley, 172.
Shurley, Sherly, or Shirly, 204.
Shoyswell, 84.
Shuckburgh, 74.
Sidney, Earls of Leicester, 298, 299.
Sidney, 297, 299.
Smith, 59, 275, 346.
Smyth, 201.
Smyth, late Bartelott, 179.
Snelling, 3.
Somerfall, 340.
Southland, 317.
Spence, 26.
Spencer, 318.
Spencer, Dukes of Marlborough, 1.
Springett, 33, 240.
Stafford, 268.
Stanley, 45, 188.

Stany, 71.
Stapley, 85.
Stone, 78, 79, 129, 347.
Stonestreet, 235.
Stonestreet, Griffin-, 233.
Stopham, 178.
Supple, 274.
Syston, or Lyston, 340.
Taylor, 306.
Temple, 3.
Thatcher, 157.
Thomas, 291, 299.
Thomason, 234.
Thorp, 348.
Threele, 132, 273.
Towers, 217.
Trayton, 80.
Tredcroft, 16, 155.
Tresham, 237.
Trevor, 174.
Turner, 86, 370.
Turnour, 368.
Tutté, 118, 289.
Wade, 230
Walleys, 173.
Walsingham, 96.

Walwin, 376.
Warnett, 129.
Wase, 125.
Webb, 101.
Wenham, 257.
West, 14.
Westbrook, 171.
Wheatley, 224.
Whitchorne, 246.
Whitfield, 15, 22.
Wildigos, 10.
Williams, 120, 261.
Wilson, 209, 333.
Wiltshire, 318.
Wimble, 60.
Wolf, 55.
Wood, 46, 189, 311.
Woodford, 201.
Woodward, 130.
Woolgar, 101.
Worge, 274.
Wright, 201.
Wrothe, 76, 206.
Wyseman, 107.
Yalwin, 195.
Yonge, 269.

166.—A Graphic and Historical Sketch of Bodyam Castle in Sussex. By WILLIAM COTTON, F.S.A. *London*, 1831. Imp. 8vo.

Dalyngrudge and Lewknor, 11.

167.—The History and Antiquities of the Castle and Town of Arundel. By the Rev. M. A. TIERNEY, F.S.A. *London*, 1834. 8vo. 2 vols. royal 8vo.

Albini, 168.
Fitz Alan, Earls of Arundel (2 Tables), folding at 192.

Howard, Dukes of Norfolk, (3 Tables), folding at 350.

168.—Visitation of Sussex, 1570. Foolscap folio. Privately printed by Sir THOMAS PHILLIPPS, Bart. The same volume contains the Visitations of Oxfordshire of 1574 and 1634.

Agmondesham *of Petworth*, 1.
Ashbornham *of Ashbornham*, 1.
Barentine *of Plompton*, 1.
Barington *of Raile*, 1.
Bartelott *of Stopham*, 2.
Bartelott *of Redland*, 2.
Bickley *of Chidham*, 2.

Burton *of East Bourton*, 12.
Bowyer *of Petworth*, 2.
Chaderton *of Eston*, 2.
Chalener *of Hampsted*, 3.
Chalener of *Childington*, 3.
Chatfield *of Bedyles*, 3.
Conuers *of Winchelsey*, 3.

Cooke *of West Burton*, 3.
Dawtrey *of The More*, 4.
Devenish *of Helingleighe*, 4.
Doninge *of Rye*, 4.
Eccleston *of Winchelsey*, 4.
Erneley *of Erneley*, 4.
Fynes *of Claverham*, 5.
Garton *of Billinghurst*, 5.
Goreinge *of Burton*, 5.
Gounter *of Racton*, 5.
Harbotle *of Goslinge*, 6.
Hensley *of Lynueld*, 6.
Hygons *of Bery*, 6.
Hobsonn *of Hastings*, 6.
Jefferay *of Chitingleighe*, 6.
Legg *of Chichester*, 6.
Lewknor *of Trotton*, 7.
Line *of Chichester*, 7.
Lunsford *of Hothley*, 7.
Midleton *of Winchelsey*, 7.
Mills *of Grattam*, 8.
Morley *of Glynd*, 8.

Michelborne and Naldrett *of Coke-feld*, 8.
Nowell *of Boniton*, 8.
Parker *of Ratton*, 8.
Peck *of Winchelsey*, 8.
Palmer *of Parham*, 9.
Playsted *of Arlington*, 9.
Riman *of Apledram*, 9.
Roberth *of Battell*, 9.
Rowse *of Rogate*, 9.
Scott *of Mote*, 9.
Selwyn *of Fryston*, 10.
Sharp *of Northiam*, 10.
Shephard *of Pesmarch*, 10.
Shirley *of Wiston*, 10.
Tawke *of Apeldram*, 10.
Temys *of London*, 10.
Theccher *of Presthawes*, 11.
Wallis *of Sussex*, 11.
Warnet *of Framfield*, 11.
Whitfield *of Winchelsey*, 11.
Wells *of Bonksted*, 12.

169.—Sussex Archæological Collections. Published by the Sussex Archæological Society. First Series. *London*, 1848-1860. 12 vols. 8vo. Second Series. *Lewes*, 1861-1865. 5 vols. 8vo.

Apsley, iv. 220.
Bodiam; see De Bodiam.
Bordé, Boord, or Board *of Cuckfield and Lingfield*, vi. 202.
Bowet, xi. 88.
Braose. v. 5. viii. 102.
Catherine *of Valois*, descendants of, vii. 27.
Culpeper, x. 154.
Dalyngruge *of Dalyngruge*, ix. 287.
De Bodiam, ix. 277.
De Wiston, v. 3.
Elphick *of Sutton*, vii. 132.
Eston, xvii. 130.
Eu, Earls of, x. 67.
Fuller *of Tanners*, xiii. 98.
Harbotell, xiv. 113.
Harrison or Harison *of Sutton*, vii. 133.
Hoese or Hussey *of Herting*, viii. 46.
Hoo, viii. 130.
Humphrey, vi. 191.
Hurdis, vii. 134.
Hussey; see Hoese.

Jeake, xiii. 78.
Kidder *of Maresfield*, ix. 130, 138.
Lewknor, iii. 92.
Monboucher, xiv. 113.
Newton *of Westby*, ix. 313.
Newton *of Cheshire*, ix. 337.
Newton *of Southover*, ix. 338.
Newton *of Lindfield*, ix. 339.
Newton *of East Mascalls*, ix. 340.
Noyes *of East Mascalls*, ix. 341.
Oxenbridge, viii. 231.
Pelham, iii. 214.
Poynings, xv. 14.
Pierpoint; see Warren.
Randolph, xiv. 114.
Scrase, viii. 14.
Wakehurst, x. 152.
Wardedieux *of Bodiam*, ix. 282.
Warren and Pierpoint, xi. 84.
Wayte, xvii. 130.
Weekes, xiv. 116.
Wilson, xi. 48, xii. 240.
Wymond, xvii. 129.

170.—Historical Notices of the Parish of Withyham, in the County of Sussex. (By the Hon. and Rev. REGINALD W. SACKVILLE-WEST, M.A.) *London*, 1857. 4to.

Cantilupe, 41.

171.—The Worthies of Sussex. By MARK ANTONY LOWER, M.A., F.S.A. *Lewes*, 1865. 4to.

Hayley, 154. | May *of Pashley*, 150.
Kempe, 108.

WARWICKSHIRE.

172.—The Antiquities of Warwickshire. By WILLIAM DUGDALE. *London*, 1656. Folio. Second edition. *London*, 1730. 2 vols. folio. Third edition. *Coventry*, 1765. Folio.

Adderley *(Wedington)*, 2 ed. ii. 1096.
Ailesbury and Somervile *(Easton)*, 610; 2 ed. ii. 828; 3 ed. 579.
Alesbury; see Piriton.
Alspath, &c. *(Mireden)*, 721; 2 ed. ii. 985; 3 ed. 697.
Archer *(Umberslade)*, 580; 2 ed. ii. 781; 3 ed. 547.
Arden, &c. *(Hampton in Arden)*, 696; 2 ed. ii. 952; 3 ed. 672.
Arden *(Cudworth)*, 675; 2 ed. ii. 925; 3 ed. 651.
Astley and Grey *(Astley)*, 70; 2 ed. i. 107; 3 ed. 74.
Astley *(Wolvey)*; 2 ed. i. 68.
Astley *(Hill Morton)*, 13; 2 ed. i. 19; 3 ed. 14.
Basset; see Stafford, Earl of.
Beauchamp *(Bobenhull)*, 32; 2 ed. i. 48; 3 ed. 34.
Beaufo; see Hugford.
Bereford and Nasford *(Barford)*, 386; 2 ed. i. 487; 3 ed. 354.
Bermingham *(Bermingham)*, 656; 2 ed. ii. 898; 3 ed. 629.
Beynvill; see Wapenbury.
Biddulph *(Birdingbury)*; 2 ed. i. 324.
Bishopsdon *(Bishopston)*, 526; 2 ed. ii. 701; 3 ed. 488.
Blithe, &c. *(Blithe)*, 755; 3 ed. 742.
Blithe *(Kingshurst)*; 2 ed. ii. 1021.

Boteler; see Sudley.
Botiller, Nevill, Gascoin, &c. *(Oversley)*, 628; 2 ed. ii. 854; 3 ed. 598.
Botreaux *(Alcester)*, 572; 2 ed. ii. 768; 3 ed. 538.
Boun or Bohun *(Coundun)*; 2 ed. i. 133.
Bracebridge *(Kingsbury)*, 759; 2 ed. ii. 1056; 3 ed. 747.
Brandeston, Montfort, &c. *(Lapworth)*, 584; 2 ed. ii. 786; 3 ed. 551.
Bretun; see Chetwode.
Brome; see Wolverdinton.
Broughton *(Little Lawford)*, 66; 2 ed. i. 100; 3 ed. 70.
Browne; see Waver.
Burdet; see Burton.
Burdet; see Camvill.
Burdet; see De Valle.
Burton, Burdet, &c. *(Bourton super Dunsmore)*, 194; 2 ed. 289.
Camvill, Burdet, and Conway *(Arrow)*, 623; 2 ed. ii. 847; 3 ed; 593.
Canning *(Foxcote)*; 2 ed. i. 634.
Cantilupe *(Aston Cantlow)*, 613; 2 ed. ii. 833; 3 ed. 583.
Cantilupe; see Cumin.
Castello *(Withibrooke)*, 139; 2 ed. i. 214; 3 ed. 145.

Castello (*Nechells*), 644; 2 ed. ii. 881; 3 ed. 616.

Catesby (*Lapworth*), 585; 2 ed. ii. 788; 3 ed. 553.

Charnells and Trussel (*Bilton*), 18; 2 ed. i. 27; 3 ed. 19.

Cherlecote, Hasele, and Lucy (*Charlecote*), 399; 2 ed. i. 507; 3 ed. 368.

Chestre, Wodlow, Herthull, &c. (*Woodlow*), 373; 2 ed. i. 469; 3 ed. 340.

Chetwin (*Grendon*), 792; 2 ed. ii. 101; 3 ed. 779.

Chetwode, Turvile, Bretun, &c. 22; ed. i. 33; 3 ed. 24.

Clinton (*Maxstoke*), 726; 2 ed. ii. 993; 3 ed. 702.

Clinton and Mountfort (*Colshill*), 728; 2 ed. ii. 1007; 3 ed. 715.

Clinton; see Stivichale.

Clodshale (*Saltley*), 646; 2 ed. ii. 884; 3 ed. 619.

Clopton (*Clopton*), 524; 2 ed. ii. 698; 3 ed. 487.

Cockain (*Pooley*), 808; 2 ed. ii. 1120; 3 ed. 807.

Coke; see Wotton.

Cokesey; see Herdebergh.

Compton (*Compton Winyate*), 424; 2 ed. i. 549; 3 ed. 394.

Comyn (*Newbold Comin*), 295; 2 ed. i. 368; 3 ed. 257.

Coningsby (*Morton Bagot*), 567; 2 ed. ii. 760; 3 ed. 533.

Conway; see Camvill.

Corbin and Lygon (*Hall End*), 807; 2 ed. ii. 1119; 3 ed. 793.

Cotes (*Honingham*), 289; 2 ed. i. 358; 3 ed. 251.

Cressy; see Piriton.

Culpeper; see Hardreshull.

Culy, &c. (*Ansty*), 80; 2 ed. i. 123; 3 ed. 85.

Cumin, Cantilupe, and West (*Smithfield*), 504; 2 ed. ii. 661; 3 ed. 466.

Curli and Nevill (*Budbroke*), 501; 2 ed. ii. 656; 3 ed. 462.

Danet; see Wotton.

De Bosco, Lovel, and Zouch (*Clifton*), 7; 2 ed. i. 9; 3 ed. 8.

De Insula or L'Isle (*Moxhull*), 686; 2 ed. ii. 938; 3 ed. 661.

De la Launde (*Langdon*), 694; 2 ed. ii. 949; 3 ed. 670.

De Valle, Burdett, and Norrys (*Ludington*), 528; 2 ed. ii. 704; 3 ed. 491.

Digby (*Colshill*), 732; 2 ed. ii. 1012; 3 ed. 720.

Dugdale, 2 ed. ii. facing 1051.

Durvassell (*Spernall*), 565; 2 ed. ii. 757; 3 ed. 531.

Erdinton (*Erdington*), 650; 2 ed. ii. 889; 3 ed. 623.

Eton and Warren (*Ratley*), 419; 2 ed. i. 539; 3 ed. 389.

Ferrers (*Badsley Clinton*), 710; 2 ed. ii. 971; 3 ed. 685.

Ferrers (*Merevale*), 784; 2 ed. ii. 1089; 3 ed. 779.

Fielding (*Bernacle*), 2 ed. i. 64.

Fisher (*Packinton Magna*), 724; 2 ed. ii. 990; 3 ed. 700.

Gough (*Edgbaston*), 2 ed. ii. 896.

Grevill (*Alcester*), 570; 2 ed. ii. 763; 3 ed. 536.

Grevill (*Milcote*), 530; 2 ed. ii. 706; 3 ed. 493.

Grey; see Astley.

Griffith; see Somervile.

Hardreshull and Culpeper (*Hartshill*), 777; 2 ed. ii. 1080; 3 ed. 764.

Harewell and Smyth (*Wootton Wawen*), 600; 2 ed. ii. 809; 3 ed. 569.

Harpur (*Chesterton*), 381; 2 ed. i. 478; 3 ed. 348.

Hasele; see Cherlecote.

Hastang and Stafford (*Lemington Hastang*), 232; 2 ed. i. 316; 3 ed. 222.

Hastings, Nevill, &c. (*Fillongley*), 740, 743; 2 ed. ii. 1024, 1029; 3 ed. 726, 728.

Hayrun (*Church Lawford*), 20; 2 ed. i. 30; 3 ed. 22.

Herdebergh, Langley, &c. (*Harborow Magna*), 63; 2 ed. i. 92; 3 ed. 66.

Herdebergh, Strange, Talbot, Cokesey, Russel, &c. (*Willey*), 49; 2 ed. i. 73; 3 ed. 52.

Herdwick (*Herdwick*), 2 ed. i. 321.

Herthull (*Baginton*), 150; 2 ed. i. 229; 3 ed. 157.

Herthull ; see Chestre.

Holden (*Pipe*), 2 ed. ii. 893.

Holt (*Aston*), 638 ; 2 ed. ii. 871 ; 3 ed. 609.

Hore, Pudsey, &c. (*Langley*), 673 ; 2 ed. ii. 922 ; 3 ed. 647.

Hore (*Stonythorpe*), 282 ; 2 ed. i. 348 ; 3 ed. 243.

Hotham (*Solihull*), 689 ; 2 ed. ii. 942 ; 3 ed. 665.

Huband (*Ipsley*), 552 ; 2 ed. ii. 737 ; 3 ed. 519.

Hugford and Beaufo (*Emscote*), 187 ; 2 ed. 278 ; 3 ed. 196.

Ingram (*Wolford Parva*), 2 ed. i. 595.

Keynes ; see Piriton.

Keyt (*Stratford-super-Avon*), 2 ed. ii. 693.

Ladbroc (*Ladbroke*), 221 ; 2 ed. i. 331 ; 3 ed. 232.

Langley, Peto, &c. (*Pinley*), 135 ; 2 ed. i. 209 ; 3 ed. 140.

Langley ; see Herdebergh.

Limesi, Pinkney and Odingsels (*Long Ichington*), 228 ; 2 ed. i. 342 ; 3 ed. 239.

Lovel ; see De Bosco.

Lovell (*Burnell's Brome*), 546 ; 2 ed. ii. 728 ; 3 ed. 510.

Lucy ; see Cherlecote.

Lygon ; see Corbin.

Macer, or Megre (*Herberbury*), 284 ; 2 ed. i. 353 ; 3 ed. 247.

Malony ; see Wapenbury.

Mancestre (*Mancester*), 775 ; 2 ed. ii. 1077 ; 3 ed. 761.

Marmion, Frevile, Ferrers, &c. (*Tamworth*), 820 ; 2 ed. ii. 1135.

Maron (*Berkswell*), 718 ; 2 ed. ii. 981 ; 3 ed. 694.

Megre ; see Macer.

Meriett (*Whitchurch*), 2 ed. i. 635.

Midlemore (*Edgbaston*), 654 ; 2 ed. ii. 894 ; 3 ed. 627.

Montfort (*Beldesert*), 592 ; 2 ed. ii. 799 ; 3 ed. 560.

Montfort ; see Brandeston.

Mountfort ; see Clinton.

Murdac (*Compton Murdak*), 433 ; 3 ed. i. 563 ; 3 ed. 404.

Nasford ; see Bereford.

Napton and White (*Napton*), 223 ; 2 ed. i. 335 ; 3 ed. 234.

Newnham, &c. (*Newnham Padox*), 57 ; 2 ed. i. 85 ; 3 ed. 61.

Nevill ; see Curli.

Nevill ; see Hastings.

Norrys ; see De Valle.

Odinsells, &c. (*Solihull*), 688 ; 2 ed. ii. 940 ; 3 ed. 664.

Odingsels ; see Limesi.

Palmer *of Compton Scorfen*, 2 ed. i. 632.

Peche (*Hampton in Arden*), 698 ; 2 ed. ii. 954 ; 3 ed. 675.

Peto (*Chesterton*), 375 ; 2 ed. i. 472 ; 3 ed. 342.

Peto ; see Langley.

Pinkney ; see Limesi.

Piriton, Keynes, Alesbury, Cressy, &c. (*Oxhill*), 471 ; 2 ed. i. 671 ; 3 ed. 430.

Pipe (*Pipe*), 653 ; 2 ed. i. 892 ; 3 ed. 626.

Pudsey ; see Hore.

Purefey (*Burton Hastings*), 36 ; 2 ed. i. 54 ; 3 ed. 39.

Ralegh (*Farnborough*), 403 ; 2 ed. i. 529 ; 3 ed. 382.

Repington (*Amington*), 825 ; 2 ed. ii. 1143 ; 3 ed. 812.

Revell ; see Wapenbury.

Rokeby (*Rugby*), 16 ; 2 ed. i. 23 ; 3 ed. 17.

Rous (*Ragley*), 627 ; 2 ed. ii. 853 ; 3 ed. 597.

Ruggeley (*Dunton*), 683 ; 3 ed. ii. 934 ; 3 ed. 658.

Russel ; see Herdelergh.

Say, &c. (*Farnborough*), 412 ; 2 ed. i. 528 ; 3 ed. 381.

Sheldon (*Weston juxta Chiriton*), 2 ed. i. 584.

Shirley (*Nether Eatendon*), 474 ; 2 ed. i. 622 ; 3 ed. 433.

Skipwith (*Newbold Revell*), 2 ed. i. 84.

Smyth ; see Harewell.

Somervile and Griffith (*Stockton*), 227 ; 2 ed. i. 341 ; 3 ed. 238.

Somervile ; see Ailesbury.

Stafford, Earl of, Basset, &c. (*Sheldon*), 725 ; 2 ed. ii. 1004 ; 3 ed. 712.

Stafford ; see Hastang.

Stanhope ; see Wotton.

Stivichale, Clinton, &c. (*Hatton*), 493 ; 2 ed. ii. 651 ; 3 ed. 454.

Strange (*Walton D'Eivile*), 443 ; 2 ed. i. 577 ; 3 ed. 411.

Strange ; see Herdebergh.

Stutevill, &c. (*Newbold-super-Avon*), 64 ; 2 ed. i. 95 ; 3 ed. 68.

Sudley, Boteler, &c. 772 ; 2 ed. ii. 1073 ; 3 ed. 759.

Talbot ; see Herdebergh.

Temple ; see Wotton.

Throckmorton (*Coughton*), 559 ; 2 ed. ii. 749 ; 3 ed. 524.

Trussel ; see Charnells.

Trussell (*Billesley*), 537 ; 2 ed. ii. 714 ; 3 ed. 500.

Turvile ; see Chetwode.

Turvill and Charnels (*Bedworth*), 78 ; 2 ed. i. 119 ; 3 ed. 83.

Underhill (*Idlicote*), 2 ed. i. 607.

Verdon (*Brandon*), 29 ; 2 ed. i. 43 ; 3 ed. 31.

Verney (*Compton Murdak*), 435 ; 2 ed. i. 566 ; 3 ed. 406.

Walgrave ; see Wolverdinton.

Wapenbury, Beynvill, Revell, Malory, &c. (*Newbold Revell*), 55 ; 2 ed. i. 82 ; 3 ed. 58.

Warren ; see Eton.

Warwick, Earldom of, 303, 311 ; 2 ed. i. 378, 387 ; 3 ed. 266, 275.

Waver and Browne (*Cester Over*), 60 ; 2 ed. i. 90 ; 3 ed. 64.

West ; see Cumin.

Whitacre (*Whitacre Superior*), 749 ; 2 ed. ii. 1039 ; 3 ed. 735.

White ; see Napton.

Willoughby (*Midleton*), 757 ; 2 ed. ii. 1054 ; 3 ed. 744.

Windsor (*Havell Grange*), 2 ed. ii. 732.

Willington (*Hurley*), 2 ed. ii. 1063.

Wodlow ; see Chestre.

Wolvardinton, Brome and Walgrave (*Wolverton*), 506 ; 2 ed. ii. 665 ; 3 ed. 467.

Wotton, Stanhope, Coke, Danet and Temple (*Derset*), 2 ed. i. 523.

Zouche (*Bulkinton*), 39 ; 2 ed. i. 56 ; 3 ed. 42.

Zouche ; see De Bosco.

173.—*Manduessedum Romanorum :* being the History and Antiquities of the Parish of Manceter, &c. By the late BENJAMIN BARTLETT, Esq., F.A.S. (Miscellaneous Antiquities, Nichols.) *London,* 1791. 4to.

Arden, 165*, folding.

Bracebridge, 166*, folding.

Guy, 163*.

Ludford, 167*.

174.—History of the Town and School of Rugby. By NICHOLAS HARRIS NICOLAS, Esq., F.S.A. *Coventry and Northampton,* 1826. 4to. Part I.

Boughton and Hume, 38.

Burnaby, 36.

Caldecott, 40-44.

Hume ; see Boughton.

Rokeby, 3.

Stafford, folding at 96.

Talboys, 33.

Wyrley, 35.

175.—Stoneleigh Abbey, from its Foundation to the present time. By the Rev. F. L. COLVILE. 1835. Imp. 8vo. *Privately printed.*

Leigh, Lords, folding at 42.

176 —The Warwickshire Antiquarian Magazine. *Warwick,* 1859. Royal 8vo. 2 parts. Pedigrees not paged.

Betham *of Rowington.*
Bracebridge *of Atherstone.*
Brookes *of Hallaton.*
Coton *of Coton.*
Dilke *of Maxstoke.*
Knight *of Barrels.*
Ferrers *of Baddesley-Clinton.*

Fetherston *of Packwood.*
Mayne *of Elmdon.*
Newdigate *of Arbury.*
Newsham *of Chadshurst.*
Stratford *of Atherstone.*
Quiney *of Shottery.*
Ward *of Barford.*

177.—Warwickshire Pedigrees selected from the Visitation of the County of Warwick, 1682 and 1683. Royal 8vo. Privately Printed, twenty copies only. A.D. 1865.

Archer *of Upton.*
Betham *of Rowington.*
Bracebride *of Atherstone.*
Brookes *of Hallaton.*
Cookes *of Harbury.*
Coton *of Coton.*
Dakins *of Maxstoke.*
Dilke *of Maxstoke.*
Dugdale *of Shustoke.*
Eboral *of Balshall.*
Farmer *of Hartshill.*
Ferrers *of Badsley Clinton.*
Fetherston *of Packwood.*
Gibson *of Combe.*

Grevil *of Beachamps-Court.*
Holbech *of Fillongley.*
Knight *of Barrels.*
Mayne *of Elmdon.*
Newdigate *of Arbury.*
Newsham *of Chadshunt.*
Norton *of Coventry.*
Parker *of Hartshill.*
Phillips *of Studley.*
Quiney *of Shottery.*
Rawlins *of Marston.*
Stratford *of Atherstone.*
Ward *of Barford.*

178.—Shakespere's Home at New Place, Stratford-upon-Avon. By J. C. M. BELLEW. *London,* 1863. 8vo.

à Combe, John; see Clopton.
Clopton; see Walker.
Clopton, Sir Hugh, and John à Combe, &c., folding at 66.
Foster; see Nash.
Hales, of High Church, Somersetshire, facing 249.

Hales, folding at 246.
Hathaway, folding at 376.
Nash and Foster, folding at 349.
Shakespere, William, folding at 38.
Walker and Clopton, 20.
Underhill, folding at 87.

WESTMORELAND.

179.—The Heraldic Visitation of Westmoreland, made in the year 1615. By Sir RICHARD ST. GEORGE, Knt., Norroy King of Arms. *London,* 1853. 8vo. and 4to.

Bellingham, 29.
Benson, 22.
Bradley, 23.
Brathwaite, 3.
Briggs, 22.

Byndlosse, 1.
Carus, 11.
Dalston, 5.
Ducket, 15.
Lankaster, 41

Laybourne, 19.
Laybourne, 50.
Laybourne, 51.
Laybourne *of Cunswick*, 19.
Levens, 24.
Lowther, 13.
Midleton *of Midleton*, 16.
Midleton *of Kirkby Lonsdale*, 41.

Musgrave, 5.
Philipson, 47.
Richmond, 40.
Stockdale, 40.
Thornborough, 26.
Warcop, 10.
Wolston, 45.

180.—Heraldic Visitation of the Northern Counties in 1530. By Thomas Tonge, Norroy, &c. *Surtees Society.* Vol. 41. 1863. See also *Cumberland, Durham, Nottingham, Northumberland, and Yorkshire.*

Thornborough, 98. | Wharton, 99.

WILTSHIRE.

181.—Aubrey's Collections for Wilts. *London,* 1821. 4to. 2 Parts. Printed by Sir Thomas Phillipps, Bart.

Anstie, ii. 6.
Long *of Wroxhall*, i. 66.
Rogers *of Bradford*, ii. 46.

Snell *of Bideston and Kingston*, i. 113.

182.—The History of Modern Wiltshire. By Sir Richard Colt Hoare, Bart., and others. *London,* 1822-1843. 6 vols. Folio.

A'Court (*Heytesbury*), I. ii. 121.
Anger; see Bruse.
Arundell *of Wardour*, IV. i. 179.
Ash (*Westbury*), III. i. 41.
Ashe (*Heytesbury*), I. ii. 118.
Ashley (*West Dean*), V. i. 24.
Astley; see Estley.
Astley; see Boreham.
Auchor; see Bruse.
Audley (*Boyton*), I. ii. 227.
Bacon *of Whiteparish*, V. ii. 45.
Badlesmere (*Heytesbury*), I. ii. 86.
Ballard *of Bishopstone*, III. iv. 3.
Barrett and Keileway *of Whelpley and Whiteparish*, V. ii. 44.
Bathurst *of Clarendon Park*, V. i. 172.
Bavent; see Scudamore.
Bavent (*Norton Bavent*), III. ii. 77.
Bayntun (*Bishopstone*), III. iv. 7.
Beach *of Warminster*, II. ii. 30.
Beauchamp (*Bishopstone*), III. iv. 5.
Beauchamp (*Downton*), III. iv. 50.

Beckford *of Fonthill*, IV. i. faces 4.
Benet *of Pyt House*, III. ii. 107.
Benett *of Norton Bavent*, III. ii. faces 78.
Bennett; see Pytt.
Berenger, &c, (*Whiteparish*), V. ii. 5, 119.
Bettesthorne, Brereton, and Compton (*Whiteparish*), V. ii. 49.
Bodenham (*Downton*), III. iv. 61.
Bokeland; see Wroth.
Bond; see Churchill.
Boreham; see Gifford.
Botreaux; see Hungerford.
Bouverie, Earl of Radnor, III. v. p. 35.
Bowle *of Idmiston*, V. i. 63.
Bowles and Davies (*Semley*), IV. ii. 36.
Bowles; see Hydes.
Brereton; see Bettesthorne.
Bristow (*Whiteparish*), V. ii. 11, 31*, 32*, 33*, 34*.
Browne, III. ii. 103.

Bruse *of Skelton and Gisbrurne, co.
York,* whence Aucher or Anger,
co. Wilts. (Fisherton Anger), II.
i. 162.
Buckler ; see Boreham.
Bulkeley *of Whiteparish,* V. ii. 28.
Bull ; see Frampton.
Burdet ; see Camville.
Burdon ; see Thorpe.
Burghersh *(Heytesbury),* I. ii. 88.
Camville, Burdet, and Stafford,
(Wilton), II. i. 153.
Cecil, Marq. of Salisbury, II. 339.
Cervington ; see Servington.
Chaldecot *of Quarlstone, &c.,* IV.
ii. 32.
Chalford and Leighton *(Westbury),*
III. i. faces 33.
Chedyok ; see Pavely.
Cheyne ; see Pavely.
Churchill, Bond, and Solers, I. ii.
253.
Clifford *of Boscumbe,* II. ii. 115.
Clifford ; see Thorpe.
Coker *of Maypowder, co. Dorset, and
Hill Deverill, co. Wilts,* I. ii. 30.
Compton ; see Bettesthorne.
Cottingtam *of Fonthill,* IV. i.
faces 4.
Croke ; see Lisle.
Dalton *of Shanks House,* IV. ii. 33.
Dauntesey *(Winterbourn Dauntsey),*
V. i. 83.
Davenant, V. ii. 85.
Davies ; see Bowles.
Davys *(Tisbury),* IV. i. 136.
De Clifford, &c. *(Winterslow),* V.
i. 44.
De Dunstanville, IV. i. 98.
De la Foyle, V. iii. 34.
De la Mere *(Fisherton de la Mere),*
I. ii. 256.
De Luveraz *(Whiteparish),* V. ii.
70.
De Plessetis, or Plessy, III. v. 12.
Duke *of Lake,* II. ii. 139.
Duncombe *of Barford,* afterwards
Lord Faversham, III. iv. 45.
Dune ; see Le Dune.
Elliott *of Winterbourn Gunner,* V.
i. 78.
Engleys or English *(Whiteparish),*
V. ii. 31.

English ; see Engleys.
Estley, or Astley *of Everley,* II. ii. 9.
Esturmy *of Wolf Hall, co. Wilts,*
I. i. 117.
Evelyn *(Everley),* II. ii. 7.
Evelyn *of West Dean,* V. i. 22.
Ewyas, &c. *(Upton Scudamore),* III.
ii. 54.
Eyre, and Matcham, V. ii. folding
at 56.
Eyre *of Brickworth, &c.,* V. ii.
folding at 56.
Eyre *of Salisbury,* V. ii. 107.
Eyres *(Boscumbe),* II. ii. 116.
Faversham, Lord; see Duncombe.
Ferne *(Dunhead St. Andrew),* IV.
i. 56.
Fitz Ellis, V. ii. 119.
Fitzhamon alias De Burstow, V. ii.
32*.
Fitzherbert ; see Martell.
Fox and Strangways, Earl of Il-
chester, V. i. 37.
Frampton ; see Hydes.
Frampton, Bull, and Polhill *(Sem-
ley),* IV. ii. 35.
Gaisford, Gibbs, and Ludlow *(West-
bury),* III. i. faces 34.
Gawen *(Barerstock),* IV. i. 100.
Gawen *(Imber),* I. ii. 165.
Gaweyn, or Gawen *(Alvediston),*
IV. ii. 84.
Gerberd *of Odstock,* III. v. 20.
Gibbs ; see Gaisford.
Giffard *(Sherrington),* I. ii. 238.
Giffard *(Boyton),* I. ii. 201.
Gifford *of Boreham,* Buckler and
Astley, III. ii. 76.
Gold *(Alvediston),* IV. ii. 94.
Goldston *of Alderbury,* V. i. 202.
Gomeldon *(Idmiston),* V. i. 62.
Gore *of Orcheston,* I. ii. 183.
Gorges *of Longford Castle,* III. v.
30.
Greene *of Standlynch,* III. iv. 50.
Greenhill *(Stockton),* I. ii. 247.
Grimsted *(Compton Chamberlain),*
IV. i. 80.
Grimsted *(West Grimstead),* V. i.
10.
Grimstead *(West Grimstead),* V.
i. 202.
Grobham and Howe, IV. i. 2.

Grosvenor, II. 178.
Grove *of Fern*, IV. i. faces 58.
Harcourt (*West Dean*), V. i. 21.
Herbert, Earl of Pembroke, II. i. 139.
Heyraz (*Whiteparish*), V. ii. 47.
Hinxman *of Little Durnford*, II. ii. 129.
Hithcock (*Whiteparish*), V. ii. 44.
Hoare *of Stourhead*, I. i. 61, 62.
Hoare, V. iii. 13.
Howe *of Berwick St. Leonard*, IV. i. 3.
Howe; see Grobham.
Hungerford, Lady Margaret, and Botreaux, I. ii. 92.
Hungerford (*Heytesbury*), I. ii. 117.
Hungerford (*Teffont Ewyas*), IV. i. 123.
Husse (*Teffont Ewyas*), IV. i. 123.
Hyde and Parker (*Tisbury*), IV. i. faces 131.
Hyde and Parker *of West Hatch*, IV. ii. 33.
Hydes, Frampton, and Bowles (*Woodford*), II. ii. 145.
Ilchester, Earls of; see Fox.
Ingham (*Codford St. Mary*), I. ii. 230.
Ingham (*West Dean*), V. i. 21.
Keileway; see Barrett.
Kent *of Boscumbe*, II. ii. 115.
Kneller (*Dunhead St. Mary*), IV. i. 32.
Lambert *of Maiden Bradley*, I. i. 111.
Lambert (*Boyton*), I. ii. 203.
Lawrence *of Cowesfield*, V. ii. faces 75.
Le Boteler (*Bramshaw*), V. ii. 103.
Le Despenser, &c. (*Winterslow*), V. i. 45.
Le Dune (*Downton*), III. iii. 46.
Leighton; see Chalford.
Le Moigne (*Maddington*), II. i. 36.
Ley (*Teffont Ewyas*), IV. i. 110.
Lisle and Croke (*Fifield Bavent*), IV. ii. 122.
Lovel (*Upton Lovel*), I. ii. 192.
Lovell; see Wroth.
Ludlow *of Hill Deverill*, I. ii. 15.
Ludlow; see Gaisford.
Lunnell; see Shuckburgh.
Lye; see Lygh.

Lygh, or Lye (*Landford*), V. ii. 84.
Malet *of Wilbury*, II. ii. faces 106.
Martell and Fitzherbert (*Berwick St. John*), IV. ii. 52.
Marvyn; see Mervyn.
Matcham; see Eyre.
Mauduit (*Warminster*), III. ii. 9.
Mautravers (*Orcheston*), I. ii. 181.
Mayne (*Teffont Ewyas*), IV. i. 112.
Mayow, V. iii. 66.
Mervyn or Marvyn *of Pertwood*, I. i. 180.
Mervyn or Marvyn *of Fonthill*, IV. i. faces 20.
Michell (*Chitterne*), I. ii. 172.
Middlecot (*Warminster*), III. ii. 43.
Middlecote, III. ii. 104.
Moels, I. ii. 91.
Molins, I. ii. 93.
Mompesson (*Boyton*), I. ii. 219.
Moore (*Heytesbury*), I. ii. 118.
Napton; see Shuckburgh.
Nelson, Earl Nelson, III. iv. faces 50; see also 72.
Nicholas (*Winterbourn Earl's*), V. i. 96 and 214.
Okeden; see Uvedale.
Pavely, Chedyok, St. Maur, Cheyne, &c. (*Westbury*), III. i. facing 3.
Payne, Tournay, and Webb, (*Semley*), IV. ii. 29.
Parker; see Hyde.
Pembroke, Earls of; see Herbert.
Penruddocke *of Compton Chamberlain*, IV. i. faces 81.
Peverell, I. ii. 91.
Phipps *of Heywood House*, III. i. faces 33.
Plessy; see De Plessetis.
Polhill; see Frampton.
Popham (*West Dean*), V. i. 21.
Powell (*Baverstock*), IV. i. 101.
Pytt, *alias* Bennett *of Pythouse*, IV. i. faces 102.
Radnor, Earls of; see Bouverie.
Ralegh *of Downton*, III. iv. 37.
Ringwood; see Ryngewood.
Romesey *of Combe Biset*, III. v. 13.
Ryngewood or Ringwood, V. ii. 31.
St. Barbe (*Whiteparish*), V. ii. 10.
St. Martin (*West Dean*), V. i. 21.
St. Maur *of Penhow Court, co. Monmouth*, I. i. 116.

St. Maur, III. i. 4; see also Pavely.

Sadleir *of Salthrop*, II. ii. 198.

Salisbury, Earls of, of the first and second Houses, VI. 40.

St. Omer (*Britford*), III. iv. 44.

Scudamore and Bavent (*Fifield Bavent*), IV. ii. 120.

Servington, or Cervington, *of Longford*, III. v. 27.

Seymer (*Salisbury*), VI. 429.

Seymour, Duke of Somerset, I. i. 117.

Seymour *of Wolf Hall, co. Wilts*, I. i. 117.

Seymour (*Whiteparish*), V. ii. 51.

Shuckburgh *of the Moot, Downton*, with Napton and Lunnell, III. iv. 54.

Solers; see Churchill.

Somerset, Dukes of; see Seymour.

Spelman (*Whiteparish*), V. ii. 74.

Stafford; see Camville.

Stantor, or Stanter *of Horningsham*, I. ii. 48.

Stapylton (*West Dean*), V. i. 21.

Stephenes *of Dutton*, III. i. 86.

Still *of East Knoyle*, I. i. 191.

Stourton *of Stourton*, I. i. 47.

Strangways; see Fox.

Stratford, V. ii. 119.

Swayne, V. iii. 49.

Temple *of Bishopstrow*, III. ii. 73.

Thatcham *of Idminston*, V. i. 58.

Thistlethwayte *of Winterslow*, V. i. 46.

Thomas, I. ii. 261.

Thorpe, Burdon, and Clifford, V. iii. 46.

Thynne *of Longleat*, I. ii. 60.

Tibtot; see Wroth.

Tichbourne (*Whiteparish*), V. ii. 31.

Toeni, or Tony (*Stratford Tony*), III. v. 5.

Tooker *of Maddington*, II. i. 37.

Topp *of Stockton*, I. ii. 242.

Tournay; see Payne.

Tregagle (*Melchet Park*), V. ii. 79.

Tregoz (*Teffont Etywas*), IV. i. 110.

Tropnell, V. ii. 118.

Truslowe (*Downton*), III. iv. 58.

Uffenham (*Downton*), III. iii. 68.

Uvedale and Okeden (*Berwick St. John*), II. ii. 60.

Vaughan *of Falstone*, III. iv. 8.

Wadman (*Imber*), I. ii. 165.

Wake, V. iii. 35.

Workedsley; see Workesley.

Waleran (*Steeple Langford*),II. i. 10.

Walerand, III. v. 73.

Warder (*Plaitford*), V. ii. 96.

Warren *of Bramshaw*, V. ii. 104.

Webb *of Odstock*, III. v. 20.

Webb; see Payne.

Westbury (*Westbury*), III. i. 19.

Whitaker (*Westbury*), III. i. 43.

Whyte (*Downton*), III. iv. 59.

Wodhull *of Little Durnford*, II. ii. 128.

Workesley, Worsley, and Workedsley (*Dunhead St. Andrew*), IV. i. 55.

Worsley; see Workesley.

Wroth, Bokeland, Tibtot, and Lovell (*Downton*), III. iv. 44.

Wyche *of Salisbury*, V. ii. folding at 29.

Wyndham *of Dinton*, IV. i. 108,

Wyndham (*Alvediston*), IV. ii. 93.

Yonge, or Young *of Durnford*, II. ii. 125.

Zouch (*Pitton*), V. i. 207.

183.—Graphical and Literary Illustrations of Fonthill Abbey, Wiltshire. By JOHN BRITTON, F.S.A. *London,* 1823. 4to.

Beckford, 42, 44, 46, 49, 50, 56, 65, 66, 68.

184.—Delineations of Fonthill and its Abbey. By JOHN RUTTER. *London*, 1823. 4to.

Beckford (three tables) at the end.

185.—Visitatio Heraldica Comitatus Wiltoniæ, Ann. 1623. *Typis Medii Montanis.* 1828. Foolscap folio, not paged. Privately printed by Sir THOMAS PHILLIPPS, Bart.

Abbot.
Alleyne.
Ashley.
Ashman.
Aubrey.
Bacon.
Baily.
Barret.
Barrett.
Bartlett.
Bartlett.
Barwick.
Baskerville.
Bayliff.
Baynard.
Baynard.
Baynton.
Bayly.
Becket.
Beckett.
Bedford.
Bellingham.
Benett *of Sarum.*
Bennet.
Bennett *of Pytthouse.*
Benson.
Bewshin.
Blacker.
Blake.
Blake.
Bower.
Bower.
Bower.
Bowle.
Breton.
Brind.
Bromwich.
Brothers.
Brouncker.
Browne.
Bruning.
Bulkeley.
Burley.
Bush.
Butler.
Button.

Calley.
Caraunte.
Carpenter.
Chafin.
Cheney.
Chivers.
Clifford.
Cordray.
Cotele.
Cusse.
Danyel.
Dauntsey.
Davy.
Day.
Diggs.
Dirdo.
Drew.
Duckett.
Duke.
Earth.
English.
Erington.
Erneily.
Eyre.
Fauxton.
Fawconer.
Ferrys.
Fisher.
Flower.
Gawen.
Gethin.
Gibbs.
Gifford.
Girdler.
Gold.
Goldston.
Gore.
Gorge.
Grove.
Grubbe.
Hall.
Harding.
Harold.
Hawker.
Hewes.
Hippesley.

Hitchcock.
Hooper.
Horsey.
Horton.
Hungerford.
Hunton.
Hutoft.
Hyde.
Ireys.
Irton.
Kent.
Keyleway.
Lambe.
Lambert.
Lapp.
Lavington.
Long.
Lovell.
Lowe.
Lowe.
Ludlow.
Lyte.
Malyn.
Markes.
Marvin.
Masculine.
Maton.
May.
Mayowe.
Mewis.
Mogradge.
Molins.
Moody.
Moore.
Moore.
Mortimer.
Mussel.
Mychell.
Nicholas.
Norborn.
Norden.
Organ.
Paulet.
Penruddock.
Phillipps.
Phillips.
Pickhayer.
Pike.
Pile.
Pinkney.
Pleydell.
Poore.
Prater.

Provender.
Prynn.
Prynn.
Pyrry.
Quintyn.
Rawleigh.
Reade *of Corsham.*
Reade *of Sutton.*
Redich.
Richmond.
Rogers.
Rolfe.
Rowsewell.
Ryley.
Sadler.
Samways.
Savage.
Scrope.
Selfe.
Seymour.
Shelley.
Sherington.
Skilling.
Skutt.
Smith.
Smith *of Corsham.*
Sneith *alias* Parker.
Snell.
Sotewell.
Souch.
South.
South.
Spatchurst.
St. Barbe.
St. John.
St. Loe.
St. Maur.
Stanter.
Staples.
Stephens.
Still.
Stokes.
Stourton.
Stradling.
Stratton.
Stylleman.
Temmes.
Thacham.
Thistlethwayte.
Thistlethwayt.
Thornhull.
Thynne.
Tichburn.

Tooker *of Maddington.*
Tooker *of Sarum.*
Topp *of Stockton.*
Topp *of Bridmore.*
Tropnell.
Truslowe.
Tutt.
Uffenham.
Valence.
Vaughan.
Vaux.
Vinour.
Warder.
Walker.
Wallis.
Walrond.
Walton.

Warnell and Ludlow.
Warre.
Weare *alias* Browne.
Webb.
Webb.
Weston.
White.
Wignoll.
Willoughby.
Wintersell.
Wroughton.
Yerbury.
Yerworth.
Yorke.
Zouch.
Young.

186.—Annals and Antiquities of Lacock Abbey, in the County of Wilts. By the Rev. W. L. Bowles, M.A., M.R.S.L., and John Gough Nichols. *London,* 1835. 8vo.

Longespé, House of, facing 149.
Romara, House of, facing 65.
Salisbury, House of, facing 39.
Salisbury, descent. of Wm. Longe-

spé, Earl of, and of Ela his Countess, from Wm. Longespé Duke of Normandy, facing 107. Vitre, Family of, &c. facing 264*.

187.—The History and Antiquities of the Manor House at South Wraxhall, and the Church of St. Peter at Biddestone, Wiltshire. Part III. of Pugin's Examples of Gothic Architecture. Third Series. *London,* 1838. 4to.

Long *of Wraxhall and Draycot, &c.*
Appendix I.

Long, Walter, Esq. *of Rood Aston,* M.P. Paternal descent of, Appendix II.

188.—The History of the Parish of Grittleton, in the County of Wilts. By the Rev. J. E. Jackson, M.A. Published by the Wiltshire Topographical Society. *London,* 1843-48. 4to.

Gore *of Grittleton,* 7. *
Greene *of Fosscote,* and of *Brook House, co. Wilts,* 14.

Houlton ; see White.
White and Houlton *of Grittleton,* folding at 8.

189.—Memoir of John Aubrey, F.R.S. By John Britton, F.S.A. Published by the Wiltshire Topographical Society. *London,* 1845. 4to.

Aubrey and Lyte, 24.

U

190.—The History of Castle Combe, co. Wilts. By G. POULETT SCROPE, Esq., M.P. *London*, 1852. 4to. Privately printed.

Badlesmere and Tiptoft, 56.
De Badlesmere, 65, 69.
De Dunstanville, 19.
Scrope *of Castle Combe*, 86, 350.

Scrope *of Cockington, co. Lincoln*, 354.
Scrope, Mr. Poulett, 358.
Tiptoft; see Badlesmere.

191.—The Wiltshire Archæological and Natural History Magazine. *Devizes*, 1854-1866. 9 vols. 8vo.

Ashe, v. 382.
Baynard *of Lackham*, iv. folding at 6.
Besill; see Hall.
Cerne and Heryng *of Draycot Cerne*, iii. folding at 178.
Darell of Littlecote, iv. folding at 226.
Essex, iv. 76.
Foster *of Marlborough*, iii. folding at 224.
Garth, ii. folding at 332.
Giffard, ii. folding at 100.
Hall, v. folding at 360.
Hall, Besill, Rogers, Horton, Long, and Yerbury, v. folding at 357.
Harding *of Boughton Gifford*, vi. facing 11.
Heryng; see Cerne.
Horton, v. folding at 232.
Horton; see Hall.

Hyde and Langford, ix. folding at 282.
Lambe *of Coulston*, iii. folding at 108.
Langford; see Hyde.
Langton *of Easton Percy*, iv. facing 77.
Long, v. 234.
Long; see Hall.
Lyte *of Easton Percy*, iv. facing 79.
Methuen, v. folding at 378.
Montagu *of Lackham*, iii. folding at 87.
Rogers, v. facing 368.
Rogers; see Hall.
Snell *of Kingston St. Michael*, iv. folding at 44.
Stourton, viii. folding at 244.
Thresher, v. 240.
Yerbury, v. folding at 369.
Yerbury; see Hall.

192.—Visitation of Wiltshire, 1677. Ex. MSS. Phillipps. *Typis Medico Montanis.* 1854. Not paged. Privately printed by Sir THOMAS PHILLIPPS, Bart. Foolscap folio.

Abbot *of Sarum*.
Ashley *of Sarum*.
Batt *of Sarum*.
Ballard *of Salisbury*.
Bowle *of Idmiston*.
Bowman *of Sarum*.
Bradford *of Sarum*.
Chafin *of Sarum*.
Coles *of Sarum*.
Dove *of Sarum*.
Elliott *of Salisbury and Winterborn Gunnor*.

Frome *of Salisbury*.
Hancocke *of Salisbury and Combe*.
Harris *of Orcheston St. George and Salisbury*.
Hearst *of Marlborough and Sarum*.
Marshall *of Salisbury and Milford*.
Pitt.
Priaulx *of Salisbury*.
Swanton *of Sarum*.
Swayne *of Sarum*.
Turberville *of Sarum*.

193.—The Monumental Brasses of Wiltshire. By EDWARD KITE. *London and Oxford,* 1860. Royal 8vo.

Baynton ; see De la Roche.
Beauchamp, Delamere, Roche, St. Amand, and Braybrooke, folding at 36.
Beauchamp ; see De la Roche.
Bettesthorne and Berkeley, 31.
Berkeley ; see Bettesthorne.
Braybrooke ; see Beauchamp.
Delamere ; see Beauchamp.

De la Roche, Beauchamp, and Baynton, 47.
Hobbes *of Malmesbury,* 79.
Long *of Semington,* 77.
Poticary *of Stockton,* folding at 76.
Roche ; see Beauchamp.
Rutland, 74.
St. Amand ; see Beauchamp.
St. Cleere *of Toodwill,* 68.

194.—Wiltshire. The Topographical Collections of JOHN AUBREY, F.R.S. An. 1659-70. Corrected and enlarged by JOHN EDWARD JACKSON, M.A., F.S.A. Published by the Wiltshire Archæological and Natural History Society. *Devizes,* 1862. 4to.

Blount; see Cheney.
Cheney, Strafford, Maltravers, Willoughby, and Blount, 401.
Dauntesey, Stradling, and Danvers *of Dauntesey,* folding at 217.
Danvers; see Dauntesey.
Essex, 239.
Gore *of Alderton,* folding at 47.
Hungerford of *Farleigh Castle,* 412.
Long *of Draycote,* 234.
Maltravers ; see Cheyney.

Power, 290.
Prynne, 71.
Rogers *of Bradford,* 22.
St. John *of Lydiard Tregoz,* folding at 170.
Snell *of Kingston St. Michael,* 132.
Stradling ; see Dauntesey.
Strafford ; see Cheney.
Willoughby ; see Cheney.
Yorke, 181.

WORCESTERSHIRE.

195.—Collections for the History of Worcestershire. By T. NASH. *London,* 1782—1789. 2 vols. folio.

Amphlett (*Hadsor*), i. 481.
Bartlet (*Longdon*), ii. 110.
Beauchamp (*Beoley*), i. 64.
Beauchamp (*Powick*), ii. 263, 264.
Berkeley (*Spechesley*), ii. 358.
Berkeley *of Cotheridge,* i. faces 258.
Bigg (*Norton*), ii. 178.
Blacket (*Iccomb*), ii. 4.
Blount, Blond, Blund, or Le Blondi, ii. faces 163, and also p. 163.
Bromley *of Upton,* ii. 445.
Bromley *of Holt,* i. 595.
Buck (*Kemsey*), ii. 19.
Child *of Northwick,* i. 99.
Cokesey (*Kidderminster*), ii. 50.

Cookes *of Norgrove,* i. faces 440.
Danet *of Elmbridge,* i. 347.
Dickens (*Churchill*), i. 191.
Dineley of *Charleton,* i. faces 272.
Foley (*Witley*), ii. faces 465.
Foliot (*Pirton*), ii. 258.
Graves (*Church Honeyborn*), i. 198.
Habington, or Abington, i. faces 588.
Hanford (*Nafford*), ii. 182.
Harewell *of Besford,* i. 77.
Haselwood (*Offenham*), ii. 203.
Hastang ; see Stafford.
Hornyold *of Blackmore Park,* i. 558.
Hugefort, or Huggeford (*Nafford*), ii. 183.

Ingram *of Upper Home*, i. 243.
Jefferies and Winnington *of Home Castle*, i. 245.
Jefferies *of Earl's Orome*, i. 267.
Jolliffe (*Oofton Hacket*), i. faces 251.
Kirkham (*Mamble*), ii. 158.
Lechmere (*Hanley Castle*), i. 560.
Lewston (*Iccomb*), ii. 3.
Lowe *of the Lowe*, ii. faces 94.
Lygon (*Madersfield*), ii. 118.
Lyttelton (*Hagley*), i. faces 493.
Meysey *of Shakenhurst*, i. faces 54.
Mortimer ; see Say.
Mucklowe and Zachary, i. faces 37.
Nanfan *of Birch Morton*, i. faces 86.
Nash *of Droitwich*, i. 327.
Pakington (*Chaddesley Corbet*), i. 186.
Pakington (*Droitwich*), i. faces 352.
Penell (*Lindridge*), ii. 94.
Percy *of Worcester*, ii. faces 317.
Percy (*Hindlip*), i. 587.
Perrot (*Fladbury*), i. 448.
Pytts (*Kyre Wyre*), i. 71.
Rous ; see Rufus.
Rufus, or Rous, ii. 85.
Rushout *of Northwick*, i. faces 99.
Russel *of Little Malvern*, ii. 141.
Russell *of Strensham*, i. 395.
Sandes, or Sandys (*Ombersley*), ii. faces 221.
Sandys ; see Sandes.

Savage *of Elmley*, i. 384, 385.
Say, Mortimer, and Talbot (*Clifton*), i. 241.
Seabright *of Besford*, i. 79.
Sholdon *of Bosly*, i. faces 64.
Sheldon *of Broadway*, i. 145.
Sheldon (*Spechesly*), ii. 357.
Shrewsbury, Earls of; see Talbot.
Somers (*Kidderminster*), ii. 54.
Stafford and Hastang *of Grafton*, i. 157.
Talbot, Earls of Shrewsbury, i. faces 158.
Talbot ; see Say.
Throckmorton (*Fladbury*), i. faces 452.
Toky and Wolmer (*Kinton*), ii. 63.
Townshend *of Elmley Lovett*, i. faces 378.
Vampage (*Nafford*), ii. 183.
Vernon *of Hanbury*, i. faces 549.
Walsh (*Abberley*), i. faces 2.
Wilson and Wingfield *of Lippard*, ii. faces 317.
Winford (*Astley*), i. 42.
Wingfield ; see Wilson.
Winnington (*Stanford*), i. 368.
Winnington ; see Jefferies.
Wolmer ; see Toky.
Wylde (*St. Peters*), ii. faces 331.
Zachary; see Mucklowe.

YORKSHIRE.

196.—Registrum Honoris de Richmond. (ROGER GALE, F.S.A.) *London*, 1722. Folio.

Brittany, Dukes of, and Earls of Richmond, folding after the preface.

197.—*Eboracum :* or the History and Antiquities of the City of York. By FRANCIS DRAKE. *London*, 1736. Folio.

Fairfax ; see Lardiner.
Fairfax, 395.
Lardiner, Leke, Thornton, Thwaites, and Fairfax, 326.

Leke ; see Lardiner.
Thornton ; see Lardiner.
Thwaites ; see Lardiner.

198.—*Monasticon Eboracense :* and the Ecclesiastical History of Yorkshire. By JOHN BURTON, M.D. *York*, 1758. Folio.

Babthorpe *of Babthorpe*, 435.
Bowes *of Babthorpe*, 438.

Ingram *of Temple Newsom*, 411.

199.—A New and Complete History of the Town of Kingston-upon-Hull. By GEORGE HADLEY, Esq. *Kingston-upon-Hull*, 1788. 4to.

De la Pole, Earls and Dukes of Suffolk and Lincoln, folding at 256.

200.—The History and Antiquities of the Deanery of Craven, in the County of York. By THOMAS DUNHAM WHITAKER, LL.D., F.S.A. *London*, 1805. 4to.

Banke *of Bank Newton*, folding at 170; 2 ed. 182.
Clifford; see Plumpton.
Clifford, 363.
Clifford *of Skipton*, folding at 209; 2 ed. 240.
Coulthurst *of Gargrave*, folding at 172; 2 ed. 184.
Currer *of Kildwick*, folding at 152; 2 ed. 161.
Dawson and Pudsey, 130; 2 ed.142.
De Aleman, Le Gras, Tempest, and Mallory, 391; 2 ed. 458.
De Killestone; 2 ed. 444.
Ferrand, 161; 2 ed. 173.
Garforth *of Steeton*, folding at 156; 2 ed. 168.
Gilliott; 2 ed. 88.
Halton *of Halton*, 121; 2 ed. 132.
Hamerton *of Hamerton, Wigglesworth, and Hellifield Peel*, folding at 118; 2 ed. 124.
Heber *of Marton and Stainton, co. York, and of Hodnet, co. Salop*, folding at 68; 2 ed. 76.
Hertlington; 2 ed. 441.
King, 179; 2 ed. 193.
Lambert, 182; 2 ed. 194.
Le Gras; see De Aleman.
Lister, 95; 2 ed. 103.
Lister *of Gisburn Park*, folding at 35; 2 ed. 38.

Malham *of Elslack*, folding at 91; 2 ed. 145.
Mallory; see De Aleman.
Marton *of Marton*, folding at 67; 2 ed. 72.
Midelton *of Midelton, Stubham, and Stockheld*, faces 206; 2 ed. 217.
Percy, as connected with Craven, folding at 29; 2 ed. at 39.
Plumpton, Rocliffe, and Clifford, 154; 2 ed. 166.
Pudsey; see Dawson.
Pudsey *of Bolton*, folding at 101; 2 ed. 110.
Radcliff, 380; 2 ed. 446.
Rocliffe; see Plumpton.
Roundell *of Screven, near Knaresborough, and Gledston House, in Craven*, folding at 71.
Swire *of Canonley*, folding at 156; 2 ed. 168.
Talbot *of Basho*, folding at 24.
Tempest *of Bracewell*, folding at 75; 2 ed. 80.
Tempest *of Broughton*, folding at 83; 2 ed. 87.
Tempest; see De Aleman.
Wilson *of Eshton*, folding at 172; 2 ed. 184.
Yorke *of Goulthwayte*, folding at. 376; 2 ed. 439.

201.—The History of Cleveland. By the Rev. JOHN GRAVES. *Carlisle*, 1808. 4to.

Beckwith *of Handale Abbey*, 345.
Bellasise, Visct. Fauconberg, &c. 57.
Bigod; see Mauley.
Bulmer, 408.
Bulmer *of Wilton*, 409.

Chaloner *of Guisbrough*, folding at 412.
Colthurst *of Upleatham*, 378.
Constable *of Dromondby*, 243.
Conyers *of Boulby*, 330.
Crathorne *of Crathorne*, 105.

Eure *of Easby, Ingleby, &c.*, 234
Forster *of Stokesley*, 225.
Fauconberg; see Bellasise.
Foulis *of Ingleby Manor*, 249.
Gower *of Stainsby*, 478.
Hall; see Trotter.
Ingram *of Temple Newsom*, 164.
Layton *of Sexhowe*, 172.
Lee *of Pinchinthorpe*, 434.
Linley *of Skutterskelfe*, 173.
Mauley, Bigod, and Ratcliffe, 298.
Marwood *of Little Busby*, 231.
Mauleverer *of Arnecliffe*, 122.
Meinell *of Whorlton Castle*, 139.
Meryton *of Castle Levington*, 92.

Meynell *of Yarum and North Kilvington*, 70.
Morley *of Normanby*, 444.
Mulgrave, Earl of; see Sheffield.
Pennyman *of Ormesby*, 440.
Ratcliffe; see Mauley.
Salvine *of Newbiggin*, 289.
Sheffield, Earl of Mulgrave, 301.
Smallwood *of Upleatham*, 378.
Stevenson; see Trotter.
Tockett *of Tockett*, 429.
Trotter *of Skelton Castle*, with Hall and Stevenson, 354.
Warton *of Beverley*, 440.
Wharton, 358.
Yoward *of Westerdale*, 269.

202.—The History and Antiquities of Doncaster. By EDWARD MILLER, Mus. D. *Doncaster.* No date. 4to.

Cooke, 206.
Copley; see Harrington.
Copley *of Sprotbrough*, 222.

Farrer, 272.
Harrington and Copley, 163.

203.—Description of Browsholme Hall, in the West Riding of the County of York. *London*, 1815. 4to. Privately printed.

Parker, folding at 24.

204.—*Loidis and Elmete:* the Lower Portions of Aredale and Wharfdale, together with the entire Vale of Calder in the County of York. By THOMAS DUNHAM WHITAKER, LL.D., F.S.A. *Leeds*, 1816. Folio.

Beaumont *of Whitley*, folding at 339.
Castleford, 263.
Dixon, folding at 130.
Dyneley *of Bramhope*, folding at 198.
Eland, 401.
Fawkes *of Farnley*, folding at 190.
Harewood, Lords of, folding at 166.
Harewood, Earls of; see Lascelles.
Lascelles, Earls of Harewood, folding at 168.
Lonsdale, Earls of; see Lowther.
Lowther, Earls of Lonsdale, folding at 360.
Mexborough, Earl of; see Savile.
Oates *of Leeds*, folding at 96.
Richardson *of Bierley, co. York and Finden Place, co. Sussex*, folding at App. 38.

Rookes *of Roydes Hall*, folding at 203.
Savile, Earls of Mexborough, folding at 272.
Sharp *of Little Horton*, faces 355.
Sheepshanks and York *of Leeds*, App. faces 31.
Smyth *of Heath in Warmfield, and Holbeck in Leeds*, folding at 360.
Stansfeld *of Stansfeld Hall*, folding at 202.
Stansfeld, 203.
Tempest *of Bracewell and Tong;* see Tong.
Tong *of Tong*, and Tempest *of Bracewell and Tong*, folding at 250.
Vavasour *of Weston*, folding at 206.

205.—Ducatus Leodiensis: or the Topography of the Town and Parish of Leeds. By RALPH THORESBY, F.R.S. London, 1715. Folio; 2nd edition, Leeds, 1816. Folio.

Akeroyd, *of Foggathorp and Leedes*, 260; 2 ed. 258.

Anderton (*Holbeck*), 184; 2 ed. 185.

Armytage *of Kirklees*, 91; 2 ed. folding at 88.

Arthington (*Leeds*), 5; 2 ed. 7.

Ashton (*Allerton Gledhow*), 131; 2 ed. 130.

Atkinson (*Leeds*), 80; 2 ed. 76.

Bathurst (*Leeds*), 13; 2 ed. 16.

Baynes (*Leeds Main Riding*), 106; 2 ed. 101.

Beckwith (*Allerton Gledhow*); see Malby.

Beeston *of Beeston*, 207; 2 ed. 205.

Bethell; see Iveson.

Bevot (*Leeds*), 20; 2 ed. 23.

Bland (*Beeston*), 208: 2 ed. 207.

Bland (*Leeds Main-Riding*), 93; 2 ed. 90.

Blythman (*Leeds*), 7; 2 ed. 9.

Bourchier (*Potter Newton*), 123; 2 ed. 122.

Boyle, Earls of Burlington, 62; 2 ed. 61.

Boyle (*Leeds*), 65; 2 ed. 64.

Brearey (*Chapel Allerton*), 126; 2 ed. 125.

Brerehaughe (*Chapel Allerton*) 125; 2 ed. 124.

Breres (*Leeds*), 71; 2 ed. 68.

Bright (*Leeds*), 78; 2 ed. 74.

Bright (*Leeds*), 78; 2 ed. 75.

Brudenell, Earls of Cardigan, 153; 2 ed. 151.

Burlington, Earls of; see Boyle.

Busfield (*Leeds*), 6; 2 ed. 5

Calverley (*Potter Newton*), 116; 2 ed. 116.

Cardigan, Earls of; see Brudenell.

Carnaby, 2 ed. 35.

Cary (*Hunslet*), 178; 2 ed. 181.

Clapham (*Cottingley*), 218; 2 ed. 218.

Clayton, 256; 2 ed. 254.

Clough (*Thorp Hall*), 225; 2 ed. 225.

Conyers (*Temple Newsom*), 226; 2 ed. 227.

Cooke (*Beeston*), 210; 2 ed. 209.

Cooke (*Leeds*), 75; 2 ed. 72.

Cookson; see Hickes.

Copley (*Leeds*), 9; 2 ed. 11.

Danby (*Farneley*), 202; 2 ed. 201.

Dickinson, 259; 2 ed. 258.

Dyneley (*Leeds*), 33; 2 ed. 35.

Everingham (*Armley*),185; 2 ed.187

Evre, Lords, 17; 2 ed. 19.

Fairfax, Lord, 67; 2 ed. 65.

Farrer (*Wortley*), 196; 2 ed. 197.

Fawkes (*Moore Allerton*), 136.

Fenton *of Leeds;* 2 ed. 221.

Fletcher (*Hunslet*), 179; 2 ed. 182.

Folkingham (*Leeds, Main Riding*), 112; 2 ed. 106.

Foxcroft *of Weet Wood*, 156; 2 ed. 155.

Freston *of Alloftes*, 124; 2 ed. 123.

Gale (*Farneley*), 203; 2 ed. 203.

Gascoigne (*Himslet*), 176; 2 ed. 179.

Greenwode (*New Lathes*), 167; 2 cd. 169.

Hardwick (*Potter Newton*), 122; 2 ed. 121.

Harebred (*Ledsham and Ledston*), 236; 2 ed. 235.

Harington (*Farneley*), 2 ed. 199.

Harrison (*Leeds*), 12; 2 ed. 13.

Hastings, Earls of Huntingdon, 2 ed. 243.

Hawkesworth *of Hawkesworth*, 2 ed. 173.

Hewley and Wolrich (*Beeston*),211; 2 cd. folding at 208.

Hickes, Idle, and Cookson, (*Moore Allerton*), 139; 2 ed. 136.

Hill (*Beeston*), 210; 2 ed. 209.

Hodgson (*Leeds*), 75; 2 ed. 72.

Hopton (*Armley*), 186; 2 ed. 187.

Howard, Dukes of Norfolk, 146; 2 ed. folding at 144.

Hungate (*Shirburn in Elmet*), 247; 2 ed. 246.

Huntingdon, Earls of; see Hastings.

Hutton *of Marske*, 173; 2 ed. folding at 176.

Ibbetson (*Red Hall*), 148; 2 ed. 146.

Idle; see Hickes.

Ingleby (*Armley*), 191; 2 ed. 192.

Ingram, Viscts. Irwin, 230; 2 ed. folding at 230.

Iveson, with Bethell (*Leeds Main Riding*), 110; 2 ed. 103.

Killingbeck (*Allerton Grange*), 134; 2 ed. 133.

Kirke (*Cookridge*), 158; 2 ed. 158

Kitchingman, 258; 2 ed. 257.

Latimer, Lord (*Cat Beeston*), 213; 2 ed. 212.

Lawson (*Leeds*), 33; 2 ed. 35.

Lawson, 250; 2 ed. 249.

Layton, 261; 2 ed. 259.

Leedes (*Leeds Main Riding*), 112; 2 ed. 105.

Leedes and Pigott (*Leeds Main Riding*), 113; 2 ed. 106.

Leghe (*Middleton*), 221; 2 ed. 221.

Leke, Earls of Scarsdale, (*Ledston*), 245; 2 ed. 244.

Lewys (*Ledston*), 243; 2 ed. 242.

Lowther (*Leeds*), 5.

Malby and Beckwith (*Allerton Gledhow*), 132; 2 ed. 131.

Matthew, Archbishop of York, 253; 2 ed. 252.

Mauliverer (*Armley*), 190; 2 ed. 191.

Mauliverer (*Potter Newton*), 118; 2 ed. 117.

Metcalf (*Leeds*), 22; 2 ed. 24.

Midgeley (*Leeds*); see Neale.

Milner *of Nun-Appleton*, and Blayds *of Leeds and of Oulton;* 2 ed. folding at 214.

Milner (*Cat Beeston*), 216.

Milner *of Pudsey*, 172; 2 ed. folding at 176.

Milnes; see Poole.

Morris (*Leeds*), 74; 2 ed. 71.

Neal and Midgeley (*Leeds*), 21; 2 ed. 23.

Nevile (*Farneley*), 200; 2 ed. 200.

Nevile *of Holbeck and Chevet*, 182; 2 ed. folding at 184.

Osborne, 2; 2 ed. 2.

Parker (*Chapel Allerton*), 128; 2 ed. 128.

Passelew (*Potter Newton*), 121; 2 ed. 120.

Pawson (*Leeds*), 77; 2 ed. 74.

Perrot (*Leeds*), 2 ed. 72.

Pickering (*Crosse Flats*), 212; 2 ed. 209.

Piers, 251; 2 ed. 250.

Pigott (*Leeds Main Riding*); see Leedes.

Portington (*Leeds Main Riding*), 99; 2 ed. 95.

Poole *of Leeds*; and Milnes *of Wakefield and Fryston*, 74; 2 ed. folding at 72.

Power, 260; 2 ed. 258.

Pudsey, 258; 2 ed. 255.

Rawden *of Rawden*, 168; 2 ed. 171.

Richardson (*Leeds*), 20; 2 ed. 22.

Rockley (*Leeds*), 25; 2 ed. 27.

Rodes (*Leeds, Main Riding*), 94; 2 ed. 90.

Rokeby, 255; 2 ed. 253.

Saltonstall (*Ledsham*), 236; 2 ed. 236.

Savile, Earls of Sussex, 152; 2 ed. 150.

Savile (*Potter Newton*), 114.

Scarsdale, Earls of; see Leke.

Scotland, Kings of; see Stuart.

Scudamore (*Leeds*), 35; 2 ed. 36.

Sharp (*Leeds*), 36; 2 ed. 37.

Simpson *of Leeds*, 2 ed. 21.

Skargill (*Thorp Hall*), 224; 2 ed. 225.

Skelton (*Leeds, Main Riding*), 110; 2 ed. 109.

Smith (*Leeds*), 21; 2 ed. 24.

Spencer (*Leeds, Main Riding*), 104; 2 ed. 98.

Stanhope (*Horsford*), 166; 2 ed. 168.

Stapleton (*Armley*), 188; 2 ed. 189.

Sterne (*Cat Beeston*), 215; 2 ed. 214.

Stuart, Kings of Scotland, 227; 2 ed. 228.

Sussex, Earls of; see Savile.

Sykes (*Leeds*), 3; 2 ed. 3.

Sykes (*Leeds*), 34; 2 ed. 36.

Tempest (*Tonge*), 205.

Thoresby (*Leeds*), 71; 2 ed. 69.

Thornhill (*Potter Newton*), 115; 2 ed. 113.

Thornton (*Leeds*), 22; 2 ed. 25.

Todd (*Leeds*), 27; 2 ed. 29.

Tomlinson (*Leeds*), 24; 2 ed. 26.

Torre *of Syndall*; 2 ed. 119.
Tottie and Walker (*Potter Newton*), 120; 2 ed. faces 119.
Wade *of New Grange*, 155; 2 ed. 154.
Walker; see Tottie.
Washington (*Leeds, Main Riding*), 102; 2 ed. 97.
Watkinson (*Leeds*), 77; 2 ed. 73.
Wentworth *of Wooley and Hickleton*, 197; 2 ed. folding at 196.

Wentworth, Earls of Strafford, 241; 2 ed. folding at 240.
Wharton, Earls and Marq. of, 252; 2 ed. 251.
Whyte, 257 2 ed. 255.
Wilson *of Leeds*, 4; 2 ed. folding at 2.
Witham (*Ledston*) 240; 2 ed. 240.
Wolrich (*Beeston*); see Hewley.
Wombwell (*Leeds*), 69; 2 ed. 67.
Wood (*Beeston*), 207; 2 ed. 206.

206.—Hallamshire. The History and Topography of the Parish of Sheffield. By JOSEPH HUNTER, F.S.A. *London*, 1819. Folio.

Ashton *of Whiteley Wood*, 208.
Bamforth *of High House*, 225.
Bright *of Banner Cross*, 205.
Bright *of Whirlow Hall*, 206.
Bright *of Carbrook and Badsworth*, 249.
Burton *of Royds Mill, Sheffield, &c.* 236.
Butler, Earl of Ormonde, 147.
Clay *of Bridge Houses*, 231.
De Busli, 24.
De Furnival, 31.
De Lovetot, 26.
Fell *of Attercliffe Forge*, 235.
Furnival; see De Furnival.
Gell *of Hopton*, 216.
Gill *of Sheffield, Norton, Car House, &c.* 234.
Green *of Thundercliffe Grange*; see Wombwell.
Hallamshire, Lords of, 23.
Hollis *of London*, 183.
Howard, Dukes of Norfolk, 100.
Jessop *of Broom Hall*, 213.
Machon *of Machon Bank*, 216.
Macro, 253.
More *of More Hall*, 281.
Morewood, *of the Oaks in Bradfield*, 274.

Mounteney *of Shiercliffe, Cowley, &c.* 227.
Norfolk, Dukes of; see Howard.
Ormonde, Earls of; see Butler.
Parker *of Woodthorpe*, 287.
Parker (*Ecclesfield*), 263.
Pegge *of Beauchief*; see Strelley.
Ratcliffe *of Sheffield Manour and The Holmes*, 192.
Rawson *of Sheffield*, 224.
Rawson *of Brookside and Wardsend*, 267.
Saunderson *of Sheffield*, 233.
Scott and Watts *of Barnes Hall*, 262.
Shiercliffe *of Ecclesfield Hall, Whitby Hall, &c.*, 264.
Shore *of Sheffield, Meersbrook, Norton, Tapton, &c.*, 219.
Shrewsbury, Earls of; see Talbot.
Sitwell *of Renishaw, &c.*, 217.
Spencer *of Attercliffe Hall and Bramley Grange*, 248.
Staniforth *of Darnall*, 252.
Strelley and Pegge *of Beauchief*, 199.
Talbot, Earl of Shrewsbury, 43.
Wadsley, 272.
Watts *of Barnes Hall* : see Scott.
Wilson *of Bromhead*, 277.
Wombwell and Green *of Thundercliffe Grange*, 265.

207.—History of Harewood. By JOHN JEWELL. *Leeds*, 1819. 12mo.

Lascelles, 17.

208.—The History of Richmond, in the County of York. By CHRISTOPHER CLARKSON, Esq., F.S.A. *Richmond,* 1821. 4to.

Ayscough, 252.
Blackburne, 257.
Cradock, 177.
Gaunt, 309.
Gower, 380.
Hutton, 267,
Norton *of St. Nicholas*, 331.
Philippe, 345.

Richmond, Earls of, 12.
Scrope *of Bolton,* folding at 345.
Scrope, 386.
Smith, 386.
Stapleton, folding at 206.
Wharton, folding at 124.
Wray, 256.
Yorke, folding at 332.

209.—The History of Richmondshire, in the North-Riding of the County of York. By THOMAS DUNHAM WHITAKER, LL.D., F.S.A. *London,* 1823. 2 vols. Folio.

Ask, i. 116.
Bindlosse *of Berwick,* ii. faces 311.
Bretagne, Ducal Family of, Earls of Richmond, i. folding at 26.
Brockholes *of Claughton,* ii. faces 449.
Butler *of Kirkland,* ii. faces 454; 455.
Clervaux and Chaytor *of Croft,* i. folding at 240.
Conyers *of Hornby Castle,* ii. folding at 42.
Dalton *of Hawkswell,* i. faces 328.
Danby, Lords of Danby and Yafforth, i. faces 254.
Danby *of Farneley and Mashamshire,* ii. folding at 98.
Darcy *of Hornby Castle,* ii. folding at 43.
Fitzhugh ; see Marmion.
Fleetwood *of Rossal,* ii. faces 444.
Graham *of Norton Conyers,* ii. faces 184.
Grantham, Lord ; see Robinson.
Harrington *of Hornby,* ii. folding at 250.
Kendal, Barons of, ii. 477.

Latimer and Neville, Lords Latimer, ii. faces 78.
Lawson *of Brough Hall,* ii. folding at 36.
Legh *(Claughton),* ii. 264.
Maire *of Lartington,* i. faces 140.
Marmion, Fitzhugh, Parr, &c., ii. 167.
Metcalfe *of Nappa,* i. faces 407.
Norton *of Norton Conyers,* ii. folding at 182.
Parr ; see Marmion.
Ravensworth, Tanfield, &c., Lords of, i. folding at 124.
Richmond, Earls of ; see Bretagne.
Robinson, Lord Grantham, ii. folding at 122.
Scrope *of Danby,* i. faces 368.
Thoresby *(Wensley),* i. 370.
Tunstall *of Thurland, Wycliffe, &c.* ii. folding at 270, 272, 273.
Wandesford *of Kirklington,* ii. folding at 140.
Wharton *of Gillingwood,* i. faces 78.
Wycliffe *of Wycliffe,* i. folding at 200.
Wyvill *of Burton Constable,* i. folding at 322.

210.—Yorkshire. An Historical and Topographical View of Wapentake, of Strafford, and Tickhill. By JOHN WAINWRIGHT. Vol. I. *Sheffield,* 1826. 4to.

Barbour ; see Bosvil.
Bosvill *of Conisborough,* 122.
Bosvil and Barbour *(Doncaster),* 90.
Carey *(Conisbrough),* 197.
Cooke *of Wheatley,* 124.

De Warren *(Conisbrough),* 195.
Fossard, 7, 25.
Frobisher *(Doncaster),* 145.
Harrington and Copley *(Doncaster),* 113.

211.—Notices relative to the Early History of the Town and Port of Hull. By CHARLES FROST, F.S.A. *London,* 1827. 4to.

De Campania, 9.
De Sculcotes, 29.
De la Pole *of Kingston-upon-Hull,* folding at 31.

De Aton, 74.
De Fortibus, 9.
Sutton *of Holderness,* facing 99.

212.—The History and Antiquities of Filey, in the County of York. By JOHN COLE. *Scarborough,* 1828. 8vo.

Bucke *of Filey.*

213. — South Yorkshire. The History and Topography of the Deanery of Doncaster. By the Rev. JOSEPH HUNTER. *London,* 1828-1831. 2 vols. Folio.

Adams *of Owston,* ii. 478.
Allott *of Bilham Grange,* ii. 366.
Allott *of South Kirkby,* ii. 450.
Anne *of Frickley,* ii. 148.
Armitage *of Doncaster,* i. 210.
Apthorpe *of Dinnington,* i. 137.
Bamford *of Pule Hill,* ii. 270.
Barnby *of Barnby,* ii. 233.
Bate *of Aston,* ii. 167.
Battie *of Warmsworth,* i. 127.
Baxter *(Bolton),* i. 384.
Beaumont *of Bretton,* ii. 249.
Beckwith *of Thurcroft;* see Mirfield.
Bellamy *(Stainton),* i. 259.
Bosvile *of Newhall,* ii. 111.
Bosvile *of Gunthwaite,* ii. 345.
Bosvile *of Chevet,* ii. 393.
Bosvile *of Clifton,* i. 123.
Bosvile *of Warmsworth,* i. 127.
Bosvile *of Braithwell,* i. 133.
Bradford *(Artesey),* i. 330.
Bright *of Ecclesal,* ii. 189.
Bright *of Badsworth,* ii. 437.
Bright *(Melton),* i. 365.
Broadhead and Brinckman, *of Bretton,* ii. 397.
Brooke *of Dodworth,* ii. 262.
Buck *of Rotherham,* ii. 178.
Burdet *of Denby,* ii. 350.
Burdet *of Birthwaite,* ii. 376.
Burton *of Kinsley,* ii. 434.
Carey, Heveningham, Newton, and Coke *(Coningsborough),* i. 115.
Childers *of Carr House,* i. 65.
Cholmley *of North Elmsal,* ii. 454.

Clarel *of Aldwick,* ii. 53.
Coke *(Coningsborough)* ; see Carey.
Cooke *of Wheatley,* i. 56.
Cooke *(second house),* i. 57.
Cooke *(third house),* i. 57.
Cooke *(fourth house),* i. 58.
Copley *of Nether Hall,* i. 51.
Copley *of Sprotborough,* i. 342.
Copley *of Skelbrook,* ii. 458.
Copley *of Wadworth,* i. 251.
Cotton *of South Haigh,* ii. 375.
Crawshaw *(Arksey),* i. 330.
Cresacre *(Barnborough),* i. 372.
Cudworth *of Eastfield,* ii. 270.
Cutler *of Stainborough,* ii. 266.
Darcy *of Aston,* ii. 164.
Darcy *of Notton,* ii. 391.
De Mauley, i. 12.
De Nevile *(Ardwick),* i. 388.
Denman *of Newhall,* ii. 75.
Despencer *(Bawtry),* i. 71.
De Warren, Earls of Warren and Surrey, i. 105.
Dolman *of Badsworth,* ii. 437.
Drax *of Woodhall,* ii. 108.
Drummond, Hay-, Earls of Kinnoul ; see Hay-Drummond.
Edmunds *of Worsborough,* ii. 290.
Ellison *of Thorne,* i. 179.
Elmhurst *of Elmhurst,* ii. 291.
Eyre *of Bramley Hall,* i. 136.
Eyre *of Laughton, Kiveton, Rampton, Grove, &c.* i. 288.
Eyre *of Oxspring,* ii. 355.
Farrer *of Barnborough Grange,* i. 378.

Fenton *of Underbank*, ii. 357.
Fitz William (*Wadley*), i. 251.
Fitzwilliam (*Arksey*), i. 330.
Fitzwilliam *of Sprotborough*, i. 339.
Fitzwilliam *of Haddlesey*, i. 339.
Fitzwilliam, Earl, ii. 93.
Fitzwilliam *of Aldwick*, ii. 56.
Fletcher *of Campsal*, ii. 464.
Foljambe *of Aldwick*, ii. 57, 60.
Fountayne and Wilson *of Melton*, i. 367.
Frank *of Campsal*, ii. 465.
Fretwell *of Hillaby*, i. 2C0.
Frobisher (*Doncaster*), i. 33.
Galway, Viscounts, ii. 414.
Gargrave *of Nostel*, ii. 214.
Gascoign, ii. 484.
Goldthorpe (*Bolton*), i. 387.
Goodwin *of Rawmarsh*, ii. 48.
Green *of Cawthorne*, ii. 234.
Green *of Alkley*, i. 80.
Gregory *of Barnby-on-the-Don*, i. 211.
Hansby *of Tickhill Castle*, i. 234.
Harrington *of Brierley*, ii. 402.
Hatfield *of Hatfield*, i. 178.
Hatfield *of Laughton en le Morthing*, i. 291.
Hay-Drummond, Earls of Kinnoul, i. 316.
Hevingham (*Coningsborough*); see Carey.
Higgins *of Skellow Grange*, ii. 482.
Horne *of Mexborough*, i. 391.
Howard *of Effingham*, Lords, ii. 11.
Hutton *of Hooton-Paynel*, ii. 143.
Ingram *of Temple Newsam*, i. 173.
Ireland *of Nostel*, ii. 215.
Jackson (*Wentworth*), ii. 79.
Jackson *of Hickleton*, ii. 13C.
Jobson *of Cudworth*, ii. 399.
Kent *of Wadworth*, i. 254.
Keresforth *of Keresforth*, ii. 258.
Killom or Kellam *of Hickleton*, ii. 135.
Kinnoul, Earls of; see Drummond-Hay.
Knight *of Langold and Firbeck*, i. 299.
Laughton *of Eastfield*, i. 246.
Laughton *of Howarth*, ii. 36.
Lee *of Hatfield*, i. 477.
Leeds, Dukes of; see Osborne.

Levett *of Melton*, i. 365.
Lewis *of Marr*, i. 361.
Lister *of Bawtry*, i. 72.
Lumley-Saunderson, Earls of Scarborough, i. 275.
Marsh *of Darton*, ii. 370.
Mauleverer *of Letwell*, i. 297.
Melton *of Aston*, ii. 162.
Metham *of Cadeby*, i. 351.
Meyrick, ii. 399.
Micklethwaite *of York*, ii. 353.
Middleham, Lords of, i. 330.
Milner *of Burton Grange*, ii. 277.
Milnes *of Great Houghton*, ii. 130.
Mirfield and Beckwith *of Thurcroft*, i. 294.
Monckton-Arundel, Visct. Galway, ii. 414.
Montfort *of Kilnhurst*, ii. 50.
More *of Barnborough*, i. 376.
Morton (*Bawtry*), i. 76.
Mounteney (*Sandal with Wheatley*), i. 55.
Nevile *of Chevet*, ii. 393.
Nevile *of Brierley*, ii. 401.
Newton (*Coningsborough*); see Carey.
Normanville *of Billingley*, ii. 127.
Osbaldeston *of Hunmanby*, ii. 413.
Osborne, Dukes of Leeds, i. 143.
Parker *of Norton, Woodthorpe, and Streetthorpe*, i. 207.
Parker *of Park Hill*, i. 303.
Pashley *of Stainton*, i. 259.
Perkins *of Fishlake*, i. 178.
Pilkington *of Chevet*, ii. 394.
Piley *of Pilley*, ii. 306.
Popeley *of Morehouse*, ii. 385.
Portington *of Barnaby-on-the-Don*, i. 214.
Ramsden *of Norton*, ii. 473.
Rasby *of Smeaton*, ii. 461.
Rawson *of Bessacarr Grange*, i. 85.
Rawson *of Pickburn*, i. 321.
Rayney *of Tyershill*, ii. 120.
Reresby *of Thribergh*, ii. 39.
Revel *of Whiston*, ii. 180.
Riccard *of Hatfield*, i. 176.
Riche *of Bullhouse*, ii. 362.
Rockley *of Rockley*, ii. 286.
Rodes *of Great Houghton*, ii. 130.
Rogers *of Netherthorpe*, i. 311.
Rokeby (*Sandal Parva*), i. 203.

Rokeby *of Skeirs*, ii. 102.
Saint Paul *of Campsal*, ii. 464.
Sandford *of Thorpe Salvin*, i. 310.
Saunderson *of Sandbeck*, i. 274.
Saunderson, Lumley- ; see Lumley-Saunderson.
Savile *of Thribergh*, ii. 41.
Savile *of Wath*, ii. 67.
Savile *of Tankersley*, ii. 301.
Savile *of Newhall*, ii. 374.
Savile *of Mexborough*, i. 393.
Saxham *(Coningsborough)*, i. 122.
Scarborough, Earls of; see Lumley.
Scrope, Lords, *of Bolton*, i. 92.
Segrave *(Letwell)*, i. 296.
Shaw *of Hallbroom*, ii. 24.
Simpson *of Stainford*, i. 184.
Skiers *of Skiers*, ii. 101.
Sotwell *of Catlinghall*, ii. 271.
Spencer and Stanhope *of Cannon Hall*, ii. 232.
Staniforth *of Firbeck*, i. 301.
Stanley, Lord Mounteagle, ii. 405.
Stead *of Onesacre*, ii. 193.
Stovin *of Tetley, Whitgift, &c.*, i. 183.
Stringer *of Whiston*, ii. 181.
Swyft *of Rotherham, Doncaster, and Streetthorpe*, i. 204.
Thelluson *(Brodsworth)*, i. 318.
Thurgoland *of Lilley*, ii. 269.
Tibetot *(Arksey with Bentley)*, i. 325.
Tolson *of Wath*, ii. 68.
Tooker *of Moor Gate*, ii. 25.
Trigott *of South Kirkby*, ii. 447.
Urswick *of Badsworth*, ii. 437.
Vavasour *of Dennaby*, i. 395.
Verelst *of Aston*, ii. 166.
Vesci *of Brampton*, ii. 179.
Vincent *of Braithwell*, i. 131.
Vincent *of Barnborough Grange*, i. 377.

Ward *of Mount Pleasant*, ii. 189.
Ward *of Upton*, ii. 445.
Warde *of Hooton Paynel*, ii. 143.
Warren and Surrey, Earls of; see De Warren.
Warton *(Wellingley)*, i. 248.
Washington *of Adwick-le-Street*, i. 353.
Waterhouse *of Coningsborough*, i. 117, 118.
Waterhouse *of Braithwell*, i. 132.
Wentworth, Earl of Strafford, ii. 267.
Wentworth *of Wolley*, ii. 388.
Wentworth *of North Elmsal*, ii. 453.
Wentworth *of South Elmsal*, ii. 456.
Wentworth *of Wentworth*, ii. 89.
Wentworth *of Bretton*, ii. 243.
West *of Rotherham and Firbeck*, i. 301.
West *of Aughton*, ii. 173.
West *of Underbank*, ii. 357.
Westby *of Ravenfield*, i. 397.
Westby *of Carhouse*, ii. 30.
Wharton *of Edlington*, i. 93.
Wheatley *of Wolley*, ii. 386.
Wilkinson *of Barnsley*, i. 384.
Wilson *of Melton ;* see Fountayne.
Winn *of Nostel*, ii. 216.
Wolstenholm *of Nostel*, ii. 215.
Wombwell *of Wombwell*, ii. 124.
Wood *of Monk Bretton*, ii. 396.
Wood *of Hemsworth*, ii. 427.
Woodruffe *of Wolley*, ii. 387.
Woodyeare *of Crook Hill*, i. 124.
Wormley *of Hatfield*, i. 175.
Wortley *of Hardwick*, i. 171.
Wortley, Lord Wharncliffe, ii. 324.
Wray *of Cusworth*, i. 349.
Wrightson *of Cusworth*, i. 350.
Wyrral *of Loversal*, i. 62.
Yarborough *of Campsmount*, ii. 466.

214.—Beverlac ; or the History and Antiquities of the Town of Beverley. By GEORGE POULSON, ESQ. *London,* 1829. 2 vols. 4to.

Anlaby *of Etton*, i. 393.
Gee, i. folding at 398.
Grimston, i. facing 432.
Hotham *of Scorboro' and Dalton*, i. folding at 351.

Legard, i. folding at 424
Thorpe *of Hoveden*, i. 393.
Warton *of Beverley Parks*, i. folding at 498.

215.—History and Antiquities of the Town and Minster of Beverley. By GEORGE OLIVER. *Beverley*, 1829. 4to.

Bassett, 564.
Bethell, 533.
De Wake, 462.
Ellerker, 508.
Gee *of Bishop Burton*, 496.
Hotham *of Scorbrough*, folding at 509.

Heron, 340.
Louvaine ; see Percy.
Machell, 562.
Percy and Louvaine, 481.
Stuteville, 459.
Warton *of Beverley Parks*, 515.

216.—Catterick Church. By the Rev. JAMES RAINE, M.A. *London*, 1834. 4to.

Burgh *of Burgh*, 22.

217.—The History and Antiquities of the Seigniory of Holderness. By GEORGE POULSON, Esq. *Hull*, 1840. 2 vols. 4to.

Aclom *of Dringhoe and Hornsea*, i. 334.
Aclom *of Skipsea*, i. 454.
Albemarle, Earls of, i. 24, 37 ; ii. 351.
Alford *of Meaux Abbey*, ii. 315.
Appleyard *of Burstwick Garth*, ii. 364.
Aveyns *of Hatfield*, i. 440.
Bee *of Skeffling*, ii. 504.
Bethell *of Rise*, i. 408.
Bilton *of Bilton*, ii. 250.
Blaydes *of High Paul*, ii. 483.
Boynton *of Barmston and Burton Agnes*, i. 196.
Brigham *of Wyton and Brigham*, ii. 368.
Brooke, Pockley, and Osbaldiston, i. 240.
Brough *of Rolleston*, i. 364.
Bryton, Galfrid de, i. 244.
Catheral *of Hollym*, ii. 394.
Carleill *of Brandsburton*, i. 277.
Cheyney *of Thorngumbald*, ii. 495.
Clapham *of Burton Pidsea*, ii. 42.
Cobb *of Ottringham*, ii. 426.
Constable *of Wassand*, i. 431.
Constable *of Fresmarsh and Catfoss*, i. 437.
Constable *of Burton Constable*, ii. 227.

Constable *of Thirntoft*, ii. 234.
Constable *of Kilnsea, Bentley and Easington*, ii. 235.
Constable *of Kirby, Knoll, and Upsall*, ii. 235.
D'Arcy *of Swine*, ii. 200.
De la See, or Sea, i. 195.
Ellerker *of Moore Grange and Risby*, i. 394.
Faulconberg *of Rise*, i. 395.
Flinton *of Garton and Flinton*, ii. 54.
Frothingham *of South Frothingham*, ii. 409.
Fulthorpe *of Sigglesthorne*, i. 420.
Garnet *of Sigglesthorne*, i. 420.
Gower *of Garton*, ii. 51.
Green *of Cawthorne and Etherdwick*, ii. 30.
Harrison *of Hornsea*, i. 319.
Hastings *of Bewick*, ii. 22.
Hatfield *of Hatfield Magna*, i. 442.
Headon *of Marton*, ii. 209.
Hildyard and Scures *of Riston*, i. 341.
Hildyard *of Arnold*, ii. 221.
Hildyard *of Ottringham*, ii. 426.
Hildyard *of Winestead*, ii. 466.
Hildyard *of Skeffling*, ii. 498.
Holme *of Paul Holme and Skeffling*, ii. 488.

Hunter *of Hayholme*, i. 355.
Hustler *of Hatfield Parva*, i. 441.
Knowles *of Bilton*, ii. 250.
Langdale *of Dowthorpe*, ii. 254.
Le Despenser *of Little Colden*, i. 370.
Lewings *of Rusholme*, i. 478.
Little *of Kilnsea*, ii. 523.
Maister *of Patrington and Winestead*, ii. 445.
Mayne and Truslove *of Rolleston*, i. 365.
Meaux *of Bewick*, ii. 20.
Melsa *of Dringhoe*, i. 463.
Melton *of Swine*, ii. 199.
Micklethwayte *of Swine*, ii. 201.
Monceaux *of Barmston*, i. 186.
Moore *of Bewick*, ii. 23.
Noel *of Hayholme*, i. 354.
Osbaldiston ; see Brooke.
Overton *of Easington*, ii. 377.
Owst *of Halsham and Kayingham*, ii. 421.
Pockley ; see Brooke.
Ricaby *of Ulram*, i. 229.
Raines *of Burton Pidsea*, ii. 45.
Raines *of Wyton*, ii. 270.
Scott *of Aldborough*, ii. 18.
Scures ; see Hildyard.

Sea ; see De la See.
Shaftsbury, Lord, ii. 201.
Shutte *of Hambleton*, ii. 70.
St. Quinton *of Brandsburton and Harpham*, i. 266.
St. Quinton, Sir William, *of Harpham*, i. 268.
Sterne *of Rise*, ii. 411.
Storr *of Hilton*, ii. 79.
Sutton *of Sutton*, ii. 70.
Sykes *of Sledmere and Roos*, ii. 91.
Thompson *of Hambleton*, ii. 63.
Thorpe *of Thorpe Garth*, ii. 513.
Tiliol *of Hatfield Parva*, i. 440.
Torre *of Rise*, i. 412.
Torre *of Syndale and Paul Holme*, ii. 491.
Topham *of Withernwick*, i. 473.
Towry *of Little Colden*, i. 371.
Truslove ; see Mayne.
Tunstall *of Wycliff*, ii. 235.
Twyer *of Ganstead*, ii. 192.
Ulf *of Aldborough*, ii. 2.
Warton *of Beverley Parks*, i. 483.
Wassand *of Wassand*, i. 433.
Wencelagh *of Brandsburton*, i. 277.
Whitehead *of Atwick*, ii. 168.
Wright *of Ploughland*, ii. 516.
Wycliffe *of Wycliffe*, ii. 239.

218.—The History and Topography of Bradford. By JOHN JAMES. *London,* 1841. Royal 8vo.

Dixon *of Heaton Royds*, 431.
Field *of Heaton*, 433.
Hird *of Low Moor;* see Wickham.
Horton *of Chadderton*, 439.
Lister *of Manningham*, 440.
Rawson *of Bradford*, 430.
Richardson *of Bierley*, 422.

Rookes *of Royds Hall*, 437.
Sharp *of Little Horton*, 426.
Smyth *of Miryshaw*, 435.
Stansfield *of Bradford*, (now *of Esholt*), 436.
Wickham *of Yorkshire*, and Hird *of Low Moor House*, 442.

219.—Pedigrees of Families of the City of York, from a Manuscript entitled "The Heraldic Visitations of Yorkshire Consolidated." By WILLIAM PAVER, Genealogist. *York,* 1842. 8vo.

Allenson *of York*, 7.
Askwith *of York*, 8.
Ayscough *of York*, 10.
Bell *of York*, 10.
Bigge *of Yorke*, 11.
Birkby *of Yorke*, 11.
Chadderton *of York*, 12.

Edmondson *of York*, 12.
Ellis *of York*, 13.
Hewley *of York*, 13.
Hildyard *of York*, 14.
Langley *of York*, 14.
Lindley *of York*, 15.
Mascall *of York*, 15.

160

Mould *of York*, 16.
Nesbit *of York*, 16.
Peirs *of York*, 17.
Pierson *of York*, 18.
Shillito *of York*, 18.
Sowray *of York*, 19.

Swinburne *of York*, 20.
Taylor *of York*, 20.
Watkinson *of York*, 21.
Wittie *of York*, 21.
Witton *of York*, 22.
Young *of York*, 22.

220.—The History and Antiquities of Cleveland. By JOHN WALKER ORD, F.G.S.L. *London*, 1846. 4to.

Allan *of Blackwell Grange*, 499.
Baliol *of Stokesley*, 395.
Bate *of Eseby*, 409.
Bowyer *of Danby*, 341.
Bruce, folding at 249.
Bulmer *of Wilton*, 385.
Carey, Lord Hunsdon, Visct. Falkland, 474.
Chaloner *of Gisborough*, 221.
Colvile *of Ernclive*, 457.
Consett *of Normanby*, 564.
Conyers and Strangwayes *of Ormesby*, 555.
Coulson *of Ayton*, 411.
Coulthurst *of Upleatham*, 350.
Crathorne *of Crathorne*, 490.
Danby, Lords of, 330.
Dundas *of Upleatham*, 351.
Everingham *of Skinningrave*, 274.
Falkland, Visct.; see Carey.
Forster *of Stokesley*, 397.
Foulis *of Ingleby*, 432.
Gower *of Stainsby*, 505.
Hale *of Tocketts*, 232.
Hunsdon, Lord; see Carey.
Hustler *of Acklam*, 529.
Ingram *of Rudby and Temple Newsom*, 466.

Lee *of Pinchinthorp*, 241.
Linley *of Skuttleskelfe*, 474.
Lowther *of Wilton*, 386.
Lumley; see Twenge.
Marwood *of Little Busby*, 408.
Mauleverer *of Arnecliffe*, 458.
Mauley, 309.
Meinell *of Whorlton*, 444.
Meinell *of Yarm*, 513.
Morley *of Normanby*, 563.
Myddleton Wharton; see Wharton Myddleton.
Peirson *of Stokesley*, 397.
Pennyman *of Ormesby*, 555.
Percy *of Kildare*, 426.
Sheffield, Earl of Mulgrave, 309.
Smallwood *of Upleatham*, 350.
Stapleton *of Myton*, &c. 558.
Steward *of Lofthouse*, 276.
Strangwayes *of Whorlton*, 447.
Strangwayes; see Conyers.
Turner *of Kirkleatham*, 368.
Twenge and Lumley, Lords of Kilton, 269.
Wharton-Myddleton *of Grinkle*, 288.
Warton *of Skelton*, 255.
Yoward *of Westerdale*, 346.

221.—*Vallis Eboracensis:* comprising the History and Antiquities of Easingwold, and its neighbourhood. By THOMAS GILL. *London*, 1852. 8vo.

De Etton, Fairfax and Neville, 257.
Fairfax; see De Etton.

Neville; see De Etton.
Scrope, Lords of Bolton, 116.

222.—The History of the Town and Township of Barnsley, in Yorkshire. By ROWLAND JACKSON. *London*, 8vo.; second Edition, *London*, 1858. 8vo.

Armitage and Wentworth, folding at 150.
Beckett; see Usher.

Clarke and Chappel *of Barnsley*, folding at 65.
Clarke; see Usher.

Chappel; see Clarke.
De Caprecuria, 50.
Halifax, folding at 145.
Keresforth *of Keresforth*, folding at 150.
Laci, Lords of Pontefract and Black-burnshire, folding at 18.

Rooke *of Barnsley*, folding at 97.
Usher, Clarke, and Beckett, folding at 113.
Wentworth; see Armitage.
Wood, folding at 81.

223.—The Early Ecclesiastical History of Dewsbury, &c. By JOHN BESWICKE GREENWOOD, M.A. *London*, 1859. 8vo.

Savile *of Lupset, Thornhill and Howley*, 214.

224.—The Visitation of the County of Yorke, begun in 1665 and finished in 1666. By WILLIAM DUGDALE, Esq., Norroy King of Arms. Surtees Society. Vol. 36. 1859. 8vo.

Adams *of Camblesforth*, 268.
Adams *of East Hardwick*, 17.
Adams *of Scausby*, 176.
Agard *of Huntington*, 217.
Allenson *of Yorke*, 230.
Anlaby *of Etton*, 334.
Anne *of Frickley*, 285.
Appleby *of Linton*, 209.
Armitage *of Keresforth Hill*, 25.
Armitage *of Kirklees*, 251.
Atkinson *of Skelton*, 364.
Austwick *of Pontfract*, 23.
Awnby *of Sherwood Hall*, 313.
Ayscough *of Skewsby*, 342-344.
Ayscough *of Yorke*, 147, 153.
Barton *of Cawton*, 124.
Bate *of Eseby*, 80.
Batte *of Okewell*, 233.
Battie *of Wadworth*, 167.
Baynes *of Mewith-head*, 44.
Beale *of Woodhouse*, 189.
Beaumont *of Whitley*, 253, 254.
Beavot *of Leedes*, 26.
Beckwith *of Acton*, 274.
Beckwith *of Handale Abbey*, 383.
Beilby *of Micklethwayt Grange*, 4.
Bellwood *of Leathley*, 213.
Belton *of Overton*, 152.
Bethell *of Ellerton and Falthrop*, 155.
Bethell *of Wrays*, 132.
Beverley *of Great Smeton*, 35.
Bigge *of Yorke*, 151.

Birkbeck *of Sheffeild and Castleford*, 312.
Bland *of Kippax Parke*, 350, 351.
Blythman *of Newlathes*, 179.
Boothe *of Cridlyng Parke*, 17.
Booth, *of Pontefract*, 358.
Bossevile *of Braywell*, 297.
Bosvile *of Warmsworth*, 276.
Bourchier *of Benningbrough*, 140.
Boynton *of Barmston*, 126.
Boynton *of Rawcliffe*, 127.
Bradford *of Arksey*, 229.
Bradley *of Acworth*, 8.
Brandling *of Leathley*, 26.
Brearey *of Yorke*, 210.
Brigham *of Brigham*, 136.
Bright *of Badsworth*, 263.
Brunskell *of Bowes*, 44.
Buck *of Carnaby*, 69.
Buck *of Flotmanby*, 70.
Bulkley *of South Emsall*, 247.
Bunny *of Newland*, 279.
Burdet *of Birthwayt*, 2.
Burgoine *of Addlethorpe*, 27.
Bushell *of Whitby*, 82.
Caley *of Brumpton*, 125.
Calverley *of Calverley*, 382.
Calverley *of Eriholme*, 61.
Carleil *of Sewarby*, 115.
Carrington *of Spaunton*, 66.
Carter *of Settrington*, 363.
Cayley *of Brumpton*, 196, 197.
Chadderton *of Yorke*, 314.

Y

Chaloner *of Gisbrough,* 201.
Chamber *of Oulston,* 366.
Chaytor *of Crofte,* 302, 303.
Cholmeley *of Braham,* 315.
Cholmeley *of Brandesby,* 220.
Cholmeley *of West Newton,* 7.
Clapham *of Beamsley,* 43.
Clayton *of Okenshaw,* 260.
Cobb *of Ottringham,* 332.
Colbye *of Bowbridge,* 47.
Colthurst *of Up Leatham,* 370.
Comyn *of Whitby,* 72.
Constable *of Burton Constable* (now Visc. Dunbar), 137.
Constable *of Catfosse,* 323.
Constable *of Cliffe,* 339.
Constable *of Everingham,* 119.
Constable *of Wassand,* 335.
Conyers *of Bowlby,* 340.
Cooke *of Wheatley,* 299.
Copley *of Batley,* 259.
Copley *of Doncaster,* 272.
Copley *of Sprodborough,* 275.
Corbet *of Kingston-upon-Hull,* 359.
Coulson *of Ayton,* 323.
Cradock *of Richmund,* 106.
Crashaw *of Bentley,* 212.
Crathorne *of Crathorne,* 145.
Craven *of Appletreewick,* 33.
Cressy *of Birkin,* 269.
Creyke *of Marton,* 328.
Crofts *of East Appleton,* 91.
Crompton *of Great Driffeild,* 322.
Crompton *of Sunderlandwyke,* 161.
Crosland *of Crosland Hill,* 188.
Crosland *of Newby,* 133.
Croston *of Threske,* 60.
Currer *of Kildwick,* 252.
Currer *of Skipton,* 231.
Cutler *of Stainebrough,* 4.
Dalton *of Hawkeswell,* 47.
Dalton *of Swyne,* 143.
Danby *of Great Leake,* 93.
Darcy *of Colburne,* 209.
Darcy *of Richmund,* 108.
Davile *of Kirkby Fleetham,* 101.
Davye *of Fockerby,* 386.
Dawney *of Cowick,* 264.
Denton *of Nawton,* 63.
Dewick *of Kingston-super-Hull,* 136.
Dodsworth *of Badsworth,* 287.
Dodsworth *of Barton,* 313.

Dodsworth *of Thorneton Watlas,* 88.
Dolman *of Pocklington,* 138.
Drake *of Rippon,* 59.
Driffeild *of Easingwold,* 384.
Eaton *of Darfield,* 287.
Edmunds *of Worsbrough,* 9.
Egerton *of Allarston,* 71.
Ellerker *of Yolton,* 295.
Ellis *of Kiddall,* 373.
Elmehirst *of Houndhill,* 199.
Empson *of Gowle,* 19.
Eyre *of Bramley,* 13.
Fairfax *of Dunsley,* 230.
Fairfax *of Mensington,* 232.
Fairfax *of Oglethorpe,* 8.
Fairfax *of Sledmer,* 229.
Fane *of Aston,* 293.
Farside *of Filingdale,* 85.
Favell *of Keirby,* 348, 349.
Fawkes *of Woodhall,* 29.
Feilding *of Starford,* 60.
Ferrand *of Flasby,* 31.
Ferrand *of Harden Beck,* 48.
Ferrand *of Westhall,* 27.
Fletcher *of Towton,* 19.
Foljambe *of Steveton,* 53.
Forster *of Rothwell,* 204.
Forster *of Stokesley,* 71.
Foulis *of Ingleby Manour,* 193.
Foxcroft *of Westwood,* 48.
Franke *of Knighton,* 79.
Franke *of Pomfret,* 3.
Frankland *of Aldwarke,* 206.
Frankland *of Thirkelby,* 78.
Fulthorpe *of Siglesthorne,* 118.
Gascoigne *of Barnbow,* 289.
Gates *of Thorne Parke,* 76.
Gee *of Bishop Burton,* 321.
Geldart *of Wigginthorpe,* 213.
Gere *of Great Barugh,* 81.
Gere *of Great Broughton,* 81.
Gibson *of Welborne,* 73.
Gill *of Carr-house,* 277.
Goodrick *of Ribstan,* 159.
Goodwin *of Rawmarsh,* 278.
Graham *of Norton Conyers,* 41.
Greene *of Bancke,* 306.
Greene *of Horsforth,* 49.
Greene *of Leversedge,* 379.
Greene *of Thundercliffe,* 1.
Greenwood *of Stapleton,* 311.
Greenwood *of West Ardesley,* 246.
Grey *of Beverley,* 333.

INDEX TO BOOKS. 224. 163

Grymston *of Drynge*, 129.
Grymston *of Frasthorpe*, 64.
Grymston *of Grymston Garth and Goodmadham*, 121.
Gyll *of Barton*, 280.
Hall *of East Lilling*, 149.
Hall *of Lenthorpe*, 214.
Hamerton *of Preston Jacklyn*, 354, 355.
Hamond *of Scarthingwell*, 378.
Hanson *of Woodhouse*, 257.
Hardy *of Wetwang*, 68.
Harrison *of Acaster*, 172.
Harrison *of Caton*, 217.
Harrison *of Allerthorpe*, 216.
Harrison *of Hornesey*, 132.
Hassell *of Hutton-upon-Darwent*, 75.
Hatfield *of Haitfield*, 270, 271.
Hatfield *of Laughton-in-le-Morthing*, 185.
Hawkesworth *of Hawkesworth*, 244.
Headlam *of Kexby*, 204.
Heber *of Hollinghall*, 54.
Heber *of Stainton*, 34
Heblethwayte *of Norton*, 205.
Hellard *of Kilham*, 118.
Herbert *of Middleton Whernho*, 165.
Herbert *of Yorke*, 148.
Hildyard *of Beverley*, 144.
Hippon *of Newhall*, 15.
Hitching *of Carleton*, 18.
Holdsworth *of Astley*, 255.
Holme *of Pall Holme*, 129.
Hopkinson *of Loftus*, 51.
Horne *of Mexburgh*, 353.
Horsfall *of Stortheshall*, 231.
Horsley *of Beckhouse*, 362.
Horsley *of Full Sutton*, 169.
Horton *of Barkisland*, 233.
Hotham *of Scarborough*, 336, 337.
Huley *of Yorke*, 161.
Humfrey *of Askerne*, 177.
Hungate *of Saxton*, 296.
Hunt *of Stainton*, 152.
Hunter *of Thorneton*, 87.
Hutchenson *of Wickham*, 83.
Hutton *of Poppleton*, 173.
Ingleby *of Lawkeland*, 46.
Ingleby *of Ripley*, 30.
Ingram *of Cattall and Thorpe*, 146.
Jackson *of Hickleton*, 5.

Jackson *of Whitby*, 117.
Jaques *of Elvington*, 162.
Jenkyn *of Grimston*, 363.
Jennings *of Rippon*, 58.
Jessop *of Bromehall*, 163.
Johnston *of Pomfret*, 6.
Kay *of Woodsome*, 171.
Kellam *of Pontefract*, 356, 357.
Keresforth *of Puell Hill*, 2.
Killingbeck *of Chapell Allerton*, 20.
Knight *of Langold*, 272.
Lacock *of Coppenthorpe*, 156.
Lacy *of Thornhill*, 299.
Lake *of Castleford*, 16.
Lambert *of Kingston-upon-Hull*, 367.
Lamont *of North Burton*, 75.
Langdale *of Snainton*, 82.
Langley *of North Grimston*, 301.
Langley *of Rathorp Hall*, 234.
Langley *of Sheriff Hutton Parke*, 300.
Langley *of Yorke*, 205.
Lawson *of Brough*, 90.
Layton *of Barroughby*, 377.
Layton *of Whitehouse*, 104.
Lee *of Pinchingthorpe*, 96.
Leedes *of Hopenthorne*, 286.
Leedes *of North Milford*, 286.
Leeke *of Horbury*, 258.
Legard *of Ganton*, 111.
Levingstoun *of Danby Forest*, 72.
Levyns *of Eske*, 330.
Lewis *of Ledston*, 290, 291.
Lindley *of Yorke*, 279.
Lister *of Linton*, 316.
Lister *of Kingston super Hull*, 128.
Lister *of Shipden Hall*, 246.
Lloyd *of Hardwick*, 365.
Lockwood *of Sowerby*, 107.
Lovell *of Skelton*, 157.
Lutton *of Knapton*, 77.
Lyster *of Arnolds Biggin*, 32.
Lyster *of Thorneton and Midhope*, 178.
Maleverer *of Arncliffe*, 97.
Manby *of Middleton*, 84.
Mares *of Sedbridge*, 45.
Marshall *of Aislaby Grange*, 316.
Marshall *of Doncaster*, 175.
Marwood *of Little Buskeby*, 160.
Mascall *of York*, 223.
Mellish *of Doncaster*, 297.

Meryton *of Castle Leventon*, 107.
Metcalfe *of Nappa*, 105.
Metcalfe *of North Allerton*, 177.
Metcalfe *of Thornborough*, 325.
Metham *of Metham*, 139.
Meynill *of North Kilvington*, 95.
Meynill *of West Dalton and Aldbrough*, 103.
Micklethwayt *of Swyne*, 280, 281.
Middleton *of Stockheld*, 57.
Monketon *of Hodroyd*, 163.
Moore *of Lower Harrop*, 54.
Moore *of Angram Grange*, 158.
More *of Austrop*, 24.
Morley *of Newton-upon-Ouse*, 176.
Morris *of North Emsall*, 267, 268.
Moreton *of Spouthouse*, 175.
Morton *of Wrath House*, 338.
Mottram *of Bishopdike Hall*, 222.
Mould *of Yorke*, 223.
Mountaigne *of Weston*, 362.
Mountney *of Rotheram*, 200.
Moyser *of Beverley*, 212.
Nary *of Malton*, 116.
Neale *of Leedes*, 234.
Nesbit *of Yorke*, 158.
Nevill *of Chevet*, 170.
Newarke *of Acham*, 194.
Newton *of Bagdale Hall*, 67.
Noell *of Hayholme*, 70.
Norcliff *of Langton*, 341.
Norton *of Sawley*, 40.
Norton *of St. Nicholas juxta, Richmond*, 102
Oglethorpe *of Brandesby*, 262.
Oglethorpe *of Oglethorpe*, 151.
Orme *of South Newbold*, 154.
Osbaldeston *of Hunmaby*, 83.
Otway *of Inyer Hall*, 385.
Palleser *of Newly*, 94.
Palmes *of Naburne*, 222.
Parker *of Brousholme*, 28.
Payler *of Thoroby*, 317.
Pearson *of Lowthorpe*, 70.
Peebles *of Dewsbury*, 367.
Peirse *of Lasenby*, 325.
Pennyman *of Ormesby*, 198.
Percehay *of Ryton*, 114.
Percy *of Stubbs Walden*, 7.
Perkinson *of Carleton*, 45.
Pinkney *of Silton Paynell*, 326.
Plumpton *of Plumpton*, 190-192.
Pockley *of Thorpe Willoughby*, 15.

Portington *of Barnby super Dun*, 168.
Portington *of Malton*, 120.
Pricket *of Allerthorpe*, 130.
Pudsey *of Lawfeild*, 29.
Ratcliffe *of Sheffoild*, 277.
Rawson *of Pickburne*, 164.
Rawson *of Shipley*, 258.
Raynes *of Apleton-in-the-Streete*, 368.
Remington *of Lund*, 123.
Reresby *of Thribergh*, 182, 183.
Rhodes *of Great Houghton*, 166.
Richardson *of North Bierley*, 50.
Ripley *of Kingston super Hull*, 130.
Robinson *of Buckton*, 117.
Robinson *of Dighton*, 208.
Robinson *of Farmanby*, 69.
Robinson *of Kirby Ravensworth*, 91.
Robinson *of Newby*, 207.
Robinson *of Rither*, 18.
Robinson *of Rokesby*, 34.
Robynson *of Thornton Riseborough*, 65.
Rokeby *of Ackworth Parke*, 372.
Rokeby *of Hotham and Skires*, 184.
Rokeby *of Moreton*, 73.
Rokeby *of Warmesworth*, 167.
Rosse *of Chapell Allerton*, 250.
Roundell *of Marston*, 208.
Rudston *of Hayton*, 131.
Ryther *of Scarcroft*, 235.
St. Quintin *of Harpham*, 135.
Saltmersh *of North Kilvington*, 94.
Salvein *of New Biggin*, 96.
Savile *of Bowlings*, 256.
Savile *of Copley*, 310.
Savile *of Methley Hall*, 346, 347.
Savile *of Mexbrough*, 181.
Scorah *of Doncaster*, 168.
Scroope *of Danby*, 36.
Scudamore *of Leedes*, 25.
Scudamore *of Overton*, 154.
Shaw *of Sheppard Castle*, 365.
Shilleto *of Yorke*, 385.
Shuttleworth *of Forcet*, 72.
Skelton *of Middleton*, 113.
Skelton *of Osmundthorpe*, 21.
Simpson *of Leedes*, 9.
Simpson *of Wetherby*, 39.
Slingar *of Catlow*, 55.
Slingsby *of Soryven*, 228.
Smallwood *of Up Leatham*, 371.

Smelt *of Kirby Fleetham*, 104.
Smith *of Sneiton*, 116.
Smithson *of Moulton*, 39.
Snawsell *of Bilton*, 150.
Sotwell *of Catlinghill*, 304, 305.
Sowray *of Yorke*, 317.
Sowtheby *of Birdsall*, 318.
Spenser *of Attercliffe*, 12.
Spenser *of Leeds*, 20.
Stables *of Tanshelfe*, 11.
Stanhope *of Hampull*, 294.
Stapleton *of Carleton*, 265.
Stapleton *of Wartre*, 110.
Stapleton *of Wighill*, 224, 226.
Stapylton *of Myton*, 141.
Stephenson *of Swynflete*, 221.
Steward *of Lofthouse*, 326.
Stillington *of Kelfield*, 215.
Stockdale *of Bilton Parke*, 58.
Stoutville *of Humanby*, 87.
Strangways *of South House*, 86.
Strickland *of Boynton*, 112.
Stringer *of Sharleton*, 282.
Sunderland *of Aykton*, 380.
Sunderland *of Harden*, 21.
Swale *of South Stainley*, 42.
Sykes *of Spoforth*, 166.
Sympson *of Ryton*, 124.
Sympson *of Sheffield*, 173.
Talbot *of Thorneton le Street*, 38.
Talbot *of Thorneton*, 236—244.
Tankard *of Whixley*, 56.
Tayler *of Coates*, 314.
Taylor *of Temple Hurst*, 16.
Taylor *of Yorke*, 214.
Tempest *of Broughton*, 360, 361.
Tempest *of Tonge*, 319.
Thomlinson *of Byrdforth*, 110.
Thomlinson *of Thorgamby*, 376.
Thomlinson *of Whitby*, 66.
Thompson *of Hambleton*, 122.
Thompson *of Kilham*, 219.
Thompson *of Kingston super Hull*, 143.
Thoresby *of Sykehouse and Leedes*, 248, 249.
Thorneton *of East Newton*, 67.
Thornhill *of Fixby*, 308, 309.
Thornton *of Tiersall*, 250.
Thorpe *of Danthorpe*, 134.
Throckmorton *of Burnebutts*, 84.
Thurgarland *of Lyley*, 261.
Tindall *of Brotherton*, 352.

Tocketts *of Tocketts*, 320.
Topham *of Aglethorpe*, 149.
Trotter *of Skelton Castle*, 99.
Tunstall *of Scargill*, 31.
Turner *of Kirk Leatham*, 324.
Vavasour *of Haselwood*, 345.
Vincent *of Baronbrough*, 202, 203.
Wade *of Kilnsay*, 32.
Wade *of Kingcrosse*, 245.
Wakefield *of Seassey*, 218.
Waller *of Sykehouse*, 369.
Walmesley *of Stayner Hall*, 14.
Wandesford *of Kirklington*, 100.
Warton *of Beverley*, 331.
Washington *of Adwicke*, 273.
Wastell *of Scorton*, 227.
Watkinson *of Yorke*, 206.
Watson *of Easthage*, 283.
Wayte *of Layburne*, 35.
Weddell *of Earswick*, 164.
Wentworth *of Broadsworth*, 3.
Wentworth *of Emsall*, 288.
Wentworth *of South Emsall*, 284.
Wentworth *of West Bretton*, 307.
Wentworth *of Wolley*, 10.
West *of Aston*, 292, 293.
Westby *of Gilthwayt*, 278.
Westby *of Ravenfield*, 174.
Wheathe *of Langtoft*, 123.
Wickham *of Bolton Percy*, 150.
Wilberfosse *of Wilberfosse*, 120.
Wilkinson *of Kirkbrigg*, 381.
Wilkinson *of Manningham*, 255.
Wilkinson *of Pontfract*, 52.
Winn *of Nostell Abby*, 298.
Wittie *of Yorke*, 221.
Witton *of Yorke*, 318.
Wombwell *of Wombwell*, 180.
Wood *of Thorpe*, 78.
Wormeley *of Rikhall*, 211.
Worsley *of Hovingham*, 62.
Wright *of Bolton-upon-Swale*, 98.
Wycliffe *of Thorpe*, 195.
Wytham *of Cliffe*, 109.
Wytham *of Garforth*, 374, 375.
Wyvell *of Bellarby*, 37.
Wyvell *of Osgodby*, 329.
Wyvell *of Constable Burton*, 89.
Yarborough *of Appleton*, 169.
Yarbrough *of Snayth*, 260.
Yarburgh *of Doncaster*, 186, 187.
Yorke *of Goulthwayt*, 92.
Yoward *of Westerdale*, 327.

166   INDEX TO BOOKS. 225—226.

225.—History of the Parish of Ecclesfield, in the County of York. By the Rev. J. EASTWOOD, M.A. *London,* 1862. 8vo.

Booth *of Brush House,* 380.
Dixon *of Page Hall,* 384.
Greaves *of Page Hall and Elmsall Lodge,* 383.

Hunter, 372.
Parkin *of Mortomley and Darley,* folding at 432.
Smith *of Barnes Hall,* 417.

226.—Heraldic Visitation of the Northern Counties in 1530. By THOS. TONGE, Norroy, &c. *Surtees Society.* Vol. 41. 1863. 8vo. *See also Cumberland, Durham, Nottinghamshire, Northumberland, and Westmoreland.*

Aclam, 65.
Anne *of Frikeley,* 9.
Ardyngton *of Ardyngton,* 21.
Aske *of Acton,* 64.
Audborough, 53.
Borton *of Whenby,* 61.
Borton, 77.
Borough, 44.
Boynton *of Sadbere,* 42.
Bullmer, 25.
Bunny, 82.
Bygode *of Setteryngton,* 67.
Calverley *of Calverley,* 85.
Cholmundeley *of Golston,* 21.
Coniers *of Maske,* 46.
Constable *of Flamborow,* 68.
Conyers, Lord, 48.
Copeley, 73.
Copeley, 81.
Danby, 87.
Delaryver *of Bransby,* 18.
Donyngton, 55.
Dransfeld, 47.
Eland *of Kingston-upon-Hull,* 69.
Ellercar *of Rosby,* 71.
Everyngham *of Birkyng,* 12.
Fayrefax *of Walton,* 57.
Fayrefax *of Steton,* 58.
Foltherop, 47.
Gascoyn *of Galtherop,* 14.
Gowre *of Stidnam,* 62.
Hastynges, 73.
Hawdonbe, 74.
Husse *of Hersewell,* 22.

Irton, 93.
Kyrkeby, 92.
Layborn, 95.
Lamplew, 94.
Malore *of Howton Coniers,* 51.
Malyvoryr *of Alderton,* 54.
Meytam *of Meytam Hall,* 63.
Middleton *of Stokell,* 87.
Musgrave, 52.
Nevill, Lord Latymer, 20.
Nevill *of Loversege,* 83.
Palmes *of Naburn,* 66.
Peke *of Wakefeld,* 81.
Percchay, 86.
Place *of Halnaby,* 49.
Plumpton *of Plumpton,* 55.
Pudsey *of Belton,* 45.
Pulleyn *of Scotton,* 13.
Roclyffe *of Coltherop,* 58.
Rokley, 76.
Salven *of Newbegynge,* 24.
Savell, 79.
Scroop, Lord, *of Bolton,* 32.
Selyngesby *of Screvyng,* 11.
Snasell, 17.
Stapilton *of Wyghell,* 16.
Tempeste, 84.
Thunstall, 95.
Vavasor, 56.
Wandysford *of Kyrkelyngton,* 50.
Wentworth *of Elmesell,* 11.
Wentworth *of West Bretton,* 85.
Wentworth, 75.

WALES.

227.—A History of the County of Brecknock. By THEO-PHILUS JONES. *Brecknock*, 1805-1809. 2 vols. 4to.

Awbrey *of Abercynrig and Palley*, ii. 607.

Awbrey *of Yniscedwin*, ii. 655.

Awbrey *of Llanelieu*, ii. 368.

Awbrey *of Tredomen, Brecon, &c.* ii. 567.

Bois, now Williams *of Velin newydd*, ii. 319.

Bourghill, Burchill, or Burfield *of Crickhowel*, ii. 441.

Brychan Brecheiniog, descendants of, i. App. 1-30, between 341 and 342.

Bullen, now Williams, *of Abercamlais*, ii. 698.

Burchill ; see Bourghill.

Burfield ; see Bourghill.

De Solariis ; see Solers.

Games *of Peytin, Newton, Aberbran, Buckland, &c.* ii. 164-169.

Gunter *of Gunterstone or Tregunter, Gileston, &c.* ii. 343.

Gwyn *of Maeslach and Garth*, ii. 262.

Havard *of Pontwilym*, ii. 127, 132.

Herbert *of Crickhowel*, ii. 451-458.

James *of Brecknock*, ii. 254.

Jeffreys *of Brecon*, ii. 117-121.

Jones *of Maesmawr ;* see Powell.

Lewis *of Llanelly ;* and Morgan *of Llangeney*, ii. 478.

Lewis *of Maesmawr ;* see Powel.

Lloyd *of Rhos Fferreg*, ii. 248.

Lloyd *of Caerau, Brecon, and Lancamddwr*, ii. 268.

Lloyd *of Millfield and Crickadarn*, ii. 303.

Madoc, now Maddocks *of Llanfrynach*, ii. 602.

Morgan *of Llangeney ;* see Lewis.

Morgan *of Penderin and Brecon*, ii. 138.

Morgan *of Ystradfellte and Dderw*, ii. 310.

Morgan *of Tymawr*, ii. 479.

Newmarch, Bernard, descendants of, i. App. 10, between 345, 346.

Parry *of Poston, co. Hereford, of*

Llandevailog tre'rgraig, *co. Brecon*, ii. 557.

Powel *of Castle Madoc*, ii. 180.

Powel *of Tyle glas*, ii. 379.

Powel, Jones, and Lewis *of Maesmawr, &c.* ii. 524.

Powel, Lords *of Llangasty tal y llyn*, ii. 550.

Powell *of Peterstone, Cantreff, &c.* ii. 585.

Powell *of Glyntarell*, ii. 687.

Price *of Brecon*, ii. 112.

Price *of Glynllech*, ii. 657.

Prichard *of Trephilip and Brecon*, ii. 322.

Rumsey *of Cwmgu and Crickhowel*, ii. 511.

Solers, or De Solariis, *of Tredustan and Pentre Solers*, ii. 377.

Stedman *of Dol y gaer*, ii. 272.

Surdwal *of Abyrescir*, ii. 205.

Turbeville, Turberville, or Turbil *of Crickhowel*, ii. 443.

Vaughan *of Yscirfechan and Trebarried*, ii. 190.

Vaughan *of Porthaml*, ii. 340.

Vaughan *of Cathedine, Brecon, Llanvillo, &c.* ii. 360.

Vaughan *of Tretower, Hergest, and Clyro*, ii. 505.

Walbeoffe or Walbieffe *of Llanhamlach*, ii. 583.

Watkins *of Brecon, Broadway, Penoyre, &c.* ii. 199.

Wilkins *of Languix, Brecknock, and Bristol*, ii. 139.

Williams *of Gwernyvet*, ii. 383.

Williams *of Eltham, afterwards of Gwernyfed*, ii. 385.

Williams, ii. 707.

Williams ; see Bullen.

Williams *of Penpont*, ii. 700.

Williams *of Aberbran*, ii. 701.

Williams *of Ffrwdgrech, afterwards of Blannant*, ii. 717.

Williams *of Velin newydd ;* see Bois.

Wynter, or Winter *of Brecon*, ii. 135-137.

228.—Glamorganshire Pedigrees. From the MSS. of Sir
    Isaac Heard, Knt. Garter King of Arms. Edited by
    Sir Thomas Phillipps, Bart. *Worcester*, 1845. Folio.

Abermarlies, 17.
Avan *of Avan*, 9, 11.
Awbrey *of Ynys Gedwyn*, 23.
Awbrey *of Gunterston*, 23.
Bach *of Lancarvan*, 35.
Basset *of Bewper*, 2.
Basset *of Lantrithyd and Boulston*, 4.
Basset *of Miskin*, 21.
Basset, 34.
Basset *of Llantrithyd*, 34.
Basset *of Tre'r Gove*, 34.
Basson and Thomas *of Brigan and Lansannwr*, 34.
Bawdrip *of Penmark*, 3.
Bevan *of Gelli Galed*, 16.
Blayne *of Llangydwyd*, 19.
Blethyn *of Shernewton*, 42.
Button *of Dyffryn Golywchi or Wolston*, 34.
Carn *of Nash*, 5.
Carn *of Ewenny*, 6.
Cradock *of Swansea*, 20.
Cradock *of Court ryd Hir*, 36.
David, 42.
David *of Ceven y Forest*, 7, 41.
Edwards, 33.
Evans *of Neath*, 11, 32.
Evans *of Cilvai and Llansamlet*, 20.
Fleming *of Monkton*, 42.
Francklen *of Gower*, 41.
Gamadge *of Lanbedrfynydd*, 44.
Gamage *of Rogiad and Coyty*, 4.
Gamage *of Newcastle and Oldcastle*, 44.
Games *of Aberbran*, 21.
Games *of Newton*, 21, 29, 37.
Gethin *of Glyntawe*, 36, 46.
Gibbon *of Trecastell*, 22, 40.
Gibbons *of Cefntreban*, 40.
Goch *of Glyn Neath*, 37.
Griffith and Herbert *of Kil-y-Bebyll*, 15.
Griffith *of Ynys Dderw*, 18.
Griffith *of Gwynedd*, 25.
Griffith *of Lansadwrn*, 25.
Gunter *of Gunterston an t Aberga-venny*, 23.

Gunter *of St. Sili*, 24.
Gwin *of Llan Issen*, 41.
Gwyn *of Lansanwr*, 1.
Gwyn *of Lliwel*, 41.
Gwyn *of Llanedern*, 41.
Gwyn *of Roath*, 41.
Gwyn, 42.
Harys *of Bryncoch*, 15.
Havard *of Pontwilim*, 29.
Herbert, 42.
Herbert *of Cogan Vach*, 42.
Hopkins *of Ynys Dawe*, 32.
Hopkins *of Machen*, 42.
Howel *of Abernant Maylan*, 20.
James *of Troy House, co. Monmouth*, 35.
Jenkins *of Hensol*, 22.
Jestyn *of Gurgan*, 28.
Jones *of Tregib*, 38.
Jones *of Abergavenny*, 36.
Kemis *of Kemis*, 30.
Kemis *of Ceven Mably*, 31.
Kemis *of Lanrumney*, 31.
Kemis *of Vayndre*, 31.
Lewis *of Van*, 6.
Lewis *of Lystalybont*, 7.
Lewis *of Glyn Taf*, 7, 30.
Lewis *of Ryd Laver*, 8.
Lewis *of Bryn Terharn*, 14.
Lewis *of Y'r Fan*, 29.
Lewis *of Pen Mark*, 30.
Lewis *of Riw 'r Perry*, 30.
Lewis *of Llustal y Bont*, 30.
Lewis *of Ely*, 34.
Llewellen *of Carwige*, 45.
Llewellyn *of Ynys Symmon*, 18.
Llewelyn *of Ynys-y-Gerwyn*, 15.
Llewelyn *of Langewydd*, 16.
Lloyd *of Prysgedwyn*, 18.
Lloyd *of Kilval*, 35.
Lloyd *of Lanvain Clydoge*, 45.
Lychwr *of Tithegston*, 21.
Lyson *of Baglan*, 31.
Madock *of Langynwyd*, 45.
Mansel *of Gower, Margam, Mudles-comb, and Swansey*, 2.
Mansel *of Brytonfery*, 12; see also Price.

Mansel, 51.
Mathew *of Llandaff*, and Trumen *of Pant y Llwyd*, 8.
Mathew *of Langyvelach*, 22.
Mathew *of Llandaff*, 27, 51.
Mathew *of Radyr*, 27.
Mathew *of Castel-y-Menych and Monks Castle*, 27.
Morgan *of Ynys-y-Dyfnant*, 19.
Morgan *of Coed-y-Gores in Lanedern*, 24.
Morgan *of Pencoed and Pencarn*, 37.
Morgan *of Mudlescum*, 38.
Morgan *of Walston*, 40.
Morgan *of Abergorki*, 46.
Morgan *of Radyr Vcha*, 46.
Mores *of Ynys y Dyfnant*, 37.
Newton, 16.
Penry *of Reeding*, 14.
Penry *of Lan Edi and Gwinleis*, 17.
Penry *of Landdarog*, 17.
Penry *of Gwinlies*, 37.
Prees *of Miskin*, 18.
Prees *of Glyn Nedd*, 19.
Prees *of Colenne*, 43.
Price *of Pen lle'r Gar*, 22.
Price and Mansel *of Brytonfery*, 32.
Price *of Lanfwyst*, 38.
Prichard *of Lanycayach*, 7.
Prichard *of Gelli Galed*, 16, 36.
Prichard *of Ynys-y-Biben*, 19.
Prichard *of Ynis Arwed*, 40.
Pryce *of Brytonfery*, 12.
Proger *of Gwern Ddy*, 37.
Popkin *of Ynysdawe*, 36.
Powel *of Pen y Fai*, 35.
Powel *of 'r Igob*, 37.
Powel *of Baydan*, 43.
Powel, 46.
Powel *of Mas Teg*, 20.
Powell *of Cluny Bedd*, 16.
Powell *of Castell Madock*, 45.
Raglan *of Carnllwyd, Llantwit,&c.* 1.
Rees *of Riwlyd Lech*, 44.

Rice *of Newton, in Carmarthenshire and Abermarlies*, 16.
Saies *of Boverton*, 33.
Says *of Lainghenydd*, 44.
Stradling *of Lantwit and Roath*, 26.
Stradling *of St. Donats*, 26.
Thomas *of Lanbradach*, 7.
Thomas *of Bettus*, 13.
Thomas *of Brigan*, 13; see also Basson.
Thomas *of Lanvihangel*, 14.
Thomas *of Lanedern*, 23.
Thomas *of Gower*, 33.
Thomas *of Baglan*, 33.
Thomas *of Brichton*, 40.
Thomas *of Marlas*, 41.
Traherne *of Castellau*, 9.
Truman *of Pant y Llwyd*; see Mathew.
Truman *of Landaff and Pant y Llwyd*, 10.
Tudor, 25.
Turberville *of Coyty*, 4.
Turberville *of Tithegstone and Penlline*, 5.
Turberville *of Llantwit Major and Sulturn*, 44.
Van *of Marcros*, 3.
Vaughan *of Tramsaran*, 39.
Vaughan *of Llandough and Glynneth*, 39.
Vaughan *of Tyle Glas*, 39.
Vaughan *of Gadlis*, 43.
Walbec *of Llanhamwlch*, 24.
Williams *of Blaen Baglan and Aberpergwm*, 12.
Williams *of Dyffryn Cleidach*, 15.
Williams *of Gwern-y-Ved*, 17.
Williams *of Bettus*, 34.
Williams *of Penrose*, 35.
Williams *of Llander Mor*, 36.
Williams *of Ryd Odyn*, 39.
Williams *of Park in Brecon*, 39.
Wogan *of Castell Gwys, in Pembrokeshire*, 39.

229. — Heraldic Visitations of Wales and part of the Marches, between the years 1586 and 1613. By LEWYS DWNN, edited by Sir Samuel Rush Meyrick. *Llandovery*, 1846. 2 vols. Impl. 4to.

Adams, i. 130, 131, 172.
Almer, ii. 355.

Angiel, i. 193.
Annwell, ii. 92.

Ap Harri, i. 56, 57.
Ap Rhys, i. 252, 263.
Arden, ii. 92.
Ashbwl, ii. 851.
Aubre, i. 285, 287.
Awbrey, ii. 39, 40, 41, 57.
Badda, i. 194.
Baker, i. 284.
Barbor, i. 79.
Barlow, i. 117, 118.
Barret, i. 68, 70, 146, 153, 154.
Bary, i. 77.
Barzey, i. 23.
Baskerville, i. 256.
Batman, i. 173, 174.
Bevan, i. 201.
Bid, i. 78.
Bierd, i. 193.
Billinges, ii. 303.
Blaeney, i. 134, 283, 284, 299.
Blane, ii. 23.
Bodvel, ii. 173, 174.
Bould, i. 246; ii. 245, 317.
Boulton, i. 133.
Bowen, i. 110, 116, 118, 119, 120, 162, 163, 166, 167, 168, 169, 170, 180, 222.
Branan, i. 274.
Brein, i. 19.
Bromeg, i. 160.
Broomfield, ii. 361.
Broughton, i. 329; ii. 315.
Bruerton, ii. 853.
Bulkley, i. 112.
Burchinshaw, ii. 300, 346.
Butler, i. 76, 132, 179, 180.
Bwl, i. 266.
Byby, ii. 288.
Byrbeck, i. 191.
Byrt, i. 88.
Cadwaladyr, ii. 228, 229, 248.
Carew, i. 71, 89.
Charles, i, 112.
Clement, ii. 266.
Clough, i. 319.
Coetmor, ii. 165, 166.
Conwy, ii. 85, 118, 295, 324, 340.
Coyny, i. 25.
Cradock, i. 143, 201.
Crowder, i. 259.
Cyffin, i. 307.
David, i. 82, 103, 104, 155, 217.
David ap Einion, i. 195.

David ab Morgan, ii. 124, 125.
David Ieuan, i. 80.
David Rytherch, i. 16, 239.
David Rys, i. 224, 225, 226.
Davids, ii. 300, 321.
Davies, i. 77, 96, 307; ii. 86, 119, 312.
Davis, i. 70, 96, 179, 195, 244.
Dawkyns, i. 145.
Daws, i. 128.
Decka, ii. 357.
Dethick, i. 133.
Devereux, i. 109.
Dwnn, i. 20, 21, 22, 26, 91, 199, 222, 294.
Dwnn of Cydwely, ii. 49, 58, 59, 61.
Dymock, ii. 313, 314.
Edward, i. 67, 152, 200.
Edward Morgan, i. 286.
Edwardes, i. 152, 327.
Edwards, i. 323, 327; ii. 232, 327, 328.
Eliot, i. 122, 204.
Elizabeth, Queen, ii. 11.
Eton, ii. 360, 362.
Evan Thomas, i. 309.
Evan ap Owen of Neuadd Wen, i. 294.
Evans, i. 306, 327; ii. 322, 323, 325, 326.
Eyton, i. 324.
Eytyn, ii. 320, 327, 357, 358.
Fferior, i. 67.
Ffolk, i. 87.
Ffylip, i. 109, 232.
Ffylips, i. 78, 92, 105, 142, 158, 171, 197, 198, 203, 208, 211.
Ffylp, i. 72.
Ffylpin, i. 67, 193.
Fylip ap Howel, i. 105.
Fletcher, ii. 121.
Foxwist, ii. 286.
Gadarn, i. 135.
Gamage, ii. 58.
Games, ii. 36, 37.
Garnons, i. 159.
George Owain Harri, i. 32, 33.
Gervys, ii. 350.
Gibbon, i. 179.
Gilbert, i. 300.
Glyn, i. 311; ii. 147, 148, 150.
Glyn Aeron, i. 27, 80.
Goch, i. 231.

Godard, i. 179.
Goodman, i. 243 ; ii. 337.
Grafton, i. 119.
Gray, ii. 214.
Grey, i. 282, 301.
Griffith, i. 281, 306, 307, 328.
Griffith ab Davydd, ii. 195.
Griffiths, i. 308.
Gronwy, i. 176.
Gruffydd, i. 29, 39, 44, 65, 242 ; ii. 73, 130, 131, 132, 144, 145, 146, 147, 154, 155, 167, 168, 175, 176, 186, 203, 213, 214, 296, 308, 322.
Grufydd, i. 151, 199, 200.
Gunter, ii. 36, 37.
Gwidigada, i. 27.
Gwinionydd, i. 27.
Gwylim, i. 138, 159.
Gwyn, ii. 172, 221, 222.
Gwynn, i, 18, 22, 31, 81, 82, 86, 92, 99, 100, 184, 185, 195, 268, 309, 310, 317.
Gwyr y Towyn, i. 59, 61.
Hampton, ii. 189.
Hanmer, ii. 311, 312, 313, 314.
Harri ap Sion, i. 62.
Harris, i. 161.
Harry ab John, ii. 196.
Hastlen, i. 26.
Havard, i. 102, 264 ; ii. 43.
Heide, i. 113.
Henry VII. ii. 88.
Herbert, i. 30, 137, 196, 292, 293, 295, 312 ; ii. 37, 38, 45, 54, 55, 58.
Hergest, i. 193.
Heton, ii. 349.
Hirvryn, i. 27.
Hobe, ii. 316.
Holant, i. 113.
Holland, ii. 117, 210, 211, 337, 338, 364.
Hookes, ii. 162.
Hope, ii. 316.
Howel, i. 177.
Hugh ap Edward, i. 309.
Hugh ap Owen, ii. 187, 188.
Hugh ap Richard, ii. 178.
Hugh ab William, ii. 251.
Hughes, i. 150, 234 ; ii. 77, 142, 148, 237, 238, 249, 252, 253, 272, 273, 282, 300.

Hulls, ii. 92.
Huw Vychan, i. 87.
Huw ap David, i. 53, 105, 215.
Humphrey, ii. 274.
Hywel, i. 265.
Iong, i. 117, 156, 162, 243.
Ireland, i. 285.
Is Kennen, i. 92.
Is Kerdyn, i. 27.
Ieuan ap Grufydd, i. 80.
Ieuan ap Howel, i. 97.
Ieuan ap Hugh, ii. 246.
Ieuan ap Robert, ii. 224.
Ieuans, i. 112.
Ievans, ii. 306, 307.
James, i. 111, 231.
James ap Owen, i. 81.
Jankins, i. 29.
Jenkyns, i. 49, 135, 192.
John ap Robert, ii. 216, 217.
John ap Huw, ii, 255, 256.
John ap Howel, ii. 94.
John ap Lewis, 215, 216.
John ap David, i. 179, 241 ; ii. 338.
John ap Hugh, i. 29.
John David ab Griffith, i. 279.
Johnes, ii. 26, 58, 290, 291, 301, 333, 348.
Johns, i. 33, 55, 56, 78, 89, 109, 123, 174, 175, 178, 189, 190, 194, 209, 212, 235.
Johns, Thomas, i. 98, 99.
Jones, i. 196, 197, 281, 304, 324, 330 ; ii. 95, 116, 305.
Jones, Thomas, of Fountain Gate, i. 45, 46.
Jordan, i. 72.
Kadwgan hên, i. 95.
Kaio, i. 26, 27.
Kannington, i. 229.
Kanon, i. 209.
Kemes, yr Anglwydd, i. 156, 164, 165.
Ketsmae, i. 228.
Kiner, i. 109.
Klement, i. 108.
Konias, ii. 295.
Konwy, ii. 296, 297, 299, 324, 340.
Kradoc, i. 145.
Kreuddyn, i. 26, 48.
Kynaston of Stocks near Ellesmere, i. 227.
Kywr, ii. 355.

Lacharn, ii. 45.
Langford, i. 325.
Lathom, ii. 340.
Laugharn, i. 73, 184.
Lee, i. 199, 201, 222.
Lewis, i. 151, 254, 255, 265, 302, 303; ii. 24, 197, 198, 199, 200, 223, 325.
Lewis, James, i. 54, 55, 195.
Lewis ap Jenkin Vychan, ii. 271, 272.
Lewis ap Henry, ii. 33, 56.
Lewis ab Owen, ii. 207.
Lewis of Harpston, ii. 24, 25.
Lewys, i. 39; ii. 30, 89.
Lewys ap Huw, i. 16.
Lewys ap Richard, i. 120.
Lewys ap Thomas, i. 35; ii. 60.
Lloyd, i. 15, 16, 17, 25, 29, 30, 36, 37, 38, 40, 41, 49, 50, 51, 52, 53, 54, 57, 64, 79, 85, 97, 105, 109, 112, 134, 140, 141, 143, 144, 145, 147, 148, 149, 166, 167, 168, 187, 188, 206, 207, 215, 216, 222, 223, 227, 228, 234, 238, 239, 242, 245, 247, 254, 260, 275, 276, 286, 288, 289, 300, 301, 302, 311, 317, 322, 323, 328.
Lloyd, ii. 25, 30, 31, 33, 34, 36, 38, 47, 53, 74, 80, 95, 96, 112, 141, 142, 185, 197, 198, 214, 225, 226, 232, 233, 238, 239, 241, 242, 243, 244, 253, 254, 268, 269, 278, 279, 310, 318, 319, 330, 332, 339, 341, 342, 344, 345, 346, 347, 348, 352, 355, 362, 363.
Llychlin, Bishop of, ii. 103.
Llywarch, ii. 139.
Longford, i. 325; ii. 356.
Lord, or Lort, i. 125.
Lougher, i. 121.
Loveline, i. 78.
Lowndes, i. 232.
Madrin, ii. 177.
Maleffant, i. 164.
Mansell, ii. 43.
Marichurch, i. 124.
Martyn, i. 75.
Mason, ii. 165.
Mathavarn, ii. 318, 319.
Maurice, i. 282, 283, 303, 318, 327.
Meil, i. 263.
Meirig, ii. 126, 127, 128, 129.

Meirig of Bodorgan, ii. 138.
Meredith, i. 285, 307, 328.
Meredydd ap Ivan, i. 183.
Meredydd ab John, ii. 273.
Meredydd ab Thomas, ii. 247.
Meyrick, i. 136, 137, 156, 178.
Middleton, ii. 290, 334, 336, 338, 348.
Moiston, ii. 307, 308, 309.
Morgan, i. 30, 103, 159, 198, 205, 218, 219, 221, 230, 233, 236, 300; ii. 71, 72, 140, 221, 297, 298.
Morgan ap Flylip, i. 241.
Morgan ap John, i. 59.
Morgan fychan, i. 80, 81.
Moris, or Morus, ii. 329.
Morris, ii. 156, 157.
Mortmer, i. 34, 35.
Morus ap Grufydd, i. 237.
Morus Vachan, i. 43.
Motton, Mutton, Mytton, ii. 257.
Myddleton, i. 69, 322.
Myles, i. 149.
Nais, i. 202.
Nannau, ii. 226, 227, 233.
Newton, i. 275.
Nicholas, i. 158.
Owen, i. 23, 62, 113, 156, 157, 247, 261, 265, 272, 286; ii. 46, 75, 132, 133, 164, 169, 170, 180, 181, 191, 192, 193, 201, 203, 205, 206, 222, 223, 336, 340.
Owen ap Meredydd, i. 95.
Owen ap William, i. 101.
Owen ap Gwallter, i. 95.
Owen Tudyr, ii. 108, 192.
Palmer, i. 147, 151.
Parry, i. 141, 332; ii. 332, 337.
Pengriffin, i. 244.
Pennant, ii. 305.
Penrhyn, i. 274, 279.
Penry, i. 24, 131, 132, 305; ii. 29, 33.
Perkyn, i. 111.
Perot, i. 74, 89, 90, 133, 134, 165.
Philip, i. 303.
Phillips, i. 85, 92, 105, 114, 115, 142, 158, 162, 193, 203, 208, 260.
Phowk, ii. 339.
Phulk, i. 87.
Pilsdon, or Puliston, ii. 150, 151, 309, 310, 359, 361.
Porter, i. 297.

Powel, i. 126, 186, 187, 223, 224, 239, 260, 264, 280, 288, 306, 331; ii. 311, 356, 361.
Powys, ii. 234, 235.
Price, i. 283, 284.
Prichard, i. 38, 240.
Prickart, i. 75.
Probert, i. 267.
Protherch, i. 142.
Pryce, i. 291, 293, 298, 313, 314, 315.
Prys, i. 44, 45, 71, 74, 77, 79, 82, 257, 258, 266.
Pryse, ii. 23, 116, 240, 288, 289, 344, 351.
Pugh, i. 271, 280.
Pughe, i. 295, 296.
Pye, i. 127.
Pyrs, ii. 122, 123, 344.
Ravenscrofft, i. 281.
Ravenscroft, ii. 315, 316.
Rayner, i. 76.
Reede, i. 68, 69, 333.
Revel, i. 155, 156.
Rhys ap Ieuan, ii. 239.
Rhys ap Thomas, ii. 32, 57, 104.
Rice, i. 210, 233 ; ii. 26.
Richard ap John, i. 315, 316; ii. 171.
Richard ap Rydderch, i. 161.
Robert ap Ieuan, ii. 220, 221.
Robert ap John, ii. 113, 245, 246.
Roberts, ii. 75, 78, 215.
Robins, ii. 290.
Robins, Bishop of Bangor, ii. 113.
Roech, Thomas lo, i. 71, 164.
Roger ap Harri, i. 211.
Rogers, i. 67, 145, 146, 229.
Rossyndale, or Rosendal, ii. 332, 333.
Rowland, ii. 184.
Rowland ap Robert, ii. 247, 248.
Rudd, i. 79, 93.
d, i. 18, 79, 91, 93, 96, 198.
Rydderch ap Richard, ii. 136, 137.
Rhys, i. 253, 266.
Rhys ap David, i. 151, 184.
Rhys ap Morgan, i. 241.
Sadler, i. 275.
Salsbri, ii. 89, 111, 114, 115, 330, 331, 332, 334, 347.
Sandde, ii 359.
Scarfe, i. 182.
Sgwrfield, i. 110, 175, 176.

Shienton, i. 205.
Siankin Davydd Sion, ii. 47.
Sion ap Rhys, i. 35.
Smith, i. 77 ; ii. 287.
Sneyd, ii. 325.
Sonlli, ii. 358.
Spencer, i. 177.
Spicer, ii. 120.
Stanley, i. 266 ; ii. 283, 284, 316.
Stedman, i. 19, 79, 80, 88.
Stepneth, i. 180.
Symmins, i. 192.
Tangerd, or Tangred, i. 128.
Thelwal, ii. 113, 335, 336.
Themelby, ii. 217.
Thicknes, ii. 188, 189.
Thomas, i. 47, 58, 60, 61, 125, 126, 159, 192, 201; ii. 151, 152, 153, 190, 271.
Tocker, i. 152, 192.
Toey, or Toy, i. 137.
Tottyl, i. 183.
Trevor, ii. 317, 318, 328, 329, 354.
Tudor Vychan, ii. 235.
Turbridge, ii. 351.
Tydyr, ii. 7, 8, 191, 192.
Vaughan, i. 127, 139, 140, 147, 148, 150, 172, 173, 190, 191, 213, 214, 226, 227, 245, 255, 280, 291, 292, 294 ; ii. 27, 55, 58, 219, 229, 230, 232, 275, 276.
Vernon, i. 153.
Voel, i. 71, 72, 177, 282.
Vychan, i. 251, 255, 258, 261; ii. 26, 27, 36, 37, 164, 175, 181.
Vychan, i. 182, 183, 204, 218, 219, 236.
Walbcof or Walbyf, ii, 37, 58.
Walter, i. 193, 228, 248 ; ii. 48.
Warren, i. 163, 181; ii. 46.
Wawgood, i. 111.,
Webb, i. 234.
Weiatt, i. 66.
Welsh, i. 124.
Wever, i. 258.
Wgan, i. 42, 43, 90, 91, 106, 107, 108, 115, 165, 179, 180, 220, 229, 293.
Wgan or Wogan, ii. 45, 55.
Whitley, ii. 323.
Whytt, or White, i. 129, 130, 161.
Wilcock, ii. 242.
Wilkin, i. 118.
William, i. 105 ; ii. 193, 194.

William ap David, i. 280, 279.
William ap Richard, ii. 149.
William ap Rhys, ii. 196.
William ap Sion, ii. 140.
Williams, i. 100, 101, 104, 122, 205, 206, 235, 243, 330; ii. 81, 82, 85, 87, 169, 204, 212, 222, 287, 303.
Winstanley, i. 257.
Wodford, i. 135.
Woods, ii. 203, 204.
Woolff, i. 11, 12, 13, 14, 104, 205.

Wynn, i. 293, 321; ii. 73, 158, 159, 160, 173, 179, 180, 207, 208, 225, 228, 230, 231, 248, 279, 280, 289, 297, 304, 319, 321, 322, 329, 341, 342, 343, 345, 346, 347, . 349, 354, 355.
Wynne, i. 328.
Yale, ii. 352
Young, ii. 314, 315.
Younge, i. 162.

230.—Pedigrees of Caermarthenshire, Cardiganshire, and Pembrokeshire, in continuation of Lewis Dwnn, to about the years 1700-10. From the MS. of JOHN PHILIPPS ALLEN LLOYD PHILIPPS, Esq., of Dale Castle, co. Pembroke. *Typis Medio Montanis*, 1859. Foolscap folio. Privately printed by Sir Thomas Phillipps, Bart.

CARMARTHENSHIRE.

Aubrey, 59.
Barrett, 61.
Bevan, 72, 73.
Bidder, 66.
Bloom, 14.
Bowen, 21, 47, 51.
Brigstock, 47.
Crow, 6.
Davies, 56.
Donne, 57, 58.
Edwards, 13.
Einion, 67.
Fleming, 53.
Griffith, 68.
Gwynn, 35, 17, 63, 24, 72, 64, 37, 16.
Herbert, 39.
Hughes, 67.
James, 54.
Jones, 7, 49, 50, 27, 69, 30, 21.
Lewes, 71, 41, 42, 44, 29.
Lloyd, 60, 12, 19, 6, 51, 36, 56, 41, 63, 71, 68, 23, 54, 14, 62, 53, 32, 63, 44, 32, 20.
Mansel, 41, 2, 11, 29.
Morgan, 50, 45, 41, 51, 2.
Mortimer, 60.
Owens 46.
Penry, 57, 34.
Perrott, 3, 146,

Phillippes, 15, 39, 40, 59, 65, 56, 44.
Powell, 52, 31, 39.
Price, 70.
Prudderch, 13.
Prys, 12.
Rice, 8.
Rudd, 3.
Thomas, 64, 66.
Vaughan, 28, 4, 1, 65, 19, 22, 38, 42, 23, 25, 17.
Williams, 33, 35, 55, 45, 72, 45, 70, 10, 37, 43.
Winter, 13.

CARDIGANSHIRE PEDI-GREES.

Birt, 100.
Bowen, 112, 98, 117.
David, 113.
Evan, 111.
Evans, 104, 105.
Gwynn, 109, 107.
Herbert, 86, 85.
Jenkin, 83, 88.
Jenkins, 115.
Jevan, 114.
John, 115, 116.
Jones, 106.
Lewes, 80, 101, 91, 87, 99, 100, 93.
Lloyd, 94, 84, 113, 88, 105, 102, 86, 87, 95, 113, 99, 79, 95, 76, 78, 90, 89, 96, 103.

Morgan, 111.
Morus, 116.
Owen, 109.
Parry, 81.
Perry, 103.
Phillipps, 99, 82.
Powell, 108.
Pryce, 73.
Prys, 77.
Rees, 110, 114.
Rhes, 101.
Stedman, 77.
Thomas, 114.
Vaughan, 74, 91, 93, 97.

PEMBROKESHIRE PEDI-
GREES.

Adams, 151.
Barlow, 139, 158.
Boulton, 123.
Bowen, 162, 121, 159, 134, 124,
119, 163, 120, 130, 138, 154,
158, 130.
Butler, 148.
Canon, 144.
Carew, 147.
Clement, 132.
Corbet, 140.
Davies, 129, 128, 135.
Dyer, 153.
Elliott, 150.
Edwards, 148.
Filbatch, 137.

Fletcher, 139.
Ford, 125.
Griffies, 130.
Harries, 134.
Jones, 151, 136, 137, 157, 140.
Jordan, 149, 162.
Langharne, 145.
Lort, 131.
Lloyd, 123, 146, 150, 156, 129, 127,
136.
Lochor, 426.
Marichurch, 120.
Martin, 141.
Meuric, 160.
Mathias, 124.
Owein, 153, 165.
Parry, 163.
Perrott, 146.
Phillipps, 120, 144, 119, 141.
Powell, 149.
Rhys, 142.
Scurfield, 142.
Simons, 127.
Tankard, 128.
Tucker, 122.
Vaughan, 122, 158.
Voel, 137.
Waring, 152.
White, 131.
Williams, 136, 161.
Wogan 153, 119, 153, 164.
Young, 163, 128.

GENERAL WORKS.

231.—Archæologia, or Miscellaneous Tracts relating to Antiquity, published by the Society of Antiquaries of London. *London,* 1770-1863, 4to. Vols. 1 to 39, Part 1.

Arundel *of Clifton,* xviii. 99.
Cavendish *of Cavendish Overhall, co.*
Suffolk, xi. 52, 62.
Drayton ; see De Prayers.
De Mauley ; see De Prayers.
De Prayers, Drayton, Lovet, and
Shirley, xxix. 407.
Grey de Wilton, Lords, xxxix. 59.
Killigrew, xviii. 99.
Lovet ; see De Prayers.

Lower, xviii. 98.
Mulgrave, Barons of, xxxi. 241.
Northumberland, Earls of, v. 207.
Palæologus, xviii. 96.
Pusey, xii. 400.
Shirley ; see De Prayers.
Stewart *of Ely,* viii. 325.
Tyrell, i. folding at 381.
Warwick, Earldom of, xxi. 200.

232.—Collectanea Topographica et Genealogica. *London,* 1835-1843. 8 vols. 8vo.

Albemarle, Earls of, vi. 264.
Alford *of Meaux Abbey, co. York,* iv. 177.
Angevin, v. 334, 345.
Arundell, vi. 16.
Ashby *of Harefield, &c.* v. 125.
Babington *of Dethick and Kingston,* ii. 94; viii. 13.
Bard *of Lincolnshire, Middlesex, and Bucks,* vi. 59, 61.
Beke *of Eresby, co. Lincoln,* iv. 331.
Bigod, i. 303.
Boteler, vii. 1.
Bowyer *of Camberwell,* iii. 151.
Broke, i. 22.
Bryan, iii. 250.
Burnard, vi. 200.
Cannynowe, i. 319.
Chamberlayne, iii. 95.
Cherry *of Camberwell,* iii. 158.
Cheslyn, iii. 314.
Cheyne, i. 409.
Clerbecke, ii. 125.
Cobham, vii. 320.
Colville, vi. 153.
Courthope *of Goudhurst, co. Kent,* and *Wyleigh, co. Sussex,* ii. 279, 393.
Dacre, i. 302.
Darell, vi. 124.
Danvers, i. 324.
Daubeney, i. 314.
Deane, iii. 190.
De Alta Ripa, vi. 124.
De Home *of Essex,* ii. 286.
Dethick, ii. 94.
Dowe, or Dove, *of Camberwell,* iii. 142.
Draper *of Camberwell,* iii. 150.
Duke *of Camberwell,* iii. 155.
Edwards *of Harlow and Arlsey,* vi. 290.
Elmerugge *of Elmerugge, &c.* v. 169.
FitzAilward, vii. 1.
FitzPaine, iii. 250, 398.
Foljambe, i. 91, 333; ii. 68.
Frechville and Musard, iv. 1, 181.
Fulham, i. 17.

Gardiner *of Peckham, and of Haling, Surrey,* iii. 14.
Gill, or Gyll, *of Hertfordshire,* viii. 274.
Girlington *of Girlington, co. York,* vi. 190.
Gorham, v. 182, 329; vi. 284; vii. 81.
Gournarde, iv. 91.
Greystock, ii. 160.
Grymes *of Camberwell,* iii. 155.
Gyll; see Gill.
Hampton *of Surrey and Sussex,* vi. 294.
Hassel *of Wyrardisbury, co. Bucks,* viii. 405.
Hammond; see Parker.
Haustead, viii. 182.
Heron *of Addiscombe, co. Surrey,* ii. 166.
Hill *of Spaxton, co. Somerset,* i. 409.
Hody, vii. 22.
Honing, vii. 394.
Ingram, viii. 140.
Lathom, vii. 1.
Leake *of Southwark,* v. 51.
Lincoln, Earls of, viii. 156.
Lunsford *of Lunsford and Wilegh, co. Sussex,* iv. 139.
Malhorne, vi. 125.
Maltravers, Baron, iii. 77.
Marton, vi. 125.
Maunsell, i. 389.
Mautravers *of Lichet, and of Crowell and Hook,* vi. 334.
Morton *of Whitehorse, Croydon,* iii. 169.
Musard; see Frechville.
Muschamp *of Camberwell,* iii. 148.
Northumberland, Earl of, vi. 275.
Ogle *of Pinchbeck, co. Lincoln,* vi. 194.
Parker *of Hammond, of Haling, co. Surrey,* iii. 16.
Percy, ii. 57; vi. 266, 370.
Ponynges, iii. 250.
Powlett *of Marrick Abbey, co. York,* v. 256.
Radcliffe, iv. 125.

Rookwood, ii. 120.
Rush, ii. 288.
St. John, i. 310.
Sackville, iii 295.
Sanford of Great Hormede, co. Herts, v. 199.
Scrope, i. 303.
Scott of Camberwell, iii. 142.
Scudamore, iv. 256.
Sheffield of Seton, co. Rutland ; and Navestock, co. Essex, i. 172 ; iv. 259.
Shelbury of Camberwell, iii. 159.
Sidenham, i. 409.

Stafford, i. 249.
Stanley, vii. 1.
Stourton, i. 312, 409.
Stumpe of Malmesbury, vii. 81.
Strangways, ii. 161.
Tracy, vi. 153.
Ufford, v. 154 ; viii. 179.
Underhill, vi. 380.
Uvedale of Marrick Abbey, co. York, v. 253.
Vernon of Camberwell, iii. 160.
Warham, iii. 2, 6.
Warren, vii. 378.
Wickham, ii. 225, 368 ; iii. 178, 345.

233.—The Topographer and Genealogist. Edited by John Gough Nichols, F.S.A. London, 1846-1858, 3 vols. 8vo.

Apuldrefield, iii. 178.
Arden, or Arderne, i. 212, 214.
Arundell of Aynho, ii. 312.
Babington, i. 133, 259, 333.
Bartholomew, iii. 221.
Bayley, i. 531.
Beke, iii. 175.
Bishop, iii. 361.
Botfield, iii. 468.
Burton of Coventry, i. 493, 579.
Clarke, ii. 10.
Clerke, ii. 9.
Clinton, i. 359.
Close, i. 557.
Collier, iii. 568.
Dalridgecourt, i. 197.
Denny, iii. 210.
Dodington, iii. 568.
D'Oyly, i. 366, 567 ; ii. 18.
Drew, ii. 209.
Ellis and FitzEllis, iii. 274.
Fitzherbert, i. 362.
Foxley, iii. 180.
Franceis, i. 361.
Fremingham, i. 516.
Freningham, iii. 178.
Gyll, ii. 560.
Hammond, i. 512.
Henlakenden, i. 228, 395 ; ii. 215.
Honywood, i. 397, 568 ; ii. 169, 256, 312, 433.
Hodilow, ii. 28.
Holman, ii. 8.
Horde, i. 33 ; ii. 515.
Howard, ii. 91.

Hurly, iii. 464.
Hustler, i. 497.
Ifield, iii. 178.
Isley, i. 517 ; iii. 196.
Kirby, ii. 13.
Knowe, iii. 220.
Kynnersley, ii. 11.
Lennard, Lord Dacre, iii. 217.
Marche, ii. 246.
Marston, ii. 14.
Meynell, i. 357. 492.
Nicholl, iii. 533.
Norres, ii. 357.
Parr, iii. 354.
Peirse, i. 510.
Pickering, i. 442.
Pimpe, i. 517.
Plomer, ii. 279.
Polhill or Polley, i. 180.
Pycheford, ii. 506.
Pitchford, ii. 509.
Preston, Viscount Tarah, ii. 471.
Rugeley, ii. 490.
Rykes, iii. 178.
St. Lawrence, iii. 178.
Sculle, iii. 178.
Siferwast, iii. 178.
Thynne, iii. 468.
Tregose, ii. 124.
Turner of Kirkleatham, i. 505.
Ufford, ii. 271.
Walerand, i. 30.
Warbleton, iii. 178.
Wykeham, iii. 49.
Yate, i. 422.

234.—A Genealogical and Heraldic Dictionary of the Landed Gentry. By John Burke, Esq. *London,* 1837-1838, 4 vols. 8vo.

The first issue of this edition bore the title of the " *History of the Commoners,*" in Four volumes, but the genealogies not being in alphabetical order the volume and page are referred to in the following Index. The figures 2, 3, and 4, refer to the second, third, and fourth editions, in which the genealogies are alphabetically arranged.

— Second Edition, *London,* 1846-48. 2 vols. royal 8vo.

A Supplement and Index followed in 1849, forming a third volume. This edition was republished in 1852, with an Addenda.

— Third Edition, *London,* 1860, 1 vol. royal 8vo.

— Fourth Edition, *London,* 1863, 1 vol. royal 8vo.

Since the death of Mr. Burke, this work has been continued by J. Bernard Burke (now Sir Bernard Burke, Ulster King-of-Arms.)

Abadam *of Middleton Hall, co. Carmarthen,* 3, 4.

Abercromby, I. iii. 1.

Abdy *of Albyns, co. Essex,* 2.

Ablett *of Llanbedr Hall, co. Denbigh,* 2.

Abney *of . Measham Hall, Derby,* 2, 3, 4.

Achmuty or Auchmuty *of Barnstown,* I. iv. 734, 2.

Ackers *of Moreton Hall, co. Chester,* 2, 3, 4.

Acroyd *of Bank Field. York,* 4 supp.

Acton *of Gatacre Park, Salop,* 3, 4.

Acton *of West Aston, co. Wicklow,* 2, 3, 4.

Acton *of Wolverton, co. Worcester,* I. iv. 686 ; 2, 3, 4.

Adair *of Bellegrove, and Rath, Qveen's Co,* 2, 3, 4.

Adair *of Heatherton Park, co. Somerset, and Colehouse, co. Devon,* 2, 3, 4.

Adair *of Loughanmore, Parkgate, co. Antrim,* 2, 3, 4.

Adam *of Blair Adam, and Barns House, co. Kinross,* 2, 3, 4.

Adams *of Ansty, co. Warwick,* I. iv. 388 ; 2, 3, 4.

Adams *of Bowdon, co. Devon,* I. iv. 443 ; 2, 3, 4.

Adams *of Hollyland, co. Pembroke,* I. iii. 630 ; 2, 3, 4.

Adams *of Northlands, co. Cavan,* 3, 4.

Adams *of Jamesbrook, co. Cork,* 3, 4.

Adams *of Annagurrah, co. Limerick,* 3, 4.

Adams *of Middleton Hall, co. Carmarthen,* 2 ; see Abadam.

Adderley *of Hams Halls, co. Warwick,* I. iii. 279 ; 2, 3, 4.

Adderley *of Burleston and Coton, co. Warwick,* I. iii. 281 ; 2, 3, 4.

Adderley *of Fillongley Hall, co. Warwick,* 3, 4.

Addison *of Chilton Lodge, co. Suffolk,* 2.

Adeane *of Babraham, co. Cambridge,* 2, 3, 4.

Agar *of Brockfield, co. York,* 2.

Aglionby *of Newbiggen Hall, co. Cumberland,* I. i. 524 ; 2.

Agnew, Vans- *of Barnbarroch,* I. iii. 436 ; 2, 3, 4.

Ainsworth *of Smithills Hall, co. Lancaster,* 2, 3, 4.

Ainsworth *of Spotland, co. Lancaster,* 2 supp.

Akers *of Malling Abbey, co. Kent,* 2, 3, 4.

Alcock *of Wilton, co. Wexford,* 2, 3, 4.

Alcock *of Ballynoe, co. Carlow,* 4.

Alcock *of Kingswood Warren, co. Surrey,* 2, 3, 4.

Aldersey *of Aldersey, co. Chester,* 2, 3, 4.

Aldworth *of Newmarket, co. Cork*, 2 supp., 3, 4.

Alen *of St. Wolston's*, I. ii. 363.

Alexander *of Ballochmyle, co. Ayr*, 4 and supp.

Alexander *of Ahilly, Buncrana, co. Donegal, and Frowick House, co. Essex*, 4.

Alexander *of Powis, co. Clackmannan*, I. ii. 170 ; 2, 3.

Alexander *of Boydstone, co. Ayr*, 3 supp. 4.

Alexander *of Westerton, Stirling*, 4.

Alington *of Swinhope, co. Lincoln*, I. i. 570 ; 2, 3, 4.

Alkin *of the Court Lodge, Kent*, 2.

Allan *of Blackwell, co. Durham, and Barton, co. York*, I. i. 39 ; 2, 3, 4.

Allanson *of Middleton Quernhow*, 2.

Allardice ; see Barclay ; 2, 3, 4.

Allen *of Cresselly, co. Pembroke*, 2, 3, 4.

Allen *of Bicton, co. Pembroke*, 2, 3, 4.

Allen *of Hoyland, co. York*, 2.

Allfrey *of Wokefield Park, co. Berks*, 2 supp., 3, 4.

Allgood *of Nunwick, co. Northumberland*, 2, 3, 4.

Allix *of Willoughby Hall ; co. Lincoln*, I. i. 482 ; 2, 3, 4.

Allix *of Swaffham House, co. Cambridge*, 2, 3, 4.

Allott *of Hague Hall, co. York*, 2 supp., 3, 4.

Alloway *of The Derries, Queen's Co.*, 2 supp., 3, 4.

Alston *of Elmdon Hall, co. Warwick*, 3, 4.

Amcotts ; see Cracroft ; 4.

Amery *of Park House, Stourbridge, co. Worcester*, 2, 3, 4.

Ames *of The Hyde, co. Bedford*, 2, 3, 4.

Amherst *of Field Gate House, co. Warwick*, 3, 4.

Amos *of St. Ibbs, co. Hertford*, 2 supp., 3.

Amphlett *of Clent House, co. Worcester*, 2, 3, 4.

Anderson *of Jesmond House, co. Northumberland, and Wallington Lodge, co. Surrey*, 2, 3, 4.

Anderson *of Grace Dieu*, 2 supp., 3, 4.

Anderson *of Havering Grange, co. Essex*, 2.

Anderton *of Euxton, co. Lancaster*, 2, 3, 4.

Andrews *of Little Lever and Rivington, co. Lancaster*, 2 supp., 3, 4.

Angerstein *of Woodlands, co. Kent*, 4.

Anguish *of Somerleyton, co. Suffolk*, I. ii. 419 ; 2.

Anketell *of Anketell Grove, co. Monaghan*, I. iv. 529 ; 2, 3, 4.

Annand *of Auchter Ellon*, 2.

Annesley *of Bletchington, co. Oxford*, I. i. 7 ; 2.

Annesley *of Arley Castle*, 2 supp., 3.

Anstruther-Thomson ; see Thomson *of Charleton ; 3, 4.*

Anstruther *of Hintlesham Hall, co. Suffolk*, 3, 4.

Antrobus *of Eaton Hall, co. Chester*, 2, 3, 4.

Arabin *of Beech Hill Park, co. Essex, and Drayton House, Middlesex*, 2 supp., 3, 4.

Arcedeckne *of Glevering Hall, co. Suffolk*, 2, 3, 4.

Archbold *of Davidstown, co. Kildare*, 2, 3, 4.

Archdall *of Castle Archdall, co. Fermanagh*, 1. ii. 107 ; 2, 3, 4.

Archer-Burton *of Woodlands, co. Hants*, 3, 4.

Archer *of Trelaske, co. Cornwall*, I. i. 576 ; 2, 3, 4.

Archibald *of Rusland Hall, co. Lancaster*, 2, 3, 4.

Arden *of Longcroft*, I. i. 636 ; 2, 3, 4.

Arkwright *of Sutton Scarsdale, co. Derby*, 3, 4.

Arkwright *of Willersley, co. Derby*, 2, 3, 4.

Arkwright *of Hampton Court, co. Hereford*, 3, 4.

Arkwright *of Mark Hall, co. Essex, and Normanton Turville, co. Leicester*, 3, 4.

Arkwright *of Dunstall, co. Stafford,* 3.

Armitage *of Atherdee, Coole, and Drumin, co. Louth,* 2, 3, 4.

Armitage *of Milnsbridge House, co. York,* 2, 3, 4.

Armistead *of Leeds,* 2 add.

Armstrong *of Garry Castle, King's Co.* I. iv. 346 ; 2, 3, 4.

Armstrong *of Castle Iver, King's Co.* I. iv. 350 ; 2, 3, 4.

Armstrong *of Killylea, co. Armagh,* 4.

Armstrong *of Ballycumber, King's Co.* I. iv. 343 ; 2, 3, 4.

Armstrong *of Mount Heaton;* see A. *of Killylea;* 2, 3, 4,

Armstrong-Mac Donnell *of New Hall,* 3, 4.

Armstrong *of Meacliffe, co. Tipperary, and Chaffpool, co. Sligo,* 3, 4.

Armstrong *of co. Clare,* 3, 4.

Armstrong *of Hemsworth, co. York,* 3. 4.

Armstrong *of Kippure Park, co. Wicklow,* 2, 3.

Armstrong *of Gallen,* I. iv. 337.

Arncy *of Chambury and Hindon,* 4 supp.

Arnold *of Ashby St. Ledger,* 2, 3 supp., 4.

Arnold *of Little Missenden Abbey, co. Bucks,* 2, 3, 4.

Arthur *of Glanomera, co. Clare,* 3, 4.

Arundel *of Trerice,* I. i. 512.

Ash *of Ashbrook, co. Londonderry,* 2, 3, 4.

Ashby *of Quenby, co. Leiceister,* I. iv. 175 ; 2, 3, 4.

Ashe *of Ashfield, co. Meath,* I. i. 577 ; 2, 3, 4.

Ashhurst *of Waterstock, co. Oxford,* 2, 3, 4.

Ashworth *of Ashworth, Elland, and Hall Carr,* 3, 4.

Askew *of Redheugh, co. Durham,* I. ii. 292 ; 2, 3, 4.

Askew *of Pallinsburn, co. Northumberland,* I. ii. 294 ; 2, 3, 4.

Aspinall *of Standen Hall, co. Lancaster,* 2, 3, 4.

Assheton *of Downham Hall, and Cuerdale, co. Lancaster,* 2, 3, 4.

Astell *of Everton Hall, co. Huntingdon,* I. i. 540 ; 2, 3, 4.

Astley *of Felfoot, co. Lancaster,* 3, 4.

Aston *of Aston, co. Chester,* 2, 3.

Atcherley *of Marton, co. Salop,* 2, 3.

Athorpe *of Dinnington, co. York,* 2, 3, 4.

Athy *of Renville, co. Galway,* 2, 3, 4.

Atkin *of Leadington, co. Cork,* 2 supp., 3, 4.

Atkins *of Firville, co. Cork,* I. iv. 567 ; 2, 3, 4.

Atkins *of Waterpark, co. Cork,* 2, 3, 4.

Atkinson, 2 supp.

Atkinson *of Lorbottle, co. Northumberland,* 2 supp., 3, 4.

Atkinson *of Rehins, co. Mayo,* 2, 3, 4.

Atkinson *of Cangort, King's Co.,* 2, 3, 4.

Atkinson *of Ashley Park, co. Tipperary,* 2, 3, 4.

Atkinson *of Angerton, co. Northumberland,* 2, 3, 4.

Atkinson *of Rampsbeck House, co. Cumberland, and Moreland, co. Westmoreland,* 3, 4.

Atthill *of Brandiston Hall, co. Norfolk,* I. i. 164 ; 2, 3, 4.

Atty *of Penley Hall, co. Warwick,* 2, 3, 4.

Attye *of Ingon Grange, co. Warwick,* 3, 4.

Aubrey *of Broom Hall, co. Salop,* 2.

Auchmuty *of Kilmore House, co. Roscommon,* 2.

Aufrere *of Foulsham, co. Norfolk,* 2 supp., 3, 4.

Austen *of Shalford, co. Surrey,* I. i. 465 ; 2, 3, 4.

Awdry *of Seend, co. Wilts,* 2, 3, 4.

Awdry *of Notton, co. Wilts,* 2, 3, 4.

Aylmer *of Courtown, co. Kildare,* 4.

Aylmer *of Lyons,* 2, 3, 4.

Aylmer *of Walworth Castle, co. Durham,* I. i. 177 ; 2, 3, 4.

Aylward *of Shankill Castle, &o. Kilkenny,* 2, 3, 4.

Aynsley *of Little Harle Tower,* I. i. 588.

Babington *of Rothley Temple, co. Leicester,* I. iv. 513 ; 2, 3, 4.

Bacon *of Friston Hall,* I. iv. 122.

Badcock *of Lincolnshire and Bucks,* I. iii. 77.

Bagge *of Stradsett, co. Norfolk,* I. iii. 227 ; 2, 3, 4.

Bagot *of Ard and Ballymoe,* 2, 3, 4.

Bagot *of Kilcoursey, King's Co.,* 2, 3, 4.

Bagot *of Pype Hall, co. Stafford,* I. i. 503 ; 2, 3.

Bagot *of Castle Bagot, co. Dublin,* 3.

Bagshawe *of The Oaks, Sheffield,* I. ii. 28 ; 2, 3, 4.

Bagwell *of Marlfield, co. Tipperary,* I. iii. 141 ; 2, 3, 4.

Baikie *of Tankerness, co. Orkney,* 3 supp., 4.

Bailey *of Aberaman, co. Glamorgan,* 3, 4.

Bailey *of Glenusk Park, co. Brecon,* 2.

Bailey *of Allertonshire,* 2 add.

Baillie *of Dochfour, co. Inverness,* 2 supp., 3, 4.

Baillie *of Redcastle, co. Ross,* 2, 3, 4.

Baillie *of Jerviswood, co. Lanark,* 2, 3.

Baily *of Hall Place, co. Kent,* 3, 4.

Bain *of Livelands, Stirling,* 4 supp.

Bainbrigge *of Lockington,* I. iv. 52 ; 2, 3, 4.

Baird *of Cambusdoon, co. Ayr,* 3, 4.

Baker *of Elemore Hall and Crook Hall, co. Durham,* I. i. 546 ; 3, 4.

Baker *of Bayfordbury, co Hertford,* 2, 3, 4.

Baker *of West Hay, co. Somerset,* 2, 3, 4.

Baker *of Fenton, Deveridge, and Hilderstone,* 4.

Baker *of Orsett Hall, co. Essex,* 3.

Baker *of Hardwicke Court, co. Gloucester,* 2, 3.

Baker *of Cottesmore, co. Rutland,* 2, 3.

Baker-Cresswell *of Cresswell,* I ii. 290.

Baldwin *of Clohina, co. Cork,* I. ii. 695 ; 2, 3, 4.

Baldwin *of Aqualate,* I. iii. 196.

Balfe *of South Park, co. Roscommon,* 4.

Balfour *of Balfour, co. Orkney,* 3, 4.

Balfour *of Balbirnie, co. Fife,* 3, 4.

Balfour *of Whittinghame, East Lothian,* 3, 4.

Balfour *of Towneley Hall, co. Louth,* 2, 3, 4.

Balfour *of Trenaby, co. Orkney,* I. iii. 133.

Balguy *of Duffield, co. Derby,* 2, 3, 4.

Ballantyne *of Holylee, Scotland;* 3, 4.

Bamford-Hesketh *of Gwyrch Castle,* I. iv. 523.

Band *of Wookey House, co. Somerset,* 2, 3, 4.

Bankes *of Corfe Castle, co. Dorset,* 4.

Bankes *of Winstanley Hall, Lancashire,* I. iv. 213 ; 2, 3, 4.

Bankes *of Kingston Hall, co. Dorset,* I. iii. 307 ; 2, 3.

Bankes *of Revesby Abbey,* I. iv. 215.

Barclay *of Mathers and Urie,* 4.

Barclay *of Leyton, co. Essex,* 4.

Barclay *of Wavertree Lodge, co. Lancaster,* 2, 3, 4.

Barclay-Allardice *of Urie and Allardice,* 2, 3, 4.

Barclay *of Bury Hill, co. Surrey,* 2, 3, 4.

Barham *of Trecwn, co. Pembroke,* 4.

Barker *of Croboy,* 4.

Barker *of Kilcooly Abbey, co. Tipperary,* 2, 3, 4.

Barker *of Fairford Park, co. Glou-cester,* 2, 3, 4.

Barnard *of Cave Castle, co. York,* I. ii. 253 ; 2, 3, 4.

Barnard *of Bartlow, co. Gloucester,* 2, 3, 4.

Barnardiston *of The Ryes, co. Suf-folk,* 2. 3, 4.

Barne *of Sotterley and Dunwich, co. Suffolk,* I. ii. 139 ; 2, 3, 4.

Barneby *of Brockhampton, co. Here-ford,* I. iv. 1 ; 2, 3, 4.

Barnett *of Stratton Park, co. Bed-ford,* 2, 3, 4.

Barnewall *of Bloomsbury, co. Meath,* 4.

Barnston *of Churton, co. Chester,* 2, 3, 4.

Barrett *of Milton House, co. Berks,* 3, 4.

Barnwell *of Mileham,* 3, 4.

Barron *of Glenview, co. Waterford,* 2, 3, 4.

Barron *of Carrig Barron, co. Waterford,* 4 supp.

Barron *of Belmont,* I. ii. 497.

Barrow *of Southwell, co. Lincoln,* 2, 3, 4.

Barry *of Lemlara, co. Cork,* 2, 3, 4.

Barry *of Ballyclough, co. Cork,* 2, 3, 4.

Barry *of Foaty and Marbury,* 2, 3, 4.

Barry *of Rocklaveston Manor, co. Notts,* 2, 3 .

Barton *of Threxton House, co. Nor-folk,* 2 supp., 3, 4.

Barton *of Stapleton Park, co. York,* I. iv. 405 ; 2, 3, 4.

Barton *of Grove, co. Tipperary,* 2, 3, 4.

Barton *of Clonelly, co. Fermanagh,* 2, 3, 4.

Barton *of The Waterfoot, co. Fer-managh,* 2, 3, 4.

Barton *of Straffan, co. Kildare,* 2, 3, 4.

Barton *of Glendalough, co. Wick-low,* 2, 3, 4.

Barton *of Rochestown, co. Tippe-rary,* 2, 3, 4.

Barton *of Greenfort, co. Donegal,* 4 supp.

Barttelott *of Stopham, co. Sussex,* I. ii. 628 ; 2, 3, 4.

Barwis *of Langrigg Hall,* 2, 3, 4.

Baskerville *of Clyro Court,* I. i. 89, 2, 3, 4.

Baskerville *of Crowsley Park, Wilts,* 2 supp., 3, 4.

Basset *of Umberleigh and Water-mouth, co. Devon,* 2, 3, 4.

Basset *of Beaupré, co. Glamorgan,* 2, 3, 4.

Basset *of Tehidy, co. Cornwall ;* 2, 3, 4.

Basset *of Bonvilstone, co. Glamor-gan,* 3, 4.

Bastard *of Kitley, co. Devon,* 2, 3, 4.

Bastard *of Charlton Marshall, co. Dorset,* 2 supp., 3, 4.

Bateman *of Knypersley Hall, co. Stafford,* I. i. 18 ; 2, 3, 4.

Bateman *of Middleton Hall, co. Derby,* I. iii. 598 ; 2, 3, 4.

Bateman *of Hartington Hall, co. Derby,* I. iii. 349 ; 2, 3, 4.

Bateman *of Guilsborough, co. North-ampton,* 3, 4.

Bateman *of Bartholey House, co. Monmouth,* 2, 3, 4.

Bateman *of Oak Park,* 2, 3.

Bates *of Denton, co. Sussex,* I. i. 556 ; 2, 3, 4.

Bates *of Milbourne, co. Northumber-land,* I. i. 623 ; 2, 3, 4.

Bathurst *of Lydney Park, co. Glou-cester ;* 2, 3, 4.

Batt *of Purdysburn and Ozier Hill,* 3, 4.

Batten *of Thorn Faulcon, co. Somer-set,* 2 supp., 3, 4.

Battersby *of Lislin and Ashgrove, co. Cavan,* 2, 3, 4.

Battersby *of Lough Bane, New-castle, &c.,* 2, 3, 4.

Batty *of Ballyhealy, co. Westmeath,* 2, 3, 4.

Baverstock *of Alton, Windsor,* 2, i. 515.

Bayly *of Norelands, co. Kilkenny,* 2.

Bayly of Ballyarthur, co. Wicklow, 2, 3, 4.

Bayly of Debsborough, co. Tipperary, 2, 3, 4.

Baynton, I. iv. 684.

Beach of Oakly Hall, co. Hants, 2, 3, 4.

Beadon of Gotten House, co. Somerset, 2 supp., 3, 4.

Beale of Heath House, co. Salop, 2, 3, 4.

Beamish of Raheroon, 3, 4.

Beamish of Kilmalooda, co. Cork, 3, 4.

Beamish of Mount Beamish, co. Cork, 3, 4.

Beamish of Willsgrove, co. Cork, 3, 4.

Bearcroft of Meer Hall, co. Worcester, 3, 4.

Beardmore of Uplands, co. Hants, 2 supp., 3, 4.

Beatson of Kilrie, 3, 4.

Beauclerk of Ardglass Castle, co. Down, 3, 4.

Beauclerk of St. Leonard's Forest, Sussex, 2.

Beauman of Hyde Park, co. Wexford, I. ii. 601 ; 2, 3, 4.

Beaumont of Barrow-upon-Trent, I. iv. 204 ; 2, 3, 4.

Beaumont of Whitley Beaumont, co. York, 1. ii. 319 ; 2, 3, 4.

Beaumont of Bretton, co. York, I. ii. 323 ; 2, 3, 4.

Becher of Hollybrook, co. Cork, 2.

Beckett of The Knoll, co. Devon, 3, 4.

Beckett of Barnsley, co. York, 2.

Beckford of Fonthill, co. Wilts. I. i. 678.

Beckford of Basing Park, co. Hants, I. ii. 599 ; 2, 3, 4.

Beckwith of Thurcroft and Trimdon, I. ii. 636 ; 2, 3, 4.

Bedingfeld of Ditchingham, co. Norfolk, I. iii. 508 ; 2, 3, 4.

Beech of Brandon Lodge, co. Warwick, 3, 4.

Beecroft of Kirkstall, co. York, 4.

Beedham of Ashfield, co. Hunts, 2.

Belgrave of Preston Hall, co. Rutland, 2, 3, 4.

Bell of Woolsington, Northumberland, 2, 3, 4.

Bell of Melling Hall, co. Lancaster, 2, 3, 4.

Bell of Thirsk, co. York, 2 supp., 4.

Bell of Bourne Park, co. Kent, 4.

Bellairs of Kirby Bellars, 3, 4.

Bellew of Stockleigh Court, co. Devon, I. ii. 532 ; 2, 3, 4.

Bence of Thorington Hall, co. Suffolk, 2, 3, 4.

Bendyshe of Barrington, co. Cambridge, 2, 3, 4.

Benett of Pyt House, co. Wilts, I. i. 248 ; 2, 4.

Bennet of Laleston, co. Glamorgan, I. ii. 23 ; 2, 3, 4.

Bennet of Rougham Hall, co. Suffolk ; 2, 3, 4.

Bennett of Thomastown, King's Co., 2, 3, 4.

Bennett of Thorpe Place, co. Surrey, 3, 4.

Bennett of Faringdon House, co. Berks : 2, 3, 4.

Bennett of Bennett's Court, co. Cork, 3, 4.

Bennett of Stourton Hall, Stourbridge, 3, 4.

Benson of Utterby House, co. Lincoln, 3, 4.

Benson of Lutwyche Hall, co. Salop, 2 supp., 3, 4.

Bent of Wexham Lodge, co. Bucks, 2, 3, 4.

Bent of Basford House, co. Stafford, I. ii. 408.

Bentinck of Terrington St. Clement, Norfolk, 3, 4.

Bentley of Birch House, co. Lancaster, 2, 3, 4.

Benyon of Englefield, co. Berks, I. iii. 683 ; 2, 3, 4.

Bere of Morebath, co. Devon, 2, 3, 4.

Bere of Timewell House, co. Devon, 2, 3, 4.

Beresford of Learmount, co. Londonderry, 2, 3, 4.

Beresford, Pack- ; see Pack.

Berington of Winsley, co. Hereford, 2 supp. 3, 4.

Berington *of Little Malvern Court, co. Worcester,* 3, 4.

Berington *of Bradwell,* I. ii. 336.

Berkeley *of Spetchley, co. Worcester,* I. i. 469 ; 2, 3, 4.

Berkeley *of Cotheridge, co. Worcester,* I. ii. 226 ; 2, 3, 4.

Bernard *of Castle Bernard, King's co.,* 2, 3, 4.

Bernard *of Palace Anne, co. Cork,* I. ii. 32 ; 2, 3, 4.

Berners *of Woolverstone Park, co. Suffolk,* 2, 3, 4.

Berney *of Morton Hall, co. Norfolk,* 2, 3, 4.

Berry *of Ballynegall, co. Westmeath,* 3.

Best *of Donnington, co. Berks,* 2 supp., 3, 4.

Best *of Eastbury House, co. Surrey,* 2, 3, 4.

Best, *late of Chilston and Wierton,* I. i. 259 ; 2, 3, 4.

Best *of Park House, co. Kent,* 2, 3, 4.

Beste *of Botleigh Grange, co. Hants,* 4.

Beswick *of Gristhorpe, co. York,* 2, 4.

Bethel *of Rise, co. York,* I. i. 451 ; 2, 3, 4.

Bethune *of Balfour,* I. iii. 376 ; 2.

Betton *of Great Berwick, co. Salop,* I. iii. 219 ; 2, 3, 4.

Betts *of Preston Hall, co. Kent,* 3, 4.

Betts *of Wrotham, co. Suffolk,* 2, 3, 4.

Bevan *of Fosbury and Trent Park,* 2, 3, 4.

Beverley *of Beverley, co. York,* 2, 3, 4.

Bewicke *of Close House, Northumberland,* I. iii. 497 ; 2, 3, 4.

Bewicke *of Hallaton Hall, co. Leicester,* 3, 4.

Bewley, I. iv. 308.

Beynon *of Carshalton Lodge, co. Surrey,* 2, 4.

Bickford *of Dunsland,* I. i. 459.

Biddulph *of Burton, co. Sussex,* 2, 3, 4.

Biddulph *of Chirk Castle, co. Denbigh,* 2, 3, 4.

Biddulph *of Biddulph,* I. iii. 280.

Biddulph *of Ledbury, co. Hereford,* I. iii. 286 ; 2, 3, 4.

Biddulph *of Burghill, co. Hereford,* 2.

Biddulph *of Armoth Castle, co. Pembroke,* 2.

Bigg, I. ii. 402.

Bigge *of Linden, Northumberland,* I. i. 630 ; 2, 3, 4.

Biggs *of Stockton,* 2, 3, 4.

Bigland *of Bigland, co. Lancaster,* I. iii. 238 ; 2, 3, 4.

Bigsby *of Suffolk and Notts,* 2 supp,

Billam *of Yorkshire,* 2 supp., 3, 4.

Bingham *of Melcombe Bingham, co. Dorset,* I. ii. 350 ; 2, 3, 4.

Birch *of Wretham, co. Norfolk,* 2, 3, 4.

Birch *of Henley Park, co. Oxford,* 3, 4.

Bird *of Dinas Mowddwy, co. Merioneth,* 2.

Bird *of Drybridge House, co. Hereford,* 2, 3, 4.

Birley *of Lancashire,* 3, 4.

Birley *of Kirkham, co. Lancaster,* 3.

Blaauw *of Beechland, co. Sussex,* 3, 4.

Blackburne *of Hale, co. Lancaster,* 2, 3, 4.

Blackburne *of Rathfarnham Castle, co. Dublin ;* 4.

Blackstone *of Castle Priory,* I. iii. 544 ; 2.

Blacker *of Carrick Blacker, co. Armagh,* I. ii. 48 ; 2, 3, 4.

Blacker *of Woodbrook, co. Wexford,* 3, 4.

Blackett *of Wylam, co. Northumberland,* I. i. 257 ; 2, 3, 4.

Blagrave *of Calcot Park, co. Berks ;* 2, 3, 4.

Blague, I. iii. 663.

Blair *of Blair, co. Ayr,* I. iv. 392 ; 2, 3, 4.

Blair *of Balthayock, co. Perth,* 2, 3, 4.

Blair *of Penninghame ;* see Stopford-Blair, 4.

Blake *of Ballinafad, co. Mayo,* 3 supp , 4.

Blake *of Horstead, co. Norfolk,* 2 supp., 3, 4.

Blake *of Swanton Abbots* ; see Jex-Blake, 3, 4.

Blake *of Renvyle, co. Galway,* 2, 3, 4.

Blake *of Ballyglunin, co. Galway,* 3, 4, and supp.

Blake, *of Towerhill, co. Mayo,* 3, 4.

Blake *of Cregg Castle, co. Galway,* 2, 3, 4.

Blake *of Danesbury, Herts,* 4.

Blake *of Furbough, co. Galway,* 2, 3, 4.

Blake *of Kiltullagh and Frenchfort, co. Galway,* 3, 4.

Blake *of Merlin Park, co. Galway,* 3.

Blakemore; see Booker.

Blakemore *of the Leys, co. Monmouth,* 2.

Blakeney *of Abbert, co. Galway,* 2, 3, 4.

Blamire *of Thackwood and The Oaks, co. Cumberland,* 2, 3, 4.

Blanchard *of Grimsargh Hall, co. Lancaster,* I. iii. 437 ; 2.

Bland *of Kippax Park, co. York,* I. iii. 326 ; 2, 3, 4.

Bland *of Blandsfort, Queen's co.,* 3, 4.

Bland *of Derriquin Castle, co. Kerry,* 2, 3, 4

Blathwayt *of Dyrham Park, co. Gloucester,* 2 supp., 3, 4.

Blaydes *of Ranby Hall, co. Notts.* I. i. 667 ; 2, 3, 4.

Blayney *of Evesham, co. Worcester,* I. iv. 6 i2 ; 2, 3, 4.

Blencowe *of Blencowe, now of Thoby Priory, co. Essex,* 3, 4.

Blencowe *of Marston St. Lawrence, co. Northampton,* I. i. 414 ; 2, 3, 4.

Blencowe *of the Hooke, co. Sussex,* 3, 4.

Blenkinsopp *of Hoppyland Castle, co. Durham,* 2, 3, 4.

Blennerhassett *of Ballyscedy, co. Kerry,* 2, 3, 4.

Blewitt *of Llantarnam, co. Monmouth,* 2.

Bliss *of Brandon Park, co. Suffolk,* 2 supp., 3, 4.

Blofeld *of Hoveton House, Norfolk,* 2 supp., 3, 4.

Blount *of Maple Durham, co. Oxford,* I. iii. 168 ; 2, 3, 4.

Blount *of Orleton, co. Hereford,* 2, 3, 4.

Bluett *of Holcombe Court, co. Devon,* 2, 3, 4.

Blundell *of Crosby, co. Lancaster,* I. ii. 527 ; 2, 3, 4.

Blundell *of Ince;* see Weld-Blundell.

Blunt *of Wallop House, co. Hants,* 2, 3, 4.

Blunt *of Kempshott Park, co. Hants,* 2, 3, 4.

Boddam *of Kirklington Hall, co. Notts,* 3, 4.

Bodenham *of Rotherwas, co. Hereford,* I. iv. 83 ; 2, 3, 4.

Bodkin *of Annagh, co. Galway,* 2 supp., 3, 4.

Bolden *of Hyning, co. Lancaster,* 2, 3, 4.

Boldero *of White House, co. Suffolk,* 3, 4.

Bolger *of Ballinabarna, co. Kilkenny,* 2, 3, 4.

Bolton *of Bective Abbey, co. Meath,* 3, 4.

Bolton *of Mount Bolton, co. Waterford,* 3, 4.

Bolton *of Curraghduff,* 2.

Bomford *of Oakley Park, co. Meath,* 2, 3, 4.

Bonar *of Bonare, Keltye, Kilgraston, and Kimmerghame,* 2 supp., 3. 4.

Bonar *of Camden, co. Kent,* 2 supp. 3, 4.

Bond *of Grange, co. Dorset,* I. i. 240 ; 2, 3, 4.

Bond *of Ardglass, co. Westmeath,* 2

Bonham *of Ballintaggart, co. Kildare,* 4.

Bontine; see Graham *of Gartmore,* 4.

Booker *of the Leys, co. Hereford, and Valindra House,* 3, 4.

Booth *of Glendon Hall, co. Northampton,* 2, 3, 4.

Borrer *of Henfield, co. Sussex,* 3, 4.

Borough *of Hulland, co. Derby, and Chetwynd Park, co. Salop,* 3, 4.

Borrowes *of Gilltown, co. Kildare,* 4.

Borthwick *of Crookston and Borthwick Castle, co. Edinburgh,* 2, 3, 4.

Bosanquet *of Forest House, co. Essex,* I. iii. 316 ; 2, 3, 4.

Bosanquet *of Broxbournbury,* co. *Herts,* 2, 3, 4.

Bosvile *of Ravenfield,* co. *York,* 2, 3, 4.

Bosville, I. i. 516.

Boswell *of Crawley Grange,* co. *Bucks,* 2, 4 supp.

Boswell *of Balmuto,* co. *Fife,* 4 supp.

Boswell *of Iver,* co. *Bucks,* 4 supp.

Boteler *of Eastry,* co. *Kent,* 2, 3, 4.

Boteler, I. i. 516.

Botfield *of Norton Hall,* co. *Northampton,* 2, 3, 4.

Botfield *of Hopton Court,* co. *Salop,* 2.

Botfield *of Decker Hill,* co. *Salop,* 2.

Boucherett *of Willingham,* co. *Lincoln,* 2, 3, 4.

Boultbee *of Springfield,* co. *Warwick,* 3, 4.

Boulton *of Moulton,* co. *Lincoln,* 2, 3, 4.

Bourke *of Thornfield,* co. *Limerick,* 2, 3, 4.

Bourke *of Carrowkeel,* co. *Mayo,* 4 supp.

Bourke *of Carraghleagh,* co. *Mayo,* 4 supp.

Bourne *of Wyersdale and Stalmine,* co. *Lancaster,* 3, 4.

Bourne *of Hickinsall,* co. *Lancaster,* 2 supp. 3, 4.

Bourne *of Hilderstone Hall,* co. *Stafford,* I. ii. 31 ; 2, 3, 4.

Bourne *of Testwood,* co. *Hants.,* 2.

Bouverie *of Delapre Abbey,* co. *Northampton,* I. ii. 7 ; 2, 3, 4.

Bowden *of Southgate and Beightonfields,* co. *Derby,* 2, 3, 4.

Bowden, Butler- *of Pleasington Hall,* co. *Lancaster,* 2, 3, 4.

Bowen *of Bowen's Court,* co. *Cork,* 4.

Bowen *of Camrose,* co. *Pembroke,* 2, 3, 4.

Bowen *of Courtwood, Queen's* co. 4.

Bowen *of Llwyngwair,* co. *Pembroke,* 4.

Bowen *of Troedyrawr,* co. *Cardigan,* 2, 3.

Bower *of Broxholme,* co. *York,* 4.

Bower *of Iwerne House,* co. *Dorset,* 2, 3, 4.

Bower *of Welham,* co. *York,* 2, 3, 4.

Bowes *of Streatham Castle,* co. *Durham,* 2, 3, 4.

Bowes *of Bradley Hall,* co. *Durham,* I. i. 181 ; 2.

Bowles *of North Aston,* co. *Oxford,* 2, 3, 4.

Boycott *of Boycott, Hinton, and Rudge,* I. iv. 470 ; 2 supp. 3, 4.

Boycott, Morse- *of Sennowe,* co. *Norfolk,* 4.

Boyd *of Ballycastle,* co. *Antrim,* 4.

Boyd *of Rosslare,* co. *Wexford,* 2, 3, 4.

Boyd *of Merton Hall,* co. *Wigton,* 2, 4 supp.

Boyd *of Middleton Park,* co. *Westmeath,* 2, 3, 4.

Boyd *of Ballymacool,* co. *Donegal,* 2, 3, 4.

Boyd *of Dunduan House,* co. *Londonderry,* 3, 4.

Boyle *of Shewalton,* co. *Ayr,* 2, 3, 4.

Boys *of East Kent,* 2 supp.

Boyse *of Bannow,* co. *Wexford,* 2, 3, 4.

Brabazon, Moore- *of Tara House,* co. *Meath,* 2 supp. 3, 4.

Brabazon *of Brabazon Park,* co. *Mayo,* 3, 4.

Brabazon *of Mornington,* co. *Meath,* 4.

Brabazon *of* co. *Louth,* 2.

Bracebridge *of Atherstone Hall,* co. *Warwick,* 2, 3, 4.

Bracebridge *of Morville,* co. *Warwick,* 3, 4.

Brackenbury *of Skendleby House,* co. *Lincoln,* 2 supp. 3, 4.

Brackenbury *of Scremby Hall,* co. *Lincoln,* 2 supp. 3, 4.

Brackenridge *of Ashfield Park,* co. *Tyrone,* 3, 4.

Braddon *of Treglith,* co. *Cornwall,* 2 add. 3, 4.

Braddon *of Skisdon Lodge,* co. *Cornwall,* 2 supp. and add. 3, 4.

Braddyll *of Conishead Priory,* 2.

Bradney, I. iii. 607.

Bradley *of Gore Court,* I. iv. 203 ; 2.

Bradley *of Slyne House,* co. *Lancaster,* 2, 3.

Bradshaigh, 4.

Bradshaw *of Barton,* co. *Derby,* I. ii. 367 ; 2, 3, 4.

Brady *of Myshall Lodge, co. Carlow,* 3, 4.

Brailsford *of Toft Hill, co. Lincoln,* I. iii. 139 ; 2.

Bramston *of Skreens, co. Essex,* I. ii. 430 ; 2, 3, 4.

Brancker, *of Liverpool,* 2 supp.

Brandling *of Gosforth,* I. ii. 39 ; 2.

Brander *of Pitgaveny, Elgin,* 2.

Brandreth *of Stullach,* I. iv. 137 ; 2.

Branfil *of Upminster Hall, co. Essex,* 2 supp. 3, 4.

Bray *of Shere, co. Surrey,* I. iii. 241 ; 2, 3, 4.

Bray *of Langford Hall, co. Cornwall,* 2, 3, 4.

Bremer *of the Priory, co. Devon,* 2.

Brereton *of Brinton, co. Norfolk,* 2, 3, 4.

Brereton *of Carrigslaney, co. Carlow,* 4. supp.

Brewster *of Wrentham, co. Suffolk,* 2 supp. 3, 4.

Brewster *of Hedingham, co. Essex,* 2 add.

Brickdale *of Birchamp House, co. Gloucester,* 2, 3, 4.

Bridger *of Buckingham House, co. Sussex,* 2, 3, 4.

Bridger *of Halnaker, co. Sussex,* 2 supp. 3, 4.

Brigham *of Foxley House, co. Chester,* 3, 4.

Brinkley *of Fortland, co. Sligo,* 3, 4.

Brisbane *of Brisbane,* I. ii. 332.

Brisco *of Coghurst, co. Sussex,* 2.

Briscoe *of Fox Hills, co. Surrey,* 4.

Briscoe *of Riverdale, co. Westmeath,* 4.

Briscoe *of Tinvane, co. Tipperary,* 3, 4.

Brise ; see Ruggles-Brise, I. i. 486 ; 4.

Bristow *of Broxmore Park, co. Wilts,* 2, 3, 4.

Bristowe *of Beesthorpe Hall, co. Notts.,* 2, 3, 4.

Bronde *of Fenton Vivian, co. Stafford,* 4.

Broadley *of Kirkella, co. York,* 2, 3, and supp. 4.

Broadley *of Welton Heuse,* 3 supp. 4.

Broadmead *of Olands, co. Somerset,* 3, 4.

Brock *of Pensax, co. Worcester,* 2, 3, 4.

Brockett *of The Ryes, co. Essex,* 2, 3, 4.

Brockholes *of Claughton, co. Lancaster,* I. iii. 384 ; 2, 3, 4.

Brocklehurst *of Tytherington, co. Chester,* 3 supp., 4.

Brocklehurst *of Hurdsfield, co. Chester,* 3 supp., 4.

Brockman *of Beachborough, co. Kent,* I. iii. 367 ; 2, 3, 4.

Brodie *of Brodie, Morayshire,* 2 supp., 3, 4.

Brodie *of Lethen, co. Nairn,* 2 supp., 3, 4.

Brodie *of East Bourne, co. Sussex,* 4 supp.

Brome *of Salop, Herts, and Kent,* I. iv. 604 ; 2, 3, 4.

Bromley *of Wootton Hall, co. Derby,* 4.

Brooke *of Mere, co. Chester,* 2, 3, 4.

Brooke *of Handford, co. Chester,* 2 add., 3, 4.

Brooke *of Sibton Park, co. Suffolk,* 4.

Brooke *of Ufford Place, co. Suffolk,* I. i. 336 ; 2, 3, 4.

Brooke *of Haughton Hall, co. Salop,* 2 supp., 3, 4.

Brooke *of Dromavana,* 4.

Brooks *of Flitwick, co. Bedford,* 2 supp. 3, 4.

Broughton *of Tunstall, co. Salop,* 2, 3.

Brouncker *of Boveridge, co. Dorset,* 2, 3, 4.

Brown *of Clonboy, co. Clare,* 2, 3, 4.

Brown *of Mount Brown, co. Limerick,* 4.

Brown *of Jarrow Hall, co. Durham,* 2, 3, 4.

Brown *of Beilby Grange, co. York,* 2, 3, 4.

Brown *of Rossington and Copgrove, co. York,* 4.

Brown *of Unthank Hall, co. Northumberland,* 4.

Brown *of Woodthorpe Hall, co. York,* 4.

Brown *of Harehills Grove, co York,* 1. iv. 34; 2, 3.

Browne *of Manulla,* 4.

Browne *of Higham Hall, co. Leicester,* 4.

Browne *of Morley Hall, co. Norfolk,* 2 supp., 3, 4.

Browne *of Janeville, co. Devon,* 2 supp., 3, 4.

Browne *of Bronwylfa, co. Flint,* 2, 3, 4.

Browne *of Browne's Hall, co. Carlow,* 2, 3, 4.

Browne *of Kilskeagh, co. Galway,* 3, 4.

Browne *of Mount Kelly, co. Galway,* 3, 4.

Browne *of Moyne, co. Galway,* 3, 4.

Browne *of Browne Hall, co. Mayo,* 2, 3, 4.

Browne *of Raheens, co. Mayo,* 3, 4.

Browne *of Braeffey, co. Mayo,* 3, 4.

Browne *of Caughley,* 3, 4.

Browne *of Salperton, co. Gloucester,* 2, 3, 4

Browne *of Rathbane, co. Limerick,* 3, 4.

Browne, I. iii. 529.

Browne *of Monkton Farleigh, co. Wilts,* 2.

Browne *of Tallantire Hall, co. Cumberland,* 2, 3.

Browne *of New Grove, co. Clare,* 2.

Browne *of Greenville and Tuam,* 3.

Bruce *of Kennet, co. Clackmannan,* I. iv. 485 ; 2 and supp.

Bruce *of Kinnaird, co. Stirling,* 2, 3, 4.

Bruce *of Miltown Castle, co. Cork,* 4.

Bruce *of Clackmannan and Cowden,* I. iv. 618.

Bruce, Knight- *of Roehampton Priory,* 2 supp., 3, 4.

Bruce *of Duffryn ;* see Pryce.

Bruce *of Scoutbush and Killroot, co. Antrim,* 2, 3, 4.

Bruckshaw *of Harry Town Hall, co. Chester,* 3, 4.

Bruen *of Oak Park, co. Carlow,* 3, 4.

Bruen *of Coollawn, co. Wexford,* 4.

Bruges *of Seend, co. Wilts,* 2, 3. 4.

Brune- Prideaux, *of Place, co. Cornwall,* I. i. 203.

Brunwin *of Bradwell, co. Essex,* 4.

Bryan *of Jenkinson, co. Kilkenny,* 3, 4.

Bryan *of Upton, co. Wexford,* 3 supp., 4.

Brydges *of Tiberton Court,* I. iv. 552.

Buchan *of Auchmacoy House, co. Aberdeen,* 3, 4.

Buchanan *of Leny ;* see Buchanan-Hamilton.

Buchanan *of Ardinconnal and Auchintorlie, co. Dumbarton,* I. iii. 654 ; 2, 3, 4.

Buchanan *of Ardoch, co. Dumbarton,* I. ii. 336 ; 2, 3, 4.

Buchanan *of Drumpellier House, co. Lanark,* 4.

Buchanan *of Hales Hall, co. Stafford,* 3 supp., 4.

Buchanan-Hamilton *of Spittal, &c.* 2 supp.

Buck *of Denholme and Glanarbeth,* 3, 4.

Buck *of Agecroft Hall, co. Lancaster,* 2.

Buck *of Moreton and Hartland Abbey, co. Devon,* 2, 3.

Buckle *of Wharton House, co. Edinburgh,* 3, 4.

Buckle *of New Hall and of Norton House,* I. ii. 575 ; 2.

Buckley *of New Hall, Salisbury,* 3, 4.

Buckley *of Ardwick and Grotton Hall,* 2 supp., 3, 4.

Buckley *of Minesteed Lodge, co. Hants,* 2.

Bucknall, Lindsey- *of Turin Castle, co. Mayo,* 2, 3, 4.

Buckston *of Bradborne, co. Derby,* I. ii. 106; 2, 3, 4.

Budgen *of Ballindoney, co. Wexford,* 4.

Budworth *of Greensted Hall, co. Essex,* 4.

Bulkeley *of Standlow,* I. iii. 336 ; 2 supp.

Bullen, Tatchell- *of Marshwood, co. Dorset*, 3, 4.

Buller *of Downes, co. Devon*, 2, 3, 4.

Buller *of Morval, co. Cornwall*, 2, 3, 4.

Buller *of Pelynt and Lanreath*, 2, 3, 4.

Bullock *of Shipdham, co. Norfolk*, I. iv. 129; 2, 3, 4.

Bullock *of Falkborne, co. Essex*, I. ii. 621; 2, 3, 4.

Bullock *of North Coker, co. Somerset*, 3, 4.

Bulteel *of Flete, co. Devon*, 2, 3, 4.

Bulwer *of Heydon, co Norfolk*, I. i. 445; 2, 3, 4.

Bunbury *of Moyle, co. Carlow*, 3, 4.

Bunbury *of Lisnavagh, co. Carlow*, 2 supp. 3, 4.

Bund *of Wick House, co. Worcester*, 2, 3.

Bunny *of Speen Hill, co. Berks*, 2, 3, 4.

Burchall *of Broadfield Court, co. Hereford*, 2 supp., 3, 4.

Burchall *of Bushey ;* see Herne ; 2, 3, 4.

Burdett *of Ballymany and Ballywater*, 2, 3, 4.

Burdett *of Hunstanton, King's Co.*, 2, 3, 4.

Burdon *of Castle Eden, Durham*, 2, 3, 4.

Burges *of Parkanaur and East Ham*, 2, 3, 4.

Burgh, Hussey de, *of Donore and Dromkeen*, 2, 3, 4.

Burke *of Knocknagur, co. Galway*, 3, 4.

Burke *of Ower, co. Galway*, 2, 3, 4.

Burke *of Beaconsfield*, 4.

Burke *of Ballydugan, co. Galway*, 2, 3, 4.

Burke *of Elm Hall, co. Tipperary*, 2, 3, 4.

Burke *of Tyaquin, co. Galway*, 2, 3.

Burke *of Prospect Villa, co. Cork*, 2 supp. 3, 4.

Burke *of Slatefield, co. Galway*, 3, 4.

Burke *of St. Clerans, co. Galway*, 2, 3, 4.

Burleigh *of Carrickfergus, co. Antrim*, 2, 3, 4.

Burley, I. iii. 527.

Burnaby *of Baggrave Hall, co. Leicester*, I. iv. 702; 2, 3, 4.

Burne *of Loynton Hall, co. Stafford*, 2 supp., 3, 4.

Burnell *of Winkburn Hall and Beauchieff Abbey*, 2, 3, 4.

Burnett *of Barns, co. Peebles*, 2 supp.

Burnes *of Montrose*, 2 supp.

Burr *of Aldermaston, co. Berks*, 3, 4.

Burr *of Gayton, co. Hereford*, 2.

Burrell *of Broomepark, Northumberland*, I. iv. 633; 2, 3, 4.

Burrell *of Stoke Park, co. Suffolk*, 4.

Burroughes *of Burlingham, co. Norfolk*, I. iii. 553; 2, 3, 4.

Burroughes *of Long Stratton, co. Norfolk*, I. iii. 554; 2, 3, 4.

Burroughs *of Rousay, co. Orkney*, 4 supp.

Burrowes *of Stradone, co. Cavan*, 2, 3, 4.

Burrowes *of Dangan Castle, co. Meath*, 4.

Burton *of Longner, co. Salop*, I. iv. 261; 2, 3, 4.

Burton *of Burton Hall, co. Carlow*, 2, 3, 4.

Burton *of Carrigaholt Castle, co. Clare*, 3, 4.

Burton *of Tunstall, co. Lancaster*, 4.

Burton *of Mount Anville*, I. iii. 269; 2.

Burton *of Suckett's Hill House*, I. iii. 312; 2 supp., 3.

Busfeild *of Upwood, co. York*, I. iv. 701; 2, 3, 4.

Bushe *of Glencairn Abbey, co. Waterford*, 3, 4.

Busk *of Ford's Grove, co. Middlesex*, 2, 3, 4.

Busvargus Family, I. iv. 296.

Butler *of Ballyline, co. Clare*, 4.

Butler *of Castle Crine, co. Clare*, 4.

Butler *of Cregg, co. Galway*, 2, 3, 4.

Butler *of Pendeford ;* see Fowler-Butler, 4.

Butler *of Priestown, co. Meath*, 2 add., 3, 4.

Butler *of Swithland*, I. i. 148.
Butler *of Warminghurst*, I. iii. 517.
Butler *of Cazenoves House, co. Mid-
dlesex*, 4 supp.
Butter *of Faskally, co. Perth*, 2, 3,
4.
Butts *of Camesworth, co. Dorset*, 2
supp. 3, 4.
Byam *of Antigua, and of Somerset-
shire*, 2, 3, 4.
Byne *of Surrey*, 2 add.
Byng *of Wrotham, co. Middlesex*, 2.
Byrne *of Cabinteely, co. Dublin*, I.
i. 462 ; 2, 3, 4.
Byrne *of Allardstown, co. Louth*, 4.
Bythesea *of The Hill, Freshford*, I.
iv. 603 ; 2, 3, 4.
Bythesea *of Week House, co. Wilts*,
I. ii. 663 ; 2.
Cadman *of Westbourne House, co.
York*, 4.
Cadogan *of Brenckburn Priory, co.
Northumberland*, 3, 4.
Cahill *of Ballyconra, co. Kilkenny*,
4 supp.
Calcott *of Caynham Court, co. Salop*,
2, 3, 4.
Calcraft *of Ancaster Hall, co. Lin-
coln*, 2, 3, 4.
Calcraft *of Rempstone, co. Dorset*, 2,
3, 4.
Caldecot *of Holton, co. Lincoln*, 3,
4.
Caldecott *of Rugby, co. Warwick*, I.
i. 620 ; 2, 3, 4.
Caldecott *of Holbrook Grange, co.
Warwick*, 3. 4.
Caldwell *of New Grange, co. Meath*,
2 supp. 3, 4.
Caldwell *of Beechlands, I. of Wight*,
3, 4.
Caldwell *of Linley Wood, co. Staf-
ford*, I. iv. 597 ; 2, 3, 4.
Callaghan *of Cork*, 2.
Callander *of Craigforth, co. Stirling*,
2 supp. 3, 4.
Calley *of Burderop, co. Wilts*, 2, 3,
4.
Calley *of Blunsdon St. Andrew,
Wilts*, 2 supp.
Calmady *of Langdon, co. Devon*, 2,
3, 4.

Calrow *of Walton Lodge, co. Lan-
caster*, 2, 3, 4.
Calthrop *of Stanhoe, co. Norfolk*, 2,
3, 4.
Calthrop *of Gosberton, co. Lincoln*,
2, 3, 4.
Calverley *of Oulton Hall, co. York*,
3, 4.
Calverley *ef the Broad, co. Sussex,
and of Ewell Castle, co. Surrey*,
I. i. 673.
Calvert *of Albury Hall, co. Herts*,
I. iii. 399 ; 2.
Calvert *of Hunsdon, co. Herts*, 2, 3.
Cambridge *of Bloxworth House, co.
Dorset*, 3 supp. 4.
Cambridge *of Whitminster, co.
Gloucester*, 2.
Cameron *of Lochiel, co. Inverness*,
2, 3, 4.
Cameron *of Worcester*, 2.
Campbell *of Ormidale, co. Argyll*,
3, 4,
Campbell *of Monzie, co. Perth*, 2,
3, 4.
Campbell *of Lochnell, co. Argyll*, 2
add. 3, 4.
Campbell *of Cessnock and Treesbanks*,
2, 3, 4.
Campbell *of Barquharrie, co. Ayr*,
I. ii. 359 ; 2, 3, 4.
Campbell *of Fairfield, co. Ayr*, I. ii.
362 ; 2, 3, 4.
Campbell *of Ardchattan Priory, co.
Argyll*, 2, 3, 4.
Campbell *of Dunoon ;* see Campbell
Wyndham, 2, 3, 4.
Campbell *of Colgrain, co. Dumbar-
ton*, 3, 4.
Campbell *of Glenfalloch, co. Perth*,
2, 3, 4.
Campbell *of Isley*, 2, 3, 4.
Campbell *of Skerrington, co. Ayr*,
2, 3, 4.
Campbell *of Barbeck*, I. i. 563 ; 2.
Campbell *of Skipness Castle, co.
Argyll*, 2, 3.
Campbell *of Gatcombe*, I. ii. 187.
Campbell *of Auchmannoch, co. Ayr*,
I. iv. 14 ; 2, 3, 4.
Campbell *of Glenlyon ;* see Gardon-
Campbell, 2 supp. 3, 4.

Campbell *of Jura, co. Argyll,* 2, 3, 4.

Campbell *of Sonachan, co. Argyll,* 4

Campbell *of Stonefield, co. Argyll,* 4.

Campbell *of Stracathro, co. Forfar,* 3. 4.

Campion *of Danny, co. Sussex,* 2, 3, 4.

Candler *of Callan,* I. i. 105 ; 2, 3, 4.

Canning *of Foxcote, co. Warwick,* I. iii. 262 ; 2, 3, 4.

Capron *of Stoke Doyle, co. Northampton,* 3, 4.

Capel *of The Grove, Painswick,* 2, 3, 4.

Cardinall *of Tendring Manor House,* 3, 4.

Cardwell *of Ellerbeck, co. Lancaster,* 4.

Carew, Pole- *of Antony, co. Cornwall,* I. i. 557 ; 2, 3, 4.

Carew *of Carew Castle and Crowcombe,* I. i. 266 ; 2, 3, 4.

Carew *of Ballinamona, co. Waterford,* I. iv. 644 ; 2, 3, 4.

Carew *of Beddington Park, co. Surrey,* 2, 3, 4.

Carey *of Careysville, co. Cork,* 2 supp. 3, 4.

Carey *of Rozel, Guernsey,* 2 supp. 3, 4.

Carleill *of Sewerby, co. Lincoln,* I. iii. 587 ; 2, 3, 4.

Carleton *of Ireland,* 3 supp. 4.

Carleton *of Market Hill, co. Fermanagh,* 2, 3, 4.

Carleton, I. iii. 259 ; 4 supp.

Carlyon *of Tregrehan, co. Cornwall,* I. iv. 22 ; 2, 3, 4.

Carn *of Nash, co. Glamorgan,* I. iv. 479 ; 2, 3, 4.

Carne *of Dimland Castle, co. Glamorgan,* 3, 4.

Carno *of Penzance, co. Cornwall,* 4 supp.

Carnegie *of Boysack and Spynie ;* see Lindsay-Carnegie, 2 supp. 3, 4.

Carpenter *of Mount Tavy, co. Devon,* 2 supp. 3, 4.

Carr *of Cocken Hall, co. Durham,* I. ii. 354 ; 2.

Carre *of Cavers ;* see Riddell-Carre.

Carrington-Smith *of St. Margaret's, co. Gloucester,* I. iv. 740.

Carroll *of Ashford, co. Wicklow,* 4.

Carroll *of Ballynure, co. Wicklow,* 2, 3, 4.

Carter *of Watlington Park, co. Oxford,* 4.

Carter *of Castle Martin, co. Kildare,* 2.

Carter *of Erris, co. Mayo,* 3.

Carthew *of Woodbridge Abbey, co. Suffolk,* 2 supp. 3, 4.

Cartwright *of Aynhoe, co. Northampton,* I. ii. 437 ; 2, 3, 4.

Cartwright *of Norwell and Normanton,* I. ii. 435 ; 2, 3, 4.

Cartwright *of Ixworth Abbey, co. Suffolk,* 2.

Carvick *of Wyke, co. York,* 2.

Cary *of Torr Abbey, co. Devon,* I. ii. 33 ; 2, 3, 4.

Cary *of Follaton, co. Devon,* I. ii. 38 ; 2, 3, 4.

Cary *of White Castle, co. Donegal,* 2 supp. 3, 4.

Cary *of Munfin, co. Wexford,* 4 supp.

Casberd *of Maes Mawr, co. Glamorgan,* 2.

Casborne *of New House, Pakenham,* 2 supp. 3, 4.

Case *of Ince, co. Lancaster,* 4.

Case *of Thingwall Hall, co. Lancaster,* 2.

Case *of Papplewick Hall, co. Notts.,* 3.

Casement *of Ballee House, co. Antrim,* 4.

Casement *of Invermore, co. Antrim,* 4.

Cassan *of Sheffield, Queen's Co.* I. i. 643 ; 2, 3, 4.

Cass *of Little Grove, co. Herts,* 3, 4.

Caswell *of Elm Grove, co. Berks,* 3, 4.

Cathcart *of Carbiston, co. Ayr,* 2 supp. 3, 4.

Cathcart *of Knockdolian, co. Ayr,* 2 supp. 3, 4.

Caton *of Binbrook, co. Lincoln*, I.
iv. 305 ; 2, 3, 4.
Cator *of Woodbastwick, Norfolk*, 3,
4.
Caulfeild *of Drumcairne, co. Tyrone*,
2, 3, 4,
Caulfeild *of Donamon Castle, co.
Roscommon*, 2, 3, 4.
Caulfeild *of Raheenduff, Queen's Co.*,
2, 3, 4.
Caulfeild *of Bloomfield, co. West-
meath*, 2, 3, 4.
Cave *of Cleve Hill, co. Gloucester*,
4.
Cay *of North Charlton, Northum-
berland*, I. i. 384 ; 2, ?, 4.
Cayley *of Wydale, co. York*, 2, 3, 4.
Chad *of Thursford Hall, co. Nor-
folk*, 4.
Chadwick *of Healey, Ridware, and
New Hall*, I. iii. 438 ; 2, 3, 4.
Chadwick *of High Bank, co. Lan-
caster*, 3, 4.
Chadwick *of Pudleston Court, co.
Hereford*, I. iv. 456 ; 3, 4.
Chadwick *of Daresbury Hall, co.
Chester*, 3, 4.
Chadwick *of Swinton Hall, co. Lan-
caster*, 2.
Chadwick, I. iii. 444.
Challen *of Shermanbury Park, co.
Sussex*, I. i. 646 ; 2, 3, 4.
Challoner *of Portnall, co. Surrey*,
2, 3, 4.
Chalmers *of Aldbar Castle, co. For-
far*, 2, 3, 4.
Chaloner *of Guisborough, co. York*,
2, 3, 4.
Chaloner *of Kingsfort, co Meath*,
3, 4.
Chamberlayne *of Maugersbury, co.
Gloucester*, 2, 3, 4.
Chamberlayne *of Stoney Thorpe, co.
Warwick*, 2, 3, 4.
Chamberlayne *of Cranbury Park,
co. Hants*, 2, 3, 4.
Chambers *of Fox Hall, co. Donegal*,
3, 4.
Chambers *of Hafod, co. Cardigan*, 4.
Chambers *of Bredgar House, co.
Kent*, I. ii. 179 ; 2.
Chambers *of Loughveagh*, 2 supp.

Chambre *of Hawthorn Hill, co. Ar-
magh*, 2, 3, 4.
Chambre *of Halhead Hall, and
Kendal*, 2 add.
Champion-Möller ; see Möller.
Champernowne *of Dartington, co.
Devon*, I. ii. 271 ; 3, 4.
Champneys *of Ostenhanger, co.
Kent*, I. iii. 555 ; 2.
Chaplin *of Blankney, co. Lincoln*,
2, 3, 4.
Chaplin *of Tathwell Hall, co. Lin-
coln*, 3, 4.
Chapman *of Whitby Strand, co.
York*, 2-supp. 3, 4.
Charlesworth *of Chapelthorpe Hall,
co. York*, 3, 4.
Charlton *of Hesleyside, co. Nor-
thumberland*, 2, 3, 4.
Charlton *of Apley Castle, co. Salop*,
2, 3, 4.
Charlton *of Chilwell, co. Notts.*, 2,
3, 4.
Charlton *of Wytheford Hall, co.
Salop*, 2.
Charlton *of Ludford, co. Hereford*,
2, 3.
Charley *of Finaghy House, co. An-
trim*, 4.
Charley *of Seymour Hill, co. An-
trim*, 4.
Charnock *of Charnock, co. Lancas-
ter*, 2.
Chauncy *of Little Munden, co.
Herts*, 2, 3 supp. 4.
Chawner *of Newton Manor House,
co. Hants*, 2, 3, 4.
Chaytor *of Spennithorne Hall, co.
York*, I. ii. 139.
Cheales *of Hayworthingham, co.
Hants*, 4.
Cheese *of Huntingdon Court, co.
Hereford*, 2, 3, 4.
Cheevers *of Killyan, co. Galway*, 2
supp. 3.
Cheney *of Badger Hall, co. Salop*,
3, 4.
Cheney *of Gaddesby, co. Leicester*,
4.
Cheney *of Monyash, co. Derby*, 2.
Cherry *of Buckland, co. Hereford*,
2, 3, 4.

Cherry *of Denford, co. Berks*, 2, 3, 4.
Chesenhall *of Arley, co. Lancaster,* 2 supp.
Chester *of Bush Hall, co. Herts,* 2, 3, 4.
Chester *of Chicheley Hall, co. Bucks,* 3, 4.
Chetwode *of Woodbrooke, Queen's Co.,* 2, 3, 4.
Chevers *of Killyan House, co. Galway,* 4.
Chichester *of Hall, co. Devon,* 2, 3, 4.
Chichester *of Calverleigh ;* see Nagle.
Child *of Bigelly House, co. Pembroke,* I. iii. 692 ; 2, 3, 4.
Child *of Newfield, co. Stafford,* 2, 3, 4.
Childe *of Kinlet, co. Salop,* I. iii. 195 ; 2, 3, 4.
Childers *of Cantley, co. York,* I. ii. 229 ; 2, 3, 4.
Chisholm, 2, 3, 4.
Chisholme *of that Ilk and Stirches, co. Roxburgh,* 4.
Cholmley *of Whitby and Howsham, co. York,* 2, 3, 4.
Cholmeley *of Brandsby, co. York,* 2, 3, 4.
Chowne *of Wheatley Lodge, co. Somerset,* 3, 4.
Christian *of Evanrigg Hall, co. Cumberland,* 2, 3, 4.
Christie *of Durie, co. Fife,* 2 supp., 3, 4.
Christmas *of Whitfield, co. Waterford,* 3, 4.
Christopher *of Bloxholm ;* see Nisbet-Hamilton, 2, 3, 4.
Christy *of Apuldrefield, co. Kent,* I. iv. 364 ; 2, 3, 4.
Chute *of The Vine, co. Hants,* I. i. 632 ; 2, 3, 4.
Chute *of Chute Hall, co. Kerry,* I. iii. 42 ; 2, 3, 4.
Clanchy *of Charleville, co. Cork,* 4.
Clapcott *of Keynstone, co. Dorset,* 4.
Clapham *of Burley Grange, co. York,* 2, 3, 4.
Clark *of Belford Hall, co. Northumberland,* I. i. 596 ; 2, 3, 4.
Clark *of Buckland Toussaints,* 2, 3, 4.
Clark *of Frimhurst, co. Surrey,* 4.

Clark *of Largantogther House, co. Londonderry,* 4.
Clarke *of Welton Place, co. Northampton,* I. iv. 254 ; 2, 3, 4.
Clarke *of Handsworth, co. Stafford,* 2, 3, 4.
Clarke *of Bridewell, co. Devon,* 2, 3, 4.
Clarke *of Knedlington Manor, co. York,* 2, 3, 4.
Clarke *of Swakeleys, co. Middlesex,* 3, 4.
Clarke *of Hyde Hall, co. Chester,* I. ii. 189 ; 2, 3, 4.
Clarke *of Ardington, co. Berks,* I. i. 110 ; 2.
Clarke *of Comrie Castle, co. Perth,* I. i. 225 ; 2.
Clarke *of Ackareidh, co. Nairn,* 4 supp.
Clavering *of Callaly, Northumberland,* I. i. 237 ; 2, 3, 4.
Clayton *of Hedgerley Park, co. Bucks,* 2, 3, 4.
Clayton *of Adlington, co. Lancaster,* 2, 3, 4.
Clayton *of Enfield Old Park, Middlesex,* 2, 3, 4.
Clayton *of Norfolk,* 2.
Cleland *of Rath-Gael, co. Devon,* I. iv. 218 ; 2, 3, 4.
Clements *of Ashfield Lodge, co. Cavan,* 2, 3 and supp., 4.
Clements *of Rathkerry, co. Cavan,* 3, 4.
Clendinning *of Thomastown, co. Mayo,* 2.
Clerk-Rattray *of Craighall Rattray, co. Perth,* I. iii. 186.
Clevland *of Tapeley Park, co. Devon,* 3, 4.
Clibborn *of Moate Castle, co. Westmeath,* 2.
Cliffe *of Bellevue, co. Wexford,* 2, 3, 4.
Clifford, I. iii. 660.
Clifford *of Frampton, co. Gloucester,* 2 supp., 3, 4.
Clifford *of Perristone and Llantilio,* 2, 3, 4.
Clifford *of Castle Annesley, co. Wexford,* 2, 3, 4.
Clifton *of Clifton and Lytham, co. Lancaster,* I. ii. 54 ; 2, 3, 4.

Clive *of Whitfield, co. Hereford,* 2 supp., 3, 4.

Close *of Drumbanagher, co. Armagh,* I. iii. 247 ; 2, 3, 4.

Clough *of Plas-Clough, co. Denbigh,* I. iii. 515; 2, 3, 4.

Clowes *of Delaford, co. Bucks,* I. iv. 724; 2, 3, 4.

Cludde *of Orleton, co. Salop,* I. i. 483 ; 2, 3, 4.

Clutterbuck *of Warkworth, co. Northumberland,* I. ii. 224 ; 2, 3, 4.

Clutterbuek *of New Ark Place, co. Gloucester,* 3, 4.

Clutton-Brock ; see Brock of Pensax ; 2 supp., 3, 4.

Clutton *of Chorlton Hall, co. Chester,* 2, 3.

Coates *of Eastwood, co. Devon,* 4.

Cobbe *of Newbridge House, co. Dublin,* 2, 3, 4.

Cochrane *of Edenmore, co. Donegal,* 4.

Coddington *of Oldbridge, co. Meath,* 2, 3, 4.

Codrington *of Wroughton, co. Wilts,* 2. 3, 4.

Coffin *of Portledge, co. Devon,* 2, 3, 4.

Cogan *of Tonade, co. Wicklow,* 4.

Coham *of Coham, co. Devon,* 2, 3, 4.

Coke *of Irusley, co. Derby,* I. iv. 268 ; 2, 3, 4.

Coke *of Lower Moor House, co. Hereford,* 2, 3, 4.

Coke *of Holkham, co. Norfolk,* I. i. 3.

Coker *of Bicester House, co. Oxford,* 2 add. 3, 4.

Colclough *of Tinterne Abbey, co. Wexford,* 3, 4.

Coldham *of Anmer Hall, co. Norfolk,* 3, 4.

Cole *of Twickenham, Middlesex,* 2, 3, 4.

Cole *of Brandrum, co. Monagahan,* 2, 3, 4.

Cole *of Holyboum, co. Hants,* 3, 4.

Cole *of Marazion, co. Cornwall,* 2 add. 3, 4.

Cole *of Stoke Lyne, co. Oxford,* I. i. 192.

Colegrave *of Downsell Hall, co. Essex,* 2 supp.

Colegrave *of Downsell Hall, co. Essex,* 3, 4.

Coles *of Ditcham, co. Hants,* 3, 4.

Coles *of Parrocks Lodge, co. Somerset,* 2, 3, 4.

Colling *of Red Hall, co. Durham,* 3, 4.

Collings *of Guernsey,* 2 add. 3, 4.

Collingwood *of Chirton and Lilburn Tower,* 3, 4.

Collingwood *of Dissington, Northumberland,* I. i. 472 ; 2, 3, 4.

Collingwood *of Cornhill House, co. Durham,* 2, 3, 4.

Collins *of Walford, co. Hereford,* 2 supp., 3, 4.

Collins *of Betterton, co. Berks,* I. iv. 616; 2, 3, 4.

Collins *of Truthan, co. Cornwall,* 2, 3, 4.

Collins *of Hatch Beauchamp, co. Somerset,* I. iii. 536 ; 2.

Collins *of Simmons Court, co. Dublin,* 2 supp.

Collinson *of The Chantry, co. Suffolk,* I. ii. 538.

Collis *of Castle Cooke ;* see Cooke-Collis, 3, 4.

Collis *of Lismore, co. Kerry,* 2 supp., 3, 4.

Collis *of Fort William, co. Kerry,* 2 supp., 3, 4.

Collyer *of Hackford Hall, co. Norfolk,* 2, 3, 4.

Colmore *of Moore End, co. Gloucester,* 3, 4.

Colquhoun *of Killermont, co. Dumbarton,* 2, 3, 4.

Colquhoun *of London,* I. ii. 345.

Colston *of Roundway Park, co. Wilts,* 2 and add., 3, 4.

Colt *of Gartsherrie, co. Lanark,* 2, 3, 4.

Colthurst-Vesey ; see Vesey *of Lucan,* 4.

Colthurst *of Dripsey Castle, co. Cork,* 2 add. 3, 4.

Colvill *of Ireland,* 2 supp.

Colville *of Lullington, co. Derby,* 2, 3, 4.

Comer *of Fitzhead, co. Somerset,* 2 add. 3, 4.

Commerell *of Strood, co. Sussex,* 2, 3, 4.

Compton *of the Manor House, Minestead,* 2, 3. 4.

Comyn *of Woodstock, and Kilcorney,* 3, 4.

Concanon *of Canownacreggy, co. Galway,* 3, 4.

Congreve *of Burton, co. Chester,* 4.

Congreve *of Mount Congreve, co. Waterford,* I. i 15 ; 3, 4.

Congreve *of Congreve, co. Stafford,* 2, 3.

Conn *of Mount Ida, co. Kilkenny,* 4.

Connellan *of Coolmore, co. Kilkenny,* 2, 3, 4.

Conner *of Manch, co. Cork,* 2 add., 3, 4.

Conner *of Ballybricken;* see Conner *of Manch.*

Conroy *of Llanbrynmair, co. Montgomery,* I. i. 491.

Constable *of Wassand, co. York,* I. i. 547 ; 2.

Constable-Maxwell ; see Maxwell, 2.

Conolly *of Castletown, co. Kildare,* I. ii. 159 ; 2, 3, 4.

Conolly *of Cottles and Midford Castle,* 2, 3, 4.

Conway *of Lower Soughton, co. Flint,* 2.

Conwy *of Bodrhyddan, co. Flint,* 2, 3, 4.

Conyers *of Copped Hall, co. Essex,* 2.

Conyngham *of Spring Hill, co. Londonderry,* 2, 3, 4.

Cooke *of Cookesborough, co. Westmeath,* 4.

Cooke-Collis *of Castle Cooke, co. Cork,* 4.

Cooke *of Cordangan, co. Tipperary,* 2 supp., 3, 4.

Cooke *of Gurrangreny,* 4.

Cooke *of Kiltinan Castle, co. Tipperary,* 2 supp., 3, 4.

Cooke *of Owston and Gwysaney,* I. ii. 276 ; 2, 3, 4.

Cooke *of The Retreat, co. Westmeath,* 2 add. 3, 4.

Cooke *of Farm Hill, co. Gloucester,* 2 supp.

Cooke *of Peak, co. York,* I. ii. 266.

Cookes *of Bentley, co. Worcester,* I. iv. 519 ; 2, 3, 4.

Cookson *of Whitehill, co. Durham,* I. ii. 506 ; 2, 3, 4.

Cookson *of Meldon Park, Northumberland,* 2, 3, 4.

Cooper *of Markrel Castle, co. Sligo,* 2, 3, 4.

Cooper *of Cooper's Hill;* see O'Hara, 3, 4.

Cooper *of Cooper Hill, co. Limerick,* 3 supp., 4.

Cooper *of Toddington Manor, co. Bedford,* I. i. 158 ; 2, 3, 4.

Cooper *of Failford, co. Ayr,* 3, 4.

Cooper *of Finchley, Middlesex,* 3 supp., 4.

Cooper *of Shrewl Costle, co. Wicklow,* 2.

Coore *of Scruton Hall, co. York,* 2, 3, 4.

Coote *of Mount Coote, co. Limerick* 2, 3, 4. ,

Cope *of Drummilly, co. Armagh,* 2 supp., 3, 4.

Cope *of Loughgall Manor, co. Armagh,* 3, 4.

Coppinger *of Ballyvolane, co. Cork,* I. ii. 326 ; 2, 3, 4.

Coppinger *of Midleton, co. Cork,* 3, 4.

Coppinger *of Leemount, co. Cork,* 2 supp., 3, 4.

Corbally *of Corbalton Hall, co. Meath,* 2, 3, 4.

Corbet *of Sundorne, co. Salop,* I. iii. 627 ; 2, 3, 4.

Corbet *of Ynysymaengwy,* I. ii. 91.

Corbett *of Elsham and Darnhall,* I. iii. 189 ; 2, 3, 4.

Corbett *of Longnor and Leighton,* 2, 3, 4.

Corbett *of Admington Hall, co. Gloucester,* 2 supp., 3, 4.

Cornewall *of Delbury, co. Salop,* 2 add. 3, 4.

Cornish *of Black Hall, co. Devon,* 3, 4.

Cornish *of Mazarion, co. Cornwall,* 2.

Cornock *of Cromwellsfort, co. Wexford,* 2, 3, 4.

Corrance *of Parham Hall, co. Suffolk,* I. iii. 370 : 2, 3, 4.

Corry *of Newry, co. Down,* 3, 4.

Corsellis *of Wyvenhoe Hall, Essex*, 3, 4.
Corstorphine *of Pittowie Hall, Fife*, 4.
Coryton *of Pentillie Castle, Cornwall*, I. i. 232 ; 2, 3, 4.
Cosby *of Stradbally, Queen's Co.*, I. iii. 153 ; 2, 3, 4.
Costello *of Edmundstown, Mayo*, 3 supp., 4.
Cotes *of Woodcote, Salop*, 2, 3, 4.
Cotgreave *of Netherleigh, Chester*, I. i. 530.
Cotton *of Etwall, Derby*, 3. 4.
Cottrell *of Hadley, Middlesex*, I. iv. 745 ; 2, 3, 4.
Coulson *of Blenkinsopp, Northumberland*, I. ii. 525 ; 2, 3, 4.
Coulthart *of Coulthart, Collyn, and Ashton-under-Lyne*, 2 supp., 3, 4.
Courtenay *of Ballyedmond, Cork*, 2, 3, 4.
Courtenay, I. ii. 306.
Cowell-Stepney ; see Stepney.
Cowper *of Carleton Hall, Cumberland*, 4.
Cox *of Ballynoe, Limerick*, 3, 4.
Cox *of Coolcliffe, Wexford*, 2, 3, 4.
Cox *of Broxwood and Eaton Bishop, Hereford*, 3, 4.
Coxwell *of Ablington ;* see Coxwell-Rogers, I. iii. 471 ; 2, 3, 4.
Coyney *of Weston Coyney, Stafford*, 2, 3, 4.
Coyney *of Weston Coyney, Stafford*, I. ii. 42.
Crackenthorpe *of Newbiggin, Westmorelaad*, 2, 3, 4.
Cracroft, now Amcotts, *of Hackthorn*, 2, 3, 4.
Cradock *of Hartforth, York*, I. iv. 256 ; 2.
Craig *of Riccarton*, 3.
Cramer *of Rathmore, Cork*, 4.
Cranstoun *of Corehouse, Lanark*, 3, 4.
Cra'ster *of Cra'ster Tower, Northumberland*, 2, 3, 4.
Craufuird *of Baidland*, 2 supp., 3, 4.
Craufurd *of Craufurdland, Ayr*, I. ii. 230 ; 2, 3, 4.
Craufurd *of Auchinames, Ayr*, I. ii. 384 ; 2, 3, 4.

Craven *of Brambridge, Hants*, 4.
Craven *of Richardstown, Louth*, 2 supp., 3, 4.
Craven *of Brockhampton Park, Gloucester*, 2, 3, 4.
Craven *of Chilton House, Wilts*, I. i. 180.
Crawford *of Crawfordsburn, Down*, 2, 3, 4.
Crawfurd *of Milton, Lanark*, 3, 4.
Crawfurd *of Crosby*, I. i. 551.
Cruwfurd *of Crawfurd, Ayr*, 2.
Crawfurd *of Saint Hill, Sussex*, 2, 3.
Crawley *of Stockwood, Bedford*, 4.
Creagh *of Bally Andrew*, 2 supp., 3, 4.
Creagh *of Dangan, Clare*, 2 supp., 3, 4.
Creagh *of Creagh Castle, Cork*, 2, 3, 4.
Creagh *of Carrigerry, Clare*, 2.
Crean *of Ballenvilla, Mayo*, 3.
Cregoe *of Trewithian, Cornwall*, 2, 3, 4.
Cree *of Ower Moigne, Dorset*, 2 supp., 3, 4.
Creighton *of Crum Castle, Fermanagh*, I. iii. 636.
Cresswell *of Cresswell, Northumberland*, I. ii. 290 ; 2, 3, 4.
Cresswell *of Pinkney Park, Wilts*, 2, 3, 4.
Creswell *of Ravenstone, Leicester*, I. iii. 475 ; 2, 3, 4.
Creyke *of Marton, York*, I. iv. 24 ; 2, 3, 4.
Crichton *of Rankeilour, Fife*, 2 supp., 3, 4.
Crigan *of Mount Pleasant, Tyrone*, 2.
Croft *of Stillington Hall, York*, 2, 3, 4.
Croft *of Aldborough Hall, York*, 4.
Croft *of Greenham Lodge, Berks*, 2 supp., 3, 4.
Crofts *of Velvetstown, Cork*, 2, 3, 4.
Crofts *of Churchtown, Cork*, 2, 3, 4.
Crofton *of Lakefield, Leitrim*, 2, 3, 4.
Croko *of Studley Priory, Oxon*, I. i. 354 ; 2, 3, 4.
Croker *of Ballynagarde, Limerick*, 2, 3, 4.

Croker *of Westmoulsey, Surrey,* I. i. 340; 3.

Crommelin *of Carrowdore Castle, Down,* I. iv. 422 ; 2, 3, 4.

Crompton *of Duffield Hall, Derby,* I. iii. 689 ; 2 supp., 3, 4.

Crompton *of Azerley Hall ;* see Stansfield *of Esholt Hall.*

Cromptou *of Hacking, Lancaster,* 2 supp.

Cromwell *of Cheshunt Park, Herts,* I. i. 428 ; 2, 3, 4.

Cronin-Coltsmann *of Glenflesk Castle, Kerry,* 4.

Crosbie *of Ballyheigue Castle, Kerry,* 2, 3, 4.

Crosbie *of Ardfert Abbey, Kerry,* 2, 3, 4.

Crosse *of Shaw Hall, Lancaster,* 2, 3, 4.

Crosse *of Broomfield, co. Somerset,* 2 add., 3, 4.

Crossley *of Scaitcliffe, Lancaster,* I. ii. 536 ; 2, 3, 4.

Crowe *of Dromore House, Clare,* 4.

Crowe *of TheAbbey, Ennis, Clare,* 3.

Cruikshank *of Langley Park, Forfar,* 3 supp , 4.

Crum-Ewing ; see Ewing, 4.

Crutchley *of Sunninghill Park, Bucks,* 2, 3, 4.

Cubitt *of Catfield Hall, Norfolk,* 2, 3, 4.

Cubitt *of Honing Hall, Norfolk,* 2, 3, 4.

Cullen *of Glenade, Leitrim,* 2, 3, 4.

Culley *of Fowberry Tower, Northumberland,* 2, 3, 4.

Cuninghame *of Lainshaw, Ayr,* 3, 4.

Cuninghame *of Caddell and Thornton,* I. ii. 526 ; 2, 3, 4.

Cuppage *of Mount Edwards, Antrim,* 4.

Cure *of Blake Hall, Essex,* 2, 3, 4.

Curling *of Maesmawr Hall, Montgomery,* 4.

Curre *of Itton Court, Monmouth,* 2, 3, 4.

Currer *of Kildwick, York,* 2, 3, 4.

Currer *of Clifton House;* see Roundell *of Gledstone,* I. iii. 94 ; 2, 3, 4.

Currie *of Bush Hill, Middlesex,* 2, 3, 4.

Curteis *of Windmill Hill, Sussex,* I. i. 314 ; 2, 3, 4.

Curtis *of East Cliffe, Devon,* 2, 3, 4.

Curtois *of The Longhills, Lincoln,* 4.

Curwin *of Workington Hall, Cumberland,* I. i. 577 ; 2, 3, 4.

Curzon *of Breedon, Leicester,* 3, 4.

Cusack *of Gerardstown and Clonard,* 2 supp., 3, 4.

Cusack *of Moyaugher, Meath,* 2.

Custance *of Weston, Norfolk,* I. i. 492 ; 2, 3, 4.

Cutcliffe *of Dunmage,* 2 supp.

Cuthbert *of Beaufront, Northumberland,* 4.

Cutler, *formerly of Yorkshire,* I. iv. 688 ; 2, 3, 4.

Cutler *of Upton, Devon,* I. iv. 690 ; 2, 3, 4.

D'Aeth *of Knowlton Court, Kent,* I. iii. 85; 2, 3, 4.

Dakeyne *of Derbyshire,* 2 supp.

Dale *of Tunstall, Durham,* 2 supp.

Dale *of Glanville's Wootton, Dorset,* 2, 3, 4.

Dale *of Ashborne, Derby,* I. iv. 115 ; 2, 3, 4.

Dalison *of Hamptons, Kent,* 2, 3, 4.

Dalton, Grant- *of Shanks House, Somerset,* 3 supp., 4.

Dalton *of Sleningford, York,* I. i. 528 ; 2, 3, 4.

Dalton *of Dunkirk Manor House, Gloucester,* 2, 3, 4.

Dalton *of Thurnham, Lancaster,* I. i. 522; 2, 3, 4.

Dalway *of Bella Hill, Antrim,* 3, 4.

Daly *of Castle Daly, Galway,* 2, 3, 4.

Daly *of Cooliney, Galway,* 3, 4.

Daly *of Dunsandle, Galway,* 2.

Dalyel *of Lingo and Ticknevin,* 3 supp., 4.

Dames *of Greenhill, King's co.* 2, 3, 4.

Daniel *of Stoodleigh, Devon,* 4.

Daniell *of New Forest, Westmeath,* 3, 4.

Danby *of Swinton, York,* I. i. 200.

Danvers *of Swithland;* see Butler Danvers.

Dane *of Killyherlin, Fermanagh,* 2, 3.

Dansey *of Easton, Hereford,* 3.

Daniel *of Tredissick, Cornwall,* 2.

Darby of Leap Castle, King's Co., 2, 3, 4.
Darby of Stoke Court, Bucks, 3, 4.
Darby of Colebrookdale, Salop, I. ii. 310; 2.
Davies of Elmley Park, Worcester, I. ii. 259.
D'Arcy of Necarn Castle; see Irvine of Castle Irvine.
D'Arcy of Hyde Park, Westmeath, 2, 3, 4.
D'Arcy of New Forest, Galway, 2, 3, 4.
D'Arcy of Kiltullagh and Clifden, I. iii. 142; 2, 3, 4.
D'Arcy of Lacken, Westmeath, 2.
Dare; see Hall-Dare.
Darell of Calehill, Kent, I. i. 133; 2, 3, 4.
Darell of Trewornan, I. i. 369.
Darley of Aldby Park, York, 2, 3, 4.
Darroch of Gourock, Renfrew, 3, 4.
Darwin of Breadsall Priory, 2, 3, 4.
Darwin of Elston Hall, Nottingham, 3, 4.
Dashwood of Stanford Park, Notts. 3, 4.
Daubeny of Cote, Gloucester, I. iv. 738; 2, 3, 4.
Daunt of Owlpen and Gortigrenane, 3, 4.
Daunt of Fahalea, Cork, 3, 4.
Daunt of Newborough, Cork, 3, 4.
Daunt of Slieveron, Cork, 3, 4.
Daunt of Tracton Abbey, Cork, 3, 4.
Daunt of Kilcascan, Cork, 3, 4.
Davenport of Capesthorne, Chester, 2, 3, 4.
Davenport of Davenport, Salop, 2, 3, 4.
Davenport of Bramall Hall, Chester, 2 add. 3, 4.
Davey of Redruth, Cornwall, 2, 3, 4.
Davidson of Cantray, Inverness, 2 add. 3, 4.
Davidson of Inchmarlo, Kincardine, 3, 4.
Davidson of Tulloch Castle, Ross, 4.
Davies of Gwysaney, Flint, 3 supp.,4.
Davies of Marrington Hall, Salop, I. ii. 642; 2, 3, 4.
Davies of Moor Court, Hereford, 2 add. 3, 4.
Davies of Alltyr Odin, Cardigan, 3, 4.

Davies of Castle Green, Cardigan, 4.
Davies of Birmingham, co. Warwick, 2 add.
Davies of Pentre, Pembroke, 2, 3, 4.
Davies, Bowen- of Maes-y-Crygie, Carmarthen, 2, 3, 4.
Davies of Elmley Park, Worcester, 2.
Davies of Vronheulog, Merioneth, 2.
Davy of Ingoldsthorpe, Norfolk, 2, 3, 4.
Davy of Lesketh How, Westmoreland, 4.
Davy of London, 2.
Davys, Campbell- of Neuadd-Fawr and Dolecoed, 4.
Dawe, or Dawes of Dilcheat, Somerset, I. iv. 577; 2, 3, 4.
Dawkins of Over Norton, 4 supp.
Dawson of Osgodby Hall, York, 2 add. 3, 4.
Dawson of Hornby Castle, Lancaster, 2, 3, 4.
Dawson of Launde Abbey, Leicester, 4.
Dawson of Groton House, Suffolk, 4.
Dawson of Moyola Park, Londonderry, 4.
Dawson of Castle Dawson, Londonderry, I. iii. 580; 2.
Dawson of Edwardston Hall, Suffolk, 2, 3.
Dawson of Castle Dawson, Londonderry, 3.
Day of Kerry, 3, 4.
Dayman of Mambury, Devon, 3, 4.
Dayrell of Lillingston Dayrell, Bucks, I. iii. 147; 2, 3, 4.
Dayrell of Shudy Camps, Cambridge, I. iii. 152; 2, 3, 4.
Deacon of Long Cross House, Glamorgan, 2.
Dealtry of Lincolnshire, 4 supp.
Dealtry of Lofthouse, York, I. i. 252; 2.
Deane of Berkeley Forest, Wexford, 3, 4.
Deane of Cromlin, Cork. I. ii. 690.
Dearden of Rochdale Manor, Lancaster, I. ii. 356; 2, 3, 4.
Dease of Turbotston, Westmeath, 3,4.
Dease, O'Reilly- of Charleville, Louth, 3, 4.
De Bingh of West Drayton, Middlesex, I. iii. 500; 2, 3, 4.

Deedes *of Sandling Park, Kent,* 2, 3, 4.
De Havilland ; see Havilland.
De Home *of Stanway Hall, Essex,* 2, 3, 4.
De la Cherois *of Donaghadee, Down,* . 2, 3. 4.
Delafield *of Fieldston,* I. i. 542 ; 2.
Delap *of Monellan, Donegal,* 2, 3, 4.
Delme *of Cams Hall, Hants,* 3, 4.
De Montmorency *of Castle Morres, Kilkenny,* 3, 4.
Dempster *of Skibo Castle, Sutherland,* 2, 3, 4.
Denham *of Fanwood Park, Fermanagh,* 2.
Denison *of Ossington, Notts,* 3, 4.
Denison *of Grimthorpe, York,* 2, 3, 4.
Denison *of Rushholme Park, Lancaster,* I. i. 383.
Denison *of Denbies, Surrey,* 2.
Denne *of Lydd, Kent,* 2, 3, 4.
Denne *of Kent and Sussex,* I. iii. 19 ; 2.
Dennis *of Fort Granite, Wicklow,* 2, 3, 4.
Dennistoun *of Denistoun, Dumbarton,* I. iii. 322 ; 2, 3, 4.
Dent *of Ribston Hall, York,* 2, 3, 4.
Dent *of Sudeley Castle, Gloucester,* 3, 4.
Dent *of Shortflatt Tower, Northumland,* 2, 3, 4.
Dering *of Lockleys, Herts,* 3, 4.
De Rinzy *of Clobernon Hall, Wexford,* 2, 3, 4.
De Teissier *of Woodcote Park, Surrey,* 3, 4.
Devenish *of Mount Pleasant, Roscommon,* 2, 3, 4.
Devenish *of Rushill, Roscommon,* 3, 4.
Devereux *of Ballyrankin House, Wexford,* 4.
De Visme *of Devonsh. and Gloucestersh,* I. iv. 320.
De Winton *of Glamorganshire,* 2, 3, 4.
De Winton *of Maesllwch Castle, Radnor,* 2, 3, 4.
De Winton *of Maesderwen, Brecon,* 2, 3, 4.
De Winton, *of Wallsworth Hall, Gloucester,* 4.

D'Eyncourt *of Bayons Manor, Lincoln,* 3, 4.
Dicey *of Claybrooke Hall, Leicester,* 3 supp., 4.
Dick *of Layer Tower, Essex,* 3.
Dickin *of Loppington, Salop,* 2, 3, 4.
Dickins *of Woolaston, Hants,* 3, 4.
Dickinson *of Kingueston, Somerset,* 3, 4.
Dickins *of Coolhurst, Sussex,* I. iv. 279 ; 2, 3, 4.
Dickinson *of Abbot's Hill, Herts,* 3, 4.
Dickinson *of Farley Hill, Berks,* 2, 3.
Dickson *of Ballyfree, Wicklow,* 3.
Dickson *of Limerick,* 2, 3, 4.
Dickson *of Woodville, Leitrim,* 3, 4.
Digby *of Osbertstown, Kildare,* I. iv. 460 ; 2, 3.
Digby *of Landenstown, Kildare,* 2.
Digby *of Sherborne Castle, Dorset,* 4.
Dilke *of Maxtocke Castle, Warwick,* 4.
Dillwyn Llewelyn *of Penllergare, Glamorgan,* 2, 3, 4.
Dimsdale *of Essenden Place, Herts,* 3, 4.
Dinsdale *of Newsham Park, Durham,* 2, 3.
Dirom *of Mount Annan, Dumfries,* 3, 4.
Disney *of the Hyde, Essex,* I. ii. 151 ; 2, 3, 4.
Disney *of Ireland,* 2, 3, 4.
Dixon *of Gledhaw, York,* I. iii. 334.
Dixon *of Unthank Hall, Northumberland,* I. iv. 671 ; 2, 3.
Dixon *of Astle Hall, Chester,* 2, 3, 4.
Dixon *of Page Hall, York,* 3, 4.
Dixon *of Seaton Carew,* 4.
Dixon *of Knells, Cumberland,* 2, 3, 4.
Dixon *of Holton, Lincoln,* 2 add. 3, 4.
Dobbin *of Armagh,* 4.
Dobbs *of Castle Dobbs, Antrim,* 2, 3, 4.
Dod *of Edge, Chester,* I. iii. 548 ; 2, 3, 4.
Dod *of Cloverley, Salop,* I. i. 297 ; 2, 3, 4.
Dodson *of Hurstpierpoint, Sussex,* 4.
Dodwell *of Glenmore, Sligo,* 3, 4.
Doherty or Docherty *of Inishowen,* 3, 4.
Dolling *of Magheralin, Down,* 2, 3, 4.

Dolman *of Pocklington, York*, 2, 4.
Dolphin *of Turoe, Galway*, 3, 4.
Dolphin *of Corr, Galway*, 3, 4.
Domville *of Lyme Hall, Chester*, 3, 4.
Donelan *of Hillswood, Galway*, 2, 3, 4.
Donelan *of Sylane and St. Peter's Well, Galway*, 3, 4.
Donelan *of Killagh, Galway*, 2, 3, 4.
Donkin *of Lower Caversham, Oxford*, I. ii. 69 ; 2.
Donnithorne *of Colne Lodge, Middlesex*, 4.
Donovan *of Ballymore, Wexford*, I. iv. 708 ; 2, 3, 4.
Donovan *of Framfield Place, Sussex*, I. i. 76 ; 2, 3, 4.
Dormer *of Ronsham, Oxford*, 2, 3, 4.
Dorrien *of Haresfoot, Herts*, 3, 4.
Dottin *of Bugle Hall, Hants*, I. i. 360 ; 2.
Douce *of West Malling, Kent*, 2, 3.
Dougal *of Glenferness, Nairn*, 4.
Dougall *of Scots' Craig, Fife*, 4.
Doughty *of Theberton Hall, Suffolk*, I. ii. 540 ; 2, 3, 4.
Doughty *of Snarford Hall, Lincoln*, 2.
Douglas- Gresley *of Salwarpe, Worcester*, 4 supp.
Douglas *of Dervoch, Antrim*, 3, 4.
Douglas *of Mountain Lodge, Armagh*, 3, 4.
Douglas *of Gyrn, Flint*, I. iv. 600.
Douglass *of Grace Hall, Down*, 2, 3, 4.
Dowdall *of Ireland*, 3, 4.
Dowdeswell *of Pull Court, Worcester*, I. i. 376 ; 2, 3, 4.
Dowdeswell *of Redmarley, Worcester*, I. iv. 544 ; 2, 3, 4.
Doyne *of Wells, Wexford*, 2, 3, 4.
Drake *of Ashe (Devon)*, 2, 3, 4.
Drake, Tyrwhitt- *of Shardeloes, Buckingham*, I. i. 580 ; 2, 3, 4.
Drake *of Stokestown, Wexford*, 3, 4.
Drake *of Roriston, Meath*, I. iv. 192 ; 2, 3, 4.
Drax *of Charborough, Dorset*, I. iv. 207 ; 2, 3, 4.
Drewe *of the Grange, Devon*, I. iv. 672 ; 2, 3, 4.
Drew *of Drewscourt, Limerick*, 3, 4.

Drew *of Strand House, Youghal, Cork*, 3, 4.
Dring *of Rockgrove, Cork*, 4.
Drinkwater *of Salford, Lancaster*, I. iii. 420 ; 2.
Drinkwater *of Shrewsbury, Salop*, I. iii. 668 ; 2.
Drinkwater *of Irwell, Lancaster*, I. iii. 669 ; 2, 3.
Drought *of Lettybrook, King's co.* 2, 3, 4.
Drought *of Whigsboro', King's co.* 3, 4.
Drummond *of Blair Drummond, Perth*, 2, 3, 4.
Drummond *of Concraig, Gloucester*, 2, 3, 4.
Drummond *of Megginch Castle, Perth*, 3, 4.
Drummond *of Cadland, Hants*, I. iii. 560 ; 2, 3, 4.
Drummond *of Stanmore, Middlesex*, I. iii. 561 ; 2, 3, 4.
Drummond *of Albury Park, Surrey*, 3.
Drury *of Knightstone, Devon*, 3, 4.
Duberly *of Gaines Hall, Huntingdon*, 2, 3, 4.
Du Boulay *of Donhead Hall, Wilts*, 4.
Du Buisson *of Glynhir, Carmarthen*, 4.
Du Cane *of Braxted, Essex*, 3, 4.
Duckett *of Duckett's Grove, Carlow*, 2, 3, 4.
Duckworth *of Over Darwen and Musbury, Lancashire*, 3, 4.
Duckworth *of Mount Erris, Roscommon*, 3, 4.
Duff *of Hatton, Aberdeen*, 3, 4.
Duff *of Wellington Lodge, Isle of Wight*, 4.
Duff *of Orton, Moray*, 3, 4.
Duff *of Fetteresso, Aberdeen*, 2, 3, 4.
Dugdale *of Merevale, Warwick*, I. i. 488 ; 2, 3, 4.
Duke *of Lake, Wilts*, I. i. 285 ; 2, 3, 4.
Duncan *of Damside, Perth*, 3, 4.
Duncombe *of Copgrove, York*, I. i. 151 ; 2.
Duncombe *of Great Brickhill, Bucks*, I. ii. 74 ; 2, 3.

Dundas *of Dundas, Linlithgow,* I. i. 642; 2, 3, 4.
Dundas *of Arniston, Mid-Lothian,* 2, 3, 4.
Dundas *of Barton Court, Berks,* I. iii. 113; 2, 3, 4.
Dundas *of Carron Hall, Stirling,* 4.
Dundas *of Duddingston,* I. iii. 178; 2, 3, 4.
Dundas *of Blair Castle, Perth,* I. ii. 368; 2, 3.
Dunlop *of That Ilk, Ayr,* I. i. 434.
Dunlop *of Drumhead, Dumbarton,* 3, 4.
Dunlop *of Corsock, Kirkcudbright,* 4.
Dunlop *of Craigton, Lanark,* 4.
Dunlop *of Monasterboice, Louth,* 4.
Dunne (O'Duinne) *of Brittas, Queen's Co.* 2, 3, 4.
Dunscombe *of King William's Town, Cork,* 3, 4.
Dunscombe *of Mount Desert, Cork,* 2, 3, 4.
Duppa *of Hollingbourne, Kent,* I. iv. 483; 2, 3, 4.
Du Pre *of Wilton Park, Bucks,* 2, 3, 4.
Durant *of Sharpham, Devon,* 4.
Durham *of Largo, Fife,* I. i. 287; 2.
Dury *of Bonsall, Derby,* 4.
Dutton *of Burland, Chester,* 3, 4.
Dykes *of Dovenby, Cumberland,* I. i. 263; 2, 3, 4.
Dymock *of Penley Hall, Flint,* I. iii. 87; 2, 3, 4.
Dymoke *of Scrivelsby, Lincoln,* I. i. 32.
Dyne *of Gore Court, Kent,* 3, 4.
Dyott *of Freeford, Stafford,* I. ii. 425; 2, 3, 4.
Eagar *of Kerry,* 4.
Eastwood *of Castletown, Louth,* 2, 3, 4.
Eaton *of Stetchworth Park, Cambridge,* 4.
Eccles *of Cronroe, Wicklow,* 2, 3, 4.
Eccles *of Fintona, Tyrone,* 4.
Echlin *of Ardquin, &c. Down,* 2, 3, 4.
Echlin *of Kirlish, Tyrone,* 4.
Eckley *of Credenhill, Hereford,* 2, 3, 4.

Edgar *of the Red House, Suffolk,* 2, 3, 4.
Edgcumbe *of Edgcumbe House, Devon,* 3, 4.
Edge *of Strelley Hall, Nottingham,* 3, 4.
Edge *of Clonbrock House, Queen's Co.* 4.
Edgell *of Standerwick Court, Somerset,* 3, 4.
Edgeworth *of Edgeworthstown, Longford,* I. iv. 753; 2, 3, 4.
Edgeworth *of Kilshreivly, Longford,* I. iv. 755; 2, 3, 4.
Edmands *of Sutton, Surrey,* 3. 4.
Edwardes *of Rhyd-y-Gors, Carmarthen,* 3, 4.
Edwardes *of Gilleston Manor, Glamorgan,* 3, 4.
Edwardes *of Sealy Ham, Pembroke,* I. ii. 313; 2, 3, 4.
Edwards *of Arlesey Bury, Bedford,* 3, 4.
Edwards *of Roby Hall,* 3, 4.
Edwards *of Pye Nest, York,* 3, 4.
Edwards *of Ness Strange, Salop,* I. ii. 78; 2, 3, 4.
Edwards *of Llandaff House, Glamorgan,* 4.
Edwards *of Old Court, Wicklow,* 2, 3, 4.
Edwards *of Nanhoron, Carnarvon,* 3, 4.
Edwards *of the Hayes, Gloucester,* 2.
Edwards *of Henlow Grange, Bedford,* 2.
Egerton-Warburton; see Warburton.
Egerton *of Tatton, Chester,* I. iii. 36; 2, 3.
Eld *of Sleighford Hall, Stafford,* 3, 4.
Elers *of Chelsea, Middlesex,* I. iv. 418; 2, 3, 4.
Eliot, *formerly of Busbridge, Surrey,* 2, 3, 4.
Eliot *of Elvet Hill, Durham,* 4.
Elliot *of Barley House, Devon,* 3, 4.
Elliot *of Binfield Park, Berks,* 2, 3, 4.
Ellis *of Ponsbourne Park, Herts,* 4.
Ellis *of Wyddial Hall, Herts,* 3, 4.

Ellis-Jervoise ; see Jervoise.

Ellis of Glasfryn, Carnarvon, 2, 3, 4.

Ellison of Hebburn, Durham, I, i. 77 ; 2, 3, 4.

Ellison of Sudbrooke Holme, Lincoln, 4.

Ellison of Boultham, Lincoln, 4.

Elmhirst of Elmhirst, York, 3, 4.

Elmhirst of West Ashby, Lincoln, 3, 4.

Elvin of East Dereham, Norfolk, 4.

Elwes of Great Billing, Northampton, I. ii. 463 ; 2, 3, 4.

Elwes of Stoke College, Suffolk, I. ii. 465 ; 2, 3, 4.

Elwon of Cleveland House, York, 4.

Elwood of Clayton Priory, Sussex, 2, 3, 4.

Elwood of Strand Hill, Mayo, 2, 3, 4.

Emeris of Louth, Lincoln, 4.

Emerson of Ulverscroft Abbey, Leicester, 3, 4.

Emery of the Grange, Banwell, Somerset, 3, 4.

Enery of Ballyconnell, Cavan, 2, 3.

Ennis of Ballinahown, Westmeath, 3, 4.

Ensor of Rollesby Hall, Norfolk, 2, 3, 4.

Entwhistle of Foxholes, Lancaster, I. iv. 41 ; 2, 3, 4.

Enys of Enys, Cornwall, I. iv. 373 ; 2, 3, 4.

Erle of Bramshott Grange, Hants, 4.

Errington of High Warden, Northumberland, 3, 4.

Errington of Sandhoe House, Northumberland, 4.

Errington of Lexden Park, Essex, 4.

Esdaile of Cothelstone House, Somerset, I. iii. 604 ; 2, 3, 4.

Estcourt of Estcourt, Gloucester, I. iv. 155 ; 2, 3, 4.

Ethelston of Wicksted Hall, Chester, 3, 4.

Ettrick of High Barnes, Durham, I. iii. 15 ; 2, 3, 4.

Eustace of Ballinglass, Kildare, 2, 3, 4.

Eustace of Castlemore, Carlow, 2, 3, 4.

Eustace of Newstown, Carlow, 3, 4.

Evans, of Hereford, 3, 4.

Evans of Tuddenham, Norfolk, 3, 4,

Evans of Eyton, Hereford, 2, 3, 4.

Evans of the Hill Court ; see Power, 2.

Evans of Allstree Hall, Derby, 2, 3, 4.

Evans of Portrane, Dublin, I. ii. 15 ; 2, 3, 4.

Evans of Ash Hill and Milltown Castle, Limerick, I. i. 593 : 2, 3, 4.

Evans of Knockaderry, Limerick, I. ii. 26 ; 2, 3, 4.

Evans of Farm Hill, Ardreigh, Kildare, 3, 4.

Evans of Lough Park, Westmeath, 3, 4.

Evans of Gartmerron House, Tyrone, 3, 4.

Evans of Carker, Cork, 4.

Evelyn of Wootton, Surrey, 3, 4.

Everard of Middleton, Norfolk, 3, 4.

Everard of Ranilestown, Meath, 4, supp.

Eversfield of Denne Park, Sussex, 4.

Ewbank of Kirton Drove, Lincoln, 3, 4.

Ewing of Strathleven, Dumbarton, 4.

Eyre of Rampton, Nottingham, I. iv. 233 ; 2, 3, 4.

Eyre of Shaw House, Berks, 4.

Eyre of Welford, Berks, 2, 3, 4.

Eyre of Wiltshire, I. iii. 290 ; 2, 3, 4.

Eyre of Lindley Hall, Leicester, 4.

Eyre of Uppercourt, Kilkenny, 4.

Eyre of Eyre Court Castle, Galway, 2, 3, 4.

Eyre of Galway, 2, 3, 4.

Eyston of East Hendred, Berks, I. i. 12 ; 2, 3, 4.

Eyton of Eyton, Salop, 2, 3, 4.

Eyton of Leeswood, Flint, 2, 3, 4.

Fagan of Feltrim, Cork, I. iv. 626 ; 2, 3.

Fairfax of Gilling Castle, York, I. ii. 113 ; 2, 3, 4.

Fairfax of Steeton and Newton Kyme, York, 2, 3, 4.

Fairholme of Chapel, Berwick, 3, 4.

Fairlie of Holmes, Ayr, 4.

Fairlie of Coodham, Ayr, 4.

Falconer *of Leighton*, 3, 4.
Falkiner *of Mount Falcon, Tippe-rary*, 3, 4.
Fallou *of Ballina House, Roscommon*, 3.
Fane *of Wormsley, Oxford*, I. iv. 92 ; 2, 3, 4.
Fanshawe *of Dengey Hall, Essex*, 2, 3, 4.
Fanshawe *of Parsloes, Essex*, 4.
Fardell *of Holbeck Lodge, Lincoln*, I. iv. 246 ; 2, 3, 4.
Farmar *of Clohass, Wexford*, I. ii. 569 ; 2, 3, 4.
Farmbrough *of Denbigh Hall, Bucks*, 4 supp.
Farmer *of Nonsuch Park, Surrey*, 3, 4.
Farnall *of Dorset and Kent*, 2, 3, 4.
Farnham *of Quorndon House, Leicester*, I. iii. 502 ; 2, 3, 4.
Farquhar *of Gilmilnscroft, Ayr*, I. iii. 22 ; 2, 3, 4.
Farquharson *of Invercauld, Aberdeen*, I. ii. 98 ; 2, 3, 4.
Farquharson *of Haughton, Aberdeen*, I. ii. 261 ; 2, 3, 4.
Farquharson *of Whitehouse, Aberdeen*, 2, 3.
Farquharson *of Baldovie, Forfar*, 3.
Farrell *of Moynalty, Meath*, 4.
Farrell *of Dalyston ;* see O'Farrell, 3, 4.
Farrer *of Ingleborough, York*, 2, 3, 4.
Farrer *of Brayfield, Bucks*, 4.
Farsyde *of Fylingdales, York*, 2, 3, 4.
Faulkner *of Castledown, Carlow*, 3, 4.
Faunce *of Sharsted, Kent*, 2, 3, 4.
Faussett *of Heppington, Kent*, 2, 3, 4.
Fawcett *of Durham*, 3, 4.
Fawkes *of Farnley, York*, 2, 3, 4.
Fazakerley *of Burwood, Surrey*, 2, 4.
Fearnley *of Hetton, Northumberland*, 3, 4.
Fellowes *of Ramsey Abbey, Huntingdon*, 2, 3, 4.
Fenton *of Underbank, York*, 2, 3, 4.
Fenton *of Castlerigg, Cumberland*, 3, 4.
Fenton *of Grinton, York*, 4 supp.
Fenwicke *of Longframlington, Northumberland*, 2, 3, 4.
Ferguson *of Raith, Fife*, 4.

Ferguson *of Kinmundy, Aberdeen*, 3, 4.
Ferguson *of Harper Lodge, Cumberland*, 2, 3, 4.
Fergusson *of Craigdarroch, Dumfries*, 2, 3, 4.
Ferrand *of St. Ives and Harden Grange, York*, I. iv. 698 ; 2, 3, 4.
Ferrers *of Baddesley Clinton, Warwick*, 1. iv. 127 ; 2. 3, 4.
Ferris *of Hawkhurst, Kent*, 2.
Fetherston *of Packwood, Warwick*, 2, 3, 4.
Fetherstonhaugh *of Hopton Court, Worcester*, 3, 4.
Fetherstonhaugh *of Kirkoswald, Cumberland*, 3, 4.
Fetherstonhaugh *of Staffield Hall, Cumberland*, 3, 4.
Fetherstonhaugh *of Carrick, Westmeath*, 4.
Fetherstonhaugh *of Bracklyn Castle, Westmeath*, I. i. 629 ; 2, 3, 4.
Fetherstonhaugh *of Rockview, Westmeath*, 4.
Ffarington *of Warden, Lancaster*, I. iii. 339 ; 2, 3, 4.
Ffarington *of Woodvale, Isle of Wight*, 3, 4.
Ffeilden *of Mollington, Chester*, 2.
Ffeilden *of Feniscrowles, Lancaster*, 2.
Ffeilden *of Witton, Lancaster*, I. ii. 444 ; 2, 3, 4.
Ffolliott *of Hollybrook House, Sligo*, 2 supp., 3, 4.
Ffoulkes *of Eriviatt, Denbigh*, 2, 3, 4.
Ffytche *of Thorpe Hall, Lincoln*, 4.
Field *of Heaton, York*, I. ii. 145 ; 2.
Finch *of Red Heath, Hertford*, 4.
Finch *of Tullamore Park, Tipperary*, 3, 4.
Finch *of Burley on the Hill, Rutland*, 4,
Findlay *of Easterhill, Lanark*, 2, 3 supp., 4.
Findlay *of Castle Toward, Argyle*, 4.
Finucane *of Stamer Park, Clare*, 2.
Finzel *of Frankfort Hall, Somerset*, 4.
Firth *of Hartford Lodge, Chester*, 2, 3, 4.
Fisher *of Cossington, Hereford*, 3, 4.
Fisher *of Chetwynd, Salop*, 3, 4.

Fitzgerald *of Glin Castle, Limerick,* I. iv. 179 ; 2, 3, 4.

Fitzgerald *of Valentia, Kerry,* 2, 3, 4.

Fitzgerald *of Holbrook, Sussex,* 3, 4.

Fitzgerald of *Turlough, Mayo,* I. iv. 312 ; 2, 3, 4.

Fitzgerald *of Adelphi, Clare,* 2, 3, 4.

Fitzgerald, Penrose- *of Corkbegg, Cork,* 3, 4.

Fitzgerald, Purcell- *of the Little Island, Waterford,* 3 supp., 4.

Fitzherbert *of Norbury, Derby ; and of Swynnerton, Stafford,* I. i. 78 ; 2, 3, 4.

Fitzhugh *of Plas Power, Denbigh,* 2, 3, 4.

Fitzmaurice *of Duagh, Kerry,* 3, 4.

Fitzpatrick *of Grantstown Manor, Queen's Co.* 4.

Fitzsimon *of Tregarthen ;* see Simons *of Hatt,* 4.

Flanagan *of Drumdoe, Roscommon,* 3, 4.

Fleming *of Stoneham, Hants,* I. ii. 372; 2, 3, 4.

Fleming *of Cumbernauld, Dumbarton,* 2, 3.

Fleming *of Barochan,* 2.

Fletcher *of Salton, Haddington,* 2, 3, 4.

Fletcher *of Garr, King's Co.* 3, 4.

Fletcher *of Dunans, Argyle,* 3, 4.

Fletcher *of Corsock,* 2, 3, 4.

Fletcher *of Kevan Ila, Monmouth,* 2, 3.

Fletcher *of Lawnswood, Stafford,* I. iv. 50; 2, 3, 4.

Flood *of Paulstown Castle, Kilkenny,* I. i. 122 ; 2, 3, 4.

Flood *of Slaney Lodge, Wexford,* 3, 4.

Floyer *of West Stafford, Dorset,* I. i. 605; 2, 3, 4.

Floyer *of Huits, Stafford,* 2, 3, 4.

Foley *of Prestwood, Worcester,* 3, 4.

Foley *of Tetworth, Huntingdon,* 3, 4.

Foljambe *of Osberton, Notts., and of Aldwarke, York,* I. iv. 438 ; 2, 3, 4.

Folliott *of Stapeley House, Chester,* 2, 3, 4.

Fonnereau *of Christ Church, Suffolk,* I. ii. 110; 2, 3, 4,

Foot *of Carrigacunna Castle, Cork,* 3, 4.

Foote *of Charlton Place, Kent,* I. i. 372.

Forbes *of Bereleigh, Hants,* 3. 4.

Forbes *of Culloden, Inverness,* I. iv. 620; 2, 3, 4.

Forbes *of Echt House, Aberdeen,* 2, 3, 4.

Forbes *of Kingerloch, co. Argyle,* 2, 3, 4.

Forbes *of Tolquhon,* 2, 3, 4.

Forbes *of Callendar, Stirling,* 3,

Forbes *of Balgowine, Aberdeen,* 3, 4.

Forbes *of Wingfield Place, co. Bucks,* 2.

Ford *of Ellell Hall, co. Lancaster,* 2, 3, 4.

Ford *of Enfield Old Park, co. Middlesex,* 3, 4.

Ford *of Abbeyfield, co. Chester,* 2, 3, 4.

Forde *of Seaforde, co. Down,* I. iv. 190; 2, 3, 4.

Fordyce, Dingwell- *of Culsh and of Bruckley Castle, Aberdeen,* 3, 4.

Forster *of Lysways Hall, co. Stafford,* 3, 4.

Forster *of Walthamstow, co. Essex,* 2.

Forster-Barham *of Trecwn, co. Pembroke,* I. iv. 550.

Forteath *of Newton, co. Elgin,* 3.

Fortescue *of Fallapit, co. Devon,* I. ii. 541 ; 2, 3, 4.

Fortescue *of Buckland Filleigh, co. Devon,* I. ii. 544 ; 2, 3.

Fortescue *of Dromisken and Ravensdale, co. Louth,* I. iv. 125 ; 2.

Fosbery *of Clorane, co. Limerick,* 2, 3, 4.

Fosbery *of Curraghbridge, co. Limerick,* 3, 4.

Fosbrooke *of Shardlow, co. Derby,* I. ii. 626 ; 2, 3, 4.

Foster *of Jamiaca, Egham, and Kempstone,* 3, 4.

Foster *of Brickhill House, co. Bedford,* I. iv. 549 ; 2, 3, 4.

Foster *of Ballymascanlan, co. Louth,* 3, 4.

Foster *of Wadsworth Banks, co. York,* 2, 3, 4.

Fountain *of Narford, co. Norfolk,* I. i. 224 ; 2, 3, 4.

Fountayne-Wilson *of Melton;* see Montagu.

Fowell *of Devonshire,* I. iv. 424 ; 2.

Fowler *of Abbey-cwm-hir,* I. ii. 375.

Fowlor *of Pendeforde, co. Stafford,* I. iv. 390 ; 2, 4.

Fowler *of Rahinston, co. Meath,* 3, 4.

Fox, Lane- *of Bramham Park, co. York,* I. ii. 493 ; 2, 3, 4.

Fox *of Grove Hill, co. Cornwall,* I. iv. 314; 2, 4.

Fox *of Kilcoursey, King's Co.* 4.

Fox *of Fox Hall, co. Longford,* 4.

Foxall *of Killcary Hall, co. Armagh,* 2, 3, 4.

Frampton *of Moreton, co. Dorset,* I. iv. 193 ; 2, 3, 4.

France *of Bostock Hall, co. Chester,* I. ii. 82 ; 2, 4,

Francklin *of Gonalston, co. Nottingham,* 2, 3, 4.

Frank *of Campsall, co. York,* I. ii. 575 ; 2, 3, 4.

Franks *of Ballyscaddane, co. Limeick,* 4.

Franks *of Carrig, co. Cork,* 3, 4.

Fraser *of Skipness Castle, co. Argyle,* 3, 4.

Fraser *of Hospitalfield, co. Forfar,* 3, 4.

Fraser *of Lovet, co. Inverness,* I. iii. 294.

Fraser *of Moniack, co. Inverness,* 2.

Fraser *of Castle Fraser, co. Ross,* 2, 3, 4.

Fraser *of Findrach, co. Aberdeen,* 3, 4.

Freeland *of Oaklands, co. Sussex,* 4.

Freeman *of Pylewell, co. Hants,* 3, 4.

Freeman *of Gaines, co. Hereford,* I. iii. 642 ; 2, 3, 4.

Freeman *of Castle Cor, co. Cork,* I. ii. 690 ; 2, 3.

Freeman *of Fawley Court, co. Oxford,* 2.

Freer *of Stratford-upon-Avon, co. Warwick,* I. iv. 752 ; 2, 3, 4.

Freke *of Hannington, co. Wilts,* 2, 3, 4.

French *of Cloomyquin, co. Roscommon,* 3, 4.

French *of Monivae Castle, co. Galway,* 3, 4.

French *of Cuskinny, co. Cork,* 3, 4.

French *of Frenchgrove, co. Mayo,* 3, 4.

French *of French Park, co. Roscommon,* I. iv. 539.

Frend *of Boskell, co. Limerick,* 3 supp., 4.

Frere *of Roydon, co. Norfolk,* 2, 3, 4.

Frere *of Twyford House, co. Herts,* 3, 4.

Frewen *of Ilmer, co. Bucks, and of Northiam, co. Sussex,* I. iv. 654 ; 2, 3, 4.

Frewen *of Brickwall, co. Sussex,* I. iii. 530 ; I. iv. 657 ; 2, 3, 4.

Frome *of Pucknoll, co. Dorset,* I. iii. 670 ; 2.

Frost *of St. John's House, co. Chester,* 4.

Fryer *of the Wergs, co. Stafford,* I. iii. 490 ; 2, 3, 4.

Fryer *of Chatteris, co. Cambridge,* 2, 3, 4.

Fulford *of Fulford, co. Devon,* I. iv. 158 ; 2, 3, 4.

Fullarton *of Killmichael, Isle of Arran,* 4.

Fuller *of Rose Hill;* see Fuller Meyrick, 2, 3, 4.

Fuller *of Neston Park, co. Wilts,* 3, 4.

Fullerton *of Thrybergh Park, co. York,* 3, 4.

Fullerton *of Ballintoy Castle, co. Antrim,* I. iv. 298 ; 2, 2, 4.

Fulton *of Braidujle, co. Antrim,* 4 supp.

Furnell *of Cahirelly, co. Limerick,* 3, 4.

Fursdon *of Fursdon, co. Devon,* 2, 3, 4.

Furse *of Halsdon, co. Devon,* 2, 3, 4.

Fydell *of Boston, co. Lincoln,* I. ii. 260; 2.

Fyffe *of Smithfield, co. Forfar,* 2, 3, 4.

Fyler *of Woodlands, Surrey,* 2, 3, 4.

Gabb *of Monmouthshire,* 2.

Gabbett *of Cahirline, Limerick,* 3, 4.

Gael *of Charlton Kings, Gloucester,* 2, 3.

Gage *of Streeve Hill, Londonderry,* 4.

Gage *of Rathlin Island, Antrim,* 3, 4.

Gaisford *of Offington, Sussex,* 4.

Galbraith *of Macrihanish, Argyle,* 2, 3.

Galbraith *of Clanabogan, Tyrone,* 4.

Gale *of Scruton, York,* I. ii. 623.

Gally-Knight *of Firbeck and Langold, York,* I. iv. 710.

Galton *of Claverbon, Warwick,* I. iv. 200 ; 2, 3, 4.

Galton *of Warley Tor, Salop,* I. iv. 201 ; 2, 3, 4.

Galton *of Hadzor House, Worcester,* I. iv. 201 ; 2, 3, 4.

Galwey *of Lota, Cork,* I. iv. 681 ; 2, 3, 4.

Gammie *of Shotover House, Oxford,* 4.

Gandy *of Heaves, Westmoreland,* 4 supp.

Gannon *of Lara, Kildare,* 3, 4.

Garde *of Ballaynecurra, Cork,* 3, 4.

Garden-Campbell *of Troup, Banff,* 3, 4.

Gardiner *of Coombe Lodge, Oxford,* 2 supp., 3, 4.

Gardiner *of Farmhill, Mayo,* 3, 4.

Gardner, Dunn- *of Chatteris, Cambridge,* 4.

Gardyne *of Middleton, Forfar,* 3, 4.

Garland *of Michaelstone Hall, Essex,* 3, 4.

Garnett *of Summerseat, Meath,* 3, 4.

Garnett *of Wyreside, Lancaster,* 3, 4.

Garnett *of Quernmore Park, Lancaster,* 2, 3, 4.

Garnier *of Rookesbury, Hants,* 2, 3, 4.

Garnons *of Colummendy, Denbigh,* I. i. 374.

Garrard *of Lamer, Herts,* I. i. 591 ; 3, 4.

Garrett *of Janeville, Carlow,* 3, 4.

Garstin *of Bragganstown, Louth,* 3, and supp., 4.

Garth *of Morden, Surrey,* I. iii. 557.

Gartshore *of Gartshore, Perth,* 3, 4.

Garvey *of Thornvale, King's Co.* 3.

Gascoigne *of Parlington, York,* 2, 3, 4.

Gaskell *of Kiddington Hall, Oxford,* 3, 4.

Gaskell *of Thorne's House, York,* 2, 3, 4.

Gaskell *of Lupset Hall, York,* 2, 3, 4.

Gason *of Richmond, Tipperary,* 2, 3, 4.

Gateacre *of Gatacre, Salop,* I. iii. 525 ; 2, 3, 4.

Gataker *of Mildenhall, Suffolk,* I. i. 589 ; 2, 3, 4.

Gaunt *of Highfield, Stafford,* 2, 3, 4.

Gaussen *of Brookman's Park, Herts,* 3, 4.

Gaussen *of Larkview House, Londonderry,* 3, 4.

Gay *of Alborough, Norfolk,* 2, 3, 4.

Gay *of Thurning Hall, Norfolk,* 3, 4.

Gennys, Henn- *of Whitleigh, Devon,* 3, 4.

Gent *of Moyns, Essex,* I. i. 370 ; 2, 3, 4.

Gentleman *of Ballyhorgan, Kerry,* 4.

Gerard *of Rocksoles, Lanark,* 3, 4.

Gerard *of Ditton Grove, Lancaster,* 2.

Gernon *of Athcarne Castle, Meath,* 3, 4.

Gervais *of Cecil, Tyrone,* 3, 4.

Gery *of Bushmead, Bedford,* I. ii. 377 ; 2, 3, 4.

Gibbard *of Sharnbrook, Bedford,* 3, 4.

Gibbings *of Gibbings Grove, Cork,* 4.

Gibbs *of Belmont, Somerset,* 3, 4.

Gibbs *of Aldenham, Herts,* 3, 4.

Gibbs *of Tyntesfield, Somerset,* 3, 4.

Gibbs *of Derry, Cork,* 3, 4.

Gibson *of Whelprigg, Westmoreland,* 2, 3, 4.

Gibson *of Shalford, Surrey, and of Sullington, Sussex,* 2, 3, 4.

Gibson *of Quernmore Park, Lancaster,* I. iii. 657 ; 2.

Gibsone *of Pentland, Edinburgh,* 3, 4.

Giffard *of Chillington, Stafford,* I. i. 206 ; 2, 3, 4.

Giffard *of Brightley, Wexford,* I. iv. 293 ; 2, 3, 4.

Gifford *of Ballysop, Wexford,* 3, 4.

Gilbert *of the Priory, Cornwall,* 2, 3, 4.

Gilbert *of Trellissick, Cornwall, and of Eastbourne, Sussex,* I. i. 323 ; 2, 3, 4.

Gilbert *of Cantley, Norfolk,* 2, 3, 4.

Gilchrist *of Ospisdale, Sutherland,* 2, 3, 4.
Gildea *of Port Royal, Mayo,* 2, 3, 4.
Gill *of Bickham Park, Devon,* 3, 4.
Gillanders *of Highfield, Ross,* 4.
Gillbanks *of Whitefield House, Cumberland,* 2, 3, 4.
Gillett, 4 supp.
Gillon *of Wallhouse, Linlithgow,* 2, 3, 4.
Gillman *of Oakmount, Cork,* 3, 4.
Gillman *of the Retreat, Cork,* 4.
Gillum *of Middleton Hall, Northumberland,* 2, 3, 4.
Gilpin *of Hockliffe Grange, Bedford,* 3, 4.
Gisborne *of Yoxall Lodge, Stafford,* 2, 3. 4.
Glanville *of Catchfrench, Cornwall,* 2, 4.
Glascott *of Alderton, Wexford,* 3, 4.
Glascott *of Killowen, Wexford,* 4.
Glasgow, Robertson- *of Montgreenan, Ayr,* 3, 4.
Glasgow *of Old Court, Cork,* 3, 4.
Gledstanes, Upton- *of Fardross, Tyrone,* 3, 4.
Glegg *of Old Withington, Chester,* 2, 3, 4.
Glegg *of Irbie and Backford, Chester,* I. ii. 235; 2, 3, 4.
Glendonwyn *of Parton, Kirkcudbright,* 3, 4.
Glover *of Mount Glover, Cork,* 3, 4.
Glynn *of Fairy Hill, Isle of Wight,* 3, 4.
Goddard *of Cliffe Pypard, Wilts,* I. iv. 323; 2, 3, 4.
Goddard *of Swindon, Wilts,* I. iv. 326; 2, 3, 4.
Godfrey *of Brook Street House, Kent,* I. i. 408; 2, 3, 4.
Godfrey *of Old Hall, Suffolk,* 2.
Godley *of Killigar, Leitrim,* 2, 3, 4.
Godman *of Park Hatch, Surrey,* 2, 3.
Godsal *of Iscoyd Park, Flint,* 3, 4.
Goff *of Hale Park, Hants,* 3, 4.
Goff *of Horetown House, Wexford,* 3, 4.
Goff *of Oakport, Roscommon,* 4.

Going *of Ballyphilip, Tipperary,* 3, 4.
Going *of Traverston, Tipperary,* 2, 3, 4.
Golding *of Maiden Erleigh, Berks,* 2, 3, 4.
Gollop *of Strode, Dorset,* I. i. 600; 2, 3, 4.
Goodall *of Dinton Hall, Bucks,* 3, 4.
Goodden *of Over Compton, Dorset,* 3, 4.
Goodford *of Chilton Cantelo, Somerset,* I. iii. 146; 2, 3, 4.
Goodhart *of Langley Park, Kent,* I. i. 369; 2.
Goodlake *of Wadley House, Berks,* 2, 3, 4.
Goodricke-Holyoake *of Tettenhall, Stafford,* I. ii. 597.
Goodwin *of Hinchley Wood, Derby,* 3, 4.
Goold *of Rosbrien, Limerick,* 3, 4.
Gorden *of Abergeldie, Aberdeen,* 2, 3, 4.
Gordon *of Culvennan, Wigton,* I. iii. 610; 2, 3, 4.
Gordon *of Cairnfield, Banff,* 2, 3, 4.
Gordon *of Pitlurg, Aberdeen,* I. iv. 45; 2, 3, 4.
Gordon *of Florida, Down,* I. iv. 376; 2, 3, 4.
Gordon *of Balmaghill, Kirkcudbright,* 2, 3, 4.
Gordon *of Haffield, Hereford,* I. ii. 219.
Gordon *of Knokespoch, Aberdeen,* 2.
Gordon *of Cairnbulg, Aberdeen,* 2, 3, 4.
Gordon *of Ffvie, Aberdeen,* 2, 3, 4.
Gordon *of Park House, Banff,* 2, 3, 4.
Gordon *of Cluny, Aberdeen,* 4.
Gore, Ormesby- *of Porkington, Salop,* I. i. 82; 2, 3, 4.
Gore, Ormsby- *of Derrycarne, Leitrim,* 4.
Gore *of Tyredagh Castle, Clare,* 2, 3, 4.
Gore *of Barrow Court, Somerset,* 4.
Goring *of Wiston, Sussex,* 3, 4.
Gosling *of Busbridge, Surrey,* 4 supp.

Gosselin *of Ware Priory, Herts,* I. i. 301 ; 2, 3, 4.
Gossett *of Eltham House, Kent,* 4.
Gossip *of Thorp Arch, York,* 2.
Gough *of Perry Hall, Stafford,* I. ii. 392 ; 2.
Goulburn *of Betchworth House, Surrey,* 2, 4.
Gould *of Frampton, Glamorgan,* 4.
Gould *of Low Trenchard, Devon,* 2, 3.
Gourlay *of Kincraig, Fife,* 2, 4.
Gow *of Fowlers Park, Kent,* 4.
Gower *of Bill Hill, Berks,* I. i. 320 ; 2, 3, 4.
Gower *of Titsey Park, Surrey,* 3, 4.
Grace *of Mantua, Roscommon,* I. ii. 350 ; 2, 3, 4.
Grace *of Gracefield, Queen's Co.* 2.
Grace *of Knole, Sussex,* 2.
Gradwell *of Dowth Hall, Meath,* 3, 4.
Græme *of Garvock, Perth,* I. iii. 125 ; 2, 3, 4.
Græme *of Orchill, Perth,* 3 supp. 4.
Græme *of Inchbraike, Perth,* 3, 4.
Graham *of Balgowan, Perth,* 3.
Graham-Clarke *of Manor House, Gloucester,* 4.
Graham *of Fintry,* I. iii. 120 ; 2, 3, 4.
Graham *of Duntrune, Forfar,* 2, 3, 4.
Graham *of Airth Castle, Stirling,* 3, 4.
Graham, Cunninghame- *of Gartmore, Perth,* 3, 4.
Graham *of Tamrawer, Stirling,* 3, 4.
Graham, Maxwell- *of Williamwood, Renfrew,* 3, 4.
Graham *of Leitchtown, Perth,* I. iv. 576 ; 2, 3, 4.
Graham *of Meiklewood, Stirling,* 2, 3, 4.
Graham *of Mossknow, Dumfries,* 2, 3, 4.
Graham *of Edmond Castle, Cumberland,* 3, 4.
Graham *of Drumgoon, Fermanagh,* 3, 4.
Grant-Duff *of Eden, Banff,* 4.
Grant *of Glenmoriston, Inverness,* 2, 3, 4.
Grant *of Kilgraston, Perth,* I. ii. 613 ; 2, 3, 4.
Grant *of Kilmurry, Cork,* 3, 4.
Grant *of the Knoll, Glamorgan,* 2, 3.

Grantham *of Ketton Grange, Rutland,* 3, 4.
Granville *of Wellesbourne, Warwick,* I. iii. 3 ; 2, 3, 4.
Grattan *of Tinnehinch, Wicklow,* 2, 3, 4.
Gratton-Guinness *of Beaumont, Dublin,* 3, 4.
Graves *of Mickleton, Gloucester,* 3, 4.
Gray *of Carntyne, Lanark,* I. iii. 8 ; 2, 3, 4.
Gray *of Darcey Lever Hall, Lancaster,* 4.
Grazebrook *of Audnam, Stafford,* 3, 4.
Greame *of Sewerby House, York,* I. ii. 590 ; 2.
Greathed *of Uddings, Dorset,* 3, 4.
Greave *of Page Hall, York,* 4.
Greaves *of Irlam Hall, Lancaster,* I. iv. 105 ; 2.
Greaves *of Avonside, Warwick,* 3, 4.
Greaves *of Staffordshire,* I. i. 386 ; 2, 4.
Greaves-Bagshawe *of Bagshawe Ridge, &c. Derby,* 4.
Green, Emmott- *of Emmott, Lancaster,* 3, 4.
Green *of Odstone Hall, Lancaster,* 2.
Green *of Greenville, Kilkenny,* 4.
Green *of Parenham, Bedford,* 3, 4.
Greene *of Slyne, Lancaster, and of Whittington, Westmoreland,* 2, 3, 4.
Greene *of Rolleston, Leicester,* I. i. 521 ; 2, 3, 4.
Greene *of Kilmanahan Castle, Waterford,* 2, 3.
Greenfield *of Brynderwen, Monmouth,* 2, 3, 4.
Greenly *of Titley Court, Hereford,* I. i. 292.
Greenway *of Barrington Grove, Gloucester,* 2, 3, 4.
Greenwell *of Greenwell Ford, Durham,* I. i. 114 ; 2, 3, 4.
Greenwell *of Broomshields, Durham,* 2, 3, 4.
Greenwood *of Keighley, York,* 2, 3, 4.
Greer *of the Grange Macgregor, Tyrone,* 2, 3, 4.
Greer *of Tullylagan, Tyrone,* 3, 4.
Greg *of Ballymenoch, Down,* 3, 4.

Greg *of Norcliffe Hall, Chester*, 2, 3, 4.

Gregor *of Trewarthenick, Cornwall*, I. ii. 617 ; 2, 3, 4.

Gregorson *of Ardtornish, Argyle*, 2,3.

Gregory *of Harlaxton ;* see Sherwin-Gregory, 4.

Gregory *of Styvichall, Warwick*, 2, 3, 4.

Gregory *of Coole Park, Galway*, 3, 4.

Gregson *of Murton and Burdon, co. Durham*, 2, 3, 4.

Grene *of Cappamurra, co. Tipperary*, 3, 4.

Grenfell *of Taplow Court, co. Bucks*, 4.

Gresley *of Nether Seale Hall, co. Leicester*, I. iii. 528.

Greswolde *of Malvern Hall, co. Warwick*, I. ii. 673 ; 2.

Greville *of North Myms Place, co. Hertford*, 3, 4.

Grey *of Chipchase Castle, co. Northumberland*, 4.

Grey *of Norton, co. Durham*, 2 supp., 3, 4.

Grey *of Styford, co. Northumberland*, 4.

Grey *of Morwick, co. Northumberland*, 2.

Griffith *of Castle Neynoe, co. Sligo*, 2 supp., 3, 4.

Griffith *of Trevalyn, co. Denbigh*, 2, 3, 4.

Grigson *of Saham Toney, co. Norfolk*, 2, 3, 4.

Grimshaw *of High Bank, co. Lancaster*, 3.

Grimshaw *of Andenshaw, co. Lancaster*, 2.

Grimston *of Grimston Garth, co. York*, I. iii. 69 ; 2, 3, 4.

Gronow *of Ash Hall, co. Glamorgan*, 3, 4.

Grote *of Dulwich Wood, co. Surrey*, I. i. 609.

Grote *of Oxfordshire*, 2.

Grove *of Ferne, co. Wilts*, 2, 3, 4.

Grove *of Zeals, co. Wilts*, 4 supp.

Grove *of Shenstone Park, co. Stafford*, 2.

Grubbe *of Eastwell, co. Wilts*, 2, 3, 4.

Grundy *of the Oaks, co. Leicester*, 2.

Grylls *of Helston, co. Cornwall*, I. ii. 338 ; 2, 3, 4.

Gubbins *of Kenmare Castle, co. Limerick*, 3, 4.

Guinness *of St. Anne's, co. Dublin*, 3, 4.

Gully *of Trevennen, co. Cornwall*, 2, 3, 4.

Gulston *of Dermydd, co. Caermarthen*, 4.

Gumbleton *of Glanatore, co. Cork*, 2 supp., 2, 3, 4.

Gun *of Rattoe, co. Kerry*, 2, 3, 4.

Gun *of Ballybunion, co. Kerry*, 2, 3, 4.

Gundry *of the Hyde, co. Dorset*, 2 add.

Gunning *of Torney's Court, co. Somerset*, 4.

Gunning *of Woolley, co. Somerset*, 4.

Gunning *of Swainswick, co. Somerset*, 4.

Gurdon *of Assington Hall, co. Somerset*, 2, 4.

Gurdon *of Letton, co. Norfolk*, I. i. 395 ; 2, 3, 4.

Gurney *of Keswick, co. Norfolk*, I. i. 484 ; 2, 3, 4.

Guthrie *of Guthrie, co. Forfar*, I. ii. 414 ; 2, 3, 4.

Guthrie *of Haukerton, co. Fife*, 2 supp.

Gwinnett *of Wistaston, co. Hereford*, 2, 3, 4.

Gwylt *of Icklingham, co. Suffolk*, 2.

Gwyn *of Baron's Hall, co. Norfolk*, 2, 3, 4.

Gwyn *of Dyffryn, co. Glamorgan*, 2, 3, 4.

Gwyn *of Ford Abbey, co. Devon*, 2.

Gwynne-Holford *of Kilgwyn, co. Caermarthen*, 2.

Gwynne *of Monachty, co. Cardigan*, 2, 3, 4.

Gwynne *of Glanlery, co. Cardigan*, 2, 3, 4.

Gyll *of Wyrardisbury, co. Bucks*, 2, 3, 4.

Hacker *of East Bridgford, co. Nottingham*, 2, 3, 4.

Hackett *of Moor Park, King's Co.* 3, 4.

Haffenden *of Hormwood, co. Kent*, I.
ii. 301 ; 2, 3.

Haggard *of West Bradeham, co. Norfolk*, 3, 4.

Hagart *of Bantaskine, Stirling*, 4 supp.

Haggitt *of Belmont, co. Hereford*, 2 supp.

Haigh *of Grainsby Hall, co. Lincoln*, 4.

Haire *of Armagh Manor, co. Fermanagh*, 3, 4.

Hale *of Alderley, co. Gloucester*, 2, 3, 4.

Hale *of King's Walden, co. Herts*, I. iii. 12 ; 2, 3, 4.

Halford *of Paddock House, co. Kent*, I. iii. 559 ; 2.

Halidy *of Squire's Hill, co. Antrim*, 3, 4.

Halkett *of Hall Hill, co. Edinburgh*, I. i. 338 ; 2, 3, 4.

Hall *of Abercarne, co. Monmouth*, I. i. 202.

Hall *of Jamaica, now of Arrow's Foot, co. York*, I. iv. 741 ; 2.

Hall *of Westbank House, co. Chester*, 2 add. 3.

Hall *of Scarboro' Hall, co. York*, 4.

Hall *of Whatton Manor, co. Nottingham*, 2, 3, 4.

Hall *of Narrow Water, co. Down*, 2, 3, 4.

Hall *of Mairwarra, co. Galway*, 3, 4.

Hall *of Grappenhall, co. Chester*, 2, 3, 4.

Halliday *of Chapel Cleeve, co. Somerset*, I. ii. 127 ; 2, 3, 4.

Hallifax *of Chadacre Hall, co. Suffolk*, 2, 3, 4.

Halsey *of Gaddesden, co. Herts*, I. ii. 619 ; 2, 3, 4.

Hambrough *of Steephill Castle, Isle of Wight*, 3, 4.

Hamerton *of Hellifield Peel, co. York*, I. i. 519 ; 2, 3, 4.

Hames *of Chagford, co. Devon*, 4.

Hamilton *of Westburn, under Duddas of Duddingston*, 4.

Hamilton *of Holmhead, co. Renfrew*, 2.

Hamilton *of Kames, co. Bute*, 2 supp.

Hamilton *of Cornacassa, co. Monaghan*, 4.

Hamilton *of Evandale, co. Lanark*, 3, 4.

Hamilton *of Orbiston and Dalzell, co. Lanark*, 3, 4.

Hamilton *of Craiglaw, co. Wigton*, 2, 3, 4.

Hamilton *of Bangour, co. Ayr*, 2, 3, 4.

Hamilton *of Barnes, co. Dumbarton*, 3 supp., 4.

Hamilton, Buchanan- *of Spittal, co. Dumbarton*, 3, 4.

Hamilton *of Sundrum, co. Ayr*, 2 supp., 3, 4.

Hamilton *of Cairn Hill, co. Ayr*, 3, 4.

Hamilton *of Rathoe House, co. Carlow*, 3, 4.

Hamilton *of Beltrim, co. Tyrone*, 2 supp., 3, 4.

Hamilton *of St. Ernans, co. Donegal*, 3, 4.

Hamilton *of Killyleagh, co. Down*, I. i. 348 ; 3, 4.

Hamilton *of Abbotstoun, co. Dublin*, 2, 3, 4.

Hamilton *of Hampton Hall, co. Dublin*, 3, 4.

Hamilton *of Hamwood, co. Meath*, 4.

Hamilton, *of Westburn*, 3 supp., 4.

Hamilton *of Raploch ;* see McNeill Hamilton, 4.

Hamlyn *of Leawood and Paschoe, Devon*, 3, 4.

Hamond *of Haling House, Surrey*, 3, 4.

Hamond *of Over Dinsdale Hall, York*, 2 supp., 4.

Hammond *of St. Alban's Court, Kent*, I. i. 130 ; 2, 3, 4.

Hammond *of Wistaston, Chester*, I. i. 367 ; 2, 3, 4.

Hamond *of Westacre, Norfolk*, 2, 3, 4.

Hanbury *of Holfield Grange, Essex*, 3, 4.

Hanbury *of Poles, Hertford*, 3, 4.

Hancocks *of Wolverley Court, Worcester*, 3, 4.

Hancocks *of Blakeshall House, Worcester*, 3, 4.

Handcock *of Cole Hill House, Longford*, 4.
Handley *of Culverthorpe Hall, Lincoln*, 2.
Handley *of Newark, Nottingham*, 2, 3, 4.
Hanford *of Woollashall, Worcester*, 2, 3, 4.
Hankey *of Fetcham, Surrey*, I. iv. 117 ; 2, 3, 4.
Hannay *of Kingsmuir, Fife*, 3, 4.
Hannay *of Kirkdale, Kirkcudbright*, 3, 4.
Hanson *of Osmondthorpe*, 2 supp., 4.
Harbin *of Newton House, Somerset*, 2, 3, 4.
Harcourt *of Ankerwycke, Berks*, I. ii. 221 ; 2, 3, 4.
Harcourt *of Nuneham Park, Oxford*, 4.
Hardcastle *of Blidworth Dale, Notts.* 3, 4.
Harden *of Crea, King's Co.* 2.
Harden *of Harrybrook, Armagh*, 4.
Harding *of Baraset, Warwick*, 2, 3, 4.
Harding *of Tamworth, Warwick*, 2 supp., 3, 4.
Harding *of Upcott, Devon*, 3, 4.
Hardy *of Letheringsett, Norfolk*, 2, 3, 4.
Hare *of Tetworth, Berks*, 4 supp.
Hare *of Docking Hall, Norfolk*, 2, 4.
Hare *of Gresford, Denbigh*, 2 add. 3, 4.
Harford *of Blaise Castle, Gloucester*, I. iv. 638 ; 2, 3, 4
Hargreaves *of Broad Oak, Lancaster*, 2, 3, 4.
Hargreaves *of Ormerod House, Lanter*, I. ii. 685.
Harland *of Sutton Hall, York*, I. iii. 194; 2, 3, 4.
Harman *of Newcastle, Longford*, 4.
Harpur *of Chilvers Coton, Warwick*, 2 supp., 3, 4.
Harries *of Priskilly, Pembroke*, I. i. 256 ; 2, 3, 4.
Harries *of Cruckton, Salop*, 2, 3, 4.
Harrington *of Worden, Devon*, I. i. 461 ; 2.
Harris *of Hayne, Devon*, I. i. 559 ; 2, 3, 4.

Harris *of Rosewarne, Cornwall*, 2.
Harrison *of Castle Harrison, Cork*, 4.
Harrison *of Ramsay and Dinton, Bucks*, 3, 4.
Harrison *of Green Bank, Westmoreland*, 2, 3, 4.
Harrison *of Winscales and Stainburn, Cumberland*, 2 supp., 3, 4.
Harrison *of Snelston Hall, Derby*, 3, 4.
Harrison *of Merton Hall, Down*, 3, 4.
Harrison, Fiske- *of Copford Hall, Essex*, 2, 3, 4.
Harrison *of Tolethorpe Hall, Lincoln*, 2, 3, 4.
Hart *of Yarnacombe, Devon*, 2.
Hart *of Kilderry, Donegal*, 3, 4.
Hartcup *of Upland Grove, Suffolk*, 2 add., 3, 4.
Hartley *of Beech Park, Dublin*, 4.
Hartley *of Bucklebury, Berks*, I. iv. 726 ; 2, 3, 4.
Hartley *of Gillfoot, Cumberland*, 2, 3, 4.
Hartopp *of Dalby, Leicester*, I. iii. 401 ; 2, 3, 4.
Harvey *of Bargy Castle, Wexford*, 2, 3, 4.
Harvey *of Kyle, Wexford*, 2, 3, 4.
Harvey *of Ickwell Bury, Bedford*, I. iv. 507 ; 2, 3, 4.
Hervey *of Castlesemple, Renfrew*, 2, 3, 4.
Harvey *of Carnousie, Banff*, 3, 4.
Harvey *of Langley Park, Berks*, 4.
Harvey *of Blurton House, Stafford*, 4.
Harvey *of Malin Hall, Donegal*, 3, 4.
Harvey *of Thorpe, Norfolk*, I. i. 399 ; 2, 3, 4.
Harwood *of Hagbourn and Streatley*, I. iii. 406 ; 2.
Hasell *of Dalemain, Cumberland*, 2 and add , 3, 4.
Hasler *of Aldingbourne, Sussex*, 2 supp., 3, 4.
Hassard *of Gardenhill, Fermanagh*, 3, 4.
Hassard *of Glenville, Waterford*, 3, 4.
Hassard *of Skea, Fermanagh*, 2, 3, 4.
Hastings *of Willesley Hall, Leicester*, 4.

Hatch *of Ardee Castle, Louth*, 3, 4.
Hatch *of the Manor, Sutton, Surrey*, 2 supp.
Hatfield *of Newton Kyme, York*, 2.
Hatfield *of Thorp Arch, York*, 2 supp., 2, 3, 4.
Hatton *of Clonard, Wexford*, 2, 3, 4.
Havers *of Thelton Hall, Norfolk*, I. i. 381; 2, 3, 4.
De Havilland *of Havilland Hall, Guernsey*, 2 supp., 3, 4.
Haviland *of Ditton Hall, Cambridge*, 2 supp., 3, 4.
Hawker *of Longparish, Hants*, I. iii. 50; 2.
Hawkesworth *of Forrest, Queen's Co.* 3, 4.
Hawkins *of Bignor Park, Sussex*, 2.
Hawkins *of Tredunnoch, Monmouth*, 2, 3, 4.
Hawkins *of Middlesex*, 2 supp., 3, 4.
Hawkins *of Alresford Hall, Essex*, 3, 4.
Hawley *of West Green House, Hants*, 2, 3, 4.
Hays *of Pitfour*, I. i. 507; 2.
Hay Macdougal *of Mackerston, Roxburgh*, I. iii. 430.
Hay-Newton *of Newton, Haddington*, 2.
Hay *of Dunse Castle, Berwick*, 3, 4.
Hay *of Hopes, Haddington*, 2, 3, 4.
Hay *of Leys, Perth*, I. i. 504; 2, 3, 4.
Hay *of Seggieden, Perth*, I. i. 509; 2, 3, 4.
Hay *of Rannes;* see Leith Hays.
Hayman *of Myrtle Grove, Cork*, 2 supp., 2, 3, 4.
Hayman *of Bye Farm, Somerset*, 2 supp.
Hayes *of Thimbleby Lodge, York*, 3, 4.
Haynes *of Thimbleby Lodge, York*, 2 supp.
Hayward *of Quedgelly House, Gloucester*, 2, 3, 4.
Haywood *of Brownhills, Stafford*, 4.
Head *of Modreeny House, Tipperary*, 3, 4.
Heale *of Highfield House, Herts*, 3, 4.
Heard *of Kinsale, Cork*, 3, 4.

Heathcote *of Connington Castle, Huningdon*, 2 supp., 4.
Heaton *of Peas Heaton, Denbigh*, 2, 3, 4.
Heber *of Hodnet, Salop*, I. iv. 132; 2, 3, 4.
Hebden *of Appleton, York*, 2.
Heddee *of Melsetter, Orkney*, 3, 4.
Heigham *of Hunston, Suffolk*, 2 supp. 3, 4.
Helyar *of Coker Court, Somerset*, 1. i. 281; 2, 3, 4.
Helyar *of Poundisford Lodge, Somerset*, 2, 3, 4.
Hemphill *of Rathkeany, Tipperary*, 4.
Hemsworth *of Abbeville, Tipperary*, 4.
Hemsworth *of Shropham Hall, Norfolk*, 2, 3, 4
Heneage *of Hainton, Lincoln*, I. iv. 103; 2, 3, 4.
Henderson, Mercer- *of Fordell, Fife*, 2 add., 3, 4.
Henderson *of Sternster, Caithness*, 3, 4.
Henderson *of Westerton, Stirling*, 2 add., 3, 4.
Henley *of Waterpery, Oxford*, 2, 3, 4.
Henley *of Leigh House, Somerset*, 2 add.
Henn *of Paradise, Clare*, 3, 4.
Hennessy *of Ballymacmoy, Cork*, 2.
Henshaw *of Sussex and Essex*, 2 supp.
Hepburn *of Colquhalzie, Perth*, 2.
Hepenstal *of Derrycassan, Longford*, 4.
Hepworth *of Pontefract, York*, 2, 3, 4.
Herbert *of Muckruss, Kerry*, 2, 3, 4.
Herbert *of Llanarth, Monmouth*, I. iv. 727; 2, 3, 4.
Herbert *of Cahirnane*, 3, 4.
Herbert *of Pill House, Tipperary*, 3, 4.
Hercy *of Cruchfield, Berks*, I. iv. 679; 2, 3, 4.
Hereford *of Sufton Court, Hereford*, I. iii. 343; 2, 3, 4.
Herne, Burchell- *of Bushey Grange, Hertford*, I. ii. 689; 2, 3, 4.
Heron *of Moore Hall, Chester*, 2, 3, 4.

Herrick *of Beaumanor, Leicester,* I. iii. 637 ; 2. 3, 4.

Herrick *of Shippool, Cork,* I. iii. 641 ; 2, 3, 4.

Hervey *of Killiane, Wexford,* 2, 3, 4.

Hesketh, Bamford- *Gwyrch Castle, Denbigh,* 2, 3, 4.

Hesketh-Fleetwood *of Rossall, Lancaster,* I. iv. 521.

Hewett *of Tyr Mab Ellis, Glamorgan,* 2, 3, 4.

Hewgill *of Harnby Grange, York,* 2, 3, 4.

Hewson *of Ennismore, Kerry,* 2.

Hext *of Trenarren, Cornwall,* I. ii. 428 ; 2 and add., 3, 4.

Hext *of Tredithy, Cornwall,* 2 add., 3, 4.

Heycock *of East Norton, Leicester,* I. iii. 643 ; 2. 3, 4.

Heyland *of Glendaragh, Antrim,* and *of Tamlaght, Derry,* 3, 4.

Heywood *of Hope End, Hereford,* 2, 3, 4.

Heywood *of Stanley Hall, York,* 2, 3, 4.

Hibbert-Ware *of Edinburgh,* I. iv. 493.

Hibbert *of Birkes Hall, Chester,* 2 3, 4.

Hibbert *of Chalfont Park, Bucks,* 2, 3, 4.

Hibbert *of Bilton Grange, Warwick,* 3, 4.

Hibbert *of Braywick Lodge, Berks,* 3, 4.

Hickie *of Kilelton, Kerry,* 2 supp., 4.

Hickman *of Thonock Hall, Lincoln,* 2, 3, 4.

Hicks *of Wilbraham Temple, Cambridge,* 2 supp., 3, 4.

Hickes *of Silton Hall, York,* I. i. 510.

Hickson *of Letterough, Kerry,* 2 supp., 3, 4.

Hickson *of Grove, Dingle, Kerry,* 2, 3, 4.

Higgins *of Skellow Grange, York,* I. ii. 155 ; 2, 3, 4.

Higgins *of Turvey House, Bedford,* 3, 4,

Higgins *of Turvey Abbey, Bedford,* 2, 3, 4.

Higgins *of Bosbury House, Hereford,* 2, 3, 4.

Higgins *of Westport, Mayo,* 2, 3, 4.

Higginson *of Lisburn, Antrim,* 3, 4.

Hildyard *of Horsley, Durham,* 4 supp.

Hildyard *of Winestead, York,* 2, 3, 4.

Hildyard *of Flintham Hall, Notts,* 2 supp., 3, 4.

Hill *of Court Hill, Salop,* I. i. 654 ; 2.

Hill *of Doneraile, Cork,* 2, 3, 4.

Hill *of Gressenhall Hall, Norfolk,* 2, 3, 4.

Hill *of Stallington Hall, Stafford,* I. ii. 318 ; 2, 3, 4.

Hills *of Colne Park, Essex,* 2, 3, 4.

Hilton *of Preston House, Kent,* 2 supp., 3, 4.

Hincks *of Breckenbrough, York,* I. iv. 366 ; 2, 3, 4.

Hinde *of Acton House, Northumberland,* I. iv. 309 : 2, 3, 4.

Hinde *of Caton and Lancaster,* 2 add.

Hingston *of Aglis, Cork,* I. iv. 43 ; 2.

Hingston *of Holbeton, Devon,* 2, 3, 4.

Hippesley *of Stoneaston, Somerset,* 3, 4.

Hippisley *of Lamborne, Berks,* I. i. 538 ; 2, 3, 4.

Hippisley *of Shobrooke Park, Devon,* 3, 4.

Hippisley *of Camely and Stanton,* 4 add. ; see Trenchard.

Hobhouse *of Hadspen House, Somerset,* I. iv. 360 ; 2, 3, 4.

Hoblyn *of Colquite ;* see Peter-Hoblyn.

Hodder *of Hoddersfield, Cork,* 2, 3, 4.

Hodges *of Hempsted, Kent,* 2, 3.

Hodgetts *of Hugley, Worcester,* 2, 3.

Hodgson *of Newly Grange, Cumberland,* 4.

Hodgson *of Houghton House, Cumberland,* 2, 3, 4.

Hodgson *of Brafferton Hall and Sand Hutton, York,* 3 supp., 4.

Hog of *Newliston, Linlithgow,* 2 supp., 3, 4.

Hogg of *Norton House, Durham,* 2, 3, 4.

Hogg of *Church View, Roscommon,* 2 supp.

Holbeck of *Farnborough, Warwick,* I. i. 659; 2, 3 and supp., 4.

Holcombe of *Pembrokeshire,* I. iv. 95.

Holden of *Aston, Derby,* 2, 3, 4.

Holden of *Palace House, Lancaster,* 2, 3, 4.

Holden of *Darley Abbey;* see Lowe of *Lockho.*

Holford of *Westonbirt, Gloucester,* 2 supp., 3, 4.

Holford of *Buckland, Brecknock,* 2, 3, 4.

Holley of *Oaklands, Devon,* 3, 4.

Hollingworth of *Hollingworth, Chester,* 2.

Hollinshead of *Hollinshead Hall, Lancaster,* 2 supp., 3, 4.

Hollis of *Shire Newton, Monmouth,* 2, 3, 4.

Hollist of *Lodsworth, Sussex,* 2, 3, 4.

Holland of *Benhall Lodge, Suffolk,* 2 supp., 3, 4.

Holme of *Lancashire;* see Bankes of *Winstanley.*

Holme of *Paull Holme, York,* I. iv. 250; 2, 3, 4.

Holmes of *St. David's, Tipperary,* 3, 4.

Holmes of *Scole House, Norfolk,* 2 add., 3, 4.

Holt of *Enfield, Middlesex,* 2 supp., 3, 4.

Hold of *Stubbylee, Lancaster,* 2, 3, 4.

Holyngworthe of *Holyngworthe, Chester,* 3, 4.

Home, Binning- of *Argaty, Perth,* 2 supp., 3, 4.

Home of *Whitfield;* see Hume of *Ninewells.*

Home of *Wedderburn;* see Milne-Home.

Home of *Broom House, Berwick,* 2 add., 4.

Homfray of *Penlyne Castle, Glamorgan,* I. i. 236; 2, 3, 4.

Homfray of *the Place, Suffolk,* 3, 4.

Honywood of *Mark's Hall, Suffolk,* 3.

Hood of *Bardon Park, Leicester,* I. iv. 166; 2, 3, 4.

Hood of *Nettleham Hall, Lincoln,* 2 add., 3, 4.

Hood of *Stonebridge, Berwick,* 2 supp., 3, 4.

Hope of *Deepdene, Surrey,* I. iv. 457; 2, 3, 4.

Hope of *Carriden, Linlithgow,* 2, 3, 4.

Hoper of *Thornhill, Sussex,* 3, 4.

Hopes of *Brampton Crofts, Westmoreland,* 2, 3, 4.

Hopkins; see Northey-Hopkins.

Hopkins of *Tidmarsh House, Berks,* 3, 4.

Hopper of *Sharow Lodge, York,* 2 and supp.

Hopper of *Walworth, Durham,* 3, 4.

Hopper-Williamson of *Shirecliffe, Durham,* 2, 3, 4.

Hopton of *Canon Frome, Hereford,* I. iv. 172; 2, 3, 4.

Hopwood of *Hopwood, Lancaster,* 2, 3, 4.

Hordern of *Oxley House, Stafford,* 2, 3, 4.

Hore of *Pole Hore, Wexford,* I. iv. 712; 2, 3, 4.

Hore of *Harperston, Wexford,* I. iv. 716; 2, 3, 4.

Horlock of *the Rocks, Gloucester,* 2.

Hornby of *Dalton, Lancaster,* I. iii. 698; 2, 3, 4.

Hornby of *Little Green, Sussex,* 3, 4.

Hornby of *Ribby Hall, Lancaster,* 2 supp., 3, 4.

Hornby of *Liverpool, Lancaster,* 2 supp., 3, 4.

Hornby of *Raikes Hall, Lancaster,* 2 supp., 3, 4.

Hornby of *St. Michael's, Lancaster,* 2 supp., 3, 4.

Horner of *Mells Park, Somerset,* 3, 4.

Hornidge of *Calverstown, Westmeath,* 3, 4.

Hornor of *the Howe, Essex,* 3, 4.

Hornyold of *Blackmore, Worcester,* I. i. 283; 2, 3, 4.

Horrocks of *Lark Hall, Lancaster,* 2.

Horton *of Howroyde, York*, 2, 3, 4.
Hosken *of Ellenglaze, Cornwall*, I. i. 94; 2, 3, 4.
Hosken-Harper *of Davenham, Cheshire*, 4.
Hoskins *of Birch House, Hereford*, 2.
Hoskins *of Higham, Cumberland*, 3, 4.
Hoskyns *of Wraxhall Abbey, Warwick*, 2, 3, 4.
Hoste *of Barwick House, Norfolk*, 2, 3, 4.
Houblon *of Hallingbury, Essex*, 2, 4.
Houghton *of Kilmanoch House, Wexford*, 3, 4.
Houlton *of Farley Castle, Somerset*, I. iv. 602 ; 2, 3, 4.
Hounsfield *of Wadsley, York*, 4.
Houstoun *of Johnstone, Renfrew*, 2, 3, 4.
Houston *of Coneywarren, Tyrone*, 2, 3, 4.
Houston-Blakiston *of Orangefield, Down*, 3, 4.
Howard *of Greystoke, Cumberland*, 2, 3, 4.
Howard *of Corby, Cumberland*, I. i. 196; 2, 3, 4.
Howard *of Broughton Hall, Flint*, 4.
Howell *of Prinknash, Gloucester*, 2, 3, 4.
Howes *of Morningthorpe, Norfolk*, I. i. 412 ; 2, 3, 4.
Howlin *of Ballyharran, Wexford*, 3, 4.
Hoy *of Harrold's Park, Essex*, 4.
Hoyle *of Ferham House, York*, 4.
Hoyle *of Kames Castle, Bute*, 4.
Hozier *of Mauldslie Castle, Lanark*, 3, 4.
Huband *of Ipsley*, 2, 3, 4.
Huddart *of Brynkir, Caernarvon*, I. ii. 348.
Huddleston *of Sawston, Cambridge*, I. ii. 582 ; 2, 3, 4.
Hugessen *of the Paddock, Kent*, 2 add., 3, 4.
Hughes *of Kinmel and Dinorben, Denbigh*, 3, 4.
Hughes *of Alltlwyd, Cardigan*, 2,3,4.
Hughes *of Donnington Priory, Berks*, 2, 3, 4.
Hughes *of Guerclas, Merioneth*, 2, 3, 4.

Hughes *of Ely House, Wexford*, 3, 4.
Hughes *of Plas Coch, Anglesey*, 2 supp., 3, 4.
Hughes *of Plas-yn-Llangoed, Anglesey*, 2 supp., 3, 4.
Hughes *of Ystrad, Denbigh*, 3, 4.
Hughes *of the Grove, Dublin*, 2, supp., 3, 4.
Huish *of Nottingham*, I. iv. 417.
Hull *of Leamcon, Cork*, 4.
Hulton *of Hulton, Lancaster*, I. iv. 29 ; 2, 3, 4.
Hume *of Ninewells, Berwick*, 2, 3, 4.
Hume *of Humewood, Wicklow*, I. iii. 388 ; 2, 3, 4.
Humffreys *of Lewyn, Montgomery*, 2, 3, 4.
Humfrey *of Wroxham House, Norfolk*, 2 supp., 3, 4.
Humfrey *of Cavanacor, Donegal*, 3, 4.
Humphrys *of Ballyhaise House, Cavan*, 3, 4.
Hungerford *of Inchodony, Cork*, 3, 4.
Hungerford *of Cahirmore, Cork*, 2, supp., 3, 4.
Hungerford *of Dingley Park, Northampton*, 2, 3, 4.
Hunt *of Pittencrieff, Fife*, 2, 3, 4.
Hunt *of Ketton, Rutland*, 4 supp.
Hunt *of Honyngham, Warwick*, 4 supp.
Hunt *of Ketton, Rutland*, 4.
Hunt *of Borcatton, Salop*, 2 add., 3, 4.
Hunt *of Shermanbury Park, Sussex*, 4.
Hunter *of That Ilk, Ayr*, I. ii. 500 ; 2, and supp., 3, 4.
Hunter *of Straidarran, Londonderry*, 3, 4.
Hunter-Arundell *of Barjarg, Dumfries*, 2, 3, 4.
Hunter *of Bonnytoun, Ayr*, 2, 3, 4.
Hunter *of Seaside and Glencarse, Perth*, 2, 3, 4.
Hunter *of Medomsley, Durham*, 2, 3, 4.
Hunter *of Blackness, Forfar*, 3, 4.
Huntley *of Boxwell, Gloucester*, I. ii. 468 ; 2, 3, 4.
Hurly *of co. Kerry*, 3 supp., 4.
Hurst *of Westbank, Lancaster*, 4.

Hurt *of Alderwasley and Kirks-worth, Derby,* 2, 3, 4.

Hussey *of Nash Court, Dorset,* 2, 3, 4.

Hussey *of Scotney Castle, Sussex,* I. i. 262 ; 2, 3, 4.

Hussey *of Wyrley Grove, Stafford,* 2 supp., 3, 4.

Hussey *of Upwood, Huntingdon,* I. ii. 358 ; 2, 3, 4.

Hussey *of Westown, Dublin,* 2, 3, 4.

Hussey *of Dingle, Kerry,* 3, 4.

Hustler *of Acklam Hall, York,* 2 supp., 3, 4.

Hutchins *of Ardnagashel and Cregane Castle, Cork,* 3 supp., 4.

Hutchinson *of Timoney, Tipperary,* 2, 3, 4.

Hutchinson *of Whitton House, Durham,* I. ii. 100 ; 2, 3, 4.

Hutchison *of Rockend, Dumbarton,* 2 add., 3, 4.

Hutton *of Marske, York,* I. iii. 303 ; 2, 3, 4.

Hutton *of Overthwaite, Westmoreland,* 2, 3, 4.

Hutton *of Gate Burton, Lincoln,* 2 add., 3, 4.

Huyshe *of Sand and Clisthydon, Devon,* I. iv. 409 ; 2, 3, 4.

Hyde *of Hyde End, Berks,* I. iv. 675 ; 2.

Hyde *of Castle Hyde, Cork,* 2, 3, 4.

Hyde *of Syndale House, Kent,* 4.

Hyett *of Painswick, Gloucester,* 2, 3, 4.

I'Anson *of Corfe Castle, Dorset,* 2 supp.

Ilbert, *of Horswell House, Devon,* I. iv. 135 ; 2, 3, 4.

Inge *of Thorpe Constantine, Stafford,* I. i. 322 ; 2, 3, 4.

Ingham *of Marton, York,* 2 supp., 3, 4.

Ingram *of Swinshead Abbey, Lincoln,* 3, 4.

Ingram *of Hoar Cross ;* see Meynell-Ingram.

Innes *of Raemoir House, Kincardine,* 2, 3. 4.

Innes *of Dromantine, Down,* 4.

Irby *of Boyland Hall, Norfolk,* I. iv. 563 ; 2, 3, 4.

Ireland *of Roberstown House, Kildare,* 2.

Ireland *of Brislington Hall, Somerset,* 4.

Ireland *of Owsden Hall, Suffolk,* 2, 3, 4.

Iremonger *of Wherwell Priory, Hants,* 2, 3.

Irton *of Irton, Cumberland,* I. iii. 675 ; 2, 3, 4.

Irvine *of Barnhinnock, Dumfries,* 4 supp.

Irvine *of Castle Irvine, Fermanagh,* 4.

Irvine *of Drum Castle, Aberdeen,* I. ii. 680 ; 2, 3, 4.

Irvine *of Inveramsay, Aberdeen,* 3, 4.

Irvine *of Killadeas, Fermanagh,* 2 supp., 3, 4.

Irvine *of Green Hill, Fermanagh,* 2, 3, 4.

Irwin *of Derrygore, Fermanagh,* 4.

Irwin *of Justustown and Calder Abbey, Cumberland,* 2, 3, 4.

Irwin *of Tanragoe, Sligo,* I. iii. 101 ; 2, 3, 4.

Isherwood *of Marple, Chester,* I. i. 101 ; 2, 3, 4.

Isted *of Ecton, Northampton,* I. ii. 462 ; 2, 3, 4.

Ives *of Bradden, Northampton,* 3, 4.

Ives *of Bentworth Hall, Hants,* 3, 4.

Izod *of Chapel Izod House, Kilkenny,* 3, 4.

Jackson *of Duddington, Northampton,* 2 supp., 3, 4.

Jackson *of Fanningstown Castle, Limerick,* 3, 4.

Jackson *of Manor House, Chester,* 3, 4.

Jackson *of Enniscoe, and Carramore, Mayo,* 2, 3, 4.

Jackson *of Ahanesk, Cork,* 4.

Jackson *of Glanbey, Waterford,* 2, 3.

Jackson *of Doncaster, York,* 2.

Jacob *of Shillingstone, Dorset,* 2.

Jacson *of Barton, Lancaster,* 2, 3, 4.

James, Grevis- *of Ightham Court, Kent,* I. i. 397 ; 2, 3, 5.

James *of Barroch and West Auckland, Cumberland,* 2, 3, 4.

James *of Otterburn, Northumberland,* 2, 3, 4.

James *of Pantsaison, Pembroke,* 2, 3, 4.

Jameson *of Windfield, Galway,* 3, 4.

Jaques *of Easby Abbey, York*, 3, 4.
Jarrett *of Camerton Court, Somerset*, 2, 3, 4.
Jarvis *of Doddington Hall, Lincoln*, 2, 3, 4.
Jeaffreson *of Dullingham House, Cambridge*, 2, 3, 4.
Jebb, *formerly of Nottinghamshire*, 2; 4 supp.
Jebb *of Walton, Derby*, 2 supp.; 4 supp.
Jeffreys *of Wem, Salop*, 2, 3, 4.
Jenkins *of Bicton Hall, Salop*, I. iii. 255; 2, 3, 4.
Jenkins *of Charlton Hill, Salop*, 2 supp. 3, 4.
Jenner *of Berkeley, Gloucester*, 2.
Jenner *of Wenvoe Castle, Glamorgan*, 2, 3, 4.
Jenney *of Bredfield, Suffolk*, I. iii. 446; 2, 3, 4.
Jennings *of Hartwell, Northampton*, I. iii. 585; 2 sup.
Jenyns *of Bottisham Hall, Cambridge*, I. iii. 582; 2, 3, 4.
Jervoise *of Herriard, Hants*; 2 add. 3, 4.
Jesse *of Llanbedr Hall, Denbigh*, 3, 4.
Jesson *of Oakwood, Stafford*, 4.
Jessop *of Doory Hall, Longford*, 2, 3, 4.
Blake, Jex-, *of Swanton Abbotts, Norfolk*, 2, 3, 4.
Jodrell *of Yeardsley, Chester*, I. i. 226; 2, 3, 4.
Johnes *of Dolaucothy, Carmarthen*, I. iv. 59; 2, 3, 4.
Johnson *of Ayscough-Fee Hall, Lincoln*, 2 supp. 3, 4.
Johnson *of Deanery, Durham*, 2, 3, 4.
Johnson *of Monks Field, Montgomery*, 2 supp., 3, 4.
Johnson *of Burleigh Field, Leicester*, 4.
Johnson *of Rockenham, Cork*, 4.
Johnston *of Shieldhall, Stirling*, 3, 4.
Johnston *of Carnsalloch, Dumfries*, 2 supp., 3, 4.
Johnston, McDowal- *of Ballywillwill, Down*, 2 supp., 3, 4.
Johnston *of Fort Johnston, Monaghan*, 2, 3, 4.
Johnston *of Magheremena Castle, Fermanagh*, 3, 4.

Johnston *of Holly Park, Down*, 4.
Johnston *of Kincardine, Perth*, 3 supp., 4.
Johnston *of Annandale, Dumfries*, 3, 4.
Johnstone *of Mainstone Court, Hereford*, 2 supp., 3.
Johnstone *of Raehills, Dumfries*, 2.
Johnstone *of Hilton-in-the-Meise*, 2 supp.
Johnstone *of Alva, Clackmannan*, I. ii. 302; 2, 3, 4.
Johnstone *of Galabank*, I. iv. 556; 2, 3, 4.
Johnstone *of Snow Hill, Fermanagh*, 2. 3, 4.
Joliffe *of Ammerdown Park, Somerset*, I. i. 517; 2, 3, 4.
Jones-Parry; see Parry.
Jones *of Lark Hill, Lancaster*, 2.
Jones *of Beneda Abbey, Sligo*, 2.
Jones *of Sandford and Barbados*, 2 supp.
Jones *of Fonmon Castle, Glamorgan*, 2, 3, 4.
Jones *of Gwynfryn, Cardigan*, 2, 3, 4.
Jones *of Gurrey, Carmarthen*, 2 add., 3, 4.
Jones *of Llwynon*; see Parry, Jones-
Jones *of Hartsheath, Flint*, 2, 3, 4.
Jones *of Llanarth Court*; see Herbert.
Jones *of Llanerchrugog Hall, Denbigh*, 3, 4.
Jones *of Nass, Gloucester*, 3, 4.
Jones *of Pantglas, co. Carmarthen*, 2 add., 3, 4.
Jones *of Trewythen, Monmouth*, 2, 3, 4.
Jones *of Wepre Hall, Flint*, 2 supp., 3, 4.
Jones *of Ystrad, Carmarthen*, 2, 3, 4.
Jones *of Chastleton, Oxford*, 3, 4.
Jones *of Badsworth Hall, York*, 3, 4.
Jones *of Bedlanamore, Dublin, and of Headfort, Leitrim*, I. iii. 267; 2, 3, 4.
Jones *of Lisselan, Cork*, 3, 4.
Jones *of Moneyglass, Antrim*, 3, 4.
Jones *of Mullinabro', Kilkenny*, 3, 4.
Jones *of Esgair Evan, Merioneth*, 3 supp., 4.

2 F

Jones *of Kelston Park, Somerset*, 4.
Jones *of Clytha, Monmouth*, 4.
Jordan *of Pigeonsford, Cardigan*, 2, 3, 4.
Joyce *of Mervue, Galway*, 2, 3, 4.
Joyce *of Rahasane, Galway*, 3, 4.
Justice *of Hinstock, Salop*, 2, 3, 4.
Kavanagh *of Borris, Carlow*, 2, 3, 4.
Kane *of Drum'seaske, Monaghan*, 4 supp.
Kay *of Fairfield, York*, 2, 3, 4.
Keane *of Beech Park, Clare*, 3, 4.
Kearney, Cuthbert- *of Garretstown, Cork*, 4.
Kearney *of Blanchville, Kilkenny*, 4.
Kearney *of Ballinvilla, Mayo*, 4 supp.
Keck *of Staughton Grange, Leicester*, 2, 3, 4.
Keigwin *of Mousehole, Cornwall*, I. iv. 287 ; 2.
Keir *of Kindrogan, Perth*, 2, 3, 4.
Kekewich *of Peamore, Devon*, 2 and supp., 3, 4,
Kelham *of Bleasby Hall, Notts*, 2 and supp., 3, 4.
Kelly *of Castle Kelly ;* see O'Kelly.
Kelly *of Kelly, Devon*, I. ii. 95 ; 2, 3, 4.
Kelly *of Newtown, Galway*, 2, 3, 4.
Kelso *of Kelsoland, Kelso*, I. ii. 534 ; 2 supp., 3, 4.
Kemmis *of Shaen, Queen's Co.*, 3, 4.
Kemmis *of Ballincour, Wicklow*, 3.
Kemp *of Lewes, Sussex*, 2, 3, 4.
Kempe *of Rosteage, Devon*, I. ii. 530 ; 2.
Kendall *of Austrey, Warwick*, 3, 4.
Kendall *of Pelyn, Cornwall*, 4.
Kennedy *of Bennane and Finnarts, Ayr*, 2, 3, 4.
Kennedy *of Dunure, Ayr*, 3, 4.
Kennedy *of Knocknalling, Ayr*, 2, 3, 4.
Kennedy *of Cultra, Down*, 3, 4.
Kennedy *of Knockgray, Kircudbright*, 2 supp., 3, 4.
Kenney *of Kilclogher, Galway*, 3, 4.
Kenney *of Correndoo, Galway*, 3, 4.
Kenney *of Ballyforan, Roscommon*, 3, 4.
Kenney *of Ballinrobe, Mayo*, 3, 4.

Kenny *of Rocksavage, Monaghan*, 2 supp.
Kenrich *of Woore Manor, Salop*, 3, 4.
Keogh *of Kilbride, Carlow*, 3, 4.
Ker *of Gateshaw, Roxburgh*, 2, 3, 4.
Ker *of Newbliss House ;* see Murray.
Kerle ; see Money.
Kerr *of Montalto, Down*, 2, 3, 4.
Kerr, Scott- *of Chatto, Roxburgh*, 2 supp., 3, 4.
Kerrich *of Geldeston Hall, Norfolk*, 2, 3, 4.
Killich *of Walton Hall, Stafford*, 4.
Kinchant *of Park Hall, Salop*, 2, 3, 4.
King *of Chadshunt, Warwick*, I. ii. 344 ; 2, 3, 4.
King *of Preston Candover, Hants*, 4.
King *of North Petherton, Somerset*, 2, 3, 4.
King *of Ballylin, King's Co.*, 3, 4.
King *of Staunton Park, Hereford*, I. ii. 211 ; 2, 3, 4.
Kingdon *of Launcells, Cornwall*, 2, 3, 4.
Kingscote *of Kingscote, Gloucester*, I. i. 280 ; 2, 3, 4.
Kinnersly *of Binfield Manor, Berks*, 4.
Kirke *of Markham, Notts*, 2 supp., 3, 4.
Kirkwood *of Woodbrooke, Roscommon*, 3, 4.
Kirsopp *of the Spital, Northumberland*, 2, 4.
Kirwan *of Blindwell, Galway*, 2, 4.
Kirwan *of Cregg, Galway*, 2, 3, 4.
Kirwan *of Castle Hackett, Galway*, 2, 3, 4.
Kirwan *of Hillsbrook, Kilkenny*, 2, 3, 4.
Kirwan *of Dalgin, Mayo*, 2, 3, 4.
Kirwan *of Moyne, Galway*, 4.
Kittermaster *of Meriden, Warwick*, 3, 4.
Knapton *of Boldre, Hants*, 4 supp.
Knatchbull *of Babington, Somerset*, 2, 3, 4.
Knight *of Firbeck and Langold, York*, 2.
Knight *of Barrels, Warwick*, 2.
Knight *of Godmersham, Kent*, I. i. 442 ; 2, 3, 4.

Knight *of Glen Parva, Leicester*, 3, 4.
Knight *of Wolverley, Worcester*, 2, 3, 4.
Knight *of Downton Castle, Hereford*, 4.
Knolles *of Killeighy and Oatlands, Cork*, 2 add., 3, 4.
Knowlys *of Heysham Hall, Lancaster*, 2.
Knox *of Rappa Castle, Mayo*, I. iv. 580 ; 2, 3, 4.
Knox-Gore *of Belleek Manor, Mayo*, I. iv. 582 ; 2, 3, 4.
Knox *of Netley Park, Mayo*, I. iv. 583 ; 2, 3, 4.
Knox *of Castlerea, Mayo*, I. iv. 670 ; 2, 3, 4.
Knox *of Mount Falcon, Mayo*, 2, 3, 4.
Knfyton *of Uphill, Somerset*, 2, 3, 4.
Kyan *of Ballymurtagh, Wicklow*, 3, 4.
Kynnersley, Sneyd- *of Loxley Park, Stafford*, I. i. 166 ; 2, 3, 4.
Kyrle *of Much Marcle, Hereford*, I. iii. 615 ; 2, 3, 4.
Labouchere *of Overstowey, Somerset*, 2, 3.
Labouchere *of Broome Hall, Surrey*, 4.
Lade *of Boughton House, Kent*, 2, 3, 4.
Lalor *of Cregg, Tipperary*, 3, 4.
Lalor, Power- *of Long Orchard, Tipperary*, 3, 4.
Lamb *of West Denton and Temmon, Northumberland*, 3, 4
Lambarde *of Sevenoaks, Kent*, 2, 3, 4.
Lambart *of Beau Parc, Meath*, 2, 3, 4.
Lambo *of Bidney and Henwood, Hereford*, 2 supp., 3, 4.
Lambert *of Boyton, Wilts*, I. i. 66.
Lambert *of Carnagh, Wexford*, I. iii. 547 ; 2, 3, 4.
Lambert *of Brookhill, Mayo*, 2, 3, 4.
Lambert *of Waterdale, Galway*, 2, 3, 4.
Lambert *of Castle Lambert, Galway*, 2, 3, 4.
Lambert *of Lyston Hall, Essex*, 2 add., 3, 4.
Lambert *of Aggard, Galway*, 3, 4.

Lamont *of Lamont, Argyle*, 3, 4.
Lamont *of Knockdow, Argyle*, 4.
Lamplugh-Raper *of Lamplugh, Cumberland*, I. iii. 160 ; 2, 3, 4.
L'Amy *of Dunkenny, Forfar*, 2, 3, 4.
Landor *of Ipsley Court, Warwick*, I. iii. 682 ; 2, 3, 4.
Lane *of King's Bromley, Stafford*, I. iii. 682 ; 2, 3, 4.
Lane *of Badgemore, Oxford*, 2, 3, 4.
Lane *of Coffleet, Devon*, 2, 3, 4.
Lane *of Ryelands, Hereford*, 2, 3, 4.
Lane-Fox *of Bramham ;* see Fox.
Langdale *of Garston House, Surrey*, 2 supp., 3, 4.
Langford- *of Trungle and Penzance, Cornwall*, 2.
Langston *of Sarsden House, Oxford*, 2, 3, 4.
Langton *of Liverpool, Lancaster*, 2.
Langton, Gore- *of Newton Park, Somerset*, I. i. 145 ; 2, 3, 4.
Laslett *of Allerton Hall, Worcester*, 2, 3, 4.
Latham *of Bradwall, Chester*, I. i. 190 ; 2, 3, 4.
La Touche *of Marlay, Dublin*, 2, 3, 4.
La Touche *of Bellvue, Wicklow*, 2, 3, 4.
La Touche *of Harristown, Kildare*, 3, 3, 4.
Lattin *of Morristown Lattin, Kildare*, I. iii. 575.
Lautour *of Hexton House, Herts*, 2, 3, 4.
Lawder *of Mough House, Leitrim*, 2.
Lawes *of Rothamsted, Herts*, 2, 3, 4.
Lawlor *of Grenagh House, Kerry*, 3, 4.
Lawrence *of Sevenhampton, Gloucester*, I. iii. 64 ; 2, 3, 4.
Lawrence *of Lisreaghan, Galway*, 2, 3, 4.
Lawson *of Aldborough, York*, I. ii. 247 ; 2, 3, 4.
Lawson *of Longhrist, Northumberland*, I. ii. 105 ; 2, 3, 4.
Lawton *of Cape View, Cork*, 3.
Lawton *of Lake Marsh, Cork*, 2.
Lawton *of Lawton, Chester*, 2, 3, 4.
Layton *of Chettisham Hall, Cambridge*, 2, 3, 4.

Lea *of Astley Hall, Worcester,* 2 supp., 3, 4.
Leader *of Dromagh Castle, Cork,* 2 supp., 3, 4.
Leader *of Mount Leader, Cork,* 2, 3, 4.
Leahy *of Shanakiel, Cork,* 2, 3, 4.
Leake *of Thorp Hall, Essex,* 2, 3, 4.
Learmouth *of Dean, Edinburgh,* 3, 4.
Leatham *of Hemsworth Hall, York,* 3, 4.
Leather *of Leaventhorpe Hall, York,* 4.
Leather *of Herringfleet, Suffolk,* 2, 3, 4.
Leche *of Carden, Chester,* I. ii. 365; 2, 3, 4.
Lechmere *of Hill House, Oxford, and of Ludford, Hereford,* 2, 3, 4.
Lechmere *of Farnhope Court, Hereford,* 2, 3, 4.
Lecky *of Ballykeally, Carlow,* 2, 3, 4.
Lecky *of Castle Lecky, Derry,* 2, 3, 4.
Lecky *of Beardiville, Antrim,* 3, 4.
Ledsam *of Chad Hill, Warwick,* 2, 3, 4.
Lee *of Hartwell, Bucks,* 2 supp., 3, 4.
Lee *of Balsdon, Devon,* 2, 3, 4.
Lee *of Grove Hall, York,* supp., 4.
Lee *of the Abbey, Knaresborough,* 2, 3, 4.
Lee *of Dillington House, Somerset,* 2, 3, 4.
Lee *of Holborough, Kent,* 3, 4.
Lee *of Dynas Powis, Salop,* 2, 3, 4.
Lee *of Coton Hall, Salop,* 3, 4.
Lee *of Barna, Tipperary,* 2, 3, 4.
Leech *of Cloonconra, Mayo,* 4.
Leech *of Rathkeale Abbey, Limerick,* 3, 4.
Leeke *of Longford, Salop,* I. iii. 506; 2, 3, 4.
Leeves *of Tortington, Sussex,* 2.
Lefevre *of Heckfield Place, Hants,* 2.
Lefroy *of Carrickglass, Longford,* 2, 3, 4.
Legge *of Malone House, Belfast,* 3, 4.
Legh *of Norbury Booth Hall, Chester,* I. ii. 44; 2, 3, 4.

Legh *of Ridge, Chester,* 2.
Legh *of Adlington, Chester,* I. iii. 453; 2, 3, 4.
Legh *of Lyme, Chester,* I. ii. 686; 2, 3, 4.
Lee *of High Legh, Chester,* 2, 3, 4.
Le Hunte *of Artramont, Wexford,* I. iii. 365; 2, 3, 4.
Le Hunt, Bainbrigge- *of Burgh, Lincoln,* 2 supp., 3, 4.
Leigh *of Stoneleigh, Warwick,* I. iii. 223.
Leigh *of West Hall High Leigh, Chester,* I. iv, 530; 2 and supp., 2, 3, 4.
Leigh *of Leatherlake House, Surrey,* I. iv. 533; 2, 3, 4.
Leigh *of Ponty Pool, Monmouth,* 2 3, 4.
Leigh *of Bardon, Devon,* I. iii. 541; 2, 3, 4, and supp.
Leigh *of Hindley Hall;* see Pemberton Leigh.
Leigh *of Luton Hoo Park, Bedford,* supp., 4.
Leigh *of Belmont, Chester,* 2, 3, 4.
Leigh *of Brownsover Hall, Warwick,* 2, 3, 4.
Leighton *of Bauseley, Montgomery,* I. i. 260; 2, 3, 4.
Leir *of Jaggard's House, Wilts,* I. iv. 578; 2, 3, 4.
Leith *of Whitehaugh;* see Forbes Leith, 2, 3, 4.
Leith-Hay *of Bannes and Leith Hall, Aberdeen,* I. ii. 136; 2, 3, 4.
Leman *of Brampton Hall, Suffolk,* 3, 4.
Lempriere *of Pelham, Hants,* 4.
Lendrum *of Magheracross, Fermanagh,* 2, 3, 4.
Lenigan *of Castle Ffogerty, Tipperary,* I. iii. 700; 2, 4,
Lennose *of Woodhead, Stirling,* 4.
Lentaigne, *Tallaght, Dublin,* 4.
Lenthall *of Bessels Leigh, Berks,* I. i. 178; 2, 3, 4.
Leslie *of Blaquhain, Aberdeen,* 2 supp., 3, 4.
Leslie *of Warthill, Aberdeen,* 2, 3, 4.
Leslie *of Ballibay, Monaghan,* I. iv. 86; 3, 4.
Leslie *of Leslie Hill, Antrim,* I. iv. 88; 2, 3, 4.

Leslie *of Glasslough, Monaghan*, I. iv. 151; 2. 3, 4.
L'Estrange *of Moystoa, King's Co.* I. iv. 640; 2.
Le Strange *of Hunstanton;* see Styleman-Le Strange.
L'Estrange *of Market Hill;* see Carleton.
Levett *of Milford Hall, Stafford*, 2, 3, 4.
Levett of *Wichnor Park, Stafford,* 2, 3, 4.
Lewin *of the Hollies, Kent,* 3, 4.
Lewin *of Cloghans, Mayo,* 2, 4.
Lewin *of the Co. Clare;* see Ross Lewin.
Lewin *of Womaston, Radnor,* 2, 3, 4.
Lewis *of Harpton Court, Radnor,* I. i. 335; 2.
Lewis *of Greenmeadow, Glamorgan,* I. iii. 386; 2, 3, 4.
Lewis *of Gilfach. Caermarthen,* 2, 3, 4.
Lewis *of Henllan, Pembroke,* 2 supp., 3, 4.
Lewis *of Stradey, Caermarthen,* 2 supp., 3, 4.
Lewis *of Gwinfe, Caermarthen,* 2 supp., 3, 4.
Lewis *of Henllys and Bodjor, Anglesey,* 2, 3, 4.
Lewis *of Kilcullen, Kildare,* 3, 4.
Lewis *of Seatown, Dublin,* 3, 4.
Lewis *of St. Pierre, Monmouth,* I. i. 221; 2, 3, 4.
Lewthwaite *of Broad Gate, Cumberland,* I. iv. 93; 2, 3, 4.
Lycester *of Toft, Chester,* I. i. 73; 2, 3, 4.
Leycester *of White Place, Berks,* 2, 3, 4.
Lillingston *of Elmdon;* see Spooner-Lillingston.
Liud *of Ryde, Isle of Wight,* 2 supp., 3, 4.
Lindesay *of Loughry, Tyrone,* 2, 3, 4.
Lindesay *of Cahoo, Dublin,* 3, 4.
Lindsay *of Belcarres, Fife,* 2, 3.
Lindow *of Ingwell, Cumberland,* 4.
Lindsay-Carnegie *of Spynie, Moray,* 3, 4.
Lindsey *of Hollymount House, Mayo,* 2, 3, 4.

Lingen *of Penlanolen, Radnor,* 2, 3, 4.
Lisle or De Lisle *of Wodyton, Isle of Wight,* 4.
Lister *of Armitage Park, Stafford,* I. i. 219.
Lister *of Burwell Park, Lincoln,* 2, 3, 4.
Lister *of Ousefleet Grange, York,* 2, 3, 4.
Lister *of Shibden Hall, York,* 4.
Little *of Bovennet House, Down,* 2.
Little *of Llanvair Grange, Monmouth,* 2, 3, 4.
Littledale *of Bolton Hall, York,* 2, 3, 4.
Littleton *of Teddesley, Stafford,* I. i. 389.
Littler *of Cheshire,* 2.
Litton *of Altmore, Tyrone,* 4.
Livingstone *of Westquarter, Stirling,* 4.
Livius *of Bedford,* 2 supp.
Llewellyn *of Tregwynt, Pembroke,* 2, 3, 4.
Lloyd *of Welcome, Warwick,* I. i. 244.
Lloyd *of Ferney Hall, Salop,* I. iii. 635.
Lloyd *of Dolobran, Warwick,* I. iv. 107; 2.
Lloyd *of Tregayan, Anglesey,* 2.
Lloyd *of Ferney Hall, Salop,* 2.
Lloyd *of Ardnagowan, Roscommon,* 2.
Lloyd *of Bronwydd, Cardigan,* 2, 4.
Lloyd *of Peniarth,* 2 supp.
Lloyd *of Brynestyn, Denbigh,* 2 supp.
Lloyd *of Plymag, Gwerclas and Bashall,* 2, 3, 4.
Lloyd *of Glansevin, Caermarthen,* 2, 3, 4.
Lloyd *of Leaton Knolls, Salop,* 2, 4.
Lloyd *of Aston, Salop,* I. iii. 346; 2, 3, 4.
Lloyd *of Dan-yr-Allt, Caermathen,* I. iv. 114; 2, 3, 4.
Lloyd *of Coedmore, Cardigan,* 2, 3, 4.
Lloyd *of Clochfaen and Plas Madog,* 3, 4.
Lloyd *of Trallwyn, Carnarvon,* 2, 3, 4.
Lloyd *of Laques, Caermarthen,* 2 supp., 3, 4.

Lloyd *of Pale, Merioneth*, 2, 3, 4.
Lloyd *of Strancally Castle, Waterford*, 4.
Lloyd *of Stockton Hall, York*, 2, 3, 4.
Lloyd *of Croghan, Roscommon*, I. iv. 89 ; 2, 3, 4.
Lloyd *of Gloster, King's Co.* I. ii. 549 ; 2, 3, 4.
Lloyd *of Castle Lloyd, Limerick*, 3, 4.
Lloyd *of Lloydsboro', Tipperary*, 2, 3, 4.
Lluellyn *of Fetcham Lodge, Surrey*, 2.
Loch *of Tittensor, Stafford*, I. ii. 202 ; 2, 3, 4.
Locke *of Rowdeford, Wilts*, 2, 3, 4.
Lockhart *of Wicketshaw, Lanark*, 4.
Lockhart *of Borthwickbrae, Selkirk*, 3, 4.
Lockyer *of Plymouth, Devon*, 2, 3, 4.
Lockwood *of Dew's Hall*; see Wood *of Bishop's Hall*.
Loftus *of Woolland, Dorset*, 2.
Loftus *formerly of Kilbride, Wicklow*, I. i. 209 ; 2, 3, 4.
Lomax *of Clayton Hall, Lancaster*, 2, 3, 4.
Lomax *of Childwickbury, Herts*, 2.
Long *of Rood Ashton, Wilts*, I. iv. 63 ; 2, 3, 4.
Long *of Preshaw, Hants*, I. iv. 72 ; 2, 3, 4.
Long *of Monkton Farleigh, Wilts*, I. iv. 67 ; 2, 3, 4.
Long *of Hampton Lodge, Surrey*, I. ii. 164 ; 2, 3, 4.
Long Wellesley *of Draycot, Wilts*, I. iii. 211.
Long *of Dunston Hall, Norfolk*, 3, 4.
Longe *of Spixworth, Norfolk*, I. iii. 361 ; 2, 3, 4.
Longe *of Catton Lodge, Norfolk*, 2.
Longfield *of Longueville, Cork*, I. i. 545 ; 2, 3, 4.
Longfield *of Waterloo, Cork*, 4.
Longfield *of Castle Mary, Cork*, 4.
Longueville *of Prestatyn, Salop*, 2, 3, 4.
Longworth *of Glynwood, Westmeath*, 3, 4.
Lopdell *of Raheen Park, Galway*, 3, 4.

Lousada *of Peak House, Devon*, 4.
Loveday *of Williamscote, Oxford*, 2, 3, 4.
Loveland *of Great Hallingbury, Hertford*, 4.
Lovell *of Lincolnshire and Bucks*, 2, 3, 4.
Lovell *of Wendover House, Bucks*, 2.
Lovett, 2 supp.
Lovett *of Liscombe and Soulbury, Bucks*, 2, 3, 4 and supp.
Lovett *of Belmont, Salop*, 2, 3. 4.
Lovibond *of Hatfield Peverell, Essex*, I. i. 163 ; 2, 3, 4.
Low *of Sunvale, Limerick*, 3, 4.
Lowe *of Locko, Derby*, 2, 3, 4.
Lowe *of Bromsgrove, Worcester*, I. iv. 38 ; 2, 3, 4.
Lowe *of Court Hill, Salop*, 3, 4.
Lowe *of Glazebrooke House, Devon*, 2.
Lowndes *of Whaddon, Bucks*, 2 supp., 3, 4.
Lowndes *of Chesham, Bucks*, 2 supp., 3. 4.
Lowndes *of Arthurlie, Renfrew*, 2, 3, 4.
Lowndes *of Hassall, Chester*, I. iv.. 333.
Lowndes *of Brightwell*; see Stone.
Lowndes *of Barrington Hall, Essex*, 4.
Lowry *of Pomeray, Tyrone*, I. iii. 140; 2, 3, 4.
Lowry *of Drumreagh, Tyrone*, 3.
Lowry *of Rochdale, Tyrone*, 3, 4.
Lowten *of Manley, Chester*, 2, 3, 4.
Lowther *of (formerly) Kilrue, Meath*, 2 add., 3, 4.
Luard *of Blyborough, Licnoln*, 2 supp., and add., 3, 4.
Luard *of the Lodge, Essex*, 4.
Lucas *of Uplands, Glamorgan*, 2. 3.
Lucas *of Hasland, Derby*, I. ii. 171 ; 2, 3, 4.
Lucas *of Stout Hall, Glamorgan*, 4.
Lucas *of Castle Shane, Monaghan*, I. iv. 144 ; 2, 3, 4.
Lucas *of Mount Lucas, King's Co.* 2, 3, 4.
Lucas *of Rathealy, Cork*, 3, 4.
Lucas *of Richfordstown, Cork*, 2, 4.
Lucy *of Charlecote, Warwick*, I. ii. 97 ; 2, 3, 4.

Ludlow *of Heywood, Wilts*, 2, 3, 4.
Lumb *of Brigham Hall, Cumberland*, 4.
Lumsdaine *of that Ilk*, 4 add.; see Sandys-Lumsdaine.
Lumsdaine *of Lathallan, Fife*, 3, 4.
Lumsden *of Cushine, Aberdeen*, 2, 3, 4.
Lumsden *of Pitcaple, Aberdeen*, 2, 3, 4.
Lumsden *of Clova, Aberdeen*, 2, 3, 4.
Lundin *of Auchtermairnie, Fife*, 2 supp.; 3, 4.
Luscombe *of Combe Royal, Devon*, 2, 3, 4.
Lushington *of Park House, Kent*, I. ii. 185; 2, 3, 4.
Luttrell *of Dunster Castle, Somerset*, I. i. 142; 2, 3, 4.
Lutwidge *of Holmrook, Cumberland*, 2 supp., 3, 4.
Luxford *of Higham, Sussex*, 3, 4.
Luxmoore *of Kerslake, Devon*, 4.
Luxmoore *of Witherdon, Devon*, 2, 3, 4.
Lyde *of Ayot, St. Lawrence;* see Ames, 2, 3, 4.
Lydekker *of Harpenden Lodge, Herts*, 3, 4.
Lyell *of Kinnordy, Forfar*, 2, 3, 4.
Lyle *of Oaks, Londonderry*, 4.
Lynch *of Barna, Galway*, 2, 3, 4.
Lynch *of Duras, Galway*, 2, 3, 4.
Lynch *of Clydagh;* see Staunton-Lynch.
Lynch *of Partry, Mayo*, 3, 4.
Llynch *of Clogher, Mayo*, 2, 3, 4.
Lynes *of Tooley Park, Leicester*, I. iv. 511; 2, 3, 4.
Lyon *of Cossins*, I. iv. 592; 2, 4.
Lyons *of Appleton Hall, Chester*, 2, 3, 4.
Lyons *of Ledestown, Westmeath*, 3, 4.
Lyons *of Old Park, Antrim*, 3, 4.
Lysley *of Mimwood, Herts*, 2 add., 3, 4.
Lysons *of Hempsted, Gloucester*, I. iii. 221; 2, 3, 4,
Lyster *of Rowton Castle, Salop*, I. iii. 53; 2, 3, 4.

Lyster *of Lysterfield, Roscommon*, 4.
Lytton *of Knebworth, Herts*, I. i. 447; 2.
M'Adam *of Waterhead, Kirkcudbright*, 3, 4.
MacAdam *of Blackwater, Clare*, 2, 3, 4.
Macalester *of Loup and Lennox, Ayr*, I. iii. 687; 2, 3, 4.
Macalister *of Glenbarr and Cour, Argyll*, 2, 3, 4.
M'Alpine *of Breandrum, Mayo*, 2.
Macartney *of Lissanoure, Antrim*, 2 supp., 3, 4.
Macartney *of the Palace, Clogher, Tyrone*, 3, 4.
Macartney *of Blacket*, 2.
Mac Braire *of Tweedhill, Berwick*, I. iv. 598; 2, 4.
M'Call *of Daldowie, Lanark*, 4 supp.
M'Call *of Braehead and Glyntown, Cork*, 2, 3.
M'Carthy *of Carrignavar, Cork*, I. ii. 606; 2, 3, 4.
M'Carthy *of Cork*, I. ii. 611.
Mac Causland *of Strabane*, I. ii. 58; 2, 3, 4.
Mac Causland *of Drenagh, Londonderry*, 4.
Mac Causland *of Bessbrook, Derry*, 4.
Mc Clintock *of Drumcar, Louth*, I. ii. 257; 2, 3, 4.
Mc Clintock, Perry- *of Seskinore, Tyrone*, 4.
Mc Clintock *of Dunmore, Donegal*, 3, 4.
Mc Clintock *of Hampstead Hall, Londonderry*, 2, 3, 4.
Mc Clure *of Belmont, Down*, 3, 4.
Mc Culloch *of Ardwall, Kirkcudbright*, 2, 3, 4.
Mac Dermott *of Coolavin, Sligo*, 2, 3, 4.
Mac Dermott *of Alderford House, Roscommon*, 2.
Macdonald *of Vallay, Inverness*, 3.
Macdonald *of Glengarry*, 3.
Macdonald *of Clanranald*, 2, 3, 4.
Macdonald *of Glenaladale, Inverness*, 4.

Macdonald *of Inchkenneth, Argyle,* 2, 3, 4.

Macdonald *of Ranathan,* 2 add., 3, 4.

M'Donald *of Dalchosnie, Perth,* 2, 3, 4.

Mac Donald *of Rammerscales, Dumfries,* 2, 3, 4.

Mac Donald *of Sandside, Caithness,* 2, 3, 4 supp.

Mac Donnell *of New Hall and Kilkee, Clare,* 2, 4.

Mac Dougall *of Mc Dougall and Dunolly, Argyle,* 2, 3, 4.

Macdowall *of Garthland, Renfrew,* 3, 4.

Macevoy *of Tobertinan, Meath,* 3, 4.

Mc Farlan *of Ballencleroche, Stirling,* 4.

Macfarlane *of Huntstown House, Dublin,* 2, 3, 4.

Macgeorge *of Nether Larg, in Galloway,* 4.

Mc Gildowny *of Clare Park, Antrim,* 2, 3, 4.

Mac Gillicuddy *of the Reeks,* 2, 3, 4.

Macgregor *of Glengyle, Perth,* 2 supp., 3, 4.

Mac Gregor *of Leragan, Rannock, Perth,* 2 supp.

Mc Grigor *of Kernock,* Stirling, 3 supp., 4.

Mac Guffie *of Crossmichael, Kirkcudbright,* 3, 4.

Machell *of Crackenthorpe,* 2, 3, 4.

Machell *of Penny Bridge, Lancaster,* 2, 3, 4.

Machen *of Eastbach Court, Gloucester,* 2, 3, 4.

Mc Kay *of Bigghouse, Argyll,* 2 supp., 3, 4.

Mackenzie *of Dundonald;* see Munro *of Teaninich.*

Mackenzie *of Portmore, Peebles,* 2, 3, 4.

Mackenzie *of Muirton, Ross,* 2, 3.

Mackenzie *of Grove House, Middlesex,* 3.

Mackenzie *of Applecross, Ross,* 2.

Mackenzie *of Ord, Ross,* 2, 3, 4.

Mackenzie *of Glack, Aberdeen,* 2 supp., 3, 4.

Mc Kerlies *of Wigtonshire,* 4.

M'Kerrell *of Hillhouse, Ayr,* I. iii. 173 ; 2, 3, 4.

Mackesy *of Aughmacart, Queen's Co.,* 4.

Mackinnon *of Mackinnon,* 2, 3, 4.

Mackinnon *of Bittacy House, Middlesex,* 4.

Mackintosh *of Mackintosh,* 2, 3, 4.

Mackintosh *of Dalmunzie, Perth,* 3, 4.

Mackie *of Bargaly, Kirkcudbright,* 3, 4.

Mc Kirdy *of Birkwood, Lanark,* 2 supp.; 3, 4.

Maclachlan *of Maclachlan, Argyll,* 2 supp., 3, 4.

Maclaine *of Lochbuy, Argyll,* 2, 3, 4.

Maclaine *of Kington House, Gloucester,* 2 supp., 3, 4.

Mc Laughlin *of Ballythomas, Queen's Co.,* 3 supp., 4.

Maclean *of Ardgour, Argyll,* 2 supp., 3, 4.

Maclean *of Pennycross, Argyll,* 2 supp., 3, 4.

Maclean *of Haremere Hall, Sussex,* 4 supp.

Macleay *of Keiss, Caithness,* 2, 3, 4.

Macleod *of Macleod,* I. iii. 476 ; 2, 3, 4.

Macleod *of Cadboll, Cromarty,* 2, 3, 4.

Macleod *of Rasay,* I. iv. 584 ; 2.

McMicking *of Miltonise, Wigton,* 2 add., 3, 4.

McMurray *of Roxborough House, Limerick,* 4.

Macnaghten *of Beardiville, Antrim,* I. ii. 307.

Macnamara *of Caddington Hall, Beds,* 4.

Macnamara *of Ayle, Clare,* 2, 3, 4.

Macnamara *of Doolen, Clare,* 2, 3, 4.

Macneil *of Barra, Inverness,* I. iv. 492 ; 2, 3.

McNeill *of Parkmount, Antrim,* 4.

McNeill-Hamilton *of Raploch, Lanark,* 4.

McNeill *of Collonsay and Gigha,* 2 and supp., 3, 4.

Maconochie *of Meadowbank, Midlothian,* 2, 3, 4.

Macpherson *of Cluny Macpherson, Inverness,* I. iii. 462 ; 2, 3, 4.

Macquarie *of Ormaig, Argyll,* 2, 3, 4.

Macqueen *of Corrybrough, Inverness,* 2, 3, 4.

Macrae *of Holmains, Dumfries,* 3, 4.

McTernan *of Heapstown, Sligo,* 4.

McVeagh *of Drewstown, Meath,* 2, 3, 4.

Madden *of Hilton, Monaghan,* 2, 3, 4.

Madden *of Inch House, Dublin,* 3, 4.

Madden *of Roslea Manor, Fermanagh,* 3, 4.

Maddison *of Partney Hall, Lincoln,* 4.

Maddock *of Naseby ;* see Ashley Maddock.

Madocks *of Glanywern, Denbigh,* 2, 3, 4.

Maesmore *of Maesmore, Denbigh,* 2 supp.

Magan *of Emoe, Westmeath,* 4.

Magan *of Clonearl, King's Co.* 2 supp. 3, 4,

Magenis *of Waringtown, Down,* 3, 4.

Magill *of Lyttleton, Westmeath,* 3, 4.

Magor *of Penventon House, Cornwall,* 2, 3, 4.

Maguire *of Gortoral House, Fermanagh,* 3, 4.

Maher *of Tullemaine Castle, Tipperary,* 2, 3, 4.

Maher *of Ballenkelle, Wexford,* 3, 4.

Maher *of Woodlands,* 2, 3, 4.

Mahony *of Dromore Castle, Kerry,* 3, 4.

Mahony *of Dunloe Castle, Kerry,* 4.

Mahony *of Castlequin, Kerry.*

Mainwaring *of Whitmore, Stafford,* I. iii. 590 ; 2, 3, 4.

Mainwaring *of Oteley Park, Salop,* I. iv. 356 ; 2, 3, 4.

Maister *of Beverley, York,* 2, 3, 4.

Maitland *of Dundrennan, Kircudbright,* 2, 3, 4.

Maitland *of Hollywich, Sussex,* I. iii. 600 ; 2.

Maitland *of Frengh, Wigton,* 3, 4.

Majendie *of Hedingham Castle, Essex,* 3, 4.

Malcolm *of Burnfoot, Dumfries,* 3, 4.

Malcolm *of Poltalloch, Argyll,* I. iv. 647 ; 2, 3, 3.

Maling *of the Elms, Worcester,* 2.

Malony *of Kiltanon, Clare,* I. iv. 766.

Malony *of Granahan, Clare,* I. iv. 768.

Mallet *of Ash, Devon,* 2 supp., 3, 4.

Mallory *of Mobberley, Chester,* 2, 3, 4.

Manley *of Manley Hall, Stafford,* I. iv. 707 ; 2, 3, 4.

Mann *of Dunmoyle, Tyrone,* 4.

Manning *of Portland Castle, Dorset,* 2 supp. ; 3, 4.

Manning *of Coldbrook Park, Monmouth,* 3, 4.

Mannoch *of Gifford's Hall, Suffolk,* 3, 4.

Mansel *of Cosgrove Hall, Northampton,* 2, 3, 4.

Mansergh *of Greenane, Tipperary,* 4.

Mansergh *of Macroney Castle, Cork,* 3, 4.

Mansfield *of Castle Wray, Donegal,* 3, 4.

Mansfield *of Morristown Lattin, Kildare,* 3, 4.

Mansfield *of Birstall House, Leicester,* I. ii. 178.

Marcon *of Wallington Hall, Norfolk,* 4.

Margesson *of Offington, Sussex,* I. i. 295 ; 2, 3, 4.

Marindin *of Chesterton, Salop,* 2 add.

Marjoribanks *of Marjoribanks, in Midlothian,* 2 supp. 3, 4.

Markham *of Becca Hall, York,* I. ii. 203 ; 2, 3, 4.

Marklove *of Lullingworth House, Gloucester,* 4.

Marlay *of Belvedere, Westmeath,* 3 supp. 4.

Marling *of Stanley Park, Gloucester,* 4.

Marriott *of Avonbank, Worcester,* I. iv. 583 ; 2, 3, 4.

Marriott, Smith- *of Horsmonden, Kent,* 2 supp. ; 3, 4.

Marsh, *Snave Manor, Kent,* 2, 3, 4.

Marsh *of Gaynes Park, Essex,* 2 supp. ; 3, 4.

Marsh *of Springmount, Queen's County,* 3, 4.

Marsh *of Ramridge, Hants,* 4.

Marshall *of Patterdale Hall, Westmoreland,* I. i. 294 ; 2, 3, 4.

Marshall *of Treworgy, Cornwall,* 2, 3, 4.

Marshall *of Broadwater, Surrey,* 4.

Marsham *of Stratton Strawless, Norfolk*, 2, 3, 4.

Marston *of Willenhall, Stafford*, 2 supp.

Marten *of Marshals Wick, Herts*, 2, 3, 4.

Martin *of Hemingstone, Suffolk*, 2,3,4.

Martin *of Worsborough Hall, York*, 2, 3, 4.

Martin *of Colston Bassett, Notts*, 2, 3, 4.

Martin, Wykeham- *of Leeds Castle, Kent*, I. i. 422; 2, 3, 4.

Martin *of Ham Court, Worcester*, 2, 3, 4.

Martin *of Anstey, Leicester*, I. iii. 469; 2, 3, 4.

Martin *of Whatton House, Lancaster*, 4.

Martin *of Bittern Lodge, Hants*, I. iv. 99; 2, 3, 4.

Martin *of Bloomfield, Sligo*, 3, 4.

Martin *of Cleveragh, Sligo*, 4.

Martin *of Ross, Galway*, 3, 4.

Martin *of Wiche, Worcester*, 3, 4.

Martin *of Ballinahinch, Galway*, 2 supp.

Martineau *of Basing Park, Hants*, 2, 3, 4.

Marton *of Capernwray, Lancaster*, I. iv. 157; 2, 3, 4.

Martyn *of Tullyra Castle, Galway*, 2, 3, 4.

Martyn *of Pertenhall, Bedford*, 3.

Mason *of Aldenham Lodge, Herts*, 3, 4.

Mason *of Necton Hall, Norfolk*, 2, 3, 4.

Mason *of Masonbrook, Galway*, 2.

Massey, *Chester*, 2 add. 3, 4.

Massey *of Pool Hall, Chester*, I. iii. 48; 2, 3, 4.

Massie *of Pulford Hall, Chester*, I. iii. 44; 2, 3, 4.

Massingberd *of Gunby, Lincoln*, I. iii. 104; 2, 3, 4.

Massingberd *of Ormsby, Lincoln*, I. i. 661; 2, 3, 4.

Massy *of Kingswell House, Tipperary*, 3 supp. 4.

Master *of the Abbey, Gloucester*, 3, 4.

Master *of Knowle Park, Gloucester*, I. i. 557; 2, 3, 4.

Master *of Barrow Green House, Surrey*, 2, 3, 4.

Matheson *of Ardross, Ross*, 2 supp. 3, 4.

Matheson *of Achany, Ross*, 2 supp.

Mathew *of Llandaff*, 2 add.

Mathew *of Tresungher*, 2, 3, 4.

Mathew *of Pentloe Hall, Essex*, 3, 4.

Matthews *of Hereford*, 2, 3, 4.

Mathias *of Lamphey Court, Pembroke*, I. iii. 542; 3, 4.

Maude *of Alverthorpe and Wakefield, York*, I. ii. 83.

Maude *of Moor House, York*, 2.

Maude *of Kendal, Westmoreland*, 2.

Mauleverer *of Arncliffe Hall, York*, 2, 3, 4.

Maunsell *of Limerick*, I. i. 306; 2, 3, 4.

Maunsell *of Fanstown Limerick*, 4.

Maunsell *of Ballywilliam, Limerick*, I. ii. 274; 2, 3, 4.

Maunsell *of Oakly Park, Kildare*, 2, 3, 4.

Maunsell *of Thorpe Malson, Northampton*, 2, 3, 4.

Maxtone *of Cultoguhey, Perth*, 2 supp., 3, 4.

Maxwell- Constable *of Everingham, York*, I. i. 325, 2, 3.

Maxwell *of Darvagel, Renfrew*, 4.

Maxwell *of Terraughty, Dumfries*, 4.

Maxwell *of Munches, Dumfries*, 4.

Maxwell *of Finnebrougue;* see Waring Maxwell, 2.

Maxwell *of Glenlee, New Galloway*, 4.

Maxwell, Perceval- *of Groomsport, Down*, 3, 4.

Maxwell *of Williamwood:* see Graham, 2.

May *of Hadlow Castle, Kent*, 2 supp., 3, 4.

Maynard *of Harsley Hall, York*, I. iii. 677; 2, and supp., 3, 4.

Mayne *of Glynch House, Monaghan*, 3, 4.

Mayne *of Powis*, 3, 4.

Mayne *of Teffont Ewyas, Wilts*, I. iv. 504.

Mayow *of Bray and Hanworth, Cornwall*, 2, 3, 4.

Meade *of Ballymartle, Cork*, 4.

Meade *of Ballyntober, Cork*, 3, 4.

Meadows *of Burgersh House, Suffolk,* I. ii. 648.

Medly *of Perfeddgoed,* 3, 4.

Meares *of Meares Court, Westmeath,* I. iii. 533 ; 2, 3, 4.

Medhurst *of Kippax Hall, York,* 3,4.

Medlycott *of Rockets Castle, Waterford,* 2, 3, 4.

De Medewe *of Witnesham Hall, Suffolk,* 2, 3, 4.

Meekins *of Glasthule House, Dublin,* 3, 4.

Meigh *of Ash Hall, Stafford,* 2, 3, 4.

Melville, Whyte- *of Bennochy, Fife,* I. ii. 659 ; 2, 3, 4.

Menzies, Stewart- *of Culdares,* 2 supp., 2, 3, 4.

Menzies *of Chesthill*; see Stewart-Menzies,

Meredith *of Pentrebychan, Denbigh,* I. iii. 425 ; 2, 3, 4.

Meredith *of Cloonalmahon, Sligo,* 2, 3, 4.

Meredith *of Dick's Grove, Kerry,* 2 add., 3, 4.

Merry *of Highlands, Berks,* 2, 3, 4.

Metcalfe *of Hawstead House, Suffolk,* 2, 3, 4.

Metcalfe *of Boxton House, Bedford,* 2.

Metge *of Athlumney, Meath,* 2 supp., 3, 4.

Methuer *of Corsham Wilts,* I. i. 392.

Meynell *of Hoar Cross, Stafford,* 2, 3, 4.

Meynell *of Meynell Langley, Derby,* 2, 3, 4.

Meynell *of North Kilvington, York,* I. i. 401 ; 2, 3, 4.

Meyrick *of Bodorgan, Anglesey,* I. iii. 631 ; 2, 3, 4.

Meyrick *of Goodrich Court, Hereford,* I. iii. 633; 2, 3, 4.

Meyrick *of Bush, Pembroke,* 4.

Michel *of Dewlish, Dorset,* I. ii. 650 ; 2, 3, 4.

Michel *of Whatcome*; see Pleydell *of Whatcome,* 3, 4.

Micklethwait *of Taverham, Norfolk,* 2, 3, 4.

Micklethwait *of Ardsley, York,* 2, 3, 4.

Middleton *of Stockeld, York,* 2, 3, 4.

Middleton *of Leam, Derby,* I. ii. 634 ; 2, 3, 4.

Milbank *of Thorp Perrow, York,* I. iv. 398 ; 2, 3, 4.

Miles *of Leigh Court, Somerset,* 2 and supp. 3.

Miles *of Kingsweston, Gloucester,* 4.

Miller *of Radway, Warwick,* I. iii. 699; 2, 3, 4.

Miller *of Collier's Wood, Surrey,* 2, 3, 4.

Miller *of Monk Castle, Ayr,* I. ii. 349 ; 2, 3, 4.

Mills *of Saxham Hall, Suffolk,* 2, 3, 4.

Mills *of Tolmers, Herts,* 3, 4.

Mills *of Lexden Park, Essex,* 2.

Milne-Home *of Milne Graden, Berwick,* 2, 3, 4.

Milnes *Beck of ingham Hall, Lincoln,* 2, 3.

Milnes *of Fryston, York,* 2, 3, 4.

Milnes *of Stubbing Edge, Derby,* 2, 3, 4.

Milward *of Thurgarton Priory, Notts,* 2, 3, 4.

Milward *of the Manor House, Lechlade, Gloucester,* 2, 3, 4.

M'Minn *of Herdstown, Down,* 4 supp.

Minchin *of Rathclough, Tipperary,* 3, 4.

Minnitt *of Anaghbeg, Tipperary,* 2, 3, 4.

Mirehouse *of Brownslade, Pembroke,* 2, 3, 4.

Mitchell, Forbes- *of Thainston, Aberdeen,* 2, 3, 4.

Mitchell *of Castlestrange, Roscommon,* 2, 3, 4.

Mitchell *of Drumreaske, Monaghan,* 4.

Mitford *of Mitford Castle, Northumberland,* I. ii. 282 ; 2, 3, 4.

Mitford *of Pitshill, Sussex,* 2, 3, 4.

Mitford *of Exbury House, Hants,* I. ii. 285 ; 2, 3, 4.

Moilliet *of Abberley Hall, Worcester,* 4.

Moir *of Leckie, Stirling,* 2 supp., 3, 4.

Moller, Le Champion- *of Butterston,* 4.

Molloy *of Clonbela, King's Co.* 4.

Molony *of Kiltanon, Clare*, 2, 3, 4.
Molony *of Granahan, Clare*, 2, 3, 4.
Molyneux *of Loseley Park, Surrey*, 2, 3, 4.
Monck *of Coley Park, Berks*, I. iv. 181; 2, 3, 4.
Monck-Mason *of Masonbrook, Galway*, I. iv. 354.
Money *of Much Marcle ;* see Kerle, I. iii. 615 ; 2, 3, 4.
Money *of Walthamstow, Essex*, 2.
Monington *of Sarnesfield ;* see Webbe Weston, 3, 4.
Monins *of Waldershare, Kent*, 2 supp., 3, 4.
Monro *of Ewell Castle, Surrey*, 2 supp., 3, 4.
Monsel *of Tervoe, Limerick*, 2, 3, 4.
Montagu *of Lackham House, Wilts*, I. ii. 52.
Montagu *of Papplewick and Melton, York*, I. ii. 268 ; 3, 4.
Monteith *of Carstairs, Lanark*, 3, 4.
Montgomerie *of Annich Lodge, Ayr*, 2, 3, 4.
Montgomery *of Garboldisham, Norfolk*, 4 supp.
Montgomery *of Milton, Northampton*, 3.
Montgomery *of Grey Abbey, Down*, I. iv. 186 ; 2, 3, 4.
Montgomery *of Benvarden, Antrim*, 3, 4.
Montgomery *of Belhavel, Leitrim*, 3, 4.
Montgomery *of Corvoy House, Donegal*, 2, 3, 4.
Montgomery *of Crilly House, Tyrone*, 4.
Montresor *of Denne Hill, Kent*, 3, 4.
Moneypenny *of Pitmilly, Fife*, 2, 3, 4.
Monypenny, Gybbon- *of Maytham Hall, Kent*, 2, 3, 4.
Moody *of Aspley Guise, Bedford*, I. ii. 560 ; 2, 3, 4.
Moody *of Kingsdon, Somerset*, 3, 4.
Moore *of Appleby Parva, Leicester*, I. i. 169 ; 2, 3, 4.
Moore *of Stockwell, Surrey*, 2, 3, 4.
Moore *of Tara House, Meath*, I. ii. 144.

Moore *of Frampton Hall, Lincoln*, 3, 4.
Moore *of Maulden, Bedford*, 4.
Moore *of Grimeshill, Westmoreland*, I. iv. 477 ; 2, 3, 4.
Moore *of Ballyhale, Kilkenny*, I. ii. 508 ; 2, 3, 4.
Moore *of Corswall, Wigton*, I. iii. 102 ; 2, 3, 4.
Moore *of Barn, Tipperary*, 2, and supp., 3, 4.
Moore, Montgomery- *of Garvey, Tyrone*, 4.
Moore *of Moore Hall, Mayo*, 2, 3, 4.
Moore *of Mooresfort, Tipperary*, 3, 4.
Moore *of Moore Fort, Antrim*, 4.
Morant *of Brokenhurst, Hants*, 4.
Morant *of Shirley House, Monaghan*, 4.
Moray *of Abercairny, Perth*, I. i. 619 ; 2, 4.
More *of Linley, Salop*, I. iii. 427 ; 2, 3, 4.
More *of Burnborough, York*, I. iii. 449.
Moreton *of Little Moreton, Chester*, I. i. 345 ; 2.
Morewood *of Alfreton, Derby*, 2, 3, 4.
Morgan *of Golden Grove, Flint*, I. ii. 163 ; 2, 3, 4.
Morgan *of Briddlesdon Park, Bucks*, 2, 3, 4.
Morgan, Grogan- *of Johnstown Castle, Wexford*, 3, 4.
Morice *of Springfield, Clare*, 3, 4.
Morland *of the Court Lodge, Lamberhurst, Kent*, 3, 4.
Morley *of Marrick Park, York*, 2 add., 3, 4.
Morony *of Milltown House, Clare*, 4.
Morrall *of Plas Yolyn, Salop*, I. ii. 595 ; 2 supp., 3, 4.
Morrell *of Headington Hill, Oxford*, 4.
Morrice *of Betshanger, Kent*, I. iii. 232 ; 2.
Morris *of the Hurst, Salop*, 2, 3, 4.
Morris *of York*, I. iv. 488 ; 2, 3, 4.
Morris, O'Connor- *of Gartnamona, King's Co.* 4.
Morris *of Dunkathel, Cork*, 4.
Morris *of Fishleigh, Devon*, 3.

Morrison of Coolegegan, King's Co. 4.

Morrogh of Old Court, Cork, 4.

Morritt of Rokeby, York, 3 supp., 4.

Morshead of Widey Court, Devon, 3 supp., 4.

Mortlock of Abingdon Hall, Cambridge, 2.

Morton of Kilmacrott House, Cavan, 2.

Moseley of Owsden, Suffolk, I, iv. 594; 2.

Moseley of Buildwas, Salop, I. i. 321; 2, 3, 4.

Moseley of Burnaston House, Derby, I. iii. 579; 2, 3, 4.

Moss, Edwards- of Roby Hall, Lancaster, 4.

Mosse of Knockfinne, Queen's Co. 2 and add.

Mostyn of Llewesog, Denbigh, 2 supp., 3, 4.

Mostyn of Kiddington, Oxford, I. iii. 381.

Mott of Barningham Hall, Norfolk, 2, 3, 4.

Moubray of Cockairny, Fife, I. i. 125; 2, 3, 4.

Moultrie of Aston Hall, Salop, 2 supp., 3, 4.

Maunsey of Castletown, Cumberland, 2 supp., 3, 4.

Mountain of the Heath, Herts, 2, 3, 4.

Moutray of Favour Royal, Tyrone, 2, 3, 4.

Mowbray of Mortimer, Berks, 3, 4.

Moysey of Bathealton Court, Somerset, 2, 3, 4.

Muckleston of Merrington, Salop, I. ii. 168.

Mudge of Sydney, Devon, 3, 4.

Mudie of Pitmuies, Forfar, 2, 3, 4.

Muirhead of Bredisholm, Lanark, 4.

Mulcaster of Cumberland, 3, 4.

Mules of Devon and Somerset, 2 supp.

Mulholland of Springvale, Down, 3, 4.

Mulholland of Eglantine, Down, 4.

Mullins of Ballyeigan, King's Co. 4.

Mulloy (O'Mulloy), I. iv. 146; 2, 3, 4.

Mulloy of Oak Park, Roscommon, 2.

Mundy of Burton, Leicester, I. i. 602.

Mundy of Markeaton, Derby, I. i. 25; 2, 3, 4.

Mundy of Shipley Hall, Derby, 2, 3, 4.

Munro of Teaninich, Ross, 2, 3, 4.

Munro of Novar, Ross, 2, 3, 4.

Murdoch, Burn- of Gartincaber, Perth, 2 supp., 3, 4.

Mure of Caldwell, Ayr, I. i. 453; 2, 3, 4.

Mure of Herringswell House, Suffolk, supp., 2, 3, 4,

Murphy of Kilbrew, Meath, 3, 4.

Murray of Philiphaugh, Selkirk, I. iii. 56; 2, 4.

Murray of Danesfield, Bucks, 2, 3, 4

Murray of Cringletie, Peebles, 3, 4.

Murray of Caw House, Londonderry, 3, 4.

Murray of Polmaise, Stirling, I. iii. 67; 2, 3, 4.

Murray of Murraythwaite, Dumfries, 2 supp., 3, 4.

Murray-Graham of Murrayshall, Perth, 2 supp., 3, 4.

Murray of Lintrose, Perth, 2, 3, 4.

Murray of Broughton, Wigton, 2, 3, 4.

Murray of Eriswell Lodge, Suffolk, 2, 3, 4.

Murray of Newbliss House, Monaghan, 3, 4.

Muskett of Clippesby House, Norfolk, I. ii. 102; 2, 3, 4.

Mussenden of Larchfield, Down, 2, 3, 4.

Musters of Colwick, Notts, 2, 3, 4.

Myddleton of Gwaynynog, Denbigh, 2, 3, 4.

Myddleton of Old Park; see Wharton Myddleton.

Mylne of Mylnefield, Perth, 3, 4.

Mynors of Treago, Hereford, I. i. 86; 2, 3, 4.

Mynors of Weatheroak, Worcester, 2, 3, 4.

Mytton of Shipton, Salop, I. iii. 671; 2, 3, 4.

Mytton of Halston, Salop, I. ii. 517; 2.

Mytton *of Cleobury North, Salop*, 2, 3, 4.

Mytton *of Garth, Montgomery*, I. ii. 523 ; 2, 3, 4.

Nagle *of Calverleigh Court, Devon*, 2, 3, 4.

Nagle *of Clogher House, Cork*, 2, 3, 4.

Naish *of Ballycullen, Limerick*, 2, 3, 4,

Nangle *of Kildalkey, Meath*, 1.

Nanney *of Maes-y-Neuadd, Merioneth*, I. ii. 180 ; 2, 3, 4.

Nanney *of Cefndeuddur, Caernarvon*, 2, 3, 4.

Naper *of Loughcrew, Meath*, I. ii. 639 ; 2, 3. 4.

Naper *of Pennard House, Somerset*, 2, 3, 4.

Nash *of Worcestershire*, 2 supp., 3, 4.

Naylor *of Leighton Hall, Montgomery*, 4.

Naylor *of Hooton Hall, Chester*, 4.

Neale *of Allesley Park, Warwick*, 2, 3, 4.

Nedham *of Jamaica*, 2 supp.

Need *of Sherwood Lodge;* see Welfitt, 2 supp., 3, 4.

Needham *of Lenton, Notts*, 2, 3, 4.

Noill *of Barnwell, Ayr*, 2, 3, 4.

Nelson *of Chaddleworth, Berks*, I. i. 365 ; 2.

Nesbitt *of Lismore House, Cavan*, 2 supp., 3, 4.

Nethercote *of Moulton Grange, Northampton*, I. ii. 93 ; 2, 3, 4.

Nettles *of Netterville, Cork*, 2, 3, 4.

Nevile *of Thorney, Notts*, I. ii. 8 ; 2, 3, 4.

Nevile *of Walcot, Northampton*, 3, 4.

Nevile *of Stubton, Notts*, 4.

Nevile *of Shelbrook Park, York*, 3 supp., 4.

Nevill *of Nevill Holt, Leicester*, 3 supp., 4.

Nevill *of Lanlliedi, Caermathen*, 2 supp.

Neville *of Borrismore House, Kilkenny*, 2, 3, 4.

Neville *of Haselour, Stafford*, 2 supp.

Neville *of Belmont Lodge, Dublin*, 2 supp.

Newcome *of Shenley, Herts*, 2, 3, 4.

Newdegate *of Harefield, Warwick*, I. ii. 697 ; 2, 3, 4.

Newdegate *of Kirk Hallam, Stafford*, 4.

Newenham *of Coolmore, Cork*, 3 supp., 4.

Newman *of Thornbury Park, Gloucester*, I. ii. 111; 2, 3, 4.

Newman *of Brands House, Bucks*, 2 supp., 3, 4.

Newman *of Barwick Court, Somerset*, 2.

Newman *of Dromore, Cork*, 3, 4.

Newport- Charlett *of Hanley Court, Worcester*, I. iv. 355.

Newton *of Newton Hall, Haddington*, I. iii. 26; 3, 4.

Newton *of Cheadle Heath, Chester*, 2, 3.

Newton *of Mickleover, Derby*, 2, 3, 4.

Newton *of Barton Grange, Somerset*, 4.

Newton *of Croxton Park, Cambridge*, 4.

Newton *of Carrickfergus, Tyrone*, 4.

Newton *of Hillmount, Londonderry*, 4.

Newton *of Dunleckney, Carlow*, 3, 4.

Niblett *of Haresfield Court, Gloucester*, 2, 3, 4.

Nicolas *of East Looe, Cornwall*, I. iv. 138; 2.

Nicolas *of London*, I. iv. 292 ; 2.

Nicholas *of Ashton Keynes, Wilts*, 3, 4.

Nicholl *of Dimlands, Glamorgan*, I. iv. 478.

Nicholl *of Tredunnock, Monmouth*, I. iv. 649 ; 2, 3.

Nicholl *of Penlline, Glamorgan*, 2.

Nicholl *of the Ham, Glamorgan*, 2, 3, 4.

Nicholl *of Merthyr Mawr, Glamorgan*, I. ii. 143 ; 2, 3, 4.

Nicholls *of Culverlands, Berks*, 2.

Nicholson *of Kinnegoe, Donegal*, 2 supp.

Nicholson *of Waverley Abbey, Surrey*, 3, 4.

Nicholson *of Roundhay Park, York*, I. iv. 615; 2, 3, 4.

Nicholson *of Balrath, Meath*, 3, 4.

Nicholson *of Thelwell, Chester*, 2.

Nicholson of EastCourt,Gloucester,2.
Nicholson of Ballow, Down, I. iii. 357 ; 2, 3, 4.
Nicholson of Roe Park, London-derry, 3, 4.
Nightingale of Embley; see Shore, 3, 4.
Nisbett of Derricairne, Leitrim, 2.
Nisbett of Cairnhill, Lanark, 2, 3, 4.
Nisbet-Hamilton, Christopher- of Dirleton, Haddington, 3, 4.
Nisbet of Southbroome House, Wilts, 2 add., 3, 4.
Nisbett of Woodhill, Donegal, 2.
Niven of Maybole, Ayr, 2.
Nixon of Fermanagh and Cavan, 4.
Nixon of Nixon Lodge, Cavan, 2.
Noel of Moxhull Park, Warwick, 2, 3, 4.
Noel of Bell Hall, Worcester, 2, 3, 4.
Norbury of Sherridge, Worcester, 2, 3, 4.
Norcliffe of Langton, York, I. ii. 630; 2 supp., 3, 4.
Norcop, Radford- of Betton Hall, Salop, 2, 3, 4.
Norman of Somersetshire, 2 supp., 3, 4.
Norman of Dencombe, Sussex, 2, 3, 4.
Norman, Lee- of Corballis, Louth, 2 supp., 3, 4.
Norman of Glengollan, Donegal, 4.
Norreys of Davyhulme Hall, Lan-caster, I. i. 310; 2, 3, 4.
Norris of Hackney, Middlesex, 2 supp., 3, 4.
North of Rougham, Norfolk, 3, 4.
North of Newton and Thurland Castle, Lancaster, 4.
Northcote of Somerset Court, Somer-set, 2, 3, 4.
Northey of Woodcote, Surrey, 2, 3, 4.
Northey- Hopkins of Oving House, Bucks, I. iv. 119 ; 2, 3.
Northmore of Cleve, Devon, 3 supp., 4.
Norwood of Kent, 4.
Notley of Combe Sydenham Hall, Somerset, 2, 3, 4.
Nourse of Weston under Penyard, 2.
Nowell of Read, now of Netherside, York, 2, 3, 4.
Noyes of East Mascalls, Sussex, 2, 3, 4.

Nugent of Clonlost, Westmeath, 3, 4.
Nugent of Portaferry, Down, 2, 3, 4.
Nugent of Bobsgrove, Cavan, 2, 3, 4.
Nunn of St. Margaret's, Wexford, 2 supp., 3, 4.
Nunn of Silverspring, Wexford, 2 supp., 3, 4.
Nuttall of Kempsey House, Worces-ter, I. iv. 487 ; 2, 3.
Oakden of Ladham House, Kent, 4.
Oakeley of Plan Tan y bwlch, Merioneth, I. i. 251.
Oakeley of Oakeley, Salop, I. i. 250 ; 2, 3, 4.
Oaks of Nowton Court, Suffolk, 2, 3, 4.
O'Brien of Ballynalacken, Clare, 4.
O'Brien of Blatherwyche ;, see Staf-ford.
O'Callaghan of Mayfort, Clare, 3.
O'Callaghan of Cadogan, Cork, 4.
O'Connell of Darrinane Abbey,Kerry, I. ii. 565 ; 2, 3, 4.
O'Conor Don, Roscommon, 2, 3, 4.
O'Conor of Mount Druid, Roscom-mon, 3, 4.
O'Connor of Dundermott, Roscom-mon, 3, 4.
O'Connor of Milton, Roscommon, 3, 4.
Odell of Carriglea, Waterford, 2, 3, 4.
O'Donel of Ross, Mayo, 2.
O'Donoghue of the Glens, Tipperary, 2, 3, 4.
O'Donovan of Clan Cathal, Cork, I. iii. 397 ; 2, 3, 4.
O'Farrell of Dalyston, Galloway, 3, 4.
O'Ferrall of Balyna, Kildare, 2, 3, 4.
O'Fflarhertie of Lemonfield, Galway, 2, 3, 4.
O'Fflarhertie, 2 add.
Ogilby of Ardnargle, Londonderry, 3, 4.
Ogilby of Altnachree Castle, Ty-rone, 4.
Ogilby of Inshewan, Forfar, 2, 3, 4.
Ogle of Eglingham, Northumberland, 2, 3, 4.
Ogle of Kirkley Hall, Northumber-land, 2, 3, 4.
O'Grady of the Grange, Antrim, 4.
O'Grady of Kilballyowen, Limerick, I. ii. 603 ; 2, 3, 4.

O'Hara *of Crebilly, Antrim*, 3 supp.,4.
O'Hara *of O'Hara Brook, Antrim*, 2, 3, 4.
O'Hara *of Annaghmore, Sligo*, 4.
Okeden *of Turnworth, Dorset*, 4.
O'Kelley *of Screen, Roscommon*, 2, 3, 4.
O'Kelley *of Gallagh, Galway*, 2, 3, 4.
O'Kelley *of Barrettstown, Kildare*, 3, 4.
O'Kelly *of Ballysax, Kildare*, 2.
O'Kelly, De Penthony-, 2.
Okeover *of Okeover, Stafford*, 2, 3, 4.
Oldfield *of Oldfield, Chester*, 2, 3, 4.
Oldfield *of Oldfield Lawn, Sussex*, 3, 4.
O'Leary, McCarthy- *of Coomlagane, Cork*, 4.
Oliphant *of Condie, Perth*, I. i. 493 ; 2, 3, 4.
Oliphant *of Broadfield House, Cumberland*, 3, 4.
Oliphant *of Gask, Perth*, I. iv. 258; 2.
Olive *of the Ton, Monmouth*, 3 supp., 4.
Oliver *of Cherrymount, Wicklow*, 2 supp., 3, 4.
Olivier *of Potterne, Wilts*, 2, 3, 4.
O'Loghlen *of Port, Clare*, 2.
Olphert *of Ballyconnell House, Donegal*, 2, 3, 4.
O'Malley *of Newcastle, Mayo*, 4.
O'Malley *of the Lodge, Mayo*, 2, 4.
O'Malley *of Spence Park, Mayo*, 2.
O'Neill *of Shanes Castle, Antrim*, 3, 4.
O'Neill *of Bunowen Castle, Galway*, I. iii. 534 ; 2.
Onley *of Stisted Hall, Essex*, 2, 3, 4.
Onslow *of Staughton House, Huntingdon*, 2 supp., 3, 4.
Onslow *of Stoke Park, Surrey*, 4.
Ord *of Fenham and Whitfield, Northumberland*, 2, 3, 4.
Ord *of Fornham, Suffolk*, 2 add., 3, 4.
Orde *of Nunnykirk, Northumberland*, I. i. 561 ; 2, 3, 4.
Orde *of Weetwood Hall, Northumberland*, 2, 3, 4.
Orlebar *of Hinwick House, Bedford*, I. i. 246 ; 2, 3, 4.
O'Reilly *of Rahattan, Wicklow*, 2.
O'Reilly *of Annagh Abbey, Cavan*, 2.

O'Reilly *of East Brefny, Queen's Co.*, 2, 3, 4.
O'Reilly *of Knock Abbey Castle, Louth*, 2, 3, 4.
O'Reilly *of Baltrasna, Meath*, 2,3,4.
O'Reilly or Reilly *of Scarvagh, Down*, 2, 3, 4.
O'Reilly *of Scarborough, York*, 3 supp., 4.
O'Reilly *of Rathaldron Castle, Meath*, 4.
Orme *of Abbeytown, Mayo*, 2 supp., 3, 4.
Orme *of Glenmore, Mayo*, 2 supp., 3, 4.
Orme *of Owenmore, Mayo*, 2, 3, 4.
Ormerod *of Tyldesley, Lancaster, and of Sedbury, Gloucester*, I. i. 112 ; 2, 3, 4.
Ormsby *of Balbinamore, Mayo*, 2, 3, 4.
Ormsby *of Gortner Abbey, Mayo*, 4 supp.
Ormsby *of Willowbank, Salop*, I. iii. 288; 2.
O'Rorke *of Ballybollan, Antrim*, 4.
Orpen *of Kerry*, I. iv. 280 ; 2, 3, 4.
Orred *of Tranmore, Chester*, 3, 4.
Osborne *of Newtown Anner, Tipperary*, 2 supp., 3, 4.
O'Shee *of Gardenmorris, Waterford*, I. ii. 120 ; 2, 3, 4.
Oswald *of Auchincruive, Ayr*, 2, 3, 4.
Oswald *of Dunnikier, Fife*, 3, 4.
Ottley *of the West Indies*, 2 add., 3, 4.
Otway *of Castle Otway, Tipperary*, 3, 4.
Owen *of Bettws Hall, Montgomery*, I. ii. 512 ; 2, 3, 4.
Owen *of Tedsmore, Salop*, I. ii. 509 ; 2, 3, 4.
Owen *of Condover, Salop*, I. ii. 515 ; 2, 3, 4.
Owen *of Woodhouse, Salop*, I. ii. 513 ; 2, 3, 4.
Owen *of Glynafon, Anglesey*, 2 add., 3, 4.
Owen *of Garthynghared, Merioneth*, 3, 4.
Owen *of Broadway Hall, Montgomery*, 2, 3, 4.
Owens *of Holestone, Antrim*, 2, 3, 4.

Owsley *of Skeffington, Leicester*, I. iii. 674.

Owen *of Glensevern, Montgomery*, I. iv. 380 ; 2.

Pack *of Avisford, Sussex*, 3, 4.

Pack-Beresford *of Finagh Lodge, Carlow*, 3, 4.

Packe *of Prestwold, Leicester*, I. i. 156 ; 2, 3, 4.

Paddon *of Thralesend, Bedford*, 3, 4.

Page *of Woodbridge, Suffolk*, 2.

Page *of Holebrook, Somerset*, 2 supp., 3, 4.

Paget *of Cranmore Hall, Somerset*, I. iii. 423 ; 2, 3, 4.

Paget *of Chipping Norton, Worcester*, 3, 4.

Paget *of Ruddington Grange, Nottingham*, 2, 3, 4.

Paget *of Ibstock, Leicester*, 4.

Paget *of Thorpe Satchville, Leicester*, 4.

Pakington *of Westwood House, Worcester*, 2.

Paley *of Langcliffe, York*, 3, 4.

Palles *of Mount Palles, Cavan*, 4 supp.

Palliser *of Derryluskan, Waterford*, 2, 3, 4.

Palmer *of Woodcourt, Somerset*, 2.

Palmer *of Kilmare, Dublin*, 2.

Palmer *of Boyne House, Kent*, 2.

Palmer *of Holme Park, Berks*, I. i. 68 ; 2, 3, 4.

Palmer *of Nazing, Essex*, 2, 3, 4.

Palmer *of Summer Hill, Mayo*, 2, 3, 4.

Palmer *of Clifton Lodge, Bedford*, 2, 3, 4.

Palmes *of Naburn, York*, I. i. 611 ; 2, 3, 4.

Papillon *of Crowhurst Park, Sussex*, I. i. 222 ; 2, 3, 4.

Pardoe *of Nash Court, Salop*, 2, 3, 4.

Pares *of Hopnell, Derby*, I. iii. 605 ; 2, 3, 4.

Parke *of Dunally, Sligo*, 2, 3, 4.

Parker *of Petteril Green, Cumberland*, I. ii. 662 ; 2, 3.

Parker *of Park Hall, Stafford*, 2.

Parker *of Inchigagin, Cork*, 2.

Parker *of Cuerden, Lancaster*, I. i. 110 ; 2, 3, 4.

Parker *of Brownsholme, York*, I. iii. 684 ; 2, 3, 4.

Parker *of Whiteway, Devon*, I. ii. 455 ; 2, 3, 4.

Parker *of Woodthorpe, York*, I. iii. 672 ; 2, 3, 4.

Parker *of Hareden, York*, 2, 3, 4.

Parker *of Hanthorpe House, Lincoln*, 4.

Parker *of Clopton Hall, Suffolk*, 4.

Parkhouse *of Eastfield Lodge, Hants*, 2, 3, 4.

Parby *of Manadon, Devon*, 4.

Parnell *of Avondale, Wicklow*, 3, 4.

Parr *of Liverpool*, 2.

Parr *of Parr, Lancaster*, 2, 3, 4.

Parr *of Ashchurch, Gloucester*, 3, 4.

Parr *of Grappenhall Heyes, Chester*, 2, 3, 4.

Parr *of Stonelands, Devon*, 2, 3, 4.

Parry, Jones- *of Madryn, Caernarvon*, 2, 3, 4.

Parry, Jones- *of Llwyn Onn, Denbigh*, 2, 3, 4.

Parry *of Noyadd Trefawr, Cardigan*, 2, 3, 4.

Parry *of Highham Court, Gloucester*, 2 supp., 3, 4.

Parsons *of Barbadoes*, 2.

Partridge *of Hockham Hall, Norfolk*, I. iii. 332 ; 2, 3, 4.

Partridge *of Bishop's Wood, Gloucester*, 2, 3, 4.

Partridge *of Horsendon House, Bucks*, 4.

Passy *of Wilhampstead*, 2 add.

Paterson *of Castle Huntly, Perth*, 2 supp., 3, 4.

Paterson *of Carpow, Perth*, 3, 4.

Pateshall *of Allensmore, Hereford*, I. i. 146 ; 2, 3, 4.

Paton *of Grandholm, Aberdeen*, 2, 3, 4.

Patrick *of Trearne, Ayr*, I. ii. 470 ; 2, 3, 4.

Patrick *of Waterside and Ladyland, Ayr*, 3, 4.

Patrick *of Danminning, Antrim*, 4.

Patrickson *of Kirklinton Park, Cumberland*, 2, 3, 4.

Patten, Wilson- *of Bank Hall, Lancaster*, I. iii. 79 ; 2, 3, 4.

Pattenson *of Ibornden, Kent*, 2, 3, 4.

Paul *of High Grove, Gloucester,* 2, 3, 4.
Pauncefote *of Preston Court, Gloucester,* 4.
Pawson *of Shawdon, Northumberland,* I. ii. 172.
Paxton *of Watford Place, Wilts,* 2, 3, 4.
Payne *of Sulby Hall, Northampton,* 2, 3, 4.
Paynter *of Boskenna, Cornwall,* I. i. 38 ; 2, 3, 4.
Paynter *of Camborne House, Surrey,* 2 supp., 3, 4.
Peach, Keighly- *of Idlicote House, Warwick,* 4.
Peacock *of South Rauceby ;* see Wilson ; 2, 3, 4.
Peacocke *of Reeves Hall, Essex,* 3, 4.
Peake *of Lleweny, Denbigh,* 2, 3, 4.
Pearce *of Ffrywdgrech, Brecon,* 2 supp., 3, 4.
Peard *of Coole Abbey, Cork,* 3, 4.
Peareth *of Usworth, Durham,* 3, 4.
Pearsall *of Willesbridge, Gloucester,* 3, 4.
Pearse *of Harlington, Bedford,* 2, 3, 4.
Pearson *of Ravensborne, Kent,* I. i. 380 ; 2.
Pease *of Hesslewood, York,* 2 supp., 3, 4.
Peck *of Cornish Hall, Denbigh, and of Temple Combe, Somerset,* 3, 4.
Peckham *of Nyton, Sussex.* 2, 3, 4.
Pedder *of Ashton Park, Lancaster,* 2, 3, 4.
Pedler *of Hoo Mavey, Devon,* I. iv. 57 ; 2.
Peel *of Peele Fold, Lancaster,* 2, 3, 4.
Peel *of Bryn-y-Pys, Flint,* 3, 4.
Peel *of Accrington, Lancaster,* 2, 3, 4.
Peel *of Aylesmore House, Gloucester,* 2, 3, 4.
Peel *of Singleton Brook, Lancaster,* 3, 4.
Peel *of Stone Hall, Pembroke,* 3, 4.
Peirse *of Thimbleby, York,* 2, 4.
Peers *of Chislehampton Lodge, Oxford,* 2.
Peirse *of Bedale, York,* 2, 3, 4.

Pelham *of Cound, Salop,* 3, 4.
Pemberton *of Barnes, Durham,* I. ii. 70.
Pemberton-Leigh *of Hindley Hall, Lancaster,* 2, 3.
Pemberton, Childe- *of Millichope, Salop,* 3, 4.
Pemberton *of Bainbridge Holme, Durham,* I. ii. 684 ; 2, 3, 4.
Pendarves *of Pendarves, Cornwall,* I. iii. 363 ; 2, 3, 4.
Penn *of Stoke Park, Bucks,* I. iii. 491 ; 2, 3, 4.
Pennant *of Downing and Bychton, Flint,* I. iii. 30 ; 2.
Pennant *of Penrhyn, Caernavon,* 2, 3, 4.
Pennant *of Bodfari, Flint,* 4.
Pennefather *of New Park, Tipperary,* I. ii. 55 ; 2, 3, 4.
Pennefather *of Ballylanigan, Tipperary,* 3, 4.
Pennyman *of Ormesby Hall, York,* 3, 4.
Penrice *of Yarmouth, Norfolk,* I. i. 362 ; 2, 3, 4.
Penrice *of Kilvrough, Glamorgan,* 3, 4.
Penrose *of Shandangan, Cork,* 2, 3, 4.
Penruddocke *of Compton Chamberlayne, Wilts,* 2, 3, 4.
Pentland *of Black Hall, Louth,* 2.
Peploe *of Garnstone, Hereford,* I. iv. 27 ; 2, 3, 4.
Peppard *of Cappagh House, Limerick,* 2, 3, 4.
Pepper *of Ballygarth, Meath,* 3, 4.
Pepper *of Lisanisky, Tipperary,* 3, 4.
Perceval *of Temple House, Sligo,* 2, 3, 4.
Percival *of Barntown, Wexford,* I. iv. 609.
Percival-Maxwell *of Finnebrogue, Down,* 2.
Percy *of Guy's Cliffe, Warwick,* 2, 3, 4.
Perkins *of Orton House, Leicester,* 2, 3, 4.
Perkins *of Sutton Coldfield, Warwick,* 3, 4.
Perrier *of Cork,* 3, 4.
Perry *of Moor Hall ;* see Watlington, 2, 3, 4.

Perry *of Bitham House, Warwick*, 4.
Perry *of Woodroof, Tipperary*, 2 supp., 3, 4.
Pershouse *of Penn, Stafford*, I. iii. 607.
Persse *of Roxborough, Galway*, 3, 4.
Peter *of Harlyn, Cornwall*, I. i. 29 ; 2, 3, 4.
Peters *of Platbridge, Lancaster*, 2 add., 3, 4.
Petre *of Colquite, Cornwall*, 2, 3, 4.
Pettiward *of Finborough Hall, Suffolk*, 4.
Peyton *of Wakehurst Place, Sussex*, 2.
Peyton *of Driney House, Leitrim*, 2, 3, 4.
Peyton *of Laheen, Leitrim*, 3, 4.
Phaire *of Killoughrum Forest, Wexford*, 2, 3.
Phelips *of Montacute, Somerset*, 2, 3, 4.
Phelips *of Briggins Park, Herts*, I. iii. 647 ; 2, 3, 4.
Philips *of Heybridge ;* see Philips *of the Heath House*, 3, 4.
Philips *of Snitterfield ;* see Philips *of the Heath House*, 3, 4.
Philips *of Bank Hall, Lancaster*, I. ii. 593 ; 2, 3, 4.
Philips *of the Heath House, Stafford*, I. ii. 591 ; 2, 3, 4.
Philipps *of Dale Castle, Pembroke*, I. iii. 511 ; 2, 3, 4.
Philipps *of Penty Park, Pembroke*, 4.
Philipps *of Aberglasney, Caermarthen*, 2, 3, 4.
Philipps *of Williamston ;* see Scurfield, 2, 3, 4.
Phillimore *of Shiplake House, Oxford*, 2 supp., 3, 4.
Phillipps *of Eaton Bishop, Hereford*, 2, 3, 4.
Phillipps de Lisle *of Garendon Park and Grace Dieu Manor, Leicester*, I. iv. 97 ; 2, 3, 4.
Phillipps *of Longworth, Hereford*, 2, 3, 4.
Phillipps *of Bryngwyn, Hereford*, I. iv. 164 ; 2, 3, 4.
Phillips *of Lawrenny Castle, Pembroke*, 2, 3, 4.

Phillips *of Witston House, Monmouth*, 2 supp., 3, 4.
Phillips *of Glenview, Cavan*, 4.
Philpotts *of Porthgwidden, Cornwall*, 4.
Phipps *of Leighton House, Wilts*, I. iv. 509 ; 2, 3, 4.
Phipps *of Dilton Court, Wilts*, 2, Pickard *of Sturminster Marshall ;* see *Cambridge*.
Pickering *of Old Lodge, Surrey*, I. ii. 191.
Pickersgill *of Netherne House, Surrey*, 4.
Pidcock *of the Platts, now of Guernsey*, 3, 4.
Pigott *of Edgmond, Salop*, I. iii. 191 ; 2, 3, 4.
Pigott *of Doddershall Park, Bucks*, I. iv, 646 ; 2, 3, 4.
Pigott *of Brockley Hall, Somerset*, 2, 3, 4.
Pigott *of Eagle Hill, Galway*, 3, 4.
Pigott *of Archer Lodge, Hants*, 2 supp., 3, 4.
Pigott *of Selvoy, Wexford*, 2 supp., 3, 4.
Pilkington *of Tore, Westmeath*, 2, 3, 4.
Pilkington *of Carrick, Queen's Co.*, 2 supp., 3, 4.
Pilkington *of Lark Lane Hall, York*, 3.
Pinfold *of Walton Hall, Bucks*, 3 supp., 4.
Pinney *of Somerton Erleigh, Somerset*, 2, 3, 4.
Piper *of Culliton, Devon*, I. iii. 310 ; 2.
Pitcairn *of Pitcairn, Perth*, 2.
Pitman *of Dunchideock House, Devon*, 2, 3, 4.
Pleydell *of Whatcombe, Dorset*, 2 add., 3, 4.
Plowden *of Plowden, Salop*, I. iii. 250 ; 2, 3, 4.
Plowden *of Ewhurst Park, Hants*, 4.
Plumer-Ward *of Gilston, Herts*, I. i. 71 ; 2.
Plummer *of Middlestead, Selkirk*, 2 supp., 3, 4.
Plumptre *of Fredville, Kent*, I. iii. 73 ; 2, 3, 4.

Pochin *of Barkby, Leicester*, I. i. 234; 2, 3, 4.

Pode *of Slade, Devon*, 2, 3, 4.

Poe *of Tipperary*, 4.

Poe *of Harley Park, Tipperary*, 2 supp., 3, 4.

Poer *of Belleville Park, Waterford*, 2, 3, 4.

Pole, Chandos- *of Radborne, Derby*, 2, 3, 4.

Pole *of Wyck Hill House, Gloucester*, 2 add.

Poley *of Boxted Hall, Suffolk*, 2, 3, 4.

Polhill *of Howbury, Bedford*, 2, 3, 4.

Pollard-Urquhart *of Castle Pollard, Westmeath*, 2, 3, 4.

Pollen *of Little Bookham, Surrey*, I. i. 575; 2, 3, 4.

Pollock *of Mountainstown, Meath*, 3, 4.

Polwhele *of Polwhele, Cornwall*, 2, 3, 4.

Ponsonby *of Hale, Cumberland*, I. i. 424; 2, 3, 4.

Poole *of Mayfield, Cork*, 2, 3, 4.

Popham *of Bagborough, Somerset*, 2, 3, 4.

Popham *of Littlecote, Wilts*, I. ii. 196; 2, 3, 4.

Popham *of Shanklin, Isle of Wight*, 4.

Popham *of Trevarno, Cornwall*, 2, 3, 4.

Porch *of Edgarley, Somerset*, I. ii. 694; 2, 3, 4.

Porcher *of Clyffe, Dorset*, 2, 3, 4.

Portal *of Laverstoke, Hants*, 2, 3, 4.

Porter *of Kilskery, Fermanagh*, 3, 4.

Porter *of Alfarthing, Surrey*, I. iii. 577.

Portman *of Bryanston, Dorset*, I. i. 62.

Postlethwaite *of the Oaks, Cumberland*, 4.

Pott *of Todrig, Selkirk*, 2, 3, 4.

Pott *of Bentham Hill, Kent*, 2, 4.

Pottinger *of Mount Pottinger, Kildare*, I. iv, 442.

Pounden *of Ballywalter House, Wexford*, 3, 4.

Powell *of Nant Eos, Cardigan*, I. i. 230; 2, 3, 4.

Powell *of Brandlesome Hall, Lancaster*, I. iii. 572; 2, 3, 4.

Powell *of Handcott House, Wilts*, I. i. 375; 2, 3, 4.

Powell *of Clonshavoy, Limerick*, 2 supp., 3, 4.

Powell *of Bellingham Lodge, Lancaster*, 3, 4.

Power *of Faithlegg, Waterford*, 4.

Power, now de la Poer, *of Gurteen, Waterford*, 4.

Power *of the Hill Court, Hereford*, I. i. 242; 2, 3, 4.

Pownall *of Pownall, Chester*, I. iv. 17; 2.

Powys *of Berwick, Salop*, 2, 3, 4.

Powys *of Westwood, Stafford*, 2, 3, 4.

Powys *of Hardwick, Oxford*, 2, 3, 4.

Poyntz *of Cowdray Park, Sussex*, I. iii. 537.

Pratt *of Ryston, Norfolk*, I. i. 231; 2, 3, 4.

Pratt *of Cabra Castle, Cavan*, I. iv. 502; 2, 3, 4.

Pratt *of Tuckbill, Stafford*, 2.

Preston *of Flasby Hall, York*, 2, 3, 4.

Preston *of Moreby, York*, 2, 3, 4.

Preston *of Westerby House, Lancaster*, I. i. 478.

Preston *of Bellinter, Meath*, 3, 4.

Preston *of Cockerham, Lancaster*, 2.

Price *of Castle Madoc, Brecknock*, I. iii. 176; 2, 3, 4.

Price *of Glangwilly, Caermarthen*, 2, 3, 4.

Price *of Saintfield, Down*, 2, 3, 4.

Price *of Norton, Radnor*, 2, 3, 4.

Price *of Plas Cadnant, Anglesey*, 2, 3, 4.

Price *of Birkenhead Priory, Chester*, 2, 3.

Prickett *of Bridlington, York*, 2, 3, 4.

Prickett *of Octon Lodge, York*, I. iii. 624.

Prideaux-Brune *of Prideaux Place, Cornwall*, 2, 3, 4.

Prideaux *of Lueson, now Luson, Devon*, I. iv. 534; 2, 3, 4.

Priestley *of White Windows, York*, 2, 3.

Priestley *of Boston, Tadcaster, York,* 2, 3.

Prime *of Walberton, Sussex,* 2, 8, 4.

Prime *of Cambridge,* I. iv. 705; 2.

Pringle *of Yair, Selkirk,* 2 supp., 3, 4.

Pringle *of Haining, Selkirk,* 2 supp., 3, 4.

Pringle *of Torwoodlee, Selkirk,* 2 supp., 3, 4.

Prior *of Rathdowney, Queen's Co.* 2, 3, 4.

Probyn *of Langhope, Gloucester,* 2, 3, 4.

Prodgers *of Monmouthshire,* 2, 3, 4.

Prothero *of Malpas Court, Monmouth,* 3, 4.

Prower *of Purton House, Wilts,* 4.

Prowett *of Oxfordshire,* 2.

Pryce *of Duffryn, Glamorgan,* 2, 3, 4.

Pryce *of Gunley, Montgomery,* I. ii. 654; 2, 3, 4.

Pryse *of Gogerddan, Cardigan,* I. iʳi. 466; 1, 3, 4.

Prytherch *of Alergole, Caermarthen,* 2 supp., 3, 4.

Pudsey *of Seisdon Hall, Stafford,* 2 supp., 3, 4.

Pugh *of Manoravon, Caermarthen,* 3, 4.

Pugh *of Llanerchydol, Montgomery,* 2, 3, 4.

Pulleine *of Crake Hall, York,* I. iv. 377; 2, 3, 4.

Puller *of Youngsbury, Herts,* 3, 4.

Purcell *of Kildare;* see Fitzgerald *of the Island,* 3 supp., 4.

Purcell *of Burton House, Cork,* 3, 4.

Purcell *of Cromlyn, Dublin,* 2.

Purcell *of Altamira, Cork,* 3, 4.

Purdon *of Tinerana, Clare,* 2, 3, 4.

Purdon *of Lisnabin, Westmeath,* 3, 4.

Purefoy *of Greenfield, Tipperary,* 3, 4.

Purnell *of Stancombe Park, Gloucester,* 2, 3, 4.

Purnell *of Kingshill, Gloucester,* 2, 3, 4.

Purton *of Faintree Hall, Salop,* 2, 3, 4.

Purvis *of Darsham, Suffolk,* I. iii. 329; 2, 3, 4.

Purvis *of Blackbrook, Hants,* 2.

Purvis *of Plawsworth, Durham,* 2.

Pusey *of Pusey, Berks,* 2, 3, 4.

Putland *of Brayhead, Wicklow,* 3, 4.

Puxley *of Dunboy Castle, Cork,* 3, 4.

Pye *of Farringdon, Stafford,* I. i. 350; 2, 3, 4.

Pye-Douglas *of Rosehill, Lanark,* I. iv. 704.

Pym *of the Hasels, Beds,* 2, 3, 4.

Pyne *of Curry Mallett, Somerset,* 2, 3, 4.

Pyrke *of Deane Hall, Gloucester,* 2, 3, 4.

Quartoch *of Norton House, Somerset,* 2, 3, 4.

Quayle *of Crogga, Isle of Man,* 2 supp., 3, 4.

Quicke *of Newton St. Cyres, Devon,* 2, 2, 4.

Rabett *of Bramfield Hall, Suffolk,* 2, 3, 4.

Radcliffe *of Hitchin Priory, Herts,* 2, 3, 4.

Radcliffe *of Warleigh, Devon,* I. ii. 27; 2, and supp, 3, 4.

Radclyffe *of Foxdenton, Lancaster,* I. iv. 399; 2, 3, 4.

Radford *of Smalley Hall, Derby,* 2 supp , 3, 4.

Radford *of Carnfield Hall, Derby,* 2.

Radford *of Tansley Wood, Derby,* 2.

Raffles *of Liverpool, Lancaster,* 2, 3, 4.

Raikes *of Welton, York,* I. iii. 461; 2, 3, 4.

Raines *of Wyton, York,* 2 supp., 3, 4.

Rait *of Anniston House, Forfar,* 2, 3, 4.

Ralston *of Ralston, Renfrew,* 2, 3.

Ram *of Ramsfort, Wexford,* 2, 3, 4.

Ramsay *of Barnton, Mid Lothian,* 2 supp., 3, 4.

Ramsay *of Whitehill, Edinburgh,* 3, 4.

Ramsay *of Barra, Aberdeen,* 4.

Ramsay *of Hill Lodge, Middlesex,* 2, 3. 4.

Ramsbotham *of Old Hall, Lancaster,* 2, 3, 4.

Ramsden *of Carlton Hall, Notts.* 2, 3, 4.

Rashleigh *of Menabilly, Cornwall,* I. i. 495; 2, 3, 4.

Rathbone *of Greenbank, Lancaster,* 2, 3, 4.

Rattray *of Craighall Rattray, Perth,* I. iii. 186; 2, 3, 4.

Rattray *of Barford House, Warwick,* 2, 3, 4.

Rawlings *of Padstow, Cornwall,* I. ii. 68; 2, 3, 4.

Rawlinson *of Graythwaite, Lancaster,* 2, 3, 4.

Rawlinson *of New Place, Hants,* 2.

Rawson *of Nidd Hall and Bradford, York,* I. ii. 47; 2, 3, 4.

Rawson *of Hope House, York,* 2.

Rawson *of Mill House, York,* 4.

Rawstorne *of Penwortham, Lancaster,* 2 and supp., 3, 4.

Raymond *of Symondsbury, Dorset,* 2, 3, 4.

Raymond *of Belchamp Hall, Essex,* 3, 4.

Raymond *of Kilmurry, Kerry,* 2 supp., 3, 4.

Read *of Hayton, York,* I. iv. 362; 3, 4.

Read, Crewke- *of Llanderiam Hall, Montgomery, and of Wern, Flint,* 2 supp., 3, 4.

Read *of Ipsden, Oxford,* 2, 3, 4.

Reade *of Rossenarra, Kilkenny,* 2, 3, 4.

Reade *of the Wood Parks, Galway,* 2, 3, 4.

Reavely *of Kinnersley Castle, Hereford,* 4.

Reay *of Gill House, Cumberland,* 2.

Rebow *of Wivenhoe Park, Essex,* 2, 3, 4.

Rede *of Ashmans, Suffolk,* 2, 3, 4,

Redington *of Kilcornan, Galway,* 2, 3, 4.

Redmond *of the Deeps, Wexford,* 3, 4.

Redmond *of Killougher, Wicklow,* 2,3.

Redmond *of Rockville, Wexford,* 2.

Redwood *of Boverton, Glamorgan,* 3.

Reed *of Crag, Northumberland,* 3, 4.

Reed *of Heathpool, Northumberland,* 3, 4.

Rees *of Killymaenllwyd, Caermarthen,* I. iii. 265; 2, 3, 4.

Reeve *of Leadenham House, Lincoln,* 2, 3, 4.

Reeves *of Burrane, Clare,* 2, 3, 4.

Reilly *of Scarvagh;* see O'Reilly, 2, 3, 4.

Remington *of the Crow Trees, Lancaster,* 3, 4.

Repington *of Armington, Warwick,* I. ii. 473.

Reveley *of Burn-y-Gwin, Merioneth,* I. iii. 123; 2, 3, 4.

Reynardson *of Holywell Hall, Lincoln,* 2 and supp., 3, 4.

Reynell *of Killynon, Westmeath,* 2, 3, 4.

Reynolds *of Norfolk, and Devon,* 3 supp., 4.

Rhodes *of Bellair and Shapwick,* 2, 3, 4.

Riall *of Old Conna Hill, Dublin,* 3, 4.

Ricardo *of Bromesberrow Place, Worcester,* 3, 4.

Ricardo *of Gatcombe, Gloucester,* I. i. 373; 2, 3, 4.

Rice *of Dane Court, Kent,* 2, 3, 4.

Rice *of Llwyn-y-Brain, Caermarthen,* 4.

Rice *of Loughor, Caermarthen,* 4.

Richards *of Solsborough, Wexford,* 4.

Richards *of Ardamine, Wexford,* 4.

Richards *of Macmine Castle, Wexford,* 4.

Richards *of Croft House, Pembroke,* 4.

Richards *of Caerynwch, Merioneth,* I. iii. 552; 2, 3, 4.

Richardson *of Aber Hirnant, Merioneth,* 2, 3, 4.

Richardson *of Poplar Vale, Monaghan,* 2 supp., 3, 4.

Richardson *of Field House, Whitby, York,* 2 supp., 3, 4.

Richardson *of Finden Place, Sussex,* I. iii. 111; 2, 3, 4.

Richardson *of Riccall Hall, York,* 2 supp., 3, 4.

Richardson *of Rich Hill, Armagh,* 4.

Richardson *of Rossfad, Fermanagh,* 4.

Richardson *of Lamleg, Antrim,* 4.

Richardson *of Waringstown, Down,* 4.

Rickaby *of Ulrome, York,* 2.

Ricketts *of Combe, Hereford,* I. i. 22; 2, 3, 4.

Rickford *of Aylesbury, Bucks,* 2.

Riddell *of Felton Park, Northumberland,* I. iii. 297; 2, 3, 4.

Riddell *of Cheeseburne Grange, Northumberland*, 2, 3, 4.
Riddell-Carre *of Cavers, Roxburgh*,4.
Ridley *of Parkend, Northumberland*, 2, 3, 4.
Rigge *of Wood Broughton, Lancaster*, I. ii. 303 ; 2, 3, 4.
Riley *of Forest Hill, Berks*, 4.
Rippon *of Waterville, Northumberland*, 2 supp., 3, 4.
Robartes *of Lantydroch, Cornwall*, I. ii. 316 ; 2, 3, 4.
Robbins *of Castle Malwood, Hants*,4.
Roberts *of Milford Haven, Pembroke*, 3, 4.
Roberts *of Coeddu, Flint*, 4.
Roberts *of Cork*, 4.
Roberts *of Ardmore, Cork*, 4.
Roberts *of Llwyndderw, Brecon*,2,3.
Roberts *of Bewdley, Worcester*, 2.
Robertson *of Chilcote, Derby*, 4.
Robertson *of Hazel Hill, Pembroke*,4.
Robertson *of Struan, Perth*, I. iv. 419 ; 2, 3, 4.
Robertson *of Prenderguest* ; see Glasgow, 3, 4.
Robertson *of Ladykirk, Berwick*, 2, 3, 4.
Robertson *of Auchleeks, Perth*, 2, 3, 4.
Robertson *of Inshes, Inverness*, 2, 3, 4.
Robertson *of Kindace, Ross*, I. ii. 76 ; 2, 3, 4.
Robertson- Walker *of Gilgarran, Cumberland*, 2, 3, 4.
Robertson *of Lude*, 2.
Robertson *of Kinlochmoidart, Inverness*, 2 add., 3, 4.
Robin *of Grove Hill, Chester*, 2.
Robinson *of Widmerpool, Nottingham*, 3, 4.
Robinson *of Silksworth, Durham*, 2 supp., 3, 4.
Robinson *of Knapton House, Norfolk*, 4.
Robinson *of Rosmead, Westmeath*, 2.
Robinson *of Sudley, Lancaster*, 2.
Robson *of Holtby, York*, 2 add., 3, 4.
Roch *of Woodbine Hill, Waterford*, 2 supp., 3, 4.
Roche *of Granagh Castle, Kilkenny*, 2, 3, 4.

Roche *of Carass, Limerick*, I. iv. 211.
Roche *of Butter Hill, Pembroke*, 2.
Roche *of Trabolgan, Cork*, 2.
Roche *of Aghado, Cork*, 2.
Rochfort *of Clogrenane, Carlow*, 2,4.
Rodd *of Trebartha, Cornwall*, I. i. 260; 2, 3, 4.
Roddam *of Roddam, Northumberland*, I. i. 675 ; 2, 3, 4.
Rodes *of Barlborough, Derby*, I. iii. 562; 2, 3, 4.
Rodger *of Hadlow Castle, Kent*, 4.
Rodon *of Vere, in the Island of Jamaica*, 3, 4.
Roe *of Gnaton Hall, Devon*, 3, 4.
Rogers *of Dowdeswell, Gloucester*, 2, 3, 4.
Rogers *of Rainscombe, Wilts*, 2, 3, 4.
Rogers *of Yarlington Lodge, Somerset*, I. iv. 625 ; 2, 3, 4.
Rogers *of Penrose, Cornwall*, I. i. 299 ; 2, 3, 4.
Rogers *of the Home, Salop*, 2, 3, 4.
Rogers *of Lota, Cork*, 2, 3, 4.
Rogers *of Stanage Park, Radnor*, 2.
Rokeby *of Arthingworth, Northampton*, I. iv. 666 ; 2, 3, 4.
Rolfe *of Heacham, Norfolk*, 2 supp., 3, 4.
Rolland *of Auchmithie, Forfar*, I. iii. 611, 2.
Rolleston *of Watnall, Notts*, 2, 3, 4.
Rolleston *of Franckfort Castle, King's County*, 2, 3, 4.
Rolls *of the Hendre, Monmouth*, 2, 3, 4.
Ronayne *of D'Laughtane, Waterford*, 2.
Rooke *of Ilford Manor, Wilts*, 4.
Rookes *of Roydes Hall*, 2.
Rooper *of Abbott's Ripton, Huntingdon*, 3, 4.
Roper *of Plas Teg, Flint*, 2, 3, 4.
Rose *of Kilrovock, Nairn*, 2, 3, 4.
Rose *of Cransley Hall, Northampton*, 4.
Rose *of Leiston Old Abbey, Suffolk*, 4.
Rose *of the Ferns, Suffolk*, 4.
Rose *of Holme, Inverness*, 2, 3, 4.
Rose *of Wolston Heath, Northampton*, 2, 3, 4.

Rose *of Ahabeg, Limerick, and Fox-hall, Tipperary*, 4.
Rose *of Glastullick (Rosshire)*, 4.
Rose *of Sandhills, Hants*, 2.
Roskell *of Lancashire*, 2.
Ross *of Cromarty*, 4.
Ross *of Rosstrevor, Down*, 2, 3, 4.
Ross- Lewin *of Ross Hill, Clare*, 2, 3, 4.
Ross *of Dalton, Dumfries*, 2 supp., 3, 4,
Ross *of Craigie and Innernethie, Perth*, I. iii. 644 ; 2.
Ross *of Rossie Castle, Forfar*, 2.
Rotch *of Lowlands, Middlesex*, 2.
Rotherham *of Crossdrum, Meath*, 4.
Rotheram *of Triermore, Meath*, 2, 3.
Rothery *of Littlethorpe, York*, 3, 4.
Rothwell *of Rockfield, Meath*, 2, 3, 4.
Rothwell *of Shantonagh ;* see Roth-well *of Rockfield*, 3, 4.
Roughsedge *of Foxghyll, Westmore-land*, 2, 3, 4.
Round *of Birch Hall, Essex*, 2, 3, 4.
Round *of Danbury Park, Essex*, 2, 3, 4.
Roundell *of Gledstone, York*, I. i. 342 ; 2, 3, 4.
Roupell *of Charlton, Kent*, 2, 3, 4.
Rous *of Courtyrala, Glamorgan*, I. i. 111 ; 2, 3, 4.
Rowan *of Mount Davys, Antrim*, 2, 3, 4.
Rowan *of Mount Davys, Antrim*, 2, Rowan, Hamilton- *of Killyleagh, Down*, 2.
Rowe *of Ballycross, Wexford*, 2, 3, 4.
Rowley *of Maperath, Meath*, 3, 4.
Rowley *of Mount Campbell, Leitrim*, 2.
Roxby *of Blackwood, York*, 3, 4.
Roy *of Nenthorn, Roxburgh*, 2, 3, 4.
Royse *of Nantenan House, Lime-rick*, 2.
Ruck- Keene *of Swyncombe House, Oxford*, 2, 3, 4.
Rudge *of Evesham, Worcester*, I. iv. 197 ; 2, 3, 4.
Rudston-Read *of Hayton, York*, 2.
Ruggles-Brise *of Spains Hall, Essex*, 2, 3, 4.
Rush *of Farthinghoe Lodge, North-ampton*, 2, 3, 4.

Rush *of Elsenham Hall, Essex*, I. ii. 61.
Rushbrooke *of Rushbrooke, Suffolk*, 2, 3, 4.
Russell *of Killough, Down*, 4.
Russell *of Stone and Comberton, Worcester*, 4.
Russell *of Aden, Aberdeen*, 2, 3, 4.
Russell *of Ashiesteel, Selkirk*, 2, 3, 4.
Russell *of Ilam Hall, Stafford*, 2, 4.
Russell *of Brancepeth, Durham*, I. i. 104 ; 2.
Russell *of King's Heath, Worcester*, 2.
Russell *of Ashford Hall, Salop*, 2.
Rust *of Alconbury House, Hunting-don*, 3, 4.
Rutherford *of Fairnington, Rox-burgh*, 4.
Rutherfurd *of that Ilk and Edger-ston, Roxburgh*, 2, 3, 4.
Rutson *of Newby Wiske, York*, 2 add., 3, 4.
Ruttledge *of Bloomfield, Mayo*, 2, 3, 4.
Ruxton *of Ardee House, Louth*, 2, 3, 4.
Ruxton *of Broad Oak, Kent*, 3, 4.
Ruxton-Fitzherbert *of Black Castle, Meath*, I. iv. 566 ; 2.
Ryan *of Inch House, Tipperary*, 2, 3, 4.
Ryan *of Ballymackeogh, Tipperary*, 4.
Ryan *of Knocklyon, Dublin*, 4.
Ryder *of Riverstown House, Kildare*, 2.
Rye *of Ryecourt, Cork*, 4.
Ryland *of Bearley and Sherborne, Warwick*. I. iv. 406.
Rynd *of Derryvolan, Fermanagh*, 4.
Rythre De *of Riverstown House, Kildare*, 3, 4.
Ryves *of Shroton House, Dorset*, 2, 3, 4.
Sadler *of Keynsham Bury, Glou-cester*, 2, 3, 4.
Sadleir *of Ballinderry, Tipperary*, 2, 3, 4.
Sadleir *of Sadlier's Wells, Tipperary*, 2.
St. Albyn *of Alfoxton, Somerset*, I. iv. 165 ; 2, 3, 4.
St. Aubyn *of Clowance, Cornwall*, 4.
St. Aubyn *of Pendrea, Cornwall*, 4.

St. Barbe *of Lymington, Hants*, I. ii. 447; 2, 3.

St. Clair *of Roslin, Edinburgh*, 3 supp., 4.

St. Clair *of Staverton Court, Gloucester*, 2, 3, 4.

St. George *of Tyrone*, 2, 3, 4.

St. George *of Headford Castle, Galway*, 2, 3, 4.

St. George *of Wood Park, Armagh*, 2, 3, 4.

St. George *of Hatley Manor, Leitrim*, 3, 4.

St. Leger *of Hayward's Hill, Cork*, I. iv. 485; 2.

St. Quintin *of Scampston Hall, York*, 4.

Salmond *of Waterfoot, Cumberland*, 2, 3, 4.

Salomons *of Burrswood and Broomhill, Kent*, 2, 3, 4.

Saltmarshe *of Saltmarshe, York*, 2, 3, 4.

Salusbury *of Byrnbella, Flint*, 2, 3, 4.

Salvin *of Croxdale, Durham*, I. i. 532; 2, 3, 4.

Salvin *of Sutton Place, Surrey*, 4.

Salvin *of Sutherland Bridge, Durham*, I. i. 537.

Salway *of Moor Park, Salop*, I. i. 152; 2, 3, 4.

Salway *of the Lodge, Salop*, I. i. 155.

Sampson *of Henbury, Gloucester*, I. iv. 188; 2, 3, 4.

Sandbach *of Hafodunos, Denbigh*, I. iv. 16; 2, 3, 4.

Sandars *of Chesterford, Essex*, 4.

Sanders *of Deer Park, Cork*, 2, 3, 4.

Sanderson *of West Tesmond, Northumberland*, 2, 3, 4.

Sandes *of Carrigafoyle, Kerry*, 2, 3, 4.

Sandes *of Sallow Gleen, Kerry*, 3, 4.

Sandes *of Greenville, Kerry*, 2, 3, 4.

Sandes *of Dunowen House, Cork*, 2.

Sandford *of Sandford, Salop*, I. ii. 665; 2, 3, 4.

Sandford *of the Isle of Rossall, Salop*, I. ii. 670; 2, 3, 4.

Sandford *of Castlerea;* see Wills-Sandford.

Sands *of Elmswood, Lancaster*, 2.

Sandys-Lumsdaine *of Lumsdaine, Berwick*, 2, and add., 3, 4.

Sandys *of Graythwaite, Lancaster*, I. i. 308; 2, 3, 4.

Sandys *of St. Nimver, Cornwall*, I. i. 658; 2.

Sandys *of St. Minver, Cornwall*, 3.

Sanford *of Nynehead Court, Somerset*, 2, 3, 4.

Sankey *of Coolmore, Tipperary*, 2, 3, 4.

Sankey *of Lurganbrae, Fermanagh*, 4.

Sargent *of Wool Lavington, Sussex*, I. iv. 723.

Sarsfield *of Doughcloyne, Cork*, 2, 3, 4.

Saunders *of Wennington Hall, Lancaster*, 2 supp., 3, 4.

Saunders *of Saunders Grove, Wicklow*, I. iv. 375; 2, 3, 4.

Saunders *of Largay, Cavan*, 2, 3, 4.

Saunderson *of Castle Saunderson, Cavan*, 2, and supp., 3, 4.

Salvage *of St. Leonards, Kent*, 2, 3, 4.

Savage *of Ballymadun, Dublin*, 2, 3, 4.

Savery *of Venn, Devon*, 2, 3, 4.

Savery *of Fowelscombe, Devon*, 2, 3, 4.

Saville *of Oaklands, Devon*, 2, 3, 4.

Sawbridge *of East Haddon, Northampton*, 2, 3, 4.

Sawbridge *of Olantigh, Kent*, 2.

Sawrey *of Broughton Tower, Lancaster*, 2, 3, 4.

Sawyor *of Heywood, Berks*, 2, 3, 4.

Say *of Tilney, Norfolk*, 2 supp., 4.

Sayer *of Pett, Kent*, I. iii. 504; 2, 3, 4.

Scarisbrick *of Scarisbrick, Lancaster*, 2 supp., 3, 4.

Scarlett *of Copped Hall, Herts*, 4.

Schank *of Barton House, Devon*, 3, 4.

Schonswar *of Ellerker, York*, 2.

Schreiber *of Henhurst, Kent*, 2, 3, 4.

Schreiber *of the Hill House, Suffolk*, 4.

Sclater *of Hoddington House, Hants*, 3, 4.

Scobell *of Nancealverne, Cornwall*, 2, 3, 4.

Scott *of Harden, Roxburgh,* I. iii. 372.

Scott *of Logie in Angusshire,* I. iv. 543 ; 2, 3.

Scott *of Betton, Salop,* I. ii. 503 ; 2, 3, 4.

Scott *of Carbrooke, Norfolk,* 2, 3, 4.

Scott *of Gala, Selkirk,* 2 supp., 3, 4.

Scott *of Stourbridge and Great Barr, Staffordshire,* I. iii. 664 ; 2, 3, 4.

Scott *of Rotherfield Park, Hants,* 4.

Scott-Chad *of Thursford Hall, Norfolk,* 4

Scott *of Melby, Zetland,* 4.

Scott *of Malleny, Mid Lothian,* I. iii. 170 ; 2 supp., 3, 4.

Scott *of Brotherton, Kincardine,* 2 supp , 3, 4.

Scott *of Raeburn, Dumfries,* I. iii. 375 ; 2, 3, 4.

Scott *of Abbotsford, Roxburgh,* 3, 4.

Scott *of Willsborough, Londonderry,* 3, 4.

Scourfield *of Williamston, Pembroke,* 4.

Scratton *of the Priory, Essex,* 3, 4.

Scrimgeour, 2 supp., and add.

Scriven *of the Priory, Surrey,* 4.

Scrivener *of Ramridge, Hants,* 3, 4.

Scrope *of Danby, York,* I. i. 450 ; 2, 3, 4.

Scrope *of Castle Combe, Wilts,* I. iii. 693 ; 2, 3, 4.

Scudamore *of Kentchurch, Hereford,* I. iii. 354 ; 2 supp., 3, 4.

Scurfield *of Ford and Hurworth upon Tees, Durham,* 2 supp., 3, 4.

Seaver *of Heath Hall, Armagh,* 2.

Sealy *of Gortnahorna House, Cork,* 2, 3, 4.

Seaman, Pierce- *of Rotherby Hall, Leicester,* 2, 3, 4.

Segrave *of Cabra, Wicklow,* 3, 4.

Selby *of Riddleston, Northumberland,* I. ii. 703 ; 2, 3, 4.

Selby *of the Mote, Kent,* 3, 4.

Selby *of Twizell House, Northumberland,* 2 add., 3, 4.

Selby *of Yearle, Northumberland,* I. ii. 706 ; 2, 3, 4.

Selby *of Cheswick House, Northumberland,* 2, 3, 4.

Sempill *of Dun Edin, Edinburgh,* 3, 4.

Senhouse *of Netherhall, Cumberland,* 2, 3, 4.

Sergison *of Cuckfield, Sussex,* 4.

Serocold *of Cherryhinton, Cambridge,* 2, 3, 4.

Seton *of Mounie, Aberdeen,* 2, 3, 4.

Seton *of Cariston, Fife,* 2, 3, 4.

Severn, Cheesment- *of Penybont Hall, Radnor,* 2, 3, 4

Severne *of Thenfold, Northampton, and of Wallop Hall, Salop,* I. i. 413 ; 2, 3, 4.

Sewell of *Queenwood Hill, Surrey,* 2 add.

Seymer *of Hanford, Dorset,* I. iii. 495 ; 2, 3, 4.

Seymour *of Knoyle, Wilts,* 2, 3, 4.

Seymour *of Ballymore Castle, Galway,* 2, 3, 4.

Seymour *of Castletown, Queen's Co.* I. iii. 200 ; 2, 3, 4.

Seys *of Tutshill, Gloucester,* 2, 3, 4.

Shafto *of Bavington Hall, Northumberland,* 4.

Shafto *of Whitworth, Durham,* I. i. 47 ; 2, 3, 4.

Shairp *of Houston, Linlithgow,* 2, 3, 4.

Shakerley *of Somerford, Chester,* I. i. 9.

Shank *of Castlerig, Fife,* 2. 3, 4.

Sharp *of Linden Hall, Lancaster,* 4.

Sharpe *of Oaklands, Sussex,* 2.

Sharpe *of Woodbridge, Suffolk,* 2.

Shaw *of Arrowe Park, Chester,* 2, 3, 4.

Shawe *of Kesgrave Hall, Suffolk,* I. i. 672 ; 2, 3, 4.

Shedden *of Paulerspury Park, Northampton,* I. iii. 351 ; 2, 3, 4.

Shedden *of Morris Hill, Ayr,* 3, 4

Shedden *of Morris Hill, Ayr,* 2 supp., and add.

Shee, Sir Martin Archer, I. i. 405.

Shekell *of Pebworth, Gloucester,* 2, 3.

Sheehy *of Corbally House, Cork,* 4.

Shelden *of Brailes House, Warwick,* 2, 3, 4.

Shelley *of Avington House, Hants,* 3, 4.

Shelton *of Rossmore House, Limerick,* 2.

Sheppard *of Frome Selwood, Somerset*, 2, 3, 4.

Sheppard *of Folkington, Sussex*, 2, 3, 4.

Sheppard *of the High House, Suffolk*, 2, 3, 4.

Sherbrooke *of Oxton, Notts*, 4.

Sheridan *of Frampton Court, Dorset*, 2, 3, 4.

Sherston *of Stoberry Park, Somerset*, 3, 4.

Sherwin-Gregory *of Bramcote Hills, Notts*, 3, 4.

Shipley *of Twyford House, Hants*, 2, 3, 4.

Shipperdson *of Pidding Hall Garth, Durham*, I. i. 108 ; 2, 3, 4.

Shirley *of Eatington, Warwick*, I. i. 49 ; 2, 3, 4.

Shore *of Norton Hall, Derby*, 2, 3, 4.

Short *of Edlington Grove, Linooln*, 2 supp., 3, 4.

Short *of Bickham, Devon*, 2 supp., 3, 4.

Shortt *of Dumfriesshire*, 2 supp., 4.

Shrubb *of Merrist Wood and Stoke, Surrey*, 2, 3, 4.

Shuckburgh *of Downton House, Wilts*, I. ii. 94.

Shuldham *of Marlesford Hall, Suffolk*, 2, 3, 4.

Shuldham *of Dunmanway, Cork*, I. i. 653 ; 2, 3, 4.

Shuldham *of Ballymulvey, Longford*, 2, 3, 4.

Shuldham, 2 add.

Shute *of Bramshaw Hill, Hants*, 2, 3, 4.

Shuttleworth *of Hodsack Park, Notts*, 2 add., 3, 4.

Shuttleworth *of Gawthorp, Lancaster*, 2, 4, 4.

Shuttleworth *of Lancaster and Durham*, I. iii. 518.

Shuttleworth *of Great Bowden, Leicester*, I. iv. 665.

Sibbald *of Westcott, Cornwall*, 3, 4.

Sibthorp *of Sibthorp, Lincoln*, 3, 4.

Sicklemore *of Wetheringsett, Suffolk*, I. iv. 743 ; 2, 3, 4.

Sidney *of Cowpen Hall, Northumberland*, 2, 3, 4.

Sier *of Ravensden, Bedford*, 3 supp., 4.

Sikes *of the Chauntry House, Notts*, I. i. 406 ; 2, 3.

Sillifant *of Combe, Devon*, 2, 3, 4.

Silvertop *of Minster Acres, Northumberland*, I. iii. 300 ; 2, 3, 4.

Simcox *of Harborne House, Stafford*, 3, 4.

Simon, Fitz- *of Tremayne and Tregarthyn, Cornwall*, 4.

Simons, Fitz- *of Anthony, afterwards of Tregarthen and Wendron, Cornwall*, 4.

Simons *of Trethowan ;* see Symons *of Hatt*, 4.

Simpson *of Mellor Lodge, Derby*, 2, 3, 4.

Simpson *of Balworth Hall, Notts*, 3, 4.

Simpson *of Knaresborough, York*, 3, 4.

Simpson *of Merklands House, Perth*, 3, 4.

Simpson *of Cloncorick Castle, Leitrim*, 2, 3, 4.

Simpson *of Whitburn, Westhouse, Durham*, 2, 3.

Simson *of Brunton, Fife*, 3, 4.

Sinclair *of Holy Hill, Tyrone*, 3, 4.

Sinclair *of Forss, Caithness*, 2, 3, 4.

Singleton *of Mell, Louth*, 3, 4.

Singleton *of Aclare, Meath*, 2, 3, 4.

Singleton *of Quinville Abbey, Clare*, 2, 3, 4.

Sitwell *of Stainsby, Derby*, 2, 3, 4.

Sitwell *of Barmour Castle, Northumberland*, 2.

Sitwell *of Ferney Hall, Salop*, 3, 4.

Sivewright *of Manor House, Berks*, 2 supp., 3, 4.

Skelton *of Papcastle, Cumberland*, 2, 3, 4.

Skene *of Rubieslaw, Aberdeen*, 2, 3, 4.

Skerrett *of Finavara, Clare*, 3, 4.

Skerrett *of Athgoe Park, Dublin*, 2, 3, 4.

Skinner *of Shirley Park, Surrey*, I. iv. 749 ; 2.

Skinner *of Fordham, Essex*, 2 add.

Skipton *of the Casino, Derry*, 4.

Skipton *of Beech Hill, Londonderry,* 2.

Skipworth *of Moortown House, Lincoln,* 2 supp., 3, 4.

Skrine *of Warleigh, Somerset,* 2, 3, 4.

Slacke *of Ashleigh, Down,* 4.

Sladen *of Hartsbourne, Herts,* 4.

Sladen *of Ripple Court, Kent,* 2, 3.

Slaney *of Hatton Grange, Salop,* I. iv. 503 ; 2, 3, 4.

Slater *of Chesterfield,* 2 add., 3, 4.

Slater *of Newick Park, Sussex,* 3, 4.

Slator *Belville House, Meath,* 2, 3, 4.

Sleeman *of Cahara House, Limerick,* 2.

Smart *of Trewhitt, Northampton,* 3, 4.

Smeaton *of Coul, Perth,* 3, 4.

Smethurst *of Chorley, Lancaster,* 4.

Smith *of Halesowen Grange, Salop,* 2, 3, 4.

Smith *of Apsley House, Bedford,* I. ii. 103 ; 2, 3, 4.

Smith *of Camer, Kent,* 2, 3, 4.

Smith *of Elmhurst, Stafford,* I. iv. 471 ; 2, 3, 4.

Smith *of Lydiate, Lancaster,* I. iv. 201 ; 2, 3, 4.

Smith *of Tresco Abbey, Cornwall,* I. i. 98 ; 2, 3, 4.

Smith *of Woodhall Park, Herts,* 3, 4.

Smith *of Selsdon, Surrey,* 3, 4.

Smith *of Dale Park, Sussex,* 3, 4.

Smith *of Ellingham Hall, Norfolk,* 2 add., 3, 4.

Smith *of Vaynol, Caernarvon,* 2, 3, 4.

Smith *of Ryhope, Durham, and of Carrowbrough, Northumberland,* 2 supp., 3, 4.

Smith *of Jordanhill, Renfrew,* I. iv. 62 ; 2, 3, 4.

Smith *of Carbeth Guthrie,* 4.

Smith *of Togston, Northumberland,* I. iii. 257 ; 2, 3.

Smith *of Camer, Kent,* 2.

Smith *of Bitteswell Hall, Leicester,* 2.

Smith *of Munslows Aston, Salop,* 2.

Smith *of Pendryffryn, Carnarvon,* 2.

Smith *of Beabey, Meath,* 2, 3, 4.

Smithwick *of Ballyngawsey, Limerick,* 4.

Smollett *of Bonhill, Dumbarton,* 2, 3, 4.

Smyth *of Heath Hall, York,* 2, 3, 4.

Smyth *of Ballynatray, Waterford,* 2, 3, 4.

Smyth *of Headborough, Waterford,* 4.

Smyth *of Ashton Court, Somerset,* 3.

Smyth *of Gaybrook, Westmeath,* 2, 3, 4,

Smyth *of Elkington, Lincoln, and of Annables, Herts,* I. ii. 652 ; 4.

Smyth *of Castle Wydenham, Cork,* 4 supp.

Smyth *of Castle Fergus, Clare,* 2.

Smyth *of Kilnalack, Cavan,* 2.

Smyth *of Drumcree House, Westmeath,* 2, 3, 4.

Smyth *of Glananea, Westmeath,* 3, 4.

Smyth *of Ballynegall, Westmeath,* 3, 4.

Smythe *of Barbavilla, Westmeath,* 2, 3, 4.

Smythe *of New Park, Roscommon,* 2, 3, 4.

Smythe *of Hilton, Salop,* 2, 3, 4.

Smythe *of Methven Castle, Perth,* I. i. 228 ; 2, 3, 4,

Snell *of Hertfordshire,* 4.

Sneyd *of Keele, Stafford,* 2, 3, 4.

Sneyd *of Ashcombe, Stafford,* I. i. 555 ; 2, 3, 4.

Soltau *of Little Efford, Devon,* 2, 3, 4.

Somerville *of Dinder House, Somerset,* 2, 3, 4.

Somerville *of Drishane, Cork,* 4.

Sotheron *of Kirklington, Notts,* I. iii. 520.

Southam *of Southam, Warwick,* 4.

Southby *of Carswell, Berks,* 2, 3, 4.

Southby *of Hodcott, Berks,* 2, 3, 4.

Southcomb *of Rose Ash, Devon,* 3, 4.

Southwell ; see Trafford, 3, 4.

Spaight *of Corbally, Clare,* 2, 3, 4.

Sparkes *of Pennyworlodd, Brecon,* 2, 3, 4.

Sparks *of Westlodge, Surrey,* 2, 3, 4.

Sparling *of Petton, Salop,* 2, 3, 4.

Sparrow *of Gosfield Place, Essex,* 2, 3, 4.

Sparrow *of Penn, Stafford,* 3, 4.

Sparrow *of Red Hill, Anglesey,* 2, 3, 4.

Spearman *of Thornley, Durham,* I. ii. 452 ; 2, 3, 4.

Spedding *of Summergrove, Cumberland,* 2, 3, 4.

Speir *of Burnbrae, Renfrew, and of Culdees, Perth,* 2, 3, 4.

Speir *of Blackstoun, Renfrew,* 3, 4.

Speirs *of Elderslie, Renfrew,* 3, 4.

Speke *of Jordans, Somerset,* 2, 3, 4.

Spencer *of Bramley Grange, York,* I. ii. 387 ; 2, 3.

Spens *of Lathallan, Stirling,* I. iv. 168 ; 2, 3, 4.

Spens *of Craigsanquhar,' Fife,* I. iv. 506 ; 2, 3, 4.

Sperling *of Dynes Hall, Essex,* 3, 4.

Spinks *of East Mousley, Surrey,* 4.

Spode *of Hawkesyard Park, Stafford,* 3, 4.

Spofforth *of Eastthorpe Hall, York,* 3, 4.

Spooner-Lillingston *of Elmdon, Warwick,* I. i. 185 ; 2, 3, 4.

Spoor *of Whitburn, Durham,* 4.

Spottiswood *of Muiresk, Aberdeen,* 2, 3.

Spottiswoode *of Spottiswoode, Berwick,* 2, 3, 4.

Spratt *of Pencil Hill, Cork,* 4.

Sproston *of Sproston, Chester,* 2 supp., 3, 4.

Spry *of Place, Cornwall,* I. iv. 691 ; 2, 3, 4.

Squire *of Barton Place, Suffolk,* 2, 3, 4.

Stacpoole *of Eden Vale, Clare,* 2, 3, 4.

Stacpoole *of Cragbrian, Clare,* 2.

Stafford *of Blatherwycke, Northampton,* I. iii. 109 ; 2, 3, 4.

Standish *of Standish, Lancaster,* I. ii. 642 ; 3, 4.

Standish *of Duxbury, Lancaster,* I. iv. 642 ; 2, 3, 4.

Standish *of Farley Hill House, Berks, and Scaleby Castle, York,* 4 supp.

Stanhope *of Revesby Abbey, Lincoln,* 3, 4.

Stanhope *of Cannon Hall, York,* I. i. 467 ; 2, 3, 4.

Stanley *of Paultons, Hants,* 3, 4.

Stanley *of Tedworth, Hants,* 4.

Stanley *of Cross Hall, Lancaster,* 2, 3, 4.

Stanley *of Dalegarth, Cumberland,* I. i. 95 ; 2, 3, 4.

Stannard *of Grange, Kilkenny,* 3.

Stanley, 2 add.

Stannard *of the Priory, Cork,* 2.

Stannus *of Carlingford, Louth,* 3, 4.

Stansfeld *of Burley Wood, York,* I. iv. 756 ; 2, 3.

Stansfield *of Esholt Hall, York,* I. iii. 59 ; 2, 3. 4.

Stanton *of Thrupp House, Gloucester,* 2 supp., 3, 4.

Staples *of Norwood, Surrey, and of Launton, Wilts,* 2 supp., 3, 4.

Staplyton *of Myton, York,* I. ii. 207 ; 2, 3, 4.

Stapylton *of Wighill, Herts,* 4.

Stapylton *of Norton, Durham,* I. ii. 210.

Starke *of Laugharne Castle, Caermarthen,* 2, 3, 4.

Starkey *of Wrenbury Hall, Chester,* 3, 4.

Starkey *of Thornton Lodge, York,* 2.

Starkie *of Huntroyde, Lancaster,* 2, 3, 4.

Starky *of Bromham, Wilts,* I. iv, 684 ; 2, 3, 4.

Staunton *of Staunton, Notts,* I. i. 526 ; 2, 3, 4.

Staunton, Lynch- *of Clydagh, Galway,* 2, 3, 4.

Staunton *of Longbridge, Warwick,* I. ii. 587 ; 2, 3, 4.

Stawell *of Rhyll House, Down,* 2, 3.

Stawell, Alcock- *of Kilbrittain Castle, Cork,* 3, 4.

Steade *of Beauchief Abbey, Derby,* I. i. 150.

Steel *of Derwent Bank, Cumberland,* 4.

Steele *of Rathbride, Kildare,* 3, 4.

Steinman *of Priory Lodge, Surrey,* 2.

Stephens, *formerly of Eastington, Gloucester,* 3, 4.

Stephens *of Tregenna, Cornwall,* I. iii. 609 ; 2, 3, 4.

Stephens, Cowell- *of Llanelly, Caermarthen,* 4.

Steuart *of Auchlunkart, Banff,* 2 supp., 3, 4.

Steuart *of Dalguise, Perth,* 2, 3, 4.

Steuart *of Ballechin, Perth,* 1. ii. 149 ; 2, 3, 4.

Steuart *of Glenormiston, Peebles,* 2, 3, 4.

Steuart *of Steuart's Lodge, Carlow,* 2, 3, 4.

Stevens *of Winscott, Devon,* 4.

Stevenson *of Uffington, Lincoln,* 2, 3, 4.

Steward *of Nottington House, Dorset,* I. iii. 586 ; 2, 3, 4.

Steward *of Norfolk,* 2, 3, 4.

Steward *of Newton Manor, Cumberland,* 4.

Stewart *of Physgill, Wigton,* 2, 3, 4.

Stewart *of Southwick,* 4.

Stewart *of Ardvorlich, Perth,* 2, 3, 4.

Stewart *of Cairnsmore, Kirkcudbright,* 2, 3, 4.

Stewart-Menzies *of Chesthill and Foss, Perth,* 2, 3, 4.

Stewart *of Drumin, now of Belladrum, Inverness,* 2, 3, 4

Stewart *of Broughton ;* see Murray Stewart, 3, 4.

Stewart *of Murdostoun, Lanark,* 4.

Stewart *of Tonderghie, Wigton,* 4.

Stewart *of Ballymenagh, Tyrone,* 3, 4.

Stewart *of Ards, Donegal,* 2, 3, 4.

Stewart *of Rockkill,* 4.

Stewart *of Hornhead, Donegal,* 4.

Stewart *of Binny, Linlithgow,* 2.

Stewart *of Lismurdie,* 2.

Stewart *of St. Fort, Fife,* I. iv. 80 ; 2, 3, 4.

Stillingfleet *of How Caple, Hereford,* 2.

Stirling *of Keir, Perth,* 3, 4.

Stirling *of Kippinross, Perth,* 3, 4.

Stodart *of Kailzie and Ormiston,* 2.

Stokes *of Mounthawk, Kerry,* 2, 3, 4.

Stokes *of Shandhawes Court, Gloucester,* 2.

Stone, Lowndes- *of Brightwell Park, Oxford,* I. iii. 258 ; 2, 3, 4.

Stone *of Streatley House, Berks,* 2, 3, 4.

Stonestreet *of Stondon, Essex,* 2, 3, 4.

Stoney *of Kyle Park, Tipperary,* 2, 3, 4.

Stoney *of Portland, Tipperary,* 2, 3, 4.

Stonor *of Stonor, Oxford,* I. ii. 440.

Stopford-Blair *of Penninghame, Wigtoun,* 3, 4.

Stopford *of Drayton House, Northampton,* 3, 4.

Storer *of Purley Park, Berks,* 2 add., 3, 4.

Storer *of Combe Court, Surrey,* 2 supp., 3, 4.

Storie *of Springfield Lodge, Surrey,* I. i. 275 ; 2.

Story *of Bingfield, Cavan,* 3, 4.

Story *of Ralagh Lodge, Tyrone,* 2.

Stothert *of Cargen, Kirkcudbright,* 2, 3, 4.

Stoughton *of Owlpen, Gloucester,* 2, 3, 4.

Strachey *of Ashwick Court, Somerset,* 2.

Strahan *of Ashurst, Surrey,* 2.

Stovin, 2 add.

Strangewayes *of Alne, York,* I. i. 665 ; 2, 3, 4.

Strangwayes *of Well, York,* I. i. 135 ; 2.

Straubeerzee, Van- *of Spenithorne, York,* 2, 3, 4.

Streatfeild *of Chiddingstone, Kent,* I. ii. 422 ; 2, and add., 3, 4.

Streatfeild *of Charts Edge, Kent,* 4.

Strelley *of Oakerthorpe, Derby,* 2, 3, 4.

Strickland *of Sizergh, Westmoreland,* I. i. 55 ; 2, 3, 4.

Strode, Chetham- *of Southill, Somerset,* I. ii. 117 ; 2, 3, 4.

Strode *of Newnham Park, Devon,* 2, 3, 4.

Strong *of Nether-Stronge, now of the Chase, Hereford,* 2, 3, 4.

Strutt *of Belper, Derby,* 2, 3, 4.

Strutt *of Derby,* 2.

Stuart *of Aldenham Abbey, Herts,* I. i. 427 ; 2, 3, 4.

Stuart *of Inchbrech, Kincardine,* 2, 3, 4.

Stuart *of Blairhall,* 4.

Stubber *of Moyne, Queen's Co.* 2, 3, 4.

Stubbs *of Cannock, Stafford,* 4.

Studdert *of Bunratty Castle, Clare,* 2, 3, 4.

Studdert *of Elm Hill, Clare,* 3, 4.

Sturt *of Critchill, Dorset*, 2, 3, 4.
Style *of Bicester House, Oxford*, 2 supp., 3, 4.
Styleman Le Strange *of Hunstanton, Norfolk*, 2, 3, 4.
Suckling *of Woodton Hall, Norfolk*, I. iii. 457 ; 2, 3.
Sulivan *of Wilmington, Isle of Wight*, 2 supp., 3, 4.
Sullivan *of Curramore, Limerick*, 4.
Sullivan *of Richings Lodge, Bucks*, I. i. 410.
Sullivan *of Chesterfield, Limerick*, 2, 3.
Sumner *of Hatchlands, Surrey*, I. i. 60 ; 4,
Sumner *of Puttenham Priory, Surrey*, I. i. 61 ; 2, 3, 4.
Surman *of Swindon Hall, Gloucester*, 2 add., 3, 4.
Surtees *of Dinsdale, Durham*, 2, 3, 4.
Surtees *of Redworth, Durham*, I. ii. 656 ; 2, 3, 4.
Surtees *of Hamsterley, Durham*, 2, 3, 4.
Surtees *of Newcastle on Tyne*, I. iv. 303.
Sutton *of Elton, Durham*, 2, 3, 4.
Sutton *of Rossway, Herts*, 2, 3, 4.
Sutton *of Shardlow Hall, Derby*, 3.
Swabey *of Langley Marish, Bucks*, 2, 3, 4.
Swain *of Wisbeach, Cambridge*, 2.
Swainson *of Shropshire and Lancashire*, 3, 4.
Swan *of Baldwinstown, Wexford*, 2 add., 3, 4.
Swann *of Fairfield, Derby*, 2.
Swetenham *of Somerford Booths, Chester*, I. ii. 459 ; 2, 3, 4.
Swettenham *of Swettenham, Chester*, I. 640 ; 2, 3, 4.
Swift *of Lynn, Westmeath*, 2, 3, 4.
Swinburne *of Pontop Hall, Durham*, 2, 3, 4.
Swinfen *of Swinfen, Stafford*, 4.
Swinnerton *of Butterton, Stafford*, I. iii. 601 ; 2.
Swinton *of Swinton, Peebles*, I. iii. 486 ; 2, 3, 4.
Swinton *of Kimmerghame, Berwick*, 3, 4.

Swire *of Cononley, York*, I. ii. 342 ; 2, 3.
Sydney *of the Bourne, Berks*, 2 supp., 3, 4.
Symes *of Ballybeg, Wicklow*, 3.
Symonds *of Pengethley, Hereford*, 2, 3, 4.
Symons *of Mynde Park, Hereford*, I. iv. 645 ; 2, 3, 4.
Symons *of Hatt, Cornwall*, 4.
Symons *of Chaddlewood, Devon*, 2, 3, 4.
Synge *of Glanmore, Wicklow*, 2, 3, 4.
Synnot *of Ballymoyer House, Armagh*, 2, 3, 4.
Synnot *of Drumcondra, Dublin*, 2 supp.
Taaffe *of Smarmore, Louth*, 3, 4.
Taafe *of Woodfield, Mayo*, 2, 3.
Tailby *of Quenby Hall, Leicester*, 4.
Tailyour *of Borrowfield, Forfar*, 2, 3, 4.
Tait *of Millrig House, Ayr*, 3, 4.
Talbot *of Ballytrent, Wexford*, 2.
Talbot *of Oakland, Worcester*, 2.
Talbot *of Talbot Hall, Wexford*, 2.
Talbot *of Margam, Glamorgan*, 3, 4.
Talbot *of Lacock Abbey, Wilts*, 2, 3, 4.
Talbot *of Mount Talbot, Roscommon*, 3, 4.
Talbot *of Temple Guiting, Gloucester*, 2, 3, 4.
Talbot *of Greenhill, Worcester*, 2, 3, 4.
Talbot *of Castle Talbot, Wexford*, I. iii. 359 ; 2, 3, 4.
Tanner *of Kingnympton Park, Devon*, 4.
Tardrew *of Amrery House, Devon*, 2, 3, 4.
Tardy *of the Grove, Essex*, 3, 4.
Tate *of Burleigh Park, Leicester*, I. ii. 488 ; 2.
Tatham *of Summerfield House, Lancaster*, 2, 3, 4.
Tattershall *of Lincolnshire, Essex, &c.* 2.
Tatlock *of Kirkby, Lancaster*, 2.
Tatton *of Wythenshaw, Chester*, I. iii. 39 ; 2, 3, 4.

Taunton *of Freeland Lodge, Oxford,* I. ii. 213 ; 2, 3. 4.

Tayleur *of Buntingsedale, Salop,* I. iv. 156 ; 2, 3, 4.

Taylor *of the Brooms, Stafford,* 2.

Taylor *of Bifrons, Kent,* I. iii. 107 ; 2, 3, 4.

Taylor-Smith *of Colpike Hall, Durham,* 2 add., 3, 4.

Taylor-Domville *of Lymme Hall, Chester,* 2 add., 3.

Taylor *of Clifton, Gloucester,* I. iv. 7.

Taylor *of Chyknell, Salop,* 2, 3, 4.

Taylor *of Kirkham Abbey, York,* 2, 3, 4.

Taylor *of Erlestoke Park, Wilts,* 3, 4.

Taylor *of Moreton Hall, Lancaster,* 3, 4.

Taylor *of Ogwell, Devon,* I. iv. 445 ; 2, 3, 4.

Taylor *of Pennington, Hants,* I. iv. 237 ; 2, 3, 4.

Taylor *of Radcliffe on Trent, Notts,* 3, 4.

Taylor *of Strensham, Worcester,* 2, 3, 4.

Taylor *of Moseley Hall, Worcester,* 2, 3, 4.

Taylor *of Todmorden Hall, Lancaster,* 2, 3, 4.

Taylor *of Ardgillan Castle, Dublin,* 3, 4.

Taylor *of Castle Taylor, Galway,* 2, 3, 4.

Taylor *of Dunkerron, Kerry,* I. iv. 288 ; 3, 4.

Tempest *of Tong, York,* 2, 3, 4.

Tempest *of Broughton Hall, York,* I. i. 474.

Temple *of Bishopstrow, Wilts,* 2, 3, 4.

Temple *of Over Dinsdale, York,* 2.

Templer *of Stover, Devon,* 3, 4.

Templer *of Shapwick, Somerset,* 2.

Templer *of Lindridge,* 4.

Tench *of Balyhaly, Wexford,* 4.

Tenison *of Kilronan Castle, Roscommon,* 2, 3, 4.

Tenison *of Fort Nelligan, Armagh,* 2, 3, 4.

Tennant *of Chapel House, York,* 2, 3, 4.

Tennent, Emerson- *of Tempo, Fermanagh,* I. ii. 21; 2, 3, 4.

Tennyson-D'Enycourt *of Bayons Manor, Lincoln,* 2, 3, 4.

Thackeray *of Clench Wharton, Norfolk,* 4.

Thackwell *of Wilton Place, Gloucester,* 3, 4.

Tharp *of Chippenham Park, Cambridge,* 4.

Thelwell *of Llanbedr, Denbigh,* 2.

Thicknesse *of Beech Hill, Lancaster,* 2, 4.

Thistlethwayte *of Southwick Park, Hants,* I. iii. 472 ; 2, 3, 4.

Thomas *of Hereford,* 2, 3.

Thomas *of Gellywernen, Caermarthen,* I. i. 628 ; 2, 3, 4.

Thomas *of Llwyn Madoc, Brecon,* 2, 3, 4.

Thomas *of Llanbradach, Glamorgan,* 4.

Thomas *of Pwllyrach, Glamorgan,* 4.

Thomas *of Welfield House, Radnor,* 2, 3, 4.

Thomas *of Ratton, Sussex,* 2, 3, 4.

Thomlinson *of Blencogo, Cumberland,* 2.

Thompson *of Kirby Hall, York,* 2, 3, 4.

Thompson *of Sheriff Hutton, York,* 2, 3, 4.

Thompson *of Annaverna, Louth,* 3, 4.

Thompson *of Clonfin, Longford,* 2, 3, 4.

Thompson *of Treveryan, Cornwall,* 2, 3, 4.

Thomson, Anstruther- *of Charleton, Fife,* 3, 4.

Thomson *of Castleton, Antrim,* 3, 4.

Thomson *of Banchory, Kincardine,* 2, 3, 4.

Thomson *of Kenfield, Kent,* 3, 4.

Thorneycroft *of Hadley Park, Salop, and of Tettenhall Wood, Stafford,* 3, 4.

Thornbrough *of Bishopsteignton, Gloucester,* I. iv. 300.

Thornhill *of Woodleys, Oxford,* 2,3,4.
Thornhill *of Thornhill and Stanton, Derby,* 2, 3, 4.
Thornhill *of Fixby and Riddlesworth, York,* 3, 4.
Thornley *of Dodworth Hall, York,* 2, 3, 4.
Thornton *of Birkin, York, and of Clapham, Surrey,* 2 supp., 3, 4.
Thornton *of Brockall, Northampton,* I. ii. 495 ; 2, 3, 4.
Thornton *of Grenville, Cavan,* 3, 4.
Thorp *of Headingly, York,* 2, 3, 4.
Thorp *of Ryton, Durham.* 2, 3, 4.
Thoyts *of Sulhamstead, Berks,* 4.
Throckmorton *of Molland, Devon,* I. ii. 161.
Thring *of Alford House, Somerset,* 4.
Thunder *of Lagore, Meath,* 3, 4.
Thurlow *of Baynards, Surrey,* 2,3, 4.
Thursby *of Abington, Northampton,* I. i. 318 ; 2, 3, 4.
Tibeaudo *of Portnehinch, Queen's Co.* 2.
Tighe *of Woodstock, Kilkenny,* I. iii. 513 ; 2, 3, 4.
Tighe *of Michelstown, Westmeath,* I. iv. 12 ; 2, 3, 4.
Tillard *of Street End House, Kent,* 2, and supp., 3, 4.
Tindal *of Chelmsford, Essex,* 3, 4.
Tipping *of Bolton, Lancaster,* 2, 3,4.
Tisdell *of Charlesfort, Meath,* 3, 4.
Tisdell *of Charleville, Louth,* 2.
Tittle *of Farm Hill, Londonderry,* 3, 4.
Todd *of Tranby Park and Halnaby, York,* 2, 3, 4.
Todd *of Buncrana Castle, Donegal,* 2.
Toke *of Godington, Kent,* 2, 3, 4.
Toll *of Perridge House, Devon,* 2,3,4.
Tollemache *of Helmingham, Suffolk,* 2, 3, 4.
Tollet *of Betley Hall, Stafford,* I. ii. 224 ; 2.
Tolson *of Bridekirke, Cumberland,* I. ii. 133 ; 2.
Tomkins *of Londonderry,* 2, 3, 4.
Tomkinson *of Willington Hall, Chester,* 2, 3, 4.
Tomlin *of Dane Court, Kent,* 2, 3, 4.
Tomline *of Orwell Park, Suffolk, and of Rily Grove, Lincoln,* 3, 4.

Tompson *of Witchingham Hall, Norfolk,* 2, 3, 4.
Tonge *of Highway, Wilts,* 3, 4.
Tooke *of Hurston Clays, Sussex,* 3,4.
Tooker *of Norton Hall, Somerset,* 2.
Topham *of Middleham Hall, York,* 2, 3, 4.
Topp *of Whitton, Salop,* 2, 3, 4.
Torkington *of Great Stukeley, Huntingdon,* 2, 3, 4.
Torre *of Syndale, York,* 2, 3, 4.
Tottenham *of Woodstock, Wicklow,* 4.
Tottenham *of Ballycurry, Wicklow,* 2, 3, 4.
Tottenham *of Glenfarne Hall, Enniskillen,* 4.
Tovey-Tennent *of Pynnacles, Middlesex, and of Poole Castle, Lanark,* 4.
Tower *of Weald Hall, Essex,* 2,3,4.
Towers *of Bushy Park, Tipperary,* 2.
Towneley *of Towneley, Lancaster,* I. ii. 262 ; 2, 3, 4.
Townsend *of Honington Hall, Warwick,* 2, 3,4 .
Townsend *of Castle Townsend, Cork,* 2, 3, 4.
Townsend *of Whitehall, Cork,* 2, 3, 4.
Townsend *of Myross Wood, Cork,* 2, 3, 4.
Townsend *of Derry, Cork,* 2, 3, 4.
Townsend *of Garrycloyne Castle, Cork,* 3, 4.
Townsend *of Woodside, Cork,* 2, 3, 4.
Townsend *of Trevallyn, Denbigh,* I. iii. 313 ; 2, 3, 4.
Townsend, 2.
Trafford *of Wroxham Hall, Norfolk,* 2 add., 3, 4.
Trafford *of Oughtrington, Chester,* 2, 3, 4.
Trafford *of Trafford, Lancaster,* I. iv. 247.
Trafford *of Swithamley, Stafford,* 3.
Traherne *of Coedriglan, Glamorgan,* 2, 3, 4.
Trail *of Ballyclough, Antrim,* 4.
Traill *of Holland, Orkney,* 4.
Traill *of Castle Hill, Caithness,* 4.
Trant *of Dovea, Tipperary,* 2, 3, 4.
Trappes *of Nidd, York,* 2.

Treby *of Goodamoor and Plympton House, Devon*, 2, 3, 4.
Tredcroft *of Warnham Court, Sussex*, 2, 3, 4.
Tredennick *of Camlin, Donegal*, 2, 3, 4.
Tregonwell *of Anderson, Dorset*, I. ii. 403; 2, 3, 4.
Tregonwell *of Cranbourne Lodge, Dorset*, 2, 3, 4.
Treherne *of Gate House, Sussex*, 3, 4.
Trelawny *of Coldrinick, Cornwall*, I. i. 368; 2, 3, 4.
Tremayne *of Heligan, Cornwall*, I. i. 193; 2, 3, 4.
Tremenheere *of Tremenheere, Cornwall*, 2, 3, 4.
Trench *of Cangort Park, King's co.* 2, 3, 4.
Trench *of Heywood, Queen's Co.* 3,
Trenchard *of Dorsetshire*, I. iv. 75; 2 add., 3, 4.
Trenchard *of Stanton, Wilts*, I. iv. 75; 2, 3, 4.
Trevanion *of Caerhayes, Cornwall*, I. i. 253; 2, 3, 4.
Trevelyan *of Netherwitton, Northumberland*, I. ii. 329; 2, 3, 4.
Tripp *of Huntspill and Samford Brett, Somerset*, 2, 3, 4.
Trist *of Bowdon and Hernaford, Devon*, 3, 4.
Trist *of Parc Behan and Carneggan, Cornwall*, 3, 4.
Tryon *of Bulwick Park, Northampton*, 3, 4.
Trotter *of Morton Hall, Midlothian*, 2, 3, 4.
Trotter *of the Bush, Midlothian*, 2, 3, 4.
Trotter *of Dreghorn, Midlothian*, 2, 3, 4.
Trotter *of Byers Green and Helmeden, Durham*, 4.
Trotter *of Ballindean, Perth*, I. iv. 524; 2, 3, 4.
Trotter *of Quansborough, Galway*, 4.
Trotter *of Downpatrick, Wicklow*, 2.
Troughton *of Walton Hall, Lancaster*, I. iv. 379; 2, 3, 4.
Troyte *of Huntsham Court, Devon*, 3, 4

Truell *of Clonmannon, Wicklow*, 2, 3, 4.
Trye *of Leckhampton Court, Gloucester*, I. i. 603; 2, 3, 4.
Tryon *of Bulwick Park, Northampton*, 4.
Tuck *of Cherry Hinton, Cambridge*, 2 supp.
Tucker *of Trematon Castle, Cornwall*, 2 supp., 3, 4.
Tucker *of Kingsnympton, Devon*, 4.
Tucker *of Coryton Park, Devon*, 2.
Tudway *of Wells, Somerset*, 2, 3, 4.
Tuffnell *of Langleys, Essex*, I. ii. 183; 2, 3, 4.
Tuite *of Sonna, Westmeath*, 3, 4.
Tunnard *of Frampton House, Lincoln*, 3, 4.
Tupper *of Guernsey*, 2 supp., 3, 4.
Turbervill *of Ewenny Abbey, Glamorgan*, 2, 3, 4.
Turbutt *of Ogston Hall, Derby*, I. i. 666; 2, 3, 4.
Turner *of Menie, Aberdeen*, 2, 3, 4.
Turner *of Glentyre, Perth*, 4.
Turnly *of Drumnasole, Antrim*, 3, 4.
Turnor *of Stoke Rochford, Lincoln*, I. i. 300; 2, 3, 4.
Turton *of Upsall, York*, 2, and add., 4.
Turville *of Bosworth Hall, Leicester*, I. ii. 644; 2, 3, 4.
Twemlow *of Peatswood, Stafford*, I. iii. 485; 2, 3, 4.
Twemlow *of Hatherton, Chester*, I. i. 334.
Twiss *of Birdhill, Tipperary*, 2, 3, 4.
Twiss *of Hoseley, Flint*, 2.
Tylden *of Milsted, Kent*, I. ii. 381; 2, 3, 4.
Tyler *of Cottrell, Glamorgan*, 2, 3, 4.
Tyler *of Newtownlimavady, Londonderry*, 4.
Tyndale *of Hayling, Hants*, I. iv. 545; 2, 3, 4.
Tyndale *of Holton, Oxford*, 4.
Tynte, Kemeys- *of Halsewell, Somerset, and of Kevanmably, Glamorgan*, I. iv. 182; 2, 3, 4.
Tyringham *of Tyringham, Bucks*, 4.
Tyrwhitt *of Nantyr, Denbigh*, I. i. 583.
Tyrrell *of Grange Castle, Kildare*, 2, 3, 4.

Tyssen-Amhnrst *of Didlington, Norfolk*, 3, 4.

Tyssen *of Northwold Lodge, Norfolk*, 2, 3, 4.

Tytler, Fraser- *of Belnain, Inverness*, 2, 3, 4.

Tytler *of Woodhouselee, Midlothian*, 3.

Unett *of the Woodlands, Stafford*, 2, 3, 4.

Unett *of Freen's Court, Hereford*, 2, 3, 4.

Uniacke *of Mount Uniacke, Cork*, 2, 3, 4.

Uniacke *of Woodhouse, Waterford*, 2, 3, 4.

Upcher *of Sheringham, Norfolk*, 2, 3, 4.

Uppleby *of Wotton House, Lincoln*, 2, 3, 4.

Upton *of Ingmire Hall, Westmoreland*, I. iv 385 ; 2, 3, 4.

Upton *of Glyde Court, Louth*, 2, 3, 4.

Urquhart *of Meldrum and Byth, Aberdeen*, I. ii. 294 ; 2, 3, 4.

Urquhart *of Craigston, Aberdeen*, I. ii. 300 ; 2, 3, 4.

Ussher *of Eastwell, Galway*, 3, 4.

Ussher *of Cappagh, Wexford*, 2, 3, 4.

Usticke *of Penwarne, Cornwall*, 2 supp.

Usticke *of Trenley House, Devon*, 3, 4.

Van Cortlandt; see Taylor *of Pnnington*, 4.

Vandeleur *of Kilrush, Clare*, 2, 3, 4.

Vanderstegen *of Cane End, Oxford*, 4.

Van Sittart *of Shottesbrook, Berks*, 2, 3, 4.

Van Sittart *of Bisham Abbey, Berks*, 2, 3, 4.

Van Sittart *of Kirkleatham, York*, 2.

Van Straubenze *of Spenithorne ;* see Straubenzee, 4.

Vassall *of Milford, Hants*, I. i. 492 ; 2.

Vavasour *of Weston, York*, I. i. 51.

Vaughan *of Nanney and Hengwrt*, I. ii. 571 ; 2. 4.

Vaughan *of Burlton Hall, Salop*, I. ii. 238 ; 2, 3, 4.

Vaughan *of Rheola, Glamorgan*, 2, 3, 4.

Vaughan *of Caethle and Penmaen Dovey, Merioneth*, 2, 3, 4.

Vaughan *of Court Field, Hereford*, 2, 3, 4.

Vaughan *of Dolymelynllyn*, 2.

Vawdry *of Cheshire*, I. i. 353 ; 2, 3, 4.

Veale *of Passaford, Devon*, 4.

Veitch *of Eliock, Dumfries*, 2, 3, 4.

Venables *of Woodhill, Salop*, 2, 3, 4.

Venables *of Leftwich, Lancaster*, 4.

Venn *of Freston Lodge, Suffolk*, 2, 3.

Vere *of Craigie Hall, Linlithgow, and of Blackwood, Lanark*, I. iii. 319 ; 2, 3, 4.

Vere *of Carlton, Notts*, 3, 4.

Vere (now Weir) *of Monaghan, Monaghan*, 2.

Vernon *of Hilton Park, Stafford*, I. iii. 622 ; 2, 3, 4.

Vernon *of Harefield Park, Middlesex*, 4.

Vernon *of Clontarf-Castle, Dublin*, 3, 4.

Vernon *of Hanbury, Worcester*, 4.

Verner *of Church Hill, Armagh*, I. iv. 56.

Vesey *of Lucan, Dublin*, 4.

Vesey *of Derrabard, Tyrone*, 3, 4.

Vignoles *of Cornahir, Westmeath*, 4.

Vigors *of Erindale, Carlow*, 2, 3, 4.

Vigors *of Burgage, Carlow*, 2, 3, 4.

Vilett *of Swindon, Wilts*, 2.

Viner, Ellis- *of Badgeworth, Gloucester*, 2, 3, 4.

Vipan *of Sutton, Cambridge*, 4.

Vivian *of Singleton, Glamorgan*, 2, 3, 4.

Vivian *of Pencalenick, Cornwall*, I. i. 407 ; 4.

Vowe *of Hallaton, Leicester*, I. ii. 91 ; 2.

Vowler *of Parnacott, Devon*, 2, 3, 4.

Vyner *of Gautby, Lincoln*, 4.

Vyner *of Newby Hall, York*, 4.

Vyse *of Stoke, Bucks*, 2, 3, 4.

Waddington *of Cavenham Hall, Suffolk*, 3, 4.

Waddell *of Easter Moffat, Lanark*, 2.

Waddy *of Clough East Castle, Wexford*, 3, 4.

Wade *of Clonebraney, Meath*, 3, 4.

Wade *of Westmeath*, 4.

Waggett *of Cork*, 2, and add.

Wait *of Woodborough, Somerset*, 2, 3, 4.

Waitman *of Westville, Lancaster*, 2, 3, 4.

Wakeman *of Graig House, Monmouth*, 2, 3, 4.

Walcot *of Bitterley Court, Salop*, 2, 3, 4.

Walcot *of Winkton, Hants*, 3, 4.

Waldie *of Hendersyde, Roxburgh*, 2, 3, 4.

Waldy *of Egglescliffe, Durham*, 2, 3, 4.

Waldron *of Ashfort House, Roscommon*, 2, 3, 4.

Wall *of Shelford, Cambridge*, 4.

Walford *of St. Vincent, Isle of Wight*, 2.

Walker-Heneage *of Compton Basset, Wilts*, I. iv. 368 ; 2, 3, 4.

Walker-Arnott *of Arlary, Kinross*, 2, 3, 4.

Walker *of Redland, Gloucester*, 2, 3, 4.

Walker *of Sand Hutton, York*, 2, and supp., 3, 4.

Walker *of Dalry, Midlothian*, 2, 3, 4.

Walker *of Gilgarran ;* see Robertson-Walker, 3, 4.

Walker *of Blythe Hall, Notts*, I. ii. 288 ; 2, 3, 4.

Walker *of Berry Hill, Notts*, 2, 3, 4.

Walker *of Tagunnan, Wexford*, 2, 3, 4.

Walker *of Crownest, York*, 3, 4.

Walker *of the Grange, Leicester*, 3, 4.

Walker, Sir G. Townshend, G.C.B., I. i. 312.

Walker *of Bushey, Herts*, 2.

Walkey *of Alphington, Devon*, 4.

Wall *of Worthy Park, Hants*, I. i. 121 ; 2, 3, 4.

Wall *of Norman Court, Hants*, 2.

Wallace *of Asholme, Knaresdale and Featherstone Castle, Northumberland*, 2 supp., 3, 4.

Wallace *of Kelly, Ayr*, I. iii. 274 ; 2.

Waller *of Farmington, Gloucester*, 3, 4.

Waller *of Cully*, 3.

Waller *of Prior Park, Tipperary*, 3, 4.

Waller *of Finoe, Tipperary*, 4.

Waller *of Castletown, Limerick*, 2, 3, 4.

Waller *of Allenstown, Meath*, 2 supp., 3, 4.

Wallington *of Gloucestershire*, 2 supp., 3, 4.

Wallington *of Dursley, Gloucester*, 2, 3, 4.

Wallis *of Drishane Castle, Cork*, 2, 3, 4.

Walmesley *of Sholley, Lancaster*, I. iii. 228 ; 2, 3, 4.

Walmesley *of Westwood House, Lancaster*, I. i. 278 ; 2, 3, 4.

Walmesley *of the Hall of Ince, Lancaster*, 2, 3, 4.

Walpole *of Freethorpe, Norfolk*, 2, 3, 4.

Walrond *of Dulford House, Devon*, I. ii. 557 ; 2, 3, 4.

Walrond *of Bradfield, Devon*, I. ii. 553 ; 2, 3, 4.

Walrond *of Calder Park, Lanark*, I. iv. 444 ; 2, 3, 4.

Walsh *of Fanningstown, Kilkenny*, 4.

Walsh *of Walsh Park, Tipperary*, 2.

Walter *of Bearwood, Berks*, 3, 4.

Walthall *of Darley Dale*, 4.

Walwyn *of Longworth, Hereford*, I. iii. 678 ; 2.

Warburton, Egerton- *of Warburton and Arley, Chester*, I. ii. 1 ; 2, 3, 4.

Warburton *of Garryhinch, King's Co.* 2, 3, 4.

Ward *of Willey, Surrey*, 2, 3, 4.

Ward *of Ogbourne St. Andrew, Wilts*, 2, 3, 4.

Ward *of Salhouse, Norfolk*, I. iv. 19 ; 2, 3, 4.

Ward *of Guilsborough, Northampton*, I. i. 379 ; 2, 3, 4.

Ward *of Fern Park, Gloucester*, 3, 4.

Ward *of Holwood, Kent*, 2, 3, 4.

Ward *of Crabborn and Coltishall Hall, Norfolk*, 2, 3, 4.

Ward *of Northwood Park, Isle of Wight*, 3, 4.

Ward *of Bangor Castle, Down*, 3, 4.

Ward *of Vianston, Down*, 2.

Warde *of Squerries, Kent*, 2 add., 3, 4.

Warde *of Clopton House, Warwick,* 2, 3, 4.
Wardlow, Clarke- *of Comrie Castle, Perth,* 2.
Wardrop *of Bridge House, Edinburgh,* 4.
Ware *of Hendon Hall, Middlesex,* 2, 3, 4.
Ware *of Woodfort, Cork,* 2, 3, 4.
Ware, Hibbert- *of Edinburgh,* 2.
Waring *of Waringstown, Down,* 2, 3, 4.
Waring-Maxwell *of Finnebrogue, Down,* 2, 3, 4.
Warner, Lee- *of Walsingham Abbey, Norfolk,* I. iv. 551; 2, 3, 4.
Warner, Lee- *of Tiblerton Court, Hereford,* I. iv. 551; 4.
Warner *of Thorpland Hall, Norfolk,* 4.
Warner *of Antigua,* 4.
Warner *of Quorn Hall, Leicester,* 4.
Warner *of Higham Hall, Essex,* 3, 4.
Warner *of Ardeer, Ayr,* I. ii. 340; 2, 3, 4.
Warre *of Hestercombe;* see Tyndale *of Haling,* 2, 3, 4.
Warren *of Killiney Castle, Dublin,* 3, 4.
Warren *of Lodge Park, Kilkenny,* 4.
Warren *of Sandford's Court, Kilkenny,* 2.
Warrener *of Conock House, Wilts,* 2.
Warrington *of Lancashire,* 2.
Warry *of Shapwick House, Somerset,* 3, 4.
Warter *of Cruck Meole, Salop,* 2, 3, 4.
Warton *of Kernsdale, Kent,* 4.
Waterhouse *of Halifax, York,* 2, 3, 4.
Waters *of Sarnau, Caermarthen,* 2, 3, 4.
Waterton *of Walton Hall, York,* 2, 3, 4.
Wathen *of Woodchester, Gloucester,* 2, 3.
Watkins *of Pernnoyre, Brecknock,* 2, 3, 4.
Watkins *of Woodfield, Worcester,* 2, 3, 4.
Watkins *of Shotton Hall, Salop,* 3, 4.
Watkins *of Badby House, Northampton,* 3, 4.

Watkins *of Yorkshire,* 2, 3, 4.
Watling *of Fron Ganol, Denbigh,* 4.
Watlington Perry- *of Moor Hall, Essex,* 4.
Watlington *of Berkshire,* 2.
Watson *of Calgarth Park, Westmoreland,* 3, 4.
Watson *of Kilmanahan Castle, Waterford,* 3, 4.
Watson *of Kilconner House, Carlow,* 3, 4.
Watson *of Lumclone, Carlow,* 3, 4.
Watson *of Clonbrogan and Buffana, Tipperary,* 2.
Watt *of Bell Vale, Lancaster,* 2.
Watts *of Danet's Hall,* 2 add.
Watts *of Hawkesdale Hall, Cumberland,* I. iii. 393; 2, 3, 4.
Watts *of Abney Hall, Chester,* 3, 4.
Watts *of Hanslope Park, Bucks,* 4.
Wauchope *of Niddrie Marischal, Midlothian,* 2, 3, 4.
Wauchope *of Edmonstone, Edinburgh,* 2, 3.
Waud *of Chester Court, York,* 2, 3, 4.
Way *of Denham, Bucks,* I. iv. 676; 2, 3, 4.
Waylen *of Devizes, Wilts,* 2 add.
Wayne *of Quorndon House, Derby,* 4.
Webb *of Newstead Abbey, Notts, and of Cowton, York,* 3, 4.
Webb *of Donnington Hall, Hereford,* 2, 3, 4.
Webb *of Woodville, Tipperary,* 2, 3, 4.
Webb *of Webbsborough, Kilkenny,* 2.
Webb *of Caheragh House, Cork,* 2, 3, 4.
Webb *of The Berrow, Worcester,* 4.
Webber *of Leckfield, Sligo, and of Kellyville, Queen's Co.,* 4.
Webster, *of Penns, Warwick,* 3, 4.
Webster *of Balruddery, Forfar,* 2 supp.
Wedderburn *of Wedderburn, Forfar,* 2, 3, 4.
Wedderburn-Colville, now Colville *of Ochiltree, Fife,* 2 supp., 3, 4.
Weedon *of Hall Court, Sussex,* 4.
Weekes *of Hampton Lodge, Sussex,* 2, 3, 4

Wegg-Prosser *of Belmont, Hereford,* 4.
Weightman or Wightham *of Burbage, Leicester,* 4.
Welch *of Arle House, Gloucester,* 2, 3, 4.
Weld *of Lulworth, Dorset,* I. i, 197; ii. 677; 2, 3, 4.
Weld-Blundell *of Ince Blundell, Lancaster,* 2, 3, 4.
Welfitt *of Sherwood Lodge, Notts,* 4.
Welfitt *of Manby Hall, Lincoln,* 2, supp.
Welles *of Grebby Hall, Lincoln,* I. ii. 516; 2, 3, 4.
Wells *of Holme Wood, Huntingdon,* 3, 4.
Wells *of Boxford, Kent,* 2.
Welwood, Clarke- *of Comrie Castle, Perth,* I. i. 276; 3, 4.
Wellwood *of Garvock, Fife,* 2.
Welman *of Norton Manor, Somerset,* I. iii. 649; 2, 3, 4.
Welsted *of Ballywalter, Cork,* 3, 4.
Wemys *of Danesfort, Kilkenny,* 2,3,4.
Wentworth *of Wentworth Castle, York,* I. ii. 81; 2, 3, 4.
Wentworth *of Woolley, York,* I. iii. 89; 2, 3, 4.
Werden *of Leyland, Lancaster,* I. iv. 330.
Were *of Wellington, Somerset,* I. iv. 140; 2.
Werge *of Hexgrave Park, Notts,* I. i. 378; 2, 3.
West *of Postern Park, Kent,* 2.
West *of Alscot Park, Gloucester,* 2, 3, 4.
West *of Braywick Lodge, Bucks,* 2, 3, 4.
West *of Harham Hall, Essex,* 2, 3, 4.
Westby *of Mowbreck and Rawcliffe, Lancaster,* I. i. 597; 2, 3, 4.
Westby *of Roebuck Castle, Dublin,* I. iii. 117; 4.
Westby *of Thornhill, Clare,* 2.
Westby *of High Park, Wicklow,* I. iii. 119; 2, 3, 4.
Westcar *of Burwood Cottage, Surrey, and Hill House,* 2, 3, 4.
Western *of Tattingstone Place, Suffolk, and of Felix Hall, Essex,* 2, and add., 3, 4.

Webbe-Weston *of Sarnesfield;* see Salvin, 2, 3, 4.
Weston *of West Horsley, Surrey,* 2, 3, 4.
Weston *of Somerby,* 2 add.
Westropp *of Attyflin, Limerick,* 2, 3, 4.
Westropp *of Coolreagh, Limerick,* 2.
Weyland *of Woodeaton, Oxford,* 2, 3, 4.
Whalley *of Somersetshire,* I. iv. 606.
Wharton *of Dryburn, Durham,* 2, 3, 4.
Wharton *of Skelton Castle, York,* 4.
Wharton-Myddleton *of Old Park, Durham,* I. i. 171; 2.
Whatman *of Vinters, Kent,* 2, 3, 4.
Whatton *of Leicestershire,* I. iv. 224; 2.
Wheble *of Bulmershe Court, Berks,* 4.
Wheeler *of Kyrewood House, Worcester,* 2, 3, 4.
Wheeler *of Otterden Place, Kent,* 2, 3, 4.
Whetham *of Kirklington Hall, Notts,* 2.
Whieldon *of Springfield House, Dorset,* I. iii. 116; 2, 3, 4.
Whippy *of Lee Place, Oxford,* 2, 3, 4.
Whitacre *of Woodhouse, York,* 2, 3, 4.
Whitaker *of Broadclough, Lancaster,* 2, 3, 4.
Whitaker *of Symonstone, Lancaster,* 2, 3, 4.
Whitaker *of the Holme, Lancaster,* 2, 3, 4.
Whitbread *of Southill, Bedford,* 2 supp., 3, 4.
Whitbread *of Loudham Park, Suffolk,* 2, 3, 4.
Whitby *of Creswell, Stafford,* 2,3,4.
Whitchurch *of Frome Selwood,* 2.
White *of Clement's Hall, Essex,* 2, 3, 4.
White *of Kellerstain, Midlothian,* 2, 3, 4.
White *of Scarnagh, Wexford,* 2,3,4.
White *of Woodlands, Dublin,* 2,3,4.
White *of Charlton Marshall, Dorset,* 2, 3.

White *of Belmont, Limerick*, 3.
White *of Exeter*, 2.
White *of Yeovil, Somerset*, 2.
Whiteford *of Thornhill, Devon*, 3, 4.
Whitgreave *of Moseley Court, Stafford*, I. iv. 558; 2, 3, 4.
Whitla *of Gobrana, Antrim*, 3, 4.
Whitmore *of Apley, Salop*, I. ii. 409; 2, 3, 4.
Whitmore *of Dudmaston, Salop*, I. ii. 412; 2, 3, 4.
Whitney *of Merton, Wexford*, 3, 4.
Whittaker *of Newcastle Court, Radnor*, 2, 3, 4.
Whittell *of Westow, York*, 2 supp., 3, 4.
Whitter *of Ashhurst, Sussex*, 4.
Whitter *of Devon*, 2, 3.
Whitting *of Sandcroft House, Somerset*, 4.
Whittingham *of Potton, Bedford*, 2.
Whittingstall *of Langley Bury, Herts*, 2.
Whittuck *of Hanham Hall, Gloucester*, 2, 3, 4.
Whyte *of Loughbrickland, Down*, 2, and add. 3, 4.
Whyte *of Newtown Manor, Leitrim*, 3, 4.
Whyte *of Redhills, Cavan*, 2, 3, 4.
Whytehead *of Crayke, York*, 2 supp. 3, 4.
Wickham *of Horsington, Somerset*, I. iv. 596; 2, 3, 4.
Wickham *of Bradford, York*, 3, 4.
Wicksted *of Betley Hall, Stafford*, I. i. 497; 2, 3, 4.
Widdrington *of Newton Hall and Hauxley, Northumberland*, 2, 3, 4.
Wight *of Brabauf Manor, Surrey*, 3, 4.
Wightwick *of Great Bloxwich, Stafford*, 2, 4.
Wilberforce *of Yorkshire*, I. iv. 720; 2, 3, 4.
Wilberforce *of Wool Lavington, Sussex*, 2.
Wilbraham *of Delamere, Chester*, I. i. 315; 2, 3, 4.
Wilbraham *of Rode*, 2, 3, 4.
Wilder *of Purley Hall and Sulham, Berks*, 2, 3, 4.

Wildman *of Newstead Abbey, Notts*, 2, 3.
Wilkins *of Maeslough Castle, Radnor*, I. ii. 216.
Wilkins *of Maesderwen, Brecon*. I. ii. 218.
Wilkins *of Clifton, Gloucester*, I. iii. 391.
Wilkinson *of White Webbs, Middlesex*, 3, 4.
Wilkinson *of Coxhoe, Durham*, I. i. 69; 2, 3, 4.
Wilkinson *of Winterburn Hall, York*, 2, 3, 4.
Wilkinson *of Harperley Park, Durham*, 2, 3, 4.
Willard *of Eastbourne, Sussex*, 2.
Willes *of Astrop House, Northampton*, 2, 3, 4.
Williams *of Ivytower, Pembroke*, I. i. 647; 2.
Williams *of Rushden Hall, Northampton*, I. ii. 14.
Williams *of Cowley Grove, Middlesex*, 2, 3.
Williams *of Herrington, Dorset*, I. i. 614; 2, 3, 4.
Williams *of Bridehead, Dorset*, I. i. 618; 2, 3, 4.
Williams *of Warfield Lodge, Berks*, 2, 3, 4.
Williams *of Llangibby Castle, Monmouth*, 2, 3, 4.
Williams *of Williamston, Kildare*, 4.
Williams *of Coldbrook Park, Monmouth*, 2, 3, 4.
Williams *of Gwernant Park, Cardigan*, 2, 3, 4.
Williams *of Temple House, Berks*, I. ii. 635; 2, 3, 4.
Williams *of Treffos, Anglesey*, 2, 3, 4.
Williams *of Malvern Hall, Warwick*, 3, 4.
Williams *of Burncoose and Caerhays Castle, Cornwall*, 4.
Williams *of Tregullow, Cornwall*, 4.
Williams *of Dendreath Castle, Merioneth*, 4.
Williams *of Cumcynfelin, Cardigan*, 4.
Williams *of Abercamlais*, 4.
Williamson *of Lawers, Perth*, 3, 4.
Williamson *of Wickham, Durham*, 2.

Willington *of Tamworth, Warwick,* I. iv. 526; 2, 3, 4.
Willington *of Killoskehane, Tipperary,* 2, 3, 4.
Willington *of Castle Willington, Tipperary,* 2, 3, 4.
Willis (De Anyers) *of Halsnead Park, Lancaster,* I. i. 43; 2, 3, 4.
Willis *of Wick House, Worcester,* 4.
Willis *of Willsgrove, Roscommon,* 2, 3, 4.
Willoughby *of Kingsbury Cliff, Warwick,* 2.
Willson *of South Rauceby, Lincoln,* 4.
Willyams *of Carnanton, Cornwall,* I. iv. 35; 2, 3, 4.
Wilshere *of Welwyn, Herts,* 4.
Wilson *of Stowlangtoft Hall, Suffolk,* 2, 3, 4.
Wilson *of Brinkcliffe Tower, York,* 3, 4.
Wilson *of Cahirconlish, Limerick,* 2, 4.
Wilson *of Knowle Hall, Warwick,* 2, 3, 4.
Wilson *of Dallam Tower, Westmoreland,* 2, 3, 4.
Wilson *of Redgrave Hall, Suffolk,* 2, 3, 4.
Wilson *of Eshton Hall, York,* I. iii. 183; 2, 3, 4.
Wilson *of Evening Hill, Cumberland,* 2, 3.
Wilson *of High Wray, Lancaster,* 2.
Wilson *of South Rauceby, Lincoln,* 3.
Windham *of Felbrigg Hall, Norfolk,* 2, 3, 4.
Windham, Smyth- *of Waghen, York,* 2, 3, 4.
Wingfield *of Tickencote, Rutland,* I. ii. 476; 2, 3, 4.
Wingfield *of Sherborne Castle;* see Digby, 4.
Wingfield *of Onslow, Salop,* I. ii. 483; 2, 3, 4.
Winn *of Nostel, York,* 3, 4.
Winstanley *of Braunston House, Leicester,* I. i. 363.; 2, 3, 4.
Winter *of Agher, Meath,* I. ii. 547; 2, 3, 4.
Wise *of Clayton, Stafford,* I. i. 19; 2, 3, 4.

Wise *of Woodcote, Warwick,* 2, 3, 4.
Wise *of Leamington, Warwick,* 2, 3, 4.
Witham *of Lartington, York,* I. ii. 5; 2, 3, 4.
Wither *of Manydown, Hants,* I. ii. 397; 2, 3, 4.
Woddrop *of Dalmarnock,* 4.
Wodehouse *of Woolmer's Park, Hertford,* 3, 4.
Wolcott *of Knowle House, Devon,* 2, 3, 4.
Wolfe *of Bishop Land, Kildare,* 3, 4.
Wolfe *of Wood Hall, Essex,* 4.
Wolferstan *of Statfold Hall, Stafford.* I. i. 187; 2, 3, 4.
Wollaston *of Shenton, Leicester,* I. iii. 415; 2, and add., 3, 4.
Wolley *of Allen Hill, Derby,* 2, 3, 4.
Wood *of Swanwick, Derby,* I. iii. 137.
Wood *of Brownshills, Stafford,* I. iv. 640.
Wood *of Hollin Hall, York,* I. iii. 691; 2, 3, 4.
Wood *of Largo, Fife,* 4.
Wood *of Bishop's Hall, Essex,* I. iv. 81; 2, 3, 4.
Wood *of Littleton, Middlesex,* 2, 3, 4.
Wood *of Thoresby, Lincoln,* 2, 3, 4.
Wood *of the Whitehouse, Hereford,* 2, 3, 4.
Wood *of Woodville, Sligo,* 2, 3, 4.
Wood *of Wirksworth Hall, Derby,* 3, 4.
Wood *of Singleton Lodge, Lancaster,* I. iii. 138; 3, 4.
Woodcock *of Rearsby House, Leicester,* 4.
Woodd *formerly of Shine Wood,* 2, 3, 4.
Woodforde *of Ansford House, Somerset,* I. iv. 760; 2, 3, 4.
Woodhouse *of Omeath Park, Louth,* 4.
Woodhouse *of Womborne Woodhouse,* I. iii. 613; 2.
Woods *of Milverton, Dublin,* 2, 3, 4.
Woods *of Wigan, Lancaster,* 2 supp., 3, 4.
Woodward *of Drumbarrow, Meath,* 3, 4.
Woodyeare *of Crook Hill, York,* I. iv. 361; 2, 3, 4.

Woolrych *of Croxley, Herts*, 2, 3, 4.
Woolryche *of Quatford Lodge, Salop*, 2 supp.
Wordsworth *of Sockbridge, Westmoreland*, 4.
Worsley *of Hovingham Hall, York*, I. iv. 607.
Worge *of Battle, Sussex*, 2.
Worley *of Long Coppice, Iver, Bucks*, 2 supp.
Wormley *of Riccall Hall, York*, 2 supp.
Worthington *of the Bryn, Chester*, 3, 4.
Worthington *of Sandiway Bank, Chester*, 2.
Wray *of Kilfield*, I. iv. 21; 2.
Wray *of Castle Wray, Donegal*, 3, 4.
Wright *of Kelvedon, Essex*, 2, 3, 4.
Wright *of Kilverstone, Norfolk*, I. ii. 614; 2, 3, 4.
Wright *of Osmaston Manor, Derby*, 2, 3, 4.
Wright *of Mapperley, Nottingham*, 2, 3, 4.
Wright *of Golagh House, Monaghan*, 3, 4.
Wright *of Gola House, Monaghan*, 2.
Wright *of Bolton-on-Swale, York*, I. ii. 678; 2.
Wright *of Mottram, St. Andrews, Chester*, I. iii. 404; 2.
Wright *of Longstone Hall, Derby*, 2 add.
Wrightson *of Cusworth, York*, 2, 3, 4.
Wroughton *of Woolley Park, Berks*, 2, 3, 4.
Wroughton *of Ibstone House, Bucks*, 2, 3.
Wrowe-Walton *of Marsden Hall, Lancaster*, 2.
Wybergh *of Clifton Hall, Westmoreland*, I. iii. 702; 2, 3, 4.
Wykeham *of Tythrop House, Oxford*, I. i. 419; 2, 3, 4.
Wylde *of Southwell, Nottingham*, 2, 3, 4.
Wyndham *of Dinton, Wilts*, 2, 3, 4.
Wyndham *of Sarum*, 2 supp., 3, 4.
Wyndham *of Cromer, Norfolk*, I. ii. 244.
Wyndowe *of Gloucestershire*, 2 supp.

Wynn *of Rug in Edeirnion, Merioneth*, 4.
Wynn *of Llangedwin, Denbigh*, 2.
Wynne *of Voelas, Denbigh*, 2 supp., 3, 4.
Wynne *of Llwyn, Denbigh*, 2, 3.
Wynne *of Peniarth, Merioneth*, I. i. 566; 2, 3, 4.
Wynne *of Haslewood, Sligo*, 2, 3, 4.
Wynne *of Garthewin, Denbigh*, I. iii. 646; 2, 3, 4.
Wynne *of Coed Coch, Denbigh*, 2, 3, 4.
Wynniatt *of Dymoch Grange, Gloucester*, 2, 3, 4.
Wyse *of the Manor of St. John, Waterford*, 3, 4.
Wyvill *of Constable Burton, York*, I. iv. 467; 2, 3, 4.
Yaldwyn *of Blackdown, Sussex*, 2 supp., 3, 4.
Yale *of Plas-yn-Yale, Denbigh*, 2, 4.
Yarborough *of Campsmount, York*, 2, 3, 4.
Yarburgh *of Heslington, York*, I. iii. 661; 2, 3, 4.
Yarde *of Whiteway, Devon*, 4.
Yarker *of Leyburn, York*, 2, 3, 4.
Yate *of Bromesberrow, Gloucester*, 2.
Yates *of Dingle Head, Lancaster*, 3, 4.
Yeatman *of Stock House, Dorset*, 2, 3, 4.
Yonge *of Puslinch, Devon*, 2, and supp., 3, 4.
Yonge *of Charnes Hall, Stafford*, 2, 3, 4.
Yonge *of Otterbourn, Hants*, 2.
Yonge, Younge, or Young *of Orlingbury*, 2 add.
York *of Wighill Park, York*, I. i. 664; 2, 3, 4.
Yorke *of Bewerley, York*, I. iv. 744; 2, 3, 4.
Yorke *of Erddig, Denbigh*, I. i. 344; 2, 3, 4.
Yorke *of Dyffryn Aled, Denbigh*, 2, 3, 4.
Yorke *of Forthampton Court, Gloucester*, 2, 3, 4.
Young *of Kingerby, Lincoln*, 2 supp., 3, 4.

Young *of Orlingbury, Northampton,* 2, 3, 4.
Young *of Cleish, Kinross,* 2, 3, 4.
Young *of Coolkeiragh, Londonderry,* 2, 3, 4.

Young *of Culdaff House, Donegal,* 3, 4.
Young *of Harristown, Roscommon,* 3 supp., 4.
Yuille *of Darleith, Dumbarton,* 3, 4.

235.—The Herald and Genealogist. Edited by JOHN GOUGH NICHOLS, F.S.A. *London.* Parts 1 to 19. 1862-1866. 8vo.

Archer, iii. 523-539.
Bate ; see Henzey.
Brettell ; see Henzey.
Bruning *of Wymering and Hambledon, Hants,* iii. 519.
Bury, Dormer, Hawtrey, and Croke, i. 338.
Carey, Lord Hunsdon, iv. 38-48.
Cary, Viscount Falkland, ii. 341, 344 ; iii. 33-54, 129-146.
Canning, i. 373-377.
Cheyne, iii. 290.
Clavering *of Callaby,* iii. 513.
Croke ; see Bury.
De Montagne, Counts, iii. 176.
Dormer ; see Bury.
Ensor and Shakespeare, ii. 205-215.
FitzCharles ; see Greene.
FitzJames ; see Waldegrave.
Fitzroy ; see Greene.
Gaynesford, i. 337.
Gifford ; see Guldeford.
Greene, Fitzroy, and FitzCharles, iii. 119.
Guldeford and Gifford, iii. 420.
Haggerston, iii. 513.
Hawtrey ; see Bury.
Heneage, iii.419.
Henzey, Brettell, and Bate, i. 421-430.
Holt, ii. 156.
Huddleston, iii. 418.
Hunloke, iii. 422.
Husey, i. 526.
Lauder, iii. 466.
Lee *of Quarrendon,* iii. 113-122, 289-295, 481-489.
Lowle or Lowell, iv. 75.
Markham, and Neville *of Holt,* iii. 516.
Mauleverer, ii. 304-11.
Mee, iii. 410.

Montague, iii. 422.
Nelson, iv. 12.
Neville *of Abergavenny ;* see Vaux.
Neville *of Holt ;* see Markham.
Norton, iii. 277-279.
Petre *of Ingatestone,* iii. 425.
Roper *of Eltham,* iii. 417.
Salvin and Strickland, iii. 428.
Sarsfield, ii. 205-215.
Scrope ; see Sheldon.
Selby *of Biddlestone,* iii. 518.
Shakespeare ; see Ensor.
Sheldon and Scrope, iii. 423.
Shelley ; see Vaux.
Simeon ; see Vaux.
Smart from Herbert, ii. 249-253.
Smith, ii. 78.
Smith, *alias* Carington, and Philpott, iii. 427.
Stanley, iii. 285.
Strickland ; see Salvin.
Sutton, ii. 491.
Taaffe, iii. 471.
Temple, iii. 386-410, 529-544 ; iv. 8-13.
Temple *of Mount Temple, co. Westmeath,* iii. 409.
Thackeray, ii. 315-328, 440-455.
Thorold, iii. 421.
Timperley, iii. 420.
Tichborne *of Tichborne, Hants,* iii. 424 ; iv. 64.
Underhill, ii. 127-132.
Vaux, Neville *of Abergavenny,* Simeon and Shelley, iii. 515.
Waldegrave and FitzJames, iii. 424.
Waldo, ii. 237-45, 312-314.
Washington, iv. 62.
Wenman, ii. 521.
West, iii. 296.
Weston, Earl of Portland, iii. 426.
Widdington *of Widdington,* iii. 514.

236.—The Royal Families of England, Scotland, and Wales, with their descendants. By JOHN BURKE, ESQ. and JOHN BERNARD BURKE, ESQ. *London,* 1851. 2 vols. Royal 8vo.

Abingdon, Earl of, ii. 135.

Adair, Sir Robert Shafto, Bart. ii. 29.

Adams, Edward, Esq. ii. 203.

Agnew, Robert Vans, Esq. i. 173.

Aikin, Eliza Constance, ii. 188.

Ailsa, Marquis of, ii. 183.

Allan, Robert Henry, Esq. i. 67.

Allan *of Blackwell Hall,* ii. 15.

Allardice, Robert Barclay, Esq. ii. 33.

Amphlett, Richard Paul, Esq. i. 135.

Anderton, William Ince, Esq. ii. 148.

Annesley, Arthur Littleton, Esq. i. 118.

Anson, Edward Hamilton, Esq. ii. 101.

Anstruther, Sir Ralph Abercrombie, Bart. ii. 56.

Ashfordby-Trenchard, Rev. John T. Craven, i. 199.

Ashurst, William Henry, Esq. i. 194.

Baker, William Robert, Esq. i. 78.

Balfour, David, Esq. i. 60.

Barneby, Thomas, Esq. i. 121.

Barrett-Lennard, Thomas, Esq., M.P. ii. 22.

Barrington, Louisa Edith, (Lady Simeon), ii. 192.

Baskerville, Thomas Baskerville, Esq. i. 18.

Bastard, Edmund Rodney Pollexfen, Esq. ii. 159.

Bates, Ralph, Esq. ii. 86.

Beckford, William, Esq. ii. 116.

Berkeley, Rev. John Rowland, ii. 51.

Berwick, Lord, i. 113.

Best, Rev. J. Wilkes, A.M. ii. 212*.

Binning-Home, George Home, Esq. i. 195.

Birch-Reynardson, Charles Thomas Samuel, Esq. ii. 146.

Blaauw, Mrs. ii. 175.

Blakiston, Sir Matthew, Bart. ii. 21.

Blathwayt, George William, Esq. i. 54.

Blois, Sir Charles, Bart. ii. 52.

Blundell-Weld, Thomas, Esq. i. 101.

Bonar, Ernest Augustus, Esq. i. 179.

Borrowes, Rev. Sir Erasmus Dixon, Bart. i. 86.

Bower, Frances Mary, i. 181.

Bowes, Thomas, Esq. ii. 137.

Bowyer, Sir George, Bart. i. 33.

Boynton, Sir Henry, Bart. ii. 114.

Brandling, Rev. Ralph Henry, ii. 71.

Branfill, Mrs. Anne Eliza, i. 111.

Braye, Baroness, ii. 6.

Breadalbane, Marquess of, i. 192.

Brickdale, John Fortescue, Esq. i. 91.

Brodie, William, Esq. i. 109.

Broke, Sir Arthur de Capell, Bart. ii. 47.

Brooke, Sir Richard, Bart. i. 24.

Brougham and Vaux, Lord, ii. 204.

Bruce, William Downing, Esq. i. 34.

Bruce-Gardyne, Thomas Macpherson, Esq. i. 189.

Bruton, John and Wrey Chichester, Esqrs. ii. 181.

Bulwer, William Earle Lytton, Esq. i. 72.

Burne, Freville Lambton, Esq. ii. 15.

Burrard, Rev. Sir George, Bart. ii. 35.

Burroughes, Rev. Ellis, ii. 8.

Burton; see Conyngham.

Butt, Mary, i. 124.

Byam, William, Esq. and Rev. Richard Burgh, i. 196.

Bythesea, Samuel William, Esq. i. 165.

Calmady, Charles Biggs, Esq. ii. 206.

Campbell, George James, Esq. ii. 73.

Campbell, Robert, Esq. ii. 85.

Carew *of Crowcombe,* ii. 151.

Cardigan, Earl of, i. 141.

Carlyon, Edward, Esq. ii. 46.

Carnegie, W. F. Lindsay, Esq. ii. 177.

Carnarvon, Earl of, ii. 43.

Cary, George Stanley, Esq. ii. 105.

Cayley, Sir Geo., Bart. i. 164.
Chadwick, Hugo Malveysin, Esq. i. 160.
Chamberlayne, Joseph Chamberlayne, i. 198.
Champion de Crespigny, Sir Claude W., Bart. i. 84.
Chandos-Pole, Edward Sacheverell, ii. 198.
Chester, Charles, Esq. ii. 68.
Chetwode, Edward Wilmot, Esq. ii. 198.
Chichester, Sir Arthur, Bart. 209.
Clanricarde, Marquis of, i. 123.
Clarke, Edward Hyde, Esq. ii. 24.
Clarke-Wellwood, Andrew, Esq. i. 64.
Clavering, Edward John, Esq. i. 82.
Clerke, Sir William Henry, Bart. ii. 182.
Cobbe, Charles, Esq. ii. 133.
Cockburn of Cockburn, ii. 185*.
Coham, William Holland Bickford, Esq. ii. 176.
Coke, D'Ewes, Esq. ii. 124.
Cole, Francis Sewell, Esq. ii. 171.
Collingwood, Edward John, Esq. ii. 189.
Conyngham and Burton, ii. 207.
Cooke, Philip Davies, Esq. i. 9.
Coote, Charles Chidley, Esq. i. 180.
Corbet, Andrew William, Esq. i. 7.
Corbet, Sir Andrew Vincent, Bart. ii. 128.
Cornewall of Delbury, ii. 199.
Cotton-Sheppard, Sir Thomas, Bart. iv. 203.
Coulthart, John Ross, Esq. ii. 212.
Cranstoun, Lord, i. 139.
Creyke, Ralph, Esq. i. 21.
Crichton-Makgill, David Maitland, Esq. i. 107.
Croft, Sir Archer Denman, Bart. ii. 16.
Cuming, Hon. Mrs. Leslie, ii. 88.
Cuningham, Sir Thomas Montgomery, Bart., ii. 60.
Currer, Frances Mary Richardson, ii. 63.
Currie; see Wodehouse.
Cusack, James William, M.D. ii. 157.
Cutler, John and George Henry, Esqrs. ii. 113.
Dale, Edward, Esq. i. 16.

Dale, Thurston, Esq. ii. 142.
Dalison; see Hammond.
Dalton, John, Esq. ii. 134.
D'Arcy, G. A. R. Esq. ii. 160.
Davenport, Wm. Sherrington, Esq. ii. 112.
Davies, Owen, i. 94.
Davies of Gwysaney, ii. 214.
Davy, Charlotte, ii. 66.
Dawes, Matthew, Esq. ii. 117.
Dawson, Gerge Pelsant, Esq. ii. 121.
Dayrell of Shudy Camps, ii. 192.
De Burgh, Hubert, Esq. i. 55
De Clifford, Baroness, ii. 185.
De la Zouch, Baroness, ii. 75.
Dennis, Thomas Stratford, Esq. ii. 55.
Dering, Cholmeley Edward, Esq. ii. 136.
De Trafford, Sir Thomas Joseph, Bart. ii. 25.
De Winton, Cann, Esq., ii. 67.
D'Eyncourt, Rt. Hon. Charles Tennyson, i. 4.
Dick-Lauder, Sir John, Bart. ii. 173.
Dimsdale, Baron, ii. 125.
Disney, John, Esq. i. 79.
Dodsworth, Sir Charles, Bart. ii. 104.
Dolman, John Thomas, Esq. i. 8.
Dormer, Noble House of, ii. 110.
Donegal, Marques of, ii. 169.
Douglas, Sir Robert, Bart. i. 185.
Downshire, Marquess of, 167.
Drew, Rev. Pierce William, i. 13, 14.
Drogheda, Marquess of, i. 158.
Duckett, John Dawson, Esq. ii. 207.
Dugdale, Wm. Stratford, Esq. i. 63.
Dunlop-Wallace, Robert Henry, Esq. i. 202.
Dunraven, Earl of, ii. 202.
East, Sir James Buller, Bart. ii. 145.
Eddy, Rev. J., M.A. i. 124.
Egerton, Wilbraham, Esq. ii. 30.
Eglinton and Winton, Earl of, i. 39.
Eld of Leighford, i. 56.
Elders, Rev. Carew Thomas, ii. 187.
Essex, Earl of, i. 172.
Ettrick, Anthony, Esq. i. 97.
Eyre, Charles, Esq. ii. 120.
Falkland, Viscount, ii. 91.
Falmouth, Viscount, ii. 58.
Farnell, Harry Burrard, Esq. ii. 182*.
Farnham, Lord, i. 1, 153.
Feilding, Lady, i. 47.

Fenwick, John, Esq. ii. 140.
Ferrers, Marmion Edward, Esq. i. 90.
Ferrers, Earl, ii. 65, 172.
Ffarington, James Nowell, Esq. i. 12.
Fitzgerald, John Francis, Knight of Glin, ii. 107.
Forbes, Lord, i. 176.
Forbes, Sir William, Bart. ii. 208.
Frampton, John, Esq. ii. 165.
French, Charlotte Emma Georgiana, i. 61.
Gatacre, Col. Edward, i. 152.
Galton, John Howard, Esq. ii. 12.
Gerard, Sir John, Bart, ii. 191.
Gilbert, Rev John Pomroy, i. 140.
Gore, Montague, Esq. i. 450.
Graeme of Garvock, ii. 174.
Graham, James Maxwell, Esq. i. 92.
Graham, Robert, Esq. ii. 37.
Graham of Fintry, ii. 122.
Gray, Rev. John Hamilton, ii. 23, 115.
Granville, Bernard, Esq. i. 44.
Greaves, Charles S., Esq. ii. 166*.
Greene, Henry, Esq. ii. 197.
Grimaldi, Marquess, ii. 167.
Grimston, Charles, Esq. i. 187.
Guildford, Earl of, i. 138.
Guthrie, John, Esq. ii. 27.
Gwynne, John, Esq. ii. 100.
Gyll, Brook Hamilton, Esq. ii. 97.
Halhead, Hilton, Esq. ii. 131.
Hall, Lady, ii. 94.
Hall, Sir John, Bart. i. 126.
Hammond and Dalison, ii. 183.
Hanford, Charles Edward, i. 103.
Harbin, George, Esq. i. 41.
Harrington, Earl of, ii. 78.
Hartley, Winchcombe Henry Howard, Esq. i. 77.
Helyer, William Hawker, Esq. i. 104.
Hepburn, Sir Thomas Buchan, Bart. ii. 84.
Herbert, John Arthur, Esq. ii. 103.
Hereford, Viscount, i 197.
Hertford, Marquess of, ii. 32.
Heytesbury, Lord, i. 182.
Hildyard, Rev. William, i. 100.
Hill, Viscount, i. 174.
Hinde, Rev. Thomas and Mrs. ii. 31.
Hippesley, Gustavus Alexander Butler, Esq. i. 186.

Hoblyn, Deeble Peter, Esq., ii. 41.
Hoghton, Sir Henry Bold, Bart. i. 125.
Holford, Mrs. A. M. E. Gwynne, i. 129.
Hony, Ven. Archdeacon, i. 154.
Horlock, Isaac John Webb, Esq. i. 190.
Hornyold, Thomas Charles, Esq. i. 177,
Hoskyns, Charles Wren, Esq. i. 66.
Howard, Philip Henry, Esq. ii. 46.
Howard de Walden, Lord, ii. 161.
Howth, Earl of, i. 171.
Huddlestone, Francis, Esq. i. 130.
Hughes, Thomas, Esq. i. 74.
Hughes of Gwerclas, i. 52.
Hunloke, Sir Henry, Bart. i. 120.
Huntingdon, Earl of, i. 36.
Huyshe, John, M.A. ii. 179.
Ibbetson, Sir Charles Henry, Bart. i. 201.
James, Demetrius Gervis, Esq. ii. 39.
Jenkyns, Mrs. i. 23.
Jodrell, John William, Esq. i. 40.
Joliffe, John Twyford, Esq. i. 70.
Kempe, Rev. Sir William Robert, Bart. i. 114.
Kempe, William, Esq. i. 143.
Landon, Charles Ginkell, Esq. ii. 72.
Langton, William Henry Powell Gore, Esq. i. 71.
Lamb, Sir Charles Montolieu, Bart. ii. 144.
Leeds, Duke of, i. 144.
Lee-Warner, Rev. Daniel Henry, i. 117.
Le Hunt, Peter Bainbrigge, Esq. ii. 123.
Leigh, Lord, i. 38.
Leigh, Egerton, Esq. ii. 138.
Leith, James Forbes, Esq. ii. 90.
Lenthall, Kyffin John William, Esq. i. 123.
Le Strange, H. L. Styleman, Esq. ii. 184.
Lethbridge, John Hesketh, Esq. ii. 106.
Lewis, Thomas, Esq. ii. 43.
Lillingston, Charles, Esq. ii. 98.
Limerick, Earl of, ii. 45.

Lind and Sherwill, i. 80.
Lindsey, Earl of, i. 166.
Lloyd, Thomas Davies, Esq. i. 42.
Lloyd, Edward Pryse, Esq. i. 191.
Lloyd, George, Esq. ii. 53.
Lloyd-Price, ii. 111.
Loftus, George Colby, Esq. i. 168.
Long, Walter, Esq. i. 159 ; ii. 153.
Lovat, Lord, ii. 63.
Lovelace, Earl of, ii. 70.
Lowndes-Stone, William F. Esq. i. 3.
Lowndes, William, Esq. i. 26.
Lowndes, William Selby, Esq. i. 55.
Lutwidge, Charles Robert Fletcher, Esq. ii. 38.
Macalister, Charles Somerville, Esq. i. 106.
MacKay, George, Esq. ii. 80.
Mackenzie, Keith William Stewart, Esq. ii. 2.
Mackenzie, Sir Evan, Bart. ii. 17.
Mackenzie, Sir James J. Randoll, Bart. ii. 162.
Mackinnon, William Alexander, ii. 18.
Mackworth, Sir Digby, Bart. i. 53.
Macleod of Macleod, i. 156.
M‘Adam, William, Esq. i. 73.
Madocks, John Edward, Esq. ii. 87.
Mainwaring, Rowland, Esq. i. 29.
Malmesbury, Earl of, ii. 61.
Mansel, Sir John Bell William, Bart. ii. 206.
Marriott, Thomas Beckett Fielding, Esq. ii. 20.
Martin, Sir Roger, Bart. i. 132.
Massereene, Viscount, ii. 1.
Mathew, Mrs. ii. 11.
Maxwell, Sir John, Bart. ii. 3.
Maxwell, Sir John Heron, Bart. ii. 74.
Menzies, Ronald Steuart, Esq. i. 68.
Methuen, Lord, i. 105.
Meynell-Ingram, Hugo Charles, Esq. i. 99.
Milford, Lord, 79.
Mills, William, Esq. i. 107.
Mitford, Robert, Esq. i. 136.
Morgan, George Robert, Esq. i. 35.
Mostyn, Thomas Arthur Bertie, Esq. ii. 132.
Mostyn, Sir Peirs, Bart. ii. 200*.

Mundy, William, Esq. i. 142.
Murray, John Nesbitt, Esq. i. 22.
Murray, John, Esq. i. 162.
Musgrave, Sir George, Bart. ii. 64.
Mynors, Peter Rickards, Esq. i. 81.
Mytton, Richard Herbert, Esq. i. 146.
Nangle, George, and Lucy Mary Tichborne, his wife, ii. 50.
Nelson, Earl, ii. 119.
Newman, Henry Wenman, Esq. i. 69.
Nicholson, Elizabeth Jane, i. 51.
Noel, Charles, Esq. i. 175.
Norreys, Sir Charles D. O. J., Bart. ii. 200.
North, Baroness, i. 115.
Northey-Hokkyns, William R., Esq. ii. 129.
Northumberland, Duke of, i. 85.
Northwick, Lord, i. 134.
Nowell of Rede and Netherside, i. 27.
Oakeley, Sir C. W. Atholl, Bart. i. 178.
Onslow, Earl of, ii. 76.
O'Reilly, James, Esq. i. 151.
Orlebar, Robert Shipton, Esq. ii. 139.
Orme, Humphrey, Esq. i. 59.
Owen, Thomas Bulkeley, Esq. i. 98.
Packe, Charles William, ii. 211.
Pakenham, Hon. and Very Rev. Henry, ii. 158.
Palmer, Sir John Henry, Bart. ii. 9.
Palmes, George, Esq. ii. 77.
Pares, Thomas, Esq. ii. 13.
Parker, Robert Townley, Esq. i. 93.
Paston-Bedingfeld, Sir Henry R. Bart. i. 148.
Paterson, George Hilton, Esq. ii. 194.
Patrick, William Charles Cochran, Esq. ii. 59.
Pearce, Lieut.-Col. William, K.H. i. 50 ; ii. 89.
Peter, William, Esq. i. 163.
Peters, Rev. Thomas, ii. 57.
Phillipps, Mrs. i. 184.
Plumptre, John Pemberton, Esq. ii. 127.
Pigot, Sir Robert, Bart. ii. 149.
Pigott, G. Grenville Wandesford, Esq. i. 147.

Poer, George Beresford, Esq. i. 200.
Polwhele, Maj. Richard Graves, i. 10.
Portman, Lord, ii. 143.
Powell, Henry Folliott, Esq. i. 32.
Price, Francis Richard, Esq. i. 87.
Prideaux, Sir Edmund Saunderson, Bart. i. 5.
Prinsep, Thomas Levett, Esq. ii. 4.
Prior, Andrew Redmond, Esq. ii. 196.
Pusey, Philip, Esq. i. 58.
Quantock, John Matthew, Esq. i. 62.
Radcliffe, F. P. Delmé, Esq. i. 37.
Rashleigh, William, Esq. i. 88.
Reade, Sir John Chandos, Bart. i. 130.
Reynardson, Charles T. S. Birch, Esq. ii. 146.
Richmond, Legh, Esq. i. 48.
Riddell, Sir W. Buchanan, Bart. ii. 164.
Riddell, Thomas, Esq. i. 45.
Robertson, William, Esq. ii. 190.
Saladin, Charles William, Esq. ii. 168.
Salisbury, Marquis of, i. 30, 31.
Salmond, James, Esq. i. 96.
Salway, John, Esq. i. 28.
Saunders. Richard, Esq. ii. 126.
Sawle, Sir Joseph Sawle Graves, Bart. i. 20.
Sawyer, Charles, Esq. ii. 92.
Saye and Sele, Lord, ii. 93.
Scudamore-Stanhope, Sir Edwin F. Bart. ii. 205*.
Scarle, John William, Esq. i. 76.
Selby, Walter, Esq. i. 49.
Seton, Alexander, Esq. ii. 186.
Shannon, Earl of, i. 170.
Sheldon, Henry James, Esq., i. 17.
Sherwill; see Lind.
Shuckburgh, Sir Francis, Bart. ii. 14.
Skelly, Francis, Esq. i. 183.
Skipwith, Sir Gray, Bart. ii. 102.
Slingsby, Sir Charles, Bart. ii. 42.
Smyth, Rev. Sir Edward Bowyer, Bart. ii. 96.
Smythe, William, Esq. ii. 5.
Sneyd, Rev. Lewis, ii. 44.

Southwell, Viscount, i. 119.
Standish, William Standish, Esq. ii. 147.
Stanhope, Earl, i. 188.
Stapleton, Hon. and Rev. Sir Francis, Bart. ii. 10.
Starkie, Le Gendre Nicholas, Esq. i. 112.
Steuart, Lady Seton, ii. 178.
Stinton, Joseph, Esq. ii. 40.
St. John, Lord, ii. 7.
Storer, Rev. John, i. 83.
Storer, Anthony Morris, Esq. ii. 169.
Stourton, Lord, ii. 170.
Stradbroke, Earl of.
Strode, Sir Edward Chetham, K.C.B. ii. 69.
Strong, George, M.D. ii. 208.
Surtees, Henry George, Esq. ii. 19.
Swettenham, Thomas J. W., Esq. i. 116.
Swinton of Swinton, ii. 25.
Tatton, Thomas William, Esq. i. 6.
Taylor, William Bewley, Esq. i. 157.
Tempest, John Plumbe, Esq. i. 19.
Thomas, Rev. Goring, Esq. i. 166.
Thornton, John, i. 193.
Thorpe, Archdeacon, ii. 155.
Tollemache, John, Esq., i. 128.
Tower, Christopher, Esq. i. 137.
Townshend, Marquis of, i. 133.
Trafford of Wrexham Hall, ii. 141.
Trelawny, Sir William L. S., Bart. ii. 180.
Trenchard, John Trenchard, i. 109.
Tylecote, Elizabeth, ii. 48.
Tyler, Charles Henry, Esq. ii. 193.
Tyrconnel, Earl of, i. 11.
Urquhart, Beauchamp Colclough, Esq. ii. 108.
Van Straubenzee, Henry, Esq. ii. 82.
Vaughan, Robert Chambre, Esq. ii. 95.
Vernon, Maj.-Gen. Henry Charles Edward, C.B. i. 57.
Vernon-Wentworth, Frederick William Thomas, i. 145.
Walcot, Rev. Charles, ii. 54.
Walker, James, Esq. i. 15.
Walker, Anna F. i. 95.

Wallace, Lieut.-Gen. Sir John, Bart. ii. 156.
Walrond, Frances, i. 75.
Walrond, Bethell, Esq. ii. 150.
Walwyn, Richard Henry, Esq. ii. 152.
Warde, Charles Thomas, Esq. i. 2.
Waterford, Marquess of, i. 108.
Waters, Thomas Methold, Esq. ii. 118.
Welby, Sir William Earle, Bart. i. 89.
Western, Charles Maxamilian Thomas, Esq.
Weeler, Sir Trevor, Bart. i. 65.
Wilder, Frederick, Esq. ii. 36.
Williamson, John Vaughan, Esq. ii. 62.
Winn, Charles, Esq. i. 149.

Wilmot, Sir John E. Eardley, Bart. ii. 154.
Winstanley, Clement, Esq. ii. 199*.
Wintrop, Rev. Benjamin, ii. 49.
Wodehouse and Currie,ii. 205.
Worsley, Sir Wm., Bart. ii. 83.
Wrangham, Rev. Geo. Walter, M.A. ii. 26.
Wyndham, John Henry Campbell, Esq. i. 161.
Wyndowe, Oliver Thomlinson, Esq. ii. 113.
Wynne, John, Esq. ii. 34.
Wyvill, Marmaduke, Esq. ii. 99.
Yarburgh, Nicholas Edmund, Esq. i. 110.
Yea, Sir William Walter, Bart. ii. 210.
Yorke, John, Esq. i. 102.

237.—Royal Descents and Pedigrees of Founders' Kin. By Sir BERNARD BURKE, Ulster King of Arms. *London.* 1858. Royal 8vo.

Queen Victoria, Seize Quartiers of.
H.R.H. Prince Albert, Seize Quartiers of.

ROYAL DESCENTS.

Adams, children of William Adams, LL.D., and the Hon. Mary Anne Adams, folding after 117.
Adeane, Henry John, Esq. 82.
Alison, Sir Archibald, Bart. 28.
Aylmer, Sir Gerald George, Bart. 39.
Barham, Rev. Charles Henry, 72.
Beach, Sir Michael Hicks Hicks-, Bart. 21.
Beamish, Lieut.-Col. North Ludlow, K.H. 50.
Brune, Charles Prideaux, Esq. 71.
Buchanan, Thomas, Esq. 38.
Bullock, George Twyte-, Esq. 117.
Caldecot, Major, *of Holton, Lincoln,* 14.
Campbell, Major General Sir John, C.B. 49.
Carlisle, Earl of, 112.
Coldclough, Mary Grey Wentworth, 59.
Collins, John Stratford, 34.

Cooper, Rev. Edward Philip, B.D. 42.
Crakenthorp and Wedd, 40.
Craven, Mrs. Augusta, 6.
Craven, Hon. Anne Hamilton, 111.
Creagh, Arthur Gethin, Esq. 29.
Cruikshank, Augustus Walter, Esq. 89.
Cullen, Viscount, 26.
Davis, Anthony, Esq. 69.
Dalzell, Robert Anstruther, Esq. 106.
Darnley, Earl of, 81.
De Pearsall *of Willsbridge, and of WartenseeCastle,* folding after 117.
De Valmer, Viscountesse, 13.
De Vesci, Viscount, 41.
Dixon *of Seaton Carew,* 78 and 79.
Domville, Sir Charles Compton, Bart. 61.
Domville, William Compton,Esq. 73.
Duckett, Sir George Floyd, Bart. 56.
Dunbar, Sir William, Bart. 30.

Dutton *of Burland Hall*, 48.
Dykes, T. L. Ballantine, Esq. 35.
Dykes *of Dykesfield* (folding), 50*.
Edwards, John Kynaston, Esq. 86.
Ellerton, John Lodge, Esq. 75.
Errol, Earl of, 24.
Evans, Thomas, Esq. 114.
Eyston, Charles John, Esq., *of East Hendred*, 102.
Falconer, William, M.A. 66.
Farnham, Lord, K.P. 36.
Farrer, James William, Esq., 67.
Fitzgerald,, Peter, Knight of Kerry, 83.
Garland, Edgar Walter, Esq., 100.
Gervis, Sir George Eliott Meyrick Tapps, Bart. 93.
Gibbs. Children of Henry Hucks Gibbs and Louisa Anne Adams, folding after 117.
Gladstone, Sir Thomas, Bart.
Gordon, Michael Francis, Esq. 90.
Gordon, Sir Home, Bart., *of Embo*, 116.
Graham, James Maxwell, Esq. 8.
Grey, Mrs. Hamilton, 9 and 68.
Hall, Roger, Esq. *of Narrow Water*, 97.
Hamilton, Charles William, Esq. *of Hamwood*, 96.
Hayward, Christie Annette, 44.
Henderson, Lieut. Gen. Douglas Mercer *of Fordell, Fife*, 25.
Hughes, Hugh Robert, Esq. *of Kinmel and Dinorben*, 11.
Hunter, David, Esq. *of Blackness*, 55.
Hurt, Francis, Esq. *of Alderwasley, Derby*, 58.
Inman, Rev. William Charles, 77.
Inchiquin, Lord, 98.
Isham, Sir Charles Edmund, Bart. 17.
Jackson, Hamilton Llewellyn, Esq. 91.
Kenny, James Christopher Fitzgerald, Esq. 45.
Kingston, William Henry Giles, Esq. 18.
Lane, John Newton and Rev. Charles, 3.
Lanesborough, Earl of, 1.
Lewis *of Lanishen, Green Meadow, and the Heath*, 53.

Lister, Matthew Henry, 99.
Lloyd, Julia Youde, 15.
Lockhart, Allan Elliott, Esq. 85.
Londonderry, Marquis of, K.P.
Maddock, George Ashby, Esq. 27.
Macdonnell, William Henry Armstrong, Esq., 113.
MacDowall, Col. Day Hort, 88.
Magan, William Henry, Esq., M.P., *of Cloncarl, King's Co.* 57.
Manning, Mary Erskine Shipley, 47.
Marley, Charles Brinsley, Esq. 115.
Mornington, Helena Countess of, 4.
Moseley, Walter, Esq. *of the Mere and Buildwas*, 62.
Nanney, John, Esq. 105.
Northmore, Thomas Welby, Esq. 84.
Oliphant, Henrietta Græme, Esq. *of Ochill*, 76.
Pack, Lieut.-Col. Arthur John Reynell-, C.B. 109.
Parry, Thomas Love Duncombe Jones, Esq. 13.
Paterson, Peter Hay, Esq. 94.
Peel, Anna Maria Cordelia, 74.
Pemberton, Richard Laurence, Esq. 51.
Pollock, Sir Hew Crawfurd, Bart. 107.
Pottinger, Sir Henry, G.C.B. 37.
Pratt, Edward Roger, Esq. 92.
Ramsden, Sir John William, Bart. 5.
Raymond, Samuel Milbank, Esq. *of Belchamp Hall, Essex*, 63.
Rollo, Lord, 19.
Rothery, Charles William, Esq. 80.
St. Germans, Earl and Countess of, 31.
Saltmarshe, Philip, Esq. *of Saltmarshe*, 104.
Scrope, Simon Thomas, Esq. *of Danby*, 103.
Shairp, Thomas, Esq. *of Houston*, 24.
Shann, family of, 7.
Shippard, Capt. William Henry, (folding), 20.
Shippardson *of Pittington Hall Garth, Durham*, 54.
Simpson, John, Esq. 34.
Smyth, John Henry Greville, Esq. *of Ashton Court*, 65.
Spottiswoode, John, Esq. 95.

Stewart, Alexander John Robert, Esq., *of Ards.* 43.
Stoughton, Thomas Anthony, Esq. 87.
Style, William Henry Marsham, Esq. 10.
Thomson, John Anstruther, Esq. *of Charlton*, 22 and 108.
Thurlow, Rev. Thomas, 2.
Tindal *of Chelmsford and Aylesbury*, 60.

Trist, John Fincher, Esq. 101 and 110.
Wallace *of Philadelphia*, 16.
Warwick, Earl of, 33.
Wedd; see Crakenthorp.
Whyte, Colonel, 52.
Williams, Thomas, Esq. 46.
Woodhouse, William Herbert, Esq. 32.

Pedigrees of Founders' Kin.

Atkinson, Charlotte Eustacia, 9.
Bund, Thomas Henry, Esq. 1.
Coldclough, Mary Grey Wentworth, 17.
Collier, Lady, 20.
Collier, Charles John T., Esq. 21.
Currer, Miss Richardson, 2.
Dykes, *of Dovenby Hall, Cumberland*, 12.
Evans, Thomas, Esq. *of Hereford*, 22.
Farnham, Lord, K.P. 7.
Harbin, George, Esq. *of Newton House, Somerset*, 5.
Howard, Frederick John, Esq. and Lady Fanny, his wife, 13.

Jacomb family, 3.
Kenney, James Christopher Fitzgerald, 10.
Knight, Joseph, Esq. 15.
Pearce, Lieut.-Colonel, K.H., *of Ffrwdgrech, Brecon*, 5.
Style, William Henry Marsham, Esq. 19.
Taylor, Herbert, Esq. 2.
Walker, Robert Onebye, Esq. 6.
Wilder *of Pinley Hall and Sulham, Berks*, 16.

238.—Archæological Journal. Published by the Archæological Institute. *London.* 8vo. 1845-1866.

Courtenay, Barons of Okehampton, and Earls of Devon, 5 tables, x. 58.

239.—Heraldic Illustrations. By JOHN BURKE, ESQ., and JOHN BERNARD BURKE, Esq. *London*, 1845. 3 vols. royal 8vo.

Allan *of Blackwell Grange, Durham*, 2, 109.
Alloway *of the Derries, Queen's Co.* 100.
Atcherley *of Marton, Salop*, 16.
Bailey *of Glanusk Park, Brecon*, 36.
Baskerville *of Clyrow Court, Radnor*, 79.
Bigg-Wither *of Manydown, Hants*, 26.
Blathwayt *of Dyrham Park, Glouc.* 33.
Bonar *of Bonare*, 118.

Botfield *of Norton Hall, Narthampton*, 31.
Bracebridge *of Morville House, Warwick*, 8.
Brodie *of Lethen*, 39.
Brown *of Janeville, Down*, 143.
Bruce-Dundas *of Blair Castle, Perth*, 121.
Bund *of Wick House, Worcester*, 22.
Burton *of Dunstall Priory, Eynsford, Kent*, 57.
Buxton *of Bellfield Dorset, and of Runton, Norfolk*, 60.

Byam *of Antigua*, 22.
Bythesea *of the Hill, Freshford, Somerset*, 20.
Cantillon *of Ballyhigue, Kerry*, 51.
Carlyon *of Tregrehan, Cornwall*, 18.
Cass *of Little Grove, East Barnet, Herts*, 142.
Chambers *of London*, 160.
Champion de Crespigny, 124.
Chapman *of Whitby Strand*, 27.
Charlton *of Chilwell Hall, Notts*, 76.
Clarke *of Welton Place, North-ampton*, 25.
Cleland *of Rath Gael House, Down*, 7.
Coham *of Coham, Devon*, 122.
Collins *of Walford, Hereford*, 97.
Cologan, 37.
Colston *of Roundway Park, Wilts*, 45.
Cooke *of Owston, York*, folding at 54.
Corbet *of Moreton Corbet, Salop*, 45.
Craufuird *of Baidland*, 42.
D'Arcy *of Hyde Park, Westmeath*, 43.
Davies *of Eton House, Kent*, 18.
Dawes *of Bolton*, 146.
Drew *of Kilwinney, &c. Cork*, 126.
East, 106.
Emery *of the Grange, Banwell, Somerset*, 108.
Erle-Drax *of Charborough Park, Dorset*, 5.
Evans *of Ashill, Limerick*, 3.
Evans *of the Hill Court, Hereford*, 50.
Evans *of Baymount, Dublin*, 87.
Eyre, 70.
Ferrand *of St. Ives, York*, 14.
Fletcher *of Water Eyton and Can-novk, Staffordshire*, 97.
Folliott *of Chester*, 34.
Gabb *of Monmouthshire*, 18.
Gale-Braddyll *of Conishead Priory, Lancaster*, 34.
Gardiner *of Coombe Lodge, Oxford*, 63.
Gurney *of Keswick, Norfolk*, 27.
Gwynne-Holford *of Buckland, Bre-con*, 32.
Gyll *of Wyrardisbury, Bucks*, 134.

Hamerton *of Hellifield Peel, York*, 15.
Hatfield *of Newton Kyme and Laughton, York*, 113.
Henshaw, 134.
Hibbert-Ware *of Edinburgh*, 10.
Higgins *of Trafalgar Park, Mayo*, 27.
Higgins *of Eastnor, Hereford*, 32.
Hogg *of Church View and Cartron, Roscommon*, 80.
Huland *of Ipsley, Warwick*, 182.
Hughes *of Gwerclas, Merioneth*, 23.
Hunter *of London*, 108.
Ingham *of Marton in Craven, York*, 103.
Irvine *of Castle Irvine, Fermanagh*, 5.
Jackson *of Enniscoe and Carramore, Mayo*, 41.
Johnson *of Ayscough Fee Hall, Lin-coln*, 133.
Johnson *of Hilton in the Merse*, 80.
Jones *of Llanarth Court, Monmouth*, 25.
Kennedy *of Knockgray, Kirkcud-bright*, 93.
King *of Staunton Park, Hereford*, 15.
Latour *of Hexton House, Herts*, 107.
Lauder, Bart. *of Fountain Hall*, 17.
Lea *of Astley Hall and Kidder-minster, Worcester*, 143.
Leathes *of Herringfleet, Suffolk*, 25.
Leche *of Carden, Chester*, 42.
Lindoe *of Norwich*, 55.
Lloyd *of Plymoq, Gwerclas and Bashall*, folding at 40.
Loveday *of Williamscote, Oxford*, 95.
Lovett *of Bath*, 138.
Maunsell *of Limerick*, 129.
Mackerrell *of Hillhouse, Ayr*, 9.
Mellor *of Chiswick, Middlesex*, 22.
Meynell *of North Kilvington, York*, 75.
Money-Kyrle *of Much Marcle, Hereford*, 64.
Mules *of Devon and Somerset*, 136.
Nichol *of Essex and of Islington, Midd.* 137.
Nicholson *of Ballow, Down*, 72.
Northumberland, Duke of, 1.
Norton *of King's Norton, Worces-ter*, 49.

Nugent *of Cranna, Galway,* 126.
Ogle *of Eglingham, Northumherland,* 111.
Oldfield *of Oldfield, Chester,* 39, 81.
O'Kelly, 46.
Parkhouse *of Eastfield Lodge, Hants,* 24.
Peel *of Accrington, Lanc.* 96.
Phillipps *of Garendon Park, Leicester,* 29.
Phillipps *of Longworth, Hereford,* 41.
Pridham *of Plymouth, Devon,* 65.
Robertson *of Inshes, Inverness,* 47.
Rodick *of Gateacre, Lanc.* 45.
Rogers *of Yarlington, Somerset,* 17.
Roskell *of Lancashire,* 99.
Rowan *of Garry, Antrim,* 36.
Sadler, 134.
Scott (Sir Walter), 11.
Shippardson *of Piddinghall Garth, Durham,* 24.
Smyth *of Gaybrook, Westmeath,* 66.
Smijth *of Hill Hall, Essex,* 74.
Spaight *of Clare and Limerick,* 57.
Standish *of Durbury Park, Lancaster,* 1.
Steward *of Norfolk,* 94.
Strutt *of Belper, Derby,* 61.
Studdert *of Bunratty Castle, Clare,* 85.
Sutherland, Duke of, 6.
Sutton *of Elton,* 19.
Synnot *of Ballymoyer House, Armagh,* 98.

Taylor *of Todmorden Hall, Lancaster,* 4.
Taylor *of Strensham Court, Worcester,* 69.
Taylor *of Pennington, Hants,* 115, and folding.
Tempest *of Tong, York,* 9.
Thomlinson *of Blencogo and Allonby, Cumberland,* 93.
Thorp *of Ryton, Durham,* 61.
Tower *of Huntsmore Park, Bucks,* 145.
Walker, 91.
Walsham *of Knill Court, Hereford,* 35.
Warrington *of Lancaster,* 8.
Welch *of Arle House, Gloucester,* 42.
Welles *of the Grange, West Moulsey, Surrey,* 48.
Wells *of East Allington, Devon,* 30.
Wentworth *of Wentworth Castle, York,* 76.
White *of Charlton Marshall, Dorset,* 26.
White *of Yeovil, Somerset,* 95.
Wilder *of Purley Hall and Sulham, Berks,* 46.
Wilkinson *of Harperley Park, Durham,* 88.
Wilson *of Knowle Hall, Warwick,* 7.
Worthington *of Sandiway Bank, Chester,* folding at 129.
Yorke *of Erddig, Denbigh,* 70.

240.—Illuminated Supplement to the Heraldic Illustrations. By JOHN BERNARD BURKE, Esq. *London,* 1851. Royal 8vo.

Berkeley *of Cotheridge, Worcester,* 12.
Goddard *of Edgbaston, Warwick,* 16.

Longcroft *of Havant, Hants,* 19.
Tregonwell *of Anderston, Dorset, and of Ashington, Somerset,* 7.

241.— The Patrician. Edited by JOHN BERNARD BURKE, Esq. *London,* 1846-1848. 6 vols. 8vo.

Baliol, iii. 174, 264.
Cradock *of Swanzy,* iv. 481.
Crawford, vi. 272.
Cromwell, i. 122.

Cusack, vi. 59.
Dyer (poet), iv. 11.
Ensor, v. 76, 77.
Grey, v. 171.

Kennedy *of Mount Kennedy, Wicklow,* v. 373.
Milton (poet), iii. 424.
Nugent, iii. 172.
Scott *of Abbotsford,* iii. 423.

Scott, iii. 425.
Spencer (poet), v. 54.
Sterne, iii. 68.
Washington, ii. 36.
Welby, iv. 67.

242.—Archæologia Cambrensis. Published by the Cambrian Archæological Association. 1st Series, 1846-1849, 4 vols. 8vo. 2nd Series, 1850-1854, 5 vols. 8vo. 3rd Series, 1855 to 1866, 11 vols. 8vo.

Bawdripp *of Odyn's Fee,* 3 S. vii. 19.
Butler, 1 S. ii. 279.
Evans, 3 S. vii. 23—28.
Griffith, 2 S. v. 41.
Gruffydd, 3 S. vi. 168.
Herbert, 3 S. vi. 272.
Holland *of Conway,* 3 S. xi., folding at 183.
Johnes, 3 S. vi. 176.
Jones *of Fonman,* 3 S. vii. 17.
Lloyd, 3 S. vi. 170, 273
Le Sore *of Odyn's Fee,* 3 S. vii. 19.

Lewis *of Penmark Place,* 3 S. vii. 20.
Lloyd, 3 S. vii. folding at 156, 314.
Morley, 3 S. ix. folding at 107.
Myddelton, 2 S. i. 135.
Pendrell, 3 S. v. 114-121, 299.
Perrot, 3 S. xi. 1-32, 101-132, 229-260, 371-381, xi. 64-72, 167-182, 311-357, 478-514.
Relfe, 3 S. ix. 104.
Umfraville *of Penmark Castle,* 3 S. vii. 21.

243.—St. James's Magazine and Heraldic and Historical Register. Edited by J. BERNARD BURKE, Esq. *London,* 1850. 2 vols. 8vo.

Alcock, *Her. Reg.* 57.
Bolton, *Her. Reg.* 50.
Boner *of Hurstperpoint, Sussex, Her. Reg.* 79.
Crawford, i. 242.
Davies *of Moor Court, Hereford, Her. Reg.* 67.

Fisher, *Her. Reg.* 88.
Hawker, *of Longparish, Hants, Her. Reg.* 85.
Marsh, i. 243.
Shuttleworth *of Hodsock Park, Notts, Her. Reg.* 68.
Waldron *of Leicestershire,* i. 496.

244.—Reports and Papers of the Architectural Societies of York, Lincoln, Northampton, Bedford, Worcester, and Leicester. *London,* 1850-1866. 8vo.

Carre *of Sleaford, Lincoln* (1863), 71.
Cromwell, Barons, *of Cromwell and Lambley* (1858), 228.
Devereux (1852-53), 445.
Hereward the Saxon (1861), folding at 18.
Tattershall, Barons (1858), 228.
Thynne (1852-3), 445.

Wac or Wake, Barons Wake (1861), fold at 18.
Wake *of Blisworth,* folding at 18.
Wake *of Clevedon, Somerset,* folding at 18.
Wake *of Clevedon,* Baronets, folding at 18.
Wake, Bart. *of Courteen Hall,* folding at 18.

245.—Visitation of the Seats and Arms of the Noblemen and Gentlemen of Great Britain. By JOHN BERNARD BURKE, Esq. *London*, 1852-1853. 2 vols. royal 8vo.

Appleton *of Waldingford, Suffolk,* i. 73.

Ashurst *of Ashurst, Lancaster,* ii. 11.

Baker *of Orsett Hall, Essex,* i. 18.

Bolton, i. 60.

Boner *of Henfield, Sussex,* i. 41.

Burke-Ryan, i. 20.

Cass *of East Barnet, Herts,* i. 38,

Coulthart *of Ashton-under-Lyne,* i. 39.

Comber *of East Newton, York,* i. 58.

Cooke *of East End House, Hants,* ii. 16.

Davies *of Farthingville, Cork,* i. 69.

Edwards *of Pye Nest, Halifax,* ii. 73.

Emeris *of Louth, Lincoln,* ii. 8.

Farmer *of Nonsuch Park, Surrey,* ii. 8.

Farnall, i. 21.

Fenwick *of Newcastle-on-Tyne,* i. 60.

Forster *of Lyswayes Hall, Stafford,* ii. 13.

Garnett *of Wyreside, Lancaster,* i. 52.

Gorham, ii. 20.

Granger *of Tattenhall Wood, Stafford,* i. 49.

Gray *of Cartyne,* ii. 36.

Greaves *of Page Hall, York,* ii. 63.

Haldane *of Gleneagles, Perth,* ii. 19.

Hartcup *of Bungay, Suffolk,* i. 18.

Hassard, ii. 14.

Hay *of Hopes, East Lothian,* ii. 10.

Hedding, ii. 61.

Jacob *of Tonbridge Wells, Kent,* ii. 28.

Jones *of Pantglas, Carmarthen,* i. 19.

Jones *of Gurrey, Glanagan,* i. 28.

Kendall *of Austrey, Warwick,* ii. 35.

Kennard *of London,* ii. 7.

Kingston *of Oakhill, Herts,* ii. 74.

Knatchbull-Hugesson *of Provender, Kent,* i. 77.

Lloyd *of Clochfaen, Llangurig, Montgomery,* ii. 55.

Luxford *of Higham, Essex,* ii. 6.

Martyn *of Pertenhall, Bedford,* ii. 23.

Maxwell *of Williamswood, Renfrew,* i. 75.

Merriman *of London,* ii. 34.

M'Gregor *of Kernock, Stirling,* ii. 1.

Moore-Stevens *of Winscot, Devon,* ii. 73.

Mosley *of Amcotts, Lancaster,* i. 29.

Mossman *of Yorkshire and Lancashire,* ii. 64.

Orred *of Tranmore, Chester,* ii. 52.

Pattinson *of West Boldon, Durham,* ii. 60.

Peacocke *of Pylewell House, Hants,* ii. 66.

Roden *of Vere, Isle of Jamaica,* i. 61.

Roundell *of Gledstone and Screven, York,* ii. 27.

Schank *of Dawlish, Devon,* ii. 17.

Scott *of the Isle of Wight,* i. 71.

Somerby, i. 50.

Sparrow *of Suffolk,* ii. 51.

Swan *of Baldwinstown, Wexford,* i. 43.

Taunton *of Freeland Lodge, Oxon,* ii. 32.

Taylor *of Borwick, Lancaster,* ii. 72.

Ternan, ii. 13.

Topham *of Middleham Hall, York,* i. 28.

Topp *of Huddersfield, York,* i. 75.

Troyte *of Huntsham Court, Devon,* ii. 74.

Walker *of Hendregadredd, Carnarvon,* i. 4.

Wallace *of Asholme, Northumberland,* i. 75.

Webster *of Penno, Warwick,* ii. 49.

Williams *of Cowley Grove, Middlesex,* i. 44.

246.—Visitation of the Seats and Arms of the Noblemen and Gentlemen of Great Britain and Ireland. By JOHN BERNARD BURKE, Esq. 2nd Series. *London.* 1854-1855. 2 vols. Royal 8vo.

Ashley-Maddock *of Naseby, Northampton,* i. 25.
Beevor *of Yorkshire and Nottinghamshire,* ii. 13.
Bellairs *of Kirkby Bellairs, Leicester,* i. 63.
Bigsby *of Suffolk and Notts.* ii. 61.
Botfield *of Norton Hall, Northampton,* i. 52.
Bourne *of Hackinsall, Lancaster,* i. 9.
Browne *of Salperton, Gloucester,* i. 1.
Brasier *of Ballyellis,* ii. 25.
Campbell *of Colgrain, Dumbarton,* i. 44.
Carmichael *of Carspherne,* i. 44.
Chapman *of Molash, Kent,* i. 17.
Cooper *of Failford, Ayr,* i. 40.
Cooper *of Little Dalby, Leicester,* ii. 72.
Coulthart *of Ashton under Lyne,* i. 18.
Creagh *of Laurentinum, Cork,* i. 63.
Dawson and Duffield, ii. 22.
Du Boulay *of Donhead Hall, Wilts,* i. 45.
Dykes *of Dovenby Hall, Cumberland,* i. 12, ii. 36.
Evans *of Plasgwyn, Anglesey,* i. 62.
Fetherston *of Hopton Court, Worcester,* i. 27.
Fitzgerald *of Tieroghan and Rathrone, Meath,* ii. 46.
Forbes *of Pitscottie,* ii. 18.
Ford *of Ellell Hall, Lancaster,* i. 21.
Garland *of Michaelstone, Essex,* ii. 34.
Gibbs *of Topsham, Devon,* ii. 53.
Gibbs *of Cork,* ii. 63.
Glover *of Mount Glover, Cork,* i. 70.
Gordon *of Sorbie,* i. 47.
Hamilton *of Barns,* i. 20.
Hamilton *of Newton,* i. 34.
Hamilton *of Gilkerscleugh,* ii. 74.
Hartley-Kennedy *of Middlesex,* ii. 29.
Hawker *of Longparish, Hants,* i. 4.

Hurly *of Tralee,* ii. 48.
Jones-Parry *of Madryn, Carnarvon,* i. 4.
Keogh, ii. 59.
Kittermaster, ii. 59.
Lammin *of Shorrolds, Fulham, Middlesex,* ii. 13.
Leatham *of High Hall, Hemsworth, York,* i. 58.
Leppington *of Middlesex,* ii. 56.
Lomax-Gaskill *of Kiddington Hall, Oxon,* ii. 52.
Mackenzie *of Craighall,* ii. 17.
Macknyghte *of Macknyghte,* i. 66.
Mayne *of Powis, Clackmannan,* i. 58.
Montgomerie *of Lainshaw and Brigend, Ayr,* i. 36.
Nolan *of Ballkealy,* i. 54.
O'Brien *of Kerry,* i. 8.
O'Daly *of Dalybrook,* ii. 45.
O'Flanagan, ii. 35.
O'Kelly *of Kilclogher Castle, Galway,* ii. 43.
Peabody, i. 11.
Pelham *of Crowhurst, Sussex,* i. 35.
Pennyman, ii. 7.
Plowden *of Lassam, Hants,* i. 6.
Richmond *of Yorkshire,* i. 11.
Roberts, i. 30.
Ross *of Renfrew,* ii. 20.
Ross *of Dalton, Dumfries,* i. 45.
Sears *of Colchester, Essex and America,* i. 5.
Spofforth *of Yorkshire,* i. 41.
Stark or Starke, ii. 79.
Stephens *of Eastington, Gloucester,* i. 49.
Sturgis, i. 9.
Taylor *of Swords, Dublin,* ii. 42.
Tighe *of Michelstown, Westmeath,* ii. 77.
Toker *of the Oaks, Kent,* ii. 15.
Troyte-Bullock *of North Coker House, Somerset,* i. 45.
Waddy *of Clougheast Castle, Wexford,* ii. 8.

Wallace *of America,* i. 31.
Waller *of Spring Grove, Middlesex,* ii. 77.

Warren *of Killiney Castle, Dublin,* ii. 9.
Williams *of Abercamlais,* i. 61.

247.—The Cambrian Journal. Published by the Cambrian Institute. 1st Series. 1854-1857, 4 vols. 8vo. 2nd Series. 1858-1863.

Byam, 2 S. v. 1-82.
Herbert *of Powys Castle, formerly of Raglan, &c.* 1 S. iv. 114-137, 162-177.
Pugh, 1 S. i. 132-140, 356-364.

248.—Midland Counties Historical Collector. *Leicester,* 1855-1856. 2 vols. 8vo.

Cutler *of Bloherby, Leicester,* ii. 306.
Hall *of Tonge, Leicester,* ii. 351.
Sharrett or Sherard *of Tonge, Leicester,* ii. 351.

249.—The East Anglian. Edited by SAMUEL TYMMS, F.S.A. *Lowestoft,* 1858-1866. Vol. I.—II. 8vo.

Albini, ii. 72.
Barlee, i. 226.
Beaumont, i. 74.
Bradbury, .i 228.
Browne, i. 182.
Castell, ii. 171.
Crabbe, ii. 259.
Dandy, ii. 164.

Dilke, i. 127.
Fincham, i. 96.
Mowbray, ii. 72.
Tey, i. 96.
Tilney, i. 96.
Vere, i. 115.
Walford, i. 127.

250.—Authorized Arms. By Sir BERNARD BURKE. *London,* 1858. Royal 8vo.

Allan *of Blackwell Grange, Durham,* 2.
Baker *of Derby,* 22.
Bower *of Broxholme, York,* 124.
Bright *of Harrow Weald, Midd.* folding at 43.
Burke *of Elm Hall, Tipperary,* folding at 138.
Clere *of London and Essex,* 4.
Coham *of Coham, Devon,* 36.
Cooper, 87.
Cowell-Stepney *of Llanelly, Carmarthen,* 174.
Eager *of Kerry,* 210-222.
Elwes *of Great Billing, Northampton,* 38.
Everard *of Middleton, Norfolk,* folding at 135.
Guinness *of St. Anne's, Dublin,* folding at 169.

Hamilton *of Glasgow,* 48.
Hamilton *of Hamwood, Meath,* 166.
Horton, 122.
Howard *of Toronto, Canada,* 60.
Jacob, 49.
Jesson *of Oakwood, Stafford,* 34.
Kenney *of Kilclougher, Galway,* folding at 67.
Leppington *of Louth, Lincoln,* 76.
Luxmore *of Kerslake, Devon,* 44.
Margery *of Kensington, Midd.* 37.
Marshall *of Belmont, Somerset,* 33.
Maxwell-Graham *of Williamswood, Renfrew,* 17.
Meade *of Ballintobber, Cork,* 10.
Michel *of Whatcombe, Dorset,* 20.
Montgomerie *of Lainshaw and Brigend, Ayr,* folding at 152.
Merse-Boycott, 177.

Mowbray *of Bishopwearmouth, Dublin*, 53.
Nangle, 199-209.
Newton *of Currickfergus*, 31.
O'Neill *of Clanboy*, folding at 112.
Ozanne, folding at 102.
Peel *of Stone Hall, Pembroke*, 42.
Phillipps *of Garendon Park, Leicester*, 165.
Rothwell *of Sharples Hall, Lancaster*, folding at 179.

Shortt, 105.
Stanier-Philip-Broade, 168.
Taylor *of Todmorden, Lanc.* 51.
Waller *of Spring Grove, Hounslow, Midd.* 29.
Webb, 171.
Whitting *of Sandcroft House, Somerset*, 129.
Willis *of Halsnead Park, Lanc.* 188.

251.—The Reliquary : Quarterly Archæological Journal and Review. *London,* 1860-1866. Nos. 1 to 25, 8vo.

Abdy, vii. 17.
Alsop, vii. 17.
Audley, vii. 18.
Babington, ii. 186.
Bagshawe, vii. 18.
Ball, vii. 18.
Bardolf, vii. 19.
Bateman, ii. 88.
Bateman *of Hartington and Middleton Hall*, vi. 105.
Bateman, Parker, & Levinge, v. 245.
Bateman, vii. 18.
Bathor, vi. 28.
Beresford, vii. 19.
Blackwall, vii. 20.
Blythe, v. 203.
Bothom, vii. 22.
Bouth, vii. 19.
Bowden, vii. 20.
Bradbery or Bradbury, vii. 21.
Bradshaw, ii. 223.
Bradshawe, vii. 22.
Brownlowe, vii. 22.
Clive, vi. 27.
Columbell, vii. 23.
Crooker, vii. 23.
Darley, vii. 23.
Ferne, vii. 23.
Fynderne, iii. 191.
Greatrakes, iv. 81-96, 220-240.

Gresley, vi. 32.
Halton, v. 64.
Harpur, ii. 6.
Hope, ii. 6.
Jones, vii. 24.
Kirke, vi. 219.
Kyrke, vii. 24.
Langford, vii. 24.
Lee, vii. 25.
Leeke, vii. 25.
Levinge ; see Bateman.
Man, vii. 26.
Mundy, vii. 26.
Milbourne, vii. 26.
Needam, vii. 27.
Newbold, vii. 27.
Parker ; see Bateman.
Pilkington, vii. 28.
Prescott, vii. 28.
Shalcross *of Shalcross*, vi. folding at 150.
Sleigh, vii. 29.
Smalley, vii. 28.
Strafford, ii. 222.
Strelly, vii. 29.
Tounrawe, vii. 30.
Vernon, vii. 30.
Welbeck, vii. 30.
Wigley, vii. 31.
Woodcock, vii. 31.

252.—Army Lists of the Roundheads and Cavaliers, &c. Edited by EDWARD PEACOCK, F.S.A. *London,* 1863. Fcp. 4to.

Doreslaer or Doreslaus, 21.

253.—Miscellanea Genealogica et Heraldica. Edited by JOSEPH JACKSON HOWARD, LL.D., F.S.A. *London*, 1866. Parts 1 and 2. Royal 8vo.

Barlor, 58.
Beresford, 36.
Burton, 38.
Blundell, 67.
Chamberlain, 24.
Cowper, 51.
Dilke, 3.
Elwes, 68-70.

Farington, 63.
Hobson, 50.
Leigh, 12, 13.
Lower, 13.
Martin, 53.
Norton, 51.
Ofspring, 52.
Smith, 52.

BERKSHIRE.

254.—Visitation of Berkshire, 1566, 1623, and 1664-5, with some additions. Privately printed by Sir THOMAS PHILLIPPS, Bart. Fcp. folio.

Aldworth *of Wargrave*, 1.
Aldworth *of Wanting*, 1.
Alford *of Hall Place, in Hurley, from Meux, York*, 1.
Allen *of Streatley*, 2.
Andrew *of Hurst, from Frefolk, Hants*, 2.
Annesley *of Maydenhead, from Annesley, Notts*, 2.
Aveline *of New Windsor and Frogmore*, 2.
Aylworth *of West Hanney*, 3.
Ayshcombe *of Lyford, Berks*, 3.
Backhouse *of Swallowfield, from Whitrige, Cambr.* 3.
Baker *of Windsor, from Bowden, Chester*, 14.
Baker *of Windsor, from Feversham, Kent*, 4.
Barker *of Newbury, from Stokesley, York*, 5.
Barker *of Wokingham*, 4.
Bacon *of Windsor, from Mere, Wilts*, 5.
Baskerville *of Bayworth, from Herefordshire*, 5.
Bathurst *of Wantage, from Horton Kirby, Kent*, 161.
Batten *of East Garston and Ardington*, 6.
Bell *of Laurence Waltham, from Eaton, Bucks*, 6.
Bennet *of Windsor, from Baldock Herts*, 6.

Berington *of Reading and Streatley, from Hereford*, 7.
Bigg *of Hurst, from Benenden, Kent*, 7.
Bisley *of Abingdon*, 7.
Blacknall *af Abingdon, from Wing, Bucks*, 7.
Blagrave *of Bulmarsh, from Uttoxeter, Staff.* 7.
Blagrave, 8.
Blanchard *of Chieveley*, 8.
Blany *of Windsor, from Keele, Montgomery*, 8.
Blore *of Reading, from Loughborough, Leicester*, 8.
Bolney *of Tylehurst, from Bolney, Sussex*, 9.
Booth *of Berkham, from Swallowferry, Derby*, 9.
Booth *of Fawler's Court, from Chisworth, Derby*, 9.
Bostock *of Abingdon, from Bostock, Chester*, 9.
Bostock (2), 10.
Bostock (3), 10.
Braham *of Windsor, from Bramhall, Suffolk*, 10.
Braybrooke *of Bright Waltham, from Suffolk*, 10.
Brickenden *of Inkpen, from Cranbrooke, Kent*, 11.
Broderwick *of Langford*, 11.
Brookes *of Wantage*, 11.

Broughton *of Wokingham, from Broughton, Staff.* 11.

Browne *of Shefford, from Wickham Brewse, Kent,* 12.

Bullock *of Arborfield,* 12.

Bulstrode *of Upton,* 12.

Bury *of Culnaham, from Hampton Poyle, Oxon.* 12.

Calton *of Milton, Berks,* 13.

Cantrell *of Okingham, from Hemingston, Suffolk,* 13.

Castillion *of Benham Valence, from Mantua and Piedmont,* 13.

Cater *of Offington,* 13.

Chamberlayne *of Donnington Castle, from Shirborne, Oxon.* 14.

Champion *of Wantage, from Horsham, Essex,* 14.

Choke *of Avington, from Ashton, Somerset,* 14.

Clarke *of Ardington,* 14.

Clifford *of Kintbury, from Boscombe, Wilts,* 15.

Collins *of Betterton,* 15.

Cotton *of Ockingham, from Exeter,* 15.

Cowper *of Bray, from Tetworth, Hunts. and Everton, Beds.* 15.

Cox *of Eaton, Hastings, from Colshill, Berks,* 15.

Dalby *of Reading,* 16.

Dancastell *of Welhouse,* 16.

Darell *of West Woodhay, from Sesay, York,* 16.

Davis *of Bere Court, from London,* 16.

BUCKINGHAMSHIRE.

255. The History of the College of Bonhommes, at Ashridge, in the County of Buckingham. *London,* 1823. Folio. *Privately printed.*

Egerton, Earls of Bridgewater, 93.

CAMBRIDGESHIRE.

256. Historical Account of Wisbeach, in the Isle of Ely. By WILLIAM WATSON, Esq., F.A.S. *Wisbeach,* 1827. Royal 8vo.

Colvile *of Carleton Colvile, Suffolk, and of Newton Colvile, Cambridgeshire,* folding at 482.
Peyton, folding at 522.

DERBYSHIRE.

257. *Vitruvius Britannicus.* History of Hardwicke Hall. By P. F. ROBINSON. *London,* 1835. Folio.

Hardwicke *of Hardwicke Hall,* 2. | Stuart, Lady Arabella, 18.

258. The History of Repton. By ROBERT BIGSBY, M.A. LL.D. *London,* 1854. 4to.

Chester, Earls of, 1.
Every *of Eggington,* 361.
Findern *of Findern,* 102.

Mercia, Kings of, 7.
Port *of Elwell,* 103.
Thacker *of Repton,* 93.

259.—Visitation of Derbyshire, 1663-4. Ex MSS. Phillipps. *Typis Medio Montanis*, 1854. Folio.

Agard *of Dunstall and Foston*, 1.
Arkney *of Willesley*, 1.
Allen *of Ightham*, 1.
Allestry *of Derby and Alveston*, 1.
Alsop *of Alsop in Dale*, 1.
Asshenhurst *of Glossopdale*, 1.
Bache *of Stanton*, 1.
Bagshaw *of Ridge*, 1.
Balidon *of Derby*, 1.
Bateman *of Haltington and Wood-house*, 1.
Bennet *of Snelston*, 1.
Beresford *of Bentley*, 1.
Bilgay, 2.
Blith *of Burchet*, 2.
Bonington *of Barrowcole*, 2.
Boothby *of Tooley Park*, 2.
Braylesford *of Semor*, 2.
Browne *of Shredicote*, 3.
Bullock *of Norton and Ouston*, 2.
Burton *of Linley & Fanshawegate*, 2.
Burton *of Bradbourn*, 2.
Buxton *of Ashborne and Yolgrave*, 2.
Charleton *of Brason*, 2.
Clarke *of Somershall*, 2.
Clarke *of Ashgate*, 2.
Colwich *of Stud*, 3.
Cooke *of Trusley*, 3.
Dakin *of Stubing*, 3.
Dalton *of Derby*, 3.
Degge *of Derby*, 3.
Draper *of Culland*, 3.
Draycot *of Derby*, 3.
Emery *of Barton Park*, 3.
Eyre *of Hassop*, 3.
Eyre *of Shalton*, 4.
Eyre *of Crankill*, 3.
Eyre *of Hassop*, 4.
Every *of Eggington*, 4.
Fitzherbert *of Tissington*, 4.
Fitzherbert *of Somershall*, 4.
Frechevile *of Staveley*, 4.
Gell *of Hopton*, 4.
Gilbert *of Lock*, 4.
Graves *of Graves*, 4.

Gregson *of Sharrowhall*, 4.
Harding *of Newton*, 4.
Harper *of Calke*, 4.
Holden *of Welne*, 4.
Hophinton, 4.
Horton, 5.
Kendall *of Smithsby*, 5.
Lee *of Ladyhole*, 5.
Low *of Denby*, 5.
Low *of Alderwasley*, 5.
Meller *of Derby*, 5.
Meverell *of Judeswall*, 5.
Milward *of Chilcot and Eton*, 5.
Morewood *of Alpeton*, 5.
Munday *of Markeaton*, 5.
Newton *of Daffield*, 5.
Osbourn *of Derby*, 5.
Pegge *of Ashbourn*, 5.
Poole *of Radbourn*, 6.
Poole *of Illege*, 6.
Poole *of Wakefordge*, 6.
Powtrell, 6.
Revell *of Ogston*, 6.
Rhodes *of Staveley Woodthorpe*, 6.
Roper *of Heanor*, 6.
Rossington *of Soopton*, 6.
Sale *of Shardelow*, 6.
Savill *of Blackwell*, 6.
Sheldon, 6.
Shore *of Snifferton*, 6.
Sitwell *of Remshaw*, 6.
Sleigh *of Ash*, 6.
Spateman, 6.
Stafford *of Botham Hall*, 7.
Tayler *of Chesterfield*, 7.
Thacker *of Repton and Hege*, 7.
Tunsted *of Tunsted*, 7.
Waklyn *of Hilton*, 7.
Wigfall *of Remshaw*, 7.
Wigley *of Middleton*, 7,
Willymott *of Chadesden*, 7.
Wolley *of Riber*, 7.
Woolhouse *of Glasswell*, 7.
Wright *of Langston*, 7.
Wright *of Unthank*, 7.

ESSEX.

260.—Suckling Papers. Weale's Quarterly Papers on Architecture. Vol. 3.

Grimston *(Bradfield)*, 85.
Poyntz *of Tortington, Gloucester*, 64.

Swynbourne *(Little Horkesley)*, 102.

GLOUCESTERSHIRE.

261.—History of Gloucester. By Rev. Thomas Dudley Fosbrooke, M.A., F.A.S. *London*, 1819. Folio.

Counsel, vi.

262.—Visitation of Gloucestershire, 1569. Ex MSS. Phillipps. *Typis Medio Montanis.* 1854. Folio.

Abingdon *of Dowdeswell*, 1.
Bagehote *of Prestbury*, 1.
Barnard *of Upton St. Leonard and Flaxley*, 1.
Bartlett *of Saintbury*, 1.
Baynham *of Westbury*, 1.
Berew *of Feld Court and Derehurst*, 2.
Bradeston *of Bradeston*, 2.
Bradway *of Poteslipe*, 2.
Bromwich *of Bromesberow*, 2.
Brayne *of Great Dean and Little Dean*, 3.
Bridgeman *of Great Dean*, 3.
Burge and Brydges, 3.
Bucke *of Alberton*, 3.
Bucke *of Bibury*, 4.
Care *alias* Carr *of Bristol*, 3.
Clopton, 4.
Compton *of Hartpury*, 4.
Daunte *of Oulpen*, 4.
Fowke *of Thornbury*, 5.
Gastrell *of Tedbury and Shipton Moygne*, 5.
Goderyche *of Charlton Kings*, 5.
Grevell *of Ebrington*, 5.
Gyse *of Elmore*, 5.
Halton *of Bristol*, 6.
Hooke *of Bristol*, 6.
Kettleby *of Sidington Lodge*, 6.
Kyngescote *of Kyngescote*, 6.
Kynne *of Sende*, 6.
Lloyd *of Holyrood Ampney*, 6.
Lawrence, 7.

Madock *of Alvington*, 7.
Mathew *of Tortworth*, 7.
Okewold *of Sudgrove and Addington*, 7.
Osbaldeston *of Long Compton, and Oddington*, 7.
Mylle *of Tremylle and Harscombe*, 8.
Partryche *of Stanley, St. Leonard and Cirencester*, 8.
Pepwall *of Bristol and Cold Ashton*, 8.
Poleyn *of King's Weston*, 8.
Raynsford *of Little Compton*, 8.
Sandford *of Stowe on the Wold*, 9.
Sheldon *of Child's Wickwayn*, 9.
Strange *of Cirencester*, 9.
Stratford *of Farmcote and Hallyng*, 9.
Vaughan *of Just*, 9.
Vele *of Longford*, 10.
Vele *of Tortworth*, 10.
Walrond *of Pukelchurch*, 10.
Walwyn *of Southam*, 10.
Watson *of Stratton*, 10.
Whitington *of St. Brevels and Cold Ashton*, 11.
Williams *of Westbury*, 11.
Wilton *of Dymoke*, 11.
Wisse *of Thornbury*, 11.
Pole *of Saperton*, 11.
Butler *of Badminton*, 12.
Whittington, Collections for, from Charters, &c. By Sir T. P.

263.—Visitation of Gloucestershire, 1583 and 1623. Printed in 1864. Folio. Privately printed by Sir Thomas Phillipps, Bart.

Abingdon *of Dowdeswell*, 1.
Acton *of Burton and Longhope*, 2.
Alye *of Tewkesbury*, 2.
Atkinson *of Stowell*, 2.
Atwood *of Deynton and Beach*, 3.

Aylworth *of Aylworth*, 3.
Bartlet *of Castle Morton, Worcester, and Saintbury, Gloucester*, with additions, 4.
Bassett *of Uley*, 4.

264.—History of the Town and Parish of Tetbury, in the County of Gloucester. By Rev. Alfred T. Lee, M.A. *London.* 1857. 8vo.

Cotes *of Cotes,* 249.

Estcourt *of Estcourt,* 196-208.

Holford *of Western Birt,* 218-220.

Huntley *of Boxwell Court,* 208-218.

Paul *of High Grove,* 221-227.

Savage *of Tetbury,* 228-237.

HAMPSHIRE.

265.—Records of the Corporation of the Borough of New Lymington in the County of Southampton. By Charles St. Barbe, F.S.A. *Printed for private circulation.* Royal 4to.

Burrard.

266.—Hampshire Visitations, 1575, 1622, and part of 1686. From the MSS. of the Rev. Wm. Bingley. Folio. Privately printed by Sir Thomas Phillipps, Bart.

Abarrow *of North Chardford,* 1.

Alexander *of Winchester, Hants,* 1.

Allen *of Forton,* 1.

Alleyn *of West Meon,* 1.

Alphe *of London,* 1.

Andrews *of Freefolk,* 2.

Arnwood *of Arnwood,* 2.

Ayleffe *of Skeres,* 2.

Bacon *of Twyford,* 2.

Bannister *of Idsworth,* 3.

Barton *of Fareham,* 3.

Baskerville *of Combe, Hereford,* 3.

Basket *of the Isle of Wight,* 3.

Bathurst *of Rye,* 3.

Bayley *of Mervelod,* 4.

Beale *of Priors Deane,* 4.

Beconshaw *of Ibsley, and Moyles Court,* 4.

Bee *of Basingstoke,* 5.

Berkeley *of Beverstone,* 5.

Bethell *of Winchester,* 5.

Betts *of Southampton,* 5.

Bilson *of Mapledurham,* 6.

Blake *of Estontowne and Andover,* 6.

Bowerman *of Brooke in the Isle of Wight,* 6.

Bowyer, 6.

Boyse *of Hinton,* 7.

Brocas and Pexall *of Beaurepaire,* 7.

Broke *of Whitchurch,* 8.

Bromfield *of Haywood, in New Forest,* 8.

Bruning *of Wymering,* 8.

Brydges, 8.

Bruges, Duke of Chandos, 9.

Brune *of Plumber,* 10.

Bulkley *of Burgate,* 10.

Bulkley *of St. Helens,* 11.

Burley *of Long Parish,* 11.

Burrard *of Lymington,* 11.

Button *of Buckland,* 12.

Chamberlain *of Lyndhurst,* 12.

Chaundler *of Hyde,* 12.

Cheeke *of Motteston,* 12.

Chute *of the Vine,* 13.

Ciampanti *of Fieldhouse,* 13.

Clarke *of Avington,* 13.

Cobbe *of Swarton,* 14.

Cole *of Lyss Abbas,* 14.

Colnet *of Combley,* 14.

Compton *of Compton,* Lisley and Ashman *of Lymington,* 14.

Compton *of Priors Deane,* 15.

Compton, 15.

Cooper, Earl of Shaftesbury, 15.

Cope *of Bedhampton,* 16.

Cope *of Bramshill,* 16.

Cotton *of Warblington,* 17.

Cowdray *of Heriard,* 17.

Cray *of Ibsley,* and Grant and Lewis, 17.

Cresville *of Odiham,* 18.

Creswell *of Farnham,* 19.

Cufaud, *alias* Cuffold *of Cuffold in Basing,* 19.

Dabridgecourt *of Stratfield Say,* 19.

Dawley *of Lainston*, 20.
Dawtry *of Hampton*, 20.
Dawtry *of Woodcote*, 20.
Deane *of Odiham and Deaneland*, 20.
De la Bere, Barry and Lister, 21.
West, Earl, De la Warr, 21.
Dennys *of Shanklin,* De Insula *of Wotton*, Brocas and Rogers *of Freefolk*, 22.
Dering *of Lyss*, 23.
Dillington, 23.
Dingley *of Wolverton*, 23.
Doddington *of Breamore*, 24.
Dowse *of Hurstborne and Wallop*, 24.
Kingston, Meux, and Drew, *of Kingston*, 25.

Edmonds *of Bossington*, 25.
Erlesman *of Westover*, 25.
Fashin *of Southampton*, 25.
Fisher *of Chilton*, 25.
Fawconer *of Hurstbourne and Kingsclue*, 26.
Fawconer *of Kingsclere*, 26.
Fielder *of East Meon*, 26.
Fielder *of Borough Court*, 27.
Fiennes and Wickham *of Ash and Deane*, 27.
Fifhide *of Alton and* Sandys *of the Vine*, 27.
Fisher *of Chilton, Candover and Tauke*, 28.
Fitzherbert, 28.
Fleming, 28.

ISLE OF MAN.

267.—A short Treatise of the Isle of Man. By JAMES CHAL-
ONER. Edited by the Rev. J. G. CUMMING, M.A.
Douglas. Printed for the Manx Society. 1864. 8vo.

Alan, Lord of Galloway, folding app. A.
Athol; *see* Derby.
Beaumont; *see* Comyn.
Comyn and Beaumont, folding app. D.

Derby and Athol, app. E.
Ergadia, folding, app. B.
Olive the Black, (Olaveson), folding app. C.

LANCASHIRE.

268.—Historical and Descriptive Account of the Town and
Chapelry of Oldham. By J. BUTTERWORTH. *Oldham.*
1817. 12mo.

Ashton, 157.
Crompton *of Crompton*, 130.
Cudworth, folding at 69.
Egerton *of Shaw*, 126.
Greaves *of Culcheth*, 74.
Gregg *of Chamber*, 72.

Horton *of Chadderton*, 158.
Radcliffe; *see* Trafford.
Shaw *of Heyside*, 111.
Tetlow, 70.
Trafford and Radcliffe, 148.

269.—History of the Ancient Chapels of Didsbury and
Chorlton, in Manchester Parish, &c. By the Rev. JOHN
BOOKER, M.A., F.S.A. *Chetham Society*, Vol. 42. 1857.
Fcap. 4to.

Barlow *of Barlow*, 294.
Hulme *of Reddish*, 226.
Longford *of Longford, Derby, and of Hough, Lanc.* 113.

Mosley *of Hulme*, 173.
Reddish *of Reddish*, 212.

270.—History of the Ancient Chapel of Birch, in Manchester Parish, &c. By the REV. JOHN BOOKER, M.A., F.S.A. *Chetham Society*, Vol. 47. 1859. Fcap. 4to.

Birch *of Birch*, folding at 102.
Birch *of Ardwick*, folding at 120.
Dickenson *of Birch*, 105.

Siddall *of Slade*, 136.
Worsley *of Platt*, folding at 67.
Worsley *of Crompton*, 68.

LEICESTERSHIRE.

271.—Historical Account of the Church of St. Margaret, Stoke Golding, Leicestershire. By T. L. WALKER. *London*, 1844. 4to. From Weale's Quarterly Papers on Architecture.

Champaigne *of Thurlestone*, 22.

LINCOLNSHIRE.

272.—English Church Furniture, &c. as exhibited in a List of the goods destroyed in the Lincolnshire Churches, A.D. 1566. Edited by EDWARD PEACOCK, F.S.A. *London*, 1866. 8vo.

Bellingham *of Manton and Brumby Wood*.
Bishop *of Hemswell*, 102.
Callis *of Little Hale and Dalderby*, 31.
Healey *of Burringham and Frodingham*, 228, 229.

Meeres *of Auburn*, 34.
Morley *of Winterton*, 164.
Morley *of Holme*, 244, 245.
Peacock *of Blyton, Scotter, and Bottesford*, 77, 78.
Turney *of Cavenby or Cainby*, 215.

273.—A Topographical Account of the Isle of Axholme. By W. PECK. *Doncaster*, 1815. 4to.

Moubray, 49—81. | Sheffield *of Butterwick*, 82—86.

274.—Read's History of the Isle of Axholme. Edited by THOMAS C. FLETCHER, 1858. (Unfinished.)

Amcotes *of Aistrop, Harrington, and Kettlethorpe*, 384.
Johnson, 64.
Popplewell, 64.

Ryther, 64.
Sheffield *of Butterwick*, 160.
Steer, 64

MONMOUTHSHIRE.

275.—Notices of Pencoyd Castle and Langstone. By OCTAVIUS MORGAN, Esq., M.P., F.R.S., V.P.S.A., and THOMAS WAKEMAN, Esq. *Newport, Printed for the Monmouthshire and Caerleon Antiquarian Association.* 4to. 1864.

Morgan *of Pencoyd*, folding at 38.

NORFOLK.

276.—Sketch of the History of Caister Castle, near Yarmouth. Edited by Dawson Turner, Esq., M.A. *London*, 1842. 8vo.

Paston, folding at 138.

277.—Norfolk Archæology. Published by the Norfolk and Norwich Archæological Society. *Norwich*, 1847-1866. 8vo.

Argentine, iii. 267.
Astley, iv. 19.
Barber, iii. 128.
Bedingfield, Sir Henry Paston, Bart. iv. folding at 134.
Berrye, iv. 16.
Blennerhasset, vii. 86.
Clifton, iii. 127.
De Caily, iii. 126.
Gawsel, iii. 126.
Hastings, vi. 76, 78, 90-97.
Heveningham *of Heveningham*, iii. folding at 284.
Le Groos, iii. folding at 90.
Le Neve, ii. folding at 396.
Littleton, iv. 19.

Manby *of Middleton in Yorkshire, of Elsham in Lincolnshire, and of Hilgay in Norfolk*, iii. folding at 130.
Mauteby, iii. 159.
Mawtby, iv. 23.
Paston, iv. folding at 1.
Paston, *descent of the marriage of Sir Thomas and Agnes Leigh*, iv. 45.
Paston, *descent of the daughters of William, Earl of Yarmouth*, iv. 52.
Pratt *of Wimbotsham*, ii. facing 142.
Shuldham, vi. 300.
Sydney *of Walsingham*, vi. 263.

278.—Visitation of Norfolk (by Harvey, 1563, transcribed by Lennard, 1618). Published by the Norfolk and Norwich Archæological Society.

Aldham, 122.
Appleyard, 38.
Audley, 129.
Bacon *of Harleston*, 24.
Baker; *see* Ladd.
Balam, 49.
Balden, 44.
Barow, 114.
Barney, 7.
Bastard, 52.
Beckham, 8.
Bedingfeld, 9, 155.
Billingford, 21.
Bolton, 101.
Brampton *of Attleburgh*, 70.
Brampton *of Brampton*, 71.
Brampton *of Setton*, 68.
Brampton *of Westwinch*, 69.
Call *of Bacton*, 22.
Carsey, 123.

Castle, 21.
Chamberleyne, 92.
Chapman, 94.
Chauncey, 113.
Clement, 11.
Colby, 95.
Coote, 85.
Copdike, 10.
Copping, 11.
Corbet, 35.
Cordall, 91.
Deane, 56.
Downe, 37.
Downe (Downes), 13.
Downing, 14.
Drake, 36.
Duck, 13.
Ensign, 40.
Everard *of Walpole*, 46.
Futter, 145.

Goldingham, 86.
Grimston, 175.
Greene, 80.
Guybon, 178.
Hart, 54.
Hast, 41.
Hethe, 75.
Hewar, 149.
Howard, 15.
Jenney, 132.
Jermy *of Antingham*, 107.
Kervile *of Watlington*, 57.
Kervile *of Wingenhale*, 189.
Ladd, alias Baker, 45.
Layer, 25.
Le Strange, 61.
Linghoke, 48.
Methwold, 82.
Nicholls, 42.
Nicolls, 43.
Osborne, 34.

Oxborough; see Hewar.
Penistone, 41.
Repps, 193.
Rokewode, 140.
Sedley, 111.
Smallpece, 115.
Smith, 87, 90.
Southwell, 124.
Steward, 19.
Thwaites, 118.
Titley, 77.
Tolwin, 78.
Warde *of Brooke*, 29.
Ward *of Postwick*, 31.
Warner, 17.
Whetnall, alias Warner, 17.
Wilkinson, 88.
Wingfield, 79.
Wodehouse *of Kimberley*, 103.
Wolsey *of Newton*, 23.
Wood *of Norwich*, 27.

NORTHAMPTONSHIRE.

279.—The History and Antiquities of Northamptonshire, compiled from the Manuscript Collections of the late learned Antiquary JOHN BRIDGES, Esq. By the Rev. PETER WHALLEY. *Oxford*, 1791. 2 vols. folio.

A fuller title than that given as No. 111, page 87.

OXFORDSHIRE.

280.—Register of the Presidents, Fellows. Demies, &c. of Magdalen College, Oxford. By J. R. BLOXAM, D:D. *Oxford*. 2 vols. 8vo.

Hayes, ii. 221.

WARWICKSHIRE.

281.—The Cistercian Abbey of Stoneley in Arden, Warwickshire, and its occupants. (By the Rev. J. M. GRESLEY.) *Ashby-de-la-Zouch*, 1854. 8vo.

Leigh *of Stoneley, Warwickshire,* | shire, folding at 26.
and Leigh and Haigh *of Lanca-* |

YORKSHIRE.

282.—Topographical History and Description of Bawtry and Thorne. By W. PECK. *Doncaster*, 1813. 4to.

Pryme, 91*-97*.

283.—History and Description of St. George's Church at Doncaster. By the Rev. JOHN EDWARD JACKSON. *London*, 1855. 4to.

Ellerker, 77.
Scorah, app. lxxvii.
Seaton *of Doncaster*, 88.

Sharp, Archbishop of York, app. lvi.

284.—A Genealogical Account of the Lords of Studley Royal in Yorkshire. By JOHN RICHARD WALBRAN, F.S.A.

Aislabie
Mallory

Tempest.

285.—Marske. A small Contribution towards Yorkshire Topography. By the Rev. JAMES RAINE, M.A. 1860, 8vo. 25 copies, from the Archæologia Æliana.

Bathurst, 75.
Bower, 80.
Cleseby, 33.
Conyers, 36.
Hutton, 11, 51.
Hutton *of Marske*, 49.

Marske, 28.
Phillip, 46.
Robinson, 84.
Rokeby, 19.
Stapylton, 12.

286.—The History of Bradford, with additions and continuation to the present time. By JOHN JAMES. 8vo. *London*, 1866. (This new issue has two more Pedigrees than those given at p. 159.)

Hailstone *of Horton Hall*, ix.

Sykes *of Driglington*, xvii.

WALES.

287.—Observation on the Snowdon Mountains, &c. By WILLIAM WILLIAMS. *London*, 1802. 8vo.

Griffith, 163—177.
Warburton, 185—187.
Williams, 178—185.

Williams, 191—193.
Yonge, 188—191.

285

INDEX TO FAMILIES.

₊ *The figures refer to the titles of the Books.*

Abadam, *Carmarthen*, 234.
Abarough, *Somerset*, 140.
Abarow, *Hampshire*, 50.
Abarrow, *Hampshire*, 50.
Abbott, *Surrey*, 162; *Wilts*, 185, 192.
Abdy, *Essex*, 48, 234; *Surrey*, 156; *London*, 102; 251.
Abell, *Bucks*, 10.
Abells, *London*, 102.
Abercromby, 234.
Abermarlies, *Glamorgan*, 228.
Abingdon, 236; *Gloucester*, 262, 263.
Abington, *Dorset*, 33.
Ablett, *Denbigh*, 234.
Abney, *Derby*, 234; *Leicester*, 80; *Stafford*, 146.
Achmuty, 234,
Ackers, *Chester*, 234.
Acland, *Devon*, 131; *Sussex*, 165.
Acroyd, *York*, 234.
Acton, *Salop*, 234; *Wicklow*, 234; *Worc.* 234; *Glou.* 263.
A Combe, *Warw.* 178.
A'Court, *Wilts*, 185.
Aclom, *York*, 217.
Aclam, *York*, 226.
Adair, *Suffolk*, 153; *Queen's co.*, 234; *Somerset*, 234; 236.
Adam, *Camb.* 16; *Kinross*, 234.
Adams, *Essex*, 48; *London*, 102; *Northamp.* 112; *Norfolk*, 107; *Warw.* 234; *Devon*, 234; *Pemb.* 230, 234; *Cavan*, 234; *Cork*, 234; *Limerick*, 234; *Carm.* 234; *York*, 213, 224; 229, 236, 237.
Adderley, *Staff.* 146; *Warw.* 172, 234.
Addison, *Durham*, 38; *Suff.* 234.
Adeane, *Camb.* 234, 237.
Agar, *York*, 234.
Agard, *York*, 224; *Derby*, 259.
Agar-Ellis, *Northamp.* 112.
Aglionby, *Cumb.* 22, 23, 234.
Agnew, Vans- 234, 236.

Agmondesham, *Surrey*, 156; *Sussex*, 168.
Aguillon, *Herts*, 54.
Aikin, 236.
Ailesbury, *Warw.* 172.
Aislabie, *York*, 284.
Ailsa, 236.
Ainsworth, *Lanc.* 234.
Akers, *Kent*, 234.
Akeroyd, *York*, 205.
Akinstall, *Camb.* 16.
Alan, *Norfolk*, 109; *Isle of Man*, 267.
Albany, *Surrey*, 156.
Albemarle, *Northamp.* 112; *Surrey*, 156, 157; *York*, 217; 232.
Albini, *Bucks*, 10, 11; *Essex*, 48, 249; *Leic.* 80; *Rutl.* 136; *Sussex*, 167.
Alchorne, *Hampshire*, 50; *Kent*, 60; *Sussex*, 165.
Alcock, *London*, 102; *Sussex*, 165; *Wexford*, 234; *Carlow*, 234; *Surrey*, 234; 243.
Alcocke, *Sussex*, 163.
Alde, *Kent*, 60.
Aldelym, *Chester*, 17.
Alder, *Durham*, 42.
Aldersey, *Chester*, 17, 234; *Kent*, 60.
Aldham, *Northamp.* 112; *Norf.* 278.
Aldworth, *Cork*, 234; *Berks*, 254.
Aleigh, *Cornwall*, 21.
Alen, 234.
Alesburge, *Bucks*, 11.
Alesbury, *Warw.* 172.
Alexander, *Hamp.* 50, 266; *Donegal*, 234; *Essex*, 234; *Ayr*, 234; *Clackmannan*, 234; *Stirling*, 234.
Alford, *Bucks*, 11; *Sussex*, 163, 165; *York*, 217; *Berks*, 254; 232.
Alfounder, *Leic.* 80.
Alfrey, *Sussex*, 165.
Alington. *Camb.* 16; *Herts*, 53, 54; *Linc.* 234.
Alison, 237.

Alkin, *Kent,* 284.
Alkstede, *Surrey,* 156.
Allan, *Durham and York,* 38, 43, 234, 220, 236, 239, 250.
Allanson, 234.
Allardice ; see Barclay and 236.
Allen, *Bucks,* 11 ; *Camb.* 16; *Chester,* 17 ; *Kent,* 60 ; *Leic.* 80 ; *Staff.* 146 ; *Somerset,* 140 ; *Sussex,* 165 ; *Pemb.* 234 ; *York,* 234 ; *Berks,* 254 ; *Derby,* 259 ; *Hamp.* 266.
Allenson, *York,* 219, 224.
Allestry, *Derby,* 259.
Allett, *Somerset,* 234.
Alleyn, *Essex,* 48 ; *Surrey,* 162 ; *Hamp.* 266.
Alleyne, *Wilts,* 185.
Allfray, *Sussex,* 165.
Allfrey, *Berks,* 234.
Allgood, *Northum.* 234.
Allin, *Berks,* 7.
Allingham, *Berks,* 7.
Allington, *Leic.* 80.
Allison, *Durham,* 37.
Allix, *Linc.* 234 ; *Camb.* 234.
Allott, *York,* 213 ; 234.
Alloway, *Queen's co.,* 234 ; 239.
Allsop, *Derby,* 27.
Alman, *Sussex,* 165.
Almer, *Wales,* 229.
Alneto, *Northamp.* 112.
Alphe, *Hamp.* 50, 266.
Alport, *Ches.* 17 ; *Staff.* 146.
Alspath, *Warw.* 172.
Alsop, *Leic.* 80, 251; *Derby,* 259.
Alsopp, *Leic.* 80.
Alston, *Herts,* 56 ; *Warw.* 234.
Alta Ripa, *Bucks,* 10, 11.
Altham, *Herts,* 54, 56 ; *Lanc.* 68.
Alwent, *Durh.* 38, 41.
Alwin, *Sussex,* 165.
Alye, *Glouc.* 263 ; *Dorset,* 33, incorrectly printed *Ayle.*
Amcoats, *Durham,* 38.
Amcotes, *Linc.* 273.
Amcotts, *see* Cracroft, 234.
Ameredith, *Devon,* 29.
Amery, *Worcester,* 234.
Ames, *Bedford,* 234.
Amherst, *Herts,* 56 ; *Kent,* 60; *Sussex,* 165 ; *Warwick,* 234.

Amory, *Devon,* 31 ; *London,* 102.
Amos, *Herts,* 234.
Amphlett, *Worcester,* 194, 23423 6.
Amundeville, *Essex,* 48.
Amy, *Cambridge,* 16.
Amyand, *Herts,* 56.
Anderson, *Bucks,* 10 ; *Durham,* 38 ; *Essex,* 48, 234 ; *Herts,* 54 ; *Lincoln,* 87 ; *Northumberland,* 120, 234 ; *Surrey,* 234 ; 234.
Anderton, *Lancaster,* 69, 71, 234 ; *York,* 205 ; 236.
Andrew, *Northampton,* 111, 112 ; *Berks,* 254.
Andrews, *Bucks,* 11 ; *Devon,* 30 ; *Durham,* 38 ; *Hampshire,* 50, 266 ; *Leicester,* 80 ; *Northampton,* 111 ; *Rutland,* 135 ; *Lancaster,* 234.
Andrewes, *Essex,* 48 ; *Leicester,* 80.
Angell, *London,* 102 ; *Surrey,* 162.
Anger, *Wilts,* 182.
Angerstein, *Kent,* 234.
Angevin, 232.
Angiel, *Wales,* 229.
Anguish, *Suffolk,* 234.
Anjou, *London,* 102.
Anketell, *Monaghan,* 234.
Anketil, *Dorset,* 33.
Anlaby, *York,* 214, 224.
Annand, 234.
Anne, *York,* 213, 224, 226.
Annesley, *Berks,* 3, 254 ; *Bucks.* 10 ; *Northampton,* 112 ; *Oxford,* 131, 234 ; 234, 236.
Annwell, *Wales,* 229.
Ansell, *Herts,* 54.
Anson, 236.
Anstey, *Sussex,* 165.
Anstie, *Wilts.* 181.
Anstruther-Thompson, 234.
Anstruther, *Suffolk,* 234 ; 236.
Anthony, *London,* 102.
Antonie, *Bucks,* 10.
Antrobus, *Cheshire,* 17, 234.
Aperdale, *Surrey,* 156.
Ap Howell, *Sussex,* 165.
Aphugh, *Berks,* 7.
Appleby, *Durham,* 38 ; *Leic.* 76, 80 ; *York,* 224.
Appleton, *Kent,* 60 ; 245.
Appleyard, *York,* 217 ; *Norfolk,* 278.
Appulton, *Kent,* 60.

Applynden, *Durham*, 38.
Ap Rees, *Bucks*, 10.
Ap Rhese, *Hunts*, 57 ; *Sussex*, 165.
Apsley, *Bucks*, 10, 13 ; *Sussex*, 163, 165, 169.
Apthorpe, *York*, 213.
Ap Harri, *Wales*, 229.
Ap Rhys, *Wales*, 229.
Apuldrefield, 233.
Apylton, *Kent*, 65.
Arabin, *Essex, and Middlesex*, 234.
Arblaster, *Staff.* 143.
Arbalester, *Staff.* 146.
Arcedeckne, *Suffolk*, 234.
Archbold, *Kildare*, 234.
Archdall, *Fermanagh*, 234.
Archer-Burton, *Hants*, 234.
Archer, *Cornwall*, 237 ; *Essex*, 48 ; *Lincoln*, 82 ; *Oxford*, 131 ; *Sussex*, 165 ; *Warwick*, 172, 177 ; 235.
Arches, *Berks*, 7.
Archibald, *Lanc.* 234.
Arden, *Wales*, 229 ; *Ches.* 19, 73 ; *Northampton*, 19, 111, 112 ; *Staff.* 143, 146 ; *Warwick*, 172 ; 233, 234.
Ardern, *Ches.* 17.
Arderne, *Ches.* 17, 19 : *Oxford*, 128, 130 ; *Sussex*, 165 ; *Staff.* 19, 233.
Ardes, *Bucks.* 10.
Ardyngton, *York*, 226.
Argentein, *Bucks.* 10.
Argentine, *Herts.* 54 ; *Norfolk*, 277.
Arkinstall, *Cambridge*, 16.
Arkney, *Derby*, 259.
Arkwright, *Derby*, 26, 234 ; *Hereford*, 234 ; *Essex*, 234 ; *Leic.* 234 ; *Staff.* 234.
Armenters, *Northampton*, 112.
Armeston, *Leic.* 80.
Armistead, *York*, 234.
Armitage, *York*, 213, 222, 224, 234 ; *Louth*, 234.
Armstrong, *Notts.* 122 ; *King's co.* 234 ; *Armagh*, 234 ; *Tipperary and Sligo*, 234 ; *Clare*, 234 ; *York*, 234 ; *Wicklow*, 234.
Armyne, *Rutland*, 136.
Armytage, *York*, 205.
Arnall, *Notts.* 122.
Arney, 234.
Arnold, *Dorset*, 33 ; *Herts*, 54 ; *Northampton*, 112 ; *Bucks*, 234 ; 234.

Arnwood, *Hamp.* 50, 266.
Arpe, *Surrey*, 156.
Arscot, *Devon*, 29.
Arsic, *Kent*, 58.
Arthington, *York*, 205.
Arthur, *Clare*, 234.
Arundel, *Dorset*, 33 ; *Essex*, 48 ; *Northampton*, 112 ; *Surrey*, 156 ; *Sussex*, 163 ; 234, 231.
Arundell, *Corn.* 21 ; *Devon*, 29 ; *Wilts*, 182 ; 232, 233.
Ash, *Londonderry*, 234 ; *Wilts*, 182 ; *Devon*, (*see* Esse), 29.
Ashbrook, *Bucks*, 13.
Ashburnham, 165.
Ashby, *Leic.* 76, 80, 234 ; *Lincoln*, 84 ; 232.
Ashbornham, *Sussex*, 168.
Ashbwl, *Wales*, 229.
Ashcomb, *Oxford*, 132.
Ashcombe, *Oxford*, 131 ; *Somerset*, 140.
Ashe, *Somerset*, 140 ; *Wilts*, 182, 191.
Ashe, *Herts*, 56 ; *Somerset*, 140 ; *Meath*, 234.
Asheldam, *Hamp.* 50.
Asheton, *Leic.* 80.
Ashfeild, *Kent*, 60.
Ashfield, *Oxford*, 128, 130, 131, 133.
Ashford, *Devon*. 29.
Ashfordby-Trenchard, 236.
Ashhurst, *Oxford*, 234.
Ashley, *Chester*, 17 ; *Northamp.* 112 ; *Suffolk*, 152 ; *Wilts*, 182, 185, 192, 246.
Ashley-Cooper, *Dorset.* 33.
Ashmall, *Durham*, 38.
Ashman, *Hamp.* 50 ; *Wilts*, 185.
Ashmole, *Staff.* 142, 146.
Ashton, *Ches.* 17 ; *Herts*, 50 ; *Lanc.* 71, 268 ; *York.* 206.
Ashurst, *Surrey*, 156 ; 236, 245.
Ashwell, *London*, 102.
Ashworth, *Oxford*, 131, 234.
Ask, *York.* 209.
Aske, *York*, 226.
Askew, *Durham*, 42, 234 ; *Northumb.* 119, 234.
Askwith, *York*, 219.
Aslacton, *Notts.* 122.
Aspale, *Suffolk*, 152.

Aspinall, *Lanc.* 234.
Aspland, *Herts*, 56.
Asshenhurst, *Derby*, 259.
Assheton, *Lanc.* 68, 234.
Astbury, *Cheshire*, 17.
Astell, *Hunts.* 234.
Astle, *Essex*, 48.
Astley, *Essex*, 48 ; *Kent*, 60 ; *Leic.* 76, 80 ; *Lanc.* 234 ; *Shrop.* 137 ; *Staff.* 143, 146 ; *Warw.* 172 ; *Wilts.* 182 ; *Norf.* 277.
Aston, *Ches.* 17, 234 ; *Herts*, 54, 56 ; *Staff.* 143, 146 ; *Surrey*, 156 ; *York*, 205.
Astrie, *Hunts*, 57.
Atcherley, *Salop*, 234, 239.
Atherton, *Lanc.* 71.
Athol, *I. of Man*, 267.
Athorpe, *York*, 234.
Athow, *Norfolk*, 107.
At Hull, *Surrey*, 156.
Athy, *Galway*, 234.
Atkin, *Cork*, 234.
Atkins, *Herts*, 54 ; *Surrey*, 156 ; *Cork*, 234.
Atkinson, *Bucks*, 13 ; *Herts*, 56 ; *London*, 102 ; *Northum.* 119, 234 ; *Mayo*, 234 ; *King's Co.* 234 ; *Cumb. and Westm.* 234 ; *York*, 205, 224 ; 237 ; *Glou.* 263.
Atmore, *Berks*, 8.
Attegar, *Herts*, 56.
Attehooke, *Hamp.* 50.
Att Fenne, *Sussex*, 163.
Att Milne, *Sussex*, 163.
Attwater, *Dorset*, 33.
Atty, *Warw.* 234.
Attye, *Warw.* 234.
Atwill, *Devon*, 29, 31.
Atwood, *Surrey*, 156, 158 ; *Glou.* 263.
Atye, *London*, 94.
Aubre, *Wales*, 229.
Aubrey, *Bucks*, 10, 13 ; *Salop*, 234 ; *Wilts.* 185, 189 ; *Carm.* 230.
Aucher, *Kent*, 60 ; *Wilts*, 182.
Auchmuty, *Roscommon*, 234.
Audborough, *York*, 226.
Audeham, *Northamp.* 112.
Audeley, *Bucks*, 7.
Audley, *Essex*, 46, 48 ; *Hunts*, 57 ; *Leic.* 80 ; *London*, 96 ; *Staff.* 145 ; *Wilts.* 182 ; 251 ; *Norf.* 278.

Aufrere, *Norf.* 234.
Aunger, *Camb.* 16.
Austen, *Hamp.* 50 ; *Herts.* 53, 54 ; *Kent*, 60 ; *London*, 102 ; *Surrey*, 156, 158, 159, 234.
Austwick, *York*, 224.
Avan, *Glam.* 227.
Aveline, *Berks*, 254.
Avelyn, *Surrey*, 158.
Avelyne, *Oxford*, 133.
Avenel, *Bucks*, 10.
Avenon, *London*, 101.
Averenges, *Herts*, 54.
Avery, *London*, 96 ; *Somerset*, 140.
Aveyns, *York*, 217.
Awbrey, *Bucks*, 10, 11 ; *Brecknock*, 227 ; *Glam.* 228 ; *Wales*, 229.
Awdry, *Wilts.* 234.
Awnby, *York*, 224.
Awsiter, *London*, 96.
Aylesbury, *Northamp.* 111, 112.
Aylesford, *Kent*, 69 ; *Surrey*, 156.
Aylesworth, *Kent*, 60.
Ayliffe, *Hamp.* 50, 266.
Aylmer, *Leic.* 80 ; *Kildare*, 234 ; *Durham*, 234 ; 234, 237.
Aylward, *Hamp.* 50 ; *Kilkenny*, 234.
Aylway, *Oxford*, 131.
Aylwin, *Sussex*, 163, 165.
Aylworth, *Berks*, 254 ; *Glou.* 263.
Aynscombe, *Sussex*, 165.
Aynsley, *Northumb.* 119, 234.
Ayote, *Northamp.* 112.
Ayre, *Camb.* 16 ; *Corn.* 21.
Ayscough, *Durham*, 38 ; *Notts.* 122 ; *York*, 208, 219, 224.
Ayshcombe, *Berks*, 254.
Ayshe, *Devon*, 31.
Ayton, *Durham*, 38.

Baber, *Somerset*, 140.
Babington, *Devon*, 29 ; *Leic.* 80 ; 234 ; *Notts.* 122, 123 ; *Staff.* 146, 232, 233 ; 251.
Babthorpe, *Herts*, 54 ; *York*, 198.
Bach, *Glam.* 228.
Bache, *Derby*, 259.
Bachellor, *Kent*, 60.
Bachesworth, *Herts*, 54.
Backhouse, *Durham*, 43 ; *Lond.* 102 ; *Berks*, 254.
Backus, *Cambridge*, 14.
Backwell, *Bucks*, 10.

Bacon, *Hamp.* 50, 266 ; *Herts*, 54 ; *Leic.* 80 ; *Norf.* 107, 278 ; *Northumb.* 119 ; *Oxford*, 133 ; *Wilts.* 182, 185 ; *Berks*, 254.

Badbye, *Kent*, 60.

Badcock, *Bucks.* 10, 234 ; *Lincoln*, 234.

Badda, *Wales*, 229.

Badlesmere, *Herts*, 54 ; *Suff.* 152 ; *Wilts*, 182, 190.

Baesh, *Herts*, 54.

Bagenhall, *Staff.* 145.

Bagehot, *Glouc.* 262.

Bagge, *Norf.* 234.

Baghott, *Leic.* 80.

Baggiley, *Ches.* 17.

Bagot, *Bucks.* 11 ; *Northamp.* 112 ; *King's co.* 234 ; *Staff.* 234 ; *Dublin,* 234.

Bagott, *Herts.* 56.

Bagshaw, *Derby,* 27, 259.

Bagshawe, *York,* 234 ; 251.

Bagwell, *Tipperary,* 234.

Baikie, *Orkney,* 234.

Baile, *Glam.* 234 ; *Brecon,* 234, 239.

Baillie, *Inverness,* 234 ; *Ross,* 234 ; *Lanark,* 234.

Baily, *Wilts,* 185 ; *Kent,* 234.

Bain, *Stirling,* 234.

Bainard, *Norf.* 109.

Bainbridge, *Durham,* 36 ; *Leic.* 80.

Bainbrigge, *Derby,* 27 ; *Leic.* 80 ; 234.

Baird, *Ayr.* 234.

Baker, *Bucks,* 10 ; *Durham,* 37, 38, 234 ; *Herts,* 56, 234 ; *Kent,* 60 ; *Notts.* 122 ; *Sussex,* 165 ; *Rutland,* 234 ; *Wales,* 229 ; *Somerset,* 234 ; *Essex,* 234 ; *Glouc.* 234, 236 ; 245, 250 ; *Berks,* 254 ; *Norf.* 278.

Baker-Cresswell, 234.

Balam, *Norf.* 278.

Balche, *Somerset,* 140.

Balden, *Norf.* 278.

Baldwin, *Cork,* 234, 234.

Baldwyn, *Hunts.* 57.

Bale, *Leic.* 80.

Balfour, *Orkney,* 234 ; *Fife,* 234 ; *East Lothian,* 234 ; *Louth,* 234 ; 236.

Balguy, *Derby,* 234.

Balidon, *Derby,* 259.

Baliol, *Durham,* 34, 38, 41 ; *Herts.* 54 ; *York,* 220 ; 241.

Ball, *Camb.* 16 ; *Kent,* 60 ; *Lond.* 102, 251.

Ballantyne, *Scotland,* 234.

Ballard, *Leic.* 80 ; *Sussex,* 165 ; *Wilts.* 182, 192.

Balliol, *Northumb.* 119.

Balston, *Essex,* 48.

Bamfield, *Devon,* 31 ; *Somerset,* 140 ; *Staff.* 146.

Bamford, *York,* 213.

Bamford-Hesketh, 234.

Bamforth, *York,* 206.

Bampfield, *Devon,* 29 ; *Oxford,* 128.

Banaster, *Leic.* 80.

Banastre, *Bucks.* 10 ; *Lanc.* 68 ; *Leic.* 80 ; *Northamp.* 112.

Banbury, *Hamp.* 50.

Bancks, *Dorset,* 33.

Band, *Somerset,* 234.

Banester, *Hamp.* 50, 266 ; *Surrey,* 162.

Banister, *Lanc.* 71 ; *Lond.* 96.

Banke, *York,* 234, 200.

Bankes, *Leic.* 80 ; *Lanc.* 69, 234 ; *Dorset,* 33, 234 ; 234.

Banks, *Lond.* 102.

Bannister, *Kent,* 60.

Barber, *Oxford,* 131, 132 ; *Norf.* 277.

Barbor, *Wales,* 229.

Barbour, *York,* 210.

Barboure, *Staff.* 146.

Barby, *Devon,* 31.

Barclay, *Essex,* 234 ; *Lanc.* 234 ; *Surrey,* 156, 234 ; 234.

Barclay-Allardice, 234.

Barcroft, *Lanc.* 68.

Bard, *Lond.* 102 ; 232.

Bardolf, *Herts,* 54 ; *Notts.* 122 ; 251.

Bardon, *Durham,* 35.

Barentine, *Sussex,* 168.

Barett, *Suffolk,* 153.

Barford, *Leic.* 80.

Bargrave, *Kent,* 60, 67.

Barham, *Kent,* 60 ; *Pemb.* 234, 236.

Baring, *Hamp.* 50.

Barington, *Sussex,* 168.

Barkeley, *Kent,* 60.

Barker, *Berks,* 7, 254 ; *Bucks,* 11 ; *Glouc.* 234 ; *Northamp.* 112 ; *Nor-*

thumb. 119; *Rutland,* 135; *Surrey,* 161; *Tipperary,* 234; 234.
Barkley, *Hamp.* 50.
Barksted, *Lond.* 102.
Barlee, 249.
Barley, *Herts.* 54, 56.
Barloe, *Hamp.* 50.
Barlor, 253.
Barlow, *Berks,* 7; *Lanc.* 71, 269; *Sussex,* 165; *Pemb.* 230; *Wales,* 229.
Barlye, *Herts.* 54.
Barnard, *Herts.* 56; *Somerset,* 140; *York,* 234; *Glouc.* 234, 262.
Barnardiston, *Northamp.* 112; *Suff.* 234.
Barnby, *York,* 213.
Barne, *Suff.* 153, 234.
Barneby, *Hereford,* 234, 236.
Barnes, *Camb.* 16; *Dorset,* 33; *Durham,* 36, 38, 43; *Kent,* 60.
Barnesley, *Staff.* 143.
Barnett, *Bedford,* 234.
Barnewall, *Meath,* 234.
Barney, *Norf.* 278.
Barnham, *Hamp.* 50; *Kent,* 60.
Barnsley, *Staff.* 146.
Barnston, *Ches.* 17, 234.
Barnwell, 234.
Baron, *Northamp.* 112.
Barow, *Norfolk,* 278.
Barre, *Bucks,* 13; *Northamp.* 112.
Barrell, *London,* 96.
Barret, *Camb.* 16, 21; *Notts,* 122; *Wilts,* 185; *Wales,* 229; *Cornwall,* 21.
Barrett, *Cornwall,* 21; *Leic.* 80; *Wilts,* 182, 185; *Carm.* 230; *Berks,* 234.
Barrett-Lennard, 236.
Barrington, *Bucks,* 10; *Essex,* 48; *Herts.* 53, 54, 236.
Barron, *Waterford,* 234, 234.
Barrow, *Camb.* 16; *Lincoln,* 234.
Barry, *Devon,* 29; *Notts.* 122, 234; *Oxford,* 131; *Cork,* 234; 234; *Bucks,* 10; *Northamp.* 112.
Bartelott, *Sussex,* 163, 168.
Barthelmew, *Hamp.* 50.
Bartholomew, 233.
Bartlett, *Worc.* 195; *Glou.* 263.
Bartlett, *Dorset,* 33; *Sussex,* 165; *Wilts* 185; *Glou.* 262.

Barton, *Notts.* 123; *York,* 224, 234; *Tipperary,* 234; *Fermanagh,* 234; *Kildare,* 234; *Wicklow,* 234; *Donegal,* 234; *Norfolk,* 234; *Hamp.* 266.
Barttelott, *Sussex,* 234.
Barwell, *Leic.* 80.
Barwick, *Wilts,* 185.
Barwis, 234.
Bary, *Wales,* 229.
Barzey, *Wales,* 229.
Baskervile, *Hamp.* 50.
Baskerville, *Northamp.* 111, 112; *Shrop.* 137; *Wilts,* 185, 234; *Wales,* 229; 234, 236; *Hereford,* 137; 239; *Berks,* 254; *Hamp.* 266.
Baskervyle, *Ches.* 17.
Basket, *Hamp.* 50, 266.
Baskett, *Dorset,* 33; *Hamp.* 50; *Sussex,* 165.
Bassano, *Derby,* 27; *London,* 102.
Basse, *London,* 102.
Basset, *Bucks,* 10; *Devon,* 29, 234; *Leic.* 76, 80; *Northamp.* 112; *Notts.* 122; *Shrop.* 137; *Staff.* 143; *Warw.* 172; *Glam.* 228, 234; *Cornwall,* 234.
Bassett, *Berks,* 7; *Corn.* 21; *Hamp.* 50; *York,* 215; *Glou.* 263.
Bassingburn, *Northamp.* 112.
Bassingburne, *Herts.* 54.
Basson, *Glam.* 228.
Bastard, *Devon,* 31, 234; *Dorset,* 234; *Corn.* 21, 236; *Norfolk,* 278.
Basynges, *Rutland,* 136.
Batchcroft, *Norfolk,* 107.
Bate, *Leic.* 80; *York,* 213, 220, 224; 235.
Bateman, *Lond.* 102; *Staff.* 145, 148, 134; *Derby,* 234; *Northamp.* 234; *Monm.* 234, 234; 251; *Berks.* 259.
Bates, *Sussex,* 234: *Northum.* 234; 236.
Bateson, *Herts,* 56.
Bath, *Leic.* 80.
Bather, 251.
Bathurst, *Bucks.* 13; *Kent,* 60; *Northamp.* 112; *Sussex,* 165; *Wilts,* 182; *York,* 205, 285; *Glouc.* 234; *Berks,* 254; *Hamp.* 266.
Batley, *Surrey,* 158.

Batman, *Wales*, 229.
Batt, *Wilts*, 192 ; 234.
Batte, *York*, 224.
Batten, *Somerset*, 234 ; *Berks*, 254.
Battersby, *Cavan*, 234; *Cornw.* 21 ; *Northumb.* 234 ; 234.
Battie, *York*, 213, 224.
Battiscomb, *Dorset*, 33.
Battishill, *Devon*, 29.
Batty, *Westmeath*, 234.
Baugh, *Oxford*, 131.
Bavent, *Wilts*, 182.
Baverstock, *Hants and Berks*, 234.
Bawdrip, *Glam.* 228, 242.
Baxter, *Durham*, 38 ; *York*, 213.
Bayles, *Essex*, 48.
Bayley, *Dorset*, 33 ; *Hamp.* 50 ; *London*, 102 ; *Sussex*, 165 ; 233.
Bayliff, *Wilts.* 185.
Bayly, *Hamp.* 50, 266 : *Wilts*, 185: *Kilkenny*, 234 : *Wicklow*, 234 : *Tipperary*, 234.
Baynard, *Wilts*, 185, 191.
Baynbrige, *Durham*, 40.
Baynbrigg, *Durham*, 38.
Baynbrigge, *Durham*, 40.
Baynes, *York*, 205, 224.
Baynham, *Glouc.* 262.
Bayning, *Lond.* 102.
Baynton, *Wilts*, 185, 193 ; 234.
Bayntun, *Wilts*, 182.
Bayton, *Sussex*, 165.
Beach, *Hamp.* 50, 234 : *Wilts*, 182, 236.
Beadon, *Somerset*, 234.
Beale, *Kent*, 60 : *Shropshire*, 234 : *Sussex*, 165 : *York*, 224 : *Hamp.* 266.
Beamish, *Cork*, 234 : 234 : 237.
Bear, *Devon*, 29.
Bearcroft, *Worc.* 234.
Beard, *Kent*, 60 : *Sussex*, 165.
Beardmore, *Hants.* 234.
Beatson, 234.
Beauclerk, *Sussex*, 165, 234 ; *Down*, 234.
Beauchamp, *Bucks*, 10 ; *Cornw.* 21 ; *Durham*, 34, 38 ; *Herts.* 54 ; *Northampton*, 112 ; *Rutland*, 135 ; *Warwick*, 172 ; *Wilts.* 182, 193 ; *Worc.* 195.
Beaulieu, *Bucks.* 10.
Beaufo, *Warw.* 172.

Beauforest, *Oxford*, 128, 130.
Beaufort, *Herts*, 54 ; *Monm.* 105 ; *Northampton*, 111, 112,
Beaufoy, *Northampton*, 112.
Beauman, *Wexford*, 234.
Beaumont, *Derby*, 27 ; *Devon*, 29 ; *Durham*, 38 ; *Herts*, 54 ; *Kent*, 60 ; *Leic.* 76, 80 ; *London*, 96, 100 ; *Stafford*, 142 ; *Surrey*, 156, 158 ; *York*, 204, 213, 224, 234, 249 ; *Isle of Man*, 267.
Beaumys, *Hunts*, 57.
Beaupre, *Norfolk,* 107.
Beausarvire, *Hamp.* 50.
Beauvoir, *Kent*, 60.
Beavot, *York*, 224.
Bebington, *Ches.* 17.
Becher, *Cork*, 234.
Becket, *Devon*, 29 ; *Wilts*, 185.
Beckett, *Wilts*, 185 ; *York*, 222, 234; *Devon*, 234.
Beckford, *Hamp.* 50, 234 ; *London*, 101 ; *Wilts*, 182, 183, 184, 234 ; 236.
Beckham, *Norfolk*, 278.
Beckingham, *Kent,* 60; *Oxford,* 128, 130.
Beckwith, *Durham*, 36 ; *York*, 201, 205, 213, 224 ; 234.
Beconshaw, *Hamp.* 266.
Bedell, *Hunts*, 57.
Bedenell, *Northumberland*, 120.
Bedford, *Bucks*, 10 ; *Durham*, 38 ; *Surrey*, 158 ; *Wilts*, 185.
Bedingfeld, *Norfolk*, 107, 234, 277, 278.
Bee, *Hamp.* 50, 266 ; *York*, 217.
Beech, *Warwick*, 234.
Beecher, *Notts*, 123 ; *Surrey*, 156.
Beecroft, *York*, 234.
Beedam, *Hunts*, 234.
Beer, *Kent*, 60.
Beeston, *Cheshire*, 17 ; *Hamp.* 50 ; *York*, 205.
Beever, 246.
Beggesovere, *Shrop.* 137.
Beilby, *York*, 224.
Beke, *Bucks*, 10 ; 232, 234.
Bekering, *Notts.* 122.
Belasyse, *Durham*, 38 ; *Herts*, 54.
Belcher, *Kent,* 60.
Belchier, *Northampton,* 111.
Beler, *Leic.* 80.

Belfield, *Herts,* 54.
Belgrave, *Leic.* 76, 80; *Rutl.* 234.
Belingham, *Sussex,* 163.
Bell, *Norfolk,* 107; *Northumb.* 119, 234; *York,* 219, 234; *Lanc.* 234; *Kent,* 234; *Berks,* 254.
Bellâ Aquâ, *Bucks,* 10.
Bellairs, *Rutland,* 136; 234, 246.
Bellamy, *Hamp.* 50; *York,* 213.
Bellasis, *Durham,* 34, 36.
Bellasise, *York,* 201.
Bellay, *Hunts,* 57.
Bellew, *Devon,* 31, 234.
Bellott, *Devon,* 31.
Bellomonte, *Herts,* 54; *Northampton,* 112.
Bellst, *Ches.* 17.
Bellwood, *York,* 224.
Bellingford, *Norfolk,* 278.
Bellingham, *Sussex,* 163, 165; *Wilts.* 185; *Westminster,* 179; *Linc.* 272.
Belmain, *Devon,* 31.
Belmeis, *Shrop.* 137.
Belson, *Bucks.* 10.
Belsonn, *Hamp.* 50.
Belton, *York,* 224.
Belwood, *Linc.* 86.
Bence, *Suffolk,* 234.
Bendyshe, *Camb.* 234.
Benet, *Bucks,* 10; *Surrey,* 162; *Wilts,* 182.
Benett, *Hamp.* 50; *Wilts,* 182, 185, 234.
Benion, *Sussex,* 163, 165.
Benger, *Kent,* 60.
Bengon, *Herts,* 65.
Bennet, *Bucks,* 10: *Devon,* 29: *Corn.* 21: *Herts,* 54, 56: *Glam.* 234: *London,* 98, 102: *Northampton,* 112: *Northumberland,* 119: *Wilts,* 185: *Suffolk,* 234: *Berks,* 254: *Derby,* 259.
Bennett, *Devon,* 31: *Leic.* 80: *Sussex,* 165: *Wilts,* 182, 185: *Surrey,* 234: *King's* 234: *Berks,* 234: *Cork,* 234; 234.
Benning, *London,* 96.
Benson, *Kent,* 60; *Linc.* 234; *Northampton,* 112; *Shropshire,* 234; *Westm.* 179; *Wilts,* 185.
Benstede, *Herts,* 54.
Bent, *Bucks,* 234 *Leic.* 80; *Staff.* 234.

Bentham, *Camb.* 14..
Bentinck, *Derby,* 27; *Norf.* 234.
Bentley, *Lanc.* 234.
Benyon, *Berks,* 7, 234; *Rutl.* 136; *Surrey,* 158; *Herts.* 56.
Bere, *Corn.* 21; *Devon,* 234; *Kent,* 60, 67.
Bereford, *Northamp.* 112; *Warw.* 172.
Berenger, *Wilts.* 182.
Beresford, *Derby,* 27; *Kent,* 60; *Leic.* 80; *Londonderry,* 234; *Somerset,* 140; 251, 253; *Derby,* 259.
Berew, *Glouc.* 262.
Berford, *Northamp.* 111.
Berington, *Berks,* 3, 7, 254; *Chesh.* 17; *Hereford,* 234; *Worc.* 234; 234.
Berkeley, *Derby,* 27; *Hamp.* 50, 266; *Leic.* 76, 80; *Worc.* 195, 234; *Wilts,* 193; 236, 240.
Berkeley-Portman, *Dorset,* 33.
Berkley, *Herts,* 54; *Somerset,* 140.
Bermingham, *Warw.* 172.
Bernard, *Bucks.* 10; *Northamp.* 111, 112; *King's co:* 234; *Cork,* 234.
Bernard-Morland, *Bucks,* 10.
Berners, *Herts,* 53; *Surrey,* 156; *Suffolk,* 244.
Berney, *Norf.* 107, 234.
Beronsaw, *Hamp.* 50.
Berowe, *Oxford,* 131.
Berry, *Berks,* 7: *Devon,* 29, 31: *Kent,* 60: *Westmeath,* 234.
Berrye, *Norf.* 277.
Bertie, *Bucks,* 10: *Dorset,* 33.
Bertram, *Northumb.* 119.
Berwick, 236.
Beryman, *Devon,* 31.
Besill, *Wilts,* 191.
Best, *Hunts,* 57: *Kent,* 60, 67, 234: *Staff.* 146: *Berks,* 234: *Surrey,* 234; 234, 236.
Beste, *Hants,* 234.
Bestwick, *Kent,* 60.
Beswick, *York,* 234.
Betham, *Warw.* 176, 177.
Bethel, *York,* 234.
Bethell, *Hamp.* 50, 266: *York,* 205, 215, 217, 224.
Bethome, *Oxford,* 132.
Bethune, 234.

Bett, *Bucks*, 10.
Bettenham, *Kent*, 60.
Bettes, *Camb.* 16 : *Hamp.* 266.
Bettesthorne, *Wilts*, 182, 193.
Bettesworth, *Hamp.* 50: *Sussex*, 163, 165.
Bettiscomb, *Dorset*, 33.
Bettison, *Notts*, 124.
Betton, *Shrop.* 234.
Betts, *Hamp.* 50: *Kent*, 234 : *Suff.* 234.
Bettsworth, *Sussex*, 165.
Betun, *Northamp.* 112.
Bethune, *Northamp.* 112.
Beumes, *Hunts.* 57.
Bevan, *Glam.* 228 : *Wales*, 229 : *Carm.* 230; 234.
Bevercotes, *Notts.* 122.
Beverley, *York*, 234.
Bevill, *Northamp.* 112 : *Hunts.* 57.
Bevot, *York*, 205.
Bewick, *Durham*, 38.
Bewicke, *Northumb.* 234 : *Leic.* 234.
Bewley, *Lond.* 102 ; 234.
Bewshin, *Wilts*, 185.
Bexwell, *Norf.* 107.
Bexley, *Bucks*, 11.
Beynon, *Surrey*, 234.
Beynvill, *Warw.* 172.
Beyvill, *Cumb.* 22, 23.
Bibbesworth, *Herts*, 64.
Bickford, 234.
Bickley, *Sussex*, 163, 165, 168.
Bickliffe, *Lond.* 102.
Bickerton, *Leic.* 80.
Bid, *Wales*, 229.
Bidder, *Carm.* 230.
Biddic, *Durham*, 34.
Biddulph, *Staff.* 143, 145, 146: *Sussex*, 163, 165, 234 : *Warw.* 172: *Denbigh*, 234 : *Hereford*, 234 : *Pemb.* 234 ; 234.
Bidulphe, *Lond.* 102.
Bierd, *Wales*, 229.
Bifleete, *Somerset*, 140.
Bigg, *Worc.* 195 ; 234, 239: *Berks*, 254.
Bigge, *Northumb.* 119, 234: *York*, 219, 224.
Biggin, *Northamp.* 112.
Bigland, *Lanc.* 71, 234.
Biggs, *Durham*, 234.
Bigod, *York*, 201 ; 232.

Bigot, *Norf.* 109.
Bigsby, *Suffolk and Notts*, 234, 246.
Bilgay, *Derby*, 259.
Bill, *Hamp.* 50.
Billam, *York*, 234.
Billers, *Herts*, 53, 54 : *Leic.* 80.
Billing, *Northamp.* 112.
Billinge, *Corn.* 21.
Billinges, *Wales*, 229.
Billingham, *Durham*, 34, 38, 40.
Billingsley, *Somerset*, 140.
Billington, *Kent*, 60.
Bilson, *Hamp.* 266.
Bilton, *York*, 217.
Bind, *Sussex*, 165.
Bindon, *Essex*, 48.
Bindloss, *Durham*, 38.
Bindlosse, *York*, 209.
Bingham, *Dorset*, 33, 234 : *Leic.* 76: *Notts.* 122.
Binning-Home, 236.
Birch, *Lanc.* 71, 270: *Norf.* 234 : *Oxford*, 234: *Sussex*, 165.
Birch-Reynardson, 236.
Birchles, *Ches.* 17.
Bird, *Ches.* 17 ; *Kent*, 60 ; *Lond.* 176 ; *Hereford*, 234 ; *Merioneth*, 234.
Birde, *Staff.* 146.
Birkbeck, *Durham*, 38, 41 ; *York*, 224.
Birkby, *York*, 219.
Birkenhead, *Ches.* 17.
Birkin, *Notts.* 123.
Birley, *Lanc.* 234.
Birsty, *Sussex*, 165.
Birt, *Card.* 230.
Birtley, *Durham*, 34, 38.
Birtwistle, *Lanc.* 68.
Bish, *Surrey*, 156.
Bishbury, *Staff.* 143.
Bishop, *Devon*, 29 ; *Dorset*, 33 ; 233 ; *Linc.* 272.
Bishopsdon, *Warw.* 172.
Bisley, *Berks*, 254.
Bisse, *Herts*, 54 ; *Somerset*, 140.
Bisshop, *Sussex*, 163.
Bix, *Kent*, 60.
Blaauw, *Sussex*, 234, 236.
Blaby, *Leic.* 80.
Blachford, *Hamp.* 50 ; *Sussex*, 165.
Blackall, *Devon*, 31.
Blackburn, *Lanc.* 68.

Blackburne, *Lanc.* 69, 234 ; *Dublin*, 234 ; *York*, 208.
Blacker, *Wilts*, 185 ; *Armagh,*, 234; *Wexford*, 234.
Blacket, *Worc.* 195.
Blackett, *Durham*, 36, 40 ; *Northumb.* 119, 234.
Blackhall, *Corn.* 21.
Blackmore, *Kent*, 60.
Blacknall, *Lond.* 102 ; *Berks*, 254.
Blackstone, *Berks*, 7 ; 234.
Blackwall, 251.
Blackwell, *Bucks*, 11 ; *Herts*, 54.
Bladen, *Rutland*, 136.
Blaeney, *Wales*, 229.
Blagrave, *Berks*, 7, 234, 254.
Blagrove, *Berks*, 3 ; *Bucks*, 13.
Blagge, *Suff.* 152.
Blague, 234.
Blair, *Ayr*, 234 ; *Perth*, 234 ; 234.
Blake, *Corn.* 21; *Durham*, 42 ; *Hamp.* 50, 266 ; *Northamp.* 112 ; *Sussex*, 163 ; *Wilts*, 185 ; *Mayo*, 234 ; *Norf.* 234 ; *Galway*, 234 ; *Herts*, 234 ; 234.
Blakeham, *Suffolk*, 152.
Blaker, *Sussex*, 165.
Blakemore, *Monmouth*, 234 ; 234.
Blakeney, *Galway*, 234.
Blakeston, *Durham*, 34, 36.
Blakiston, *Durham*, 38 ; 236.
Blamire, *Cumb.* 234.
Blanchard, *Somerset*, 140 ; *Lanc.* 234 ; *Berks*, 254.
Bland, *York*, 205, 224, 234 ; *Queen's Co.* 234 ; *Kerry*, 234.
Blandy, *Berks*, 7.
Blanks, *Bucks*, 10.
Blane, *Wales*, 229.
Blany, *Berks*, 254.
Blathwayt, *Glou.* 234 ; 236, 237.
Blaydes, *Notts.* 234 ; *York*, 217.
Blaykeston, *Durham*, 40.
Blayne, *Glam.* 228.
Blayney, *Worc.* 234.
Blaxton, *Durham*, 41.
Blencowe, *Cumb.* 22, 23 ; *Essex*, 234 ; *Northamp.* 111, 112, 234 ; *Sussex*, 234.
Blenkinsop, *Durham*, 38 ; *Northumb.* 119.
Blenkinsopp, *Durham*, 234.
Blenkinsoppe, *Durham*, 40.

Blennerhasset, *Suffolk*, 153 ; *Norf.* 277.
Blennerhassett, *Kerry*, 234.
Blethyn, *Glam.* 228.
Blewett, *Somerset*, 140.
Blewitt, *Monmouth*, 234.
Bligh, *Corn.* 21.
Blinckarne, *Lond.* 96.
Bliss, *Leic.* 77, 80 ; *Suffolk*, 234.
Blith, *Derby*, 259.
Blithe, *Warw.* 172.
Blofeld, *Norf.* 234.
Blois, 236.
Bloom, *Carm.* 230.
Blomefield, *Norf.* 107.
Blomer, *Kent*, 60.
Blondell, *Kent*, 60.
Blore, *Berks*, 254.
Blosse, *Lond.* 96.
Blount, *Bucks*, 13 ; *Dorset*, 33 ; *Herts*, 54 ; *Hereford*, 234 ; *Leic.* 80 ; *Oxford*, 234 ; *Sussex*, 163, 165 ; *Wilts*, 194 ; *Worc.* 195.
Bludder, *Surrey*, 156, 162.
Bluet, *Devon*, 29.
Blewett, *Devon*, 234.
Blundell, *Lanc.* 69, 71, 234, 253.
Blundell-Weld, 236.
Blunt, *Bucks*, 13 ; *Kent*, 60 ; *Herts*, 53 ; *Leic.* 76 ; *Hants*, 234 ; *Oxf.* 131 ; *Sussex*, 163.
Blythe, 251.
Blythman, *York*, 205, 224.
Bockett, *Berks*, 7.
Boddam, *Notts.* 234.
Bode, *Kent*, 60.
Bodenham, *Rutland*, 135, 136 ; *Hereford*, 234 ; *Wilts*, 182.
Bodkin, *Galway*, 234.
Bodiam, *Sussex*, 169.
Bodle, *Essex*, 48 ; *Leic.* 80.
Bodleigh, *Devon*, 29.
Bodvel, *Wales*, 229.
Bogan, *Devon*, 31 ; *Corn.* 21.
Bohun, *Bucks*, 10 ; *Norf.* 109 ; *Surrey*, 156 ; *Sussex*, 163.
Boileau, *Hamp.* 50.
Bois, *Breck.* 227.
Boivile, *Leic.* 76.
Bokeland, *Wilts.* 182.
Bokenham, *Suffolk*, 152.
Boketon, *Northamp.* 112.
Bolam, *Northumb.* 119.

Bolbeck, *Northumb.* 119.
Bold, *Chester*, 17 ; *Lanc.* 69, 71.
Bolden, *Lanc.* 234.
Boldero, *Suffolk*, 152, 234.
Bolebec, *Bucks.* 10 ; *Herts.* 54.
Boleyne, *Herts.* 54.
Bolger, *Kilkenny*, 234.
Bolles, *Herts.* 56.
Bolney, *Berks.* 254.
Bolton, *Hunts.* 57 ; *Waterford*, 234 ;
  234 ; *Meath*, 234 ; 243, 245 ; *Nor-*
  folk, 278.
Bomford, *Meath*, 234.
Bonar, *Kent*, 234 ; 234, 236, 239,
  243, 245.
Bonatre, *Corn.* 21.
Bond, *Corn.* 21 ; *Dorset*, 33, 234 ;
  Westmeath, 234 ; *Wilts.* 182.
Bonfoy, *London*, 96.
Bonham, *Essex*, 48 ; *Hamp.* 50 ;
  Kildare, 234.
Bonington, *Derby.* 259.
Bonithon, *Corn.* 21.
Bonnell, *London*, 76.
Bonner, *Somerset*, 140.
Bontine, 234.
Bonvile, *Devon*, 29 ; *Somerset*, 138.
Bonville, *Sussex*, 165.
Booker, *Hereford*, 234.
Booth, *Berks.* 3, 254 ; *Cheshire*, 17 ;
  Durham, 34, 36, 38 ; *Kent*, 60 ;
  Lanc. 71, 75 ; *Northamp.* 234 ;
  Sussex, 165 ; *York*, 224, 225.
Boothe, *Durham*, 40 : *York*, 224.
Boothby, *Derby*, 27, 259 ; *Leic.* 80 ;
  Staff. 146 ; *Surrey*, 158.
Bootle, *Lanc.* 71.
Boord, *Sussex*, 165.
Boraw, *Bucks.* 10 ; *Leic.* 80.
Borde, *Sussex*, 169.
Bordon, *Durham*, 35.
Boreham, *Wilts*, 182.
Borlace, *Bucks*, 10
Borlace-Warren, *Bucks*, 10.
Borlase, *Bucks.* 9.
Borough, *Camb.* 16 ; *Derby*, 27,
  234 ; *Herts*, 54 ; *Northumb.* 119 ;
  Shrop. 234 ; *York*, 226.
Borrer, *Sussex*, 234.
Borrowes, *Kildare*, 234, 236.
Borthwick, *Edinburgh*, 234.
Borton, *York*, 226.
Bosanquet, *Herts.* 56, 234 ; *Essex*,
  234.

Bosavern, *Corn.* 21.
Boscawen, *Bucks.* 10 ; *Corn.* 21 ;
  Surrey, 158.
Boseville, *Bucks*, 11.
Bosom, *Notts.* 122.
Bosseville, *York*, 224.
Bossawsach, *Corn.* 21.
Bostock, *Ches.* 17 ; *Hamp.* 50 ;
  Berks. 254.
Bosustowe, *Corn.* 21.
Bosvil, *York*, 210.
Bosvile, *Kent*, 60 ; *York*, 213, 224,
  234.
Bosvill, *York*, 210.
Bosville, *Kent*, 60, 62 ; 234.
Boswell, *Bucks.* 11, 234 ; *Fife*, 234.
Boteler, *Bucks*, 10, 11 ; *Herts.* 53,
  54 ; *Kent*, 234 ; *Notts.* 122 ;
  Somerset, 140 ; *Surrey*, 156, 162 ;
  Warw. 172, 232, 234 ; *Northamp.*
  112.
Botfield, *Northamp.* 234 ; *Shrop.*
  234 ; 233, 232, 246.
Bothom, 251.
Bothby, *London*, 96, 99.
Bothe, *Lanc.* 71.
Botiller, *Northamp.* 112 ; *Notts.*
  122 ; *Warw.* 172.
Bottetourt, *Bucks*, 10 ; *Rutland*,
  136.
Botreaux, *Herts.* 54 ; *Shrop.* 137 ;
  Warw. 172 ; *Wilts*, 182.
Botry, *Northamp.* 112.
Boucherett, *Linc.* 234.
Bouchier, *Berks.* 7.
Bouge, *Leic.* 80.
Boughton, *Leic.* 80 ; *Warw.* 174.
Bould, *Wales*, 229.
Boultbee, *Warw.* 234.
Boulton, *Surrey*, 156 ; *Leic.* 234 ;
  Pemb. 230 ; *Wales*, 229.
Boun, *Leic.* 80 ; *Warw.* 172 ; *Notts.*
  122.
Bourchier, *Devon*, 29 ; *Somerset*,
  138 ; *York*, 205, 224.
Boureman, *Somerset*, 140.
Bourghill, *Breck.* 227.
Bourke, *Limerick*, 234 ; *Mayo*, 234.
Bourne, *Derby*, 27 ; *Hamp.* 50 ;
  Kent, 60 ; *Leic.* 80 ; *Hants.* 234 ;
  Oxford, 129, 130, 131 ; *Somerset*,
  140 ; *Lanc.* 234 ; *Staff.* 234 ; 246.
Bourstal, *Herts.* 53.

Bouth, 251.
Bouverie, *Surrey*, 156 : *Wilts*, 182 : *Northampton*, 234.
Bovil, *Herts*, 54.
Bowcher, *Somerset*, 140.
Bowden, *Derby*, 27, 234 : *Leic.* 80 : *Lanc.* 234 ; 251.
Bowen, *Carm.* 230 : *Cardig.* 230, 234 : *Pemb.* 230, 234 : *Wales*, 229 : *Queen's co.* 234 : *Cork*, 234.
Bower, *Derby*, 27 : *Dorset*, 33, 234 : *Durham*, 36, 38, 43 : *Devon*, 29 : *Somerset*, 140 : *Wilts*, 185 : *York*, 234 ; 236, 250, 285.
Bowerman, *Devon*, 29 : *Hamp.* 266.
Bowes, *Durham*, 34, 36, 38, 40, 43, 234 : *Staff.* 146 : *York*, 198 ; 236.
Bowet, *Sussex*, 169.
Bowle, *Kent*, 60 : *Wilts*, 182, 185, 192.
Bowles, *Herts*, 54 : *Northamp.* 112 : *Wilts*, 182 : *Oxford*, 234.
Bowman, *Wilts*, 192.
Bownest, *Herts*, 56.
Bowreman, *Hamp.* 50.
Bowrne, *Oxford*, 128.
Bowser, *Bucks*, 13.
Bowyer, *Bucks*, 10 : *Hamp.* 50, 266 : *Herts*, 56 ; *London*, 91 : *Staff.* 145, 146 : *Surrey*, 156, 162 : *Sussex*, 163, 165, 168 : *York*, 220 ; 232, 236.
Boycott, 234.
Boyd, *Antrim*, 234 : *Wigton*, 234 : *Westmeath*, 234 : *Donegal*, 235 ; *Londonderry*, 234, *Wexford*, 234.
Boydell, *Ches.* 17.
Boyle, *York*, 235 : *Ayr*, 234.
Boyne, *Essex*, 48.
Boynton, *Durham*, 38 : *York*, 217, 224, 226 ; 236.
Boys, *Essex*, 48 ; *Hamp.* 50 ; *Kent*, 60, 234 ; *Somerset*, 140 ; *Sussex*, 165.
Boyse, *Wexford*, 234 ; *Hamp.* 266.
Boyvill, *Cumb.* 22, 23.
Boyville, *Leic.* 80.
Bozon, *Leic.* 80.
Brabazon, *Berks*, 7 ; *Leic.* 80 : *Meath*, 234 ; *Mayo*, 234 ; *Louth*, 234.
Bracebride, *Warw.* 177.
Bracebridge, *Leic.* 80 ; *Warwick*, 172, 173, 176, 234 ; 239.

Brackenbury, *Durham*, 34, 40 ; *Linc.* 234.
Brackenridge, *Tyrone*, 234.
Bradbridge, *Surrey*, 162 ; *Sussex*, 163.
Bradbruge, *Sussex*, 165.
Bradbury, 249, 251.
Bradden, *Northamp.* 112.
Braddon, *Cornw.* 234.
Braddyll, *Lanc.* 68, 70 ; 234.
Bradeston, *Glouc.* 262.
Bradford, *Wilts*, 192 ; *York*, 213, 224.
Bradgate, *Leic.* 80.
Bradley, *Kent*, 60 ; *Westm.* 179 ; *York*, 224 ; *Lanc.* 234 ; 234.
Bradney, *Berks*, 7 ; *Staff.* 143 ; 234.
Bradshaigh, *Lanc.* 71 ; 234.
Bradshaw, *Ches.* 17 ; *Derby*, 27, 234 ; *Herts*, 56 ; *Leic.* 80, 251.
Bradshawe, 251.
Bradway, *Glou.* 262.
Bradwell, *Ches.* 17.
Brady, *Carlow*, 234.
Braham, *Berks*, 254.
Brahm, *Surrey*, 158.
Brailsford, *Linc.* 234.
Braithwaite, *Westm.* 179.
Brakyn, *Camb.* 16.
Brakenbury, *Durham*, 38.
Brakynbury, *Durham*, 44.
Bramston, *Essex*, 48, 234 ; *Hamp.* 50.
Brampton, *Norf.* 107, 278.
Branan, *Wales*, 229.
Brancker, *Lanc.* 234.
Brand, *Herts*, 54 ; *Sussex*, 165.
Brander, *Surrey*, 158 ; *Elgin*, 234.
Brandeston, *Warw.* 172.
Brandling, *Durham*, 38, 36 ; *York*, 224 ; 234, 236.
Brandon, *Rutland*, 135.
Brandreth, *Staff.* 146 ; 234.
Branfil, *Essex*, 234 ; 236.
Braose, *Northamp.* 112 ; *Surrey*, 156 ; *Sussex*, 163, 169 ; *Bucks*, 10.
Brasey, *Oxford*, 131.
Brasier, 246.
Brasse, *Durham*, 38.
Brathwaite, *Westm.* 179.
Bray, *Bucks.* 10 ; *Corn.* 21, 234 ; *Northamp.* 111, 112 ; *Oxf.* 131 ; *Staff.* 143 ; *Surrey*, 156, 158, 234.

Braybroke, *Northamp.* 111.
Braybrook, *Northamp.* 112.
Braybrooke, *Herts,* 54 ; *Wilts,* 193 ;
    Berks, 254.
Braybuff, *Hamp.* 50.
Braye, 236.
Braylesford, *Derby,* 259.
Brayn, *Leic.* 76.
Brayne, *Glou.* 262.
Breadalbane, 236.
Brearey, *York,* 205, 224.
Brecknock, *Bucks,* 13.
Brein, *Wales,* 229.
Breose, *Bucks,* 10.
Bremer, *Devon,* 234.
Brerehaughe, *York,* 205.
Breres, *York,* 205.
Brereton, *Bucks,* 10 ; *Chesh.* 17 ;
    Hamp. 50 ; *Somerset,* 140 ; *Staff.*
    146 ; *Surrey,* 162 ; *Wilts,* 182 ;
    Norf. 234 ; *Carlow,* 234.
Brerewood, *Bucks,* 10.
Bresworth, *Berks,* 7.
Bretagne, *York,* 209.
Breton, *Kent,* 60 ; *Leic.* 77, 80 ;
    Northamp. 112 ; *Wilts,* 185.
Brett, *Dors.* 33 ; *Kent,* 60 ; *Leic.*
    80 ; *Staff.* 146.
Brettell, 235.
Bretton, *Hamp.* 50.
Bretun, *Warw.* 172.
Brewster, *Suffolk,* 234 ; *Essex,* 234.
Brice, *Somerset,* 140.
Brickdale, *Glouc.* 234 ; 236.
Brickenden, *Berks,* 254.
Bridger, *Sussex,* 163, 164, 165, 234.
Bridges, *Herts,* 56 ; *Kent,* 60 ;
    Somerset, 140.
Bridgewater, *Northampton,* 111,
    112.
Bridgman, *Hamp.* 50 ; *Glouc.* 262.
Brierwood, *Bucks,* 13.
Brigham, *Chesh.* 234 ; *Oxf.* 131 ;
    York, 217, 224.
Briggs, *Leic.* 80 ; *Norfolk,* 107 ;
    Westminster, 179.
Brigginshaw, *London,* 96.
Bright, *Durham,* 38 ; *York,* 205, 206,
    213, 224 ; 250.
Brightwell, *Bucks,* 10.
Brigstock, *Carm.* 230.
Brigstocke, *Hamp.* 50.

Brinckman, *York,* 213.
Brind, *Wilts,* 185.
Brindley, *Staff.* 145.
Brinkley, *Sligo,* 234.
Brinsley, *Notts.* 122.
Brisbane, 234.
Brisco, *Cumb.* 22 ; *Sussex,* 234.
Briscoe, *Herts,* 54 ; *Surrey,* 234 ;
    Westmeath, 234.
Brise, *Essex,* 48, 234.
Bristed, *Dorset,* 33.
Bristow, *Durham,* 38 ; *Herts,* 53, 54 ;
    Wilts, 182, 234.
Bristowe, *Notts.* 234.
Brittany, *Herts,* 54 ; *York,* 196.
Broad, *Hamp.* 50.
Broade, *Staff.* 145, 234.
Broadhead, *York,* 213.
Broadley, *York,* 234 ; 234.
Broadmead, *Somerset,* 234.
Broc, *Shrop.* 137.
Brocas, *Hamp.* 50, 266 ; *Leic.* 80 ;
    Surrey, 156.
Brock, *Bucks,* 10 ; *Chesh.* 17 ; *Worc.*
    234.
Brocket, *Herts,* 54, 56.
Brockett, *Durham,* 41 ; *Essex,* 234.
Brockholes, *Hamp.* 50 ; *Lanc.* 234 ;
    Lond. 93 ; *York,* 209.
Brockhull, *Kent,* 60.
Brockman, *Kent,* 60, 234.
Brocklehurst, *Chester,* 234.
Broderwick, *Berks,* 254.
Brodie, *Moray,* 234 ; *Nairn,* 234 ;
    Sussex, 234 ; 236, 239.
Broadnax, *Hamp.* 50 ; *Kent,* 60 ;
    Sussex, 163, 165.
Brodrepp, *Dorset,* 33.
Brodrick, *Surrey,* 156.
Brograve, *Herts,* 53, 54, 56 ; *Kent,*
    60.
Brokas, *Hamp.* 50.
Broke, 232, 236 ; *Hamp.* 266.
Brokesby, *Leic.* 80.
Brome, *Bucks,* 13 ; *Kent,* 60, 232 ;
    Oxford, 131 ; *Salop,* 234 ; *Herts,*
    234 ; *Warw.* 172.
Bromfield, *Hamp.* 266.
Bromhead, *Leic.* 77.
Bromley, *Chesh.* 17 ; *Durham,* 38 ;
    Derby, 234 ; *Herts,* 54, 56 ;
    Kent, 60 ; *Worc.* 195 ; *Bucks,* 11.

Bromeg, *Wales*, 229.
Brompton, *Shrop.* 137.
Bromwich, *Wilts*, 185 ; *Glouc.* 262.
Bronker, *Lond.* 96.
Brook, *Staff.* 143.
Brooke, *Chesh.* 17, 234 ; *Hamp.* 50 ; *Kent*, 60 ; *Leic.* 80 ; *Northamp.* 111 ; *Somerset*, 140 ; *Surrey*, 158 ; *Sussex*, 165 ; *York*, 213, 217 ; *Suff.* 234 ; *Shrop.* 234 ; 234, 236.
Brookes, *Warw.* 176, 177 ; *Berks*, 254.
Brooker, *Kent*, 60.
Brooks, *Bedford*, 234.
Brookshank, *Lond.* 100.
Broome, *Herts*, 56.
Broomfield, *Wales*, 229.
Brothers, *Wilts*, 185.
Brough, *York*, 217 ; *Notts.* 124.
Brougham, *Cumb.* 22 ; 236.
Broughton, *Chesh.* 17 ; *Devon*, 29 ; *Herts*, 54 ; *Hunts*, 57 ; *Somerset*, 140 ; *Staff.* 146 ; *Warw.* 172 ; *Wales*, 229 ; *Shrop.* 234 ; *Berks*, 254.
Brouncker, *Dorset*, 234 ; *Wilts*, 185.
Brown, *Devon*, 29 ; *Essex*, 48 ; *Kent*, 60 ; *Rutland*, 135 ; *Surrey*, 156 ; *Clare*, 234 ; *Durham*, 234 ; *York*, 234 ; *Northumb.* 234.
Browne-Willis, *Bucks*, 10.
Browne, *Derby*, 27, 259 ; *Dorset*, 33 ; *Herts*, 54 ; *Hunts*, 57 ; *Kent*, 60 ; *Leic.* 80, 234 ; *London*, 96 ; *Northamp.* 111 ; *Oxford*, 131 ; *Rutland*, 136 ; *Surrey*, 156, 158 ; *Sussex*, 163, 165 ; *Warw.* 172 ; *Wilts*, 182, 185, 234 ; *Norfolk*, 234 ; *Devon*, 234 ; *Flint*, 234 ; *Carlow*, 234 ; *Galway*, 234 ; *Mayo*, 234 ; *Glouc.* 234 ; *Limerick*, 234 ; *Cumb.* 234 ; *Clare*, 234 ; 234 ; 239, 246, 249 ; *Berks*, 254.
Brownlow, *Linc.* 82.
Brownlowe, 251.
Bruce, *Herts*, 56 ; *York*, 220 ; *Clackmannan*, 234 ; *Stirling*, 234 ; *Cork*, 234 ; *Surrey*, 234 ; *Antrim*, 234 ; 234, 236, 239.
Bruckshaw, *Chester*, 234.
Brudenell, *Bucks*, 10, 11, 13 ; *Leic.* 80 ; *Northamp.* 111 ; *York*, 205.
Brudnell, *Hamp.* 50 ; *Rutland*, 135.

Brüen, *Chesh.* 17 ; *Carlow*, 234 ; *Wexford*, 234.
Bruere, *Northamp.* 112 ; *Surrey*, 156.
Bruerton, *Wales*, 229.
Bruges, *Wilts*, 234 ; *Hamp.* 266.
Brune, *Dorset*, 33 ; *Corn.* 234 ; 237 ; *Hamp.* 266.
Brunskell, *York*, 224.
Brunskill, *London*, 96 ; *Durham*, 38.
Bruning, *Wilts*, 185 ; 235 ; *Hamp.* 266.
Brunwin, *Essex*, 234.
Brurwood, *Bucks*, 13.
Brus, *Durham*, 37, 38.
Bruse, *Wilts*, 182.
Bruton, 236.
Bruyn, *Bucks*, 10 ; *Leic.* 76, 80.
Bryan, *Dorset*, 33 ; *Kent*, 60, 67 ; *Sussex*, 165 ; 232 ; *Kilkenny*, 234 ; *Wexford*, 234.
Bryant, *Surrey*, 156.
Brychan, *Breck.* 227.
Brydges, *Herts.* 54 ; *Kent*, 60 ; 234 ; *Glouc.* 262 ; *Hamp.* 266.
Bryton, *York*, 217.
Buccleuch, *Lanc.* 69.
Buchan, *Aberdeen*, 234.
Buchanan, *Dumbarton*, 234 ; *Lanark*, 234 ; *Staff.* 234 ; 234 ; 237.
Buck, *Camb.* 16 ; *Durham*, 38 ; *Herts.* 54 ; *Kent*, 60 ; *Worc.* 195 ; *York*, 213, 224 ; *Lanc.* 234 ; *Devon*, 234 ; 234.
Bucke, *York*, 212 ; *Glouc.* 262.
Buckeridge, *Berks*, 7.
Buckingham, *Bucks*, 10, 13 ; *Essex*, 46 ; *Northamp.* 112.
Buckinghamshire, *Bucks*, 10.
Buckland, *Northamp.* 112.
Buckle, *Surrey*, 156, 158 ; *Sussex*, 165 ; *Edinburgh*, 234 ; 234.
Buckler, *Dorset*, 33 ; *Wilts*, 182.
Buckley, *Wilts*, 234 ; *Hants*, 234.
Bucknall, *Mayo*, 234.
Bucknell, *Herts*, 54.
Buckston, *Derby*, 27, 234.
Buckworth, *Camb.* 16.
Budgen, *Surrey*, 156, 158 ; *Wexford*, 234.
Budokeside, *Devon*, 29.
Budworth, *Essex*, 234.
Bufkin, *Kent*, 60 ; *Sussex*, 165.

Bugan, *Corn.* 21.
Bugg, *Notts.* 122 ; *Leic.* 76.
Buggin, *Herts,* 56.
Buisly, *Rutland,* 136.
Bulkler, *Hamp.* 50.
Bulkeley, *Chester,* 17 ; *Staff.* 146 ; *Wilts.* 182, 185.
Bulkley, *York,* 224 ; *Wales,* 229 ; *Hamp.* 266.
Bull, *Oxford,* 131 ; *Wilts,* 182.
Bullen, *Bucks,* 227 ; *Dorset,* 234.
Buller, *Corn.* 21, 234 ; *Devon,* 234 ; 234 ; *Somerset,* 140.
Bulleyne, *Bucks,* 11.
Bullingham, *Rutland,* 136.
Bullmer, *York,* 226.
Bullon, *Devon,* 29.
Bullock, *Norfolk,* 234 ; *Essex,* 48, 234 ; *Somerset,* 234 ; 237 ; *Berks,* 254 ; *Derby,* 259.
Bulmer, *Durham,* 34, 36, 38 ; *Norfolk,* 107 ; *York,* 201, 220.
Bulman, *Sussex,* 165.
Bulstrode, *Berks.* 3, 254 ; *Bucks,* 10, 13.
Bulteel, *Devon,* 234.
Bulwer, *Herts,* 56 ; *Norfolk,* 234, 236.
Bulwer-Lytton, *Herts,* 56.
Bunbury, *Chesh.* 17 ; *Carlow,* 234.
Bunce, *Kent,* 60.
Bund, 234 ; 237 ; 239.
Bungay, *Kent,* 60.
Bungey, *Sussex,* 165.
Bunny, *Berks,* 234 ; *Durham,* 36, 38 ; *York,* 224, 226.
Burchall, *Hereford,* 234 ; 234.
Burchill, *Breck.* 227.
Burchinshaw, *Wales,* 229.
Burdet, *Leic.* 76, 80 ; *Northamp.* 112 ; *Warw.* 172 ; *Wilts,* 182 ; *York,* 213, 224.
Burdett, *Leic.* 80 ; *King's Co.* 234, 234.
Burdon, *Durham,* 38, 234 ; *Notts.* 122 ; *Wilts,* 182.
Burell, *Cornw.* 21.
Bures, *Surrey,* 156.
Burfield, *Breck.* 227.
Burford, 137.
Burganey, *Chesh.* 17.
Burgate, *Oxford,* 133.
Burgatt, *Surrey,* 158.
Burge, *Glouc.* 262.

Burges, 234.
Burgess, *Corn.* 21.
Burgh, *Lincoln,* 83 ; *Notts.* 122 ; *York,* 216 ; 234.
Berghersh, *Bucks,* 10 ; *Rutland,* 136; *Wilts,* 182.
Burghley, *Herts,* 56.
Burgoin, *Devon.* 29.
Burguine, *York,* 224.
Burgoyne, *Camb.* 16.
Burke, *Galway,* 234 ; *Tipperary,* 234 ; *Cork,* 234 ; *Bucks,* 234 ; 234 ; 245 ; 250.
Burlacy, *Bucks,* 10, 11.
Burland, *Dorset,* 33.
Burleston, *Durham,* 38.
Burleigh, *Antrim,* 234.
Burley, *Hamp.* 50, 266 ; *Wilts,* 185; 234.
Burlington, *York,* 205.
Burnaby, *Berks,* 7 ; *Northamp.* 111 ; *Warw.* 174 ; *Leic.* 234.
Burnard, 232.
Burnby, *Devon,* 31.
Burne, *Staff.* 234 ; 236.
Burneby, *Devon,* 29.
Burnel, *Bucks,* 13 ; *Shrop.* 137 ; *Surrey,* 156.
Burnell, *London,* 96 ; *Notts.* 123 ; 234.
Burnett, *Surrey,* 158 ; *Peebles,* 234.
Burnes, 234.
Burnopp, *Durham,* 38.
Burnynghill, *Durham,* 38.
Burr, *Kent,* 60 ; *Berks,* 234 ; *Hereford,* 234.
Burrard, *Hamp.* 50, 236, 265, 266.
Burrell, *Rutl.* 136; *Surrey,* 156 ; *Sussex,* 163, 164, 165 ; *Northum.* 234 ; *Suffolk,* 234.
Burroughes, *Norfolk,* 234 ; 236.
Burroughs, *Orkney,* 234.
Burrow, *Leic.* 80.
Burrowes, *Cavan,* 234 ; *Meath,* 234.
Burslem, *Staff.* 145.
Burt, *Kent,* 60.
Burton, *Derby,* 27, 259 ; *Leic.* 76, 80 ; *Rutland,* 135, 136 ; *Surrey,* 156,162; *Sussex,* 165, 168 ; *Warw.* 172 ; *York,* 206, 213 ; 233 ; *Shrop.* 234 ; *Carlow,* 234 ; *Clare,* 234 ; *Lanc.* 234 ; 234 ; 236 ; 239 ; 253.
Burvargus, *Corn.* 21.
Burwell, *Durham,* 38.

Bury, *Camb.* 16; *Devon,* 29, 81, 235; *Berks,* 254.
Buryngton, *Devon,* 81.
Busbridge, *Sussex,* 165.
Busby, *Bucks,* 10; *Durham,* 38.
Busfeild, *York,* 234.
Busfield, *York,* 205.
Bush, *Wilts,* 185.
Bushe, *Waterford,* 234.
Bushell, *York,* 224.
Busk, *Midd.* 234.
Busking, *Sussex,* 165.
Bussew, *Rutland,* 136.
Bustard, *Oxford,* 130.
Busvargus, 234.
Buswell, *Leic.* 80.
Butcher, *Berks,* 7.
Butler, *Bucks,* 10; *Camb.* 15, 16; *Devon,* 29; *Dors.* 33; *Durh.* 36, 38, 40; *Herts,* 54, 56; *Kent,* 60; *Lanc.* 71; *Northamp.* 111, 112; *Notts.* 122; *Oxf.* 128, 130, 131; *Sussex,* 163, 165; *Wilts,* 185; *York,* 206, 209; *Wales,* 229; *Pemb.* 230; *Clare,* 234; *Galway,* 234; *Meath,* 234; *Midd.* 234; 234, 242; *Glou.* 262.
Butt, *Herts,* 56; 236.
Butter, *Perth,* 234.
Butterwicke, *Sussex,* 165.
Button, *Hamp.* 50, 266; *Wilts,* 185; *Glam.* 228.
Butts, *Kent,* 60; *Sussex,* 165; *Dorset,* 234.
Buxton, 239; *Derby,* 259.
Bwl, *Wales,* 229.
Byam, *Antigua and Somerset,* 234, 236; 239; 247.
Byby, *Wales,* 229.
Byde, *Herts,* 54, 56.
Byerley, *Durham,* 38; *Leic.* 80.
Byers, *Durham,* 38.
Bygode, *York,* 226.
Byll, *Corn.* 21.
Bynchestre, *Durham,* 38.
Bynd, *Surrey,* 162.
Byndlos, *Sussex,* 165.
Byndlosse, *Westm.* 179.
Byne, *Surrey,* 156, 158, 234; *Sussex,* 163, 165.
Byng, *Herts,* 54; *Midd.* 234.
Byrbeck, *Wales,* 229.
Byrchet, *Kent,* 60.

Byrd, *Corn.* 21; *Leic.* 80.
Byrde, *Essex,* 46.
Byrne, *Dublin,* 234; *Louth,* 234.
Byron, *Notts.* 122, 126.
Byrt, *Wales,* 229.
Byrte, *Dorset,* 33; *Kent,* 60.
Bysh, *Surrey,* 162.
Byshe, *Surrey,* 156.
Bysshe, *Sussex,* 165.
Bysshopp, *Sussex,* 165.
Bythesea, *Sussex,* 165; *Wilts,* 234; 236; 239.

Caarleton, *Sussex,* 165.
Cabell, *Devon,* 31.
Cadman, *Kent,* 60; *York,* 234.
Cadogan, *Bucks,* 10; *Northum.* 234.
Cadurcis, *Northamp.* 112.
Cadwell, *Kent,* 60.
Cadwaladyr, *Wales,* 229.
Cæsar, *Herts.* 54; *Kent,* 60; *Lond.* 100.
Cage, *Camb.* 16; *Kent,* 60.
Cahill, *Kilkenny,* 234.
Calcraft, *Salop,* 234; *Linc.* 234; *Dorset,* 33, 234.
Calclough, *Staff.* 145.
Calcott, *Leic.* 80; *Oxford,* 130.
Caldecot, *Linc.* 234; 237.
Caldecote, *Chesh.* 17; *Leic.* 80.
Caldecott, *Warw.* 174, 234.
Caldwell, *Kent,* 60; *Leic.* 80; *Staff.* 146, 234; *Meath,* 234; *Isle of Wight,* 234.
Call, *Norfolk,* 278.
Callaghan, *Cork,* 234.
Callander, *Stirling,* 234.
Caley, *York,* 224.
Callard, *Devon,* 29.
Calley, *Wilts,* 185, 234.
Callcott, *Oxford,* 128.
Callis, *Essex,* 48; *Linc.* 234.
Calmady, *Devon,* 234; 236.
Calrow, *Lanc.* 234.
Calthorp, *Norf.* 107; *Somerset,* 140.
Calthorpe, *Norf.* 107.
Calthrop, *Norf.* 107; *Linc.* 234.
Calton, *Hunts,* 57; *Berks,* 254.
Calveley, *Chesh.* 17.
Calverd, *Herts,* 56.
Calverley, *Durham,* 36; *Northumb.* 118; *Linc.* 234; *York,* 205, 224, 226, 234.

Calvert, *Bucks*, 10 ; *Herts*, 54, 56, 234 ; *Surrey*, 156.
Calwodeley, *Devon*, 29.
Calz, *Notts*. 122, 123.
Cambell, *Lond.* 101.
Camber, *Sussex*, 165.
Cambo, *Northumb.* 119.
Cambridge, *Dorset*, 134 ; *Glouc.* 234.
Camell, *Surrey*, 158.
Cameron, *Worc.* 234 ; *Inverness*, 234.
Cammel, *Dorset*, 33.
Camoys, *Sussex*, 163.
Campbell, *Hamp*, 50 ; *Argyle*, 234 ; *Perth*, 234 ; *Ayr*, 234 ; *Dumbarton*, 234 ; *Forfar*, 234 ; 234 ; 236 ; 237 ; 246.
Campion, *Sussex*, 164, 165, 234.
Campton, *Hamp.* 50.
Camvile, *Leic.* 80.
Camvill, *Northamp.* 112 ; *Warw.* 172.
Camville, *Wilts*, 182.
Candler, *Northamp.* 112 ; 234.
Canning, *Lond.* 101 ; *Warw.* 172, 234 ; 235.
Cannynge, *Lond.* 97.
Cannynowe, 232.
Canon, *Herts*, 56 ; *Pemb.* 230.
Cantelup, *Notts*, 122.
Cantalupe, *Notts*, 123.
Cantilupe,- *Bucks*, 10 ; *Leic.* 80 ; *Northamp.* 111 ; *Sussex*, 170 ; *Warw.* 172.
Cantillon, 239.
Cantrell, *Derby*, 28 ; *Berks*, 254.
Capel, *Hamp.* 50 ; *Glouc.* 234 ; *Herts*, 53, 54, 55, 56 ; *Lond.* 98.
Capell, *Somerset*, 140.
Capes, *Northamp.* 112.
Capron, *Northamp.* 234.
Caraunte, *Wilts*, 186.
Cardigan, *York*, 205, 236.
Cardinall, 234.
Cardwell, *Lanc.* 234.
Care, *Glouc.* 262.
Carew, *Corn.* 21, 234 ; *Devon*, 29, 31 ; *Surrey*, 156, 158, 162, 234 ; *Wales*, 229 ; 234 ; *Waterford*, 234 ; *Pemb.* 230, 236.

Carey, *Devon*, 29 ; *York*, 209, 210, 213, 220 ; *Cork*, 234 ; *Guernsey*, 234 ; 235.
Carington, *Bucks*, 11 ; *Chesh.* 17 ; *Essex*, 48 ; *Herts*, 56 ; *Leic.* 80 ; 235.
Carkeredge, *Kent*, 60.
Carleil, *York*, 224.
Carleill, *York*, 217 ; *Linc.* 234.
Carleton, *Bucks*, 13 ; *Camb.* 16 ; *Cumb.* 22, 23 ; *Notts.* 122 ; *Oxf.* 128, 130, 131 ; *Surrey*, 156 ; *Ireland*, 234 ; *Fermanagh*, 234 ; 234.
Carlele, *Durham*, 38.
Carlisle, 237.
Carlyon, *Corn.* 234 ; 236 ; 239.
Carmichael, 246.
Carmino, *Cornwall*, 20.
Carmond, *Berks*, 3.
Carn, *Glam.* 228, 234.
Carnaby, *Durham*, 38 ; *Northumb.* 120 ; *York*, 205.
Carnagie, 236.
Carnarvon, *Herts*, 54 ; 236.
Carne, *Berks*, 7 ; *Cornwall*, 234 ; *Glam.* 234.
Carnegie, 234.
Carnsew, *Cornwall*, 20.
Carpenter, *Wilts*, 185 ; *Devon*, 234.
Carr, *Durham*, 38, 234 ; *Linc.* 84 ; *Northumb.* 120 ; *Sussex*, 165 ; *Glouc.* 262.
Carre, 234 ; 244. ·
Carrell, *Sussex*, 163, 165.
Carrill, *Sussex*, 165.
Carrington, *York*, 224.
Carrington-Smith, *Glouc.* 234.
Carroll, *Wicklow*, 234.
Carrow, *Durham*, 38.
Carrowe, *Durham*, 34.
Carryll, *Sussex*, 165.
Carsey, *Norf.* 278.
Cartell, *Kent*, 60.
Carter, *Bucks*, 10, 13 ; *Herts*, 56 ; *Kent*, 60 ; *Northamp.* 112 ; *Surrey*, 156 ; *York*, 224 ; *Oxford*, 234 ; *Kildare*, 234 ; *Mayo*, 234.
Carthew, *Suffolk*, 234.
Cartwright, *Dorset*, 33 : *Northamp.* 111, 112, 234 : *Notts*, 122 ; *Suffolk*, 234 ; 234.
Carus, *Westmorcland*, 179.

Carvick, *York*, 234.
Carwardine, *Essex*, 48.
Carwithan, *Devon*, 29.
Cary, *Bucks*, 10: *Devon*, 29, 31, 234: *Durham*, 42: *Hamp.* 50: *Herts*, 54: *Somerset*, 140: *York*, 205: *Donegal*, 234: *Wexford*, 234; 235; 236.
Caryl, *Surrey*, 156.
Casbard, *Glam.* 234.
Casborne, 234.
Case, *Lanc.* 69, 234: *Notts.* 234.
Casement, *Antrim*, 234.
Cass, *Herts*, 234; 239; 245.
Cassan, *Queen's Co.* 234.
Castell, *Camb.* 16; 249.
Castello, *Norf.* 107: *Shrop.* 137: *Warw.* 172.
Castillon, *Berks*, 254.
Castle, *Hunts*, 57: *Shrop.* 137: *York*, 204: *Norf.* 278.
Castleford, *York*, 204.
Caswall, *Essex*, 48.
Caswell, *Lond.* 96: *Berks*, 234.
Cater, *Berks*, 3, 254.
Cathcart, *Ayr*, 234.
Catheral, *Chesh.* 17: *York*, 217.
Catherine of Valois, *Sussex*, 169.
Catesby, *Northamp.* 111,112: *Warw.* 172.
Caton, *Linc.* 234.
Cator, *Norf.* 234.
Catleyn, *Norf.* 107.
Catteral, *Lanc.* 68.
Caulfeild, *Roscommon*, 234: *Queen's Co.* 234: *Westmeath*, 234: *Tyrone*, 234.
Cave, *Bucks*, 11: *Glouc.* 234: *Leic.* 76, 80: *Northamp.* 111, 112: *Oxf.* 128, 130: *Surrey*, 158.
Cavendish, *Derby*, 26, 27; 231.
Caulx, *Somerset*, 140.
Cawley, *Sussex*, 163, 165.
Cay, *Northumb.* 234.
Cayley, *York*, 224, 234; 236.
Cecil, *Herts*, 53, 54, 56: *Northamp.* 111, 115, 116: *Rutl.* 135, 136: *Surrey*, 156: *Wilts*, 182.
Cerne, *Wilts*, 191.
Cervington, *Wilts*, 182.
Chacomb, *Northamp.* 112.
Chad, *Norf.* 234.

Chaderton, *Sussex*, 168.
Chadderton, *Lanc.* 75: *York*, 219, 224.
Chadwick, *Derby*, 27: *Lanc.* 70, 71, 234: *Staff.* 146: *Hereford*, 234: *Cheshire*, 234; 234; 236.
Chafin, *Dorset*, 33: *Wilts*, 185, 192.
Chaker, *Bucks*, 10.
Chaldecot, *Wilts*, 182.
Chaldecott, *Dorset*, 33.
Chalener, *Sussex*, 168.
Chalford, *Wilts*, 182.
Chalderton, *Camb.* 16.
Chalke, *Somerset*, 140.
Challen, *Sussex*, 163, 234.
Challenor, *Sussex*, 164, 165.
Challonor, *Surrey*, 234.
Challons, *Devon*, 29.
Chalmers, *Forfar*, 234.
Chaloner, *York*, 201, 220, 224, 234; *Meath*, 234; *Bucks*, 10.
Chamber, *Durham*, 36, 38; *Leic.* 80; *York*, 224.
Chamberlain, *Oxf.* 128; *Hamp.* 266; 253.
Chamberlaine, *Leic.* 80; *Oxf.* 131.
Chamberlayn, *Camb.* 16; *Herts*, 54.
Chamberlayne, *Glouc.* 234; *Hunts*, 234; *Warw.* 234; 232; 236; *Berks*, 254.
Chamberleyne, *Norf.* 278.
Chamberlyn, *Hamp.* 50.
Chambers, *Kent*, 60, 234; *Lond.* 96, 100; *Donegal*, 234; *Cardigan*, 234; 234; 239.
Chambre, *Kent*, 60; *Leic.* 80; *Northamp.* 112; *Armagh*, 234; *Cumb.* 234.
Champagne, *Leic.* 80.
Champaigne, *Leic.* 271.
Champaine, *Leic.* 76.
Champanti, *Hamp.* 50.
Champayne, *Dorset*, 33.
Champernon, *Devon*, 32; *Leic.* 80.
Champernowne, *Devon*, 31, 234.
Champion, *Hamp.* 50; *Lond.* 104; 236; 239; *Berks*, 254.
Champion-Moller, 234.
Champness, *Somerset*, 140.
Champneys, *Kent*, 60, 234.
Chancellor, *Durham*, 34.
Chandler, *Durham*, 38; *Hamp.* 50.

Chandos, *Herts*, 54, 56; *Surrey*,
158; 236.
Chance, *Chesh.* 17.
Chanworth, *Bucks*, 11.
Chaplin, *Linc.* 234.
Chapman, *Camb.* 15; *Kent*, 60;
Leic. 77; *Sussex*, 163, 165; *York*,
234; 239; 246; *Norf.* 278.
Chappel, *York*, 222.
Chappell, *Somerset*, 140.
Charlemagne, *Lanc.* 69.
Charles, *Devon*, 29; *Wales*, 229.
Charlesworth, *York*, 234.
Charleton, *Kent*, 60; *Sussex*, 165;
Derby, 259.
Charley, *Antrim*, 234.
Charlton, *Northumb.* 234; *Salop*,
234; *Notts.* 234; *Hereford*, 234;
239.
Charman, *Suffolk*, 152.
Charnels, *Leic.* 76.
Charnell, *Leic.* 80.
Charnells, *Leic.* 80; *Warw.* 172.
Charnock, *Lanc.* 234.
Charron, *Durham*, 38; *Northumb.*
119.
Chase, *Herts*, 56.
Chastillon, *Northamp.* 112.
Chatfield, *Sussex*, 163, 165, 168.
Chatham, *Leic.* 80.
Chaucer, *Bucks*, 10.
Chaunceler, *Durham*, 38.
Chauncey, *Northamp.* 111; *Norf.*
278.
Chauncy, *Herts*, 53, 54, 234;
Northamp. 112.
Chaundler, *Hamp.* 266.
Chaunterell, *Dorset*, 33.
Chaunceux, *Northamp.* 112.
Chawner, *Hants*, 234.
Chaworth, *Northamp.* 112; *Notts.*
122.
Chaytor, *Durham*, 34, 38, 43; *York.*
224, 234.
Cheales, *Hants*, 234.
Checkford, *Dorset*, 33.
Chedyok, *Wilts*, 182.
Cheek, *Berks*, 3; *Somerset*, 140.
Cheeke, *Hamp.* 50, 266.
Cheefney, *York*, 217.
Cheese, *Hereford*, 234.
Cheevers, *Galway*, 234.
Cheke, *Berks*, 17.

Chelrey, *Herts*, 54.
Chelworth, *Somerset*, 140.
Chenduit, *Northamp.* 112.
Cheney, *Bucks*, 11; *Kent*, 60;
Northamp. 112; *Wilts*, 185, 194;
Shrop. 234; *Leic.* 234; *Derby*,
234.
Chenow, *Essex*, 48.
Chequers, *Bucks*, 10.
Cherlecote, *Warw.* 172.
Chernocke, *Bucks*, 10.
Cherry, *Berks*, 7, 8, 234; *Hereford*,
232; 234.
Cheselden, *Leic.* 80.
Chesenhall, *Lanc.* 234.
Cheshunt, *Northamp.* 112.
Chesilden, *Rutl.* 135.
Cheslyn, *Leic.* 80; 232.
Chester, *Bucks*, 11, 234; *Chesh.* 17;
Herts, 54, 56, 234; *Kent*, 65;
Lanc. 71; *Leic.* 80; 236; *London*,
104; *Northamp.* 112; *Derby*, 258.
Chesterfield, *Bucks*, 10; *Derby*, 27;
Herts, 54.
Chestre, *Warw.* 172.
Cheswick, *Durham*, 42.
Chetham, *Lanc.*,71, 75.
Chetwode, *Beds.* 2; *Bucks*, 10;
Chesh. 17; *Northamp.* 111, 112;
Warw. 172; *Queen's Co.* 234; 236.
Chetwood, *Staff.* 146.
Chetwin, *Warw.* 172.
Chevercourt, *Leic.* 80.
Cheverel, *Dorset*, 33; *Leic.* 80.
Chevers, *Galway*, 234.
Cheyne, *Northamp.* 111, 112; *Wilts*,
182; 232; 235.
Cheyney, *Devon*, 29; *Herts*, 54;
Kent, 58, 60; *York*, 217.
Cheyney, *Kent*, 60.
Cheytor, *Durham;* 36, 40.
Chichele, *Northamp.* 111; *Oxf.* 127.
Chicheley, *Camb.* 16; *Surrey*, 158.
Chichester, *Devon*, 29, 234; *Staff.*
143; *Sussex*, 164, 165; 234; 236.
Chichley, *Essex*, 48.
Chidiock, *Dorset*, 33.
Chilborne, *Kent*, 60.
Chilcot, *London*, 96; *Somerset*, 140.
Child, *Herts*, 54; *Staff.* 145, 234;
Worc. 195; *Pemb.* 195.
Childe, *Shrop.* 234.
Childers, *York*, 213, 234.

Chippingdale, *Leic.* 80.
Chisim, *Sussex*, 165.
Chisholm, *Kent*, 60 ; 234.
Chisholme, *Roxburgh*, 234.
Chivers, *Wilts*, 184.
Choke, *Berks*, 254.
Chokes, *Northamp.* 112.
Cholmley, *York*, 213, 234.
Cholmeley, *Linc.* 82 ; *York*, 224, 234.
Cholmondeley, *Chesh.* 17.
Cholmundeley, *York*, 226.
Chowne, *Kent*, 60 ; *Sussex*, 164, 165 ; *Somerset*, 234.
Christian, *Cumb.* 22, 234 ; *Leic.* 80.
Christie, *Fife*, 234.
Christmas, *Waterford*, 234.
Christopher, 234.
Christy, *Kent*, 234.
Chudleigh, *Devon*, 29 ; *Dorset*, 33.
Churchill, *Bucks*, 10 ; *Dorset*, 33 ; *Herts*, 54 ; *Northamp.* 112 ; *Wilts*, 182.
Churchar, *Sussex*, 165.
Churcher, *Sussex*, 163.
Chute, *Hamp.* 50, 266 ; *Kent*, 60 ; *Kerry*, 234.
Ciampanti, *Hamp.* 266.
Cioches, *Northamp.* 112.
Clanchy, *Cork*, 234.
Clanford, *Northamp.* 112.
Clanricarde, 236.
Clapcott, *Dorset*, 234.
Clapham, *York*, 206, 217, 224, 234.
Clapton, *Leic.* 80.
Clare, *Berks*, 7 ; *Bucks*, 10 ; *Dorset*, 33 ; *Hamp.* 50 ; *Herts*, 54 ; *Surrey*, 156.
Clarel, *York*, 213.
Clarell, *Northamp.* 112.
Clarenaulx, *Leic.* 76.
Clarendon, *Essex*, 48.
Clark, *Kent*, 60 ; *Somerset*, 140 ; *Northumb.* 234 ; *Surrey*, 234 ; *Londonderry*, 234 ; 234 ; *Sussex*, 165.
Clarke, *Berks*, 7, 234 ; *Herts*, 56 ; *Kent*, 60 ; *Leic.* 80 ; *Northamp.* 112, 234 ; *Suffolk*, 153 ; *Surrey*, 156 ; *Sussex*, 165 ; *York*, 222, 234 ; *Staff.* 234 ; *Devon*, 234 ; *Middlesex*, 234 ; *Chesh.* 234 ; *Perth*, 234 ; *Nairn*, 234 ; 233 ; 236 ; 239 ; *Berks*, 254 ; *Derby*, 259 ; *Hamp.* 266.

Clarke-Jervoise, *Leic.* 80 ; *Hamp.* 50.
Clavell, *Dorset*, 33.
Clavelshey, *Somerset*, 140.
Claver, *Bucks*, 10.
Clavering, *Durham*, 34, 37, 38, 42 ; *Northamp.* 112 ; *Northumb.* 234 ; 235 ; 236.
Clavil, *Dorset*, 33.
Claxton, *Durham*, 34, 36, 38, 40 ; *Somerset*, 140.
Clay, *Notts*, 123 ; *York*, 205.
Clayton, *Berks*, 7 ; *Bucks*, 11, 234 *Lanc.* 69, 71, 234 ; *Northumb.* 119 ; *Staff.* 145 ; *Surrey*, 156 ; *York*, 205 ; 224 ; *Middlesex*, 234 ; *Norf.* 234.
Cleaver, *Bucks*, 10.
Cleiveland, *Leic.* 77, 80.
Cleland, *Devon.* 234 ; 239.
Clement, *Wales*, 229 ; *Pemb.* 230 ; *Norf.* 278.
Clements, *Cavan*, 234.
Clendinning, *Mayo*, 234.
Clendon, *Northamp.* 111.
Clennell, *Northumb.* 120.
Clerbecke, 232.
Clere, *Norf.* 107 ; 250.
Clerk, *Lond.* 96.
Clerk-Rattray, *Perth*, 234.
Clerke, *Bucks*, 10 ; *Hamp.* 50 ; *Herts*, 54 ; *Kent*, 60, 67 ; *Leic.* 80 ; *Sussex*, 165 ; 233 ; 236.
Clervaux, *Durham*, 43 ; *York*, 209.
Cleseby, *York*, 285.
Cleveland, *Chesh.* 18.
Clevland, *Devon*, 234.
Cleybrooke, *Kent*, 60.
Clibborn, *Westmeath*, 234.
Cliderowe, *Herts*, 54.
Clieveland, *Chesh.* 17.
Clifden, *Northamp.* 112.
Cliffe, *Wexford*, 234.
Clifford, *Bucks*, 11 ; *Durham*, 37 ; *Kent*, 58 ; *Herts*, 56 ; *Northum.* 119 ; *Notts*, 122 ; *Shrop.* 137 ; *Wilts*, 182, 185 ; *York*, 200 ; *Glouc.* 234 ; *Wexford*, 234 ; 234 ; *Berks*, 254.
Clifton, *Lanc.* 71, 234 ; *Hunts*, 57 ; *Notts*, 122, 125 ; *Surrey*, 162 ; *Norfolk*, 227.
Clippesley, *Norf.* 107.

Clinton, *Dors.* 33; *Herts,* 54; *Warw.* 172; 233.
Clitherow, *London,* 101.
Clitherowe, *Herts,* 54.
Clive, *Ches.* 17; *Kent,* 60; *Hereford,* 234; 251.
Cloberry, *Devon,* 29.
Clodshall, *Warw.* 172.
Clopton, *Durham,* 36, 38; *Suffolk,* 149, 155; *Warw.* 178, 172; *Leic.* 80; *Glouc.* 262.
Close, *Armagh,* 234; 233.
Clothall, *Sussex,* 163, 165.
Clotterbooke, *Herts,* 56.
Clotworthy, *Devon.* 29.
Clough, *Denb.* 234; *York,* 205; *Wales,* 229.
Clowes, *Bucks,* 234.
Cludde, *Shrop.* 234.
Clutterbuck, *Herts,* 54, 56; *Glouc.* 234; *Northumb.* 234.
Clutton, *Chesh.* 234.
Clutton-Brock, 234.
Coates, *Devon,* 234.

Cobb, *Hamp.* 50; *Kent,* 60; *Oxf.* 131, 132; *York,* 217, 224.
Cobbe, *Dublin,* 234; 236; *Hamp.* 266.
Cobham, *Herts,* 54; *Northamp.* 112; *Surrey,* 161; 232.
Cock, *Herts,* 53, 54, 56.
Cockain, *Warw.* 172.
Cockburn, 236.
Cockes, *Somerset,* 140.
Cocket, *Norf.* 107.

Cocks, *Herts,* 54; *Surrey,* 156.
Cockshott, *Leic.* 80.
Cockram, *Dorset,* 33.
Cockrane, *Donegal,* 234.
Code, *Cornwall,* 20.
Coddington, *Meath,* 234.
Codington, *Surrey,* 158.
Codrington, *Wilts,* 234.
Coetmor, *Wales,* 229.
Coffin, *Devon,* 234.
Cogan, *Oxf.* 128, 130; *Somerset,* 140; *Wicklow,* 234.
Coghill, *Oxf.* 131.
Coghull, *Chesh.* 17.
Coham, *Devon.* 234; 236; 239; 250.
Cokaine, *Derby,* 27.

Coke, *Derby,* 28; 234; *Herts,* 54; *Leic.* 80; *Northamp.* 112; *Norf.* 107, 234; *York,* 213; *Warw.* 172; *Hereford,* 234; 236.
Cokefeld, *Notts.* 122.
Coker, *Dors.* 33; *Northamp.* 112; *Wilts.* 182; *Oxf.* 234.
Cokesey, *Oxf.* 133; *Warw.* 172; *Worc.* 195.
Colby, *Norf.* 278.
Colbye, *York,* 224.
Colclough, *Staff.* 142, 145; *Wexford,* 234, 237.
Colborne, *Somerset,* 140.
Colbrand, *Leic.* 80; *Sussex,* 165.
Colbrond, *Sussex,* 163.
Coldham, *Herts,* 56; *Surrey,* 156; *Sussex,* 163, 165.
Cole, *Devon,* 29; *Leic.* 80; *Somerset,* 140; *Surrey,* 162; *Sussex,* 165; *Middlesex,* 234; *Monaghan,* 234; *Hants,* 234, 266; *Cornwall,* 234; *Oxf.* 234, 236.
Coleclough, *Staff.* 146.
Colebrook, *Sussex,* 165.
Colebrooke, *Bucks,* 10; *Sussex,* 163.
Colegrave, *Essex,* 234.
Colepeper, *Kent,* 60; *Northamp.* 112; *Sussex,* 165.
Coles, *Northamp.* 112; *Wilts,* 192; *Hants,* 234; *Soms.* 234.
Coleworth, *Northamp.* 112
Colet, *Bucks,* 11.
Colfe, *Kent,* 60, 61.
Colins, *Devon,* 29.
Colles, *Soms.* 140.
Collet, *Lond.* 96.
Colleton, *Devon,* 29, 31.
Collett, *Kent,* 60.
Colley, *Durham,* 38.
Collier, *Dorset,* 33; *Kent,* 60; *Staff.* 146; 233; 237.
Colling, *Durham,* 234.
Collings, *Devon.* 31; *Guernsey,* 234.
Collingwood, *Durham,* 38, 234; *Northumb.* 120, 234; 236.
Collins, *Kent,* 60; *Sussex,* 165; *Hereford,* 234; *Berks,* 234, 254; *Corn.* 234; *Soms.* 234; *Dublin,* 234; 237; 239.
Collinson, *Suffolk,* 234.
Collis, *Kerry,* 234.
Colly, *Rutland,* 135.

Collyer, *Norfolk*, 234,
Collyns, *Devon*, 31.
Colmore, *Durham*, 36; *Glou.* 234;
    Somerset, 140
Colnet, *Hamp.* 266.
Colnett, *Hamp.* 50.
Cologan, 239.
Colquhoun, *Dumbarton*, 234; *Lond.*
    234.
Colston, *Somerset*, 139; *Wilts*, 234;
    239.
Colt, *Hamp.* 50; *Lanark*, 234.
Colthurst, *York*, 201, 224; *Cork*, 234.
Columbell, 251.
Colvile, *Camb.* 16, 256; *York*, 220.
Colvill, *Ireland*, 234.
Colville, *Northamp.* 112; *Derby*, 234,
    232.
Colwell, *Kent*, 60; *Sussex*, 165.
Colwich, *Derby*, 259.
Comb, *Somerset*, 140.
à Combe, *Warw.* 178.
Combe, *Herts*, 54.
Combemartin, *Northamp.* 112.
Comber, *Sussex*, 165; 245.
Comberford, *Staff.* 143, 147.
Combre, *Sussex*, 163.
Comer, *Somerset*, 234.
Comin, *Leic.* 80.
Commerell, *Sussex*, 165, 234.
Compton, *Hamp.* 50, 265; *Northamp.*
    111; *Notts.* 122; *Somerset*, 140;
    Sussex, 165; *Warw.* 172; *Wilts*,
    182; *Glou.* 262.
Comyn, *Durham*, 36; *Herts*, 54;
    London, 96; *Warw.* 172; *York.*
    224; *Isle of Man*, 267.
Conant, *Kent*, 59.
Concanon, *Galway*, 234.
Congreave, *Staff.* 146.
Congreve, *Berks*, 7; *Ches.* 234; *Staff.*
    234; *Waterford*, 234.
Coniers, *Durham*, 34; *York*, 226.
Coningsby, *Herts*, 53, 54, 56; *Norf.*
    107; *Warw.* 172.
Conn, *Kilkenny*, 234.
Connellan, *Kilkenny*, 234.
Conner, *Cork*, 234.
Conroy, *Montgomery*, 234.
Consett, *York*, 220.
Constable, *Kent*, 60; *Sussex*, 165;
    York, 201, 217, 224, 226, 234.
Constable-Maxwell, 234.

Constantine, *Dorset*, 33.
Conolly, *Kildare*, 234; 234.
Contry, *Kent*, 67.
Conuers, *Sussex*, 168.
Conway, *Hamp.* 50; *Flint*, 234;
    Warw. 172.
Conwy, *Flint*, 234; *Wales*, 229.
Conyers, *Bucks*, 13; *Durham*, 36,
    38, 40; *Essex*, 48, 234; *Leic.* 80;
    Notts. 122; *York*, 201, 205, 209,
    220, 224, 226, 285.
Conyngham, *Londonderry*, 234, 236.
Cooke, *Devon*, 29; *Herts*, 56; *Kent*,
    60; *Leic.* 80; *Sussex*, 163, 165,
    168; *York*, 202, 205, 210, 213,
    224, 234, 239; *Westmeath*, 234;
    Tipperary, 234; *Glou.* 234; 234;
    236, 245; *Derby*, 259.
Cooke-Collis, 234.
Cookes, *Oxf.* 127; *Warw.* 177;
    Wilts, 195; *Worc.* 234.
Cookson, *York*, 205; *Durham*, 234;
    Northumb. 234.
Cooper, *Durham*, 36, 38; *Notts.* 122,
    123; *Sussex*, 165; *Sligo*, 235;
    Limerick, 234; *Bedford*, 234; *Ayr*,
    234; *Midd.* 234; *Wicklow*, 234;
    234; 237; 246; 250; *Hamp.* 266.
Coore, *York*, 234.
Coote, *Limerick*, 234; 236; *Norf.*
    278.
Copdike, *Norf.* 278.
Copdow, *Essex*, 48.
Cope, *Hamp.* 50, 266; *London*, 95;
    Staff. 146; *Northamp.* 112; *Ar-
    magh*, 234.
Copeley, *York*, 226.
Copleston, *Devon*, 29.
Coplestone, *Devon*, 31; *Dorset*, 33.
Copley, *Hamp.* 50; *Notts.* 122;
    Surrey, 156, 158, 162; *Sussex*,
    163, 165; *York*, 202, 205, 213,
    224, 226.
Coppin, *Herts.* 54; *Kent*, 60.
Copping, *Norf.* 278.
Coppinger, *Cork*, 234.
Corbally, *Meath*, 234.
Corbet, *Bucks.* 10; *Norf.* 107, 278;
    Northamp. 112; *Northumb.* 119;
    Shrop. 137, 234, 239; *York*, 224:
    224.
Corbett, *Kent*, 60; *Leic.* 80; *Glou.*
    234; 234.

Corbin, *Warw.* 172.
Corbyn, *Staff.* 143.
Cordall, *Norfolk*, 278.
Cordray, *Wilts*, 185.
Corham, *Hamp.* 50.
Cormick, *Herts.* 56.
Cornewall, 236.
Corney, *Oxf.* 131.
Cornish, *Devon*, 234 ; *Cornw.* 234.
Cornock, *Wexford*, 234.
Cornwall, *Bucks*, 10 ; *Northamp.* 112.
Corona, *Chesh.* 17.
Corrance, *Suffolk*, 234.
Corry, *Down*, 234.
Corsellis, *Essex*, 48, 234.
Corstorphine, *Fife*, 284.
Cortingstock, *Notts*, 122.
Cory, *Norf.* 108.
Coryton, *Cornwall*, 234.
Cosby, *Queen's Co.* 234.
Cost, *Northamp.* 111.
Costello, *Mayo*, 234.
Cosyn, *Durham*, 38.
Cotele, *Wilts*, 185.
Cotes, *Leic.* 80 ; *Salop*, 234 ; *Warw.* 172 ; *Glouc.* 264.
Cothercote, *Shrop.* 137.
Cotgreave, *Chesh.* 234.
Coton, *Leic.* 80 ; *Warw.* 176, 177.
Cottam, *Kent*, 60.
Cottesford, *Oxf.* 129, 131.
Cottingham, *Ches.* 17.
Cottington, *Somerset*, 140.
Cottingtam, *Wilts.* 182.
Cottle, *Devon.* 29.
Cotton, *Camb.* 16 ; *Ches.* 17 ; *Derby*, 27, 234 ; *Hamp.* 50, 266 ; *Hunts.* 57 ; *Kent*, 60 ; *Leic.* 76, 80 ; *Staff.* 143, 146 ; *York*, 213 ; 236 ; *Berks.* 254.
Cottrell, *Midd.* 234.
Cottrell-Dormer, *Bucks*, 10.
Couchman, *Kent*, 60.
Coudray, *Ches.* 17.
Coulson, *Northumb.* 119 ; 234 ; *York*, 220, 224.
Coulthart, 234, 236, 245, 246.
Coulthurst, *York*, 200, 220.
Coumbemartyn, *Northamp.* 111.
Coundon, *Durham*, 38.
Counsel, *Glouc.* 261.
Couper, *Berks*, 3.

Courci, *Northamp.* 112.
Courtenay, *Bucks.* 10 ; *Cornw.* 20 ; *Devon*, 29 ; Cork, 234 ; 234 ; 238.
Courthop, *Kent*, 60.
Courthope, *Sussex*, 165 ; 232.
Coutry, *Kent*, 60.
Coventry, *Sussex*, 165.
Covert, *Kent*, 60 ; *Surrey*, 266 ; *Sussex*, 165.
Coward, *Somerset*, 140.
Cowdray, *Bucks.* 10 ; *Hamp.* 266.
Cowdrey, *Hamp.* 50.
Cowell-Stepney, 234, 250.
Cowper, *Chesh.* 17 ; *Cumb.* 234 ; *Herts.* 54 ; 56 ; *Kent*, 60 ; *Leic.* 80 ; *Surrey*, 156 ; *Sussex*, 163, 165 ; *Berks*, 254 ; 253.
Cowton, *Durham*, 43.
Cox, *Berks*, 254 ; *Derby*; 27 ; *Leic.* 80 ; *Somerset*, 140 ; *Sussex*, 165 ; *Limerick*, 234 ; *Wexford*, 234 ; *Hereford*, 234.
Coxe, *Herts*, 54.
Coxwell, 234.
Coyney, *Staff.* 146, 234.
Coyny, *Wales*, 229.
Cozens, *Kent*, 60.
Crabbe, 249.
Cracroft, *Camb.* 16 ; *Linc.* 234.
Crackenthorpe, *Westm.* 234.
Cradock, *Durham*, 38 ; *Leic.* 77, 80 ; *Sussex*, 165 ; *York*, 208, 224 ; *Glouc.* 228 ; 234 ; *Wales*, 229 ; 241.
Cradocke, *Leic.* 80.
Craford, *Kent*, 60.
Craig, 234.
Crakenthorpe, *Herts*, 56 ; 237.
Cramer, *Cork*, 234 ; *Suffolk*, 152.
Cranach, *Chesh.* 17.
Crane, *Northamp.* 112 ; *Suffolk*, 155.
Cranesley, *Northamp.* 111.
Cranford, *Northamp.* 112.
Cranmer, *Notts*, 122 ; *Suffolk*, 152 ; *Surrey*, 156.
Cranstoun, *Lanark*, 234 ; 236.
Crashaw, *York*, 224.
Cras'ter, *Northumb.* 234.
Crathorne, *York*, 201, 220, 224.
Craufuird, 234 ; 239.
Craufurd, *Ayr*, 234.
Craven, *York*, 224 ; *Hants*, 243 ;

Louth, 234; *Glouc.* 234; *Wilts.* 234; 287.
Crawford, *Down*, 234; 241.
Crawfurd, *Lanark*, 234; *Ayr*, 234; *Sussex*, 234; 243.
Crawshaw, *York*, 213.
Crawley, *Northamp.* 112; *Bedf.* 234.
Cray, *Hamp.* 266.
Craye, *Camb.* 16.
Crayford, *Kent*, 60.
Creagh, *Clare*, 234; *Cork*, 234; 234; 237; 246.
Crean, *Mayo*, 234.
Cregoe, *Cornw*, 234.
Cree, *Dorset*, 234.
Creighton, *Fermanagh*, 234.
Creke, *Camb.* 16; *Herts*, 54.
Creon, *Leic.* 80.
Cresacre, *York*, 213.
Crespin, *Hunts*, 57.
Cressener, *Essex*, 48.
Cressi, *Bucks*, 10.
Cresswell, *Northumb.* 119, 234; *Wilts*, 234.
Creswell, *Hamp.* 50, 266; *Northamp.* 112; *Leic.* 234.
Cressy, *Herts*, 54; *Northamp.* 112; *Notts.* 122, 125; *Warw.* 172; *York*, 224.
Cresvile, *Hamp.* 266.
Crevequer, *Herts*, 54.
Crew, *Northamp.* 111.
Crewe, *Chesh.* 17; *Derby*, 17; *Leic.* 80; *Northamp.* 112; *Staff.* 142.
Crews, *Northamp.* 113.
Creyke, *York*, 224, 234; 236.
Crichton, *Fife*, 234; 236.
Crigan, *Tyrone*, 234.
Criol. *Leic.* 80; *Herts*, 54.
Crips, *Sussex*, 165.
Cripps, *Kent*, 60.
Crocker, *Devon*, 29.
Croft, *Leic.* 80; *York*, 234; *Berks*, 234; *Durham*, 43; 236.
Croftes, *Suffolk*, 152.
Crofts, *York*, 224; *Cork*, 234.
Crofton, *Leitrim*, 234.
Croke, *Bucks*, 10, 11, 13; *Wilts*, 182; *Oxf.* 234; 235.
Croker, *Limerick*, 234; *Surrey*, 234.
Cromer, *Sussex*, 165.
Crommelin, *Down*, 234.

Crompe, *Kent*, 60.
Crompton, *Derby*, 27, 234; *York*, 224; *Lanc.* 234, 268; 234.
Cromwell, *Bucks*, 11; *Herts*, 54, 56, 234; *Hunts*, 57; 241; 244.
Cronin-Coltsmann, *Kerry*, 234.
Crooke, *Oxf.* 131.
Crooker, 251.
Cropley, *Hunts*, 57; *London*, 96.
Crosbie, *Kerry*, 234; *London*, 97.
Crosier, *Durham*, 36, 38.
Crosland, *York*, 224.
Crosse, *Bucks*, 10; *Lanc.* 234; *Somerset*, 234.
Crossley, *Lanc.* 70, 71, 234.
Croston, *York*, 224.
Crouch, *Herts*, 54.
Crow, *Carm.* 230.
Crowder, *Wales*, 229.
Crowe, *Surrey*, 158; *Clare*, 234.
Crowmer, *Kent*, 58.
Croxall, *Staff.* 143.
Croxton, *Chesh.* 17.
Croyser, *Durham*, 34, 40.
Crue, *Ches.* 17.
Crum-Ewing, 234.
Cruis, *Devon*, 31.
Cruikshank, *Forfar*, 234; 287.
Crump, *Sussex*, 165.
Crumwell, *Notts*, 122.
Crutchley, *Bucks*, 234.
Cruwys, *Devon*, 29.
Crux, *Kent*, 60.
Cryche, *Notts*, 122.
Cubitt, *Norfolk*, 234.
Cuddon, *Suffolk*, 153.
Cudworth, *York*, 213; *Lanc.* 268.
Cuffe, *Somerset*, 140.
Cuffold, *Hamp.* 50, 266.
Cuiley, *Leic.* 76.
Cukeney, *Notts*, 122.
Culey, *Leic.* 80.
Cullen, *Leitrim*, 234; 237.
Culley, *Northumb.* 234.
Culliford, *Dorset*, 33; *Somerset*, 140.
Cullum, *Suffolk*, 149, 152.
Culme, *Devon*, 29.
Culpeper, *Kent*, 60, 67 : *Northamp.* 112; *Sussex*, 165, 169; *Warw.* 172.
Culworth, *Northamp.* 112.
Culy, *Warw.* 172.

Cumin, *Northumb.* 119; *Warw.* 172.
Cuming, 236.
Cuningham, 236.
Cuninghame, *Ayr,* 234; 234.
Cuppage, *Antrim,* 234.
Cupper, *Somerset,* 140.
Cure, *Essex,* 234.
Curl, *Leic.* 80.
Curli, *Warw.* 172.
Curling, *Kent,* 60; *Montgomery,* 234.
Curre, *Monm.* 234.
Currie, *Chesh.* 17; *Midd.* 234; 236.
Currer, *York,* 200, 224, 234; 234;
  236; 237.
Curson, *Oxford,* 130, 131.
Cursone, *Oxford,* 128.
Curteis, *Kent,* 60; *Sussex,* 165, 234.
Curtis, *Devon,* 234.
Curtois, *Lincoln,* 234.
Curwen, *Cumb.* 22, 23, 24, 234.
Curwyn, *Cumb.* 23.
Curzon, *Derby,* 27; *Leic.* 234.
Cusack, *Meath,* 234; 234; 236; 241.
Cusse, *Wilts,* 185.
Cust, *Linc.* 82.
Custance, *Norfolk,* 234.
Cutcliffe, 234.
Cuthbert, *Durham,* 34; *Northumb.*
  234.
Cutler, *Leic.* 80; *London,* 97; *York,*
  213, 224, 234; *Devon,* 234; 236;
  248.
Cuttes, *Camb.* 16.
Cutts, *Bucks,* 10.
Cyffin, *Wales,* 229.

D'Abernon, *Surrey,* 156.
Dabridgecourt, *Hamp.* 50; 266.
Daccomb, *Dorset,* 33.
Dackombe, *Dorset,* 33.
Dacombe, *Dorset,* 33.
Dacre, *Cumb.* 22, 23; *Essex,* 48;
  Herts, 53, 54, 56; 232; *Northumb.*
  119.
Dacres, *Herts,* 54.
Dade, *Kent,* 60.
D'Aeth, *Kent,* 60, 234.
Dakeyne, *Derby,* 27, 234.
Dakin, *Derby,* 259.
Dakins, *Warw.* 177.
Dalbiac, *Sussex,* 165.
Dalbridgecourt, 283.

Dalby, *Berks,* 254.
D'Aldone, *Kent,* 64.
Dale, *Derby,* 27, 234; *Durham,* 38,
  234; *Dorset,* 234; *Rutland,* 136;
  236.
Dalden, *Durham,* 38.
Dalison, *Kent,* 60, 234; 236.
Dalrymple, *Sussex,* 165.
Dalston, *Cumb.* 22; *Westm.* 179.
Dalton. *Camb.* 16; *Lanc.* 71, 234;
  Wilts, 182; *York,* 209, 224, 234;
  Somerset, 234; *Glouc.* 234, 236;
  Derby, 259.
Dalway, *Antrim,* 234.
Daly, *Galway,* 234.
Dalyel, 234.
Dalyngruge, *Sussex,* 169.
Dalyngrudge, *Sussex,* 166.
Dalzell, 237.
Damer, *Dorset,* 33.
Dames, *King's Co.* 234.
D'Amorie, *Surrey,* 156.
Dammartin, *Surrey,* 156.
Danby, *Northamp.* 112; *York,* 205,
  209, 220, 224, 226, 234.
Dancastell, *Berks,* 254.
Dandy, 249.
Dane, *Kent,* 60; *Fermanagh,* 234;
  Somerset, 140.
Danet, *Leic.* 80; *Warw.* 172; *Worc.*
  195.
Daneys, *Rutland,* 136.
Daniel, *Chesh.* 17; *Herts,* 56, 60;
  Devon, 234; *Cornwall,* 234; *Suf-
  folk,* 156.
Daniell, *Chesh.* 17; *Westmeath,* 234.
Dannet, *Leic.* 80.
Dannett, *Leic.* 80.
Dansey, *Hereford,* 234.
Danvers, *Berks,* 7; *Bucks,* 10; *Leic.*
  76, 80; *Northamp.* 111, 112;
  Wilts, 194; 232; 234; *Oxford,*
  128, 130, 131, 132, 134.
Danyel, *Wilts,* 185.
Dapifer, *Norfolk,* 109.
Darby, *King's Co.* 234; *Bucks,* 234;
  Shrop. 234.
D'Arci, *Herts,* 54.
Darcy, *Durham,* 38; *York,* 209, 213,
  224; *Notts.* 122.
D'Arcy, *York,* 217; *Westmeath,* 234,
  239; *Galway,* 234; 234; 236.

Dare, *Essex*, 48; 234.
Darell, *Herts*, 54; *Kent*, 60, 284; *Wilts*, 191; 232; 234; *Berks*, 254.
Darker, *Northamp.* 112.
Darley, *York*, 234; 251.
Darlington, *Durham*, 34, 37.
Darnley, 237. .
Darroch, *Renfrew*, 234.
Darrell, *Sussex*, 165.
Darwin, *Derby*, 27; *Notts.* 234; 234.
Dashwood, *Bucks*, 10, 11; *Notts.* 234.
Daubeney, 232.
Daubeny, *Glouc.* 234.
Daunt, *Cork*, 234; 234.
Daunte, *Glouc.* 262.
Dauntesey, *Wilts*, 182, 194.
Dauntsey, *Herts*, 54; *Wilts*, 185.
Davenant, *Wilts*, 182.
Davenport, *Chesh.* 17, 234; *Durham*, 38; *Shrop.* 234; 236.
Daventre, *Northamp.* 112.
Davey, *Cornw.* 234.
David, *Glam.* 228; *Card.* 230; *Wales*, 229.
David ap Einion, *Wales*, 229.
David Ieuan, *Wales*, 229.
David ab Morgan, *Wales*, 229.
David Rys, *Wales*, 229.
David Rytherch, *Wales*, 229.
Davids, *Wales*, 229.
Davidson, *Inverness*, 234; *Kincardine*, 234; *Ross*, 234; *Northumb.* 119.
Davie, *Kent*, 60.
Davies, *Cornw.* 20; *Hamp.* 50; *Sussex*, 165; *Wilts*, 182; *Wales*, 229; *Carm.* 230; *Pemb.* 230; *Flint*, 234; *Worc.* 234; *Shrop.* 234; *Hereford*, 234; *Card.* 234; *Warw.* 234; *Merioneth*, 234; 234; *Chesh.* 17; *Somerset*, 140; 236; 239; 243; 245.
Davile, *York*, 224.
Davils, *Devon*, 29.
Davis, *Chesh.* 17; *Wales*, 229; *Somerset*, 139; 237; *Berks*, 254.
Davison, *Durham*, 34, 37, 38.
Davy, *Devon*, 29, 31; *Norfolk*, 234; *Wilts*, 185; *Westm.* 234; *Lond.* 234; 236.
Davye, *Devon*, 31; *York*, 224.

Davys, *Wilts*, 182; 234.
Dawes, *Leic.* 80; *Northumb.* 118; *Somerset*, 234.
Dawkins, 234.
Dawkyns, *Wales*, 229.
Dawley, *Hamp.* 50, 266.
Dawney, *Bucks*, 11; *York*, 224.
Daws, *Wales*, 229.
Dawson, *Berks*, 7; *Durham*, 36; *Leic.* 80, 234; *York*, 200, 234; *Lanc.* 234; *Suffolk*, 234; *Londonderry*, 234; *Surrey*, 158; 236; 246.
Dawtrey, *Sussex*, 168.
Dawtry, *Hamp.* 50, 266; *Sussex*, 163, 165.
Day, *Wilts*, 185; *Kerry*, 234.
Daye, *Camb.* 16.
Daykins, *Durham*, 43.
Dayman, *Devon*, 234.
Dayncourt, *Notts.* 112.
Dayrell, *Bucks*, 10, 234; *Camb.* 234; 236.
Dayvell, *Bucks*, 11.
Deacon, *Glam.* 234.
De Acstede, *Surrey*, 156.
De Albini, *Essex*, 48.
De Aldelym, *Chesh.* 17.
De Aleman, *York*, 200.
De Alta Ripa, *Hamp.* 50; *Sussex*, 163, 165; 232.
Dealtry, *Linc.* 234; *York*, 234.
De Amory, *Leic.* 76.
De Amundeville, *Essex*, 48.
Deane, *Hamp.* 50, 266; *Kent*, 60; *Wexford*, 234; *Cork*, 234; 232; *Staff.* 143; *Norfolk* 278.
Deans, *Berks*, 7.
De Appleby, *Leic.* 76.
Dearden, *Lanc.* 234.
Dearham, *Durham*, 36, 38.
De Aspale, *Suffolk*, 152.
Death, *Kent*, 60.
De Aton, *York*, 211.
Dease, *Westmeath*, 234; *Louth*, 234.
De Aumari, *Leic.* 80.
De Aubernon, *Devon*, 29.
D'Avrenches, *Kent*, 66.
De Bagott, *Herts*, 56.
De Badlismere, *Wilts*, 190.
De Beauchamp, *Bucks*, 10.
De Beggesovere, *Shrop.* 137.
De Bella, *Notts.* 122.
De Blakeham, *Suffolk*, 152.

De Blurton, *Staff.* 142.
De Bodiam, *Sussex*, 169.
De Bohun, *Shrop.* 137.
De Bois, *Leic.* 76, 80.
De Bosco, *Warw.* 172.
De Boulay, 246.
De Boys, *Essex*, 48.
De Bradeston, *Surrey*, 156.
De Brahm, *Surrey*, 158.
De Branche, *Surrey*, 156.
De Breose, *Surrey*, 156.
De Broc, *Shrop.* 137; *Surrey*, 156.
De Builli, *Notts.* 125.
De Bures, *Surrey*, 156.
De Burgh, *Bucks*, 10; *Herts*, 54; *Norfolk*, 109; *Northamp.* 111; *Midd.* (misprinted De Bingh), 234; 236.
De Burghersh, *Kent*, 64.
De Burgo, *Kent*, 58.
De Burstow, *Surrey*, 156.
De Busli, *York*, 206.
De Caily, *Norfolk*, 277.
De Campania, *York*, 211.
De Camvile, *Leic.* 76.
De Capell, *Sussex*, 165.
De Caprecuria, *York*, 222.
De Castello, *Shrop.* 137.
Decka, *Wales*, 229.
De Clare, *Hamp.* 50.; *Northamp.* 111.
De Clifford, *Wilts*, 182; *Northumb.* 119; *Rutland*, 136; 236.
De Corono, *Chesh.* 17.
De Cothercote, *Shrop.* 137.
De Cotton, *Leic.* 76.
De Crevecœur, *Kent*, 66.
De Creonn, *Surrey*, 156.
De Cuiley, *Leic.* 76.
De Daventre, *Northamp.* 112.
De Denum, *Durham*, 38.
De Donzi, *Suffolk*, 154.
De Dunstanville, *Wilts*, 182, 190.
Dee, *London*, 93; *Sussex*, 165.
Deedes, *Kent*, 234.
Deene, *Leic.* 80.
D'Eincourt, *Rutland*, 136.
Deiri, *Lanc.* 69.
D'Eschalers, *Herts*, 54.
De Esseby, *Linc.* 76.
De Etton, *York*, 221.
De Exherst, *Kent*, 60.
De Fay, *Surrey*, 156.

De Ferrars, *Leic.* 80.
De Fortibus, *York*, 211.
De Frevile, *Staff.* 144.
De Furnival, *York*, 206.
De Gatton, *Kent*, 60; *Surrey*, 156.
Degge, *Staff.* 142; *Derby*, 259.
De Grenville, *Bucks*, 10.
De Grey, *Bucks*, 10.
De Goodhurst, *Kent*, 60.
De Haia, *Sussex*, 165.
De Hastings, *Leic.* 76.
De Haviland, 234.
De Hemegrave, *Suff.* 151, 152.
De Hethe, *Suff.* 151.
De Hoese, *Sussex*, 165.
De Home, *Essex*, 232, 234.
De Houby, *Leic.* 76.
De Ickworth, *Suff.* 152.
De Insula, *Hamp.* 50; *Warw.* 172.
De Isney, *Dorset*, 33; *Essex*, 48.
De Kendale, *Sussex*, 165.
De la Bere, *Hamp.* 266.
De la Chambre, *Sussex*, 164, 165.
De la Cherois, *Down*, 234.
Delafield, 234.
De la Foyle, *Wilts*, 182.
Delahay, *Northamp.* 112; *Rutland*, 136.
Delahyde, *Berks*, 3, 7.
De Lacy, *Lanc.* 71; *Shrop.* 137.
De la Launde, *Warw.* 172.
De la Lee, *Herts*, 54, 56.
De la Mare, *Herts*, 54; *Northamp.* 111.
Delamere, *Wilts*, 182, 193.
Delamore, *Hamp.* 50.
Delap, *Donegal*, 234.
De la Pole, *Bucks*, 10; *Northamp.* 112; *York*, 199, 211; *Oxf.* 133.
De la Poyle, *Surrey*, 156.
De la Roche, *Wilts*, 193.
Delaryver, *York*, 226.
De la See, *York*, 217.
De la Val, *Northumb.* 120.
De la Warr, *Hamp.* 50.
De la Warre, *Northamp.* 111; *Hamp.* 266.
Delawood, *Herts*, 56.
De la Zouch, *Leic.* 76; 236.
De Lerling, *Norf.* 107.
De Lichborowe, *Northamp.* 112.
De Ligne, *Linc.* 82; *Suff.* 152.
De Limesi, *Norf.* 107.

De Lisle, *Norf.* 107.
Dell, *Bucks*, 10.
Delme, *Hants*, 234.
Delme-Ratcliffe, *Herts*, 56.
De Lovetot, *York*, 206.
De Luveraz, *Wilts*, 182.
Delves, *Chesh.* 17 ; *Devon*, 31.
De Lysors, *Notts.* 125.
De Masey-Massie, *Chesh.* 17.
De Mauley, *York*, 213 ; 231.
De Maureward, *Leic.* 76.
De Meduana, *Kent*, 58.
De Michelgrove, *Sussex*, 163.
De Millom, *Cumb.* 23.
De Montalt, *Chesh.* 19.
De Montagne, 235.
De Montmorency, *Kilkenny*, 234.
Dempster, *Sutherland*, 234.
Denbigh, *Leic.* 80.
Dene, *Hamp.* 50 ; *Northamp.* 111.
Denefield, *Hamp.* 50.
De Neville, *York*, 213.
Denew, *Kent*, 60.
Denham, *Fermanagh*, 234.
Denman, *York*, 213.
Denison, *Notts.* 234 ; *York*, 234 ;
    Lanc. 234 ; *Surrey*, 234.
Denmead, *Hamp.* 50.
Denne, *Kent*, 60, 234 ; *Sussex*, 234.
Dennet, *Sussex*, 163.
Dennis, *Devon*, 29 ; *Wicklow*, 234 ;
    236.
Dennistoun, *Dumbarton*, 234.
Denny, *Herts*, 53, 54 ; 233.
Dennys, *London*, 29 ; *Hamp.* 266.
Denom, *Northumb.* 119.
De Norwich, *Suff.* 153.
Dent, *Durham*, 38, 41 ; *York*, 234 ;
    Glouc. 234 ; *Northumb.* 234.
Denton, *Bucks*, 10; *Kent*, 60; *York*,
    224 ; *Oxf.* 129, 130, 132.
Denys, *Hamp.* 50 ; *Northamp.* 112.
De Odingsells, *Leic.* 76.
De Pearsall, 237.
De Plessetis, *Wilts*, 182.
De Poictou, *Lanc.* 71, 74.
De Prayers, 231.
De Quiney, *Leic.* 76.
De Quincey, *Staff.* 142.
Derby, *Derby*, 27 ; *Dorset*, 33 ; *Herts*,
    54, 56 ; *Leic.* 80 ; *Northamp.* 112 ;
    Sussex, 165 ; *Isle of Man*, 267.
De Rede, *Suff.* 152.

Derham, *Essex*, 48.
De Ridlesworth, *Norf.* 107.
De Ridware, *Leic.* 76.
De Rillestone, *York*, 200.
Dering, *Hamp.* 50, 266 ; *Herts*,
    56,234; *Kent*,60; *Sussex*,165,236.
De Rinzy, *Wexford*, 234.
De Risby, *Suff.* 152.
De Roches, *Hamp.* 50.
De Rohaud, *Leic.* 80.
De Roos, *Notts.* 112.
De Ros, *Northamp.* 111.
De Rosier, *Kent*, 60.
Derwentwater, *Cumb.* 22; *Essex*, 48.
De Sancto Philiberto, *Berks*, 8.
De Saxham, *Suff.* 152.
De Sculcotes, *York*, 211.
De Segrave, *Kent*, 66.
De Shapwick, *Devon*, 30.
De Shepey, *Leic.* 76.
Desmond, *Devon*, 29.
De Solariis, *Breck.* 227.
De Sopesfeld, *Suff.* 152.
Despenser, *Northamp.* 112 ; *York*,
    213 ; *Rutland*, 136.
De Staunton, *Leic.* 76.
De Stirap, *Notts.* 125.
De Temple, *Leic.* 76.
De Teissier, *Surrey*, 234.
Dethick, *Derby*, 27 ; *Durham*, 34,
    36, 38 ; *Norf.* 107 ; *Wales*, 229 ;
    232.
De Tonbridge, *Surrey*, 156.
De Tocka, *Staff.* 143.
De Trafford, 236.
De Turre, *Linc.* 86.
De Tynten, *Devon*, 30.
De Upton, *Shrop.* 137.
De Valoines, *Norf.* 109.
De Valle, *Warw.* 172.
De Valmer, 237.
Devenish, *Sussex*, 163, 168 ; *Ros-
    common*, 234.
De Vere, *London*, 95.
Devereux, *Bucks*, 10 ; *Herts*, 54 ;
    Leic. 80 ; *Northamp.* 112 ; *Wales*,
    229 ; 244.
De Vesci, 237.
De Veteriponte, *Northumb.* 119.
De Visme, *Devon and Glam.* 234.
De Vivonia, *Dorset*, 33.
Devon, *Bucks*, 10 ; *Northamp.* 112 ;
    Surrey, 156.

Devonshire, *Derby*, 27.
De Wake, *York*, 215.
De Walden, *Bucks*, 13.
De Walshall, *Leic.* 76.
De Walshaon, *Suffolk*, 152.
De Warmwell, *Dorset*, 33.
De Warren, *York*, 210, 213.
Dewe, *Berks.* 7.
Dewes, 239.
De Wellesburgh, *Leic.* 70.
De Welton, *Northamp.* 111.
Dewhurst, *Herts*, 56.
De Wichard, *Leic.* 70.
Dewick, *York*, 224.
De Wililey, *Shrop.* 137.
De Windsore, *Surrey*, 156.
De Winton, *Glam.* 234; *Radnor*, 234; *Brecon.* 234; *Glou.* 234; 236.
De Wiston, *Sussex*, 169.
De Worting, *Hamp.* 50.
Deyer, *Hunts*, 57.
Deyncourt, *Bucks*, 10; *Linc.* 234; 236.
Dicey, *Leic.* 234.
Dick, *Essex*, 234; 236.
Dickens, *Worc.* 195.
Dickenson, *Lanc.* 270.
Dicker, *Sussex*, 165.
Dickin, *Shrop.* 234.
Dickins, *Sussex*, 165, 234; *Staff.* 143.
Dickinson, *Berks*, 7, 234; *Herts.* 56, 234; *Northamp.* 112; *York*, 205; *Somerset*, 139, 234; *Notts.* 123.
Dickonson, *Hamp.* 50.
Dickson, *Wicklow*, 234; *Limerick*, 234; *Leitrim*, 234.
Dig, *Kent*, 60.
Digby, *Bucks*, 10, 13; *Dorset*, 33, 234; *Leic.* 80; *Warw.* 172; *Kildare*, 234; *Rutl.* 135, 136; *Staff.* 146.
Digges, *Surrey*, 162.
Diggles, *Lanc.* 75.
Diggs, *Wilts*, 185.
Dilke, *Warw.* 176, 177, 234; 249; 253.
Dillington, *Hamp.* 50, 266; *Leic.* 80.
Dillon, *Devon*, 29; *Northamp.* 112.
Dillwyn-Llewelyn, *Glam.* 234.
Dimsdale, *Herts.* 54, 56, 234, 236.
Dine, *Kent*, 60.

Dineley, *Worc.* 195.
Dingley, *Hamp.* 50, 266; *Kent*, 60.
Dinham, *Devon*, 29.
Dinsdale, *Durham*, 234.
Diot, *Staff.* 146.
Dirdo, *Wilts*, 185.
Dirom, *Dumfries*, 234.
Disney, *Dorset*, 33; *Essex*, 48, 234. *Ireland*, 234; 236.
Dixie, *Leic.* 80.
Dixon, *London*, 96; *Durham*, 36. 234; *Kent*, 60; *Leic.* 80; *York*, 204, 218, 225, 234; *Northumb.* 234; *Chesh.* 234; *Cumb.* 234; *Linc.* 234, 237.
Dixwell, *Kent*, 60.
Dobbin, *Armagh*, 234.
Dobbs, *Antrim*, 234.
Dobell, *Sussex*, 165.
Dobree, *Kent*, 60.
Dockwra, *Cumb.* 16; *Herts*, 53, 54.
Dod, *Chesh.* 17, 234; *Shrop.* 234.
Dodding, *Lanc.* 70.
Doddington, *Somerset*, 140.
Dodington, 233.
Dodson, *Sussex*, 234.
Dodsworth, *Durham*, 36, 38; *York*, 224; 236.
Dodwell, *Sligo*, 234.
Doherty, 234.
Doily, *Bucks*, 10.
D'Oilly, *Northamp.* 112.
Dokenvelt, *Berks*, 7.
Dolling, *Dorset*, 33; *Down*, 234.
Dolman, *York*, 213, 224, 234; 236.
Dolphanby, *Durham*, 38.
Dolphin, *Galway*, 234.
Dolshills, *Surrey*, 156.
Dom, *Kent*, 60.
Domville, *Chesh.* 17, 234; 237.
Donaldson, *Durham*, 42.
Done, *Ches.* 17.
Donegal, *Sussex*, 165; 236.
Donelan, *Galway*, 234.
Donham, *Notts.* 126.
Doning, *Sussex*, 163.
Doninge, *Sussex*, 168.
Donkin, *Oxf.* 163.
Donne, *Devon*, 29; *Carm.* 220.
Donnithorne, *Midd.* 234.
Donovan, *Wexford*, 234; *Sussex*, 234.
Donynge, *Sussex*, 165.

2 s

Donyngton, *York*, 226.
Doon, *Kent*, 60.
Dorchester, *Dorset*, 33.
Doresleur or Doroslaüs, 252.
Dormer, *Bucks*, 10; *Herts*, 54, 56;
    Northamp. 112; *Oxf.* 234; 235;
    236.
Dorrien, *Herts*, 234.
Dorril, *Surrey*, 156, 158.
Dottin, *Hamp.* 50, 234.
Doubleday, *Durham*, 38.
Douce, *Kent*, 60, 234; *Sussex*, 165.
Dougal, *Nairn*, 234.
Dougall, *Fife*, 234.
Doughty, *Hamp.* 50; *Suffolk*, 234;
    Lincoln, 234.
Douglas-Gresley, *Worc.* 234.
Douglas-Hamilton, *Rutland*, 136.
Douglass, *Down*, 234.
Douglas, *Antrim*, 234; *A,magh*,
    234; *Flint*, 234; 236.
Doune, *Carm.* 230.
Dove, *Wilts*, 192.
Dovre, *Durham*, 38.
Dowdall, *Ireland*, 234.
Dowdeswell, *Worc.* 234.
Dowe, 232.
Dowel, *Kent*, 60.
Downe, *Northamp.* 112; *Surrey*,
    156; *Norfolk*, 278.
Downes, *Chesh.* 17; *Durham*, 36.
Downing, *Norf.* 278.
Downshire, *Herts*, 54; 236.
Dowriche, *Devon*, 31.
Dowrish, *Devon*, 29.
Dowse, *Hamp.* 50, 266.
Dowthwaite, *Durham*, 38.
D'Oyley, *Northamp.* 112; *Bucks*, 10.
D'Oyley, 233.
Doyley, *Oxf.* 128, 129, 130, 131,
    132.
Doyne, *Wexford*, 234.
Drake, *Bucks*, 10, 234; *Chesh.*
    17; *Devon*, 29, 234; *Herts*, 54,
    56; *Kent*, 60; *York*, 224; *Meath*,
    234; *Wexford*, 234; *Surrey*, 156,
    162; *Norfolk*, 278.
Dransfeld, *York*, 226.
Draper, *Durham*, 38, 41; *Kent*, 60;
    Leic. 80; *London*, 91; 232;
    Notts. 122; *Derby*, 259.
Drax, *Dorset*, 234; *London*, 96,
    100; *York*, 213.

Dray, *Kent*, 60.
Draycott, *Staff.* 142; *Derby*, 259.
Drayton, *Bucks*, 10; *Northamp.*
    111; 231.
Drew, *Devon*, 29, 31; *Hamp.* 50,
    266; *Wilts*, 185; 233; *Limerick*,
    234; *Cork*, 234, 239; 236.
Drewe, *Devon*, 234.
Driffield, *York*, 224.
Dring, *Cork*, 234.
Drinkwater, *Lanc.* 234; *Shrop.* 234.
Drogheda, 236.
Drought, *King's Co.*, 234.
Drummond, *Perth*, 234; *Glouc.*
    234; *Hants.* 234; *Midd.* 234;
    Surrey, 234; *York*, 213.
Drurey, *Camb.* 16.
Drury, *Essex*, 48; *Norf.* 107;
    Northamp. 112; *Sussex*, 165;
    Devon, 234; *Suffolk*, 149, 152;
    Sussex, 163.
Dryden, *Northamp.* 111, 112.
Duberly, *Hunts*, 234.
Dublin, *Bucks*, 10.
Du Bois, *Norfolk*, 107.
Du Boulay, *Wilts*, 234.
Du Buisson, *Carm.* 234.
Du Cane, *Essex*, 48, 234.
Duck, *Devon*, 31; *Durham*, 38;
    Northamp. 112; *Norfolk*, 278.
Duckenfield, *Chesh.* 17.
Ducket, *Westm.* 179.
Duckett, *Wilts*, 185; *Carlow*, 234;
    236; 237.
Duckworth, *Lanc.* 234; *Roscommon*,
    234; *Surrey*, 156.
Ducy, *Staff.* 146.
Dudley, *Berks*, 7; *Durham*, 36, 38;
    Leic. 80; *Northamp.* 111, 112.
Dudlow, *Kent*, 60.
Duff, *Aberdeen*, 234; *I. of Wight*,
    234; *Moray*, 234.
Duffield, *Bucks*, 9, 11; 246.
Dugdale, *Warw.* 172, 179, 234;
    236.
Duke, *Devon*, 29; *Wilts*, 182, 185,
    234; 232; *Suffolk*, 153; *Surrey*,
    162.
Dukenfield, *Berks*, 7.
Dukenfield, *Berks*, 75.
Dunbar, 237.
Duncan, *Perth*, 234.
Duncannon, *Surrey*, 158.

Duncomb, *Surrey*, 156.
Duncombe, *Bucks*, 10, 11 ; 234 ; *Herts*, 54 ; *Leic.* 80 ; *Wilts*, 182 ; *York*, 234 ; *Surrey*, 158.
Duncumb, *Leic.* 80.
Dundas, *Berks*, 7, 234 ; *York*, 220 ; *Linlithgow*, 234 ; *Mid Lothian*, 234 ; *Stirling*, 234 ; *Perth*, 234 ; 234.
Dune, *Wilts*, 182.
Dunlop, *Dumbarton*, 234 ; *Kirkcudbright*, 234 ; *Lanark*, 234 ; *Louth*, 234 ; *Ayr*, 234.
Dunmoll, *Sussex*, 165.
Dunne, *Derby*, 27 ; *Queen's Co.* 234.
Dunraven, 236.
Dunscombe, *Cork*, 234.
Dunstanville, *Surrey*, 156.
Dunster, *Herts*, 54.
Duport, *Leic.* 80.
Duppa, *Kent*, 234.
Du Pre, *Bucks*, 234.
Du Quesne, *Essex*, 48.
Durant, *Devon*, 234 ; *Hamp.* 50 ; *Oxf.* 131 ; *Rutl.* 135.
Duranthorp, *Leic.* 80.
Duras, *Northamp.* 112.
Durham, *Fife*, 234.
Durward, *Essex*, 47.
Durwassell, *Warw.* 172.
Dury, *Derby*, 234.
Duston, *Northamp.* 112.
Dutton, *Chesh.* 17, 234 ; 237.
Dwnn, *Wales*, 229.
Dycer, *Lond.* 96, 100.
Dyer, *Devon*, 31 ; *Pemb.* 230 ; *Somerset*, 139, 140 ; 241.
Dyke, *Sussex*, 165 ; *Surrey*, 158.
Dykes, *Cumb.* 234 ; 237 ; 246.
Dymock, *Wales*, 229 ; *Flint*, 234.
Dymoke, *Linc.* 85, 234.
Dyne, *Kent*, 60 ; 234 ; *Sussex*, 165.
Dyneley, *York*, 204, 205.
Dynham, *Devon*, 31 ; *Bucks*, 10 ; *Oxf.* 129.
Dyott, *Staff.* 142, 143, 234.
Dyve, *Chesh.* 17 ; *Northamp.* 112.

Eagar, *Kerry*, 234 ; 250.
Eagles, *Bucks*, 11.
Earle, *Lanc.* 69.
Earlsman, *Hants.* 50.
Earth, *Wilts.* 185.

East, *Berks*, 7 ; 236 ; 239.
Eaton, *Chesh.* 17 ; *Essex*, 48 ; *York*, 224 ; *Camb.* 234.
Eastwood, *Louth*, 234.
Eboral, *Warw.* 177.
Eccles, *Essex*, 48 ; *Wicklow*, 234 ; *Tyrone*, 234.
Eccleston, *Sussex*, 168.
Echingham, *Northamp.* 112.
Echlin, *Down*, 234 ; *Tyrone*, 234 ;
Eckley, *Hereford*, 234.
Eddy, 236.
Eden, *Durham*, 34, 37, 40, 41 ; *Suffolk*, 155.
Edgar, *Suffolk*, 234.
Edgbury, *Kent*, 60.
Edgcombe, *Devon*, 29.
Edgcumbe, *Devon*, 234.
Edge, *Notts*, 234 ; *Queen's Co.* 234 ; *Staff.* 146.
Edgell, *Somerset*, 234.
Edgeworth, *Longford*, 234.
Edingham, *Kent*, 60.
Edmands, *Surrey*, 234.
Edmed, *Kent*, 60.
Edmondes, *Northamp.* 112.
Edmonds, *Hamp.* 50, 266 ; *Devon*, 29 ; *Sussex*, 165.
Edmondson, *York*, 219.
Edmundes, *Sussex*, 163.
Edmunds, *York*, 213, 224.
Edolphe, *Kent*, 60.
Edward, *Wales*, 229.
Edward Morgan, *Wales*, 229.
Edwardes, *Wales*, 229 ; *Carm.* 234 ; *Glam.* 234 ; *Pemb.* 234.
Edwards, *Camb.* 16 ; *Derby*, 27 ; *Devon*, 31 ; *Hunts*, 57 ; *Leic.* 80 ; *Glam.* 228, 234 ; *Wales*, 229 ; *Carm.* 230 ; *Pemb.* 230 ; 232 ; *Sussex*, 165 ; *Beds.* 234 ; *York*, 234 ; *Shrop.* 234 ; *Wicklow*, 234 ; *Carn.* 234 ; *Glouc.* 234 ; 234 ; *Rutl.* 136 ; 237 ; 245.
Edwin, *Surrey*, 156.
Effingham, *Hamp.* 50 ; *Surrey*, 156.
Egerley, *Oxf.* 128, 130.
Egerton, *Chesh.* 17, 234 ; *Herts*, 54 ; *Northamp.* 111, 112 ; *Lanc.* 71, 268 ; *York*, 224 ; 236 ; *Bucks*, 255.
Egerton-Warburton, 234.
Eggerdon, *Dors.* 33

Egleston, *Durham*, 38.
Eglinton, 236.
Einion, *Carm*. 230.
Ekins, *Dors*. 33 ; *Northamp*. 111, 112 ; *Northumb*. 119.
Eland, *Lanc*. 71 ; *York*, 204, 226
Elcocke, *Chesh*. 17.
Eld, *Staff*. 234, 146 ; 236.
Eldred, *Suffolk*, 152.
Elers, *incorrectly printed* Elders, 236 ; *Midd*. 234.
Elfred, *Sussex*, 165.
Elgar, *Essex*, 48.
Eliot, *Hamp*. 50; *Devon*, 31 ; *Wales*, 229 ; *Surrey*, 156, 234 ; *Durham*, 234.
Eliott, *Surrey*, 158.
Elizabeth, Queen, *Wales*, 229.
Elkington, *Leic*. 80.
Ellacot, *Devon*, 29.
Ellacott, *Devon*, 31.
Ellercar, *York*, 226.
Ellerker, *York*, 215, 217, 224, 283.
Ellerton, 237.
Elliot, *Devon*, 234 ; *Berks*, 234 ; *Sussex*, 163.
Elliott, *Wilts*, 182, 192 ; *Pemb*. 230.
Ellis, *Herts*, 56, 234 ; *Kent*, 60 ; *Sussex*, 165 ; *York*, 219, 224 ; *Carn*. 234 ; 233.
Ellis-Jervoise, 234.
Ellison, *Durham*, 38, 234; *Linc*. 234 ; *York*, 213 ; *Northumb*. 119.
Elmeden, *Durham*, 38.
Elmhirst, *York*, 224, 234; *Linc*. 234.
Elmhurst, *York*, 213.
Elmerugge, 232.
Elmes, *Bucks*, 10 ; *Northamp*. 111.
Elphick, *Sussex*, 169.
Elsley, *Kent*, 60.
Elson, *Sussex*, 163, 165.
Elstob, *Durham*, 34, 36, 38.
Elstobbe, *Durham*, 40.
Elryngton, *Kent*, 64.
Elton, *Chesh*. 17.
Elvin, *Norfolk*, 234.
Elwes, *Herts*, 54 ; *Northamp*. 234, 250 ; *Suffolk*, 234 ; 253.
Elwill, *Surrey*, 156.
Elwin, *Kent*, 60.
Elwis, *Herts*, 53.
Elwon, *York*, 234.

Elwood, *Sussex*, 234 ; *Mayo*, 234.
Elwyn, *Kent*, 60.
Emeris, *Linc*. 234 ; 245.
Emerson, *Durham*, 43 ; *Leic*. 234.
Emery, *Somerset*, 234 ; *Derby*, 259.
Emildon, *Durham*, 38.
Emily, *Surrey*, 156, 158.
Emmot, *Lanc*. 60.
Empson, *York*, 224; *Northamp*. 112.
Emson, *Northamp*. 112.
Emyley, *Northamp*. 112.
Endesore, *Staff*. 142.
Enery, *Cavan*, 234 ; 239.
Engaine, *Herts*, 54; *Northamp*. 111, 112.
Engham, *Kent*, 60.
England, *Norfolk*, 108 ; *Northamp*. 112.
Engleys, *Wilts*, 182.
English, *Wilts*, 182, 185.
Ennis, *Westmeath*, 234.
Ensign, *Norfolk*, 278.
Ensor, *Norfolk*, 234 ; 235 ; 241.
Entwhistle, *Lanc*. 234.
Entwisle, *Lanc*. 71.
Enyon, *Northamp*. 112.
Enys, *Corn*. 234.
Epplyngden, *Durham*, 38.
Erdington, *Leic*. 76, 80.
Erdinton, *Warw*. 172.
Ergadia, *Isle of Man*, 266.
Erington, *Wilts*, 185.
Erle, *Dors*. 33 ; *Hants*, 234 ; 239.
Erleston, *Hamp*. 266.
Ermitage, *Chesh*. 17.
Erneley, *Sussex*, 168.
Ernely, *Wilts*, 185.
Ernley, *Sussex*, 163, 165.
Errington, *Durham*, 38 ; *Northumb*. 119, 234 ; *Essex*, 234.
Errol, 237.
Esdaile, *Somerset*, 234.
Espec, *Leic*. 80 ; *Rutl*. 136.
Espinesse, *Kent*, 60.
Esse, *Devon*, 29 ; *Somerset*, 140.
Esseby, *Northamp*. 112 ; *Leic*. 76.
Essex, *Bucks*, 10 ; *Herts*, 56 ; *Lanc*. 71 ; *Leic*. 76 ; *Northamp*. 112 ; *Wilts*, 191, 194 ; 236.
Estcourt, *Glouc*. 234, 264.
Estday, *Kent*, 60.
Estleigh, *Essex*, 48.
Estley, *Wilts*, 182.

Eston, *Devon*, 29; *Sussex*, 169.
Estsax, *Linc.* 87.
Esturmy, *Wilts*, 182.
Estwick, *Leic.* 80.
Estwicke, *Hamp.* 50.
Ethelston, *Chesh.* 234.
Eton, *Warw.* 172; *Wales*, 229.
Etterick, *Hamp.* 50.
Ettericke, *Dorset*, 33.
Ettrick, *Durham*, 234; 236.
Ettricke, *Durham*, 38.
Elton, *Notts.* 123.
Eu, *Sussex*, 169.
Eure, *Durham*, 34; *York*, 201.
Eureaux, *Dorset*, 33.
Eustace, *Norfolk*, 109; *Kildare*, 234; *Carlow*, 234.
Evan, *Card.* 230.
Evan Thomas, *Wales*, 229.
Evan ap Owen, *Wales*, 229.
Evans, *Derby*, 27, 234; *Card.* 230; *Glam.* 228; *Wales,-*229; *Hereford*, 234; *Norfolk*, 234; *Dublin*, 234; *Limerick*, 234; *Kildare*, 234; *Westmeath*, 234; *Tyrone*, 234; *Cork*, 234; 234; 237; 239; 242, 246.
Evelegh, *Devon*, 29.
Evelyn, *Sussex*, 165; *Wilts*, 182; *Surrey*, 156, 158, 159, 234.
Everard, *Berks*, 3; *Leic.* 80; *Norfolk*, 234, 250, 278; *Meath*, 234.
Evering, *Kent*, 60.
Everingham, *York*, 205, 220, 226; *Notts.* 122, 123.
Eversfield, *Sussex*, 165, 234.
Every, *Somerset*, 140; *Derby*, 258, 259.
Evington, *London*, 96.
Evre, *York*, 205.
Ewbank, *Linc.* 234.
Ewbanke, *Durham*, 36, 38.
Ewens, *Somerset*, 140.
Ewer, *Herts*, 54.
Ewing, *Dumbarton*, 234.
Ewre, *Oxford*, 131.
Ewyas, *Wilts*, 182.
Eyleston, *of Eyleston*, omitted 122, 2 ed. i. 339.
Eyr, *Notts.* 122; 236.
Eyre, *Bucks*, 10; *Cornwall*, 21; *Essex*, 48; *Leic.* 80, 234; *London*, 96; *Northamp.* 112; *Wilts*, 182;

185, 234; *York*, 213, 224; *Berks*, 234; *Notts.* 122, 123, 234; *Kilkenny*, 234; *Galway*, 234; 239; *Derby*, 259.
Eyres, *Wilts*, 182.
Eyrick, *Leic.* 80.
Eyston, *Berks*, 3, 7, 234; 237.
Eyton, *Leic.* 80; *Northamp.* 112; *Wales*, 229; *Salop*, 234; *Flint*, 234.
Eytyn, *Wales*, 229.

Faber, *Somerset*, 140.
Fagan, *Cork*, 234.
Fagg, *Sussex*, 163, 165.
Fairclough, *Herts*, 53.
Fairfax, *York*, 197, 205, 221, 224, 226, 234.
Fairholme, *Berwick*, 234.
Fairlie, *Ayr*, 234.
Falconer, *Leic.* 80; 234; 237.
Falkiner, *Tipperary*, 234.
Falkland, *York*, 220; 236.
Fallon, *Roscommon*, 234.
Falmouth, 236.
Falwesle, *Northamp.* 112.
Fane, *Dorset*, 33; *Hamp.* 50; *Sussex*, 165; *York*, 224; *Oxford*, 234; *Rutland*, 136.
Fanshawe, *Herts*, 54; *Essex*, 234; *Surrey*, 156.
Fardell, *Linc.* 234.
Farendon, *Sussex*, 165.
Farewell, *Somerset*, 140.
Farindon, *Surrey*, 156.
Farington, *Lanc.* 69, 70; *Sussex*, 165, 253.
Farmar, *Wexford*, 234.
Farmbrough, *Bucks*, 234.
Farmer, *Leic.* 80; *London*, 96; *Warw.* 177; *Surrey*, 234; 245.
Farmour, *Leic.* 80.
Farnall, *Dorset and Kent*, 234; 245.
Farnell, 236.
Farnham, *Leic.* 76, 80, 234; 236; 237.
Farquhar, *Ayr*, 234.
Farquharson, *Dorset*, 33; *Aberdeen*, 234; *Forfar*, 234.
Farr, *Suffolk*, 153.
Farrand, *York*, 200.
Farrant, *Surrey*, 162.
Farrell, *Meath*, 234; 234.
Farren, *Leic.* 80.

Farrent, *Leic.* 80.
Farrer, *Durham*, 38 ; *York*, 202, 205, 213, 234 ; 237 ; *Bucks*, 234.
Farringdon, *Devon*, 29.
Farrington, *Sussex*, 163.
Farside, *York*, 224.
Farsyde, *York*, 234.
Fartho, *Northamp.* 111.
Farynton, *Lanc.* 71.
Fashin, *Hamp.* 50, 266.
Fasset, *Surrey*, 158.
Fastolft, *Suffolk*, 153.
Fauconberg, *Northamp.* 112 ; *York*, 201.
Fauconer, *Sussex*, 163.
Faulconberg, *York*, 217.
Faulconer, *Leic.* 76.
Faulkner, *Carlow*, 234.
Faunce, *Kent*, 234.
Faunt, *Leic.* 76, 80.
Fauntleroy, *Dors.* 33.
Faussett, *Kent*, 60, 234.
Fauxton, *Wilts*, 185.
Favel, *Northamp.* 111.
Favell, *Northamp.* 112 ; *York*, 224.
Faversham, *Northamp.* 112 ; *Wilts.* 182.
Fawcett, *Durham*, 38, 234.
Fawconer, *Bucks*, 10 ; *Wilts*, 185 ; *Hamp.* 266.
Fawkener, *Hunts.* 57 ; *Rutl.* 135.
Fawkes, *York*, 204, 205, 224, 234.
Fawknor, *Hamp.* 50.
Fawne, *Derby*, 27.
Fawsley, *Northamp.* 112.
Fayrefax, *York*, 226.
Fayrehare, *Durham*, 38.
Fazakerley, *Surrey*, 234.
Fearnley, *Northumb.* 234.
Featherstone, *Herts*, 54.
Featherstonhaugh, *Cumb.* 22 ; *Durham*, 34, 36.
Feilde, *Herts*, 54.
Feilden, *Chesh.* 17.
Feilding, *Leic.* 80 ; *Rutl.* 135 ; *York*, 224 ; 236.
Felbrigg, *Norfolk*, 107.
Fell, *Hamp.* 50 ; *York*, 206.
Fellowes, *Hamp.* 50 ; *Hunts.* 234.
Felton, *Durham*, 38 ; *Northamp.* 112.
Fenner, *Sussex*, 165.
Fenton, *York*, 205, 213, 234 ; *Cumb.* 234 ; *Notts.* 122 ; *Staff.* 145.

Fenwick, *Durham*, 38 ; 236 ; *Northumb.* 119 ; 245.
Fenwicke, *Northumb.* 120, 234.
Ferby, *Kent*, 60.
Ferguson, *Fife*, 254 ; *Aberdeen*, 234 ; *Cumb.* 234.
Fergusson, *Dumfries*, 234.
Fermanagh, *Bucks*, 10.
Fermor, *Northamp.* 111, 112 ; *Sussex*, 165.
Ferne, *Linc.* 86 ; *Wilts*, 182 ; *Staff.* 142, 146 ; 151.
Ferrand, *York*, 200, 224, 234 ; 239.
Ferrariis, *Norfolk*, 109.
Ferrars, *Leic.* 80 ; *Northamp.* 112.
Ferrers, *Bucks*, 10 ; *Derby*, 25 ; *Dorset*, 33 ; *Herts*, 54 ; *Leic.* 77 ; *Northamp.* 111 ; *Warw.* 172, 176, 177, 234 ; *Staff.* 142, 143 ; *Surrey*, 156 ; 236.
Ferrier, *Norfolk*, 108.
Ferris, *Sussex*, 163, 165 ; *Kent*, 234.
Ferrys, *Wilts*, 185.
Ferte, *Northamp.* 112.
Fetherston, *Sussex*, 165 ; *Warwick*, 176, 177, 234 ; 246.
Fetherstonhaugh, *Camb.* 23, 234 ; *Durham*, 40 ; *Worc.* 234 ; *Westmeath*, 234 ; *Northumb.* 119.
Fettiplace, *Rutland*, 136.
Fettyplace, *Berks*, 3, 5.
Fetyplace, *Berks*, 6 ; *Oxford*, 133.
Feversham, *Kent*, 60.
Fevre, *Herts*, 56.
Ffarington, *Lanc.* 234 ; *I. of Wight*, 234 ; 236.
Ffeilden, *Chesh.* 234 ; *Lanc.* 234.
Ffolliott, *Sligo*, 234.
Ffoulkes, *Denbigh*, 234.
Ffytche, *Linc.* 234.
Fferior, *Wales*, 229.
Ffolk, *Wales*, 229.
Ffylip, *Wales*, 229.
Ffylips, *Wales*, 229.
Ffylp, *Wales*, 229.
Ffylpin, *Wales*, 229.
Field, *Herts*, 56 ; *York*, 234, 218.
Fielder, *Hamp.* 266.
Fielding, *Leic.* 80 ; *Warw.* 172 ; *Northumb.* 119.
Fiennes, *Bucks*, 10 ; *Herts.* 54 ; *Leic.* 80 ; *Northamp.* 112 ; *Oxford*, 131 ; *Hamp* 266.

Fiencs, *Surrey*, 156.
Fifield, *Kent*, 60.
Fifhide, *Hamp.* 266.
Filbatch, *Pemb.* 230.
Filiol, *Dorset*, 33.
Filmer, *Herts*, 54, 56 ; *Kent*, 60.
Finch, *Herts*, 56, 234 ; *Kent*, 60 ; *London*, 96 ; *Northamp.* 112 ; *Sussex*, 165 ; *Rutland*, 234 ; *Tipperary*, 234 ; *Surrey*, 156, 162.
Fincham, *Camb.* 16 ; *Norfolk*, 107, 110 ; 249.
Findern, *Derby*, 258.
Findley, *Lanark*, 234 ; *Argyll*, 234.
Fines, *Berks*, 7, 11.
Fines, *Kent*, 60.
Fineux, *Kent*, 60.
Finucane, *Clare*, 234.
Finzel, *Somerset*, 234.
Fiott, *Bucks*, 10.
Firebrace, *Leic.* 80.
Firth, *Chesh.* 234.
Fisher, *Hamp.* 50, 266 ; *Kent*, 60 ; *Warw.* 172 ; *Wilts*, 185 ; *Hereford*, 234 ; *Salop*, 234 ; 243.
Fitch, *Essex*, 48.
Fitton, *Chesh.* 17 ; *Leic.* 80 ; *Northumb.* 119.
Fitz, *Camb.* 16 ; *Devon*, 29.
Fitz Aer, *Shrop.* 137.
Fitz Ailward, 232.
Fitz Alan, *Dorset*, 33; *Northamp.* 112. *Sussex*, 167 ; *Essex*, 48 ; *Shrop.* 137 ; *Surrey*, 156.
Fitz Aucher, *Sussex*, 163.
Fitz Charles, 235.
Fitz Duncan, *Cumb.* 23 ; *Northamp.* 112.
Fitz Ellis, *Wilts*, 182.
Fitz Flal, *Essex*, 48.
Fitz Gerald, *Essex*, 48.
Fitzgerald, *Limerick*, 234 ; *Kerry*, 234 ; *Sussex*, 234 ; *Mayo*, 234 ; *Clare*, 234 ; *Cork*, 234 ; *Waterford*, 234 ; 236 ; 237, 246.
Fitz Gerold, *Herts*, 54 ; *Northamp.* 112.
Fitz Gilbert, *Hamp.* 50.
Fitzhamon, *Wilts*, 182 ; *Surrey*, 156.
Fitzherbert, *Dorset*, 33 ; *Leic.* 76, 80 ; *London*, 93 ; *Wilts*, 182 ; 233 ; *Derby*, 234; *Stafford*, 234; *Oxford*, 131 ; *Shrop.* 137 ; *Derby.* 259 ; *Hamp.* 266.

Fitzhugh, *Hamp.* 50 ; *York*, 209 ; *Denbigh*, 234 ; *Notts.* 122.
Fitz James, *Dorset*, 33 ; 235.
Fitz John, *Northamp.* 112.
Fitz Maurice, *Bucks*, 11 ; *Kerry*, 234.
Fitz Nigel, *Bucks*, 10.
Fitz Odo, *Shrop.* 187.
Fitz Pain, *Surrey*, 156.
Fitz Paine, 232.
Fitz Piers, *Bucks*, 10 ; *Northamp.* 111 ; *Surrey*, 156.
Fitzpatrick, *Queen's Co.* 234.
Fitx Pons, *Sussex*, 165.
Fitz Randolph, *Notts.* 122.
Fitz Roy, *Northamp.* 112 ; 235.
Fitz Richer, *Norfolk*, 109.
Fitz Robert, *Shrop.* 137.
Fitz Roger, *Sussex*, 163.
Fitz Sewin, *Northamp.* 112.
Fitzsimon, 234.
Fitzwalter, *Essex*, 48 ; *Herts*, 54 ; *Northamp.* 112.
Fitz Warin, *Shrop.* 137.
Fitzwarine, *Somerset*, 138.
Fitzwilliam, *Northamp.* 111, 112 ; *York*, 213 ; *Notts.* 122.
Flamock, *Corn.* 20.
Flamvile, *Leic.* 80.
Flanagan, *Roscommon*, 234.
Flanders, *Leic.* 80.
Fleete, *Kent*, 60.
Fleetwood, *Bucks*, 10 ; *London*, 89 ; *York*, 209 ; *Lanc.* 71.
Fleming, *Bucks*, 13 ; *Hamp.* 50, 234, 266 ; *Herts*, 54 ; *Glam.* 228 ; *Carm.* 230 ; *Dumbarton*, 234; 234 ; *Lanc.* 71 ; *Shrop.* 137.
Flemying, *Bucks*, 10.
Flemyng, *Essex*, 48.
Fletcher, *Cumb.* 22, 23 ; *Kent*, 60 ; *York.* 205, 213, 224 ; *Wales*, 229 ; *Pemb.* 230 ; *King's Co.* 234 ; *Argyle*, 234 ; *Monmouth*, 234 ; *Staff.* 234 ; 234.
Fletcher-Vane, *Cumb.* 23.
Fletewood, *Staff.* 146.
Flint, *Kent*, 60.
Flinton, *York*, 217.
Flood, *Kilkenny*, 234 ; *Wexford*, 234.
Flower, *Camb.* 16; *Hamp.* 53 ; *Wilts*, 185, *Notts.* 112 ; *Rutland*, 135.
Floyer, *Devon*, 29 ; *Dorset*, 33, 234 ; *Staff*, 143, 234 ; *Somerset*, 140.

Flud, *Kent,* 60.
Fludd, *Kent,* 60.
Flyer, *Herts,* 53, 54, 56; *Staff.* 146.
Flytche, *Essex,* 48.
Foche, *Kent,* 60.
Foden, *Staff.* 146.
Fogge, *Kent,* 60, 66.
Foley, *Worc.* 195, 234; *Hunts.* 234; *Staff.* 142, 143.
Foliot, *Dorset,* 33; *Herts,* 54; *Northamp.* 111, 112; *Worc.* 195; *Notts.* 122.
Folkes, *Kent,* 60.
Folkingham, *York,* 205.
Folliott, *Chesh.* 234, 239.
Foljambe, *Derby,* 27; *York,* 213, 224, 234; *Notts.* 122, 234; *232.*
Foltherop, *York,* 226.
Folville, *Hunts,* 57; *Leic.* 80.
Fonnereau, *Suffolk,* 234.
Foot, *Cork,* 234.
Foote, *Kent,* 60, 234.
Forbes, *Hants,* 234; *Inverness,* 234; *Aberd.* 234; *Argyle,* 234; *Stirling,* 234; *Bucks,* 234; 234; 236; 246.
Forcer, *Durham,* 34, 38.
Ford, *Chesh.* 17; 234; *Devon,* 29, 31; *Sussex,* 163, 165; *Pemb.* 230; *Lanc.* 234; *Midd.* 234; 246.
Forde, *Devon,* 29; *Down,* 234.
Fordyce, *Aberdeen,* 234.
Forester, *Derby,* 27; *Herts,* 54.
Forser, *Durham,* 40.
Forster, *Berks,* 3; *Durham,* 38, 42; *Hunts,* 57; *Kent,* 60; 67; *Sussex,* 163, 165; *York,* 201, 220, 224; *Staff.* 234; *Essex,* 234; 245.
Forster-Barham, 234.
Fort, *Somerset,* 140.
Forteath, *Elgin,* 234.
Fortescue, *Devon,* 29, 234; *Herts,* 54, 56; *Leic.* 80; *Louth,* 234; *Oxf.* 133.
Fortibus, *Herts,* 54.
Fosbery, *Limerick,* 234.
Fosbrooke, *Derby,* 234.
Fossard, *York,* 210.
Foster, *Bucks,* 10; *Leic.* 80; *Sussex,* 165; *Warw.* 178; *Wilts,* 191; *Jamaica,* 234; *Surrey,* 234; *Bedf.* 234; *York,* 234; *Louth,* 234; *Rutl.* 136; *Somerset,* 140.
Fotherby, *Durham,* 41; *Kent,* 60.

Fotherley, *Herts,* 54.
Foucher, *Leic.* 80.
Foulkes, *Chesh.* 17.
Foulis, *York,* 201, 220, 224.
Foulshurst, *Northamp.* 112.
Fountain, *Devon,* 29; *Norf.* 234; *Herts,* 53.
Fountayne, *Devon,* 31; *York,* 213.
Fountayne-Wilson, 234.
Fowberge, *Hunts,* 57.
Fowel, *Devon,* 29.
Fowell, *Devon,* 234.
Fowke, *Berks,* 7; *Staff.* 146; *Glouc.* 262.
Fowle, *Kent,* 60; *Sussex,* 165.
Fowlehurst, *Northamp.* 111.
Fowler, *Kent,* 60; *Norf.* 107; *Sussex,* 165; *Staff.* 143, 234; *Meath,* 234; 234; *Staff.* 146.
Fowne, *Derby,* 27.
Fownes, *Somerset,* 139.
Fox, *Bucks,* 11; *Derby,* 27; *Dors.* 33; *Leic.* 80; *Northamp.* 112; *Wilts,* 182; *York,* 234; *Corn.* 234; *King's Co.* 234; *Longford,* 234; *Somerset,* 139.
Foxall, *Armagh,* 234.
Foxcroft, *York,* 205, 224.
Fox-Lane, *Sunderland,* 156.
Foxle, *Berks,* 8.
Foxley, *Northamp.* 112; 233; *Berks,* 8.
Foxton, *Camb.* 16.
Foxwist, *Wales,* 229.
Foyle, *Hamp.* 50.
Frampton, *Dorset,* 33, 234; *Wilts,* 182; 236.
France, *Chesh.* 234.
Franceis, *Devon,* 29; 233.
Francis, *Somerset,* 140.
Franck, *Sussex,* 165.
Francklen, *Glam.* 228.
Francklin, *Notts,* 234.
Frank, *Herts,* 54, 56; *York,* 213, 234.
Frankcheyney, *Devon,* 29.
Franke, *York,* 224.
Frankland, *Bucks,* 10; *York,* 224; *Sussex,* 163.
Franklyn, *Herts,* 54.
Franks, *Cork,* 234; *Limerick,* 234.
Fraser, *Argyle,* 234; *Inverness,* 234; *Forfar,* 234; *Ross,* 234; *Aberdeen,* 234.

Fray, *Bucks*, 13 ; *Herts*, 54.
Freake, *Somerset*, 140.
Frebody, *Sussex*, 165.
Frecheville, 232 ; *Notts.* 122; *Derby*, 259.
Frederick, *Surrey*, 156.
Freeland, *Essex*, 48 ; *Hamp.* 50 ; *Sussex*, 165, 234.
Freeman, *Northamp.* 112 ; *Sussex*, 165 ; *Hants*, 234 ; *Hereford*, 234 ; *Cork*, 234 ; *Oxf.* 234 ; *Oxf.* 134 ; *Surrey*, 156.
Freer, *Warw.* 234.
Freke, *Dorset*, 33 ; *Wilts*, 234.
Freman, *Herts*, 54.
Fremingham, 233.
French, *Derby*, 27 ; *Galway*, 234 ; *Roscommon*, 234 ; *Cork*, 234 ; *Mayo*, 234 ; 236.
Frend, *Limerick*, 234.
Freningham, 233.
Frere, *Hamp.* 50 ; *Norfolk*, 234 ; *Herts*, 234 ; *Oxf.* 128, 130.
Freston, *York*, 205.
Fretwell, *York*, 213.
Frevile, *Durham*, 38.
Frevill, *Durham*, 34.
Freville, *Herts*, 54 ; *Surrey*, 156.
Frewen, *Leic.* 80 ; *Bucks*, 234 ; *Sussex*, 234.
Frobisher, *York*, 210, 213.
Frodsham, *Chesh.* 17.
Frome, *Bucks*, 10 ; *Wilts*, 192 ; *Dors.* 234.
Fromond, *Surrey*, 156.
Fromonds, *Surrey*, 156.
Frost, *Chesh.* 234.
Frothingham, *York*, 217.
Frowick, *Herts*, 54, 53 ; *Surrey*, 156.
Fry, *Devon*, 29 ; *Dorset*, 33 ; *Somerset*, 140.
Fryer, *Camb.* 234 ; *Staff.* 234.
Fulford, *Devon*, 29, 234 ; *Dors.* 33.
Fulham, 232 ; *Surrey*, 156.
Fuller, *London*, 96 ; *Sussex*, 165, 169, 234 ; *Wilts*, 234 ; *Hamp.* 50 ; *Surrey*, 156.
Fullarton, *Arran*, 234.
Fullerton, *York*, 234 ; *Antrim*, 234.
Fulleshurst, *Chesh.* 17.
Fullwood, *Leic.* 80.
Fulthorp, *Durham*, 34.
Fulthorpe, *Durham*, 36, 38 ; *York*, 217, 224.

Fulton, *Antrim*, 234.
Fulwer, *Hamp.* 50.
Furnell, *Limerick*, 234.
Furnival, *Herts*, 54 ; *Northamp.* 112 ; *York*, 206.
Fursdon, *Devon*, 234.
Furse, *Devon*, 234.
Fursland, *Devon*, 29, 31.
Furtho, *Northamp.* 112.
Futter, *Norfolk*, 278.
Fydell, *Linc.* 234.
Fyffe, *Forfar*, 234.
Fyler, *Dorset*, 33 ; *Surrey*, 234.
Fyiip ap Howel, *Wales*, 229.
Fyncham, *Norfolk*, 110.
Fynderne, 251.
Fynes, *Sussex*, 165, 168.
Fytch, *Essex*, 48.

Gabb, *Monm.* 234, 239.
Gabbett, *Limerick*, 234.
Gadern, *Wales*, 229.
Gael, *Glouc.* 234.
Gage, *Leic.* 80 ; *Sussex*, 164, 165 ; *Londonderry*, 234 ; *Antrim*, 234 ; *Suffolk*, 151, 152.
Gaisford, *Sussex*, 234 ; *Wilts*, 182.
Gainsford, *Oxf.* 128, 130; *Surrey*, 156.
Galbraith, *Argyle*, 234; *Tyrone*, 234.
Gale, *Devon*, 29 ; *Lanc.* 70, 239 ; *York*, 205, 234.
Gally-Knight, 234.
Galley, *Somerset*, 140.
Galton, *Warw.* 234 ; *Shrop.* 234 ; *Worc.* 234 ; 236.
Galway, *York*, 213.
Galwey, *Cork*, 234.
Gamadge, *Glam.* 228.
Gamage, *Glam.* 228 ; *Wales*, 229.
Games, *Lond.* 94 ; *Glam.* 228 ; *Wales*, 229 ; *Bucks*, 227.
Gammie, *Oxf.* 234.
Gamul, *Chesh.* 17.
Gamull, *Staff.* 146.
Gandy, *Westm.* 234.
Gannon, *Kildare*, 234.
Gape, *Herts*, 54, 56.
Garde, *Cork*, 234.
Garden-Campbell, 234.
Gardiner, *Berks*, 7 ; *Bucks*, 11 ; *Hamp.* 50 ; *Herts*, 53, 54 ; *Oxf.* 234, 239 ; *Camb.* 234 ; *Mayo*, 234 ; 232 ; *Surrey*, 156.

Gardner, *Camb.* 16 ; *Sussex,* 165.
Gardyne, *Forfar,* 234.
Garfield, *Lond.* 96.
Garforth, *York,* 200.
Gargrave, *York,* 213.
Garland, *Devon,* 31 ; *Essex,* 234 ; 237 ; 246.
Garnet, *York,* 217.
Garnett, *Durham,* 36, 38 ; *Meath,* 234 ; *Lanc.* 234 ; 245.
Garneys, *Suffolk,* 153.
Garnon, *Northamp.* 111.
Garnons, *Wales,* 229; *Denbigh,* 234.
Garnier, *Hants,* 234.
Garrard, *Herts,* 54, 56, 234.
Garret, *Surrey,* 156.
Garrett, *Carlow,* 234.
Garstin, *Louth,* 234.
Garth, *Durham,* 38, 41 ; *Sussex,* 165 ; *Wilts,* 191 ; *Surrey,* 234, 156, 158.
Garthe, *Surrey,* 162.
Garton, *Sussex,* 163, 165, 168.
Gartshore, *Perth,* 234.
Garvey, *King's Co.* 234.
Garway, *Sussex,* 163.
Gascoign, *York,* 213, 226.
Gascoigne, *Durham,* 38 ; *Herts,* 56 ; *York,* 205, 224, 234 ; *Notts,* 122.
Gascoyn, *York,* 226.
Gaskell, *Oxf.* 234 ; *York,* 234.
Gason, *Sussex,* 165 ; *Tipperary,* 234.
Gastrell, *Northamp.* 112 ; *Glouc.* 262.
Gateacre, *Salop,* 234.
Gatacre, 236.
Gataker, *Suffolk,* 234.
Gatigang, *Durham,* 38.
Gates, *York.* 224.
Gatesdene, *Herts,* 54.
Gatton, *Kent,* 66.
Gatwick, *Surrey,* 156.
Gaunt, *Leic.* 80 ; *Northamp.* 112; *York,* 208 ; *Staff.* 234.
Gauntkort, *Northamp.* 111.
Gaussen, *Herts,* 234 ; *Londonderry,* 234.
Gavell, *Surrey,* 156.
Gawdy, *Herts,* 54.
Gawen, *Wilts.* 182, 185 ; *Somerset,* 140.
Gawsell, *Norfolk,* 107, 277.

Gay, *Devon,* 29 ; *Norfolk,* 234.
Gayer, *Berks.* 3.
Gaynesford, 235.
Gaynsford, *Bucks.* 13 ; *Hamp.* 50 ; *Kent,* 60 ; *Surrey,* 156, 159.
Gayton, *Northamp.* 112.
Gaywood, *Staff.* 146.
Geare, *Devon,* 29.
Geddyng, *Suffolk,* 152.
Gee, *Leic.* 80 ; *Sussex,* 165 ; *York,* 214, 215, 224 ; *Surrey,* 158.
Geere, *Devon,* 31.
Geldart, *York,* 224.
Gelderidge, *Sussex,* 165.
Gell, *York,* 206 ; *Derby,* 259.
Gennys, *Devon,* 234.
Gent, *Essex,* 48, 234 ; *Northamp.* 112.
George Owain Harri, *Wales,* 229.
Gentleman, *Kerry,* 234.
Gerberd, *Wilts,* 182.
Gerard, *Berks,* 3 ; *Bucks,* 10 ; *Chesh.* 17 ; *Dorset,* 33 ; *Essex,* 48 ; *Lancaster,* 71, 234 ; *Lanark,* 234 ; 236.
Gere, *York,* 224.
Germin, *Hunts,* 57.
Gernon, *Northamp.* 112 ; *London,* 91 ; *Meath,* 234.
Gervis, 237.
Gervais, *Camb.* 16 ; *Tyrone,* 234.
Gerveis, *Leicester,* 80.
Gervys, *Wales,* 229.
Gery, *Bedford,* 234 ; *Leicester,* 80.
Gethin, *Wilts,* 185 ; *Glam.* 228.
Ghiaues, *Northamp.* 112.
Gibbard, *Bedford,* 234.
Gibbings, *Cork,* 234.
Gibbon, *Kent,* 60 ; *Glam.* 228 ; *Wales,* 229.
Gibbons, *Glam.* 228 ; *Oxf.* 130.
Gibbs, *Devon.* 32 ; *Kent,* 60 ; *Wilts,* 182, 185 ; *Herts,* 234 ; *Somerset,* 234 ; *Cork,* 234 ; 237 ; 246.
Gibons, *Oxford,* 128.
Gibson, *Warw.* 177 ; *York,* 224 ; *Surrey and Sussex,* 234 ; *Westm.* 234 ; *Lanc.* 234 ; *Northumb.* 119.
Gibsone, *Edinburgh,* 234.
Giddy, *Sussex,* 165.
Giffard, *Bucks,* 10 ; *Devon,* 29 ; *Hamp.* 50 ; *Leic.* 77 ; *Norf.* 109 ; *Wilts,* 182, 191 ; *Staff.* 234 ; *Wexford,* 234.

Gifford, *Durham*, 36, 38 ; *Hamp.* 50 ;
  Leic. 80 ; *Northamp.* 112 ; *Wilts,*
  182, 185 ; 235 ; *Wexford,* 234 ;
  Staff. 146.
Gigger, *Dorset,* 33.
Gilbert, *Devon,* 29, 31; *Kent,* 60 ;
  Northamp. 112 ; *Sussex,* 165, 234 ;
  Wales, 229 ; *Corn.* 244 ; *Norf.*
  234 ; 236 ; *Derby,* 259.
Gilborne, *Kent,* 60.
Gilchrist, *Sutherland,* 234.
Gildart, *Kent,* 60.
Gildeford, *Durham,* 38.
Gildea, *Mayo,* 234.
Giles, *Devon,* 29, 31.
Gill, *Devon,* 234 ; *Herts,* 56 ; *York,*
  206, 224 ; 232.
Gille, *Herts,* 56.
Gillanders, *Ross,* 234.
Gillbanks, *Cumb.* 234.
Gillett, 234.
Gillon, *Linlithgow,* 234.
Gillman, *Cork,* 234.
Gilliott, *York,* 200.
Gillow, *Kent,* 60.
Gillum, *Northumb.* 234.
Gilpin, *Durham,* 34 ; *Bedford,* 234.
Gilman, *Staff.* 146.
Gipps, *Kent,* 60 ; *Suff.* 152.
Girlington, 232.
Girdler, *Wilts,* 185 ; *Staff.* 143.
Gisborne, *Derby,* 27 ; *Staff.* 234.
Gisnes, *Northamp.* 112.
Glanville, *Devon,* 31 ; *Cornw.* 234.
Glapthorne, *Cumb.* 16.
Glascott, *Wexford,* 234.
Gladstone, 237.
Glasgow, *Cork,* 234 ; *Ayr,* 234.
Glasier, *Chesh.* 17.
Gledstanes, *Tyrone,* 234.
Glegg, *Chesh.* 17, 234.
Glendonwyn, *Kirkcudbright,* 234.
Glisson, *Somerset,* 140.
Glothian, *Herts,* 56.
Glover, *Leic.* 80 ; *Cork,* 234 ; *Sur-*
  rey, 156, 158 ; 246.
Glydd, *Surrey,* 156 ; *Kent,* 60.
Glyn, *Dorset,* 33 ; *Wales,* 229.
Glyn Acron, *Wales,* 229.
Glynn, *Hamp.* 50, 234 ; *Somerset,*
  140 ; *Surrey,* 156.
Goade, *Bucks,* 13.
Gobion, *Herts,* 54 ; *Leic.* 80.

Goble, *Sussex,* 163.
Gobyon, *Northumb.* 119.
Goch, *Sussex,* 165 ; *Glam.* 228 ;
  Wales, 229.
Godard, *Wales,* 229.
Goddard, *Hamp.* 50 ; *Leic.* 80 ;
  Wilts, 234 ; *Warw.* 240.
Goderyche, *Glouc.* 262.
Godfrey, *Kent,* 60, 234 ; *Suffolk,* 234.
Godley, *Leitrim,* 234.
Godman, *Sussex,* 165 ; *Surrey,* 234.
Godolphin, *Bucks,* 10.
Godsal, *Flint,* 234.
Godsalve, *Norfolk,* 107.
Godwine, *Devon,* 29.
Godwyn, *Somerset,* 140.
Goff, *Hants,* 234 ; *Wexford,* 234 ;
  Roscommon, 234
Going, *Tipperary,* 234.
Gokin, *Kent,* 60.
Golafre, *Bucks,* 10 ; *Northamp.* 112.
Golborne, *Chesh.* 17.
Gold, *Wilts,* 182, 185.
Golding, *Berks,* 234.
Goldingham, *Norfolk,* 278.
Goldington, *Bucks,* 10 ; *Leic.* 80.
Goldsmith, *Hamp.* 50.
Goldston, *Wilts,* 182, 185.
Goldthorpe, *York,* 213.
Goldwill, *Norfolk,* 107.
Gollop, *Dorset,* 33, 234.
Gomeldon, *London,* 96 ; *Wilts,* 182.
Gonville, *Norfolk,* 107; *Suffolk,* 153.
Gooch, *Suffolk,* 153.
Goodall, *Leic.* 80 ; *Bucks,* 234.
Goodchild, *Durham,* 38.
Goodday, *Essex,* 48 ; *Suffolk,* 152.
Goodden, *Dorset,* 33, 234.
Goodford, *Somerset,* 234.
Goodhurst, *Kent,* 60.
Goodhart, *Kent,* 234.
Goodlad, *Hamp.* 50.
Goodlake, *Berks,* 234.
Goodman, *Leic.* 80 ; *Wales,* 229.
Goodrick, *Camb.* 16 ; *York,* 224.
Goodricke-Holyoake, *Staff.* 234.
Goodridge, *Devon,* 31.
Goodwin, *Bucks,* 9, 11 ; *Sussex,*
  165 ; *York,* 213, 224 ; *Derby,* 234.
Goodwyn, *Bucks,* 10 ; *Camb.* 16 ;
  Hamp. 50 ; *Herts,* 56.
Goodyer, *Herts,* 56.
Goold, *Limerick,* 234.

Gordon, *Aberdeen*, 234; 246; *Wigton*, 234; *Banff*, 234; *Down*, 234; *Kirkcudbright*, 234; *Hereford*, 234; 237.

Gore, *Herts*, 54; *Kent*, 58; *Leic.* 80; *Northamp.* 112; *Wilts*, 182, 185, 188, 194; *York*, 221; *Clare*, 234; *Somerset*, 234; *Shrop.* 234; *Leitrim*, 234; 236; *Surrey*, 156.

Goreinge, *Sussex*, 168.

Gorge, *London*, 96; *Wilts*, 185; *Somerset*, 140.

Gorges, *Bucks*, 11; *Dorset*, 23; *Hamp.* 50; *Wilts*, 182.

Gorham, 232; 245.

Goring, *Sussex*, 163, 165, 234.

Gorram, *Shrop.* 137.

Gosling, *Surrey*, 234.

Gosselin, *Herts*, 56, 234.

Gosset, *Bucks*, 13; *Kent*, 234.

Gossip, *York*, 234.

Gostelow, *Northamp.* 112.

Goswick, *Durham*, 42.

Gott, *Herts*, 56; *Sussex*, 165.

Gottes, *Camb.* 16.

Gough, *Essex*, 48; *Herts*, 56; *Warw.* 172; *Staff.* 143, 234; *Somerset*, 140.

Goulburn, *Surrey*, 234.

Gould, *Bucks.* 13; *Devon*, 31; 234; *Dorset*, 33; *Herts*, 54; *Glam.* 234; *Somerset*, 139.

Goulding, *Kent*, 60.

Gouldsmith, *Kent*, 60.

Gouldwell, *Camb.* 16.

Goulston, *Herts*, 54, 56.

Gounter, *Sussex*, 163, 168.

Gourlay, *Fife*, 234.

Gournarde, 232.

Gournay, *Somerset*, 140.

Goushill, *Notts*, 122.

Gove, *Devon*, 29.

Gow, *Kent*, 234.

Gower, *Durham*, 38; *Northamp.* 112; *York*, 201, 208, 217, 220; *Berks*, 234; *Surrey*, 234.

Gowre, *York*, 226.

Gozelin, *Northamp.* 112.

Grace, *Hunts*, 57; *Roscommon*, 234; *Queen's Co.* 234; *Sussex*, 234.

Gradwell, *Meath*, 234.

Græme, *Perth*, 234; 236.

Grafton, *Chesh.* 17; *Essex*, 48; *Northamp.* 112; *Wales*, 229.

Graham, *Cumb.* 22, 23, 234; *York*, 209, 224; *Perth*, 234; *Forfar*, 234; *Stirling*, 234; *Renfrew*, 234; *Dumfries*, 234; *Fermanagh*, 234; 236; 237.

Graham-Clarke, *Glouc.* 234.

Granado, *Herts*, 56.

Grand, *Essex*, 48.

Grandison, *Kent*, 66.

Grange, *Camb.* 16.

Granger, *Staff.* 245.

Grant, *Northamp.* 112; *Inverness*, 234; *Cork*, 234; *Glam.* 234.

Grant-Duff, *Banff*, 234.

Grantham, *York*, 209; *Rutl.* 234.

Granville, *Warw.* 234; 236.

Grattan, *Wicklow*, 234.

Gratton-Guinness, *Dublin*, 234.

Gratwick, *Sussex*, 163, 165.

Gratwicke, *Sussex*, 163.

Graves, *Worc.* 195; *Glouc.* 234; *Derby*, 259.

Gray, *Bucks*, 11; *Hamp.* 50; *Leic.* 80; *Sussex*, 165; *Wales*, 229; *Lanc.* 234; *Lanark*, 234; 236; 237; 245.

Graystanyes, *Durham*, 38.

Grazebrook, *Staff.* 234.

Greame, *York*, 234.

Greathed, *Dorset*, 234.

Greatrakes, 251.

Greave, *York*, 234.

Greaves, *Kent*, 60; *York*, 225, 245; *Lanc.* 234; 268; *Staff.* 234; *Warw.* 234; 236.

Greaves-Bagshawe, *Derby*, 234.

Grebbel, *Kent*, 60.

Green, *Berks*, 7; *Bucks*, 10; *Chesh.* 17; *Essex*, 48; *Leic.* 80; *Northamp.* 112; *York*, 206, 213, 217; *Lanc.* 234; *Kilkenny*, 234; *Bedf.* 234.

Greenacres, *Lanc.* 68.

Greene, *Dorset*, 33; *Herts*, 54, 56; *Leic.* 80, 234; *Northamp.* 111; *Wilts*, 182, 188; *York*, 224; *Lanc.* 234; *Westm.* 234; *Waterford*, 234; 235; 236; *Norfolk*, 278; *Northumb.* 119; *Somerset*, 140.

Greenfield, *Monm.* 234.

Greenhill, *Bucks*, 11; *Wilts*, 182.

Greenland, *Kent,* 60.
Greenly, *Hereford,* 234.
Greenway, *Glouc.* 234.
Greenwell, *Durham,* 38 ; 234.
Greenwode, *York,* 205.
Greenwood, *York,* 224, 234 ; *Oxf.* 131.
Greer, *Tyrone,* 234.
Greg, *Down,* 234 ; *Chesh.* 234.
Gregg, *Chesh.* 17 ; *Lanc.* 268.
Gregor, *Corn.* 234.
Gregorson, *Argyle,* 234.
Gregory, *Leic.* 80 ; *Linc.* 82 ; *York,* 213 ; *Warw.* 234 ; *Galway,* 234 ; 234 ; *Notts,* 122.
Gregson, *Durham,* 42, 234 ; *Derby,* 259.
Grelley, *Rutland,* 136.
Greme, *Cumb.* 22.
Grendon, *Staff.* 143.
Grene, *Tipperary,* 234 ; *Staff.* 146.
Grenfell, *Bucks,* 234.
Grentemaisnell, *Leic.* 80.
Grentemaisnil, *Herts,* 54 ; *Northamp.* 112.
Grentmesnill, *Leic.* 77.
Grenville, *Bucks,* 10, 11 ; *Devon,* 29 ; *Herts,* 56.
Greseley, *Bucks,* 10.
Gresham, *Sussex,* 165 ; *Rutland,* 136 ; *Surrey,* 156.
Greslei, *Herts,* 54.
Gresley, *Leic.* 80, 234 ; 251 ; *Staff.* 145.
Greswolde, *Warw.* 234.
Greveson, *Durham,* 87.
Grevil, *Warw.* 177.
Grevill, *Warw.* 172 ; *Northamp.* 111.
Greville, *Bucks,* 10 ; *Herts,* 54, 234.
Grey, *Chesh.* 17 ; *Derby,* 27 ; *Dors.* 33 ; *Durham,* 38, 42, 234 ; *Kent,* 58 ; *Leic.* 76, 79, 80 ; *Northamp. Sussex,* 163, 165 ; *Warw.* 172 ; *York,* 224 ; *Wales,* 229 ; *Northumb.* 119, 234 ; 241 ; *Notts.* 122 ; *Oxford,* 133 ; *Rutland,* 136 ; *Somerset,* 138 ; *Staff.* 142, 146.
Grey-Egerton, *Chesh.* 17.
Grey de Ruthyn, *Bucks,* 10.
Grey de Wilton, 231.
Greystock, 232 ; *Northumb.* 119.
Grice, *Norfolk,* 108.
Griffies, *Pemb.* 230.
Griffeth, *Oxford,* 131.

Griffin, *Chesh.* 17 ; *Leic.* 80 ; *Northamp.* 111, 112 ; *Sussex,* 165.
Griffith, *Durham,* 38 ; *Leic.* 80 ; *Warw.* 172 ; *Glam.* 228 ; *Wales,* 229, 287 ; *Carm.* 230 ; *Sligo,* 234 ; *Denbigh,* 234, 242 ; *Staff.* 143.
Griffith ab Davydd, *Wales,* 229.
Griffiths, *Wales,* 229.
Grigson, *Norfolk,* 234.
Griling, *Kent,* 60.
Grimaldi, 236.
Grimsditch, *Herts,* 56.
Grimshaw, *Lanc.* 68, 234.
Grimstead, *Wilts,* 182.
Grimsted, *Wilts,* 182.
Grimston, *Herts,* 54, 56 ; *York,* 214, 234, 236 ; *Essex,* 260 ; *Norfolk,* 278.
Groby, *Leic.* 80.
Grobham, *Wilts,* 182.
Gronow, *Glam.* 234.
Gronwy, *Wales,* 229.
Grosvenor, *Chesh.* 17 ; *Wilts,* 182 ; *Staff.* 143, 146.
Grote, *Surrey,* 234 ; *Oxford,* 234.
Grove, *Kent,* 58 ; *Wilts,* 182, 185, 234 ; *Staff.* 234.
Grubb, *Bucks,* 10.
Grubbe, *Wilts,* 185, 234.
Grufydd, *Wales,* 229.
Gruffydd, *Wales,* 229 ; 242.
Grundy, *Leic.* 234.
Grylls, *Cornw.* 234.
Grymes, 232.
Grymston, *Essex,* 48 ; *York,* 224.
Gubbins, *Limerick,* 234.
Guildford. *Northamp.* 112 ; 236 ; *Surrey,* 156.
Guilford, *Hamp.* 50.
Guinness, *Dublin,* 234, 250.
Gulafre, *Bucks,* 10.
Guldeford, *Bucks,* 11 ; 235.
Guldene, *Dorset,* 33.
Gull, *Kent,* 60.
Gully, *Corn.* 234.
Gulston, *Caermarthen,* 234.
Gumbleton, *Cork,* 234.
Gun, *Kerry,* 234.
Gundry, *Dorset,* 234.
Gunning, *Somerset,* 234.
Gunter, *Berks,* 3 ; *Hamp.* 50 ; *Sussex,* 163, 165 ; *Breck.* 227 ; *Glam.* 228 ; *Wales,* 289.
Gurdon, *Somerset,* 234 ; *Norfolk,* 234.

Gurney, *Norfolk*, 234, 239.
Guthrie, *Forfar*, 234 ; *Fife*, 234 ; 236.
Guy, *Hamp.* 50; *Sussex*, 165 ; *Warw.* 173.
Guybon, *Norfolk*, 107, 278.
Guyney, *Rutland*, 136.
Gwidigada, *Wales*, 229.
Gwin, *Glam.* 228.
Gwinionydd, *Wales*, 229.
Gwinnett, *Hereford*, 234.
Gwylim, *Wales*, 229.
Gwylt, *Suffolk*, 234.
Gwyn, *Norfolk*, 234 ; *Glam.* 228, 234 ; *Devon*, 234 ; *Breck.* 227 ; *Wales*, 229.
Gwynn, *Card.* 230 ; *Carm.* 230 ; *Wales*, 239 ; *Surrey*, 156.
Gwynne, *Cardiff*, 234 ; 236.
Gwyr y Towyn, *Wales*, 229.
Gwynne-Holford, *Carm.* 234 ; 239 ;
Gyll, *Bucks*, 10, 13, 234, 239; *Herts*, 56 ; *York*, 224 ; 232; 233 ; *Devon*, 38 ; 236.
Gynes, *Northamp.* 112.
Gyse, *Glou.* 262.

Habergham, *Lanc.* 68.
Habington, *or* Abington, *Worc.* 195.
Hacket, *Leic.* 80.
Hackett, *Surrey*, 158 ; *King's Co.* 234.
Hacker, *Dorset*, 33 ; *Notts.* 234.
Hadd, *Kent*, 60.
Haddon, *Rutland*, 136.
Hadham, *Durham*, 38.
Hadsley, *Herts*, 56.
Haffenden, *Kent*, 234.
Haggard, *Norfolk*, 234.
Hagart, *Stirling*, 234.
Hagger, *Camb.* 16.
Haggerston, *Durham*, 34, 42; *Hamp.* 50; 235.
Haggitt, *Hereford*, 234.
Hagthorp, *Durham*, 34.
Hagthorpe, *Durham*, 38, 40.
Haigh, *Linc.* 234; *Lanc.* 281.
Haire, *Fermanagh*, 234.
Hailstone, *York*, 286.
Hakewell, *Devon*, 29, 31.
Haldane, *Perth*, 245.
Hale, *Bucks*, 10, 13 ; *Herts*, 54, 56, 234 ; *York*, 220.

Hales, *Kent*, 58, 60 ; *Oxf.* 134 ; *Somerset*, 140 ; *Warw.* 178.
Halford, *Leic.* 80; *Rutland*, 135 ; *Kent*, 234.
Halhead, 236.
Haliday, *Antrim*, 234.
Halifax, *York*, 222.
Halkett, *Edinburgh*, 234.
Hall, *Camb.* 16 ; *Cheshire*, 17, 234 ; *Durham*, 36, 38, 40; *Essex*, 48 ; *Kent*, 60, 67 ; *Leic.* 80, 248 ; *Northumb.* 119 ; *Oxf.* 131 ; *Rutl.* 136; *Sussex*, 165 ; *Wilts*, 185, 191; *York*, 201, 224, 234 ; *Jamaica*, 234 ; *Monm.* 234 ; *Notts*, 234 ; *Down*, 234 ; *Galway*, 234 ; 236 ; 237.
Hallamshire, *York*, 206.
Halle, *Kent*, 60.
Hallett, *Kent*, 60.
Halliday, *Somerset*, 234.
Hallifax, *Suffolk*, 234.
Halliman, *Durham*, 36, 38.
Hallowell, *Surrey*, 158.
Halsey, *Herts*, 54, 56, 234.
Halsted, *Lanc.* 68.
Halswell, *Somerset*, 140.
Halton, *Derby*, 25 ; *York*, 200 ; 251; *Glou.* 262.
Hambrough, *Isle of Wight*, 234.
Hamerton, *York*, 200, 224, 234, 239.
Hames, *Kent*, 60 ; *Devon*, 234.
Hamilton, *Berks*, 7 ; *Bucks*, 11 ; *Essex*, 48 ; *Hamp.* 50 ; *Rutland*, 136; *Renf.* 234; *Bute*, 234; *Monaghan*, 234 ; *Lanark*, 234 ; *Wigton*, 234 ; *Ayr*, 234 ; *Dumbarton*, 234; *Carlow*, 234 ; *Tyrone*, 234 ; *Donegal*, 234 ; *Down*, 234 ; *Dublin*, 234; *Meath*, 234 ; 234 ; 237 ; 246 ; 250.
Hamlyn, *Devon*, 234 ; *Hamp.* 50.
Hammond, *Kent*, 60, 234 ; *Suffolk*, 152 ; 232 ; 233 ; *Chesh.* 234 ; 236.
Hamon, *Kent*, 60.
Hamond, *Camb.* 16 ; *Lond.* 96 ; *York*, 224, 234 ; *Surrey*, 234 ; *Norfolk*, 234.
Hampden, *Bucks*, 10, 11 ; *Herts*, 56.
Hamper, *Sussex*, 163.
Hampton, *Lond.* 96 ; *Wales*, 229 ; 232 ; *Sussex*, 164.

Hampshire, *Oxf.* 131.
Hamson, *Oxf.* 131.
Hanbury, *Hamp.* 50; *Herts,* 234;
  Essex, 234; *Monm.* 105, 106.
Hancock, *Durham,* 38; *Somerset,*
  140; *Longford,* 234.
Hancock, *Durham,* 38; *Somerset,* 140.
Hancocke, *Wilts,* 192.
Hancocks, *Worc.* 234.
Hand, *Chesh.* 17.
Handcock, *Devon,* 29.
Handlo, *Bucks,* 10.
Handley, *Notts,* 122, 124, 234;
  Linc. 234.
Handslope, *Northamp.* 112.
Handvile, *Kent,* 60.
Hanford, *Worc.* 195, 234; 236.
Hanham, *Dorset,* 33.
Hanington, *Kent,* 60.
Hankey, *Essex,* 48; *Sussex,* 234.
Hanmer, *Bucks,* 10; *Wales,* 229.
Hannay, *Fife,* 234; *Kirkcudbright,*
  234.
Hansard, *Durham,* 34, 38.
Hansby, *York,* 213.
Hanson, *York,* 224, 234.
Harbart, *Durham,* 38.
Harbin, *Somerset,* 234; 236; 237.
Harbord, *Norfolk,* 107; *Northamp.*
  112.
Harborough, *Leic.* 80.
Harbotel, *Durham,* 38.
Harbotell, *Notts,* 122; *Sussex,* 169.
Harbotle, *Sussex,* 168.
Harbottle, *Northumb.* 119.
Harbourne, *Oxf.* 131.
Harby, *Herts,* 54; *Northamp.* 112.
Harcourt, *Bucks,* 10, 13; *Berks,*
  234; *Chesh.* 17; *Herts,* 54; *Leic.*
  80; *Northamp.* 112; *Surrey,* 158;
  Wilts, 182; *Oxf.* 234.
Harden, *King's Co.* 234; *Armagh,* 234.
Harding, *Durham,* 38; *Surrey,* 156;
  Wilts, 185, 191; *Warw.* 234;
  Devon, 234; *Derby,* 259.
Hardinge, *Durham,* 40; *Derby,* 28;
  Surrey, 156.
Hardman, *Lanc.* 69.
Hardres, *Kent,* 66.
Hardreshull, *Northamp.* 112; *Warw.*
  172.
Hardware, *Chesh.* 17.
Hardwick, *Kent,* 60; *Leic.* 76; *York,*
  205.

Hardwicke, *Herts,* 54; *Derby,* 257.
Hardy, *Dorset,* 33; *Kent,* 60; *Nor-
  folk,* 234; *York,* 224.
Hare, *Herts,* 54; *Norfolk,* 107, 234;
  Berks, 234; *Denbigh,* 234.
Harebred, *York,* 205.
Harecourt, *Staff.* 146.
Harewell, *Worc.* 195; *Wilts,* 172.
Harewood, *York,* 204.
Harford, *Glouc.* 234.
Hargreaves, *Lanc.* 234.
Harington, *Leic.* 76; *Rutland,* 135;
  York, 205.
Harkshaw, *Somerset,* 140.
Harlakenden, *Essex,* 48; *Kent,* 58,
  60; (incorrectly printed Henla-
  kenden) 233.
Harland, *York,* 234.
Harle, *Northumb.* 119.
Harlestone, *Kent,* 60, 67.
Harley, *Derby,* 27; *Leic.* 80.
Harlstone, *Kent,* 60.
Harman, *Oxford,* 128, 130; *Long-
  ford,* 234.
Harold, *Herts,* 54; *Wilts,* 185.
Harper, *Derby,* 259.
Harpur, *Derby,* 27; *Leic.* 80; *Staff.*
  143; *Warw.* 172, 234; 251.
Harpyn, *Durham,* 38, 34.
Harries, *Pemb.* 230, 234; *Shrop.*
  234.
Harrington, *Cumb.* 22, 23; *Lanc.*
  68, 71; *Leic.* 80; *Surrey,* 156;
  York, 202, 209, 210, 213; *Devon,*
  234; 236.
Harringworth, *Leic.* 80.
Harris, *Devon,* 29, 234; *Hamp.* 50;
  Surrey, 162; *Wilts,* 192; *Wales,*
  229; *Corn.* 234.
Harrison, *Bucks,* 10, 234; *Durham,*
  38; *Hamp.* 50; *Herts,* 54, 56;
  Lanc. 69; *Linc.* 82, 234; *Sussex,*
  169; *York,* 205, 217, 224; *Cork,*
  234; *Westm.* 234; *Cumb.* 234;
  Derby, 234; *Down,* 234; *Essex,*
  234.
Harri ap Sion, *Wales,* 229.
Harry ab John, *Wales,* 229.
Harrys, *Devon,* 31.
Harrowby, *Herts,* 56.
Hart, *Kent,* 60; *Surrey,* 158; *Devon,*
  234; *Donegal,* 234; *Norfolk,* 278.
Harte, *Leic.* 80.
Hartcup, *Suffolk,* 234, 245.

Hartgill, *Somerset*, 139, 140.
Hartley, *Berks*, 7, 234 ; *Cumb.* 234 ; *Dublin*, 234 ; 236 ; 246.
Hartopp, *Leic.* 80, 234.
Harty, *Kent*, 60.
Harvey, *Camb.* 16 ; *Essex*, 48, *Kent*, 60 ; *Leic.* 80 ; *London*, 96 ; *Northamp.* 111, 112 ; *Surrey*, 156 ; *Wexford*, 234 ; *Bedford*, 234 ; *Renfrew*, 234 ; *Banff*, 234 ; *Berks*, 234 ; *Suffolk*, 234 ; *Staff.* 234 ; *Donegal*, 234 ; *Norfolk*, 234.
Harvy, *Somerset*, 140.
Harwedon, *Northamp.* 111.
Harwood, 234.
Harys, *Glam.* 228.
Hasele, *Warw.* 172.
Hasell, *Cumb.* 22, 23, 234.
Haselwood, *Leic.* 80 ; *Worc.* 195.
Hasler, *Sussex*, 234.
Hasling, *Kent*, 60, 67.
Haslington, *Chesh.* 17.
Hassal, *Chesh.* 17.
Hassard, *Fermanagh*, 234 ; *Waterford*, 234.
Hassard, 245.
Hassel, *Bucks*, 10, 232,
Hassell, *Bucks*, 13 ; *York*, 224,
Hast, *Norfolk*, 278.
Hastang, *Warw.* 172 ; *Worc.* 195.
Hastings, *Bucks*, 10, 11 ; *Leic.* 76, 80, 234 ; *Northamp.* 111, 112 ; *Notts.* 122 ; *Oxford*, 128, 130 ; *Shrop.* 137 ; *Warw.* 172 ; *York*, 205, 217 ; *Northumb.* 119 ; *Norfolk*, 277.
Hastlen, *Wales*, 229.
Hastynges, *York*, 226.
Hatch, *Devon*, 29 ; *Louth*, 234 ; *Surrey*, 234.
Hatcher, *Rutland*, 136.
Hatfield, *York*, 213, 217, 224, 234, 239.
Hathaway, *Warw.* 178.
Hatley, *Camb.* 16.
Hatton, *Chesh.* 17 ; *Northamp.* 111; *Wexford*, 234.
Havard, *Breck.* 227 ; *Glam.* 228 ; *Wales*, 229.
Havelland, *Dorset*, 33.
Havens, *Essex*, 48.
Havers, *Norfolk*, 107, 234.
Haversham, *Bucks*, 10.

Haviland, *Camb.* 234.
Havilland, *Guernsey*, 234.
Haughton, *Chesh.* 17.
Haule, *Kent*, 60.
Haustead, 232.
Hausted, *Northamp.* 112.
Hauton, *Northamp.* 112.
Haw, *Staff.* 146.
Hawdonbe, *York*, 226.
Haweis, *Cornw.* 20.
Hawford, *Camb.* 16.
Hawker, *Wilts*, 185 ; *Hamp.* 234, 243, 246.
Hawkesworth, *London*, 96 ; *York*, 205, 224 ; *Queen's Co.* 234.
Hawking, *Kent*, 60.
Hawkins, *Berks*, 7 ; *Surrey*, 156 ; *Sussex*, 234 ; *Monm.* 234 ; *Midd.* 234 ; *Essex*, 234.
Hawles, *Dorset*, 33.
Hawley, *Hamp.* 50 ; 234; *Northamp.* 112 ; *Sussex*, 165.
Hawtayne, *Sussex*, 165.
Hawte, *Hamp.* 50.
Hawthorne, *Berks*, 7.
Hawtrey, *Bucks*, 10, 11 ; *Oxford*, 131 ; 235.
Hawtton, *Oxford*, 128, 130.
Hawyk, *Durham*, 38.
Hay, *Sussex*, 164, 165 ; *Berwick*, 234 ; *Haddington*, 234 ; *Perth*, 234 ; *East Lothian*, 245.
Hay-Drummond, *York*, 213.
Hay-Macdougal, *Roxburgh*, 234.
Hay-Newton, *Haddington*, 234.
Haydock, *Hamp.* 50 ; *Lanc.* 68.
Haydon, *Devon*, 29.
Hayes, *Berks*, 8 ; *Leic.* 80 ; *York*, 234 ; *Oxford*, 280.
Hayley, *Sussex*, 171.
Hayman, *Somerset*, 234 ; *Cork*, 234.
Haynes, *York*, 234.
Hayrun, *Warw.* 172.
Hays, 234.
Hayter, *Dorset*, 33.
Hayton, *Bucks*, 10.
Hayward, *Kent*, 60 ; *Berks*, 7 ; *Somerset*, 140 ; *Glouc.* 234 ; 237.
Haywood, *Staff.* 234.
Head, *Tipperary*, 234.
Headlam, *Durham*, 41; *York*, 224.
Headon, *York*, 217.
Heale, *Herts*, 234.

Healey, *Linc.* 272.
Heard, *Cork,* 234.
Hearne, *Bucks,* 13.
Hearst, *Wilts,* 192.
Heath, *Durham,* 34, 36, 38 ; *Surrey,* 156 ; *Sussex,* 165.
Heathcote, *Derby,* 27 ; *Staff.* 145 ; *Hamp.* 50 ; *Leic.* 80 ; *Hunts,* 234.
Heaton, *Denbigh,* 234.
Heber, *Northamp.* 112 ; *Shrop.* 234 ; *York,* 200, 224.
Hebborne, *Durham,* 34, 38, 40 ; *Northumb.* 120.
Hebden, *York,* 234.
Heblethwayte, *York,* 224.
Heddee, *Orkney,* 234.
Hedding, 245.
Hedlam, *Durham,* 38.
Hedley, *Northumb.* 119.
Hedworth, *Durham,* 34, 38, 40, 44.
Heide, *Wales,* 229.
Heigham, *Suff.* 152, 434.
Heighington, *Durham,* 36, 38.
Helder, *Herts,* 54.
Hele, *Devon,* 29, 31 ; *Surrey,* 156.
Helgot, *Shrop.* 137.
Hellard, *York,* 224.
Hellesby, *Chesh.* 17.
Hellier, *Hamp.* 50.
Helton, *Dorset,* 33.
Helyar, *Somerset,* 234.
Helyer, 236.
Hemegrave, *Suff.* 152.
Hemphill, *Tipperary,* 234.
Hemsworth, *Norfolk,* 234 ; *Tipperary,* 234.
Heneage, *London,* 93 ; *Linc.* 234 ; 235.
Henden, *Kent,* 60.
Hendley, *Kent,* 60.
Henderson, *Fife,* 234 ; *Caithness,* 234 ; *Stirling,* 234, 237.
Henley, *Dorset,* 33 ; *Hamp.* 50 ; *Somerset,* 140, 234 ; *Oxford,* 234.
Henn, *Clare,* 234.
Henning, *Dorset,* 33.
Hennessy, *Cork,* 234.
Henry, *Chesh.* 17.
Henny VII. *Wales,* 229.
Henscott, *Devon,* 29.
Henshaw, *Chesh.* 17 ; *Sussex,* 163, 165, 234 ; *Essex,* 234 ; 239.
Hensley, *Sussex,* 168.

Henslie, *Leic.* 80.
Henville, *Dorset,* 33.
Henzey, 235.
Hepburn, *Perth,* 234 ; 236.
Hepden, *Sussex,* 165.
Hepenstal, *Longford,* 234.
Hepple, *Northumb.* 119.
Hepworth, *York,* 234.
Herbert, *Bucks,* 10 ; *Hamp.* 50 ; *Hunts,* 57 ; *Monm.* 105, 106; 234; *Northamp.* 112 ; *Sussex,* 165 ; *Wilts,* 182 ; *York,* 224 ; *Breck.* 227 ; *Glam.* 228 ; *Carm.* 230 ; *Card.* 230; *Wales,* 229 ; *Kerry,* 234 ; *Tipperary,* 234 ; 234 ; 236 ; 242 ; 247.
Hercy, *Notts,* 122, 126 ; *Oxf.* 131; *Rutland,* 126 ; *Berks,* 234.
Herdebergh, *Warw.* 172.
Herdwick, *Warw.* 172.
Herdwicke, *Leic.* 80.
Hereford, *Lanc.* 71 ; *Leic.* 80 ; *Hereford,* 234 ; 236.
Hereward, 244.
Hergest, *Wales,* 229.
Heriz, *Notts,* 122.
Herle, *Devon,* 29 ; *Leic.* 76, 80 ; *Somerset,* 140.
Herling, *Norfolk,* 107.
Hern, *London,* 100.
Herne, *Hunts,* 57 ; *Herts,* 234.
Heron, *Durham,* 34, 38, 40, 42 ; *Chesh.* 234 ; *Northumb.* 119 ; *Notts.* 124 ; 232 ; *Herts,* 54 ; *York,* 215.
Heronville, *Staff.* 142.
Herrick, *Leic.* 80, 234 ; *Cork,* 234.
Hertford, *Bucks,* 10; *Hamp.* 50; 236.
Herthull, *Warw.* 172.
Hertwell, *Northamp.* 111.
Hertlington, *York,* 200.
Hervey, *Bucks,* 10 ; *Essex,* 48 ; *Northamp.* 112 ; *Suffolk,* 152, 154 ; *Surrey,* 156 ; *Wexford,* 234.
Hervy, *Kent,* 60.
Herward, *Hamp.* 50.
Heryng, *Wilts,* 191.
Heselrig, *Leic.* 76.
Hesilrige, *Leic.* 80.
Hesketh, *Lanc.* 71 ; *Denbigh,* 234.
Hesketh-Fleetwood, *Lanc.* 234.
Heslop, *Durham,* 38.
Hester, *Oxford,* 131.

Hethe, *Suffolk*, 152 ; *Norfolk*, 278.
Hetley, *Hunts*, 57.
Heton, *Wales*, 229.
Heveningham, *Suffolk*, 153 ; *Norfolk*, 277.
Hever, *Sussex*, 165.
Hevingham, *York*, 213.
Hewar, *Norfolk*, 107, 278.
Hewett, *Hamp.* 50 ; *Herts*, 54 ; *Leic.* 80 ; *Glam.* 234.
Hewes, *Wilts*, 185.
Hewgill, *York.* 234.
Hewish, *Somerset*, 140.
Hewitt, *Herts*, 56.
Hewley, *York*, 205, 219.
Hewson, *Kerry*, 234.
Hext, *Devon*, 29 ; *Somerset*, 140 ; *Corn.* 234.
Heycock, *Leic.* 234.
Heydon, *Herts*, 54.
Heyford, *Northamp.* 112.
Heygate, *Herts*, 56 ; *Leic.* 80.
Heyland, *Antrim and Derry*, 234.
Heyraz, *Wilts*, 182.
Heyrick, *Leic.* 80.
Heysham, *Herts*, 54, 56.
Heytesbury, 236.
Heywood, *Lanc.* 71 ; *Hereford*, 234 ; *York*, 234.
Hibbert, *Chesh.* 17, 234; *Bucks*, 234; *Berks*, 234 ; *Warw.* 234.
Hibbert-Ware, *Edinburgh*, 234 ; 239.
Hibbins, *Herts*, 56.
Hick, *Northumb.* 119.
Hickes, *Durham*, 38 ; *York*, 205, 234.
Hickie, *Kerry*, 234.
Hickman, *Bucks*, 10 ; *Linc.* 83, 234.
Hicks, *Hamp.* 50 ; *London*, 94 ; *Camb.* 234.
Hickson, *Kerry*, 234.
Hide, *Herts*, 54.
Higgens, *Sussex*, 165.
Higgins, *Sussex*, 163 ; *York*, 213, 234 ; *Bedford*, 234 ; *Hereford*, 234, 239 ; *Mayo*, 234, 239.
Higginson, *Antrim*, 234.
Higham, *Essex*, 48 ; *Camb.* 16 ; *Sussex*, 165.
Hildesley, *Berks*, 3 ; *Oxford*, 128, 130.

Hildyard, *Durham*, 38, 234 ; *York*, 217, 219, 224, 234 ; *Notts.* 234 ; 236.
Hill, *Devon*, 29 ; *Hamp.* 50 ; *Herts*, 54 ; *Kent*, 60 ; *Leic.* 80 ; *Somerset*, 140 ; *Staff.* 143, 146, 234 ; *Sussex*, 165 ; *York*, 205 ; 232 ; *Shrop.* 234 ; *Cork*, 234 ; *Norfolk*, 234 ; 236.
Hillersdon, *Devon*, 29, 31.
Hilliard, *Durham*, 36.
Hills, *Essex*, 48, 234.
Hilton, *Durham*, 34, 36, 38, 39, 43, 44 ; *Kent*, 60, 234 ; *Leic.* 80 ; *Sussex*, 163, 165 ; *Northumb.* 118.
Hincks, *York*, 234.
Hinde, *Northumb.* 234 ; *Lanc.* 234 ; 236.
Hingston, *Devon*, 234 ; *Cork*, 234.
Hinson, *Lond.* 96.
Hinton, *Berks*, 3 ; *Chesh.* 17 ; *Sussex*, 163.
Hinxman, *Wilts*, 182.
Hippesley, *Bucks*, 11; *Somerset*, 140. 234 ; 236.
Hippisley, *Wilts*, 185 ; *Berks*, 234 ; *Devon*, 234 ; 234.
Hippon, *York*, 224.
Hird, *York*, 218.
Hirvryn, *Wales*, 229.
Hitch, *Oxf.* 128, 130.
Hitchcock, *Wilts*, 182, 185.
Hitching, *York*, 224.
Hoare, *Bucks*, 10 ; *Wilts*, 182.
Hobart, *Bucks*, 10 ; *Norf.* 107.
Hobbes, *Wilts*, 192 ; *Surrey*, 162.
Hobbs, *Somerset*, 140 ; *Hamp.* 50.
Hobe, *Wales*, 229.
Hobhouse, *Soms.* 139, 234.
Hoblyn, 234 ; 236.
Hobson, *Hamp.* 50 ; 253.
Hobsonn, *Sussex*, 168.
Hoby, *Bucks*, 10.
Hockenhull, *Chesh.* 17.
Hodder, *Cork*, 234.
Hodesak, *Notts*, 122.
Hodges, *Lond.* 96 ; *Leic.* 80 ; *Northamp.* 112 ; *Somerset*, 140 ; *Kent*, 234.
Hodgetts, *Worc.* 234.
Hodgson, *Durham*, 36, 38 ; *Kent*, 60 ; *Sussex*, 165 ; *York*, 205, 234; *Cumb.* 234.

Hodilow, 233.
Hodnet, *Shrop.* 137.
Hody, *Dorset*, 33 ; 232.
Hoese, *Sussex*, 163, 169.
Hog, *Linlithgow*, 234.
Hogg, *Durham*, 234 ; *Roscommon*, 234, 239.
Hoghton, *Lanc.* 68, 71 ; 236.
Holand, *Herts*, 54 ; *Northamp.* 111, 112.
Holant, *Wales*, 229.
Holbeam, *Devon*, 29.
Holbeach, *Somerset*, 140.
Holbech, *Northamp.* 112 ; *Warw.* 177.
Holbeck, *Warw.* 234.
Holbrooke, *Kent*, 60, 67.
Holcomb, *Devon*, 29.
Holcombe, *Pemb.* 234.
Holcot, *Hunts*, 57.
Holcroft, *Chesh.* 17 ; *Hamp.* 50 ; *Lanc.* 71.
Holden, *Derby*, 27, 234, 259 ; *Kent.* 60 ; *Lanc.* 68, 234; *Leic.* 80 ; 235 ; *Staff.* 147 ; *Warw.* 172.
Holden-Rose, *Northamp.* 112.
Holdsworth, *York*, 224.
Holdenby, *Northamp.* 111, 112.
Holes, *Herts*, 54.
Holford, *Camb.* 16 ; *Chesh.* 17 ; *Glous.* 234, 264; *Breck.* 234, 236.
Holgate, *Essex*, 48.
Holland, *Camb.* 16 ; *Norfolk*, 107 ; *Oxf.* 133 ; *Sussex*, 165 ; *Wales*, 229 ; *Suffolk*, 234 ; 242.
Holled, *Leic.* 80.
Holles, *Derby*, 27 ; *Herts*, 54 ; *Surrey*, 156.
Holley, *Devon*, 234.
Holliday, *Lond.* 96.
Hollingbery, *Kent*, 60.
Hollinshed, *Chesh.* 17.
Hollis, *Norfolk*, 107 ; *Notts*, 122 ; *York*, 206 ; *Monm.* 234.
Hollingworth, *Chesh.* 234.
Hollinshead, *Lanc.* 234.
Hollist, *Sussex*, 234.
Holloway, *Berks*, 3 ; *Oxf.* 131.
Holman, *Northamp.* 112 ; *Surrey*, 156, 158 ; 233.
Holme, *Lanc.* 234 ; *Chesh.* 17 ; *York*, 217, 224, 234.

Holmes, *Camb.* 16 ; *Durham*, 88 ; *Hamp.* 50 ; *Tipperary*, 234 ; *Norfolk*, 234 ; *Sussex*, 163.
Holowell, *Hamp.* 50.
Holt, *Hamp.* 50 ; *Chesh.* 17 ; *Lanc.* 68; *Oxf.* 130 ; *Warw.* 172 ; *Midd.* 234; *incorrectly printed* Hold, 234 ; 235.
Holte, *Camb.* 16 ; *Oxf.* 128.
Holyngworthe, *Chesh.* 234.
Holway, *Devon*, 31 ; *Somerset*, 140.
Home, *Perth*, 234 ; *Berwick*, 234 ; 234.
Homfray, *Glam.* 234 ; *Suffolk*, 234.
Hone, *Devon*, 29.
Honford, *Chesh.* 17 ; *Lanc.* 72.
Honing, 232.
Hony, 236.
Honychurch, *Devon*, 29.
Honywood, *Essex*, 48 ; *Kent*, 60 ; *Sussex*, 165 ; *Suffolk*, 234 ; 233.
Hoo, *Herts*, 54, 56 ; *Norfolk*, 107 ; *Staff.* 146, 147 ; *Sussex*, 163, 169.
Hood, *Bucks*, 10 ; *Leic.* 80, 234 ; *Linc.* 234 ; *Berwick*, 234.
Hooke, *Hamp.* 50 ; *Sussex*, 165 ; *Glouc.* 262.
Hookes, *Wales*, 229.
Hooper, *Kent*, 60 ; *Somerset*, 140 ; *Wilts*, 185.
Hooton, *Chesh.* 17.
Hope, *Berks*, 7 ; *Derby*, 27 ; *Wales*, 229 ; *Surrey*, 234 ; *Linlithgow*, 234 ; 251.
Hoper, *Devon*, 29 ; *Sussex*, 234.
Hopes, *Westm.* 234.
Hophinton, *Derby*, 259.
Hopkins, *Bucks*, 10 ; *Staff.* 146, 147 ; *Surrey*, 156 ; *Glam.* 228 ; *Berks*, 234 ; 234.
Hopkinson, *York*, 224.
Hopper, *Kent*, 60 ; *York*, 234 ; *Durham*, 234.
Hopton, *Rutl.* 136 ; *Somerset*, 140 ; *Suffolk*, 153 ; *York*, 205 ; *Hereford*, 234.
Hopwood, *Lanc.* 71, 234.
Hord, *Oxford*, 131.
Horde, 233.
Hore, *Warw.* 172 ; *Wexford*, 234.
Hordern, *Staff.* 234.
Horkett, *Hamp.* 50.

Horlock, *Glouc.* 234 ; 236.
Horne, *Kent*, 60 ; *York*, 213 ; 224.
Hornby, *Lanc.* 234 ; *Sussex*, 234.
Horner, *Somerset*, 140, 234 ; *Herts*, 56.
Hornidge, *Westmeath*, 234.
Hornor, *Essex*, 234.
Hornyold, *Worc.* 195, 234 ; 236.
Horrocks, *Lanc.* 234.
Horseman, *Oxford*, 128, 130.
Horsey, *Dorset*, 33 ; *Herts*, 54, 56 ; *Wilts*, 185.
Horsfall, *York*, 224.
Horsley, *Durham*, 38 ; *Northumb.* 119 ; *York*, 224.
Horsmonden, *Kent*, 60.
Horspoole, *Kent*, 60 ; *Sussex*, 165.
Horton, *Wilts*, 185, 191 ; *York*, 218, 224, 234 ; 250 ; *Derby*, 259 ; *Lanc.* 268.
Hosatus, *Sussex*, 163, 165.
Hose, *Dorset*, 33.
Hosier, *Northamp.* 112.
Hosken, *Cornw.* 234.
Hosken-Harper, *Chesh.* 234.
Hoskins, *Dorset*, 33 ; *Surrey*, 156, 158, 162 ; *Hereford*, 234 ; *Cumb.* 234.
Hoskyns, *Warw.* 234 ; 236.
Hoste, *Norfolk*, 234.
Hotham, *Warw.* 172 ; *York*, 214, 215, 224.
Hothum, *Northamp.* 111.
Hotot, *Northamp.* 111 ; *Notts*, 122.
Houblon, *Essex*, 48 ; 234.
Houby, *Leic.* 76, 80.
Hough, *Chesh.* 17.
Hougham, *Kent*, 59, 60.
Houghton, *Hamp.* 50 ; *Lanc.* 69 ; *Rutl.* 135, 136 ; *Suffolk*, 152 ; *Sussex*, 165 ; *Wexford*, 234.
Houlton, *Wilts*, 188 ; *Somerset*, 234.
Hound, *Camb.* 16.
Hounsfield, *York*, 234.
Hourd, *Somerset*, 140.
Houstonn, *Renfrew*, 234.
Houston, *Tyrone*, 234.
Houston-Blakiston, 234.
Hovell, *Norfolk*, 107.
Howard, *Bucks*, 11, 13 ; *Cumb.* 22, 23, 234 ; *Durham*, 38 ; *Essex*, 48 ; *Hamp.* 50 ; *Herts*, 56 ; *Kent*, 60 ;

Norfolk, 107, 278 ; *Northumb.* 119 ; *Staff.* 144 ; *Surrey*, 156 ; *Sussex*, 163, 167 ; *York*, 205, 206, 213 ; *Flint*, 234 ; 233 ; 236 ; 237 ; *Canada*, 250.
Howe, *Herts*, 54, 56 ; *Wilts*, 182.
Howel, *Glam.* 228 ; *Wales*, 229.
Howell, *Kent*, 60 ; *Glouc.* 234.
Howes, *Norfolk*, 234.
Howland, *Surrey*, 156.
Howlin, *Wexford*, 234.
Howper, *Somerset*, 140.
Howth, 236.
Hoy, *Essex*, 234.
Hoyle, *York*, 234 ; *Bute*, 234.
Hozier, *Lanark*, 234.
Huband, *Warw.* 172 ; 234.
Hubert, *Leic.* 80.
Hubble, *Kent.* 60 ; *Sussex*, 165.
Huckmore, *Devon*, 29, 31.
Huddart, *Carn.* 234.
Huddisfield, *Devon*, 29.
Huddleston, *Cumb.* 22 ; *Camb.* 234 ; 235 ; 236.
Huddy, *Somerset*, 140.
Hudleston, *Camb.* 16 ; *Cumb.* 22, 23.
Hudson, *Leic.* 80.
Hugeson, *Kent*, 60.
Hugesson, *Kent*, 234.
Hugford, *Warw.* 172.
Hugefort or Huggeford, *Worc.* 195.
Hugh ap Edward, *Wales*, 229.
Hugh ap Richard, *Wales*, 229.
Hugh ap Owen, *Wales*, 229.
Hugh ab William, *Wales*, 229.
Hughes, *Bucks*, 10 ; *Kent*, 60 ; *Oxford*, 131 ; *Somerset*, 140 ; *Carm.* 230 ; *Wales*, 229 ; *Denbigh*, 234 ; *Card.* 234 ; *Berks*, 234 ; *Merioneth*, 234, 239 ; *Wexford*, 234 ; *Anglesey*, 234 ; *Dublin*, 234 ; 236.
Huish, *Devon*, 29 ; *Notts*, 234.
Huit, *Stafford*, 146.
Huland, *Warw.* 239.
Hulcote, *Northampton*, 112.
Huley, *York*, 224.
Hulgrave, *Chesh.* 17.
Hulke, *Kent*, 60.
Hull, *Devon*, 29 ; *Durham*, 38, 40 ; *Surrey*, 156 ; *Cork*, 234.
Hullock, *Hunts*, 57.
Hulls, *Wales*, 229.
Hulme, *Lanc.* 71, 269.

Hulse, *Berks,* 3 ; *Chesh.* 17 ; *Hamp.* 50 ; *Kent,* 60.
Hulton, *Hamp,* 50 ; *Lanc.* 71, 234.
Hume, *Warw.* 174 ; *Berwick,* 234 ; *Wicklow,* 234.
Humet, *Rutl.* 136.
Humez, *Rutl.* 136.
Humffreys, *Montg.* 234.
Humfines, *Dorset,* 33.
Humfrey, *Northamp.* 111, *York,* 224 ; *Norfolk,* 234 ; *Donegal,* 234.
Humphrey, *Camb.* 16 ; *Leic.* 80 ; *Sussex,* 169 ; *Wales,* 229.
Humphry, *Sussex,* 165.
Humphrys, *Cavan,* 234.
Hungate, *York,* 205, 224.
Hungerford, *Berks,* 7 ; *Dorset,* 33 ; *Hamp.* 50 ; *London,* 94 ; *Somerset,* 141 ; *Oxf.* 131 ; *Surrey,* 156 ; *Wilts.* 182, 185, 194 ; *Cork,* 234 ; *Northamp.* 234.
Hunloke, 235, 236.
Hunsdon, *Herts,* 54 ; *York,* 220.
Hunt, *Devon,* 31 ; *Kent,* 60 ; *Rutl.* 135 ; *Somerset,* 139 ; *Suffolk,* 153 ; *York,* 224 ; *Fife,* 234 ; *Rutl.* 234; *Warw.* 234 ; *Sussex,* 234 ; *Shrop.* 234.
Huntbach, *Staff.* 143, 146.
Hunter, *Berks,* 7 ; *Durham,* 38, 234 ; *Herts,* 56 ; *Leic.* 80 ; *York,* 217, 224, 225 ; *Ayr,* 234 ; *Londonderry,* 234 ; *Dumfries,* 234 ; *Fife,* 234 ; *Forfar.* 234 ; 237 ; *London,* 239.
Huntingdon, *Oxf.* 131 ; *York,* 205 ; 236.
Huntley, *Gloucester,* 234, 264.
Hunton, *Wilts,* 185.
Hurdis, *Sussex,* 169.
Hurlbatt, *Hamp.* 50.
Hurleston, *Chesh.* 17.
Hurly, *Sussex,* 165 ; 233 ; *Kerry,* 234 ; 246.
Hurst, *Rutl,* 136 ; *Devon,* 9 ; *Lanc.* 234.
Hurt, *Derby,* 27, 234 ; 237.
Hurte, *Staff.* 146.
Husee, *Dorset,* 33.
Husey, *Dorset,* 33 ; 235.
Husse, *Wilts,* 182 ; *York,* 226.
Hussey, *Dorset,* 33, 234 ; *Hamp.*

50 ; *Kent,* 60 ; *Linc.* 84, 88 ; *Notts.* 122 ; *Rutl.* 136 ; *Staff.* 143, 234 ; *Surrey,* 156, 158 ; *Sussex,* 169, 163, 165, 234 ; *Hunts,* 234 ; *Dublin,* 234 ; *Kerry,* 234.
Hustler, *York,* 217, 220, 234 ; 233.
Hutchins, *Cork,* 234.
Hutchinson, *Durham,* 38, 234 ; *Essex,* 48 ; *Herts,* 54 ; *Notts,* 122 ; *York,* 224 ; *Tipperary,* 234 ; *Dumbarton,* 234.
Hutoft, *Wilts,* 185.
Hutton, *Cumb.* 22, 23 ; *Durham,* 34, 36, 38, 40 ; *Leic.* 80 , *York,* 205, 208, 213, 224, 234, 285 ; *Linc.* 234 ; *Westm.* 234.
Huw ap David, *Wales,* 229.
Huw Vychan, *Wales,* 229.
Huxley, *Chesh.* 17.
Huyshe, *Devon,* 234. 236.
Hyde, *Berks,* 3, 6, 234 ; *Chesh.* 17 ; *Dorset,* 33 ; *Hamp.* 50 ; *Herts,* 56 ; *Lanc.* 71 ; *Leic.* 80 ; *Rutl.* 136 ; *Wilts,* 182, 185, 191 ; *Cork,* 234 ; *Kent,* 234.
Hydes, *Wilts,* 182.
Hygons, *Sussex,* 163, 168.
Hyett, *Somerset,* 140 ; *Glouc.* 234.
Hywel, *Wales,* 229.

l'Anson, *Dorset,* 33, 234.
Ibbetson, *York,* 205 ; 236.
Idle, *York,* 205.
Ickworth, *Suffolk,* 152.
Iermonger, *Berks,* 3.
Ieuan ap Grufydd, *Wales,* 229.
Ieuan ap Howel, *Wales,* 229.
Ieuan ap Hugh, *Wales,* 229.
Ieuan ap Robert, *Wales,* 229.
Ieuans, *Wales,* 229.
Ievans, *Wales,* 229.
Ifield, 233.
Ilchester, *Wilts,* 182 ; *Somerset,* 139.
Ilbert, *Devon,* 234.
Ile, *Durham,* 43, 38.
Iliffe, *Leicester,* 80.
Illingworth, *Notts,* 122.
Imworth, *Northamp.* 112.
Inchiquin, 237.
Incledon, *Devon,* 31.
Inge, *Staff.* 234, 143, 146.
Ingham, *York,* 234, 239 ; *Wilts,* 182.

Inglose, *Rutland*, 136.
Ingleby, *York*, 204, 224.
Inglose, *Rutland*, 136.
Ingoldsby, *Bucks*, 10.
Ingpen, *Hamp*. 50.
Ingram, *Warw*. 172; *Wilts*, 195;
 York, 198, 201, 205, 213, 220,
 224; *Lincoln*, 234; 232; 234;
 Surrey, 158.
Inguersby, *Northamp*. 112.
Ingwardeby, *Leicester*, 30.
Inman, 237.
Innes, *Kincardine*, 234; *Down*, 234;
 Berks, 7.
Inslie, *Leicester*, 80.
Inskipp, *Sussex*, 165.
Iong, *Wales*, 229.
Irby, *Bucks*, 13; *Lincoln*, 88; *Nor-
 folk*, 234.
Ireland, *Lancaster*, 71, 69; *York*,
 213; *Wales*, 229; *Kildare*, 234;
 Somerset, 234; *Suffolk*, 234.
Iremonger, *Hamp*. 50, 234.
Ireys, *Wilts*, 185.
Irish, *Somerset*, 140.
Ironside, *Dorset*, 33; *Durham*, 38.
Irton, *Cumberland*, 22, 23, 234;
 Hamp. 50; *Wilts*, 185; *York*,
 226.
Irvine, *Dumfries*, 234; *Aberdeen*,
 234; *Fermanagh*, 234, 239.
Irwin, *Fermanagh*, 234; *Cumb*. 234;
 Sligo, 234.
Isaak, *Devon*, 31.
Isaake, *Devon*, 31.
Isham, *Northamp*. 111, 112; *Somer-
 set*, 140; 237.
Isherwood, *Chesh*. 17, 234.
Is Kennen, *Wales*, 229.
Is Kerdyn, *Wales*, 229.
Isley, 233.
Isney, *Essex*, 48.
Isted, *Sussex*, 185; *Northamp*. 234.
Ithell, *Camb*. 16.
Ivery, *Somerset*, 140.
Ives, *Norfolk*, 108; *Northamp*. 112,
 234; *Hants*. 234.
Iveson, *York*, 205.
Ivye, *Oxford*, 131.
Iwardby, *Bucks*, 10.
Izod, *Kilkenny*, 234.

Jackson, *Durham*, 38; *Herts*, 56;

London, 96; *Somerset*, 140; *York*,
 213, 224, 234; *Northamp*. 234;
 Limerick, 234; *Cheshire*, 234;
 Mayo, 234, 239; *Cork*, 234; *Wa-
 terford*, 234; 237; *Northumb*.118.
Jackman, *Hunts*, 57.
Jacob, *Kent*, 60, 245; *London*, 96;
 Dorset, 234; 250.
Jacomb, 237.
Jacson, *Lancaster*, 234.
Jakes, *Leicester*, 80.
Jakson, *Durham*, 38.
James, *Durham*, 34, 36, 38; *Hamp*.
 50; *Kent*, 60, 67, 234; *Somerset*,
 140; *Surrey*, 156, 162; *Breck*.
 227; *Glam*. 228; *Wales*, 229;
 Carm. 230; *Cumb*. 234; *North-
 umb*. 234; *Pemb*. 234; 236.
James ap Owen, *Wales*, 229.
Jameson, *Galway*, 234.
Jankins, *Wales*, 229.
Janson, *Northamp*. 112.
Janssen, *Dorset*, 33.
Jaques, *York*, 224, 234.
Jarrett, *Somerset*, 234.
Jarvis, *Camb*. 16; *Leic*. 80; *Linc*.
 234; *Staff*. 146.
Jawdrell, *Camb*. 16; *Hunts*, 57.
Jeaffreson, *Camb*. 234.
Jeake, *Sussex*, 169.
Jeames, *Berks*, 7.
Jebb, *Notts*, 234; *Derby*, 234.
Jee, *Leicester*, 80.
Jefferay, *Sussex*, 164, 165, 168.
Jefferies, *Worcester*, 195.
Jefferson, *Durham*, 38.
Jeffreys, *Bucks*, 10; *Leicester*, 80;
 Breck. 227; *Shrop*. 234.
Jekyll, *Bucks*, 10; *Herts*, 54;
 Northamp. 112.
Jemmett, *Kent*, 60.
Jeninges, *Staff*, 146.
Jenison, *Durham*, 38; *Notts*, 124.
Jenkenson, *Oxf*. 131.
Jenkin, *Kent*, 60; *Sussex*, 165;
 Card. 230.
Jenkins, *Glam*. 228; *Card*. 230;
 Shrop. 234.
Jenkinson, *Bucks*, 10; *Suss*. 165,
 164.
Jenkyn, *Herts*, 54; *York*, 224.
Jenkyns, *Wales*, 229; 236.
Jenman, *Sussex*, 163.

Jennens, *Leicester*, 80 ; *Northamp.* 112.
Jenner, *Berks*, 7 ; *Sussex*, 165 ; *Glouc*, 234 ; *Glam.* 234.
Jenney, *Suffolk*, 234 ; *Norfolk*, 278.
Jennings, *Herts*, 54 ; *Kent*, 60 : *Somerset*, 140 ; *Northamp.* 234 ; *York*, 224.
Jenyns, *Camb.* 234.
Jephson, *Hamp*, 50.
Jerman, *Sussex*, 163.
Jermin or Jermyn, *Sussex*, 165.
Jermy, *Norfolk*, 278.
Jerningham, *Norfolk*, 107 ; *Suffolk*, 153.
Jerrard, *Somerset*, 140.
Jerveis, *Leicester*, 80.
Jervis, *Leicester*, 80.
Jervoise, *Bucks*, 10 ; *Leic.* 80 ; *Hamp.* 50, 234.
Jesse, *Essex*, 48 ; *Denbigh*, 234.
Jesson, *Staff.* 234, 250.
Jessop, *Dorset*, 33 ; *York*, 206, 224 ; *Longford*, 234.
Jestyn, *Glam.* 228.
Jevan, *Card.* 230.
Jevon, *Staff.* 143.
Jewell, *Devon*, 29.
Jex, *Norfolk*, 234.
Jobson, *York*, 213.
Jocelin, *Herts*, 53.
Jocelyn, *Essex*, 48 ; *Herts.* 54.
Jodrell, *Berks*, 13 ; *Chesh.* 17, 234 ; 236.
John, *Card.* 230.
John ap David, *Wales*, 229.
John David ab Griffith, *Wales*, 229.
John ap Howel, *Wales*, 229.
John ap Hugh, *Wales*, 229.
John ap Huw, *Wales*, 229.
John ap Lewis, *Wales*, 229.
John ap Robert, *Wales*, 229.
Johnes, *Wales*, 229 ; *Carm.* 234 ; 242.
Johns, *Wales*, 229.
Johnson, *Durham*, 36, 38, 234 ; *Kent*, 60 ; *Lanc.* 68, 71 ; *Linc.* 86 ; 234, 239, 274 ; *London*, 16, 100 ; *Norfolk*, 108 ; *Northumb.* 119 ; *Rutland*, 135 ; *Montgomery*, 234 ; *Leic.* 235 ; *Cork*, 234 ; 239.

Johnston, *York*, 224 ; *Stirling*, 234 ; *Dumfries*, 234 ; *Down*, 234 ; *Monaghan*, 234 ; *Fermanagh*, 234 ; *Perth*, 234.
Johnstone, *Hereford*, 234 ; *Dumfries*, 234 ; *Clackmann*, 234 ; *Fermanagh*, 234 ; 234.
Joliffe, *Somerset*, 234 ; 236.
Jolliffe, *Worcester*, 195.
Jones, *Hamp.* 50 ; *London*, 96 ; *Monm.* 105, 234, 239 ; *Oxford*, 131, 132, 234 ; *Somerset*, 140, 234 ; *Breck.* 227 ; *Glam.* 228, 234 ; *Wales*, 229 ; *Pemb.* 230 ; *Carm.* 230, 234, 245 ; *Cardiff*, 230, 234 ; *Lanc.* 234 ; *Sligo*, 234, *Barbadoes*, 234 ; *Flint*, 234 ; *Denbigh*, 234 ; *Glouc.* 234 ; *York*, 234 ; *Dublin*, 234 ; *Leitrim*, 234 ; *Cork*, 234 ; *Antrim*, 234 ; 245 ; 246 ; *Kilkenny*, 234 ; *Merioneth*, 234 ; 242 ; 251.
Jordan, *Kent*, 60 ; *Staff.* 143 ; *Surrey*, 158 ; *Wales*, 229 ; *Pemb.* 230 ; *Cardiff*, 234.
Joyce, *Galway*, 234.
Judd, *Kent*, 60.
Jull, *Kent*, 60.
Juxon, *Kent*, 60 ; *Sussex*, 163.
Justice, *Shrop.* 234.

Kadwell, *Kent*, 60.
Kadwgan hên, *Wales*, 229.
Kaio, *Wales*, 229.
Kannington, *Wales*, 229.
Kanon, *Wales*, 229.
Kane, *Monaghan*, 234.
Kavanagh, *Carlow*, 234.
Kay, *York*, 224, 234.
Kaye, *Hunts*, 57.
Keane, *Clare*, 234.
Kearney, *Kilkenny*, 234 ; *Mayo*, 234 ; *Cork*, 234.
Kearsley, *London*, 96.
Keate, *Berks*, 6 ; *Herts*, 54, 56.
Keble, *Leic.* 76, 80 ; *Northamp.* 112.
Keck, *Leic.* 234.
Kederminster, *Bucks*, 13.
Kedwelley, *Hamp.* 50.
Keigwin, *Cornwall*, 234.
Keileway, *Wilts*, 182.
Keir, *Perth*, 234.
Kekewich, *Devon*, 234.

Kelham, *Notts.* 234.
Kellam, *York*, 224, 213.
Kelley, *Devon*, 31.
Kelloway, *Hamp.* 50.
Kelly, *Devon*, 29, 234; *Galway*, 234;
  234.
Kelsall, *Chesh.* 17.
Kelso, *Kelso*, 234.
Kelsolt, *Notts*, 122.
Kemes yr Anglwydd, *Wales*, 229.
Kemis, *Glam.* 228.
Kemmis, *Queen's Co.* 234; *Wicklow*,
  234.
Kemp, *Surrey*, 162; *Sussex*, 165,
  234.
Kempe, *Cornwall*, 20; *Hamp.* 50;
  Kent, 60; *London*, 96; *Sussex*,
  163, 165, 171; *Devon*, 234; 236.
Kempton, *Camb.* 16.
Kendal, *Devon*, 29; *Durham*, 34,
  38; *York*, 209.
Kendale, *Herts*, 54; *Sussex*, 165.
Kendall, *Devon*, 31; *Durham*, 40;
  Leic. 80; *Warw.* 234, 245; *Corn.*
  234; *Derby*, 259.
Kenion, *Oxford*, 132.
Kenisham, *Devon*, 29.
Kenn,. *Northamp.* 112; *Somerset*,
  140.
Kennard, *London*, 245.
Kennedy, *Ayr*, 234; *Down*, 234;
  Kirkcudbright, 234, 239; 241.
Kennet, *Durham*, 38.
Kenney, *Galway*, 234, 250; *Ros-
  common*, 234; *Mayo*, 234; 237.
Kenny, *Monaghan*, 234; 237.
Kenrick, *Surrey*, 156, 158; *Shrop.*
  234.
Kent, *Northamp.* 112; *Rutland*, 135;
  Suffolk, 152; *Wilts*, 182, 185;
  York, 213.
Kentish, *Herts*, 54.
Kenwrick, *Kent*, 60; *Northamp.* 112.
Kenyon, *Lanc.* 71; *Oxf.* 131.
Keogh, *Carlow*, 234; 246.
Ker, *Roxburgh*, 234; 234.
Keresforth, *York*, 213, 222, 224.
Kerr, *Down*, 234; *Roxburgh*, 234.
Kervile, *Norf.* 107, 278.
Kerle, 234.
Kerrich, *Norfolk*, 234.

Kestell, *Cornwall*, 20.
Kettleby, *Glouc.* 262.
Ketsmae, *Wales*, 229.
Keverell, *Berks*, 7.
Keyleway, *Wilts*, 185.
Keylway, *Dorset*, 33.
Keynes, *Dorset*, 33; *Northamp.* 111,
  112; *Warw.* 172.
Keyt, *Warw.* 172.
Klement, *Wales*, 229.
Kibblewhite, *Berks*, 7.
Kidder, *Sussex*, 169.
Kildare, *Devon*, 29.
Killich, *Staff.* 234.
Killingbeck, *York*, 205, 224.
Killigrew, 231.
Killinghall, *Durham*, 34, 38; *Nor-
  thumb.* 118.
Killom, *York*, 213.
Kiner, *Wales*, 229.
Kinchant, *Shrop.* 234.
King, *Bucks*, 10, 11, 13; *Leic.* 80;
  Surrey, 156; *York*, 200; *Warw.*
  234; *Hamp.* 234; *Somerset*, 234;
  King's Co. 234; *Hereford*, 234,
  239.
Kingdon, *Cornw.* 234.
Kingesley, *Herts*, 54.
Kingscote, *Glouc.* 234.
Kingsley, *Chesh.* 17; *Kent*, 60.
Kingsmill, *Hamp.* 50.
Kingston, *Hamp.* 50; *Leic.* 80;
  Somerset, 140; 237; *Herts*, 245.
Kingstone, *Sussex*, 165.
Kingswell, *Hamp.* 50.
Kinleside, *Sussex*, 165.
Kinnoul, *York*, 213.
Kinnersley, *Berks*, 234.
Kirby, 233.
Kirkbride, *Cumb.* 22, 23.
Kirkby, *Leic.* 80; *Hamp.* 50.
Kirke, *York*, 205; *Notts.* 234; 251.
Kirketon, *Notts.* 122.
Kirkham, *Devon*, 29, 31; *Worc.* 195.
Kirkwood, *Roscommon*, 234.
Kirsopp, *Northumb.* 234.·
Kirton, *Northampton*, 112.
Kirwan, *Galway*, 234; *Kilkenny*,
  234; *Mayo*, 234.
Kitchingham, *York*, 205.
Kittermaster, *Warw.* 234, 246.
Klement, *Wales*, 229.

Knapman, *Devon*, 31.
Knapp, *Bucks*, 10.
Knyfton, *Somerset*, 234.
Knyvett, *Bucks*, 13.
Konias, *Wales*, 229.
Konwy, *Wales*, 229.
Kradoc, *Wales*, 229.
Kreuddyn, *Wales*, 229.
Kryell, *Hunts*, 57.
Kyme, *Linc.* 84.
Kymer, *Dorset*, 33.
Kyan, *Wicklow*, 234.
Kynaston, *Wales*, 229.
Kyngescote, *Glouc.* 262.
Kynne, *Northamp.* 112; *Glouc.* 262.
Kynnersley, *Staff.* 234; 233.
Kynnesman, *Northamp.* 111.
Kyrke, 251.
Kyrkeby, *York*, 226.
Kyrle, *Hereford*, 234.
Kytson, *Suffolk*, 151, 152.
Kywr, *Wales*, 229.

Labouchere, *Somerset*, 234; *Surrey*, 234.
Lacharn, *Wales*, 229.
Lacock, *York*, 224.
Lacon, *Norfolk*, 108.
Laci, *York*, 222.
Lacy, *Lanc.* 71; *Leic.* 80; *Oxf.* 131; *Staff.* 143; *Somerset*, 140; *Shrop.* 137; *York*, 224.
Lad, *Kent*, 60.
Ladbroc, *Warw.* 172.
Ladbroke, *Surrey*, 156.
Ladd, *Norfolk*, 278.
Lade, *Sussex*, 165; *Kent*, 234.
Lake, *Bucks*, 10; *Herts*, 54; *Kent*, 60; *York*, 224.
La Leye, *Northamp.* 112.
Lalor, *Tipperary*, 234.
Lamb, *Kent*, 60; *Northamp.* 112; *Sussex*, 165; *Northumb.* 234; 236.
Lambard, *Kent*, 60.
Lambarde, *Kent*, 67, 234.
Lambart, *Meath*, 234.
Lambe, *Durham*, 38; *Wilts*, 185, 191; *Hereford*, 234.
Lambert, *Durham*, 36, 38, 40; *Hamp.* 50; *Surrey*, 156, 158; *Wilts*, 182, 185, 234; *York*, 200, 224; *Wexford*, 234; *Mayo*, 234; *Galway*, 234; *Essex*, 234.

Lambton, *Durham*, 34, 36, 37, 38, 40.
Lammin, *Midd.* 246.
Lamont, *York*, 224; *Argyll*, 234.
Lampard, *Surrey*, 156.
Lamplew, *York*, 226.
Lamplugh, *Cumb.* 22, 23, 234.
Lamport, *Northamp.* 112.
L'Amy, *Forfar*, 234.
Lancaster, *Lanc.* 69, 71; *Somerset*, 140; *Rutl.* 136.
Lancelyn, *Chesh.* 17.
Lande, *Devon*, 31.
Landon, *Herts*, 56; 236.
Landor, *Warw.* 234.
Lane, *Bucks*, 10; *Northamp.* 112; *Rutl.* 136; *Staff.* 143, 234; *Oxf.* 234; *Devon*, 234; *Hereford*, 234, 237.
Lane-Fox, 234.
Lanesborough, 237.
Langdale, *York*, 217, 224; *Surrey*, 234.
Langesford, *Devon*, 31.
Langford, *Bucks*, 7; *Devon*, 29; *Herts*, 54; *Notts*, 122; *Wilts*, 191; *Wales*, 229; *Corn.* 234; 251.
Langham, *Leic.* 13; *Sussex*, 165.
Langharne, *Pemb.* 230.
Langhorne, *Lond.* 94.
Langley, *Lanc.* 71; *Northamp.* 112; *Warw.* 172; *York*, 219, 224.
Langport, *Northamp.* 112.
Langrish, *Hamp.* 50.
Langston, *Oxf.* 234.
Langton, *Durham*, 34, 38; *Linc.* 85; *Lanc.* 71, 234; *Northamp.* 112; *Wilts*, 191; *Somerset*, 234; 236.
Langworth, *Kent*, 60.
Lanion, *Corn.* 20.
Lankaster, *Westm.* 179.
Lante, *Devon*, 31.
Lanvallei, *Herts*, 54.
Lany, *Leic.* 80.
Lapp, *Wilts*, 185.
Larder, *Devon*, 29; *Dorset*, 33.
Lardiner, *York*, 197.
Larkworthy, *Devon*, 31.
Larkyn, *Camb.* 16.
Lascelles, *York*, 204, 207.
Lascells, *Notts*, 122.
Laslett, *Worc.* 234.
Lassells, *Leic.* 80.

2 x

Lathbury, *Leic.* 80.
Latham, *Camb.* 16 ; *Chesh.* 17, 234 ;
   Lanc. 69, 71.
Lathom, *Chesh.* 17, 19 ; *Lanc.* 73 ;
   232 ; *Wales,* 229.
Lathorpe, *Staff.* 146.
Latimer, *Bucks,* 10 ; *Dorset,* 33 ;
   Durham, 38 ; *Leic.* 80 ; *Norfolk,*
   107 ; *Northamp.* 111, 112 ; *York,*
   205, 209.
Laton, *Durham,* 38.
La Touche, *Dublin,* 234 ; *Kildare,*
   234 ; *Wicklow,* 234.
Latour, *Herts,* 239.
Lattin, *Kildare,* 234.
Latton, *Berks,* 3 ; *Surrey,* 156.
Latus, *Camb.* 22, 23.
Latymer, *Lond.* 98.
Lauder, 235, 239.
Laughton, *York,* 213.
Laugham, *Wales,* 229.
Laurence, *Dorset,* 33 ; *Leic.* 80.
Lautour, *Herts,* 234.
Lavington, *Wilts,* 185.
Law, *Leic.* 80 ; *Sussex,* 165.
La Warre, *Rutland,* 136.
Lawder, *Leitrim,* 234.
Lawes, *Herts,* 54, 56, 234.
Lawlor, *Kerry,* 234.
Lawndey, *Herts,* 54.
Lawrence, *Camb.* 16 ; *Leic.* 80 ;
   Wilts, 182 ; *Glouc.* 234, 262 ;
   Galway, 234.
Lawrens, *Hamp.* 50.
Lawson, *Camb.* 22 ; *Durham,* 38, 40,
   42 ; *Northumb.* 119, 234; *York,*
   205, 209, 224, 234.
Lawton, *Chesh.* 17, 234 ; *Staff.*
   142 ; *Cork,* 234.
Layborn, *York,* 226.
Laybourne, *Westm.* 179.
Layer, *Norfolk,* 278.
Layton, *Camb.* 234 ; *York,* 201, 205,
   224.
La Zouch, *Herts,* 54.
La Zouche, *Leic.* 80 ; *Shrop.* 137.
Lea, *Worc.* 234, 239.
Leach, *Devon,* 31.
Leacroft, *Derby,* 25 ; *Staff.* 146.
Leadbitter, *Northumb.* 119.
Leader, *Cork,* 234.
Leahy, *Cork,* 234.
Leake, *Norfolk,* 108 ; 232 ; *Essex,* 234.

Leaper, *Derby,* 27.
Learmonth, *Edinb.* 234.
Leatham, *York,* 234, 246.
Leather, *York,* 234 ; *Suffolk,* 234.
Leathes, *Suffolk,* 153, 239.
Le Boteler, *Wilts,* 182.
Leche, *Chesh.* 17, 234, 239.
Lechford, *Surrey,* 156.
Lechmere, *Bucks,* 11 ; *Oxf.* 234 ;
   Heref. 234 ; *Worc.* 195.
Lecky, *Carlow,* 234 ; *Derry,* 234 ;
   Antrim, 234.
Le Despencer, *Rutland,* 136 ; *Wilts,*
   182 ; *York,* 217.
Ledet, *Herts,* 54 ; *Northamp.* 111,
   112.
Ledgard, *Sussex,* 165.
Ledsam, *Warw.* 234.
Le Dune, *Wilts,* 182.
Lee, *Berks,* 7 ; *Bucks,* 10, 12, 13,
   234 ; *Chesh.* 17, 234 ; *Durham,* 36,
   38 ; *Devon,* 32, 234 ; *Herts,* 53,
   54, 56 ; *Kent,* 60, 234; *Oxf.* 128,
   130 ; *Sussex,* 163, 165 ; *York,* 201,
   213, 220, 224, 234 ; *Wales,* 229 ;
   Somerset, 234 ; *Shrop.* 234 ; *Tippe-*
   rary, 234 ; 235 ; 236 ; 251 ; *Derby,*
   259 ; *Surrey,* 158.
Leech, *Sussex,* 165 ; *Mayo,* 234 ;
   Limerick, 234.
Leedes, *Camb.* 16 ; *York,* 205, 224.
Leeds, *Hamp.* 50 ; *York,* 213 ; 236.
Leek, *Notts.* 122, 124.
Leeke, *Rutland,* 136 ; *York.* 224 ;
   Salop, 234 ; 251.
Leeson, *Northamp.* 111, 112.
Leete, *Hunt,* 57.
Leetes, *Camb.* 16.
Leeves, *Sussex,* 234.
Le Fevre, *Hants,* 56, 234.
Le Fleming, *Shrop.* 137.
Lefroy, *Kent,* 60 ; *Longford,* 234.
Leftwich, *Chesh.* 17.
Leg, *Hamp.* 50.
Legard, *York,* 214, 224 ; *Leic.* 80.
Legg, *Sussex,* 168.
Legge, *Camb.* 16 ; *Belfast,* 234.
Legh, *Chesh.* 17, 234 ; *Lanc.* 68, 71 ;
   York, 209.
Leghe, *York,* 205.
Legard, *Leic.* 80.
Le Grand, *Essex,* 48.
Le Gras, *York,* 200.

Le Groos, *Norfolk*, 277.
Le Gross, *Norfolk*, 107.
Le Grys, *Norfolk*, 108.
Le Hart, *Devon*, 29.
Le Hunt, *Derby*,27 ; *Linc.* 234 ; 236.
Le Hunte, *Wexford*, 234.
Leicester, *Chesh.* 17 ; *Kent*, 60 ; *Leic.* 76, 80 ; *Northamp.* 112 ; *Sussex*, 165.
Leigh, *Chesh.* 17, 234 ; *Corn.* 21 ; *Devon*, 21, 234 ; *Hamp.* 50 ; *Lanc.* 69 ; *Leic.* 80 ; *Somerset*, 140 ; *Staff.* 143 ; 281 ; *Sussex*, 165 ; *Warw.* 175, 234, 281 ; *Surrey*, 156, 157, 158, 160, 234 ; *Monm.* 234 ; *Bedford*, 234 ; 234 ; 236 ; 253.
Leighton, *Montgomery*, 234 ; *Wilts*, 182.
Leir, *Wilts*, 234.
Leith, *Aberdeen*, 234 ; 234 ; 236.
Leke, *York*, 197, 205.
Leland, *Sussex*, 165.
Le Lou, *Northamp.* 112.
Leman, *Herts*, 54 ; *London*, 98 ; *Suffolk*, 234, 153.
Le Mareschal, *Herts*, 54.
Lemins, *Kent*, 60.
Le Morgne, *Wilts*, 182.
Lemons, *Kent*, 60.
Lempriere, *Hants*, 234.
Lench, *Oxf.* 128.
Le Neve, *Essex*, 48 ; *Norfolk*, 277.
Lendrum, *Fermanagh*, 234.
Lenigan, *Tipperary*, 234.
Lennard, *Essex*, 48 ; 233.
Lennose, *Stirling*, 234.
Le Noreis, *Lanc.* 72, 73.
Lenox, *Sussex*, 165.
Lentaigne, *Dublin*, 234.
Lenthall, *Berks*, 3, 7, 234 ; *Oxf.* 131 ; 236.
Le Palmer, *Shrop.* 137.
Leppington, *Midd.* 246 ; *Linc.* 250.
Le Poer, *Northamp.* 111.
Le Power, *Sussex*,175.
Lescher, *Essex*, 48.
Leslie, *Aberdeen*, 234 ; *Antrim*, 234 ; *Monaghan*, 234.
L'Estrange, *Norfolk*, 107 ; *King's Co.* 234 ; 234.
Le Strange, *London*, 103 ; *Shropshire*, 137 ; 234 ; 236 ; *Norf.* 278.

Le Sore, 242.
Lethieullier, *Kent*, 60.
Lethbridge, 236.
Leukenor, *Northamp.* 112.
Levens, *Westm.* 179.
Leventhorpe, *Herts*, 53, 54.
Lever, *Lanc.* 71.
Levermore, *Devon*, 29, 31.
Leversage, *Chesh.* 7.
Leversedge, *Kent*, 60 ; *Somerset*, 140.
Leveson, *Northamp.* 112 ; *Staff.* 143, 146.
Levesey, *Kent*, 60.
Levett, *Sussex*, 165 ; *York*, 213 ; *Staff*, 234.
Levitt, *Sussex*, 163, 165.
Levinge, *Leic.* 80 ; 251.
Levingstoun, *York*, 224.
Levins, *Oxford*, 128.
Levinz, *Oxford*, 130.
Levyns, *York*, 224.
Le Warre, *Leic.* 89 ; *Rutland*, 136 ; *Somerset*, 140.
Lewen, *Dorset*, 33 ; *Surrey*, 156.
Lewes, *Somerset*, 140 ; *Sussex*, 163 ; 165 ; *Card.* 230 ; *Carm.* 230.
Lewin, *Kent*, 60, 234 ; *Mayo*, 234 ; . *Radnor*, 234 ; 234.
Lewings, *York*, 217.
Lewis, *Bucks*, 10 ; *York*, 213, 224 ; *Breck.* 227 ; *Wales*, 229 ; *Radnor*, 234 ; *Glam.* 228, 234 ; *Carm.* 234 ; *Pemb.* 234 ; *Anglesey*, 234 ; *Kildare*, 234 ; *Dublin*, 234 ; *Monmouth*, 234 ; 236 ; 237 ; 242.
Lewis ap Henry, *Wales*, 229.
Lewis ap Jenkyn Vychan, *Wales*, 229.
Lewis ab Owen. *Wales*, 229.
Lewkenor, *Hamp.* 50.
Lewknor, *Sussex*, 163, 165, 166, 168, 169.
Lewknore, *Northamp.* 111.
Lewston, *Dorset*, 33 ; *Wors.* 195.
Lowthwaite, *Cumb.* 23, 234.
Lewys, *Dorset*, 33 ; *York*, 205 ; *Wales*, 229.
Lewys ap Huw, *Wales*, 229.
Lewys ap Thomas, *Wales*, 229.
Lewys ap Richard, *Wales*, 229.
Lexington, *Northamp.* 112.
Ley, *Staff.* 142 ; *Wilts*, 182.

Leybourn, *Shrop.* 137.
Leycester, *Chesh.* 17, 234 ; *Berks,* 234 ; *Northamp.* 112.
Leye, *Northamp.* 111.
Libbe, *Oxf.* 131.
Lickland, *Somerset,* 140.
Liddel, *Durham,* 34, 37.
Liddell, *Durham,* 36, 38.
Lifield, *Surrey,* 158.
Light, *Oxf,* 128.
Lightbowne, *Lanc.* 75.
Ligne, *Suffolk,* 152.
Lilburn, *Durham,* 34.
Lilburne, *Durham,* 36.
Lillingston, *Hamp.* 50 ; 234 ; 236.
Lillyng, *Northamp.* 112.
Limbrey, *Hamp.* 50.
Limerick, 236.
Limesi, *Herts,* 54 ; *Norfolk,* 109 ; *Northamp.* 111 ; *Warw.* 172.
Limsey, *Leic.* 80.
Lincoln, *Lanc.* 71 ; *Leic.* 80 ; *Northamp.* 112 ; 232.
Lind, *Hamp.* 50, 234 ; 236.
Linde, *Somerset,* 140.
Lindesay, *Tyrone,* 234 ; *Dublin,* 234
Lindley, *York,* 219, 224.
Lindoe, *Norfolk,* 239.
Lindow, *Cumb.* 234.
Lindsay, *Fife,* 234.
Lindsay-Carnagie, *Moray,* 234.
Lindsey, *Mayo,* 234 ; 236.
Line, *Sussex,* 168.
Linley, *Notts,* 122 ; *York,* 201, 220.
Lingen, *Radnor,* 234.
Linghoke, *Norfolk,* 278.
Lipping, *Bucks,* 10 ; *Sussex,* 165.
Lippincot, *Devon,* 29.
Lisle, *Dorset,* 33 ; *Durham,* 34 ; *Hamp.* 50, 234 ; *Northamp.* 112 ; *Northumb.* 119, 120 ; *Somerset,* 140 ; *Wilts,* 182.
Lisley, *Hamp.* 50.
Lister, *Durham,* 38 ; *Hamp.* 50 ; *York,* 200, 213, 218, 224, 234 ; *Linc.* 234 ; *Stafford,* 234 ; 237 ; *Leic.* 80.
Litchfield, *Bucks,* 10.
Littcote,. *Oxf.* 128.
Little, *Herts,* 56 ; *York,* 217 ; *Down,* 234 ; *Monm.* 234.
Littleboys, *Sussex,* 165.

Littledale, *York,* 234.
Littler, *Chesh.* 17, 234.
Littleton, *Leic.* 76 ; *Stafford,* 234 ; *Norfolk,* 277.
Litton, *Tyrone,* 234 ; *Surrey,* 162.
Livingstone, *Stirling,* 234.
Livius, *Bedf.* 234.
Lizures, *Northamp.* 112.
Llewellen, *Glam.* 228
Llewellyn, *Glam.* 228 ; *Pemb.* 234.
Lewelyn, *Glam.* 228.
Lloyd, *Hamp.* 50 ; *Herts,* 56 ; *Kent,* 60 ; *Lanc.* 70 ; *Northamp.* 112 ; *York,* 224, 234 ; *Breck.* 227 ; *Glam.* 228 ; *Pemb.* 230 ; *Card.* 230, 234 ; *Carm.* 230, 234 ; *Wales,* 229 ; *Warw.* 234 ; *Shrop.* 234 ; *Roscommon,* 234 ; *Anglesey,* 234 ; *Denbigh,* 234 ; *Carn.* 234 ; *Merioneth,* 234 ; *Waterford,* 234 ; *King's Co.* 234 ; *Tipperary,* 234 ; *Limerick,* 234 ; 236 ; 237 ; 239 ; 242 ; *Montgomery,* 245 ; *Glouc.* 262 ; *Surrey,* 162 ; *Sussex,* 163.
Lluellyn, *Surrey,* 234.
Llychlin, Bishop of Wales, 229.
Llywarch, *Wales,* 229.
Lobb, *Hamp.* 50.
Loch, *Staff.* 234.
Lochor, *Pemb.* 230.
Locke, *Wilts,* 234.
Lockett, *Derby,* 27.
Lockhart, *Lanark,* 234 ; *Selkirk,* 234 ; 237.
Lockwood, *Essex,* 48 ; *York,* 224 ; 234.
Lockyer, *Devon,* 234.
Lodbroke, *Leic.* 80.
Loder, *Berks,* 7.
Lodge, *Berks,* 7.
Loftie, *Kent,* 60.
Loftus, *Dorset,* 234 ; *Wicklow,* 234, 236.
Lomax, *Herts,* 56, 234 ; *Lanc.* 234 ; *Oxf.* 246.
Lone, *Kent,* 63.
Londonderry, 237.
Long, *Berks,* 7 ; *Dorset,* 33 ; *Hamp.* 50, 234 ; *Somerset,* 140 ; *Sussex,* 165 ; *Surrey,* 159, 234 ; *Norfolk,* 234 ; *Wilts,* 181, 185, 187, 191, 193, 194, 234 ; 236.
Longcroft, *Hamp.* 240.

Longe, *Devon*, 31; *Norfolk*, 234.
Longespe, *Herts*, 54; *Wilts*, 186.
Longspe, *Northamp.* 112.
Longford, *Wales*, 229; *Lanc.* 269.
Longfield, *Cork*, 234.
Longueville, *Bucks*, 10; *Northamp.* 112; *Shrop.* 234.
Longworth, *Westmeath*, 234.
Lonsdale, *York*, 204.
Lopdell, *Galway*, 234
Loraine, *Northumb.* 119.
Lord, *Kent*, 60; *Wales*, 229.
Lort, *Pemb.* 230; *Wales*, 229.
Lostock, *Chesh.* 17.
Lottisham, *Somerset*, 140.
Loudham, *Notts.* 122.
Louet, *Bucks*, 10.
Lougher, *Wales*, 229.
Lound, *Camb.* 16.
Lousada, *Devon*, 234.
Louthe, *Hunts*, 57.
Louraine, *York*, 215.
Lovat, 236.
Lovatt, *Staff.* 145.
Love, *Camb.* 16; *Hamp.* 50; *Kent*, 60; *Sussex*, 165.
Loveday, *Norfolk*, 108; *Oxford*, 234, 239.
Loveden, *Berks*, 3.
Loveis, *Devon*, 29.
Lovekin, *Essex*, 48.
Lovel, *Northamp.* 111; *Warw.* 172; *Wilts.* 182.
Lovelace, *Kent*, 60; 236.
Loveland, *Herts*, 234.
Loveline, *Wales*, 229.
Lovell, *Bucks*, 10, 234; *Cumb.* 24; *Dors.* 33; *Herts*, 54; *Lond.* 91; *Norfolk*, 107; *Northamp.* 112; *Rutland*, 136; *Warw.* 172; *Wilts*, 182, 185; *York*, 224.
Lovet, 231; *Bucks*, 10.
Lovetot, *Herts*, 54; *Notts.* 122.
Lovett, *Northamp.* 111, 112; *Bucks*, 10, 234; 234; *Salop.* 234; 239; *Surrey*, 158.
Lovibond, *Essex*, 48, 234.
Low, *Limerick*, 234; *Derby*, 159.
Lowe, *Chesh.* 17; *Derby*, 27, 234; *Kent*, 60; *Notts.* 123; *Wilts.* 185; *Worc.* 195, 234; *Shrop.* 234; *Devon*, 234.
Lower, *Cornw.* 23; 231; 253.

Lowes, *Northumb.* 119.
Lowin, *Kent*, 60.
Lowis, *Devon*, 31.
Lowle, or Lowell, 235.
Lowman, *Devon*, 29, 31.
Lowndes, *Bucks*, 10, 234; *Kent*, 60; *Chesh.* 234; *Renfrew*, 234; *Essex*, 234; *Wales*, 229; 236.
Lowry, *Tyrone*, 234.
Lowten, *Chesh.* 234.
Lowther, *Cumb.* 23; *Westm.* 179; *York*, 204, 205, 220; *Meath*, 234.
Loyzelure, *Durham*, 88.
Luard, *Linc.* 234; *Essex*, 48, 234.
Lucar, *Somerset*, 140.
Lucas, *Derby*, 27, 234; *Suffolk*, 152; *Glam.* 234; *Monaghan*, 234; *King's Co.* 234; *Cork*, 234.
Lucian, *Northamp.* 112.
Luck, *Sussex*, 165.
Luckyn, *Herts*, 54, 56.
Lucy, *Bucks*, 10; *Cumb.* 23; *Herts.* 54; *Northamp.* 112; *Warw.* 234, 172.
Ludford, *Leic.* 80; *Warw.* 173.
Ludlow, *Hamp.* 50; *Shrop.* 137; *Wilts.* 182, 185, 234.
Luke, *Hunts*, 57.
Lukin, *Oxford*, 131.
Lumb, *Cumb.* 234.
Lumen, *Devon*, 29.
Lumley, *Herts*, 56; *Northamp.* 111, 112; *York*, 220, 213; *Surrey*, 156, 161; *Durham*, 34, 37, 38, 44.
Lumsdaine, *Fife*, 234; 234.
Lumsden, *Aberdeen*, 234.
Lunard, *Essex*, 48.
Lund, *Camb.* 16.
Lundin, *Fife*, 234.
Lunell, *Northamp.* 112.
Lunnell, *Wilts*, 182.
Lunsford, *Sussex*, 165, 168; 232.
Lupus, *Norfolk*, 107; *Northamp.* 112.
Luscombe, *Devon*, 31, 234.
Lushington, *Kent*, 60, 234.
Luson, *Suffolk*, 153.
Luther, *Hamp.* 50; *Sussex*, 165.
Lutterell, *Notts.* 122.
Lutton, *Devon*, 29, 31; *York*, 224.
Luttrell, *Devon*, 31; *Somerset*, 234.
Lutwich, *Stafford*, 146.

Lutwidge, *Camb.* 234; 236.
Luxford, *Sussex*, 234; *Essex*, 245.
Luxmoore, *Devon*, 234, 250.
Lybbe, *Oxford*, 128, 130.
Lychwr, *Glam.* 228.
Lyde, *Herts.* 54, 234; *Oxf.* 131.
Lydeat, *Staff.* 146.
Lydekku, *Herts*, 234.
Lydiat, *Staff.* 142.
Lydiate, *Lanc.* 69.
Lye, *Wilts*, 182.
Lyell, *Forfar*, 234.
Lygh, *Wilts*, 182.
Lyght, *Oxf.* 130.
Lygon, *Warw.* 172; *Worc.* 195.
Lyle, *Londonderry*, 234.
Lymbergh, *Dorset*, 33.
Lymme, *Chesh.* 17.
Lynch, *Kent*, 60; *Galway*, 234; *Mayo*, 234; 234.
Lyndsay, *Sussex*, 165.
Lyndhurst, *Hamp.* 50.
Lyne, *Hamp.* 50.
Lynford, *Bucks*, 10.
Lynes, *Leic.* 234.
Lynn, *Devon*, 31.
Lynne, *Camb.* 16; *Devon*, 29; *Northamp.* 111; *Rutland*, 136.
Lyon, 234.
Lyons, *Northamp.* 111, 112; *Chesh.* 234; *Westmeath*, 234; *Antrim*, 234.
Lys, *Hamp.* 50.
Lysley, *Herts*, 234.
Lyson, *Glam.* 228.
Lysons, *Glouc.* 234.
Lyssley, *Hamp.* 50.
Lyster, *York*, 224; *Shrop.* 234; *Roscommon*, 234.
Lyston, *Sussex*, 165.
Lytcott, *Oxford*, 130.
Lyte, *Somerset*, 140; *Wilts*, 185, 189, 191.
Lyttelton, *Worc.* 195.
Lytton, *Herts*, 53, 54, 56, 234.

M'Adam, *Kirkcudbright*, 234; 236.
Mac Adam, *Clare*, 234.
Macalister, *Ayr*, 234; *Argyll*, 234; 236.
M'Alpine, *Mayo*, 234.
Macartney, *Tyrone*, 234; *Antrim*, 234; 234.

Mac Braire, *Berwick*, 234.
M'Call, *Lanark*, 234; *Cork*, 234.
M'Carthy, *Cork*, 234.
Mac Causland, *Londonderry*, 234; *Derry*, 234; 234.
Maccaree, *Kent*, 60.
Macclesfield, *Staff.* 146.
Mc Clintock, *Louth*, 234; *Tyrone*, 234; *Donegal*, 234; *Londonderry*, 234.
Mc Clure, *Down*, 234.
Mc Culloch, *Kirkcudbright*, 234.
Mac Dermott, *Sligo*, 234; *Roscommon*, 234.
Macdonald, *Inverness*, 234; *Argyle*, 234; 234.
Mac Donald, *Dumfries*, 234; *Caithness*, 234.
M'Donald, *Perth*, 234.
Mac Donnell, *Clare*, 234; 237.
Mac Dougall, *Argyle*, 234.
Macdowall, *Renfrew*, 234, 237.
Mace, *Devon*, 31; *Kent*, 60.
Macer or Megre, *Warw.* 172.
Macevoy, *Meath*, 234.
Mc Farlan, *Stirling*, 234.
Macfarlane, *Dublin*, 234.
Macgeorge, *Galloway*, 234.
Mc Gildowny, *Antrim*, 234.
Mac Gillicuddy, 234.
M'Gregor, *Stirling*, 245.
Macgregor, *Perth*, 234.
Mac Gregor, *Stirling*, 234.
Mc Grigor, *Stirling*, 234.
Mac Guffie, *Kirkcudbright*, 234.
Machell, *Durham*, 36, 38; *York*, 215; *Lanc.* 234; 234.
Machen, *Glouc.* 234.
Machon, *Durham*, 38; *York*, 206.
Mc Intosh, *Herts*, 56.
Mc Kay, *Argyle*, 234; 236.
Makenzie, *Peebles*, 234; *Ross*, 234; *Midd.* 234; *Aberdeen*, 234; 234; 236; 246.
Mc Kerlies, *Wigton*, 234.
M'Kerrell, *Ayr*, 234.
Mackerrell, *Ayr*, 239.
Mackesy, *Queen's Co.* 234.
Mackinnon, *Midd.* 234; 234; 236.
Mackintosh, *Perth*, 234; 234.
Mackie. *Kirkcudbright*, 234.
Mc Kirdy, *Lanark*, 234.
Macknyghte, 246.

Mackworth, *Bucks,* 10, 11; *Rutland,* 135, 136.

Maclachlan, *Argyle,* 234.

Maclaine, *Argyll,* 234; *Glouc.* 234.

Maclane, *Berks,* 7.

Mc Laughlin, *Queen's Co.* 234.

Maclean, *Argyll,* 234; *Sussex,* 234.

Macleay, *Caithness,* 234.

Macleod, *Cromarty,* 234; 234; 236.

Mc Micking, *Wigton,* 234.

Mc Murray, *Limerick,* 234.

Macnaghten, *Antrim,* 234.

Macnamara, *Bedford,* 234; *Clare,* 234.

Macneil, *Inverness,* 234.

Mc Neill, *Antrim,* 234; *Lanark,* 234; 234.

Maconochie, *Midlothian,* 234.

Macpherson, *Inverness,* 234.

Macquaire, *Argyll,* 234.

Macqueen, *Inverness,* 234.

Macre, *Dumfries,* 234.

Macro, *York,* 206.

Mc Ternan, *Sligo,* 234.

Mc Veagh, *Meath,* 234.

Macworth, 236.

Madan, *Herts,* 56; *Leic.* 80.

Madden, *Monaghan,* 234; *Dublin,* 234; *Fermanagh,* 234.

Maddison, *Durham,* 34, 36, 38; *Linc.* 234.

Maddock, 234; 237.

Madock, *Glam.* 228; *Glouc.* 262.

Madoc now Maddocks, *Breck.* 227.

Madocks, *Denbigh,* 234; 236.

Madokes, *Durham,* 36.

Madrin, *Wales,* 229.

Madysonne, *Durham,* 40.

Maesmore, *Denbigh,* 234.

Magan, *Westmeath,* 234; *King's Co.* 234; 237.

Magenis, *Down,* 234.

Magill, *Westmeath,* 234.

Magnaville, *Herts,* 54.

Magor, *Cornw.* 234.

Maguire, *Fermanagh,* 234.

Maher, *Tipperary,* 234; *Wexford,* 234; 234.

Mahony, *Kerry,* 234.

Mainwaring, *Chesh.* 17; *Staff.* 145, 234; *Shrop.* 234; 236.

Maior, *Leic.* 80.

Maire, *Durham,* 34, 38; *York,* 209.

Maister, *York,* 217, 234.

Maisnell, *Northumb.* 118.

Maisterson, *Chesh.* 17.

Maitland, *Kirkcudbright,* 234; *Sussex,* 234; *Wigton,* 234.

Majendie, *Essex,* 234.

Makepeace, *Northamp.* 112.

Malby, *York,* 205.

Malcolm, *Dumfries,* 234; *Argyll,* 234.

Maleffant, *Wales,* 229.

Maleverer, *York,* 224.

Malet, *Durham,* 41; *Somerset,* 140; *Wilts,* 182.

Malham, *York,* 200.

Malhorn, 232.

Malie, *Dorset,* 33.

Maling, *Worc.* 234.

Mallet, *Devon,* 31, 234.

Mallock, *Devon,* 29.

Mallory, *Camb.* 16; *Chesh.* 17, 234; *York,* 200, 284; *Northamp.* 111.

Malmesbury, 236.

Malony, *Warw.* 172; *Clare,* 234.

Malore, *York,* 226.

Malory, *Leic.* 76, 80.

Malpus, *Chesh.* 17.

Maltravers, *Dorset,* 33; *Sussex,* 163; *Wilts,* 194; 232.

Maluval, *Notts,* 123.

Malvelyn, *Leic.* 80.

Malvoisin, *Shrop.* 137.

Malyn, *Wilts,* 185.

Malyvoryr, *York,* 226.

Man, *Kent,* 60; 251.

Manby, *Norfolk,* 108, 277; *York,* 224.

Mancestre, *Warw.* 172.

Manchester, *Lanc.* 71.

Mandeville, *Bucks,* 10; *Dorset,* 33; *Northamp.* 112.

Maners, *Durham,* 42.

Maningham, *Camb.* 16; *Kent,* 60.

Manley, *Chesh.* 17; *Staff.* 146, 234; *Kent,* 60.

Manlor, *Staff.* 146.

Mann, *Tyrone,* 234.

Manners, *Derby,* 26; *Durham,* 42; *Hamp.* 50; *Herts,* 56; *Leic.* 80; *Linc.* 82; *Northamp.* 112; *Rutl.* 135.

Manning, *Devon,* 31; *Dorset,* 234; *Sussex,* 165; *Monm.* 234; *Kent,* 60; 237.

Manningham, *Kent*, 67.
Manny, *Northamp.* 112.
Mannoch, *Suffolk*, 234.
Mansel, *Dorset*, 33 ; *Northamp.* 112, 234 ; *Glam.* 228 ; *Carm.* 230 ; 236.
Mansell, *Wales*, 229.
Manship, *Surrey*, 156.
Manseigh, *Tipperary*, 234 ; *Cork*, 234.
Mansfield, *Donegal*, 234 ; *Kildare*, 234 ; *Leic.* 234.
Mantell, *Kent*, 60 ; *Sussex*, 165.
Manwaring, *Chesh.* 17.
Manwood, *Kent*, 59, 60.
Maplesden, *Kent*, 60.
Marbury, *Chesh.* 17.
March, *Camb.* 16 ; *Durham*, 34, 38 ; *Hamp.* 50.
Marche, *Durham*, 40 ; *Kent*, 60 ; 233.
Marcon, *Norfolk*, 234.
Mares, *York*, 224.
Mareschal, *Herts*, 54 ; *Surrey*, 156.
Margery, *Middl.* 250.
Margesson, *Sussex*, 165, 234.
Margetson, *Surrey*, 158.
Marichurch, *Pemb.* 230 ; *Wales*, 229.
Marindin, *Shrop.* 234,
Marjoribanks, *Midlothian*, 234.
Markes, *Northamp.* 112 ; *Wilts*, 185.
Markham, *Northamp.* 111 ; *Notts*, 122, 124 ; *York*, 234 ; 235.
Marklove, *Glouc.* 234.
Markwick, *Sussex*, 165.
Marlborough, *Bucks*, 10 ; *Herts*, 54 ; *Northamp.* 112 ; *Sussex*, 165.
Marlay, *Westmeath*, 234.
Marler, *Kent*, 60.
Marley, *Durham*, 38 ; 237.
Marlott, *Sussex*, 165.
Marlow, *Essex*, 48.
Marling, *Glouc.* 234.
Marmion, *Leic.* 76, 80 ; *Northamp.* 111, 112 ; *Warw.* 172 ; *York*, 209.
Marmyon, *Oxf.* 134.
Marney, *Bucks*, 10 ; *Essex*, 47, 48.
Maron, *Warw.* 172.
Marriott, *Worc.* 234 ; *Kent*, 234 ; 236.
Marsey, *Notts*, 122.
Marsh, *Kent*, 60, 234 ; *Lond.* 96 ;

York, 213 ; *Essex*, 234 ; *Hants*, 234 ; *Queen's Co.* 234 ; 233.
Marshal, *Hamp.* 50 ; *Somerset*, 140.
Marshall, *Devon*, 29 ; *Durham*, 38 ; *Hunts*, 57 ; *Leic.* 80 ; *Northamp.* 112 ; *Sussex*, 165 ; *Wilts*, 192 ; *York*, 224 ; *Westm.* 234 ; *Corn.* 234 ; *Surrey*, 234 ; *Somerset*, 250.
Marsham, *Kent*, 60 ; *Norfolk*, 234.
Marske, *York*, 285.
Marston, *Leic.* 80 ; 233 ; *Staff.* 234 ;
Martell, *Wilts*, 182.
Martin, *Devon*, 29 ; *Dorset*, 33 ; *Durham*, 38 ; *Hamp.* 50, 234 ; *Northamp.* 112 ; *Oxford*, 131 ; *Suffolk*, 155 ; *Sussex*, 163 ; *Pemb.* 230 ; *Suffolk*, 234 ; *York*, 234 , *Notts*, 234 ; *Kent*, 234 ; *Worc.* 234 ; *Leic.* 234 ; *Lanc.* 234 ; *Sligo*, 234 ; *Galway*, 234 ; 236 ; 253.
Martineau, *Hants*, 234.
Martival, *Leicester*, 80.
Marton, *York*, 200 ; 232 ; *Lanc.* 234.
Martyn, *Bucks*, 10 ; *Camb.* 16 ; *London*, 104 ; *Somerset*, 140 ; *Sussex*, 165 ; *Wales*, 229 ; *Bedford*, 234 ; 245 ; *Galway*, 234.
Martyne, *Durham*, 36.
Marvin, *Wilts*, 185.
Marvyn, *Wilts*, 182.
Marwood, *Devon*, 29 ; *York*, 201, 220, 224.
Maryon, *London*, 94.
Mascall, *Sussex*, 165 ; *York*, 219, 224 ; *Durham*, 38.
Masculine, *Wilts*, 185.
Mason, *Kent*, 60 ; *Leic.* 80 ; *Wales*, 229 ; *Herts*, 234 ; *Norfolk*, 234 ; *Galway*, 234.
Massereene, 236.
Massey, *Camb.* 16 ; *Chesh.* 17, 234.
Massie, *Chesh.* 17, 234.
Massingberd, *Linc.* 234.
Massy, *Chesh.* 17 ; *Tipperary*, 234.
Master, *Derby*, 27 ; *Kent*, 60, 67 ; *Glouc.* 234 ; *Surrey*, 234.
Matcham, *Wilts*, 182.
Matham, *Herts*, 54.
Mathavarn, *Wales*, 229.
Matheson, *Ross*, 234.
Mathew, *Devon*, 29 ; *Glam.* 228 ;

Hamp. 50; *Essex*, 234; 234;
236; *Glouc.* 262.
Mathewe, *Northamp.* 111.
Mathias, *Pemb.* 230, 234.
Maton, *Wilts*, 185.
Matthew, *Durham*, 34; *Northamp.*
112; *Sussex*, 165; *York*, 205.
Matthews, *Hereford*, 234.
Maude, *Kent*, 60; *York*, 234;
Westm. 234.
Maudeley, *Somerset*, 140.
Mauduit, *Northamp.* 112; *Wilts.*182.
Mauley, *York*, 201, 220.
Mauleverer, *York*, 210, 213, 220,
234; 235.
Mauliverer, *York*, 205.
Maunsell, *Berks*, 3; 232; *Limerick*,
234, 239; *Kildare*, 234; *North-
amp.* 234.
Maundeville, *Norfolk*, 107.
Maunser, *Sussex*, 165.
Mauntell, *Northamp.* 112.
Maureward, *Leic.* 76, 80.
Maurice, *Wales*, 229.
Mautravers, *Wilts.* 182; 232.
Mauteby, *Norfolk*, 277.
Mawtby, *Norfolk*, 277.
Maxe, *Northamp.* 112.
Maxtone, *Perth*, 234.
Maxwell, *Renfrew*, 234, 245; *Gal-
loway*, 234; *Dumfries*, 234; *Down*,
234; *York*, 234; 234; 236; 250.
Maw, *Linc.* 86.
Mawdley, *Somerset*, 140.
May, *Bucks*, 11; *Hamp.* 50; *Kent*,
60, 234; *Leic.* 80; *Sussex*, 163,
165, 171; *Wilts*, 185.
Maydwell, *Essex*, 48.
Maye, *Somerset*, 140.
Maynard, *Derby*, 27; *Essex*, 48;
Herts, 53, 54; *Northamp.* 112;
York, 234.
Mayne, *Warw.* 176, 177; *Wilts.*
182, 234; *York*, 217; *Herts*, 54;
Monaghan, 234; 234; 246.
Mayo, *Herts.* 56; *Lond.* 96, 99.
Mayow, *Wilts*, 182; *Cornw.* 234.
Mayowe, *Wilts*, 185.
Meaburne, *Durham*, 38.
Mead, *Bucks*, 10.
Meade, *Camb.* 16; *Leic.* 80; *Cork*,
234, 250.
Meadows, *Suffolk*, 234.

Meares, *Westmeath*, 234.
Meale, *Bucks*, 13.
Meautys, *Herts.* 54.
Meaux, *York*, 217.
Medley, *Sussex*, 164, 165.
Medly, 234.
Medlycott, *Somerset*, 139; *Water-
ford*, 234.
Medhope, *Oxford*, 131.
Medhurst, *York*, 234.
De Medowe, *Suffolk*, 234.
Mee, 235.
Meekins, *Dublin*, 234.
Meere, *Dorset*, 33.
Meeres, *Hamp.* 50; *Notts.* 122;
Sussex, 165; *Linc.* 272.
Meetkerke, *Herts.* 54.
Meetkirke, *Herts.* 56.
Meggs, *Dorset*, 33; *Lond.* 96.
Megre, *Warw.* 172.
Meigh, *Staff.* 234.
Meignell, *Leic.* 76, 80.
Meil, *Wales*, 229.
Meinell, *York*, 201, 220.
Meireg, *Wales*, 229.
Meisnell, *Durham*, 38.
Melbourne, *Northamp.* 112.
Melhuish, *Devon*, 29.
Mellent, *Northamp.* 112.
Meller, *Dorset*, 33; *Hamp.* 50;
Derby, 259.
Mellish, *Notts.* 125; *York*, 224.
Mellor, *Derby*, 27; *Midd.* 239.
Melsa, *York*, 217.
Melton, *York*, 213, 217.
Melville, *Fife*, 234.
Melward, *Sussex*, 165.
Menifie, *Devon*, 31.
Mennis, *Kent*, 60.
Menvill, *Durham*, 38.
Menzies, 234, 236.
Meoles, *Chesh.* 17.
Merbury, *Chesh.* 17.
Mercia, *King's Co.* 258.
Merclesden, *Lanc.* 58.
Mere, *Chesh.* 17.
Meredith, *Chesh.* 17; *Denbigh*, 234.
Sligo, 234; *Kerry*, 234; *Wales*,
229.
Meredydd ap John, *Wales*, 229.
Meredydd ap Ivan, *Wales*, 229.
Meredydd ap Thomas, *Wales*, 229.
Meres, *Sussex*, 165.
2 Y

Meriett, *Warw.* 172.
Merifield, *Somerset*, 140.
Mering, *Notts*, 122.
Merland, *Surrey*, 156.
Merlay, *Northumb.* 119.
Merlott, *Sussex*, 163.
Merrick, *Lond.* 96.
Merriman, *Berks*, 7 ; *Lond.* 245.
Merriweather, *Kent*, 60.
Merry, *Berks*, 234.
Merryweather, *Kent*, 60.
Merse-Boycott, 250.
Merston, *Surrey*, 156.
Merton, *Chesh.* 17.
Mervyn, *Sussex*, 163, 165 ; *Wilts*, 182.
Meryton, *York*, 201, 224.
Meschens, *Northumb.* 118.
Meschines, *Northamp.* 112.
Mese, *Oxford*, 131.
Metcalf, *York*, 205.
Metcalfe, *Durham*, 38 ; *York*, 209 ; 224; *Suffolk*, 152, 234 ; *Bedf.* 234.
Metge, *Meath*, 234.
Metham, *York*, 213, 224.
Methuen, *Wilts*, 119, 234, 236.
Methwold, *Norfolk*, 278.
Meuric, *Pemb.* 230.
Meux, *Hamp.* 50 ; *Herts*, 56.
Meverell, *Derby*, 259.
Mewis, *Wilts*, 185.
Mexborough, *York*, 204.
Meynell, *York*, 201, 234, 239 ; *Derby*, 27, 234 ; *Staff.* 234, 236 ; 233.
Meynill, *York*, 224.
Meyrick, *York*, 213 ; *Wales*, 229; *Anglesey*, 234 ; *Hereford*, 234 ; *Pemb.* 234.
Meysey, *Worc.* 195.
Meysnil, *Leic.* 80.
Meytam, *York*, 226.
Michel, *Dorset*, 33, 234, 250.
Michelborne, *Sussex*, 164, 165, 168.
Michell, *Sussex*, 163, 165 ; *Wilts*, 182.
Mickleham, *Surrey*, 156.
Mickleton, *Dorset*, 38.
Micklethwait, *Norfolk*, 234 ; *York*, 234.
Micklethwayte, *York*, 217, 224.
Middlecot, *Wilts*, 182.
Middlecote, *Wilts*, 182.
Middleham, *York*, 213.

Middleton, *Durham*, 34, 36, 38, 42 ; *Kent*, 60; *Northumb.* 119, 121 ; *Notts*, 123 ; *Rutland*, 136 ; *Sussex*, 163, 164, 165 ; *York*, 224, 226, 234; *Derby*, 234 ; *Wales*, 229.
Midelton, *York*, 200.
Midford, *Durham*, 38.
Midgeley, *York*, 205.
Midlemore, *Warw.* 172.
Midleton, *Durham*, 40 ; *Sussex*, 168 ; *Westm.* 179.
Mighells, *Suffolk*, 150.
Milbank, *York*, 234.
Milbanke, *Durham*, 38.
Milbourne, 251.
Milburn, *Somerset*, 140.
Mildenhall, *Kent*, 60.
Mildmay, *Essex*, 48 ; *Herts*, 53 ; *Hamp.* 50 ; *Lond.* 96 ; *Northamp.* 112 ; *Somerset*, 139.
Miles, *Leic.* 80 ; *Somerset*, 234 ; *Glouc.* 234.
Milford, 236.
Mill, *Sussex*, 165.
Mille, *Sussex*, 163.
Miller, *Essex*, 48 ; *Hamp.* 60 ; *Herts*, 54, 56 ; *Sussex*, 163, 165 ; *Warw.* 234 ; *Surrey*, 234 ; *Ayr*, 234.
Milles, *Kent*, 60.
Millington, *Chesh.* 17.
Millot, *Durham*, 34, 36, 38, 40.
Millett, *Berks*, 7.
Mills, *Herts*, 56, 234 ; *Essex*, 234 ; *Sussex*, 168 ; *Suffolk*, 152, 234 ; 236.
Milne-Horne, 234.
Milner, *Kent*, 60 ; *Lond.* 96 ; *York*, 205, 213.
Milnes, *Derby*, 27, 234 ; *Notts*, 124 ; *York*, 205, 213, 234 ; *Linc.* 234.
Milneton, *Chesh.* 17.
Milton, *Bucks*, 13 ; 241.
Milward, *Somerset*, 140 ; *Notts*, 234; *Glouc.* 234 ; *Derby*, 259.
M'Minn, *Down*, 234.
Minchin, *Tipperary*, 234.
Minnitt, *Tipperary*, 234.
Minors, *Staff.* 146.
Minshull, *Berks*, 10 ; *Chesh.* 17 ; *Devon*, 31 ; *Lanc.* 72 ; *Sussex*, 165.
Mintern, *Dorset*, 33.
Mirehouse, *Pemb.* 234.
Mirfield, *York*, 213.

Mirfine, *Kent*, 60.
Missenden, *Bucks*, 10; *Northamp.* 112.
Mitchael, *Somerset*, 140.
Mitchel, *Essex*, 48.
Mitchell, *Aberdeen*, 234; *Roscommon*, 234; *Monaghan*, 234.
Mitford, *Berks*, 7; *Northamp.* 119, 234; *Sussex*, 234; *Hants*, 234; 236.
Mobberley, *Chesh.* 17.
Moeles, *Somerset*, 140.
Moels, *Herts*, 54; *Wilts*, 182.
Mohun, *Devon*, 22, 30, 31; *Dorset*, 33; *Northamp.* 112.
Mogradge, *Wilts*, 185.
Moilliet, *Worc.* 234.
Moir, *Stirling*, 234.
Moiston, *Wales*, 229.
Molam, *Dorset*, 33.
Moleyns, *Somerset*, 140.
Molford, *Devon*, 29.
Molines, *Oxf.* 131.
Molins, *Bucks*, 10; *Wilts*, 182, 185.
Molyneux, *Bucks*, 7; *Lanc.* 71; *Surrey*, 158, 234; *Sussex*, 165.
Moller, 234.
Mollesley, *Staff.* 143.
Molley, *King's County*, 234.
Molony, *Clare*, 234.
Mompesson, *Dorset*, 33; *Hamp.* 50; *Wilts*, 182.
Monboucher, *Durham*, 38; *Northumb.* 119; *Notts*, 122; *Sussex*, 169.
Monceaux, *York*, 217.
Monchensie, *Bucks*, 10.
Monchensey, *Bucks*, 10.
Monck, *Northumb.* 119; *Berks*, 234.
Monck-Mason, *Galway*, 234.
Monckton, *Kent*, 60.
Moncton, *Notts*, 125; *York.* 213.
Money, *Essex*, 234; 234; *Hereford*, 239.
Moningham, *Hamp.* 50.
Monington, 234.
Monins, *Kent*, 60, 234.
Monk, *Hamp.* 50; *Kent*, 60; *Sussex*, 165.
Monke, *Berks*, 7; *Sussex*, 165.
Monketon, *York*, 224.
Monoux, *London*, 103.
Monox, *Herts*, 56.
Monro, *Herts*, 56; *Surrey*, 234.

Monsel, *Limerick*, 234.
Monson, *Herts*, 54, 56.
Montacute, *Bucks*, 10; *Dorset*, 33; *Herts*, 54; *Northamp.* 112; *Surrey*, 156; *Sussex*, 163; *Somerset*, 140.
Montagu, *Wilts*, 191, 234; *York*, 234; *Bucks*, 23; *Northamp.* 111.
Montague, *Devon*, 29; *Lanc.* 69; *Sussex*, 163; 235.
Montaigne, *Norfolk*, 109.
Montalt, *Northamp.* 112; *Chesh.* 17
Monte, *Northamp.* 112.
Monteith, *Lanark*, 234.
Montfitchet, *Herts*, 54; *Lond.* 91.
Montford, *Norfolk*, 109.
Montfort, *Warw.* 172; *York*, 213; *Surrey*, 156.
Montgomerie, *Ayr*, 234; 246; 250.
Montgomery, *Norfolk*, 234; *Northamp*, 234; *Down*, 234; *Antrim*, 234; *Leitrim*, 234; *Donegal*, 234; *Tyrone*, 234.
Montresor, *Kent*, 234.
Monypenny, *Kent*, 60, 234; *Fife*, 234.
Moody, *Hamp.* 50; *Wilts*, 185; *Bedford*, 234; *Somerset*, 234.
Moorcroft, *Durham*, 38.
Moore, *Berks*, 3, 7; *Derby*, 27; *Dorset*, 33; *Hamp.* 50; *Kent*, 60; *Leic.* 77, 80, 234; *Oxf.* 128; *Somerset*, 140; *Surrey*, 156, 158, 234; *Wilts*, 182, 185; *York*, 217, 224; *Meath*, 234; *Linc.* 234; *Bedford*, 234; *Westm.* 234; *Kilkenny*, 234; *Wigan*, 234; *Tipperary*, 234; *Tyrone*, 234; *Mayo*, 234; *Antrim*, 234.
Moore-Stephens, *Devon*, 245.
Morant, *Hants*, 234; *Monaghan*, 234.
Moray, *Perth*, 234.
Mordaunt, *Leic.* 80; *Hamp.* 50; *London*, 92; *Norfolk*, 107; *Northamp.* 111, 112.
More, *Devon*, 29; *Herts*, 53, 54; *Oxf.* 130; *Surrey*, 156; *Sussex*, 165; *York*, 206, 213, 224, 234; *Shrop.* 234.
Morecroft, *Oxf.* 131.
Mores, *Berks*, 4; *Kent*, 58; *Glam.* 228.

Moreton, *Chesh.* 17, 234; *Northamp.* 112; *Staff.* 146; *York*, 224.
Morewick, *Northamp.* 112.
Morewood, *Derby*, 27, 234, 259; *York*, 206.
Morgan, *Dorset*, 33; *Durham*, 36; *Herts*, 54; *Monm.* 106, 275; *Northamp.* 112; *Somerset*, 140; *Surrey*, 156; *Breck.* 227; *Glam.* 228; *Wales*, 229; *Card.* 230; *Carm.* 230; *Flint*, 234; *Bucks*, 234; *Wexford*, 234; 236.
Morgan ap Flylip, *Wales*, 229.
Morgan ap John, *Wales*, 229,
Morganfychan, *Wales*, 229.
Moris or Morus, *Wales*, 229.
Morice, *Clare*, 234.
Morland, *Bucks*, 10; *Durham*, 38; *Kent*, 60, 234.
Morle, *Herts*, 54.
Morley, *Hamp.* 50; *Northamp.* 112; *Sussex*, 163, 164, 165, 168; *York*, 201, 220, 224, 234; 242; *Linc.* 272.
Mornington, 237.
Morpeth, *Durham*, 38.
Morony, *Clare*, 234.
Morrall, *Shrop.* 234.
Morrell, *Oxf.* 234,
Morrice, *Kent*, 234.
Morris, *Leic.* 77, 80; *Hamp.* 50; *York*, 205, 224, 234; *Shrop.* 234; *King's Co.* 234; *Devon*, 234; *Cork*, 234; *Wales*, 229.
Morrison *Herts*, 54, 55; *King's Co.* 234.
Morrogh, *Cork*, 234.
Morrist, *York*, 234.
Morshead, *Devon*, 234.
Mortimer, *Bucks*, 10; *Herts*, 54; *Rutland*, 136; *Shrop.* 137; *Surrey*, 156; *Wilts*, 185; *Worc.* 195; *Carm.* 230.
Mortlock, *Camb.* 234.
Mortmer, *Wales*, 229.
Morton, *Dorset*, 33; *Leic.* 80; *Surrey*, 162; *Sussex*, 165; *York*, 213, 224; 232; *Cavan*, 234.
Morus ap Grufydd, *Wales*, 229.
Morus Vachan, *Wales*, 229.
Morus, *Card.* 230.
Moryson, *Herts*, 53.
Moseley, *Lanc.* 70; *Staff.* 146;

Suff. 234; *Shrop.* 234; *Derby*, 234; 237.
Mosley, *Lanc.* 71, 245, 269.
Moss, *Lanc.* 234.
Mosse, *Queen's Co.* 234.
Mossman, *York and Lanc.* 245.
Mossock, *Durham*, 41.
Mostyn, *Denbigh*, 234; *Oxford*, 234; 236.
Moton, *Leic.* 76, 80.
Mott, *Berks*, 7; *Norfolk*, 234.
Motton, *Wales*, 229.
Mottram, *York*, 224.
Moubray, *Derby*, 27; *Rutl.* 136; *Fife*, 234; *Linc.* 273.
Mould, *York*, 219, 224.
Moulton, *Kent*, 67.
Moultrie, *Shrop.* 234.
Mounsey, *Cumb.* 234.
Mount Faltrel, *Northamp.* 112.
Mountaigne, *Durham*, 38; *York*, 224.
Mountchensy, *Herts*, 54.
Mountain, *Herts*, 234.
Mounteagle, *Leic.* 76.
Mountford, *Staff.* 146.
Mountfort, *Warw.* 172.
Mounteney, *Herts*, 54; *Leic.* 80; *York*, 206, 213.
Mountfitchet, *Bucks*, 13.
Mountgomery, *Northamp.* 111.
Mountney, *York*, 224.
Moutray, *Tyrone*, 234.
Mowbray, *Berks*, 234; *Bucks*, 11; *Durham*, 38; *Hamp.* 50; *Herts*; 54, 56; *Leic.* 80; *Linc.* 86, *Northamp.* 112; *Notts.* 125; *Sussex*, 163; 249; 250.
Moyle, *Bucks*, 10; *Kent*, 60; *Oxford*, 129.
Moyne, *Berks*, 7; *Hunts*, 57.
Moys, *Surrey*, 156.
Moyser, *York*, 224.
Moysey, *Somerset*, 234.
Mucegros, *Northamp.* 112.
Muckleston, *Shrop.* 234.
Mucklowe, *Worc.* 195.
Mudge, *Devon*, 234.
Mudie, *Forfar*, 234.
Muirhead, *Lanark*, 234.
Mulcaster, *Kent*, 60; *Cumb.* 234; *Surrey*, 158.

Mules, *Devon and Somerset,* 234, 239.
Mulgrave, *York,* 201; 231.
Mulholland, *Down,* 234.
Mullins, *King's Co.* 234.
Mulloy, 234; *Roscommon,* 234.
Mulsho, *Leic.* 76.
Mulso, *Bucks,* 10; *Northamp.* 111.
Multon, *Cumb.* 23; *Kent,* 60.
Munchensi, *Surrey,* 156; *Northamp.* 112.
Munck, *Devon,* 29.
Munday, *Derby,* 259.
Mundeford, *Norf.* 107.
Mundy, *Herts,* 54; *Leic.* 80; *Derby,* 234; 236; 251.
Munro, *Ross,* 234.
Murdac, *Warw.* 172.
Murdak, *Northamp.* 112.
Murdoch, *Perth,* 234.
Mure, *Ayr,* 234; *Suff.* 234.
Murphy, *Meath,* 234.
Murray, *Bucks,* 10, 234; *Herts,* 56; *Northumb.* 119; *Meath,* 234; *Selkirk,* 234; *Peebles,* 234; *Londonderry,* 234; *Stirling,* 234; *Dumfries,* 234; *Perth,* 234; *Wigton,* 234; *Suffolk,* 234; *Monaghan,* 234; 236.
Musard, *Berks,* 6; *Bucks,* 10; 232.
Muschamp, *Durham,* 42; *Surrey,* 156; 232.
Musgrave, *Cumb.* 22, 23; *Durham,* 38; *Kent,* 60; *Westm.* 179; *York,* 226; 236.
Muskham, *Notts,* 122.
Muskett, *Norfolk,* 234.
Mussel, *Wilts,* 185.
Mussenden, *Northamp.* 112; *Down,* 234.
Musson, *Shrop.* 137.
Musters, *Notts,* 122, 234.
Muttlebury, *Somerset,* 140.
Mychell, *Wilts,* 185.
Myddelton, *York,* 220; *Denbigh,* 234; *Wales,* 229; 234.
Myddelton, 242.
Mydleton, *Durham,* 40.
Myldemore, *Dorset,* 33.
Myles, *Wales,* 229.
Mylne, *Perth,* 234.
Mylner, *Kent,* 60.
Mylford, *Devon,* 31.

Mylle, *Glouc.* 262.
Mynn, *Sussex,* 156.
Mynors, *Stafford,* 143; *Hereford,* 234; *Worc.* 234; *Wales,* 234; 236.
Mytton, *Shrop.* 234; *Montgomery,* 234; 236.
Nagle, *Devon,* 234; *Cork,* 234.
Nailour, *Hunts,* 57.
Nais, *Wales,* 229.
Naish, *Limerick,* 234.
Naldrett, *Sussex,* 163, 165, 168.
Nanfan, *Worc.* 195.
Nangle, *Meath,* 234; 236; 250.
Nannan, *Wales,* 229.
Nanney, *Merioneth,* 234; *Carn.* 234; 237.
Naper, *Meath,* 234; *Somerset,* 234.
Napier, *Bedf.* 1; *Dorset,* 33.
Napper, *Dorset,* 33; *Somerset,* 140; *Oxford,* 131.
Napton, *Leic.* 80; *Warw.* 172; *Wilts,* 182.
Narborough, *Kent,* 60.
Nary, *York,* 224.
Nasford, *Warw.* 172.
Nash, *Northamp.* 112; *Surrey,* 158; *Sussex,* 163, 165; *Warw.* 178; *Worc.* 195, 234.
Naunton, *Leic.* 80.
Naylor, *Kent,* 60; *Montgomery,* 234; *Chesh.* 234.
Neal, *Leic.* 76; *York,* 205.
Neale, *Bucks,* 11; *Hamp.* 50; *York,* 224; *Warw.* 234; *Leic.* 80.
Neave, *Essex,* 48.
Nedham, *Herts,* 54; *Leic.* 80; *Northamp.* 112; *Jamaica,* 234.
Need, 234.
Needham, *Notts,* 234; 251.
Neile, *Durham,* 38.
Neill, *Ayr,* 234.
Nele, *Leic.* 80; *Rutl.* 136.
Nelson, *London,* 96; *Wilts,* 182; *Berks,* 234; 235; 236.
Nerwyt, *Essex,* 48.
Nesbit, *York,* 219, 224.
Nesbitt, *Cavan,* 234.
Nesham, *Durham,* 38.
Nethercote, *Northamp.* 234.
Nethersole, *Kent,* 60.
Nettles, *Cork,* 234.

Nevil, *Herts*, 53 ; *Surrey*, 156.
Nevile, *Somerset*, 140 ; *York*, 205, 213, 234 ; *Notts*, 234 ; *Northamp.* 234.
Nevill, *Bucks*, 10 ; *Cumb.* 23 ; *Durham*, 38, 44 ; *Kent*, 60 ; *Leic.* 80, 234 ; *Monm.* 106 ; *Northamp.* 111, 112 ; *Notts*, 122 ; *Warw.* 172 ; *York*, 224, 226 ; *Carm.* 234.
Neville, *Bucks*, 13 ; *Durham*, 38 ; *Essex*, 48 ; *Herts*, 54, 56 ; *Linc.* 86 ; *Sussex*, 163 ; *York*, 221 ; *Staff.* 234 ; *Dublin*, 234 ; *Kilkenny*, 234 ; 235.
Nevinson, *Kent*, 60.
Newbold, 251.
Newborow, *Somerset*, 140
Newbottle, *Northamp.* 111.
Newburgh, *Dorset*, 33.
Newbury, *Sussex*, 165.
Newcastle, *Sussex*, 165.
Newce, *Herts*, 56.
Newcomb, *Devon*, 31.
Newcombe, *Devon*, 29 ; *Herts*, 54, 56, 234.
Newcourt, *Devon*, 29.
Newdegate, *Warw.* 234 ; *Staff.* 234.
Newdigate, *Leic.* 80 ; *Surrey*, 156 ; *Warw.* 176, 177.
Newenham, *Cork*, 234.
Newington, *Kent*, 60 ; *Sussex*, 165.
Newland, *Surrey*, 156.
Newman, *Dorset*, 33 ; *Kent*, 60 ; *London*, 96 ; *Somerset*, 140, 234 ; *Sussex*, 165 ; *Bucks*, 234 ; *Glouc.* 234 ; *Cork*, 234 ; 236.
Newmarch, *Bucks*, 10 ; *Northamp.* 111 ; *Breck.* 227.
Newmarsh, *Linc.* 86.
Newnham, *Chesh.* 17 ; *Northamp.* 112 ; *Warw.* 172.
Newport, *Herts*, 54 ; *Northamp.* 112.
Newport-Charlett, *Worc.* 234.
Newsham, *Warw.* 176, 177.
Newton, *Chesh.* 17, 234 ; *Devon*, 31 ; *Leic.* 80 ; *Linc.* 82 ; *Somerset*, 140 ; 234 ; *Sussex*, 164, 165, 169 ; *York*, 213, 224 ; *Wales*, 229 ; *Glam.* 228 ; *Haddington*, 234 ; *Camb.* 234 ; *Tyrone*, 234 ; *Londonderry*, 233 ; *Carlow*, 234 ; 250 ; *Derby*, 259.
Newarke, *York*, 224.

Neyrnut, *Bucks*, 10.
Niblett, *Glouc.* 234.
Nichol, *Essex and Midd.* 239.
Nicholas, *Wilts*, 182, 185, 234 ; *Surrey*, 156 ; *Wales*, 229 ; *Hamp.* 50.
Nichole, *Essex*, 48.
Nicholl, *Herts*, 53, 56 ; 233 ; *Glam.* 234 ; *Monm.* 234.
Nicholls, *Bucks*, 13 ; *Leic.* 80 ; *Berks*, 234 ; *Norfolk*, 278.
Nicholson, *Durham*, 38, 42 ; *Kent*, 60 ; *Donegal*, 234 ; *Surrey*, 234 ; *York*, 234 ; *Meath*, 234 ; *Chester*, 234 ; *Glouc.* 234 ; *Down*, 234, 239 ; *Londonderry*, 234 ; 236.
Nicolas, *Cornwall*, 234 ; *London*, 234.
Nicolls, *Norfolk*, 278.
Nightingale, 234.
Nightingall, *Camb.* 16.
Nind, *Berks*, 7.
Nisbet, *Haddington*, 234 ; *Wilts*, 234.
Nisbett, *Leitrim*, 234 ; *Lanark*, 234 ; *Donegal*, 234.
Nisell, *Kent*, 60.
Niven, *Ayr*, 234.
Nixon, *Cavan*, 234.
Noble, *Devon*, 29 ; *Leic.* 80 ; *Staff.* 146.
Nodes, *Herts*, 54.
Noel, *Leic.* 80 ; *Lond.* 94 ; *Rutl.* 135 ; *Suffolk*, 152 ; *York*, 217 ; *Worc.* 234 ; *Warw.* 234 ; 236.
Noell, *Sussex*, 165 ; *York*, 224.
Noion, *Staff.* 153.
Nolan, 246.
Nooke, *Berks*, 3.
Noone, *Leic.* 80.
Norborn, *Wilts*, 185.
Norbury, *Worc.* 234.
Norcliff, *York*, 224.
Norcliffe, *York*, 234.
Norcop, *Shrop.* 234.
Norden, *Sussex*, 165 ; *Wilts*, 186.
Norfolk, *Bucks*, 11 ; *Herts*, 54 ; *Northamp.* 112 ; *Notts*, 122 ; *York*, 206.
Norland, *Herts*, 56.
Norman, *Staff.* 142 ; *Somerset*, 234 ; *Sussex*, 234 ; *Louth*, 234 ; *Donegal*, 234.

Normanvill, *Rutland*, 136.
Normanville, *York*, 213.
Norres, *Lanc.* 72, 73 ; 233.
Norreys, *Berks*, 8 ; *Herts*, 54 ; *Kent*, 60 ; *Lanc.* 69, 71, 234, 236.
Norris, *Berks*, 7 ; *Bucks*, 10, 13 ; *Devon*, 29 ; *Hamp.* 50 ; *Oxf.* 131, 133 ; *Somerset*, 140 ; *Midd.* 234.
Norrys, *Warw.* 172.
North, *Hamp.* 50 ; *Northamp.* 112 ; *Notts*, 122 ; *Suffolk*, 153 ; *Surrey*, 156 ; *Sussex*, 165 ; *Norfolk*, 234 ; *Lanc.* 234 ; 236.
Northampton, *Bucks*, 10 ; *Lanc.* 71 ; *Northamp.* 112.
Northcot, *Devon*, 31.
Northcote, *Devon*, 29 ; *Somerset*, 234.
Northey, *Bucks*, 10, 234 ; *Kent*, 60 ; *Surrey*, 156, 158, 234 ; 236.
Northmore, *Devon*, 234 ; 237.
Northover, *Somerset*, 140.
Northumberlànd, *Essex*, 48 ; *Northumb.* 119 ; 231 ; 232 ; 236 ; 239.
Northwick, 236.
Northwode, *Kent*, 66.
Northwood, *Kent*, 60.
Norton, *Camb.* 16 ; *Durham*, 38 ; *Hamp.* 50 ; *Herts*, 56 ; *Kent*, 60 ; *Warw.* 177 ; *York*, 208, 209, 224 ; 235 ; 253 ; *Worc.* 239.
Norwich, *Leic.* 80 ; *Northamp.* 111 ; *Oxf.* 133 ; *Suffolk*, 153.
Norwode, *Bucks*, 13.
Norwood, *Kent*, 60, 234.
Notbene, *Kent*, 60.
Notley, *Somerset*, 234.
Nottingham, *Kent*, 60.
Nourse, *Bucks*, 13 ; *Oxf.* 131 ; 234.
Nowell, *Essex*, 48 ; *Kent*, 60 ; *Lanc.* 68, 71 ; *Sussex*, 165, 168 ; *York*, 234 ; 236.
Nowers, *Bucks*, 10 ; *Leic.* 80.
Noye, *Sussex*, 165 ; *Cornw.* 20.
Noyes, *Sussex*, 169, 234.
Nugent, *Westmeath*, 234 ; *Cavan*, 234 ; *Down*, 234 ; *Galway*, 239 ; 241.
Nunn, *Wexford*, 234.
Nuthal, *Chesh.* 17.
Nuttall, *Worc.* 234.

Oakden, *Kent*, 234.

Oakeley, *Merioneth*, 234 ; *Salop*, 234 ; 236.
Oakes, *Suffolk*, 152.
Oaks, *Suffolk*, 234.
Oates, *York*, 204.
O'Brien, *Northamp.* 112 ; *Clare*, 234 ; 234 ; 246.
O'Callaghan, *Clare*, 234 : *Cork*, 234.
O'Connell, *Kerry*, 234.
O'Conor, *Roscommon*, 234.
O'Connor, *Roscommon*, 234.
Ocstede, *Surrey*, 156.
O'Daly, 246.
Odell, *Oxf.* 131 ; *Waterford*, 234.
Odingsels, *Herts*, 54 ; *Leic.* 76 ; 80 ; *Norfolk*, 107 ; *Notts*, 122.
Odingsells, *Warw.* 172.
Odinsells, *Warw.* 172.
O'Donel, *Mayo*, 234.
O'Donoghue, *Tipperary*, 234.
O'Donovan, *Cork*, 234,
O'Farrall, *Kildare*, 234.
O'Farrell, *Galloway*, 234.
O'Flanagan, 246.
O'Flarhertie, *Galway*, 234 ; 234.
Ofspring, 253.
Oglander, *Dorset*, 33 ; *Hamp.* 50.
Ogilby, *Londonderry*, 234 ; *Tyrone*, 234 ; *Forfar*, 234.
Ogle, *Durham*, 42 ; *Lanc.* 69 ; *Northumb.* 119, 120, 234, 239 ; 232.
Ogellthorpe, *Oxf.* 128.
Oglethorp, *Oxf.* 130.
Oglethorpe, *Surrey*, 156 ; *York*, 224.
O'Grady, *Antrim*, 234 ; *Limerick*, 234.
O'Hara, *Antrim*, 234 ; *Sligo*, 234.
Okenden, *Hamp.* 50 ; *Dorset*, 33 ; *Wilts*, 182.
Okeover, *Derby*, 27 ; *Leic.* 80 ; *Staff.* 234.
O'Kelley, *Roscommon*, 234 ; *Galway*, 234 ; *Kildare*, 234.
O'Kelly, *Kildare*, 234 ; 234 ; 239 ; 246.
Okewold, *Glouc.* 262.
Olaveson, *Isle of Man*, 267.
Oldershaw, *Leic.* 80.
Oldfield, *Chesh.* 17, 234, 239 ; *Sussex*, 234.
Oldmixon, *Somerset*, 140.
O'Leary, *Cork*, 234.

Oliphant, *Perth*, 234 ; *Cumb.* 234 ; 237.
Olive, *Monm.* 234.
Oliver, *Chesh.* 17 ; *Kent*, 60 ; *Wicklow*, 234.
Olivier, *Wilts*, 234.
Olliver, *Sussex*, 165.
Olney, *Bucks*, 10.
O'Loughlen, *Clare*, 234.
Olphert, *Donegal.*
Olton, *Chesh.* 17.
O'Malley, *Mayo*, 234.
Ombersley, *Kent*, 60.
Oneby, *Leic.* 77, 80.
Onebye, *Leic.* 77.
O'Neill, *Antrim*, 234 ; *Galway*, 234 ; 250.
Oneley, *Sussex*, 163, 165.
Onley, *Essex*, 48, 234; *Northamp.* 112.
Onslow, *Surrey*, 156, 162, 234 ; *Hunts*, 234 ; 236 ; *Sussex*, 163.
Onslowe, *Herts*, 54.
Orby, *Surrey*, 156.
Ord, *Durham*, 34, 38 ; *Leic.* 80 ; *Northumb.* 119, 234 ; *Suffolk*, 234.
Orde, *Durham.* 36, 38, 42 ; *Northumb.* 234.
Orfeur, *Cumb.* 22.
Organ, *Wilts*, 185.
Orkney, *Bucks*, 11.
Orlebar, *Bedf.* 234 ; 236.
O'Reilly, *Wicklow*, 234; *Cavan*, 234; *Queen's Co.* 234 ; *Louth*, 234; *Meath*, 234 ; *Down*, 234 ; *York*, 234 ; 236.
Orme, *Northamp.* 112 ; *Staff.* 142, 146 ; *Sussex*, 163 ; *York*, 224 ; *Mayo*, 234 ; 236.
Ormerod, *Chesh.* 17 ; *Lanc.* 68, 71, 234; *Glouc.* 234 ; *Somerset*, 140.
Ormonde, *Bucks*, 10 ; *York*, 206.
Ormsby, *Durham*, 43 ; *Mayo*, 234 ; *Shrop.* 234.
Orange, *Somerset*, 140.
O'Rorke, *Antrim*, 234.
Orpen, *Kerry*, 234.
Orreby, *Chesh.* 17.
Orred, *Chesh.* 234, 245.
Orrell, *Camb.* 16 ; *Lanc.* 71.
Orton, *Leic.* 80.
Osbaldeston, *Lanc.* 71 ; *Oxf.* 131 ; *Sussex*, 165 ; *York*, 213, 217, 224; *Glouc.* 162.
Osborne, *Devon*, 32 ; *Essex*, 48 ;

Herts. 54 ; *Kent*, 60, 67 ; *Northamp.* 111 ; *York*, 205, 213 ; *Tipperary*, 234 ; *Norfolk*, 278.
Osbourn, *Derby*, 259.
O'Shee, *Waterford*, 234.
Osmond, *Devon*, 31.
Oswald, *Ayr*, 234 ; *Fife*, 234.
Oteby, *Herts*, 56.
Otgar, *Lond.* 96.
Otho, or Other, *Surrey*, 158.
Ottley, *West Indies*, 234.
Otway, *York*, 224 ; *Tipperary*, 234.
Oulton, *Chesh.* 17.
Ouseley, *Bucks*, 10, 11.
Outhorpe, *Notts*, 122.
Overton, *Leic.* 80 ; *Somerset*, 140 ; *York*, 217.
Owein, *Pemb.* 230.
Owen, *Hamp.* 50 ; *Northamp.* 112 ; *Somerset*, 140 ; *Sussex*, 163 ; *Oxf.* 128, 130 ; *Wales*, 129 ; *Card.* 230 ; *Montgomery*, 234 ; *Shrop.* 234 ; *Anglesea*, 234 ; *Merioneth*, 234 ; *Antrim*, 234 ; 236.
Owen ap Gwalter, *Wales*, 229.
Owen ap Meredydd, *Wales*, 229.
Owen ap William, *Wales*, 229.
Owen Tydyr, *Wales*, 229.
Owens, *Carm.* 230.
Owst, *York*, 217.
Ower, *Kent*, 60.
Owsley, *Leic.* 234.
Oxborough, *Norfolk*, 278.
Oxenbridge, *Bucks*, 13 ; *Hamp.* 50, 51 ; *Herts*, 56 ; *Sussex*, 169.
Oxenden, *Kent*, 60.
Oxenford, *Northamp.* 111, 112.
Oxenham, *Sussex*, 165.
Oxford, *Kent*, 60 ; *Herts*, 54 ; *Norfolk*, 107.
Ozanne, 250.

Pabenham, *Bucks*, 11 ; *Northamp.* 112.
Pace, *Leic.* 10.
Pack, *Sussex*, 234, 237.
Pack-Beresford, *Carlow*, 234.
Packe, *Leic.* 80, 234, 236.
Packenham, *Kent*, 60.
Paddon, *Bedford*, 234.
Paganell, *Bucks*, 10 ; *Surrey*, 156.
Paganell, *Northamp.* 112 ; *Rutland*, 136.

Page, *Berks.* 8; *Chesh.* 17; *Herts.* 56; *Lond.* 96; *Sussex*, 163, 165; *Suffolk*, 235; *Somerset*, 234.
Paget, *Dorset*, 33; *Leic.* 80, 234; *Staff.* 143; *Somerset*, 234; *Worc.* 234; *Notts.* 234.
Pagitt, *Lond.* 96.
Paginton, *Bucks*, 10.
Paisley, *Essex*, 48.
Pakenham, *Linc.* 82; *Norfolk*, 107, *Northamp.* 112; 236.
Pakington, *Worc.* 195,234; *Bucks*,10.
Palæologus, 231.
Palgrave, *Norfolk*, 108.
Palleser, *York*, 224,
Paley, *York*, 234.
Palles, *Cavan*, 234.
Palliser, *Waterford*, 234.
Palmer, *Berks*, 7, 234; *Herts*, 56; *Kent*, 60, 234; *Leic.* 80; *Northamp.* 111; *Somerset*, 140, 234; *Sussex*, 163, 165, 168; *Shrop.* 137; *Warw.* 172; *Wales*, 229; *Dublin*, 234; *Essex*, 234; *Mayo*, 234; *Bedford*, 234; 236.
Palmerston, *Leic.* 80.
Palmes, *Hamp.* 50; *Leic.* 80; *Notts*, 122; *Rutland*, 135; *York*, 224, 226, 234; 236.
Palton, *Somerset*, 140.
Panton, *Sussex*, 165.
Papillon, *Essex*, 48; *Kent*, 60; *Sussex*, 234.
Paramor, *Kent*, 60.
Paramore, *Leic.* 80.
Paramour, *Kent*, 60.
Parbo, *Kent*, 60.
Parby, *Down*, 234.
Pardoe, *Shrop.* 234.
Pares, *Derby*, 234; 236.
Pargiter, *Northamp.* 112; *Staff.* 146.
Park, *Northamp.* 112.
Parke, *Durham*, 38; *Sligo*, 234.
Parker, *Devon*, 29, 234; *Herts*, 54; *Lanc.* 68, 234; *Lond.* 96, 99; *Staff.* 145, 146, 148, 234; *Surrey*, 161; *Sussex*, 165, 168; *Warw.* 177; *York*, 203, 205, 206, 213, 224, 234; *Wilts.* 182; *Cumb.* 234; *Cork*, 234; *Linc.* 234; *Staff.* 234; 232; 236; 251.
Parkes, *Staff.* 147.
Parkhouse, *Hunts*, 234, 239.
Parkin, *York*, 225.

Parkhurst, *Surrey*, 156, 162; *Northamp.* 112.
Parkins, *Herts*, 54.
Parkinson, *Durham*, 38.
Paris, *Hunts*, 57; *Norfolk*, 107:
Parmiger, *Hamp.* 50.
Parnell, *Sussex*, 165; *Wicklow*, 234.
Parr, *Herts*, 56; *Kent*, 60; *Leic.* 80; *Northamp.* 112; *York*, 209; *Lanc.* 234; *Glouc.* 234; *Chesh.* 234; *Devon*, 234; 233.
Parris, *Camb.* 16.
Parry, *Breck*, 227; *Wales*, 229; *Card.* 230, 234; *Pemb.* 230; *Carn.* 234; *Glouc.* 234; *Denbigh*, 234; 237.
Parry-Price, *Chesh.* 18.
Parsonne, *Camb.* 16.
Parsons, *Barbadoes*, 234.
Partryche, *Glouc.* 262.
Parvish, *Surrey*, 156.
Partridge, *Bucks*, 224; *Norfolk*, 234; *Glouc.* 234,
Pashley, *York*, 213.
Paslew, *Lanc.* 68.
Pasmere, *Devon*, 31.
Passelew, *York*, 205.
Passemere, *Devon*, 29.
Passy, 234.
Paston, *Oxf.* 133; 236; *Norfolk*, 276, 277.
Pate, *Leic.* 80.
Pateshull, *Herts*, 54; *Northamp.* 112; *Hereford*, 234.
Paterson, *Perth*, 234; 236, 237.
Paton, *Aberdeen*, 234.
Patrick, *Ayr*, 234; *Antrim*, 234; *Herts*, 56; 236.
Patrickson, *Cumb.* 234.
Patten, *Lanc.* 69, 234.
Pattenson, *Cumb.* 22, 23; *Kent*, 60, 234.
Pattinson, *Durham*, 245.
Pattison, *Durham*, 38.
Paul, *Sussex*, 165; *Glouc.* 234, 264.
Paule, *Durham*, 38.
Paulet, *Bucks*, 13; *Devon*, 29; *Wilts*, 185.
Pauncefote, *Glouc.* 234.
Pauncefoote, *Somerset*, 140.
Pauncefort, *Bucks*, 11.
Pavely, *Derby*, 25; *Northamp.* 111, 112; *Notts*, 122; *Wilts.* 182.
Pawlet, *Devon*, 29.

Pawlett, *Hamp.* 50; *London*, 96; *Somerset*, 140.
Pawson, *York*, 205; *Northumb.* 234.
Paxton, *Herts*, 56; *Wilts*, 234.
Pay, *Sussex*, 165.
Payler, *Kent*, 60; *York*, 224.
Payne, *Hunts*, 57; *Kent*, 60; *Somerset*, 140; *Suffolk*, 152; *Sussex*, 165; *Wilts*, 182; *Northamp.* 234.
Paynter, *Kent,* 60; *Cornw.* 234; *Surrey*, 234.
Payton, *Camb.* 16.
Paynell, *Leic.* 80; *Northamp.* 112.
Peabody, 246.
Peach, *Warw.* 234.
Peachey, *Sussex*, 163, 165; *Herts*, 54.
Peacock, *Durham*, 38; 234; *Linc.* 272.
Peacocke, *Essex*, 234; *Hamp.* 245.
Peake, *Denbigh*, 234.
Pearce, *London*, 96; *Brecon*, 234; 236; 237.
Peard, *Cork*, 234.
Peareth, *Durham*, 38, 234; *Northamp.* 112.
Pearsall, *Glouc.* 234.
Pearse, *Bedford*, 234.
Pearson, *Kent*, 60; *York*, 224.
Pease, *Durham*, 43; *York*, 234.
Peche, *Derby*, 27; *Leic.* 80; *Warw.* 172.
Peck, *Leic.* 80; *Sussex*, 165, 168.
Peckham, *Sussex*, 163, 165, 234.
Pedder, *Lanc.* 234.
Pedler, *Devon*, 234.
Pedwardyn, *Northamp.* 111.
Peebles, *York*, 224.
Peel, *Lanc.* 234, 239; *Flint*, 234; *Glouc.* 234; *Pemb.*234; 237; 250.
Peek, *Kent*, 60.
Peers, *Oxford*, 234.
Pegge, *Derby*, 27, 259; *York*, 206.
Peirce, *Kent*, 60.
Peirs, *Kent*, 60; *Sussex*, 165; *York*, 219.
Peirse, *York*, 224, 234; 233.
Peirson, *York*, 220.
Peke, *Kent*, 60; *York*, 226.
Pekeryng, *Cumb.* 24.
Pelham, *Dorset*, 33; *Hamp.* 50; *Herts*, 54; *Sussex*, 164, 165, 169, 246; *Shrop.* 234.

Pellatt, *Sussex*, 163, 165.
Pellew, *Herts*, 56.
Pelsant, *Leic.* 80.
Pelsett, *Camb.* 16.
Pemberton, *Durham*, 34, 36, 38, 234; *Northamp.* 111; *Lanc.* 234; *Shrop.* 234; 237.
Pembroke, *Herts*, 54; *Leic.* 80; *Surrey*, 156; *Northamp.* 112; *Wilts*, 182.
Pembruge, *Leic.* 80; *Shrop.* 137.
Pendarves, *Cornw.* 234.
Pendock, *Notts.* 122.
Pendrell, 242.
Penell, *Worc.* 195.
Pengriffin, *Wales*, 229.
Peniston, *Oxford*, 130.
Penistone, *Norfolk*, 278.
Penn, *Bucks*, 10, 11, 234.
Pennant, *Wales*, 229; *Flint*, 234; *Carn.* 234.
Penne, *Dorset*, 33; *Herts*, 54.
Pennefather, *Tipperary*, 234.
Pennington, *Cumb.* 22, 23; *Somerset*, 140.
Pennyman, *York*, 201, 220, 224, 234; 246.
Pennystone, *Oxford*, 128.
Penrhyn, *Wales*, 229.
Penrice, *Herts*, 54; *Norfolk*, 234; *Glam.* 234.
Penris, *Hamp.* 50.
Penrose, *Cork*, 234.
Penruddock, *Wilts*, 185.
Penruddocks, *Wilts*, 182, 234.
Pentland, *Louth*, 234.
Penny, *Wales*, 229; *Glam.* 228; *Carm.* 230.
Peper, *Hamp.* 50.
Pepis, *Camb.* 16.
Peploe, *Hertf.* 234.
Peppard, *Limerick*, 234.
Pepper, *Leic.* 80; *Meath*, 234; *Tipperary*, 234.
Pepsall, *Hamp.* 50.
Pepwell, *Glouc.* 262.
Pepys, *Norfolk*, 107.
Percehay, *York*, 224, 226.
Percival, *Somerset*, 140; *Sligo*, 234; *Wexford*, 234; *Down*, 234;
Percivall, *Somerset*, 140.
Percy, *Bucks*, 10; *Cumb.* 23; *Durham*, 38; *Essex*, 48; *Leic.* 80; *Nor-*

thamp. 112 ; *Northumb.* 119 ; *Sussex*, 163 ; *Worc.* 195 ; *Warw.* 234 ; *York*, 200, 215, 220, 224 ; 232.
Perfect, *Berks*, 7.
Perient, *Herts*, 54.
Perin, *Leic.* 80.
Perkes, *Staff.* 146.
Perkins, *Leic.* 80, 234 ; *York.* 213 ; *Warw.* 234.
Perkinson, *Durham*, 34, 40 ; *York*, 224.
Perkyn, *Wales*, 229.
Perkynson, *Durham*, 38.
Perne, *Camb.* 16.
Perot, *Wales*, 229.
Perott, *Berks*, 7.
Perriam, *Devon*, 29.
Perrier, *Cork*, 234.
Perrot, *Oxf.* 128, 131 ; *Worc.* 195 ; *York*, 205 ; 242.
Perrott, *Bucks*, 11 ; *Oxford*, 130 ; *Carm.* 230 ; *Pemb.* 230.
Perry, *Berks*, 7 ; *Essex*, 48 ; *Herts.* 56 ; *Somerset*, 140 ; *Card.* 230 ; *Warw.* 234 ; *Tipperary*, 234 ; 234,
Pershall, *Kent*, 60.
Pershouse, *Staff.* 143, 146, 234.
Persse, *Galway*, 234.
Pert, *Herts*, 56.
Peryent, *Herts*, 56.
Pery, *Devon*, 29.
Pescod, *Hamp.* 50.
Pesmeade, *Hamp.* 50.
Pestell, *Leic.* 80.
Peter, *Devon*, 31 ; *Cornw.* 234 ; 236.
Peters, *Bucks*, 13 ; *Lanc.* 234 ; 236.
Petley, *Kent*, 60.
Peto, *Warw.* 172.
Petre, *Devon*, 29; *Essex*, 48 ; *Surrey*, 156 ; *Corn.* 234 ; 235.
Pett, *Kent*, 60.
Pettiward, *Suff.* 234.
Pettit, *Kent*, 60.
Petitt, *Kent*, 60.
Pettus, *Norfolk*, 107.
Petty, *Oxford*, 128, 130, 131.
Pettyfer, *Northamp.* 112.
Peverel, *Derby*, 25 ; *Dorset*, 33 ; *Northamp.* 111, 112 ; *Sussex*, 163; *Shrop.* 137.
Peverell, *Norfolk*, 109 ; *Wilts*, 182.
Pexall, *Leic.* 80.
Pexsall, *Hamp.* 50.

Peyton, *Sussex*, 234 ; *Leitrim*, 234 ; *Camb.* 256 ; *Bucks*, 11 ; *Kent*, 60.
Peyver, *Herts*, 54.
Peyvre, *Bucks*, 13.
Phaire, *Wexford*, 234.
Phelip, *Herts*, 54.
Phelips, *Somerset*, 234 ; *Herts*, 234.
Phelps, *Leic.* 80.
Phetiplace, *Oxford*, 131.
Pheffard, *Surrey*, 156.
Philibert, *Berks*, 8.
Philip, *Wales*, 229.
Philippe, *York*, 208.
Philips, *Somerset*, 140 ; *Lanc.* 234 ; *Staff.* 234 ; 234.
Philipps, *Pemb.* 234 ; *Carm.* 234 ; 234.
Philipson, *Westm.* 179.
Phillimore, *Berks*, 7 ; *Oxford*, 234.
Phillip, *Durham*, 38 ; *York*, 285.
Phillips, *Wales*, 229 ; *Wilts*, 185 ; *Warw.* 177 ; *Pemb.* 234 ; *Monm.* 234 ; *Cavan*, 234.
Phillipps, *Leic.* 80, 250 ; *Wilts*, 185 ; *Hamp.* 50; *Card.* 230 ; *Pemb.* 230 ; *Hereford*, 234, 239 ; *Leic.* 234, 239 ; 236.
Phillippes, *Carm.* 230.
Philpott, 235.
Philpotts, *Corn.* 234.
Phipps, *Bucks*, 11 ; *Wilts*, 182, 234 ; *Sussex*, 165.
Phowk, *Wales*, 229.
Phulk, *Wales*, 229.
Picot, *Northamp.* 112.
Pickard, 234.
Pickersgill, *Surrey*, 234.
Pickford, *Shrop.* 137.
Pickhaver, *Wilts*, 185.
Pickering, *Leic.* 80 ; *Northumb.* 111 ; *York*, 205 ; *Sussex*, 165 ; 233 ; *Surrey*, 234.
Pictavensis, *Lanc.* 69.
Pidcock, *Guernsey*, 234.
Pierce, *Somerset*, 140.
Piercy, *Dorset*, 33.
Piers, *Camb.* 16 ; *Dorset*, 33 ; *York*, 205.
Pierson, *York*, 219.
Pierpoint, *Sussex*, 169 ; *Shrop.* 137.
Pierpont, *Notts*, 122.
Pigeon, *Hamp.* 50 ; *Kent*, 60.
Pigge, *Northamp.* 112.

Pigot, *Bucks,* 10 ; *Camb.* 16 ; *Notts.* 122 ; 236.
Pigott, *Bucks,* 10, 234 ; *Herts,* 56 ; *Sussex,* 165 ; *York,* 205 ; *Shrop,* 234 ; *Somerset,* 234 ; *Galway,*234 ; *Hants,* 234 ; *Wexford,* 234 ; 236.
Pike, *Wilts,* 185.
Pikering, *Hants,* 57.
Pilcher, *Kent,* 60.
Pile, *Wilts,* 185.
Piley, *York,* 213.
Pilfold, *Sussex,* 165, 163.
Pilkington, *Durham,* 34, 38, 40 ; *Herts,* 53, 54 ; *Lanc.* 71 ; *Leic.* 80 ; *York,* 213, 234 ; *Westmeath,* 234 ; *Queen's Co.* 234 ; 251.
Pilsdon, *Wales,* 229.
Pimpe, 233.
Pinchon, *Surrey,* 158.
Pindar, *Linc.* 86.
Pine, *Somerset.* 140.
Pinfold, *Bucks,* 11, 234.
Pinke, *Oxf.* 131.
Pinkeney, *Herts,* 54 ; *Northamp.* 111, 112.
Pinkney, *Warw.* 172 ; *Wilts,* 185 ; *York,* 224.
Pinney, *Somerset,* 234.
Piot, *Staff.* 146.
Pipe, *Leic.* 80 ; *Staff.* 142, 143, 146 ; *Warw.* 172.
Piper, *Devon,* 234.
Piriton, *Northumb.* 119 ; *Warw.* 172.
Pister, *Hamp.* 50.
Pitcairn, *Perth,* 234.
Pitchford, 233.
Pitfield, *Lond.* 96.
Pitt, *Bucks,* 13 ; *Dorset,* 33 ; *Hamp.* 50 ; *Leic.* 80 ; *Somerset,* 140 ; *Wilts,* 192 ; *Rutland,* 136.
Pittesford, *Northamp.* 112.
Pix, *Kent,* 60.
Place, *Durham,* 36, 38 ; *York,* 226.
Plantagenet, *Berks,* 7 ; *Bucks,* 10 ; *Essex,* 48 ; *Herts,* 56 ; *Lanc.* 74 ; *Northamp.* 111 ; *Notts,* 125.
Platt, *Surrey,* 156.
Player, *Hamp.* 50.
Playse, *Durham,* 34, 40.
Playsted, *Sussex,* 168.
Playters, *Suffolk,* 153.
Playz, *Herts,* 54.
Plecy, *Dorset,* 33 ; *Surrey,* 158.

Pledgerd, *Camb.* 16.
Plescy, *Surrey,* 156.
Plessington, *Rutland,* 135.
Plessitis, *Hamp.* 50.
Plessis, *Northumb.* 119.
Plessy, *Wilts,* 182.
Pleydell, *Berks,* 3, 4 ; *Dorset,* 33, 234 ; *Wilts,* 185.
Plomer, *Herts,* 54, 56, 234 ; 233.
Plott, *Berks,* 3.
Plot, *Staff.* 143.
Plowden, *Northamp.* 112 ; *Oxf.* 131 ; *Hants,* 234, 246 ; *Shrop.* 234.
Plumbe, *Leic.* 80 ; *Lanc.* 71.
Plumleigh, *Devon,* 31.
Plumer, *Herts,* 54, 56.
Plummer, *Selkirk,* 234.
Plumpton, *Derby,* 27 ; *Herts,* 54 ; *Northamp.* 111, 112 ; *York,* 200, 224, 226.
Plumptre, *Kent,* 60, 234 ; *Notts,* 122 ; 236.
Pochin, *Leic.* 80, 234.
Pockley, *York,* 217, 224.
Pocklington, *Notts,* 123.
Pocock, *Berks,* 7 ; *Durham,* 37.
Pode, *Devon,* 234.
Poe, *Tipperary,* 234.
Poer, *Waterford,* 234 ; 236.
Poher, *Northamp.* 112.
Pointingdon, *Devon,* 29.
Pole, *Derby,* 27, 234 ; *Herts,* 54 ; *Glouc.* 234, 262 ; *Sussex,* 163.
Poleyn, *Glouc.* 262.
Polhill, *Kent,* 60 ; *Sussex,* 165 ; *Wilts,* 182 ; 233 ; *Bedford,* 234.
Pollard, *Durham,* 34 ; *Devon,* 29 ; *Oxf.* 131 ; *Somerset,* 140 ; *Westmeath,* 234.
Pollen, *Hamp.* 50 ; *Surrey,* 234.
Polley, *Herts,* 56 ; *Kent,* 60.
Pollock, *Meath,* 234 ; 237.
Polsted, *Surrey,* 162 ; *Sussex,* 165.
Polwhele, *Corn.* 20, 234 ; 236.
Pomerai, *Devon,* 32.
Pomeray, *Devon,* 31.
Ponsonby, *Cumb.* 23, 234 ; *Surrey,* 158.
Ponynges, 232.
Poole, *Chesh.* 17 ; *Hamp.* 50 ; *Kent,* 60 ; *York,* 205 ; *Cork,* 234 ; *Derby,* 259.
Pooley, *Camb.* 16.

Poore, *Wilts*, 185.
Pope, *Kent*, 60; *Leic.* 76; *Northamp.* 112; *Oxf.* 127, 128, 130, 131; *Sussex*, 165.
Popeley, *York*, 213.
Popham, *Hamp.* 50, 234; *Leic.* 80; *Somerset*, 140, 234; *Wilts*, 182, 234; *Corn.* 234.
Popkin, *Glam.* 228.
Popplewell, *Linc.* 86, 274.
Porcas, *Kent*, 60.
Porch, *Somerset*, 234.
Porcher, *Dorset*, 234.
Porker, *Kent*, 60.
Port, *Kent*, 58; *Derby*, 258.
Portal, *Hants*, 234.
Porte, *Staff.* 146.
Porter, *Cumb.* 22; *Durham*, 36, 38, 40; *Kent*, 60; *Linc.* 82; *Sussex*, 165; *Wales*, 229; *Fermanagh*, 234; *Surrey*, 234.
Portman, *Dorset*, 33, 234; *Somerset*, 140; 236.
Portington, *York*, 205, 213, 224.
Post, *Kent*, 60.
Postlethwaite, *Cumb.* 234.
Poto, *Bucks*, 10.
Poticany, *Wilts*, 193.
Potkyn, *Camb.* 16.
Pott, *Selkirk*, 234; *Kent*, 234.
Potter, *Derby*, 27.
Pottinger, *Kildare*, 234; 237.
Pounde, *Hamp.* 50.
Pounden, *Wexford*, 234.
Poulteney, *Herts*, 54.
Poultney, *Herts*, 53; *Leic.* 76, 80.
Poutrell, *Notts*, 122.
Powel, *Chesh.* 17; *Breck.* 227; *Glam.* 228; *Wales*, 229.
Powell, *Bucks*, 13; *Leic.* 80; *Lond.* 96; *Oxf.* 131; *Sussex*, 165; *Wilts*, 182, 234; *Breck.* 227; *Glam.* 228; *Card.* 230, 234; *Carm.* 230; *Pemb.* 230; *Lanc.* 234; *Limerick*, 234; 236.
Power, *Leic.* 80; *Oxf.* 128, 130; *Sussex*, 163, 165; *Wilts*, 194; *York*, 205; *Waterford*, 234; *Hereford*, 234.
Powke, *Staff.* 143.
Powis, *Herts*, 56; *Northamp.* 112; *Sussex*, 165; *Shrop.* 137.
Powlett, *Berks*, 7; *Sussex*, 165; 232.

Pownall, *Chesh.* 234.
Powney, *Berks*, 8.
Powtrell, *Derby*, 259.
Powys, *Wales*, 229; *Staff.* 234; *Shrop.* 234; *Oxf.* 234.
Poyner, *Herts*, 54.
Poynings, *Surrey*, 156; *Sussex*, 165, 169.
Poyntington, *Devon*, 31.
Poyntz, *Dorset*, 33; *Herts*, 54; *Oxf.* 128; *Sussex*, 163, 165, 234; *Essex*, 260.
Praed, *Bucks*, 11.
Praers, *Chesh.* 17.
Pragiter, *Northamp.* 111.
Prater, *Wilts*, 185.
Pratt, *Leic.* 80; *Hunts*, 57; *Norfolk*, 234, 277; *Staff.* 234; *Cavan*, 234; *Berks*, 4; 237.
Prayers, *Northamp.* 111.
Prees, *Glam.* 228.
Prendreth, *Kent*, 60.
Prescott, *Durham*, 38, 43; *Herts*, 56; 251.
Prestland, *Chesh.* 17.
Prestley, *Herts*, 54.
Preston, *Devon*, 29; *Durham*, 40; *Herts*, 54; *Lanc.* 71, 234; *Somerset*, 140; *York*, 234; *Meath*, 234; 233; *Northamp.* 112; *Kent*, 60.
Prestwich, *Lanc.* 71.
Prestwiche, *Leic.* 80.
Prestwood, *Devon*, 29, 31.
Priaulx, *Wilts*, 192.
Price, *Berks*, 7; *Chesh.* 17, 234; *Herts*, 56; *Breck.* 227, 234; *Glam.* 228; *Wales*, 229; *Carm.* 230, 234; *Down*, 234; *Radnor*, 234; *Anglesey*, 234; 236.
Prichard, *Breck.* 227; *Glam.* 228; *Wales*, 229.
Prickart, *Wales*, 229.
Pricket, *York*, 224.
Prickett, *York*, 234.
Pride, *Berks*, 7; *Herts*, 56.
Prideaux, *Devon*, 29, 32, 234; *Corn.* 234; 236.
Pridham, *Devon*, 239.
Priestley, *York*, 234.
Prime, *Sussex*, 234; 234.
Prince, *Devon*, 30.
Pringle, *Selkirk*, 234.
Prinsep, 236.

Prior, *Queen's Co.* 234; 236.
Probert, *Wales,* 229.
Probyn, *Glouc.* 234.
Proctor, *Bucks,* 10; *Camb.* 16; *Northumb.* 120.
Prodgers, *Monm.* 234.
Proger, *Glam.* 228.
Protherch, *Wales,* 229.
Prothero, *Monm.* 234.
Provender. *Wilts,* 185.
Proude, *Kent,* 60.
Prouse, *Devon,* 29, 31.
Prouz, *Devon,* 31.
Prowse, *Devon,* 31; *Northamp.* 112; *Somerset,* 140.
Prowz, *Devon,* 29.
Prudderch, *Carm.* 230.
Prower, *Wilts,* 234.
Prowett, *Oxf.* 234.
Pryce, *Glam.* 228, 234; *Wales,* 229; *Card.* 230; *Montg.* 234.
Prye, *Devon,* 29, 31.
Pryme, *York,* 282.
Prynn, *Wilts,* 185.
Prynne, *Wilts,* 194.
Prys, *Wales,* 229; *Card.* 230; *Carm.* 230.
Pryse, *Wales,* 220; *Card.* 234.
Prytherch, *Carm.* 234.
Puckeringe, *Herts,* 54.
Pudsey, *Oxf.* 131; *Staff.* 146, 234; *Warw.* 172; *York,* 200, 205, 224, 226.
Pugh, *Wales,* 229; *Carm.* 234; *Montg.* 234; 247.
Pughe, *Wales,* 229.
Puleston, *Northamp.* 112
Pulford, *Chesh.* 17.
Pulleine, *York,* 234.
Puller, *Herts,* 234.
Pulleyn, *York,* 226.
Pulteney, *Leic.* 80.
Pultney, *Herts,* 53.
Pulter, *Derby,* 27; *Herts,* 53, 54; *Hunts,* 57.
Pulton, *Leic.* 77; *Northamp.* 111.
Punshon, *Durham,* 36, 38, 40.
Purcell, *Staff.* 146; *Cork,* 234; *Dublin,* 234; 234.
Purdon, *Clare,* 234; *Westmeath,* 234.
Purefey, *Leic.* 76; *Warw.* 172.
Purefoy, *Bucks,* 10; *Leic.* 80; *Northamp.* 112; *Tipperary,* 234.

Purtrell, *Glouc.* 234.
Purton, *Shrop.* 234.
Purvis, *Northumb.* 119; *Suffolk,* 234; *Hants,* 234; *Durham,* 234.
Pusey, *Berks,* 3, 234; 231; 236,
Putt, *Devon,* 29.
Puttenham, *Hamp.* 50.
Putland, *Wicklow,* 234.
Puxley, *Cork,* 234.
Pybus, *Dorset,* 33.
Pycheford, 233.
Pycot, *Herts,* 54.
Pye, *Berks,* 7; *London,* 96; *Wales,* 229; *Staff.* 234; *Lanark,* 234.
Pyke, *Dorset,* 33; *Somerset,* 140.
Pym, *Herts,* 54; *Kent,* 60; *Bedford,* 234.
Pymme, *Somerset,* 140.
Pynchon, *Bucks,* 13.
Pyncombe, *Devon,* 31.
Pyne, *Devon,* 29; *Somerset,* 140, 234.
Pyrke, *Glouc.* 234.
Pyrry, *Wilts,* 185.
Pytt, *Wilts,* 182.
Pytts, *Worc.* 195.
Pyott, *Staff.* 143.
Pyrs, *Wales,* 229.

Quarles, *Essex,* 48.
Quartoch, *Somerset,* 234; 236.
Quayle, *Isle of Man,* 234.
Quesne, *Essex,* 48.
Quicke, *Devon,* 234.
Quincy, *Leic.* 80; *Northamp.* 112; *Herts,* 54.
Quiney, *Warw.* 176, 177.
Quinton, *Kent,* 60.
Quintyn, *Wilts,* 185.

Rabett, *Suffolk,* 234.
Raby, *Chesh.* 17.
Radbard, *Somerset,* 140.
Radcliff, *York,* 200.
Radcliffe, *Dorset,* 33; *Durham,* 38; *Essex,* 48; *Herts,* 56, 234; *Devon,* 234; *Kent,* 60; *Lanc.* 68, 71, 268; *Northumb.* 120; *Sussex,* 165; 236; 232.
Radclyffe, *Durham,* 38; *Lanc.* 234; *Rutland,* 136.
Radeclive, *Lanc.* 68.
Radford, *Dorset,* 33; *Derby,* 234.

Radnor, *Wilts*, 182.
Raffles, *Lanc.* 234.
Rafton, *Durham*, 37.
Raglan, *Glam.* 228.
Ragon, *Northamp.* 112.
Rahn, *Essex*, 48.
Raikes, *York*, 234.
Raines, *Sussex*, 165 ; *York*, 217, 234.
Rainsford, *Herts*, 56 ; *Oxford*, 128.
Rait, *Forfar*, 234.
Ralfe, *Kent*, 60 ; *Sussex*, 165.
Ralegh, *Devon*, 29 ; *Warw.* 172 ; *Wilts*, 182.
Raleigh, *Somerset*, 140.
Ralston, *Renfrew*, 234.
Ram, *Wexford*, 234.
Ramey, *Norfolk*, 108.
Rampton, *Notts.* 123.
Ramsay, *Midlothian*, 234 ; *Midd.* 234 ; *Edinb.* 234 ; *Aberdeen*, 234.
Ramsbotham, *Lanc.* 234.
Ramsden, *Notts.* 234 ; *York*, 213 ; 237.
Rand, *Durham*, 38.
Randolph, *Kent*, 60 ; *Sussex*, 169.
Randyll, *Staff.* 143.
Raper, *Sussex*, 165.
Rasby, *York*, 213.
Rashleigh, *Cornwall*, 234 ; 236.
Rastall, *Notts.* 124.
Ratcliff, *Durham*, 34.
Ratcliffe, *Durham*, 40 ; *York*, 201, 206, 224.
Rathbone, *Lanc.* 234.
Ratinden, *Northamp.* 112.
Rattray, *Perth*, 234 ; *Warw.* 234.
Ravenscroft, *Sussex*, 165 ; *Wales*, 229.
Ravenscrofft, *Wales*, 229.
Ravensworth, *Durham*, 38 ; *York*, 209.
Rawden, *York*, 205.
Rawe, *Durham*, 38.
Rawleigh, *Wilts*, 185.
Rawles, *Dorset*, 33.
Rawling, *Herts*, 54.
Rawlings, *Cornwall*, 234.
Rawlinson, *Lanc.* 234 ; *Hants*, 234.
Rawlins, *Warw.* 177.
Rawson, *York*, 206, 213, 218, 224, 234.
Rawstone, *Essex*, 48.

Rawstorne, *Lanc.* 234.
Rayman, *Sussex*, 165.
Rayment, *Herts*, 56.
Raymes, *Northumb.* 119.
Raymond, *Essex*, 48, 234 ; *Herts*, 54 ; *Dorset*, 534 ; *Kerry*, 234 ; *Somerset*, 104, 237.
Rayleigh, *Essex*, 48.
Rayne, *Durham*, 38.
Rayner, *Wales*, 229.
Raynes, *York*, 224.
Rayney, *York*, 213.
Raynsford, *Northamp.* 112 ; *Oxford*, 130 ; *Glouc.* 262.
Raynton, *London*, 96.
Rayson, *Leic.* 80.
Read, *Norfolk*, 107 ; *Northumb.* 120 ; *York*, 534 ; *Flint and Montg.* 234 ; *Oxford*, 234.
Reade, *Durham*, 42 ; *Herts*, 54, 56 ; *Kent*, 60 ; *Wilts*, 185 ; *Galway*, 234 ; *Kilkenny*, 234 ; 236.
Reams, *Norfolk*, 109.
Reavely, *Hereford*, 234.
Reay, *Cumb.* 234.
Rebow, *Essex*, 48, 234.
Reddish, *Lanc.* 269.
Rede, *Bucks*, 10 ; *Suffolk*, 152, 153, 234.
Redesdale, *Northumb.* 119.
Redich, *Wilts*, 185.
Redington, *Galway*, 234.
Redman, *Bucks*, 10.
Redmond, *Wicklow*, 234 ; *Wexford*, 234.
Redvers, *Bucks*, 10.
Redwood, *Glam.* 234.
Redyshe, *Berks*, 3.
Reed, *Durham*, 38 ; *Northumb.* 119, 234.
Reede, *Wales*, 229.
Rees, *Glam.* 228 ; *Carm.* 230, 234.
Reeve, *Linc.* 234.
Reeves, *Surrey*, 158, 234 ; *Clare*, 234.
Redheugh, *Durham*, 38.
Reilly, 234.
Reinbudcurt, *Northamp.* 112.
Reinbudccurt, *Herts*, 54.
Reigne, *Linc.* 80.
Relfe, *Sussex*, 165 ; 242.
Remington, *York*, 224 ; *Lanc.* 234.
Rempeston, *Notts*, 122.

Rempston, *Dorset*, 33.
Rennell, *Berks*, 7 ; *Hamp.* 50.
Repington, *Warw.* 172, 234.
Repps, *Norfolk*, 107.
Reresby, *York*, 224.
Reveley, *Merioneth*, 234 ; *Durham*, 42 ; *Northumb.* 119.
Reve, *Sussex*, 165.
Revel, *Northumb.* 119 ; *York*, 213 ; *Wales*, 229.
Revell, *Leic.* 80 ; *Warw.* 172 ; *Derby*, 259.
Rovenscroft, *Wales*, 229.
Revett, *Bucks*, 10 ; *Herts*, 54.
Reynardson, *Linc.* 234 ; 236.
Reynell, *Devon*, 29, 31 ; *Sussex*, 165 ; *Westmeath*, 234.
Reynes, *Surrey*, 158.
Reynolds, *Bucks*, 10 ; *Norfolk and Devon*, 234.
Rhese, *Sussex*, 165.
Rhodes, *Devon*, 30 ; *York*, 224 ; 234 ; *Derby*, 259.
Rhys, *Wales*, 229 ; *Pemb.* 230.
Rhys ap David, *Wales*, 229.
Rhys ap Ieuan, *Wales*, 229.
Rhys ap Morgan, *Wales*, 229.
Rhys ap Thomas, *Wales*, 229.
Riall, *Dublin*, 234.
Ricaby, *York*, 217.
Riccard, *York*, 213.
Ricardo, *Worc.* 234 ; *Glouc.* 234.
Rice, *Hamp.* 50 ; *Wales*, 229 ; *Glam.* 228 ; *Kent*, 234 ; *Carm.* 230, 234.
Rich, *Essex*, 48 ; *Hamp.* 50 ; *Lond.* 95.
Richard ap John, *Wales*, 229.
Richard ap Rydderch, *Wales*, 229.
Richards, *Berks*, 7 ; *Hamp.* 50 ; *London*, 96 ; *Somerset*, 140 ; *Wexford*, 234 ; *Pemb.* 234 ; *Merioneth*, 234.
Richardson, *Durham*, 36, 38 ; *Kent*, 60 ; *Norfolk*, 107 ; *Surrey*, 158 ; *Sussex*, 163, 165, 234 ; *York*, 204, 205, 218, 224, 234 ; *Merioneth*, 234 ; *Antrim*, 234 ; *Monaghan*, 234 ; *Armagh*, 234 ; *Down*, 234 ; *Fermanagh*, 234.
Riche, *York*, 213.
Richmond, *Cumb.* 22 ; *Herts*, 54 ; *Lanc.* 70 ; *Sussex*, 165 ; *Westm.* 179 ; *Wilts*, 185 ; *York*, 208, 209 ; 236 ; 246.

Rickaby, *York*, 234.
Ricketts, *Hamp.* 50 ; *Hereford*, 234.
Rickford, *Bucks*, 234.
Riddell, *Durham*, 34, 36, 42 ; *Northumb.* 234 ; *Roxburgh*, 234 ; 236.
Ridell, *Durham*, 38.
Ridel, *Northamp.* 111.
Rider, *Herts*, 56 ; *Hamp.* 50 ; *Kent*, 60.
Rideware, *Notts.* 122.
Ridge, *Sussex*, 165, 163.
Ridley, *Northumb.* 119, 234.
Ridisare, *Leic.* 76.
Ridware, *Derby*, 27.
Rigby, *Lanc.* 71.
Rigge, *Lanc.* 234.
Riggs, *Hamp.* 59 ; *Sussex*, 163, 165.
Riley, *Berks*, 234.
Riman, *Sussex*, 168.
Ringer, *Bucks*, 13.
Ringwood, *Hamp.* 50 ; *Wilts*, 182.
Ripariis, *Northamp.* 112.
Ripley, *York*, 224.
Rippon, *Northumb.* 234.
Risby, *Suffolk*, 152.
Risdon, *Devon*, 29, 31.
Risley, *Bucks*, 10 ; *Northamp.* 112.
Rishton, *Sussex*, 163, 165.
Ritherton, *Somerset*, 140.
Rivers, *Hamp.* 50.
Rivett, *Camb.* 16 ; *Somerset*, 140.
Robartes, *Cornw.* 234.
Robbins, *Hants*, 234.
Robert ap Ieuan, *Wales*, 229.
Robert ap John, *Wales*, 229.
Roberth, *Sussex*, 168.
Roberts, *Devon*, 29 ; *Hamp.* 50 ; *Kent*, 60 ; *Leic.* 77, 80 ; *Lond.* 94 ; *Sussex*, 165 ; *Wales*, 229 ; *Pemb.* 234 ; *Flint*, 234 ; *Cork*, 234 ; *Brecon*, 234 ; *Worc.* 234 ; 246.
Robertson, *Derby*, 234 ; *Perth*, 234 ; *Berwick*, 234 ; *Pemb.* 234 ; *Ross*, 234 ; *Cumb.* 234 ; 234 ; 236 ; *Inverness*, 234, 239.
Robin, *Chesh.* 234.
Robins, *Wales*, 229.
Robinson, *Durham*, 31, 234 ; *Herts*, 53, 54, 56 ; *Kent*, 60, 67 ; *Leic.* 80, 234 ; *Staff.* 143 ; *York*, 209, 224, 285 ; *Lanc.* 234 ; *Westmeath*, 234 ; *Notts.* 234 ; *Norfolk*, 234.
Robotham, *Herts*, 54.

Robson, *Durham,* 36, 38; *York,* 234.
Robye, *Hamp.* 50.
Robynson, *York,* 224.
Roch, *Waterford,* 234.
Rochdale, *Surrey,* 156.
Roche, *Kilkenny,* 234; *Limerick,* 234; *Pemb.* 234; *Cork,* 234; *Wilts,* 193.
Rochfort, *Carlow,* 234.
Rockley, *York,* 205, 213.
Rocliffe, *Derby,* 27; *York,* 200.
Roclyffe, *York,* 226.
Rodd, *Cornw.* 234.
Roddam, *Northumb.* 234.
Rode, *Chesh.* 17; *Staff.* 146.
Roden, *Jamaica,* 245.
Rodes, *Derby,* 234; 27; *York,* 205, 213.
Rodger, *Kent,* 234.
Rodham, *Northumb.* 120.
Rodick, *Lanc.* 239.
Rodington, *Shrop.* 137.
Rodney, *Somerset,* 140.
Rodon, *Jamaica,* 234.
Rodville, *Leic.* 80.
Roe, *Devon,* 234.
Roech, *Wales,* 229.
Roger ap Harri, *Wales,* 229.
Rogers-Harrison, *Herts,* 56.
Rogers, *Dorset,* 33; *Herts,* 56; *Hamp.* 50; *Wilts,* 181, 185, 191, 194, 234; *London,* 96; *York,* 213; *Wales,* 229; *Glouc.* 234; *Somerset,* 234, 239; *Cornwall,* 234; *Cork,* 234; *Shrop.* 234; *Radnor,* 234.
Rokeby, *Durham,* 44; *Kent,* 60; *Warw.* 172,174; *York,* 205, 213, 224, 285; *Northamp.* 234.
Rokes, *Bucks,* 11.
Rokesley, *Herts,* 54.
Rokewode, *Norfolk,* 278.
Rokley, *York,* 226.
Rolfe, *Hamp.* 50; *Kent,* 60; *Wilts,* 185; *Norfolk,* 234.
Rolland, *Forfar,* 234.
Rolle, *Devon,* 29.
Rolles, *Oxford,* 131.
Rolleston, *Notts,* 234; *King's Co.* 234.
Rollo, 237.
Rolls, *Monm.* 234.
Rolt, *Herts,* 54.
Rolte, *Kent,* 60.

Romaine, *Durham,* 37.
Romara, *Wilts,* 186.
Romelli, *Northamp.* 112.
Romesey, *Wilts,* 182.
Romsey, *Hamp.* 50; *Somerset,* 140.
Ronayne, *Waterford,* 234.
Rooe, *Hunts,* 57; *Leic.* 80.
Rooke, *Kent,* 60; *Wilts,* 234; *York,* 222.
Rookes, *York,* 204, 218; 234.
Rookwood, 232.
Roope, *Devon,* 31.
Rooper, *Hunts,* 234.
Roos, *Berks,* 7; *Hamp.* 50; *Herts,* 54; *Notts,* 122.
Rootes, *Sussex,* 165.
Rope, *Chesh.* 17.
Roper, *Durham,* 38; *Kent,* 60; *Flint,* 234; 235; *Derby,* 259.
Ros, *Northamp.* 111, 112.
Roscarrock, *Cornwall,* 20.
Rose, *Northamp.* 112, 234; *Sussex,* 163, 165; *Nairn,* 234; *Suffolk,* 234; *Inverness,* 234; *Limerick,* 234; *Tipperary,* 234; *Ross-sh.* 234; *Hants,* 234; *Staff.* 147.
Rosel, *Notts,* 122.
Rosier, *Kent,* 60.
Roskell, *Lanc.* 234, 239.
Roskimer, *Devon,* 29.
Ross, *Leic.* 80; *Cromarty,* 234; *Clare,* 234; *Dumfries,* 234, 246; *Perth,* 234; *Forfar,* 234; *Down,* 234; 246.
Rosse, *Somerset,* 140; *York,* 224.
Rossington, *Derby,* 259.
Rossyndale, *Wales,* 229.
Rotch, *Midd.* 234.
Rotherfeld, *Hamp.* 50.
Rotherham, *Meath,* 234.
Rotheram, *Meath,* 234.
Rothery, *York,* 234; 237.
Rothwell, *Meath,* 234; 234; *Lanc.* 250.
Roughsedge, *Westm.* 234.
Round, *Essex,* 48, 234; *Kent,* 60.
Roundell, *York,* 200, 224, 234, 245.
Roupell, *Kent,* 234.
Rous, *Hamp.* 50; *Hunts,* 57; *Suffolk,* 153; *Warw.* 172; *Worc.* 195; *Glam.* 234.
Rouse, *Devon,* 29.
Rouswell, *Somerset,* 140.

Row, *London*, 96.
Rowan, *Antrim*, 234, 239 ; *Down*, 234.
Rowe, *Devon*, 31 ; *Durham*, 38 ; *London*, 100, 101 ; *Sussex*, 165 ; *Wexford*, 234.
Rowed, *Surrey*, 158.
Rowland, *Wales*, 229.
Rowlatt, *Herts*, 54.
Rowley, *Meath*, 234; *Leitrim*, 234.
Rowse, *Sussex*, 168.
Rowsewell, *Wilts*, 185.
Roxby, *York*, 234.
Roy, *Dorset*, 33 ; *Roxburgh*, 234.
Roynon, *Somerset*, 140.
Royse, *Limerick*, 234.
Ruck, *Kent*, 60.
Ruck-Keene, *Oxford*, 234.
Rudd, *Durham*, 38 ; *Wales*, 229 ; *Carm.* 280.
Rudge, *Worc.* 234.
Rudiard, *Hamp.* 50 ; *Staff.* 146.
Ruding, *Leic.* 80.
Rudston, *Camb.* 16 ; *York*, 224, 234.
Rufus, *Worc.* 195.
Rugeley, *Staff.* 146 ; 233.
Rugge, *Norfolk*, 107.
Ruggeley, *Staff.* 142 ; *Warw.* 172.
Ruggles, *Essex*, 48, 234.
Rumelli, *Northamp.* 112.
Rumsey, *Breck.* 227.
Rush, *Essex*, 48, 234 ; *Northamp.* 112, 234 ; 232.
Rushall, *Staff.* 143.
Rushbrooke, *Suffolk*, 234.
Rushout, *Worc.* 195 ; *Rutland*, 136.
Ruskin, *Leic.* 80.
Russel, *Warw.* 172 ; *Worc.* 195 ; *Dorset*, 33.
Russell, *Bucks*, 10, 11 ; *Dorset*, 33 ; *Herts*, 54, 56 ; *Lanc.* 71 ; *Northamp.* 111, 112 ; *Worc.* 195, 234; *Sussex*, 165 ; *Down*, 234; *Aberdeen*, 234 ; *Selkirk*, 234 ; *Staff.* 234 ; *Durham*, 234 ; *Salop*, 234.
Rust, *Hunts*, 234.
Ruthall, *Bucks*, 10.
Rutherford, *Roxburgh*, 234.
Rutherforth, *Essex*, 48.
Rutington, *Notts*, 122.
Rutland, *Leic.* 80 ; *Northamp.* 112 ; *Wilts*, 193.
Rutson, *York*, 234.
Rutten, *Kent*, 59, 60.

Rutter, *Chesh.* 17.
Ruttledge, *Mayo*, 234.
Ruxton, *Kent*, 234 ; *Louth*, 234 ; *Meath*, 234.
Ryan, *Tipperary*, 234 ; *Dublin*, 234.
Rydderch, *Wales*, 229.
Ryder, *Herts*, 54, 56 ; *Kildare*, 234.
Rydeware, *Leic.* 80.
Rye, *Cork*, 224.
Rykes, 233.
Ryland, *Warw.* 234.
Ryley, *Wilts*, 185.
Ryman, *Sussex*, 163.
Rynd, *Fermanagh*, 234.
Ryngewood, *Wilts*, 182.
Ryther, *Linc.* 86, 274 ; *Surrey*, 162 ; *York*, 224.
Rythre, *Kildare*, 234.
Ryves, *Dorset*, 33, 234.

St. Albyn, *Somerset*, 234.
St. Amand, *Bucks*, 10 ; *Wilts*, 193.
St. Andrew, *Northamp.* 112 ; *Notts*, 122.
St. Aubyn, *Somerset*, 140 ; *Corn.* 234.
St. Barbe, *Hamp.* 50, 234 ; *Wilts*, 182, 185.
St. Clair, *Edinburyh*, 234 ; *Glouc.* 234.
St. Cleere, *Wilts*, 193.
St. Clere, *Northamp.* 112.
St. George, *Camb.* 16 ; *Tyrone*, 234 ; *Galway*, 234 ; *Armagh*, 234 ; *Leitrim*, 234.
St. Germans, 237,
St. John, *Hamp.* 50 ; *Hunts*, 57 ; *Leic.* 80 ; *Lond.* 94 ; *Northamp.* 111, 112 ; *Surrey*, 156 ; *Sussex*, 163, 165 ; *Wilts*, 185, 194 ; 232 ; 236.
St. Lawrence, 233.
St. Leger, *Devon*, 29 ; *Herts*, 56 ; *Kent*, 60 ; *Cork*, 234.
St. Loe, *Dorset*, 33 ; *Wilts*, 185.
St. Martin, *Wilts*, 182.
St. Maur, *Wilts*, 182, 185.
St. Medard, *Northamp.* 111.
St. Nicholas, *Leic.* 80.
St. Omer, *Wilts*, 182.
St. Philibert, *Suffolk*, 152.
St. Quintin, *York*, 224, 234.
St. Quinton, *York*, 217.
St. Walery, *Bucks*, 10.

Sabin, *Kent*, 60.

Sacheverell, *Leic.* 80; *Notts*, 122; *Oxf.* 131.

Sackett, *Kent*, 60.

Sackvill, *Sussex*, 165.

Sackville, *Bucks*, 10, 11; *Kent*, 63; *Oxf.* 133; 232.

Sadleir, *Hamp.* 50; *Herts*, 53, 54, 56; *Wilts*, 182; *Tipperary*, 234.

Sadler, *Wilts*, 185; *Glouc.* 234; *Wales*, 229; 239.

Saies, *Glam.* 228.

Sainsbury, *Berks*, 7.

Sainthill, *Devon*, 29.

Saint Paul, *York*, 213.

Saker, *Kent*, 60.

Saladin, 236.

Salceto, *Northamp.* 112.

Sale, *Derby*, 259.

Salisbury, *Herts*, 54; *Leic.* 80; *Somerset*, 140; *Wilts*, 182, 186; 236.

Salkeld, *Dorset*, 33; *Cumb.* 22.

Salmon, *Hamp.* 50; *Notts*, 122.

Salmond, *Cumb.* 234; 236.

Salomons, *Kent*, 234.

Salsbri, *Wales*, 229.

Salter, *Bucks*, 13, *Dorset*, 33.

Saltmarsh, *Durham*, 34.

Saltmarshe, *York*, 234; 237.

Saltmersh, *York*, 224.

Saltonstall, *Herts*, 54; *Northamp.* 112; *York*, 205.

Salusbury, *Herts*, 54; *Flint*, 234.

Salven, *York*, 226.

Salvein, *York*, 224.

Salvin, *Durham*, 34, 36, 38, 234; *Surrey*, 234; 235.

Salvine, *York*, 201.

Salway, *Shrop.* 234; 236.

Samborne, *Hamp.* 50; *Somerset*, 140.

Sambrooke, *Herts*, 54.

Samford, *Somerset*, 140.

Samon, *Hamp.* 50.

Sampford, *Dorset*, 33.

Sampson, *Durham*, 38; *Glouc.* 234.

Samuel, *Devon*, 29.

Samways, *Dorset*, 33; *Wilts*, 185.

Samwell, *Northamp.* 111, 112.

Sandbach, *Chesh.* 17; *Denb.* 234.

Sandde, *Wales*, 229.

Sandars, *Essex*, 234.

Sander, *Surrey*, 156.

Sanders, *Herts*, 56; *Kent*, 60; *Staff.* 143, 146; *Surrey*, 156; *Cork*, 234.

Sanderson, *Durham*, 36, 38; *Northumb.* 234.

Sandes, *Camb.* 16; *Surrey*, 156; *Worc.* 195; *Kerry*, 234; *Cork*, 234.

Sandford, *Bucks*, 13; *Camb.* 16; *Lanc.* 75; *Shrop.* 137, 234; *York*, 213; 234; *Glouc.* 262.

Sandham, *Sussex*, 163, 165.

Sands, *Kent*, 60; *Surrey*, 156; *Lanc.* 234.

Sandys, *Berks*, 7; *Cornw.* 20, 234; *Kent*, 60; *Northamp.* 112; *Somerset*, 140; *Worc.* 195; *Lanc.* 234; *Berwick*, 234.

Sanford, *Devon*, 31; 232; *Somerset*, 234.

Sankey, *Tipperary*, 234; *Fermanagh*, 234.

Sapcotts, *Devon*, 29; *Hunts*, 57.

Sare, *Kent*, 60.

Sargent, *Sussex*, 163, 234.

Saris, *Sussex*, 165.

Sarsfield, *Cork*, 234; 235.

Saunder, *Surrey*, 158.

Saunders, *Berks*, 7; *Bucks*, 10; *Herts*, 54; *Leic.* 80; *Northamp.* 112; *Lanc.* 234; *Wicklow*, 234; *Cavan*, 234; 236.

Saunderson, *Notts.* 122, 125; *York*, 206, 213; *Cavan*, 234.

Savage, *Chesh.* 17; *Dorset*, 33; *Hamp.* 50; *Kent*, 60, 234; *Leic.* 80; *Oxf.* 128, 130; *Sussex*, 165; *Wilts*, 185; *Worc.* 195; *Dublin*, 234; *Glouc.* 264.

Savell, *York*, 226.

Saverey, *Devon*, 29.

Savery, *Devon*, 31, 234.

Savile, *Herts*, 56; *Leic.* 80; *Lanc.* 71; *York*, 204, 205, 213, 223, 224.

Savill, *Essex*, 48; *Derby*, 259.

Saville, *Notts*, 123; *Devon*, 234.

Savin, *Kent*, 60.

Sawbridge, *Northamp.* 112, 234; *Kent*, 234.

Sawle, 236.

Sawrey, *Lanc.* 234.

Sawyer, *Berks*, 7, 234; 236.

Saxham, *Suffolk*, 152 ; *York*, 213.
Say, *Bucks*, 10 ; *Herts*, 54 ; *Oxf.*
131 ; *Warw.* 172 ; *Worc.* 195 ;
Norfolk, 234.
Saye and Sele, 236.
Sayer, *Kent*, 60, 234 ; *Durham*, 38.
Says, *Glam.* 228.
Scalers, *Herts*, 54.
Scarborough, *Durham*, 34, 37, 38 ;
York, 213.
Scardeville, *Hamp.* 50 ; *Sussex*, 165.
Scarfe, *Wales*, 229.
Scarisbrick, *Lanc.* 71, 234.
Scarlett, *Herts*, 234.
Scarsdale, *Leic.* 80 ; *York*, 205.
Scawen, *Bucks*, 13 ; *Surrey*, 156,
158.
Schank, *Devon*, 234, 245.
Schonswar, *York*, 234.
Schreiber, *Kent*, 234 ; *Suffolk*, 234.
Sclater, *Hamp.* 50, 234.
Scobell, *Corn.* 234.
Scoles, *Berks*, 7.
Scorah, *York*, 224, 283.
Scot, *Staff.* 146 ; *Surrey*, 156.
Scotland, *Leic.* 80 ; *York*, 205.
Scott, *Bucks*, 13 ; *Dorset*, 33 ; *Es-
sex*, 48 ; *Kent*, 60 ; *Staff.* 143,
234 ; *Sussex*, 165, 168 ; *York*, 206,
217 ; 232 ; *Roxburgh*, 234 ; *Angus*,
234 ; *Shrop.* 234 ; *Norfolk*, 234 ;
Selkirk, 234 ; *Hamp.* 234, 245 ;
Zetland, 234 ; *Midlothian*, 234 ;
Kincardine, 234 ; *Dumfries*, 234 ;
Londonderry, 234 ; 239 ; 241.
Scourfield, *Pemb.* 234.
Scrase, *Sussex*, 165, 169.
Scrimshire, *Notts*, 122.
Scratton, *Essex*, 234.
Scrimgeour, 234.
Scriven, *Surrey*, 234 ; *Camb.* 16.
Scrivener, *Hants*, 234.
Scroop, *York*, 226.
Scroope, *Hamp.* 50 ; *Oxf.* 131 ; *York*,
224.
Scrope, *Durham*, 34 ; *Leic.* 80 ;
Notts, 122 ; *Rutland*, 136 ; *Wilts*,
185, 190, 234 ; *York*, 208, 209,
213, 221, 234 ; 232 ; 235 ; 237.
Scruteville, *Durham*, 36.
Scudamore, *Hereford*, 52, 234 ;
Kent, 60 ; *Wilts*, 182 ; *York*, 205,
224 ; 232 ; 236.

Sculle, 233.
Scurfield, *Durham*, 38, 234 ; *Pemb.*
230.
Scures, *York*, 217.
Sea, *York*, 217.
Seabright, *Worc.* 195.
Searle, 236.
Sears, *Essex*, 246.
Seaton, *York*, 283.
Seaver, *Armagh*, 234.
Seaward, *Devon*, 32.
Sealy, *Cork*, 234.
Seaman, *Leic.* 234.
Sebright, *Herts*, 54.
Sedborough, *Somerset*, 140.
Sedgwick, *Camb.* 16 ; *Durham*, 38.
Sedley, *Herts*, 64 ; *Leic.* 80 ; *Nor-
folk*, 278.
Segar, *Devon*, 31.
Segrave, *Bucks*, 11 ; *Derby*, 27 ;
Leic. 80 ; *Northamp.* 112 ; *York*,
213 ; *Wicklow*, 234.
Sefton, *Lanc.* 71.
Seinliz, *Northamp.* 111.
Selby, *Bucks*, 10 ; *Durham*, 36, 38,
42 ; *Kent*, 60, 234 ; *Northumb.*
234 ; 235 ; 236.
Selfe, *Wilts*, 185.
Selling, *Kent*, 60.
Selsey, *Herts*, 54 ; *Sussex*, 163.
Selwin, *Sussex*, 165.
Selwyn, *Sussex*, 168.
Selyngesby, *York*, 226.
Semare, *Northamp.* 111.
Semphill, *Edinburgh*, 234.
Senhouse, *Cumb.* 234.
Sergison. *Sussex*, 234.
Sergeant, *Leic.* 80 ; *Sussex*, 165.
Serleby, *Notts*, 122.
Serocold, *Camb.* 234.
Servington, *Wilts*, 182.
Seton, *Berks*, 7 ; *Durham*, 38 ; *Aber-
deen*, 234 ; *Fife*, 234 ; 236.
Severn, *Radnor*, 234.
Severne, *Northamp.* 112, 234 ; *Shrop.*
234.
Seward, *Devon*, 29.
Sewell, *Surrey*, 234.
Sewster, *Camb.* 16.
Seymer, *Dorset*, 33, 234 ; *Wilts*,
182.
Seymor, *Oxford*, 128.
Seymour, *Bucks*, 10 ; *Cumb.* 23 ;

Devon, 29, 31 ; *Oxford,* 130 ; *Wilts,* 182, 185, 234 ; *Galway,* 234 ; *Queen's Co.* 234.
Seys, *Glouc.* 234.
Seyntclerc, (incorrectly printed Leyntclere), *Leic.* 80.
Seyton, *Northamp.* 111.
Sgargill, *Camb.* 16.
Sgwrfield, *Wales,* 229.
Shacklock, *Lanc.* 75.
Shaa, *Somerset,* 140.
Shadwell, *Sussex,* 165.
Shadforth, *Durham,* 38.
Shaftesbury, *Dorset,* 33.
Shafto, *Durham,*38, 234 ; *Northumb.* 234.
Shaftoe, *Durham,* 34, 36, 40.
Shairp, *Linlithgow,* 234 ; 237.
Shaftsbury, *York,* 217.
Shakerley, *Chesh.* 17, 234 ; *Kent,* 60 ; *Northamp.* 112.
Shakespeare, 235.
Shakespere, *Warw.* 178.
Shakspere, *Essex,* 47.
Shalcross, 251.
Shank, *Fife,* 234.
Shann, 237.
Shannon, 236.
Shapcote, *Devon,* 31.
Shapcott, *Devon,* 29.
Shardelow, *Suffolk,* 152.
Shareshull, *Staff.* 143.
Sharington, *Norfolk,* 107.
Sharowe, *Bucks,* 10, 13.
Sharp, *Kent,* 60 ; *Northamp.* 112 ; *Lanc.* 234 ; *Sussex,* 165, 168 ; *York,* 204, 205, 218, 283.
Sharpe, *Berks,* 7 ; *Leic.* 80 ; *Sussex,* 234 ; *Suffolk,* 234.
Sharrett, *Leic.* 248.
Shaw, *Herts,* 54, 56 ; *York,* 213, 224 ; *Lanc.* 268.
Shawe, *Kent,* 60 ; *Suffolk,* 234.
Sheddon, *Northamp.* 234 ; *Ayr,* 234.
Shee, 234.
Sheepshanks, *York,* 204.
Sheehy, *Cork,* 234.
Sheffield, *Linc.* 86, 273, 274 ; *London,* 96 ; *York,* 201, 220 ; 232.
Sheinton, *Wales,* 229.
Shekell, *Glouc.* 234.
Shelbury, *London,* 96 ; 232.
Shelden, *Warw.* 234.

Sheldon, *Sussex,* 165; *Warw.* 172 ; *Worc.* 195 ; 235 ; 236 ; *Derby,* 259 ; *Glouc.* 262.
Shelley, *Sussex,* 163, 164, 165 ; *Hants,* 234 ; 235 ; *Wilts,* 185.
Shelton, *Staff.* 142, 146 ; *Limerick,* 234.
Shenton, *Leic.* 80.
Shepard, *Oxford,* 131.
Shepey, *Leic.* 76, 80.
Shephard, *Sussex,* 168.
Sheppard, *Sussex,* 163, 165, 234; *Somerset,* 234 ; *Suffolk,* 234.
Sherard, *Leic.* 80, 248 ; *Rutland,* 135.
Sherbrook, *Notts,* 123.
Sherbrooke, *Notts,* 234.
Sherburn, *Lanc.* 68.
Sherburne, *Lanc.* 71 ; *Herts,* 53.
Sherd, *Chesh.* 17.
Sheridan, *Dorset,* 234.
Sherington, *Wilts,* 185.
Sherman, *Camb.* 16 ; *Leic.* 80.
Sherrington, *Bucks,* 10.
Sherston, *Somerset,* 139, 234.
Sherwerd, *Herts,* 56.
Sherwill, 236.
Sherwin, *Notts,* 234.
Sherwood, *Berks,* 6.
Shienton, *Wales,* 229.
Shiercliffe, *York,* 206.
Shiffner, *Sussex,* 165.
Shillingford, *Devon,* 29 ; *Oxford,* 131.
Shilleto, *York,* 224.
Shillito, *York,* 219.
Shipley, *Hamp.* 50, 234.
Shipman, *Notts,* 122.
Shippard, 237.
Shippardson, *Durham,* 38 ; 237 ; 239.
Shipperdson, *Durham,* 234.
Shipward, *Leic.* 80.
Shirley, *Essex,* 48 ; *Leic.* 80 ; *Northamp.* 111, 112 ; *Sussex,* 163, 165, 168 ; *Warw.* 172, 234 ; *Staff.* 142 ; 231.
Shore, *York,* 206 ; *Derby,* 234, 259.
Shoreditch, *London,* 91.
Short, *Kent,* 60 ; *Staff.* 146 ; *Linc.* 234 ; *Devon,* 234.
Shorter, *Bucks,* 13.
Shortt, *Dumfries,* 234 ; 250.

Shotbolt, *Herts*, 53.
Shottesbrooke, *Berks*, 3.
Shouldham, *Norfolk*, 107.
Shovell, *Kent*, 60.
Shoyswell, *Sussex*, 165.
Shrewsbury, *Worc.* 195 ; *York*, 206.
Shrubb, *Surrey*, 234.
Shuckburgh, *Northamp.* 112 ; *Wilts.* 182, 234 ; *Sussex*, 165 ; 236.
Shudd, *Surrey*, 156.
Shuldham, *Suffolk*, 234 ; *Cork*, 234 ; *Longford*, 234 ; 234 ; *Norfolk*, 277.
Shurley, *Sussex*, 164, 165.
Shute, *Hants*, 234.
Shutes, *Camb.* 16.
Shutte, *York*, 217.
Shuttleworth, *Lanc.* 68, 70, 234 ; *Notts*, 125, 234 ; *Durham*, 234 ; *Leic.* 234 ; *York*, 224 ; 242.
Siankin, *Wales*, 229.
Sibbald, *Cornwall*, 234.
Sibthorp, *Linc.* 234.
Sibthorpe, *Notts*, 122.
Sicklemore, *Suffolk*, 234.
Siddall, *Lanc.* 270.
Sidenham, *Somerset*, 140 ; 232.
Sidley, *Kent*, 60.
Sidney, *Kent*, 60 ; *Sussex*, 163, 165 ; *Northumb.* 234.
Sier, *Bedf.* 234.
Siferwast, 233.
Sikes, *Notts*, 124, 234.
Silver, *Hamp.* 50.
Silvertop, *Durham*, 38 ; *Northumb.* 234.
Sillifant, *Devon*, 234.
Simcox, *Staff.* 234.
Simeon, *Hamp.* 50, 235.
Simon, *Cornwall*, 234.
Simons, *Kent*, 60 ; *Pemb.* 230 ; *Cornwall*, 234.
Simpson, *Durham*, 38, 234 ; *Hamp.* 50 ; *Kent*, 60 ; *York*, 205, 213, 224, 234 ; *Derby*, 234 ; *Notts*, 234 ; *Perth*, 234 ; *Leitrim*, 234 ; 237.
Simson, *Fife*, 234.
Sinclair, *Tyrone*, 234 ; *Caithness*, 234.
Singleton, *Louth*, 234 ; *Meath*, 234 ; *Clare*, 234.
Sion ap Rhys, *Wales*, 229.

Sitsilt, *Herts*, 56.
Sitwell, *York*, 206 ; *Derby*, 234, 259 ; *Northumb.* 234 ; *Shrop.* 234.
Sivewright, *Berks*, 234.
Skargill, *York*, 205.
Skeffington, *Kent*, 60 ; *Leic.* 80, 81 ; *Staff.* 143.
Skeggs, *Hunts*, 57.
Skelly, 236.
Skelton, *Cumb.* 22, 23, 24, 234 ; *York*, 205, 224.
Skene, *Aberdeen*, 234.
Skennerton, *Northamp.* 112.
Skepper, *Durham*, 36, 38.
Skerrett, *Clare*, 234 ; *Dublin*, 234.
Skiers, *York*, 213.
Skilling, *Hamp.* 50 ; *Wilts*, 185.
Skinner, *Devon*, 29 ; *Dorset*, 33 ; *Kent*, 60 ; *Somerset*, 140 ; *Surrey*, 156, 158, 234 ; *Essex*, 234.
Skipton, *Derry*, 234 ; *Londonderry*, 234.
Skipwith, *Leic.* 80 ; *Warw.* 172 ; 236.
Skipworth, *Linc.* 234.
Skrimshire, *Staff.* 146.
Skrine, *Somerset*, 234.
Skrymsher, *Leic.* 80.
Skutt, *Wilts*, 185.
Skynner, *Devon*, 31.
Slacke, *Down*, 234.
Slade, *Hunts*, 57.
Sladen, *Herts*, 234 ; *Kent*, 234.
Slader, *Devon*, 29.
Slaney, *Shrop.* 234.
Slanning, *Devon*, 29.
Slater, *Essex*, 48 ; *Sussex*, 234 ; 234.
Slator, *Meath*, 234.
Slegge, *Camb.* 16.
Sleeman, *Limerick*, 234.
Sleigh, 251 ; *Derby*, 259.
Slingar, *York*, 224.
Slingsby, *York*, 224 ; 236.
Slocock, *Berks*, 7.
Slocomb, *Bucks*, 13.
Slorey, *Leic.* 80.
Slymer, *Dorset*, 33.
Small, *Dorset*, 33.
Smalle, *Leic.* 80.
Smallpece, *Norfolk*, 278.
Smalley, *Leic.* 80 ; 251.
Smallwood, *York*, 201, 220, 224.

Smart, *Durham,* 38 ; *Leic.* 80 ; *Northamp.* 234 ; 235.

Smeaton, *Perth,* 234.

Smethurst, *Lanc.* 234.

Smethwick, *Chesh.* 17.

Smelt, *York,* 224.

Smith, *Berks,* 7 ; *Bucks,* 11 ; *Chesh.* 17 ; *Dorset,* 33 ; *Durham,* 36, 37, 38, 234 ; *Essex,* 48 ; *Herts.* 54, 56, 234 ; *Kent,* 60, 234 ; *Lanc.* 69, 234 ; *Leic.* 80, 234 ; *London,* 96 ; *Oxford,* 127, 128 ; *Somerset,* 140 ; *Staff.* 146, 234 ; *Surrey,* 156, 234 ; *Sussex,* 165, 234 ; *Wilts,* 185 ; *York,* 205, 208, 224, 225 ; *Wales,* 229 ; *Shrop.* 234 ; *Bedf.* 234 ; *Cornw.* 234 ; *Norf.* 234, 278 ; *Camb.* 234 ; *Northumb.* 234 ; *Renfrew,* 234 ; *Meath,* 235 ; 235 ; 253.

Smijth, *Essex,* 46, 48, 239 ; *Bucks,* 13, 10.

Smithe, *Surrey,* 162.

Smithes, *Somerset,* 140.

Smithson, *York,* 224.

Smithwick, *Limerick,* 234.

Smollett, *Dumbarton,* 234.

Smyth, *Bucks,* 11 ; *Devon,* 31 ; *Herts,* 54, 56, 234 ; *Leic.* 80 ; *Northamp,* 112 ; *Oxford,* 130 ; *Surrey,* 158 ; *Sussex,* 163, 165 ; *Warw.* 172 ; *York,* 204, 218 ; 234 ; *Waterford,* 234 ; *Somerset,* 234 ; *Westmeath,* 234, 239 ; *Linc.* 234 ; *Cork,* 235 ; *Clare,* 234 ; *Cavan,* 234 ; 236 ; 237.

Smythe, *Durham,* 38 ; *Hamp.* 50 ; *Kent,* 60 ; *Westmeath,* 234 ; *Roscommon,* 234 ; *Shrop.* 234 ; *Perth,* 234 ; 236.

Snagg, *Herts,* 54.

Snape, *Oxford,* 130.

Snappe, *Oxford,* 128, 130.

Snasell, *York,* 226.

Snawsell, *York,* 224.

Sneide, *Staff.* 146.

Sneith, *Wilts,* 185.

Snell, *Berks,* 3 ; *Bucks,* 10 ; *Herts,* 54, 234 ; *Leic.* 80 ; *Wilts,* 181, 185, 191, 194.

Snelling, *Sussex,* 165.

Snellinge, *Devon,* 31.

Sneyd, *Staff.* 145, 234 ; *Wales,* 229 ; 236.

Soame, *Herts,* 54.

Solly, *Kent,* 60.

Solers, *Breck.* 227 ; *Wilts,* 182.

Soltau, *Devon,* 234.

Somaster, *Devon,* 29, 31.

Somerby, 245.

Somer, *Kent,* 60.

Somerfall, *Sussex,* 165.

Somerford, *Chesh.* 17 ; *Staff.* 146.

Someri, *Northamp.* 112 ; *Rutl.* 136.

Somerie, *Surrey,* 156.

Somers, *Herts,* 54 ; *Worc.* 195.

Somerset, *Durham,* 38 ; *Somerset,* 140 ; *Wilts,* 182.

Somervile, *Warw.* 172 ; *Staff.* 143.

Somerville, *Somerset,* 139, 234 ; *Cork,* 234.

Somery, *Leic.* 76.

Sommers, *Surrey,* 156.

Sompter, *Hamp.* 50.

Sonde, *Surrey,* 156.

Sondes, *Kent,* 60.

Sonibanck, *Oxford,* 131.

Sonlli, *Wales,* 229.

Soresby, *Derby,* 27.

Sotehill, *Derby,* 27.

Sotewell, *Wilts,* 185.

Sotheron, *Notts,* 234.

Sotherton, *Norfolk,* 107.

Sotwell, *York,* 213, 224.

Souch, *Wilts,* 185.

Soulby, *Leic.* 80.

South, *Hamp.* 50 ; *Wilts,* 185.

Southam, *Warw.* 234.

Southampton, *Northamp.* 112.

Southby, *Berks,* 7, 234.

Southcot, *Devon,* 31.

Southcote, *Devon,* 29 ; *Surrey,* 156.

Southcomb, *Devon,* 234.

Southill, *Leic.* 76, 80.

Southland, *Kent,* 60 ; *Sussex,* 165.

Southmedde, *Devon,* 31.

Southwell, *Norfolk,* 107, 278 ; *Surrey,* 156 ; *Suffolk,* 152 ; 234 ; 236.

Southworth, *Lanc.* 71 ; *Somerset,* 140.

Sowle, *Hamp.* 50.

Sowray, *York,* 219, 224.

Sowtheby, *York,* 224.

Spaight, *Clare,* 234, 239.

Sparham, *Norfolk,* 107.

Sparkes, *Brecon*, 234.
Sparkhauke, *Herts*, 54.
Sparks, *Surrey*, 234.
Sparling, *Shrop.* 234.
Sparrow, *Essex*, 48, 234 ; *Suffolk*, 234, 245 ; *Anglesey*, 234.
Spatchurst, *Wilts*, 185.
Spateman, *Derby*, 259.
Speake, *Somerset*, 140.
Spearman, *Northumb.* 119 ; *Durham*, 38, 234.
Spedding, *Cumb.* 234.
Speir, *Renfrew*, 234.
Speirs, *Renfrew*, 234.
Speke, *Somerset*, 234.
Spelman, *Wilts*, 182.
Spence, *Sussex*, 164, 165.
Spencer, *Bucks*, 10, 13 ; *Herts*, 53, 54 ; *Kent*, 60 ; *Northamp.* 111, 112 ; *Sussex*, 155 ; *York*, 205, 206, 213, 234 ; *Wales*, 229 ; 241.
Spens, *Stirling*, 234 ; *Fife*, 234.
Spenser, *York*, 224.
Sperling, *Essex*, 234.
Spicer, *Herts*, 54 ; *Wales*, 229.
Spigurnell, *Bucks*, 10.
Spinks, *Surrey*, 234.
Spiruwin, *Norfolk*, 109.
Spode, *Staff.* 234.
Spofforth, *York*, 224, 246.
Spooner, *Warw.* 234.
Spoor, *Durham*, 234.
Spottiswood, *Aberdeen*, 234.
Spottiswoode, *Berwick*, 234 ; 237.
Spracklyn, *Kent*, 60.
Spratt, *Co.* 234.
Spring, *Suffolk*, 155.
Springett, *Kent*, 60 ; *Sussex*, 164, 165.
Sprinte, *Hamp.* 50.
Sproston, *Chesh.* 234.
Sprott, *Staff.* 142.
Spurstow, *Chesh.* 17.
Spurway, *Devon*, 31.
Spry, *Cornw.* 234.
Squibb, *Dorset*, 33.
Squire, *Suffolk*, 234.
Stables, *York*, 224.
Stace, *Rutland*, 136.
Stacey, *Kent*, 60 ; *Herts*, 56.
Stacpoole, *Clare*, 234.
Stafferton, *Berks*, 8.

Stafford, *Berks*, 7 ; *Bucks*, 10 ; *Dorset*, 33 ; *Essex*, 46 ; *Kent*, 60 ; *Leic.* 76, 80 ; *Northamp.* 111, 112, 234 ; *Rutland*, 135 ; *Staff.* 146 ; *Suffolk*, 153 ; *Sussex*, 165 ; *Warw.* 172, 174 ; *Wilts*, 182 ; *Worc.* 195 ; 232 ; *Derby*, 259.
Stagg, *Dorset*, 33.
Stamford, *Leic.* 80 ; *Staff.* 143.
Stampe, *Oxford*, 130, 131.
Standard, *Oxford*, 131.
Standish, *Lanc.* 71, 234, 239 ; *Berks*, 234 ; *York*, 234, 236.
Standysh, *Berks*, 3.
Stanford, *Leic.* 80 ; *Staff.* 146.
Stanhope, *Bucks*, 10 ; *Derby*, 27 ; *Herts.* 54 ; *Linc.* 88, 234 ; *Notts*, 122, 123 ; *Surrey*, 156 ; *Warw.* 172 ; *York*, 205, 213, 224, 234, 236.
Stanier-Philip-Broade, 168.
Staniforth, *York*, 206, 213.
Stanley, *Chesh.* 17 ; *Cumb.* 23, 234 ; *Derby*, 27 ; *Herts*, 54, 56 ; *Kent.* 60 ; *Lanc.* 70, 234 ; *Hants*, 234 ; *Leic.* 80 ; *Northamp.* 112 ; *Staff.* 142, 143, 146 ; *Sussex*, 163, 165 ; *York*, 213 ; *Wales*, 229 ; 232 ; 234 ; 235 ; *London*, 96.
Stannard, *Norfolk*, 107 ; *Kilkenny*, 234 ; *Cork*, 234.
Stannus, *Louth*, 234.
Stanshall, *Berks*, 3.
Stansfeld, *York*, 204, 234.
Stansfield, *Lanc.* 68 ; *Notts*, 125 ; *York*, 218, 234.
Stanter, *Wilts*, 185, 182.
Stanton, *Leic.* 80 ; *Shrop.* 137 ; *Glouc.* 234.
Stany, *Sussex*, 165.
Stapeley, *Chesh.* 17.
Stapilton, *Herts*, 54 ; *York*, 226.
Stapleford, *Notts.* 122.
Staplehill, *Devon*, 29, 31.
Staples, *Wilts*, 185, 234 ; *Surrey*, 234.
Stapleton, *Hamp.* 50 ; *Norfolk*, 107 ; *Notts*, 126 ; *York*, 205, 208, 220, 224, 236.
Stapley, *Sussex*, 164, 165.
Stapylton, *Berks*, 7 ; *Wilts*, 182 ; *York*, 224, 234, 285 ; *Durham*, 234 ; *Herts*, 234.

Staresmore, *Leic.* 76, 80.
Starke, *Carm.* 234 ; 246.
Starkey, *Chesh.* 17, 234; *Kent*, 60 ;
 Leic. 80 ; *York*, 234.
Starkie, *Chesh.* 17 ; *Lanc.* 68, 71,
 234 ; 236.
Starky, *Wilts*, 234.
Staunton, *Hamp.* 50 ; *Leic.* 76, 80 ;
 Notts, 122, 234 ; *Galway*, 234 ;
 Warw. 234.
Staveley, *Devon*, 29 ; *Leic.* 80.
Staverton, *Berks*, 3 ; *Hamp.* 50.
Stawell, *Down*, 234 ; *Cork*, 234.
Stead, *York*, 213.
Steade, *Derby*, 234.
Steavens, *Berks*, 7.
Stedman, *Card.* 30 ; *Breck.* 227 ;
 Wales, 229.
Steede, *Kent*, 60.
Steel, *Cumb.* 234.
Steele, *Chesh.* 17 ; *Leic.* 80 ; *Kil-
 dare*, 234.
Steer, *Linc.* 86. 274.
Steere, *Surrey*, 158 ; *Sussex*, 163.
Steinman, *Surrey*, 234.
Stenton, *Notts*, 123.
Stephenes, *Wilts*, 182.
Stephens, *Berks*, 7 ; *Kent*, 60 ; *Leic.*
 80 ; *Wilts*, 185; *Glouc.* 234,
 246 ; *Cornw.* 234 ; *Carm.* 234.
Stephenson, *York*, 224.
Stepneth, *Wales*, 229.
Sterne, *Camb.* 16 ; *Herts*, 56; *York*,
 205, 217 ; 241.
Steuart, *Banff*, 234 ; *Perth*, 234 ;
 Peebles, 234 ; *Carlow*, 234 ; 236.
Stevens, *Devon*, 234.
Stevenson, *Durham*, 38 ; *York*, 201 ;
 Linc. 234.
Steward, *Camb.* 16 ; *Herts*, 54, 56 ;
 Kent, 60; *Norfolk*, 107, 234, 239,
 278 ; *Northamp.* 112 ; *York*, 220,
 224 ; *Dorset*, 234 ; *Cumb.* 234.
Stewart, *Wigton*, 234 ; *Perth*, 234 ;
 Kirkcudbright, 234 ; *Inverness*,
 234; *Lanark*, 234 ; *Tyrone*, 234 ;
 Donegal, 234 ; *Linlithgow*, 234 ;
 Fife, 234 ; 234 ; 231 ; 237.
Stewkley, *Hamp.* 50.
Steyning, *Somerset*, 140.
Still, *Dorset*, 33 ; *Somerset*, 140 ;
 Wilts, 182, 185.
Stillingfleet, *Dorset*, 33, 234.

Stillington, *York*, 224.
Stillwell, *Surrey*, 156.
Stinton, 236.
Stirap, *Notts*, 122.
Stirling, *Perth*, 234.
Stivichale, *Warw.* 172.
Stockdale, *Westm.* 179 ; *York*, 224.
Stocker, *Somerset*, 140.
Stockett, *Kent*, 60.
Stockton, *Chesh.* 17 ; *Leic.* 80.
Stockwith, *Hamp.* 50.
Stodart, 234.
Stoke, *Dorset*, 33 ; *Leic.* 80.
Stokeport, *Chesh.* 17.
Stokes, *Bucks*, 11 ; *Camb.* 16 ; *Kent*,
 60 ; *Northamp.* 111 ; *Wilts*, 185 ;
 Kerry, 234 ; *Glouc.* 234.
Stompe, *Oxford*, 128.
Stone, *Bucks*, 10 ; *Kent*, 60 ; *Somer-
 set*, 140 ; *Sussex*, 165 ; *Berks*,
 234 ; *Oxford*, 234.
Stonehewer, *Durham*, 38.
Stonehouse, *Kent*, 60.
Stoner, *Oxf.* 128.
Stones, *Hunts*, 57.
Stonehurst, *Sussex*, 165 ; *Essex*,
 234.
Stoney, *Tipperary*, 234.
Stonhouse, *Bucks*, 11.
Stonor, *Bucks*, 10, 13 ; *Herts*, 56 ;
 Oxford, 130, 234.
Stopford, *Wigton*, 234 ; *Northamp.*
 234.
Stopham, *Sussex*, 165.
Storer, *Berks*, 234 ; *Surrey*, 234 ;
 236.
Storeton, *Chesh.* 17.
Storcy, *Cavan*, 234 ; *Tyrone*, 234.
Storie, *Surrey*, 234.
Storr, *York*, 217.
Story, *Durham*, 38.
Stotesbury, *Northamp.* 111, 112.
Stotevill, *Camb.* 16 ; *Notts*, 122.
Stothert, *Kirkcudbright*, 234.
Stoughton, *Kent*, 60 ; *Glouc.* 234 ;
 Surrey, 156 ; *Sussex*, 163 ; 237.
Stourton, *Leic.* 80 ; *Wilts*, 182, 185,
 191 ; 232 ; 236.
Stoutville, *York*, 224.
Stovin, *Linc.* 86 ; *York*, 213 ; 234.
Stowe, *Berks*, 7.
Stowford, *Devon*, 29.
Strabolgi, *Norfolk*, 107.

Strabolgie, *Northumb.* 119.
Strabolgy, *Notts*, 122.
Strachey, *Somerset*, 234.
Stradbroke, 236.
Stradling, *Wilts*, 185, 194 ; *Glam.* 228.
Strafford, *Northamp.* 112 ; *Wilts*, 194 ; 251.
Strahan, *Surrey*, 234.
Straithmore, *Durham*, 38.
Strange, *Berks*, 7 ; *Rutl.* 136 ; *Shrop.* 137 ; *Warw.* 172 ; *Glouc.* 262.
Strangewayes, *Dorset*, 33 ; *York*, 234.
Strangeways, *Durham*, 42 ; *Hamp.* 50 ; 232.
Strangwayes, *York*, 220, 234.
Strangways, *Herts*, 56 ; *Wilts*, 182 ; *York*, 224.
Strangman, *Essex*, 47 ; *Kent*, 60.
Stratford, *Northamp.* 112 ; *Warw.* 176, 177 ; *Wilts*, 182 ; *Glouc.* 262.
Stratton, *Wilts*, 185.
Straubenzee, *York*, 234.
Streatfeild, *Kent*, 60, 234.
Streatfield, *Derby*, 27.
Strechlegh, *Devon*, 29.
Strete, *Leic.* 80.
Strethay, *Staff.* 143,
Strelley, *Derby*, 27, 234 ; *Leic.* 80 ; *York*, 206 ; *Wilts*, 185 ; 251.
Stretley, *Oxf.* 128, 130.
Stretton, *Leic.* 80.
Streynsham, *Kent*, 60.
Strickland, *York*, 224 ; *Westm.* 234 ; 235.
Stringfellow, *Hamp.* 50.
Stringer, *Kent*, 60 ; *Notts*, 122 ; *York*, 213, 224.
Strobridge, *Devon*, 31.
Strode, *Devon*, 29, 31, 234 ; *Dorset*, 33 ; *Hamp.* 50 ; *Herts*, 54, 56 ; *Somerset*, 140, 234 ; 236.
Strong, *Herts*, 54 ; *Hereford*, 234 ; 236.
Strongbow, *Herts*, 54.
Strother, *Northumb.* 119.
Strowell, *Somerset*, 140.
Strutt, *Derby*, 27, 234, 239 ; *Essex*, 48.
Stuart, *Derby*, 257.

Stuart, *Hamp.* 50 ; *Shrop.* 137 ; *York*, 205 ; *Herts*, 234 ; *Kincardine*, 234 ; 234.
Stubber, *Queen's Co.* 234.
Stubbs, *Stafford*, 234.
Studdert, *Clare*, 234, 239.
Studley, *Kent*, 60.
Stukeley, *Devon*, 29.
Stumpe, 232.
Sture, *Devon*, 29, 31.
Sturgeon, *Suffolk*, 152.
Sturges, *Hamp.* 50.
Sturgis, 246.
Sturt, *Surrey*, 158 ; *Dorset*, 234.
Stutevill, *Northamp.* 112 ; *Warw.* 172.
Stuteville, *Cumb.* 22 ; *Leic.* 80 ; *York*, 215.
Stutteville, *Northumb.* 119.
Stydolf, *Surrey*, 156.
Style, *Oxf.* 234 ; *Kent*, 60, 237.
Styleman, *Norfolk*, 234.
Stylleman, *Hamp.* 50 ; *Wilts*, 185.
Suckling, *Suffolk*, 153 ; *Norfolk*, 234.
Sudeley, *Glouc.* 49.
Sudley, *Warw.* 172.
Suffolk, *Oxf.* 133 ; *Suffolk*, 153.
Suliard, *Kent*, 60.
Sulivan, *Isle of Wight*, 234.
Sullivan, *Bucks*, 10, 234 ; *Limerick*, 234.
Sulyard, *Essex*, 48.
Sumer, *Kent*, 60.
Sumery, *Herts*, 54.
Sumner, *Surrey*, 234.
Sunderland, *Bucks*, 10 ; *York*, 224.
Supple, *Sussex*, 165.
Surdwal, *Breck.* 229.
Surman, *Glouc.* 234.
Surrenden, *Hamp.* 50.
Surtees, *Durham*, 34, 36, 38, 40, 234 ; *Northumb.* 234 ; 234.
Sussex, *York*, 205.
Sutherland, 239.
Sutton, *Camb.* 16 ; *Chesh.* 17 ; *Leic.* 76, 80 ; *Northamp.* 112 ; *Notts*, 122, 123 ; *Oxf.* 127 ; *Rutl.* 136 ; *Shrop.* 127 ; *Durham*, 234 ; *Herts*, 234 ; *Derby*, 234 ; *York*, 211, 217 ; 235 ; 239.
Swabey, *Bucks*, 11, 234.
Swain, *Dorset*, 33 ; *Camb.* 234.
Swainson, *Shrop.* and *Lanc.* 234.

Swainston, *Durham*, 41.
Swale, *York*, 224.
Swan, *Kent*, 60; *Wexford*, 234, 245.
Swanley, *Lond.* 96.
Swann, *Derby*, 234.
Swanton, *Wilts*, 192.
Swayne, *Dorset*, 33; *Wilts*, 192, 182.
Swetenham, *Chesh.* 17; 234.
Swettenham, *Chesh.* 17, 234, 236.
Swift, *Westmeath*, 234.
Swillington, *Leic.* 80; *Notts*, 122.
Swinburn, *Durham*, 38.
Swinburne, *Durham*, 38, 234; *Northumb.* 119; *York*, 219.
Swinfen, *Stafford*, 234.
Swinhoe, *Durham*, 42.
Swinnerton, *Staff.* 234.
Swinton, *Peebles*, 234; *Berwick*, 234, 236.
Swire, *York*, 200, 234.
Swyft, *York*, 213.
Swynbourne, *Essex*, 259.
Swynerton, *London*, 96.
Swynfen, *Leic.* 80; *Staff.* 143.
Swynnerton, *Northamp.* 112; *Chesh.* 17.
Sydenhale, *Northamp.* 112.
Sydenham, *Dorset*, 33; *Somerset*, 140.; 232.
Sydnam, *Somerset*, 140.
Sydney, *Surrey*, 156; *Berks*, 234; *Norfolk*, 277.
Sydnor, *Suffolk*, 153.
Sykes, *York*, 205, 217, 224, 285.
Sylvester, *Chesh.* 17.
Symcotts, *London*, 96.
Symes, *Wicklow*, 234.
Symmins, *Wales*, 229.
Symonds, *Camb.* 16; *Dorset*, 33; *Devon*, 31; *Hereford*, 234.
Symons, *Hereford*, 234; *Devon*, 234; *Cornw.* 234.
Sympson, *Durham*, 38; *Kent*, 60; *York*, 224.
Synge, *Wicklow*, 234.
Synnot, *Armagh*, 234, 239; *Dublin*, 234.
Syston, *Sussex*, 165.

Taafe, *Mayo*, 234.
Taaffe, *Louth*, 234; 235.
Tailgebose, *Norfolk*, 109.
Tailard, *Leic.* 80.

Tailbois, *Durham*, 38; *Northumb.* 118.
Tailby, *Leic.* 234.
Tailyour, *Forfar*, 234.
Tait, *Ayr*, 234.
Talbot, *Bucks*, 10; *Dorset*, 33; *Durham*, 38; *Hamp.* 50; *Leic.* 80; *Staff.* 144; *Rutl.* 136; *Warw.* 172; *Worc.* 195, 234; *York*, 200, 206, 224; *Wilts*, 234; *Wexford*, 234; *Glam.* 234; *Roscommon*, 234; *Glouc.* 234.
Talboys, *Warw.* 174.
Talk, *Hamp.* 50.
Talke, *Hamp.* 50.
Talmach, *Suffolk*, 152.
Talmache, *Surrey*, 156.
Tame, *Hamp.* 50; *Northamp.* 112.
Tamworth, *Leic.* 80; *Rutl.* 136.
Tanfield, *Northamp.* 111, 112.
Tangerd, *Wales*, 229.
Tankard, *York*, 224; *Pemb.* 230.
Tanke, *Hamp.* 50.
Tanner, *Cornw.* 20; *Devon*, 234.
Tappenden, *Kent*, 60.
Tarbock, *Lanc.* 71.
Turboks, *Lanc.* 69.
Tardrew, *Devon*, 234.
Tardy, *Essex*, 234.
Tarleton, *Chesh.* 17; *Lanc.* 69.
Tasborough, *Suffolk*, 153.
Tash, *Bucks*, 10.
Tate, *Leic.* 80, 234; *Northamp.* 111; *Surrey*, 159.
Tatten, *Chesh.* 17.
Tattershall, *Essex*, 234; 244.
Tatteshall, *Leic.* 80.
Tatlock, *Lanc.* 234.
Tatton, *Chesh.* 234; 236.
Taunton, *Cornw.* 20; *Oxford*, 234, 245.
Taver, *Camb.* 16.
Taverner, *Herts*, 53, 54.
Tawke, *Sussex*, 163, 168.
Tawley, *Devon*, 31.
Taylboys, *Notts*, 122.
Taylarde, *Hunts*, 57.
Tayler, *York*, 224.
Tayleur, *Shrop.* 234.
Taylor, *Bucks*, 7; *Camb.* 16; *Kent*, 60, 234; *Oxford*, 131; *Sussex*, 165; *York*, 219, 224, 234; *Staff.* 234; *Durham* 234 *Chesh.* 234;

Glouc. 234; *Shrop.* 234; *Wilts,* 234; *Lanc.* 234, 250, 239; *Devon,* 234; *Hants,* 234, 239; *Notts,* 234; *Worc.* 234, 239; *Dublin,* 234; *Galway,* 234; *Kerry,* 234; 236; 237; 245; *Dublin,* 246; *Derby,* 259.
Teasdale, *Durham,* 38.
Tecon, *Herts,* 54.
Temmes, *Wilts,* 185.
Temple, *Bucks,* 10; *Leic.* 76, 80; *Northamp.* 112; *Surrey,* 156; *Sussex,* 165; *Wilts,* 182, 234; *York,* 234, 235; *Warw.* 172.
Templer, *Devon,* 234; *Somerset,* 234; 234.
Tempest, *Durham,* 34, 36, 37, 38; *York,* 200, 204, 205, 224, 234, 239, 284; *Lanc.* 71; 236.
Tempeste, *York,* 226.
Temys, *Sussex,* 168.
Tench, *Wexford,* 234.
Tenche, *Kent,* 60.
Tendering, *Essex,* 48.
Tenison, *Roscommon,* 234; *Armagh,* 234.
Tennant, *Staff.* 143; *York,* 234; *Fermanagh,* 234.
Tennyson, *Linc.* 234.
Ternan, 245.
Terry, *Notts,* 122; *Kent,* 60.
Tetlow, *Lanc.* 268.
Teverey, *Notts,* 122.
Tey, 249.
Teynham, *Kent,* 60.
Thacker, *Derby,* 258, 259.
Thackeray, *Norfolk,* 234; 235.
Thackwell, *Glouc.* 234.
Thame, *Leic.* 80.
Thanet, *Leic.* 80; *Northamp.* 112.
Tharp, *Camb.* 234.
Thatcham, *Wilts,* 182, 185.
Thatcher, *Kent,* 60; *Sussex,* 163, 156.
Thelwal, *Wales,* 229.
Thelwell, *Denbigh,* 234.
Themelby, *Wales,* 229.
Theccher, *Sussex,* 168.
Theed, *Northamp.* 112.
Thelluson, *York,* 213.
Thicknes, *Wales,* 220.
Thicknesse, *Lanc.* 23.
Thickbrome, *Leic.* 80.
Thimblethorp, *Oxford,* 131.

Thirkeld, *Durham,* 38; *Northumb.* 118.
Thirland, *Notts,* 126.
Thirlwall, *Northumb.* 119.
Thistlethwayt, *Wilts,* 185.
Thistlethwayte, *Wilts,* 182, 185; *Hants,* 234.
Thoates, *Cumb.* 24.
Thomas, *Kent,* 60; *London,* 96; *Suffolk,* 152; *Sussex,* 163, 165, 234; *Wilts,* 182; *Glam.* 228, 234; *Card.* 230; *Carm.* 230, 234; *Wales,* 229; *Hereford,* 234; *Brecon,* 234; *Radnor,* 234; 236.
Thomason, *Sussex,* 165.
Thometon, *York,* 224.
Thomlinson, *Durham,* 36, 38, 40; *Cumb.* 234, 239; *York,* 224.
Thompson, *Berks,* 7; *Bucks,* 10; *Essex,* 48; *Herts,* 56; *Kent,* 60; *Northumb.* 118; *Rutland,* 136; *Surrey,* 162; *York,* 217, 224, 234; *Cornw.* 234; *Louth,* 234; *Longford,* 234; 237.
Thomson, *Kent,* 60, 67, 234; *Herts,* 56; *Antrim,* 234; *Fife,* 234; *Kincardine,* 234.
Thoresby, *Norfolk,* 107; *York,* 205, 209, 224.
Thorn, *Devon,* 29.
Thornborough, *Westm.* 179, 180.
Thornburgh, *Hamp.* 50.
Thorneycroft, *Shrop. and Staff.* 234.
Thornbrough, *Glouc.* 234.
Thorneton, *York,* 224.
Thorngrafton, *Northumb.* 119.
Thornhill, *Kent,* 60; *York,* 205, 224, 234; *Derby,* 234; *Oxford,* 234.
Thornhaugh, *Notts,* 122.
Thornhull, *Dorset,* 33; *Wilts,* 185.
Thornhurst, *Dorset,* 33.
Thornley, *York,* 234.
Thornton, *Camb.* 16; *Chesh.* 17; *Herts,* 56; *Northamp.* 111, 112, 234; *Northumb.* 119; *York,* 197; 205, 224, 234; *Surrey,* 234; *Cavan,* 234; 236.
Thornycroft, *Chesh.* 17.
Thorold, *Camb.* 16; *London,* 101; 235.
Thoroton, *Notts,* 122.
Thorowgood, *London,* 96.

Thorp, *Durham*, 38, 234, 239 ;
Northamp. 112 ; *Sussex*, 165 ;
York, 234.
Thorpe, *Berks*, 7 ; *Northumb.* 119 ;
Wilts, 182 ; *York*, 214, 217, 224 ;
236.
Thoyts, *Berks*, 234.
Threel, *Sussex*, 163, 165.
Threlkeld, *Cumb.* 22, 23.
Thresher, *Wilts*, 191.
Throckmorton, *Herts*, 53, 54; *Hunts*,
57 ; *Northamp.* 111, 112 ; *Oxford*,
130 ; *Surrey*, 158 ; *Warw.* 172 ;
Worc. 195; *York*, 224 ; *Devon*,
234.
Throgmorton, *Bucks*, 10 ; *Oxford*,
128.
Thring, *Somerset*, 234.
Thunder, *Meath*, 234.
Thunstall, *York*, 226.
Thurban, *Bucks*, 11.
Thurbane, *Bucks*, 10.
Thurgarland, *York*, 224.
Thurgoland, *York*, 213.
Thurbarne, *Kent*, 59.
Thurland, *Surrey*, 162.
Thurlow, *Surrey*, 156, 234 ; 237.
Thursby, *Durham*, 38 ; *Northamp.*
234 ; *Kent*, 60.
Thurstanton, *Chesh.* 17.
Thurston, *Kent*, 60.
Thwaites, *York*, 197 ; *Norfolk*, 278.
Thynne, *Essex*, 48 ; 233 ; *Wilts*,
182, 185 ; 244.
Tibeaudo, *Queen's Co.* 234.
Tibetot, *York*, 213.
Tibtot, *Wilts*, 182.
Tichborne, *Hamp.* 50, 235 ; *Kent*,
60 ; *Surrey*, 162.
Tichbourne, *Wilts*, 182.
Tichburn, *Wilts*, 185.
Tichesey, *Surrey*, 156.
Tighe, *Kilkenny*, 234 ; *Westmeath*,
234, 246.
Tilghman, *Kent*, 60.
Tildesley, *Lanc.* 71.
Tiliol, *York*, 217.
Tillard, *Kent*, 234.
Tillesley, *Kent*, 60.
Tilliol, *Cumb.* 22.
Tilly, *Kent*, 60.
Tilney, *Camb.* 16 ; *Linc.* 88 ; 249.
Tilston, *Chesh.* 17.

Timms, *Kent*, 60.
Timperley, 235.
Tindal, *Essex*, 234 ; 237.
Tindale, *Norfolk*, 107 ; *Northumb.*
119.
Tindall, *York*, 224.
Tinker, *Rutland*, 136.
Tipping, *Berks*, 7 ; *Bucks*, 10, 11 ;
Lanc. 234; *Oxford*, 129.
Tiptoft, *Herts*, 54 ; *Rutland*, 136 ;
Wilts, 190.
Tirrell, *Surrey*, 162.
Tirrick, *Staff.* 146.
Tirwhit, *Northamp.* 112.
Tisdell, *Meath*, 234 ; *Louth*, 234.
Tison, *Northumb.* 118.
Tisted, *Hamp.* 50.
Titherleigh, *Hamp.* 50.
Titherington, *Chesh.* 17.
Titley, *Norfolk*, 278.
Tittle, *Londonderry*, 234.
Tixall, *Staff.* 142.
Tocker, *Wales*, 229.
Tocketts, *York*, 224.
Todd, *York*, 205, 234 ; *Donegal*, 234.
Todenham, *Devon*, 29.
Todeni, *Leic.* 80 ; *Norfolk*, 109.
Toeni, *Wilts*, 182.
Tocy, *Wales*, 229.
Toke, *Herts*, 56 ; *Kent*, 60, 234.
Toker, *Kent*, 15.
Tokett, *York*, 201.
Toky, *Worc.* 195.
Tolcthorpe, *Rutland*, 136.
Toll, *Devon*, 234.
Toller, *Rutland*, 136.
Tollemache, *Suffolk*, 234 ; 236.
Tollet, *Staff.* 234.
Tolson, *Kent*, 60 ; *York*, 213 ; *Cumb.*
234.
Tolwin, *Norfolk*, 278.
Tomlinson, *Leic.* 80 ; *York*, 205 ;
Chesh. 234.
Tomlin, *Kent*, 234.
Tomline, *Suffolk and Linc.* 234.
Tompson, *Norfolk*, 234.
Tong, *Kent*, 58 ; *York*, 204.
Tonge, *Berks*, 7 ; *Durham*, 34, 36,
38, 40, 44 ; *Kent*, 60.
Tonstall, *Surrey*, 162.
Tony, *Herts*, 54.
Toode, *Durham*, 38.
Tooke, *Herts*, 54 ; *Sussex*, 234.

Tooker, *Wilts,* 182, 185 ; *York,* 213 ; *Somerset,* 234.
Toone, *Leic.* 80.
Toose, *Somerset,* 140.
Topesfield, *Suffolk,* 152.
Topham, *York,* 217, 224, 234, 245.
Topp, *Wilts,* 182, 185 ; *Shrop.* 234 ; *York,* 245.
Torkyngton, *Hunts,* 57.
Torkington, *Hunts,* 234.
Tornay, *Kent,* 60.
Torre, *Linc.* 86 ; *York,* 305, 217, 234.
Torriano, *Berks,* 7.
Tothill, *Devon,* 29, 31.
Tottie, *York,* 205.
Tottyl, *Wales,* 229.
Tottenham, *Wicklow,* 234 ; *Enniskillen,* 234.
Touchet, *Chesh.* 17.
Tounley, *Lanc.* 71, 234.
Tounrawe, 251.
Tournay, *Wilts,* 182 ; *Dorset,* 33.
Tovey, *Midd. and Lanark,* 234.
Tower, *Essex,* 234 ; *Bucks,* 10, 13, 239 ; 236.
Towers, *Camb.* 16 ; *Rutland,* 136 ; *Sussex,* 165 ; *Tipperary,* 234.
Townley, *Lanc.* 68.
Towneley, *Lanc.* 234.
Townsend, *Warw.* 234 ; *Cork,* 234 ; *Denbigh,* 234 ; 234.
Townshend, *Chesh.* 17 ; 236 ; *Herts,* 54 ; *Worc.* 195.
Towry, *York,* 217.
Tracy, *Bucks,* 10 ; *Glouc.* 49 ; *Lond.* 96 ; 232.
Trafford, *Chesh.* 17, 234 ; *Lanc.* 70, 71, 234, 268 ; *Northamp.* 112 ; *Staff.* 146, 234 ; *Norfolk,* 234 ; 236.
Traherne, *Glam.* 228, 234.
Trail, *Antrim,* 234.
Truill, *Orkney,* 234 ; *Caithness,* 234.
Traut, *Tipperary,* 234.
Trappes, *York,* 234.
Traylebew, *Chesh.* 17.
Trayne, *Durham,* 38.
Trayton, *Sussex,* 165.
Treaunt, *Northamp.* 112.
Treby, *Dorset,* 234.
Tredcroft, *Sussex,* 163, 165, 234.
Treddennick, *Donegal,* 234.

Tredenham, *Herts,* 53.
Tredway, *Rutland,* 136.
Trefusis, *Cornw.* 20.
Tregagle, *Wilts,* 182.
Tregarthyn, *Cornw.* 20.
Tregian, *Cornw.* 20.
Tregonwell, *Dorset,* 33, 234, 240.
Tregos, *Sussex,* 163.
Tregose, 233.
Tregoz, *Wilts,* 182.
Trehampton, *Linc.* 87.
Treherne, *Sussex,* 234.
Trelawney, *Bucks,* 10 ; *Devon,* 29.
Trelawny, *Cornw.* 234 ; 236.
Tremayne, *Devon,* 29, 31; *Cornw.* 234.
Tremenheere, *Cornw.* 234.
Trench, *Kent,* 60 ; *King's Co.* 234 ; *Queen's Co.* 234.
Trenchard, *Dorset,* 33, 234, 236.
Tresham, *Northamp.* 111, 117 ; *Sussex,* 165.
Treswallen, *London,* 96.
Trevanion, *Cornw.* 20, 234.
Trevellian, *Devon,* 29.
Trevelyan, *Northumb.* 119, 234.
Trevilian, *Somerset,* 140.
Trevor, *Bucks,* 10 ; *Sussex,* 165 ; *Wales,* 229.
Trey, *Devon,* 31.
Trigose, 233.
Trigott, *York,* 213.
Tripp, *Kent,* 67 ; *Somerset,* 234.
Trippe, *Kent,* 60.
Trist, *Northamp.* 111, 112 ; *Cornw.* 234 ; *Devon,* 234 ; 237.
Tritton, *Kent,* 60.
Trollop, *Durham,* 36, 38.
Trollope, *Rutland,* 135 ; *Durham,* 34, 40.
Tropnell, *Wilts,* 182, 185.
Trosse, *Devon,* 32.
Trotter, *Durham,* 36, 234 ; *York,* 201, 224 ; *Midlothian,* 234 ; *Galway,* 234 ; *Wicklow,* 234.
Troughear, *Hamp.* 50.
Troughton, *Lanc.* 234.
Troutbeck, *Chesh.* 17 ; *Herts,* 54.
Trowle, *Camb.* 16.
Troyte, *Devon,* 234, 245 ; 246.
Truell, *Wicklow,* 234.
Truman, *Glam.* 228.
Trumball, *Bucks,* 13.
Trusbut, *Northamp.* 112.

Trusbutt, *Norfolk*, 107.
Truslove, *York*, 217.
Truslowe, *Wilts*, 182, 185.
Trussel, *Chesh.* 17 ; *Leic.*76 ; *Warw.* 172 ; *Northamp.* 112.
Trussell, *Hamp.* 50 ; *Northamp.* 111 ; *Warw.* 172.
Tryce, *Hunts*, 57.
Trye, *Glouc.* 234.
Trymnell, *Leic.* 80.
Tryon, *Northamp.* 234 ; *Surrey*, 156.
Tryst, *Northamp.* 112.
Tryvet, *Kent*, 64.
Tuberville, *Berks*, 7.
Tuchett, *Chesh.* 17.
Tuck, *Camb.* 234.
Tucker, *Corn.* 20, 234 ; *Devon*, 29, 234 ; *Kent*, 60, 67 ; *Pemb.* 230.
Tudenham, *Norfolk*, 107 ; *Northamp.* 112.
Tudway, *Somerset*, 234.
Tudor, *Glam.* 228.
Tudor Vychan, *Wales*, 229.
Tuffnell, *Essex*, 234.
Tufnaile, *Essex*, 48.
Tufton, *Kent*, 60 ; *Northamp.* 112 ; *Leic.* 80.
Tuite, *Westmeath*, 234.
Tuke, *Notts*, 122.
Tunnard, *Linc.* 234.
Tunstal, *Lanc.* 71.
Tunstall, *Durham*, 34, 36, 38, 40 ; *York.* 209, 217, 224.
Tunsted, *Derby*, 259.
Tupper, *Guernsey*, 234.
Turbervill, *Dorset*, 33 ; *Hunts*, 57 ; *Glam.* 234.
Turberville, *Glam.* 228 ; *Breck.* 227 ; *Dorset*, 33 ; *Wilts*, 192.
Turbridge, *Wales*, 229.
Turbutt, *Derby*, 234.
Turgis, *Surrey*, 156.
Turner, *Derby*, 27 ; *Kent*, 60 ; *Leic.* 80; *Lond.* 96; *Oxf.* 129 ; *Sussex*, 163, 165 ; *York*, 220, 224 ; 233 ; *Aberdeen*, 234 ; *Perth*, 234.
Turnham, *Shrop.* 137.
Turney, 272.
Turnly, *Ant.* 234.
Turnor, *Linc.* 82, 234.
Turnour, *Sussex*, 163, 165 ; *Surrey*, 156.
Turpin, *Camb.* 16 ; *Leic.* 80.

Turton, *Staff.* 142, 143, 146 ; *York*, 234.
Tutt, *Hamp.* 50 ; *Sussex*, 163, 165 ; *Wilts*, 185.
Turvile, *Leic.* 76, 78, 80 ; *Warw.* 172 ; *Notts*, 122.
Turvill, *Warw.* 172.
Turville, *Bucks*, 10 ; *Leic.* 80, 234 ; *Northamp.* 112.
Tweddell, *Durham*, 38 ; *Northumb.* 119.
Twemlow, *Staff.* 145, 234 ; *Chesh.* 234.
Twemlowe, *Chesh.* 17.
Twenge, *York*, 220.
Twentyman, *Notts*, 124.
Twigge, *Derby*, 27.
Twisden, *Kent*, 60, 66.
Twistleton. *Leic.* 80.
Twiss, *Tipperary*, 234 ; *Flint*, 234.
Twyer, *York*, 217.
Twyne, *Hamp.* 50.
Twynhoe, *Dorset*, 33.
Twysden, *Kent*, 60.
Tybetot, *Rutland*, 136.
Tydyr, *Wales*, 229.
Tyghall, *Berks*, 3.
Tylden, *Kent*, 60, 234.
Tylecote, 236.
Tyler, *Glam.* 234 ; *Londonderry*, 234 ; 236.
Tylliol, *Durham*, 38.
Tyllington, *Hamp.* 50.
Tyndale, *Hamp.* 234 ; *Oxford*, 234.
Tynte, *Somerset*, 140, 234.
Typping, *Oxf.* 128, 130, 131.
Tyrconnel, 236.
Tyrell, *Essex*, 48;
Tyringham, *Bucks*, 10, 234 ; *Hunts.* 57 ; *Leic.* 80 ; *Northamp.* 112.
Tyrrel, *Bucks*, 10.
Tyrrell, *Bucks*, 10, 13 ; *Kildare*, 234.
Tyrringham, *Bucks*, 11.
Tyrwhitt, *Denbigh*, 234.
Tyssen, *Essex*, 48 ; *Herts*, 56 ; *Lond.* 100 ; *Norfolk*, 234.
Tytherleigh, *Hamp.* 50.
Tytherley, *Dorset*, 33.
Tytler, *Inverness*, 234 ; *Midlothian*, 234.

Uffenham, *Wilts*, 182, 185.

Ufford, *Oxf.* 133; *Suffolk,* 152; 232;
233. ·
Ulf, *York,* 217.
Umfraville, *Durham,* 38; *Northumb.*
119; 242.
Unett, *Staff.* 234; *Hereford,* 234.
Underhill, *Warw.* 172, 178; 232;
235.
Uniacke, *Cork,* 234; *Waterford,*
234.
Unton, *Berks,* 3.
Unwin, *Bucks,* 13.; *Hamp.* 50.
Unwyne, *Staff.* 146.
Upcher, *Norfolk,* 234.
Uppleby, *Linc.* 234.
Upton, *Devon,* 29, 31; *Kent,* 60;
Shrop. 137; *Somerset,* 140;
Westm. 234; *Louth,* 234.
Urquhart, *Aberdeen,* 234, 236.
Urrey, *Hamp.* 50.
Ursey, *London,* 93.
Urswick, *York,* 213.
Usher, *York.* 222.
Ussher, *Galway,* 234; *Wexford,*
234.
Usticke, *Cornw.* 234; *Devon,* 234.
Uthwatt, *Bucks,* 11.
Uvedall, *Hamp.* 50.
Uvedale, *Dorset,* 33; *Surrey,* 156,
161; *Wilts,* 182, 232.
Uxbridge, *Dorset,* 33.

Vachell, *Berks,* 3; *Bucks,* 10.
Vaile, *Kent,* 60.
Valence, *Bucks,* 10; *Linc.* 83; *Nor-
thumb.* 119; *Wilts,* 185.
Valoines, *Herts,* 54.
Vampage, *Worc.* 195.
Van, *Monm.* 106; *Glam.* 228.
Vanacker, *Herts,* 54.
Van Corslandt, 234.
Vandeleur, *Clare,* 234.
Vanderstegen, *Oxf.* 234.
Vane, *Durham,* 34, 37, 38, 41;
Notts, 125.
Van Sittart, *Bucks,* 11; *Berks,* 234;
York, 234.
Van Straubenzee, 234; 236.
Vasey, *Durham,* 36, 38.
Vassall, *Hants,* 234.
Vaughan, *Hamp.* 50; *London,* 91;
Somerset, 140; *Wilts,* 182, 185;
Buck. 227; *Pemb.* 230; *Card.*

230; *Carm.* 230; *Wales,* 229;
Glam. 228, 234, *Shrop.* 234;
Merioneth, 234; *Hereford,* 234;
234; *Glouc.* 262.
Vauncy, *Herts,* 54.
Vaux, *Bucks,* 10; *Cumb.* 23; *Herts,*
54; *Leic.* 80; *Northamp.* 111;
Wilts, 185; 235.
Vavasor, *York,* 226.
Vavasour, *York,* 204, 213, 224, 234;
Linc. 86; *Northamp.* 111.
Vawdrey, *Chesh.* 17.
Vawdry, *Chesh.* 234.
Vazie, *Oxf.* 131.
Veale, *Devon,* 234.
Veitch, *Dumfries,* 234.
Vele, *Glouc,* 262.
Venables, *Chesh.* 17; *Hamp.* 50;
Shrop. 234; *Linc.* 234.
Venn, *Suffolk,* 234.
Venour, *Berks,* 7; *Kent,* 60.
Ventris, *Camb.* 16.
Verdon, *Leic.* 76, 80; *Warw.* 172.
Vere, *Bucks,* 10, 13; *Glouc.* 49;
Herts, 54; *Kent,* 60; *Norfolk,* 107;
Northamp. 111; *Lanark and Lin-
lithgow,* 234; *Notts,* 234; *Mona-
ghan,* 234; 249.
Verelst, *York,* 213.
Vernai, *Somerset,* 140.
Verney, *Bucks,* 10; *Hamp.* 50;
Herts, 54, 56; *Northamp.* 111;
Rutland, 135; *Somerset,* 140;
Surrey, 158; *Warw.* 172.
Vernon, *Bucks,* 10; *Chesh.* 17;
Herts, 54, 56; *Leic.* 80; *North-
amp.* 112; *Northumb.* 119; *Shrop.*
137; *Staff.* 143, 234; *Worc.* 195,
234; *Wales,* 229; 232; *Middle-
sex,* 234; *Dublin,* 234; 236;
251.
Verner, *Armagh,* 234.
Verulam, *Herts,* 56.
Vesci, *York,* 213.
Vescy, *Northumb.* 119; *Camb.* 16.
Vesey, *Dublin,* 234; *Tyrone,* 234.
Veteriponte, *Cumb.* 23.
Vieleston, *Northamp.* 112.
Vignoles, *Westmeath,* 234.
Vigors, *Carlow,* 234.
Vilers, *Notts,* 122.
Vilett, *Wilts,* 234.

Villiers, *Herts*, 54; *Leic.* 76, 80; *Rutland*, 135; *Staff.* 146.
Vincent, *Leic.* 76, 80; *Surrey*, 156, 158; *York*, 213, 224.
Viner, *Glouc.* 234.
Vinour, *Wilts*, 185.
Violett, *Kent*, 60.
Vipan, *Camb.* 234.
Vipont, *Rutland*, 136; *Northumb.* 119.
Vise, *Staff.* 146.
Vitre, *Wilts*, 186.
Vivian, *Glam.* 234; *Corn.* 234.
Voel, *Pemb.* 232; *Wales*, 229.
Von Rahn, *Herts*, 56.
Vowe, *Leic.* 80, 234.
Vowel, *Devon*, 29.
Vowler, *Devon*, 234.
Vychan, *Wales*, 229.
Vyne, *Oxford*, 131.
Vyse, *Northamp.* 112; *Bucks*, 234.
Vyner, *Linc.* 234; *York*, 234.
Vyvyan, *Cornw.* 20.

Waddell, *Lanark*, 234.
Waddington, *Suffolk*, 234.
Waddy, *Wexford*, 234, 246.
Wade, *Lanc.* 72; *Sussex*, 165; *York*, 205, 224; *Meath*, 234; *Westmeath*, 234
Wadham, *Devon*, 29; *Dorset*, 33; *Hamp.* 50; *Oxford*, 127; *Surrey*, 156.
Wadland, *Leic.* 80.
Wadman, *Wilts*, 182.
Wadsley, *York*, 206.
Wage, *Kent*, 60.
Waggett, *Cork*, 234.
Wahul, *Bedford*, 2.
Wainman, *Oxford*, 130.
Wait, *Somerset*, 234.
Waitman, *Lanc.* 234.
Wake, *Bucks*, 10; *Cumb.* 22; *Herts*, 54; *Leic.* 76, 80; *Northamp.* 111, 112; *Wilts*, 182; *York*, 224; 244.
Wakebrigge, *Derby*, 27.
Wakefield, *York*, 224.
Wakehurst, *Sussex*, 169.
Wakelyn, *Northamp.* 112; *Derby*, 259.
Wakeman, *Devon*, 31; *Monm.* 234.
Walbec, *Glam.* 228.

Walbeof, *Wales*, 229.
Walbeoffe, *Breck*, 227.
Walcot, *Berks*, 7; *Shrop.* 234; *Hamp.* 234; 236.
Walcote, *Leic.* 80.
Walcott, *Berks*, 7.
Waldegrave, *Herts*, 54; 235.
Waldgrave, *Norfolk*, 107.
Waldie, *Roxburgh*, 234.
Walden, *Hunts*, 57.
Waldo, 235.
Waldron, *Leic.* 80, 243; *Somerset*, 140; *Roscommon*, 234.
Waldy, *Durham*, 234.
Wale, *Northamp.* 112; *Camb.* 234.
Waleran, *Wilts*, 182.
Walerand, *Wilts*, 182; 233.
Walford, *Isle of Wight*, 234; 249.
Walgrave, *Warw.* 172.
Walker, *Durham*, 38; *Herts*, 54, 56, 234; *Leic.* 77, 80, 234; *London*, 96; *Notts*, 122, 234; *Somerset*, 140; *Staff.* 146; *Wilts*, 185, 234; *York*, 205, 234; *Kinross*, 234; *Glouc.* 234; *Midlothian*, 234; 234; 236; 237; 239; 245; *Warw.* 178.
Walkey, *Devon*, 234.
Wall, *Hamp.* 50, 234; *Lanc.* 71.
Wallace, *Northumb.* 119, 234, 245; *Ayr*, 234; 236; 237; 246.
Wallascott, *Oxford*, 131.
Waller, *Bucks*, 10, 11; *Derby*, 27; *Devon*, 29; *Hamp.* 50; *Herts*, 54, 56; *Kent*, 60; *York*, 224; *Glouc.* 234; *Tipperary*, 234; *Limerick*, 234; *Meath*, 234; 234; *Midd.* 246, 250.
Wallers, *Leic.* 80.
Wallescott, *Rutl.* 136.
Walleys, *Sussex*, 165.
Wallington, *Glouc.* 234.
Wallis, *Dorset*, 33; *Sussex*, 168; *Wilts*, 185.
Wallop, *Hamp.* 50; *Northamp.* 112.
Wallur, *Bucks*, 11.
Walmesley, *Essex*, 48; *Lanc.* 68, 69, 70, 234; *York*, 224; *Surrey*, 156.
Walpole, *Norfolk*, 107, 234.
Walrcand, 232.
Walrond, *Devon*, 29, 31, 234; *So-*
3 c

merset, 140; *Wilts*, 185; *Lanark*, 234; 236; *Glouc.* 262.

Walsh, *Leic.* 80; *Somerset*, 140; *Worc.* 195; *Kilkenny*, 234; *Tipperary*, 234.

Walsham, *Suff.* 152; *Hereford*, 239.

Walshe, *Bucks*, 10.

Walshall, *Leic.* 76, 80.

Walsingham, *Kent*, 60; *Surrey*, 156; *Sussex*, 165.

Walter, *Camb.* 16; *Hamp.* 50; *Kent*, 60; *Wales*, 229; *Berks*, 234.

Walters, *London*, 96; *Monm.* 105.

Walthall, *Chesh.* 17; *Derby*, 27; 234.

Waltham, *Devon*, 29, 31.

Walthew, *Kent*, 60.

Walton, *Durham*, 38; *London*, 101; *Somerset*, 140; *Wilts*, 185.

Walwyn, *Hereford*, 234; 236; *Glouc.* 262.

Walur, *Notts*, 122.

Walwin, *Sussex*, 165.

Walworth, *Northumb.* 118.

Wandesford, *York*, 209, 224.

Wandysford, *York*, 226.

Wapenbury, *Warw.* 172.

Warbleton, 233.

Warburton, *Chesh.* 17, 234; *Herts*, 54, 56; *King's Co.* 234; *Wales*, 287.

Warcop, *Cumb.* 24; *Westm.* 179.

Warcup, *Oxford*, 130.

Warcupp, *Oxford*, 131.

Warcuppe, *Oxford*, 128.

Ward, *Berks*, 3; *Camb.* 16; *Chesh.* 17; *Durham*, 36, 38; *Kent*, 60, 234; *Leic.* 80; *London*, 94, 96; *Northamp.* 111, 234; *Northumb.* 119; *Rutland*, 136; *Staff.* 146; *Sussex*, 163; *Warw.* 176, 177; *York*, 213; *Surrey*, 234; *Wilts*, 234; *Norfolk*, 234, 278; *Glouc.* 234; *I. of Wight*, 234; *Down*, 234.

Warde, *Durham*, 38; *Herts*, 56; *Leic.* 80; *Norfolk*, 107, 278; *York*, 213; *Kent*, 234; *Warw.* 234; 236.

Wardedieux, *Sussex*, 169.

Wardell, *Durham*, 38.

Warder, *Wilts*, 182, 185.

Wardlow, *Perth*, 234.

Wardrop, *Edinburgh*, 234.

Ware, *Midd.* 234; *Cork*, 234; *Edinburgh*, 234.

Wareing, *Chesh.* 17.

Warham, 232; *Dorset*, 33; *Hamp.* 50.

Waring, *Pemb.* 230; *Down*, 234.

Warmouth, *Northumb.* 120.

Warnell, *Wilts*, 185.

Warnet, *Sussex*, 168.

Warnett, *Sussex*, 164, 165.

Warner, *Norfolk*, 234, 278; *Hereford*, 234; *Antigua*, 234; *Leic.* 234; *Ayr*, 234; *Essex*, 234.

Warnford, *Hamp.* 50.

Warr, *Devon*, 29.

Warre, *Somerset*, 140; *Wilts*, 185; *Hamp.* 234.

Warren, *Bucks*, 10, 11; *Chesh.* 17; *Essex*, 48; *Kent*, 60; *London*, 96; *Norfolk*, 109; *Northumb.* 119; *Surrey*, 156, 158, 159; *Sussex*, 163, 169; *Warw.* 172; *Wilts*, 182; *York*, 213; *Wales*, 229; 232; *Dublin*, 234; 246; *Kilkenny*, 234.

Warrener, *Wilts*, 234.

Warrington, *Lanc.* 234, 239.

Warry, *Somerset*, 234.

Warter, *Shrop.* 234.

Warton, *York*, 201, 213, 214, 215, 217, 220, 224; *Kent*, 234.

Warwick, *Bucks*, 10; *Cumb.* 22; *Northamp.* 112; *Warw.* 172; 231; 237.

Waschet, *Chesh.* 17.

Wase, *Leic.* 80; *Sussex*, 163, 165.

Washington, *Northamp.* 112; *York*, 205, 213, 224; 235; 241.

Wassand, *York*, 217.

Wassenes, *Notts*, 126.

Wastal, *Northumb.* 119.

Wastell, *York*, 224.

Wasteneys, *Chesh.* 17.

Wastney, *Notts*, 122.

Waterer, *Surrey*, 162.

Waterford, 236.

Waterhouse, *Bucks*, 10; *Herts*, 53, 54; *York*, 213, 234.

Waters, *Carm.* 234; 236.

Waterton, *Linc.* 86; *York*, 234.

Wathen, *Glouc.* 234.

Watkins, *Dorset*, 33 ; *Somerset*, 140 ; *York*, 224, 234 ; *Breck.* 227, 234 ; *Worc.* 234 ; *Shrop.* 234 ; *Northamp.* 234.
Watkinson, *Derby*, 27 ; *York*, 205, 219, 224.
Watling, *Denbigh*, 234.
Watlington, *Berks*, 7, 234 ; *Herts*, 56 ; *Essex*, 234.
Watmere, *Kent*, 60.
Watmoughe, *Kent*, 60.
Watnow, *Notts*, 122.
Watson, *Camb.* 16 ; *Essex*, 41 ; *Durham*, 42, 36, 38 ; *Hamp.* 50 ; *Northumb.* 119 ; *York*, 224 ; *Westm.* 234 ; *Waterford*, 234 ; *Carlow*, 234 ; *Tipperary*, 234 ; *Glouc.* 262.
Watt, *Lanc.* 234.
Watton, *Kent*, 60, 67.
Watts, *Herts*, 54 ; *Northamp.* 112 ; *Somerset*, 140 ; *York*, 206 ; *Cumb.* 234 ; *Chesh.* 234 ; *Bucks*, 234 ; 234.
Wauchope, *Midlothian*, 234 ; *Edinburgh*, 234.
Waud, *York*, 234.
Wauncy, *Northamp.* 112.
Waver, *Warw.* 172.
Wawgood, *Wales*, 229.
Way, *Bucks*, 234.
Waylen, *Wilts*, 234.
Wayne, *Derby*, 234.
Wayneman, *Oxford*, 128.
Wayte, *Hamp.* 50 ; *Sussex*, 169 ; *York*, 224.
Weare, *Wilts*, 185.
Webb, *Bucks*, 10 ; *Dorset*, 33 ; *Kent*, 60 ; *London*, 96 ; *Surrey*, 156, 158 ; *Sussex*, 165 ; *Wilts*, 182, 185 ; *Wales*, 229 ; *Notts*, 234 ; *York*, 234 ; *Hereford*, 234 ; *Tipperary*, 234 ; *Kilkenny*, 234 ; *Cork*, 234 ; *Worc.* 234 ; 250.
Webbe, *Devon*, 31; *Camb.* 16.
Webber, *Queen's Co.* 234.
Webster, *Warw.* 234, 245 ; *Forfar*, 234.
Wecherlin, *Kent*, 60.
Wedd, *Herts*, 56 ; 237.
Weddell, *York*, 224.
Wedderburn, *Forfar*, 234.
Wedgewood, *Staff.* 146.

Wedgwood, *Staff.* 145.
Weedon, *Sussex*, 234.
Weekes, *Sussex*, 169, 234 ; *Devon*, 31.
Weeler, 236.
Weever, *Chesh.* 17.
Wegg-Prosser, *Hereford*, 234.
Weiatt, *Wales*, 229.
Weightman, *Leic.* 234.
Welbeck, 251.
Welbury, *Durham*, 38.
Welby, *Notts*, 123 ; *Rutland*, 136 ; *Linc.* 82 ; 236 ; 241.
Welch, *Glouc.* 234, 239.
Weld, *Chesh.* 17 ; *Dorset*, 33, 234 ; *Herts*, 54 ; *Lond.* 91, 96, 97, 100 ; *Lanc.* 234.
Welfitt, *Notts*, 234 ; *Linc.* 234.
Welisburne, *Berks*, 3.
Welles, *Northumb.* 119 ; *Linc.* 234 ; *Staff.* 143 ; 239.
Wellesburgh, *Leic.* 76.
Weller, *Kent*, 60.
Wellis, *Staff.* 146.
Wells, *Dorset*, 33 ; *Hamp.* 50 ; *Leic.* 80 ; *Sussex*, 168 ; *Hunts*, 234 ; *Kent*, 234 ; *Devon*, 239.
Welsh, *Leic.* 76 ; *Wales*, 229.
Welton, *Northamp.* 111.
Welwood, *Perth*, 234.
Welman, *Somerset*, 234.
Wellwood, *Fife*, 234.
Welsted, *Cork*, 234.
Wemys, *Kilkenny*, 234.
Wencelagh, *York*, 217.
Wendy, *Cumb.* 16.
Wenham, *Sussex*, 165.
Wenlock, *Kent*, 60.
Wenman, *Bucks*, 10 ; *Oxf.* 131, 235.
Wentworth, *Herts*, 56 ; *Leic.* 80 ; *Northamp.* 112 ; *York*, 205, 213, 222, 224, 226, 234, 239.
Werden, *Chesh.* 17 ; *Lanc.* 234.
Were, *Somerset*, 234.
Werge, *Notts*, 234.
West, *Bucks*, 10, 11, 234 ; *Dorset*, 33 ; *Hamp.* 50 ; *Herts*, 54 ; *Rutland*, 136 ; *Sussex*, 163, 165 ; *Warw.* 172 ; *York*, 213, 224 ; *Essex*, 234 ; *Kent*, 234 ; *Glouc.* 234 ; 235.

Westby, *Lanc.* 71, 234; *Dublin*, 234; *Clare*, 234; *Wicklow*, 234; *York*, 213, 224.
Westbury, *Wilts*, 182.
Westbrook, *Surrey*, 156; *Sussex*, 165.
Westbrooke, *Sussex*, 163.
Westcar, *Surrey*, 234.
Westcote, *Devon*, 29.
Westmoreland, *Essex*, 48.
Western, *Essex*, 48, 234; *Suffolk*, 234; *Herts*, 56; 236.
Weston, *Staff.* 142, 146; *Surrey*, 156, 158, 159, 234; 234; 235; *Wilts*, 185.
Westropp, *Limerick*, 234.
Westrow, *Hamp.* 50.
Wettenhall, *Chesh.* 17.
Wevell, *Kent*, 60.
Wever, *Wales*, 229.
Weyland, *Berks*, 13; *Oxf.* 234; *Norfolk*, 107.
Weymouth, *Essex*, 48.
Wgan, *Wales*, 229.
Whalley, *Hamp*, 50; *Hunts*, 57; *Lanc.* 68; *Leic.* 80; *Notts*, 122; *Somerset*, 234.
Wharton, *Bucks*, 10, 11; *Durham*, 36, 38, 234; *Northamp.* 112; *Oxf.* 131; *Westm.* 180; *York*, 201, 205, 208, 209, 213, 220, 234.
Whatman, *Kent*, 234.
Whatton, *Leic.* 80, 234; *Notts*, 122.
Wheate, *Oxf.* 131.
Wheathe, *York*, 234.
Wheathill, *Leic.* 80.
Wheatley, *Sussex*, 165; *York*, 213, 224.
Wheble, *Berks*, 234.
Wheeler, *Kent*, 60, 234; *Worc.* 234.
Whelden, *Kent*, 60.
Wheler, *Lond.* 91; *Durham*, 38.
Whellesburgh, *Leic.* 80.
Whelock, *Chesh.* 17.
Whelton, *Northamp.* 112.
Whetham, *Notts*, 234.
Whethill, *Bucks*, 13.
Whetnall, *Norfolk*, 278.
Whichcote, *Herts*, 54.
Whieldon, *Dorset*, 234.
Whippy, *Oxf.* 234.
Whitacre, *Warw.* 172; *York*, 234.

Whitaker, *Dorset*, 33; *Lanc.* 68, 234; *Wilts*, 182.
Whitaphe, *Leic.* 80.
Whitbread, *Berks*, 10; *Bedford*, 234; *Suffolk*, 234.
Whitbrooke, *Hunts*, 57.
Whitby, *Staff.* 234; *Derby*, 27.
Whitchurch, *Hamp.* 50; 234.
Whitchorne, *Sussex*, 165.
White, *Berks*, 3; *Dorset*, 33, 234, 239; *Durham*, 36, 38, 40; *Essex*, 48, 234; *Hamp.* 50; *Kent*, 60; *London*, 104; *Notts*, 122; *Surrey*, 156; *Warw.* 172; *Wilts*, 185, 188; *Pemb.* 230; *Midlothian*, 234; *Wexford*, 234; *Dublin*, 234; *Limerick*, 234; *Devon*, 234; *Somerset*, 234, 239.
Whiteford, *Devon*, 234.
Whitehead, *Hamp.* 50; *York*, 217.
Whitehall, *Staff.* 143.
Whitelock, *Oxf.* 134.
Whitfeld, *Herts*, 54; *Kent*, 60.
Whitfield, *Dorset*, 33; *Northumb.* 119; *Sussex*, 165, 168.
Whitgrave, *Staff.* 146.
Whitgreave, *Staff.* 234.
Whitgift, *Surrey*, 161.
Whithed, *Hamp.* 50.
Whithull, *Leic.* 80.
Whiting, *Leic.* 80.
Whitington, *Somerset*, 140; *Glouc.* 262.
Whitla, *Antrim*, 234.
Whitley, *Berks*, 7; *Wales*, 229.
Whitlock, *Devon*, 29.
Whitmore, *Chesh.* 17; *Lond.* 91; *Shrop.* 234.
Whitney, *Wexford*, 234.
Whittaker, *Kent*, 60; *Radnor*, 234.
Whittell, *York*, 234.
Whitter, *Sussex*, 234; *Devon*, 234.
Whittewrong, *Berks*, 10.
Whitting, *Somerset*, 234, 250.
Whittingham, *Durham*, 34, 38; *Northamp.* 112; *Northumb.* 120; *Bedf.* 234.
Whittingstall, *Herts*, 234.
Whittington, *Staff.* 142; *Glouc.* 262.
Whitton, *Oxf.* 128, 130; *Kent*, 60.
Whittuck, *Glouc.* 234.
Whitwange, *Northumb.* 120.
Whitwick, *Staff.* 146.

Whityngham, *Herts*, 54.
Whorwood, *Oxf.* 131; *Staff.* 143.
Whyddon, *Devon*, 29.
Whyghte, *Devon*, 81.
Whyte, *Berks*, 7; *Wilts*, 182;
  York, 205; *Down*, 234; *Leitrim*,
  234; *Cavan*, 234, 237.
Whytehead, *York*, 234.
Whytehed, *Durham*, 38.
Whytt, *Wales*, 229.
Wichard, *Leic.* 76, 80.
Wichalse, *Devon*, 29; *Kent*, 60.
Wickham, *Leic.* 80; *Oxf.* 131;
  Somerset, 139, 234; *York*, 218,
  224, 234; 232.
Wicks, *Lond.* 96.
Wicksted, *Chesh.* 17; *Staff.* 234.
Widdington, 235.
Widdrington, *Durham*, 38; *Nor-
  thumb.* 119, 234.
Wideville, *Northamp.* 112.
Widmerpole, *Notts*, 122.
Wigfall, *Derby*, 259.
Wiggett, *Hamp.* 50.
Wight, *Northamp.* 112; *Surrey*, 156,
  234.
Wightman, *Leic.* 80.
Wightwick, *Staff.* 143, 234.
Wigland, *Chesh.* 17.
Wigley, *Leic.* 80; 251; *Derby*, 259.
Wignoll, *Wilts*, 185.
Wigsall, *Surrey*, 158.
Wigston, *Leic.* 80.
Wikes, *Somerset*, 140.
Wilberforce, *York*, 234; *Sussex*,
  234.
Wilberfosse, *York*, 224.
Wilbore, *Camb.* 16.
Wilbraham, *Chesh.* 17, 234; *Lanc.*
  69; *Northamp.* 112; *Staff.* 146;
  234.
Wilcock, *Kent*, 60; *Wales*, 229.
Wilcocks, *Bucks*, 11; *Leic.* 80.
Wilcox, *Leic.* 80.
Wilde, *Kent*, 60; *Suffolk*, 150.
Wilder, *Berks*, 7, 234, 239; 236;
  237.
Wildes, *Kent*, 60.
Wildigos, *Sussex*, 165.
Wilding, *Lond.* 96, 100.
Wildman, *Notts*, 234.
Wileman, *Leic.* 80.
Wililey, *Shrop.* 137.

Wilkes, *Bucks*, 10; *Camb.* 16;
  Devon, 31; *Staff.* 143, 146.
Wilkie, *Durham*, 42.
Wilkin, *Breck.* 227, 234; *Radnor*,
  234; *Glouc.* 234.
Wilkinson, *Derby*, 27; *Durham*, 36,
  38, 234, 239; *Kent*, 60; *York*,
  213, 224, 234; *Midd.* 234; *Nor-
  folk*, 278.
Wilks, *Surrey*, 158.
Willaby, *Herts*, 56.
Willard, *Sussex*, 234.
Willes, *Berks*, 7; *Northamp.* 112,
  234.
Willesford, *Devon*, 31.
Willett, *Dorset*, 33.
Willey, *Durham*, 38.
William, *Wales*, 229.
William ap David, *Wales*, 229.
William ap Richard, *Wales*, 229.
William ap Rhys, *Wales*, 229.
William ap Sion, *Wales*, 229.
Williams, *Berks*, 7, 234; *Bucks*, 10,
  13; *Devon*, 29; *Dorset*, 33, 234;
  Hamp. 50; *Herts*, 54, 56; *Hunts*,
  57; *Linc.* 82; *Monm.* 105, 106,
  234; *Oxf.* 131; *Sussex*, 163, 165;
  Glam. 228; 237; *Wales*, 229,
  287; *Carm.* 230, 234; *Breck.*
  227; *Northamp.* 234; *Midd.* 234,
  245; *Kildare*, 234; *Card.* 234;
  Anglesey, 234; *Warw.* 234; *Corn.*
  234; *Merioneth*, 234; 234; 246;
  Glouc. 262.
Williamson, *Durham*, 34, 36, 38,
  234; *Kent*, 60; *Notts*, 122; *Perth*,
  234, 236.
Willington, *Warw.* 172, 234; *Tip-
  perary*, 234.
Willis, *Bucks*, 10; *Hamp.* 50; *Herts*,
  54; *Lanc.* 234, 250; *Worc.* 234;
  Roscommon, 234.
Willmot, *Oxford*, 131.
Willoughby, *Devon*, 29, 31; *Dorset*,
  33; *Hamp.* 50; *Herts*, 54; *Kent*,
  60; *Northamp.* 111; *Notts.* 122,
  123, 126; *Warw.* 172, 234;
  Wilts, 185, 194.
Willson, *Linc.* 234.
Willyams, *Cornwall*, 234.
Willy, *Durham*, 38.
Willymot, *Herts*, 54.
Willymott, *Derby*, 259.

Wilmot, *Derby*, 27 ; *Leic.* 80 ; 236.
Wilmott, *Hamp.* 50 ; *Kent*, 60.
Wilsford, *Kent*, 60.
Wilsher, *Herts*, 56.
Wilshere, *Herts*, 54, 234.
Wilson, *Durham*, 37, 38 ; *Herts*, 54 ; *Kent*, 60 ; *Leic.* 80 ; *London*, 94 ; *Northumb.* 119 ; *Surrey*, 156 ; *Sussex*, 165, 169 ; *Worc.* 195 ; *York*, 200, 205, 206, 213, 234 ; *Suffolk*, 234 ; *Limerick*, 234 ; *Warw.* 234, 239 ; *Cumb.* 234 ; *Lanc.* 234 ; *Linc.* 234.
Wilton, *Northamp.* 112 ; *Glouc.* 262.
Wiltshire, *Berks*, 10 ; *Essex*, 48 ; *Hamp.* 50 ; *London*, 96 ; *Sussex*, 165.
Wimble, *Sussex*, 165.
Wimondefold, *Notts*, 122.
Winch, *Berks*, 8.
Winchcombe, *Berks*, 3, 7.
Winchelsea, *Northamp.* 112.
Winchester, *Berks*, 7 ; *Kent*, 60 ; *Northamp.* 112.
Wincoll, *Leic.* 80.
Windham, *Norfolk*, 234 ; *York*, 234.
Windsor, *Bucks*, 11, 13 ; *Essex*, 48 ; *Hamp.* 50 ; *Kent*, 60 ; *Surrey*, 156, 158 ; *Warw.* 172.
Winford, *Worc.* 195.
Wing, *Kent*, 60.
Wingate, *Herts*, 54.
Wingfield, *Hunts*, 57 ; *Norfolk*, 107, 278 ; *Northamp.* 111, 114 ; *Rutland*, 135, 136, 234 ; *Shrop.* 234 ; 234 ; *Worc.* 195.
Winlowe, *Bucks*, 10.
Winn, *York*, 213, 224, 234, 236.
Winne, *Kent*, 60.
Winnington, *Worc.* 195 ; *Chesh.* 17 ; *Herts*, 56.
Winstanley, *Lanc.* 70 ; *Leic.* 80, 234 ; *Wales*, 229 ; 236.
Winter, *Leic.* 80 ; *Carm.* 230 ; *Meath*, 234.
Wintersoll, *Wilts*, 185.
Wintershall, *Oxford*, 130.
Wintershull, *Oxford*, 128.
Winterton, *Surrey*, 156 ; *Sussex*, 163.
Winthrop, *Herts*, 56.
Wintrop, 236.
Wirley, *Staff.* 146.

Wise, *Camb.* 16 ; *Devon*, 29 ; *Staff.* 234 ; *Warw.* 234.
Wiseman, *Berks*, 6, 7 ; *Herts*, 56.
Wiston, *Staff.* 142.
Wisse, *Glouc.* 262.
Witham, *York*, 205, 234.
Withen, *Kent*, 60.
Wither, *Hamp.* 50, 234.
Wittewrong, *Herts*, 56.
Wittewronge, *Herts*, 54.
Wittie, *York*, 219, 224.
Witton, *Surrey*, 158 ; *York*, 219, 224.
Witts, *Surrey*, 158.
Wivell, *Devon*, 29.
Wiverton, *Notts*, 122.
Woddrop, 234.
Wodehouse, *Norfolk*, 107, 278 ; *Herts*, 234 ; 236.
Wodford, *Wales*, 229.
Wodhull, *Northamp.* 112 ; *Wilts*, 182.
Wodlow, *Warw.* 172.
Wogan, *Pemb.* 230 ; *Glam.* 228.
Wolcott, *Devon*, 234.
Wolf, *Sussex*, 163, 165.
Wolfe, *Devon*, 31 ; *Essex*, 234 ; *Kildare*, 234 ; *Northamp.* 112 ; *Leic.* 76, 80.
Wolferstan, *Staff.* 143, 234.
Wolff, *Hamp.* 50.
Wolffe, *Surrey*, 158.
Wollacomb, *Devon*, 29.
Wollaston, *Bucks*, 11 ; *Leic.* 80, 234 ; *Staff.* 146.
Wolley, *Herts*, 54 ; *Derby*, 234, 259.
Wolmer, *Worc.* 195.
Wolrich, *Staff.* 146 ; *York*, 205.
Wolsey, *Norfolk*, 278.
Wolston, *Devon*, 31 ; *Westm.* 179.
Wolstenholm, *York*, 213.
Wolvardinton, *Warw.* 172.
Wolveridg, *Hamp.* 50.
Wolverston, *Staff.* 146.
Wolverton, *Corn.* 20 ; *Northamp.* 111, 112.
Wombwell, *Kent*, 60, 67 ; *York*, 205, 206, 213, 224.
Wood, *Camb.* 16 ; *Chesh.* 17 ; *Devon*, 29 ; *Essex*, 48, 234 ; *Hamp.* 50 ; *Leic.* 87 ; *Northamp.* 112 ; *Notts*, 122 ; *Staff.* 145, 146, 234 ; *Suffolk*, 152 ; *Surrey*, 156 ; *Sussex*,

165; *York*, 205, 213, 222, 224, 234; *Derby*, 234; *Fife*, 234; *Midd.* 234; *Linc.* 234; *Hereford*, 234; *Sligo*, 234; *Lanc.* 234; *Norfolk*, 278.
Woodcock, *Leic.* 80, 234; 251.
Woodd, 234.
Woodford, *Leic.* 76, 80; *Sussex*, 165.
Woodforde, *Somerset*, 234.
Woodhall, *Herts*, 54, 56.
Woodhouse, *Norfolk*, 107; *Staff.* 143, 146; *Louth*, 234; 234; 237.
Woodhull, *Northamp.* 111.
Woodman, *Northamp.* 119.
Woodnoth, *Chesh*, 17.
Woodroffe, *Surrey*, 156.
Woodruffe, *York*, 213.
Woods, *Wales*, 229; *Dublin*, 234; *Lanc.* 234.
Woodward, *Kent*, 60; *Lond.* 96; *Sussex*, 165; *Meath*, 234.
Woodyeare, *York*, 213, 234.
Woolff, *Wales*, 229.
Woolgar, *Sussex*, 165.
Woolhouse, *Dorset*, 33; *Derby*, 259.
Woolrych, *Herts*, 234.
Woolryche, *Shrop.* 234.
Wordsworth, *Westm.* 234.
Worge, *Sussex*, 165, 234.
Workesley, *Wilts*, 182.
Worleston, *Chesh.* 17.
Worley, *Bucks*, 234; *Kent*, 60.
Wormeley, *York*, 224.
Wormley, *York*, 213, 234.
Wornele, *Somerset*, 140.
Worsley, *Hamp.* 50; *Lanc.* 68, 270; *Northamp.* 111; *York*, 224, 234; 236; *Wilts*, 182.
Worth, *Chesh.* 17; *Devon*, 29; *Somerset*, 140.
Worthal, *Devon*, 29.
Worthington, *Chesh.* 234, 239.
Worting, *Hamp.* 50.
Wortley, *Durham*, 36; *York*, 213.
Wotton, *Bucks*, 10; *Devon*, 31; *Rutland*, 136; *Warw.* 172.
Wraight, *Kent*, 60.
Wrangham, 236.
Wray, *Durham*, 38; *Oxf.* 131; *York*, 213, 208; 234; *Donegal*, 234.
Wren, *Northumb.* 119.
Wrenbury, *Chesh.* 17.
Wrenn, *Durham*, 36.

Wrenne, *Durham*, 40.
Wrey, *Devon*, 29.
Wright, *Berks*, 7; *Chesh.* 17, 234; *Derby*, 27, 259, 234; *Durham*, 36, 37, 38; *Essex*, 48, 234; *Hamp.* 50; *Kent*, 60; *Herts*, 56; *Leic.* 77, 80; *Lond.* 96; *Norfolk*, 107, 234; *Staff.* 146; *Sussex*, 165; *York*, 217, 224, 234; *Notts*, 234; *Monaghan*, 234.
Wrighte, *Bucks*, 10; *Leic.* 80; *Northamp.* 112.
Wrightson, *York*, 213, 234.
Wroth, *Lond.* 94; *Wilts*, 182.
Wrothe, *Sussex*, 165; *Somerset*, 140.
Wrottesley, *Essex*, 48; *Staff.* 143.
Wroughton, *Wilts*, 185; *Berks*, 234; *Bucks*, 234.
Wrowe-Walton, *Lanc.* 234.
Wyat, *Kent*, 60.
Wybergh, *Westm.* 234.
Wyche, *Wilts*, 182.
Wycker, *Surrey*, 158.
Wycliffe, *Durham*, 36, 38; *York*, 209, 217, 224.
Wyclyff, *Durham*, 44.
Wydville, *Chesh.* 17; *Northamp.* 111.
Wyke, *Somerset*, 140; *Surrey*, 156.
Whykeham-Martin, *Northamp.* 112.
Wykeham, *Bucks*, 10; *Oxford*, 127, 234; 233.
Wykes, *Devon*, 29.
Wylde, *Hamp.* 50; *Northamp.* 112; *Worc.* 295; *Staff.* 143; *Notts*, 234.
Wylme, *Chesh.* 17.
Wylmeldon, *Surrey*, 156.
Wymond, *Sussex*, 169.
Wynard, *Devon*, 32.
Wyndham, *Bucks*, 10, 13; *Cumb.* 23; *Dorset*, 33; *Hamp.* 50; *Herts*, 56; *Norfolk*, 107, 234; *Wilts*, 182, 234; 236.
Wyndout, *Herts*, 56.
Wyndsor, *Sussex*, 163.
Wyndowe, *Glouc.* 234; 236.
Wynington, *Chesh.* 17.
Wynn, *Wales*, 229; *Merioneth*, 234; *Denbigh*, 234.
Wynne, *Wales*, 229; *Denbigh*, 234; *Merioneth*, 234; *Sligo*, 234; 236.
Wynniatt, *Glouc.* 234.
Wynter, *Breck.* 227.

Wynyard, *Hamp.* 50.
Wyot, *Dorset*, 33.
Wyrdham, *Berks*, 3.
Wyrley, *Northamp.* 111, 112 ; *Staff.* 143 ; *Warw.* 174.
Wyrral, *York*, 213.
Wyse, *Staff.* 145 ; *Waterford*, 234.
Wyseman, *Sussex*, 163, 165 ; *York*, 213.
Wytham, *York*, 224.
Wyvell, *Surrey*, 162 ; *York*, 224.
Wyvile, *Leic.* 80.
Wyvill, *Durham*, 38 ; *York*, 209, 234 ; 236.

Yaldwyn, *Sussex*, 163, 234.
Yale, *Wales*, 229 ; *Denbigh*, 234.
Yalwin, *Sussex*, 165.
Yarborough, *Hamp.* 50 ; *York*, 213, 224.
Yarbrough, *York*, 224.
Yarburgh, *York*, 224, 234, 236.
Yard, *Devon*, 29, 81.
Yarde, *Leic.* 80 ; *Down*, 234.
Yarker, *York*, 234.
Yate, *Berks*, 3 ; *Oxford*, 128, 130, 131 ; *Glouc.* 234 ; 233.
Yates, *Lanc.* 234.
Yea, 236.
Yeatman, *Dorset*, 33 ; 234.
Yeland, *Durham*, 38.

Yeo, *Devon*, 29, 31.
Yerbury, *Wilts*, 185, 191.
Yerworth, *Devon*, 29 ; *Wilts*, 185.
Yngoe, *Essex*, 47.
Yong, *Hamp.* 50.
Yonge, *Devon*, 31, 234 ; *Hamp.* 50, 234 ; *Staff.* 234 ; *Sussex*, 165 ; 234 ; *Wales*, 287.
York, *Kent*, 60 ; *Lanc.* 69 ; *York*, 234.
Yorke, *Herts*, 54 ; *Wilts*, 185, 194 ; *York*, 200, 208, 224, 234 ; *Denbigh*, 234, 239 ; *Glouc.* 234, 236.
Young, *Devon*, 29 ; *Durham*, 38 ; *Kent*, 60 ; *Sussex*, 163 ; *Wilts*, 182, 195 ; *York*, 219 ; *Pemb.* 230 ; *Wales*, 229 ; *Linc.* 234 ; *Northamp.* 234 ; *Kinross*, 234 ; *Londonderry*, 234 ; *Donegal*, 234 ; *Roscommon*, 234.
Younge, *Wales*, 229.
Yoward, *York*, 201, 220, 224.
Yuille, *Dumbarton*, 234.

Zachary, *Worc.* 195.
Zouch, *Derby*, 27 ; *Devon*, 29 ; *Leic.* 76, 80 ; *Northamp.* 112 ; *Surrey*, 156, 159 ; *Wilts*, 182, 185.
Zouche, *Berks*, 7 ; *Bucks*, 10 ; *Leic.* 80 ; *Northamp.* 111, 112 ; *Shrop.* 137 ; *Sussex*, 163 ; *Warw.* 172.

THE END.